THE POLITICS OF CRIME AND CONFLICT

The Politics of
CRIME
and CONFLICT

A Comparative History of Four Cities

TED ROBERT GURR
PETER N. GRABOSKY
RICHARD C. HULA

with contributions by

David Peirce
Leif Persson
Sven Sperlings

 SAGE PUBLICATIONS   Beverly Hills • London

For information address:

SAGE PUBLICATIONS, INC.
275 South Beverly Drive
Beverly Hills, California 90212

SAGE PUBLICATIONS LTD
St George's House / 44 Hatton Garden
London E C 1N 8ER

Printed in the United States of America

Library of Congress Cataloging in Publication Data

Gurr, Ted Robert, 1936-
    The politics of crime and conflict.

    Includes index.
    1. Crime and criminals—History—Case studies.   2. Offenses against public safety—History—Case studies.   3. Criminal justice, Administration of—History—Case studies.   4. Crime prevention—History—Case studies.
I. Grabosky, Peter N., 1945-   joint author.
II. Hula, Richard C., 1947-   joint author.   III. Title
HV6251.G86   364   76-45429
ISBN 0-8039-0677-3

FIRST PRINTING

CONTENTS

THE POLITICS OF CRIME AND CONFLICT

This is an inquiry into the problems of crime and conflict in four of the world's principal cities since the beginning of the nineteenth century. The three Western cities are London, Stockholm, and Sydney. Calcutta has been included to provide a Third World contrast to the Western experience.

We are particularly concerned about the interdependence between crime and conflict and the policies and institutions by which public order is defined and established—hence "the politics of crime and conflict." The ultimate aim is to provide a better understanding of what lies behind the apparent decline of public order in almost all the large cities of the West. The historical and comparative data are not likely to satisfy those who want answers to the immediate, practical question of what kinds of policies "work," because the measures that were effective prove to have been very different from one time to another. One of many conclusions not fully anticipated at the outset of this study is that public order depends more on basic socioeconomic and political circumstances than on conditions controlled by the law, the police, the courts, or the prisons.

We offer here a general description and interpretation of subjects usually studied separately and in narrower compass. The principal method is conventional historiography, but the coverage is inevitably superficial by most historians' standards because we have chosen to survey four societies over nearly two centuries. The concepts and hypotheses are mainly those of comparative political science, with particular reference to elites and contending class interests. The subject matter is traditionally that of sociology and criminology. By strict disciplinary standards, the study no doubt resembles one of those odd creatures portrayed in medieval bestiaries, part fish, part fowl, and part beast. We hope that it will be accepted as a contribution to a new, or at least rare, species of interdisciplinary study in which historical materials are used comparatively to formulate and test general theories germane to critical social issues.

A multiplying clan of social theorists has taken up the critical examination of ideological biases and unexamined premises in the empirical and theoretical scholarship of others. We shall be explicit about the values that inform this study. The principal contributors to this study prefer social order, however defined by the ordinary people of the societies we examined, to disorder. We have varying degrees of skepticism, though, about whether public order as defined and policed by governing elites has coincided with popular views. As the first line of social defense, we prefer tolerant, humanitarian policies, that is, conciliation and accommodation as the preferred methods of conflict management, and the avoidance of brutalizing punishment when dealing with offenders. We also recognize that in some social circumstances, humanitarian policies are not wholly effective or popular. None of us, though, advocates solutions of the kinds advocated on the extreme left or extreme right. One reason is the principled conviction that a substantial level of disorder is more tolerable than the annihilation of civil liberties in the service of revolution or reaction. The other reason is the skeptical conclusion, borne out by the results of this study, that draconian policies are no more certain to ensure public order than are humanitarian approaches. When faced with a choice between liberal policies that do not work very well and authoritarian solutions that have no better prospect of working, we much prefer the liberal alternatives.

The idea for a comparative historical study such as this was first advanced in 1971 by Prof. Marvin Wolfgang of the University of Pennsylvania and Drs. George Weber and Saleem Shah of the Center for Studies of Crime and Delinquency. The strategy of the study, including its general approach and the focus on urban crime and conflict, was devised by the senior author in collaboration with Prof. Louis H. Masotti, director of the Center for Urban Affairs at Northwestern University. The study subsequently was funded by the National Institute of Mental Health in all but its final phase, from 1972 through 1975. The senior author completed work on the manuscript in 1976 while supported by a Common Problems Senior Fellowship awarded by the German Marshall Fund of the United States.

The collaboration that produced this study requires a word of explanation. Peter N. Grabosky, Richard C. Hula, and David Peirce were appointed as research fellows of the Center for Urban Affairs and assumed primary responsibility for the studies of Sydney, Calcutta, and London, respectively. Prof. Masotti provided advice and administrative oversight for the project during most of its lifespan. Background papers on Stockholm were prepared on subcontract with the Institute of Criminology of the University of Stockholm by Leif Persson, Sven Sperlings, and a number of their students. Later Prof. Grabosky added to these papers and synthesized them. I prepared the conceptual framework of the study and carried out the comparative analysis, supervising and in some instances contributing to the city studies as well. All the Western cities were visited at least once and usually several times in the course of research. Although unavoidable political circumstances prevented us from doing field work in Calcutta, we had invaluable advice from Ramkrishna Mukherjee, Research Professor of Sociology at the Indian Statistical Institute, Calcutta. Of course, Prof. Mukherjee bears no responsibility for our conclusions about his native city.

Some of the qualities but none of the liabilities of this work are due to the advice and criticisms of other scholars, whom we thank. The theoretical and comparative sections of the work have been scrutinized in whole or part by Wesley Skogan and Frederick DuBow of Northwestern University, Neal Milner of Northwestern and the University of Hawaii, and Richard Rose of Strathclyde University, Scotland. The study of Calcutta was read with close critical attention by David H. Bayley of the University of Denver and John McLane of Northwestern, as well as by Prof. Mukherjee. Among the Australian scholars who aided the project, we would like particularly to thank Greg Woods and Gordon Hawkins of the Sydney University Law School. For comments on the Stockholm manuscript, thanks are due to Karsten Aström, Leif Lenke, Ingemar Rexed, and Hanns von Hofer of the Institute of Criminology at the University of Stockholm. The London manuscript was evaluated by David Thomas and Nigel D. Walker of the Institute of Criminology, University of Cambridge. Inevitably during this close collaboration, the contributors often reviewed one another's findings and reinforced one another's interpretations; thus we have only ourselves to blame for the errors and perversities that critics will no doubt find.

This study has also relied on the talents and sustained labors of a number of people whose names appear nowhere else in the book. Tina Peterson was responsible for managing and analyzing the enormous archive of data we compiled on crime. The indicators of crime and the correlation analyses are principally her work, and she also contributed a background paper surveying other quantitative historical studies of crime. For more than two years Virginia Nicodemus managed the project's multifarious fiscal and clerical business, aided and abetted by Gaye Haverkos and Katherine Dolan. Erika Gurr constructed nearly one hundred graphs and tracked down many an obscure source and reference. A background paper by Mark Wynn reviewed for us some of the contemporary sociological and criminological literature on the definitions and causes of crime. Michael Stohl made available a collection of data on civil conflict in London. A number of others, students and secretaries, graphic artists and computer technicians, and many patient librarians at institutions scattered half-way around the globe, have given a helping hand to this enterprise. In the final stages Rhoda Blecker, our editor at Sage, worked intercontinental miracles in coordinating tightly scheduled copy-editing, revisions, and proofreading. We thank them all. A special word of acknowledgement deservedly goes to our publishers, George McCune and Sara Miller McCune, for making it possible to bring the study out quickly and in several different editions, the better to reach its potential audience.

Ted Robert Gurr

Part I

PROBLEMS AND POLICIES OF

URBAN PUBLIC ORDER

Ted Robert Gurr

INTRODUCTION TO THE COMPARATIVE STUDY OF URBAN PUBLIC ORDER

Western civilization is centered on its cities, and Western people have come to judge their collective progress and well-being not only by their material and cultural accomplishments but by the civility and security of urban life. Reformers and social historians alike have celebrated the diminution of violence, venality, robbery, and riot in the nineteenth and early twentieth century histories of most European cities. North Americans have had fewer grounds for self-congratulation, but by and large they have accepted the European view that the citizens of the "good city" are as orderly as its municipal parks and public buildings. In the past generation, however, such optimism has been badly shaken by an apparent renaissance of disorder. By whatever indices one chooses—crime statistics or journalistic accounts, sociological treatises or public outcry—there has been a pronounced increase in crime and strife in most large Western cities. The phenomenon is by no means confined to Western cities either, though people of the world's poorer regions seem to be less alarmed perhaps because they have not thought themselves quite so close to the gates of the heavenly city.

To present a comparative history of urban public order, we describe problems of public order in London, Stockholm, Sydney, and Calcutta during the past century and a half, with particular attention to the evolution of the public policies and institutions that define and control disorder. These four cities were chosen partly because of their diverse cultural, demographic, and developmental traits, but mainly because each presents distinctive problems of public order. London, resting on Roman and Anglo-Saxon foundations, has the longest tradition of urban civilization. It is the largest of the four, and

3

has led a double life: In the first half of the nineteenth century it was reputedly noisome and turbulent, ridden with vice and crime; yet by the end of the Victorian era it was known as one of the most civil and orderly cities of Europe. London thus poses two particular questions. One involves the extent to which the objective evidence either supports the conventional historical view (that the city became more orderly in the nineteenth century) or justifies the contemporary fear of rising disorder. The other asks whether it is possible to identify the altered circumstances and policies that contributed to the establishment of public order in the last century and the apparent renaissance of disorder in recent decades.

Stockholm, a smaller and newer city, is included as much because of its contemporary characteristics as for its historical background. Swedish society is notably prosperous, homogeneous, and egalitarian. The courts and penal institutions of Sweden have been leaders in innovative sentencing and rehabilitation practices. Politically the Swedish working class has been an effective, usually dominant political force since the 1920s. According to many theories of the etiology of disorder, these conditions should make contemporary Stockholm an exceptionally orderly city. The more problematic issue, though, is whether and how social programs and disorder have been linked over time. Did the incidence of crime in Stockholm decline in response to improving social conditions, or was it relatively low at the outset? Has institutional innovation contributed to the alleviation of crime, or was the low level of crime a precondition for official experimentation?

The two remaining cities in the study share legal systems and institutions of public order that derive from the English tradition but have virtually nothing else in common. Sydney was founded as a penal colony at the edge of a howling antipodean wilderness in 1788. Its problems as well as policies of public order were imported, so to speak, but after those rough beginnings we can trace in Sydney the evolution of distinctive patterns of criminality and public response to them. Sydney, like the new cities of North America, can be thought of as a vast social experiment. The opportunity existed to create a civil and orderly urban society, equipped with great resources and constrained by little except the cultural baggage of its citizens. The questions concern whether and how Sydneysiders have dealt with, and avoided, the problems of disorder that have beset most of the cities of Europe and North America.

Calcutta was chosen because it is so fundamentally dissimilar in history and prospects from the three Western cities; it does not typify Third World cities. A good case can be made that Calcutta, of the major cities of the world, has been least favored by circumstance. It was founded on a pestilent swamp by foreigners bent on exploiting

Bengal's wealth, and for nearly three centuries it served as a conduit through which that wealth was exported. In the twentieth century it has been swelled by a surplus rural population and waves of refugees who have far exceeded the city's waning economic opportunities and have overwhelmed its limited capacity to provide urban services. It has been wracked by famine, protracted revolutionary warfare, and chronic communal rioting. If one takes a pessimistic view of the urban prospect, one can paraphrase a remark made by Mayor Kenneth Gibson of Newark about American cities: Wherever the cities of the world are going, Calcutta will get there first. Yet Calcutta survives; somehow its people and rulers have evolved ways of living with endemic problems of public order.

We do not necessarily promise to answer all these specific questions because they may prove intractable. Nonetheless they dictated our choice of cities, influenced the kinds of information we sought, and suggested some kinds of analyses and interpretations of that information.

This study also has objectives that extend well beyond the ideographic analysis of public order in four cities. One general issue is whether there is historical warrant for the common scholarly and official view that crime and civil strife regularly declined in the nineteenth century in Western cities, then increased on some relative scale in mid-twentieth century. We assume that such a pattern exists as a working hypothesis for the three Western cities in the study; there is no conventional wisdom that would lead us to expect to find the same circumstances in Calcutta. It will be equally interesting to determine whether these trends—if they exist at all—are characteristic of all types of disorder, or only of some. This issue also stimulates us to ask whether there are distinctive patterns of change in disorder. We assume that changes have not been random, but there are three different ways in which systematic change could have taken place. One is that the incidence of disorder has changed gradually and continuously. The second is that changes have been abrupt and discontinuous but nonetheless cumulative. The last is that change is episodic, comprising recurring waves of rising and declining disorder. No one pattern of change will be universal. We want to know which patterns are characteristic of which kinds of crime and strife, at which times and in which societies. Particularly, have any of the cities experienced historically any great short-run increases in common crime that are analogous, in magnitude or character, to the apparent rise in crime since 1950?

The second general objective is to assess the relative importance of political and institutional factors in the creation and maintenance of public order. Crime and civil strife do not occur in a political vacuum. Both are defined by elites, with varying degrees of reference to or disregard of the views of other classes. Formally, the prevailing definitions of disorder encompass actions that are legally proscribed. In practice, disorder consists of actions that are resented and reported by citizens, policed by law enforcement agencies, and prosecuted and sanctioned by courts and penal institutions. One cannot understand the trends and patterns of criminality or strife without examining this institutional context. Therefore we want to identify major changes in the interests of rulers, legal codes, police systems and operations, and judicial and penal procedures. Suppose now that we do find distinctive patterns of change in policies and institutions of public order that account for historical and contemporary trends in public disorder. Are there trends toward either expanding or selectively limiting the scope of "disorderly" behavior? Are the police more or less numerous and active now than a century ago? Have judicial and penal policies become consistently more humane and rehabilitative, and more or less effective over time?

By studying the institutions that define and respond to disorder, we begin to deal with the matter of explanation. There are clear historical trends in the magnitude of serious crime in all the cities. There also are evolutionary changes in the character and issues of civil strife. The ultimate theoretical purpose of this kind of study is to understand better the underlying conditions—the socioeconomic and political causes—of these changes. One theoretical approach to crime, promoted especially by critical sociologists like Richard Quinney, is to seek its explanation, hence the origins of changes in its incidence, in the interests of the elites and institutions that selectively define and prosecute it.[1] A parallel argument attributes civil strife to the inequity and repression visited by rulers on the ruled.[2] These political explanations, as we label them, suggest that changes in disorder may be preceded by changes in the composition and interests of elites, especially as observable in changing policies and institutions of public order. To anticipate a conclusion, the hypothesis is only a partial explanation. It accounts for some important changes in the manifestations of civil strife, especially as regards the working class, and also for a number of short-term fluctuations in the official records of crime and punishment. But we find no long-term developments in the policies and institutions of public order that can explain the eruption of mass protest in the last quarter-century or, more important, the long-term trends in common crime. This is in fact one of the principal substantive findings of our study. The similar long-term trends in serious crime to be observed in three of the four cities apparently signify real changes in the social behavior of large numbers of people. And the policies of public order that seem to have "controlled" this behavior in some eras have had no visible effects in others.

Another large class of proposed explanations assumes the objective reality of crime as well as strife, and attributes both phenomena to the socioeconomic rather than the political conditions of society. The socioeconomic sources of disorder include the pressures of population growth and density, patterns of cultural, class, and residential separation, the ebb and flow of economic well-being, and inequities and constrained opportunities in the distribution of money and influence. We find that the inhabitants of the four cities often had good cause to blame some kinds of disorder on such conditions. Comparative study demonstrates that episodes of increased disorder have often followed an increase in some kinds of societal strains, not just in one city but in different times and places. The connection between increasing societal strain and growing disorder is particularly evident in Calcutta. In the three Western cities, by contrast, the evidence is contradictory. The gradual social and economic improvements that paralleled the development of urban public order in the nineteenth century and the first third of the twentieth have continued apace, while at the same time crime and strife increased. Thus on our evidence, either the nature of social causality in Western societies has altered in some fundamental way since World War II, or the celebrated social and economic improvements in urban life in the nineteenth and early twentieth centuries were only indirectly or coincidentally linked to the decline of disorder.

Neither the political nor the socioeconomic approaches to the explanation of public order consistently account for the historical experience of the four cities. The response of officials to burgeoning disorder, though, has seldom been either self-critical or socially reformist. Instead they have designed new mechanisms of control and tinkered with old ones. When disorder is seen to increase, legal and penal codes are revised and police forces are established, expanded, and nationalized; judicial procedures are modified, new penal institutions are established, and alternative strategies of treatment are brought into play. Times of crisis in public order are a stimulus to innovation, and in case after case we can see how officials perceived and responded to episodes of disorder. The next question is whether new policies designed to enhance public order were as efficacious as their advocates hoped or claimed them to be. Even in historical analysis the answers are vexingly tenuous.

General questions about the trends and conditions of public disorder, and the origins and effects of policies of order maintenance, cannot be answered conclusively with information from London, Stockholm, Sydney, and Calcutta. Since three of the cities are Western, the applicability of our generalizations to the cities of the Third World is hypothetical at best. Moreover three of the cities have legal codes and institutions of public order in the English tradition, which simplifies some kinds of comparison but makes it likely that certain observations and conclusions are relatively limited in application. Nonetheless the studies provide sufficient comparative and historical perspective to suggest that most of the prevailing popular, official, and academic explanations of public disorder and how to reduce it are time-bound and culture-bound, which is to say that they are applicable under some conditions and not under others. To make better sense of the subject we need more general theory about the underlying and immediate conditions of public order and disorder. No such theory is proposed here, but the final chapter suggests a general framework for theory, and results of our comparison of the four cities give some substance to it. At the same time the framework reveals the limits even of as broad a comparative study as this one.

It is customary to mention earlier studies that pose the questions or set the procedures of the research at hand. We cannot follow this practice because there has been virtually no comparative historical research on the trends and politics of public order, urban or otherwise. Social scientists have made many comparative studies of civil conflict and some of crime, but few of these works have a historical dimension. The historians interested in public order usually have focused on a single era in a single society. A few scholars, sociologists as well as historians, have traced the changing patterns of disorder and the evolution of policies and institutions of public order over a longer period. For example, we have identified some twenty studies of the changing incidence of crime in Western societies, but only four span a century or more, and only one refers to several societies.

Since the comparative history of public order lacks a distinctive research tradition, we have had to devise one, but we have relied on something other than conventional wisdom in choosing and interpreting the data on which we based our conclusions. Social scientists hold contending conceptions of crime and public order, attach different degrees of significance to data on crime, and have proposed diverse theories about the causes of disorder. The chapter that follows reviews some prevailing conceptual disputes and formulates our views on the meanings and measures of disorder.

NOTES TO CHAPTER I.1

1. See Richard Quinney, *The Social Reality of Crime* (Boston: Little, Brown, 1970) and *Critique of Legal Order* (Boston: Little, Brown, 1973); and also Austin Turk, *Criminality and Legal Order* (Skokie, Ill.: Rand-McNally, 1969).

2. This was Karl Marx's view, of course, and it is characteristic of those who write in the Marxist tradition. Among the contemporary non-Marxist theorists who take a similar theoretical approach to group conflict are Ralf Dahrendorf, *Class and Class Conflict in Industrial Society* (Stanford: Stanford University Press, 1959) and Johan Galtung in various writings.

CONCEPTIONS AND
MEASURES OF DISORDER

In ordinary English usage "disorder" connotes a threatening lack of predictability in the behavior of others in one's social environment. It refers particularly to the individual and collective acts that are called deviance, crime, and civil strife. There is no point in proposing a universal, denotative definition of social disorder because the objective behaviors so labeled vary from time to time and place to place. In common and historical usage, though, the term is usually associated with actions that threaten the values and interests of the dominant groups in society. Members of such groups wield greatest influence in defining common views of what constitutes "disorder," and theirs are the voices most likely to be heared in historical records.

This study is concerned specifically with *public disorder*, that is, manifestations of social disorder that are the objects of concerted public efforts at control. Public disorder, so defined, has normative, formal, and behavioral facets. In a normative sense, public disorder consists of the threatening activities that large or influential groups think ought to be under public control. The formal boundaries of public disorder are prescribed in legal codes. In practice, public disorder refers to individual and collective actions that are in fact policed and prosecuted. The policies of public order are those which are designed to create and maintain the prevailing conceptions of order; the institutions of public order are the agencies—security and civil police, courts, prisons, training schools—through which policies are implemented.

There is some social disorder in all societies, and it is valid to ask how much and why. But these questions are secondary to our primary interest in understanding the extent to which governments

9

assume responsibility for controlling social disorder and the policies they devise for doing so. In Western societies the processes by which this is accomplished are intrinsically political. Some groups' changing conceptions of order become influential enough to change the legal boundaries of disorderly behavior and, either as a consequence or independently, the practical scope of control activities is adjusted to accommodate the new views. Political leaders and the bureaucracies responsible for maintaining order have a large measure of influence on these processes, but elites and institutions outside government also can act decisively in politicizing social disorder, depending on the times and the nature of the polity. Thus the norms reflected in legal and practical efforts at control are not necessarily as narrow as those of a political elite, nor often as encompassing as the views of the "public" tapped by opinion surveys; rather, they are an amalgam of the norms of various politically influential groups in a society. Since such norms may be diverse and contradictory, their practical consequences for policies of public order share these characteristics. Among the consequences of diversity and change in groups' concerns about disorder are varying and inconsistent patterns of official action.

Both individual and collective actions, "crime" and "civil strife," are included within the ambit of public disorder as it is defined here. It may be asked whether it is useful to study them together, especially since the prevailing empirical tradition is to treat them as distinct phenomena. Behaviorally they are distinct, of course, in the sense that "crime" consists of an aggregate of individual acts, chiefly for individual motives, whereas "civil strife" consists of collective actions entailing some collective objectives. In social and political reality, though, these behaviors often are treated as if they were similar. Both threaten some peoples' sense of well-being, and both lead to concerted demands for the reestablishment of "order." In most contemporary societies the same legal codes define and proscribe crime and various kinds of collective action, and the same or similar institutions of public order are maintained to deal with both conditions.

In a scientific sense we would be justified in juxtaposing crime and civil strife if they tended to occur together, or if there were general theories indicating that they have common antecedents. The evidence on the empirical question of their covariance is fragmentary and inconclusive. The broadest relevant historical study shows that crime and collective violence were generally unrelated in France between 1831 and 1861. In the country as a whole, the incidence of crimes against persons and property varied over time quite independently of the more abrupt variation in collective violence, and comparisons of departments in specific years showed no significant correlations between their levels of crime and collective violence.[1] Contrary evidence comes from a study of much smaller scope, which indicated that in Southern cities in the United States the rise of civil rights demonstrations coincided with a marked short-run decline in violent crimes among blacks.[2] As for theoretical connections between crime and strife, perspectives as diverse as Marxism and structural-functional analysis imply some fundamental similarity in their social origins.[3] We make no a priori assumption about the connections between crime and strife. Both faces of disorder are examined in this study, first because many private citizens and officials respond to them as though they were similar, and second because we think it is worth asking whether and how each has affected the other, and the policies of public order, in the four cities.

CONCEPTIONS OF CRIME

Crime is a complex and culturally relative concept. The activities characterized as crime vary so greatly with respect to perpetrator, purpose, character, and societal response that any search for a valid universal definition of criminal behavior is chimerical. In primitive societies there may be little or no "crime" in the Western sense of formally proscribed behavior that is collectively punished. In the Comanche Indian tribe, for example, behavior contrary to societal norms was ordinarily dealt with through personal means. Homicide committed by someone outside the family required private revenge; wife-stealing was settled by paying off the husband or by revenge against the "thief." Excessive sorcery was the only Comanche "crime" for which the punishment—lynching—was collectivity imposed.[4] Criminal codes—even in more complex societies—vary widely, both among such societies and within them over time. Bloch contended that "there is no such thing as crime in the absolute sense. . . . Definitions as to what is a crime differ greatly from culture to culture and at different times in history. . . ."[5] In ancient Egypt it was criminal to cause the death of a cat; in medieval Europe to dispute the teachings of the Roman Catholic Church; in seventeenth-century England to play at sports on Sunday; and in contemporary South Africa to have sexual relations with someone of another race.

There is a basis for a formal definition of crime that is generally applicable, though. Michael and Adler have argued that "the only possible definition of crime . . . [is] behavior which is prohibited by the criminal code."[6] Such a formal definition is useful for cross-cultural research in that it obviates a search for objectively comparable behaviors and requires instead that we use the standards of the time and place studied. The possibility remains that some of these standards may be universals, or at least so pervasive that they can be treated as constants. Nettler argues, for example, that people have a "timeless desire to be able to move about freely without being robbed or beaten" and that attacks on one's person and property are universally condemned as "wrongs in themselves." Of course all victims of such acts abhor them, and assault and theft seem to be the contemporary criminal activities that figure most prominently in the average person's fear of crime.[7] But "crime" means both more and less than these kinds of acts, socially and legally: "more" because many other kinds of acts are also defined and sanctioned as crime, and "less" because not all attacks on one's person and belongings are labeled and treated as crime.

Murder is a leading candidate for universal condemnation. Contemporary opinion seems to be virtually unanimous that "murder" is a crime and deserves punishment. But that agreement is a function of the use of the label. Some people in every society take others' lives, deliberately or accidentally, directly or indirectly. Unacceptable life taking is ordinarily labeled "murder," and other forms of life taking have different labels—"justifiable use of force," "involuntary manslaughter," and "execution." In Western societies there is something like consensus that deliberate, unprovoked life taking by private individuals is reprehensible, but across societies there are cultural and legal differences regarding what constitutes justifiable provocation.

Much the same argument can be made about "theft," the other candidate for universal crime. Certain ways of acquiring goods are generally rejected and labeled "crime" in contemporary societies; principally these are the private seizure of valuable commodities by force or stealth and without compensation. But the gray area is considerable: businessmen may be able to sell misrepresented or shoddy goods, or charge excessive interest, without penalty. A good many individuals and groups in Western societies subscribe to the notion that other people's property represents ill-gotten gains; thus actions the victims resentfully call "theft" are believed by the takers to be self-righteous retributive or distributive justice. When powerless people seize others' goods their acts are called theft. When politically powerful people seize others' goods, the seizures may be labeled graft, licensing fees, taxation, or nationalization, depending on how they are justified. Our point is not that all such actions should be labeled "theft," but that theft, like murder and all other categories of crime, is an evaluative concept whose precise substantive meaning can be determined only by reference to particular cultures and legal systems.

The cultural relativity of crime is accepted by the substantial majority of contemporary sociologists and criminologists. Virtually none would allege that crime consists of transgressions of the revealed will of God, despite the prevalence of that view in the

Puritanical, Fundamentalist, and Talmudic religious traditions in which a good many Americans, including sociologists and criminologists, have been raised.[8] Some scholars accept, or at least are especially concerned with, Lombrosian theories that crime results from the physiological and mental aberrations of offenders. For most, however, the cultural relativity of crime is a fundamental assumption.[9] It is an assumption of this study also, and one of its implications is that direct comparisons of the levels of criminality across societies are of dubious validity. In fact few such comparisons are made here. Rather, we want to learn how each society's self-defined problems of criminality have changed over time. Such changes, in legal definitions and reports of crime, can be validly compared across societies in ways not applicable to "objective" behavior.

If definitions of crime vary with social and political circumstances, questions about the connection arise. There are two contending academic interpretations of the social origins of criminal law. One is that crime consists of acts that offend strong collective sentiments, that criminal law is the embodiment of moral consensus in a society. Criminal actions occur because individuals have not internalized social norms about proper behavior. In a recent statement of the functional view, Nettler says: "The criminal law . . . *expresses* moral beliefs, it *codifies* them, and it attempts to *enforce* them."[10] In the countervailing view, which is also the newer one, crime consists of acts that offend the perceptions and, especially, threaten the interests of powerful groups in society. Criminal law is the embodiment of the interests of elites, and criminal behavior is a manifestation of nonelite interests. There is an almost dialectical opposition between these two views, which Chambliss has labeled the "functional" and "conflict" theories of crime.[11] Unfortunately most of the research done in these two traditions assumes rather than tests the correctness of the interpretations. From an empirical point of view the accuracy and fruitfulness of the two interpretations surely varies among types of crime and among societies—and indeed they may be equally appropriate. Murder can threaten simultaneously the security of elites and the moral sensibilities of virtually everyone in society. And murder can be perpetrated by individuals who have an objective interest in revenge or gain through murder, although they would be dissuaded from the act if they were adequately socialized in the prevailing norms of society.

This study's assumptions about the nature of crime and criminal law derive from both the functional and conflict traditions. We said earlier that crime is a socially subjective phenomenon. In all societies some men commit assault and homicide, acquire goods by force or fraud, take drugs and alcohol, have extramarital intercourse, slander and disobey their rulers, and otherwise offend their neighbors' sensibilities. Crime is the Western label for acts that violate the norms of society's more influential members so seriously that the acts are legally prohibited and punishments are prescribed for those found guilty. "Deviance" is a somewhat larger and less distinct set of behaviors that violate widely held norms or morality but are not necessarily subject to formal prohibition.

In England, Sweden, and New South Wales, criminal law and prevailing norms appear to have been in approximate agreement about crimes of violence and acquisition, and probably about "serious" crime in general, for most of recent history. The generalization is less applicable to so-called victimless crimes. Influential people in these societies have repeatedly sought to impose standards of conduct on the consumption of alcohol and on gambling, prostitution, and public behavior that runs against the grain of common practice. Generally the moralistic elements have prevailed legally, but the apparent decline in most of the proscribed behaviors probably says more about selective enforcement and practical caution than it does about popular acceptance of legal standards.

In societies having diverse cultural groups, and also in highly stratified societies, conceptions of deviance may differ significantly from one group to another, hence have no close or necessary correspondence to criminality as legally defined. Thus legal definitions typically are a reflection of one group's views about unacceptable behavior. Calcutta can be characterized as such a society throughout most of its history, although more than two distinct groups have been involved and different elites have held power at different times.

In brief, it cannot be assumed a priori that the legal definitions of crime and the control policies used to implement these definitions reflect either social consensus or the interests of an elite. Each assumption presumes an answer to what should be a set of empirical questions about the degree of consensus in any given society on what disorder is, who is threatened by it, and what ought to be done about it. These are among the "political" questions that studies of this kind should address.

CONCEPTIONS OF CIVIL STRIFE

Whereas most crime is viewed with distaste even by the scholars who debate its nature, civil strife is the object of much more ambivalent social and academic attitudes. We mean by the latter overt, collective confrontations between contending groups in a society, including communal and political clashes, economic strikes, antigovernment riots and demonstrations, rebellions, revolutionary movements, and terrorist campaigns. This definition is more inclusive than most others in academic use because it includes nonviolent and nonpolitical strife such as strikes, but it raises few questions of interpretation or objective comparison.[12]

Unlike crime, which exists by reference to prevailing social conceptions and legal definitions, the collective events here labeled civil strife have an objective, behavioral reality: They involve open physical or symbolic combat between groups whose interests conflict. What is problematic about such events is not their reality but the valence of social attitude and political response toward them. Social attitudes toward civil strife depend on whose interests are being advanced or threatened by collective action: One group's "political violence" is another group's "legitimate protest."[13] Rulers' attitudes and response are more uniform, and most such occurrences in the societies we studied are or have been illegal and suppressed whenever they occurred, insofar as governments could suppress them.

The degree of acceptability and the legal status of civil strife nonetheless have changed significantly over time in the four cities, and so have its typical forms and rates of incidence. Strikes and demonstrations are common and widely accepted techniques for promoting group interests in all these societies in the second half of the twentieth century. But in the nineteenth century, when these forms of group action first became common, rulers feared them— sometimes with reason—as fundamental threats to social order, and strenuously attempted to suppress them. The transition from suppression to sufferance and compromise came about more or less rapidly and in quite different circumstances. In Sweden and New South Wales, for example, the urban working classes early and quickly gained political influence within the parliamentary system, and the view of economic strikes as essential and threatening did not long prevail. In Calcutta, by contrast, the strike and the demonstration were widely used in the twentieth century in the service of revolutionary goals, hence were suppressed as long as Bengal remained under colonial rule. That tradition persists in Calcutta, where political strikes and demonstrations are still more intense and ominous events than they are in the other three cities.

A potential for civil strife exists wherever group interests are in conflict, which means virtually everywhere. We make no assumptions about whether the condition is socially desirable or undesirable, though. The citizens and rulers of the four cities evidently have had divergent and changing views on that issue themselves. Thus it is important to determine how popular and official views of strife have changed over time, and under what circumstances. There are certain constants: "Revolutionary" acts of strife will always be anathema to elites and those who identify with them, whereas groups having no effective means to influence those who control their lives are likely to favor collective protest and attack more than those possessing some political power. What does change markedly over time is the extent to which particular kinds of strife become tolerated, and by whom.

THE MEANINGS OF DATA ON DISORDER

Civil strife being quite visible, its occurrence and approximate magnitude are easily detected in societies for which there are numerous official, journalistic, and historical sources. Problems arise mainly with respect to the bias and coverage of the source materials. There is seldom any doubt that reported events did happen, even though their true character may be distorted by the historical records. It also is likely that accounts of most socially consequential events in the four cities have found their way into the records we used.[14]

Unlike custodians of information on illiteracy, employment, hospital beds, tax receipts, and most other social indicators, those responsible for criminal acts seek to conceal data on crime. Admittedly the evidence of homicide is difficult to conceal, and the victims of burglary and robbery generally are aware that the crimes have occurred. Victims of theft do not necessarily report their losses to the police, though, and the much more numerous "victimless" crimes come to official attention only through active police surveillance. The clandestine nature of "crime as legally defined" is compounded by the selective attention given by police to certain kinds of offenders and offenses. Add to this the nonuniform practices of statistical bureaus and courts, and one has ample grounds for agreement with Daniel Bell's assertion that criminal statistics in the United States are about as reliable "as a woman giving her 'correct' age."[15] Presumably there is some correlation between women's self-reports and their true ages, which implies that self-reports (and crime statistics) can be used as indicators rather than precise measures of what they purport to be about. Austin Turk is representative of scholars who reject even this possibility. He dismisses "official crime statistics and data obtained from and about persons identified publicly as criminals" as "simply not directly relevant" for identifying and studying patterns of criminal behavior.[16]

Despite the extreme skepticism of some critics, the conventional approach to official crime statistics is to acknowledge the manifold sources of "error" in the processes by which they are generated, then to treat them as approximate indicators of objective criminal behavior. This is not entirely an act of faith. Various unofficial studies have been made of crimes of violence and acquisition, mostly in the United States but also in Britain. They include observation of delinquents, self-reports of criminal activity, and opinion surveys of victimization. When the results are compared with official statistics, it is evident that the latter substantially understate the total volume of criminal behavior by ratios from 2:1 to 10:1. But the comparisons also show that the *relative* frequency of crimes mentioned in victimization surveys corresponds closely to the *relative* frequency of crimes known to the police. Moreover, as Nettler concludes in a summary of such studies, "the social conditions associated with high rates of serious crimes known to the police are also, with some qualifications, associated with high rates of victimization."[17] In other words, the various sources of official and unofficial information on crimes of violence and acquisition all seem to reflect the same underlying behavioral realities.

According to Thorsten Sellin, the "best" kinds of official indicators are those which are closest to the source of crime from the standpoint of administrative procedure, that is, those based on reports of "crime known to police." Reported crimes will be fewer in number than the total of all criminal acts, but more numerous than arrests, and still more numerous than cases brought to trial and cases resulting in conviction. Data on some kinds of crime also are said to be much more accurate than data on others: Reports of homicides are thought to be more precise than reports of crime against property, and data on both are more accurate than reports of "victimless" crimes. More recent data are generally claimed to be more accurate than historical data because of standardization of reporting procedures. Data from some countries are said to be a good deal more reliable than data from others, given irregularities and inconsistencies in the processes by which crime information is categorized and summarized.[18] The principal authority on crime data in the United States has said that the country has collected "the worst crime statistics of any major country in the Western world,"[19] but Swedish consultants to this study claim that Swedish data on the subject are quite accurate.

Much of the debate over the "accuracy" of crime statistics results from attempts to assess the "true" extent of criminal behavior. Perhaps that is the wrong avenue to explore; certainly it seems to be the wrong issue to try to settle with official crime statistics. In this study we are concerned with two equally important questions, which are more readily answered with the data available. First, we are concerned with the extent of crime *as a social and political reality*. Hence we are especially interested in how much popular and official concern there is about crime, and how much public effort is directed at it. Table I.2.1 summarizes information on the availability, reliability, and meanings of data on criminality in Western societies. The column specifying the significance of the measures reveals that public and especially official concern are precisely the kinds of conditions most directly represented by the more widely available indicators of

Table I.2.1 Data and Indicators of Criminality in Western Societies

Data	Source	Availability of comparative data[a]	Prima facie significance of indicators[b]	Validity of information[c]
Criminal behavior	Self-reports	Scattered questionnaire studies, mostly in the U.S. after 1960, mostly of juveniles	Extent of individual criminal behavior	Honesty of respondents is doubtful, but self-reports show crime rates much higher than police records
Victimization	Surveys of victims	A few sample surveys, mostly in U.S. cities, after 1960	Impact of crime on ordinary citizens	Presumably good for victims of assault and theft; imply "true" crime rates two to ten times greater than police records
Crimes known to police	Police records	Reported for serious crimes in many Western societies beginning in mid- to late nineteenth century, for minor offenses somewhat later	Extent of citizen and police concern with crime	For crimes with victims, markedly influenced by citizen trust in police; for crimes without victims, a function of police surveillance; for both a function of recording systems
Arrests	Police records	Similar to above, "Crimes known to police"	Extent of police action against suspected criminals	Generally good but affected by recording and reported practices
Committals to trial	Higher court records	Serious crimes only, usually reported or knowable pre-1800[d]	Extent of official concern with serious crime	Good except where cases are shifted among jurisdictions or between higher and lower courts

Table I.2.1 (continued)

Court convictions	Higher court records	Same as above, "committals to trial"d	Extent of official sanctions against serious crime	Good
Cases disposed of summarily	Lower court records	Minor crimes only; not reported consistently until late nineteenth or early twentieth centuries	Extent of official sanctions against minor crime	Variable, affected by recording and reporting practices
Executions	Administrative records	Same as "Court convictions," above	Severity of official sanctions against crime	Excellent
Prison population	Administrative records	National and some local jurisdictions from late nineteenth century, some earlier data	Impact of sanctions on convicted criminals	Good in twentieth century, incomparable during much of 1800s because of extensive use of workhouses, transportation, etc.

a. These judgments are based on first-hand knowledge of the countries and cities studied, and selective reading of the literature, but they gloss over great differences among countries. In England and Wales the first national crime statistics, on committals to trial for serious offenses, were compiled beginning in 1805; detailed and comprehensive data are available after 1856. In the United States, which has lagged far behind most other Western nations in this regard, national compilation of "uniform" crime statistics dates only from 1933. Before that, data are available only for some states and cities, though certain of these series extend back into the eighteenth century.

b. This column suggests the simplest and most direct interpretation of indicators constructed from the comparative data. By "indicators" we mean aggregated data expressed as a ratio to population (e.g., "murders per 100,000").

c. "Validity" refers to the accuracy with which the indicators are likely to measure the conditions listed under "Prima facie significance."

d. The activities of higher courts before the introduction of national reporting systems can be determined by analysis of court records and reports. This laborious process has been carried out only in a few countries and jurisdictions.

crime. This is not a novel insight. Bloch used American data on delinquency to demonstrate that they index public and official attitudes at least as much as delinquent behavior,[20] and much of the critical and revisionist literature in criminology suggests that crime statistics reflect the interests of the public order system. It is remarkable that there have been so few attempts to act on that insight by analyzing what crime data signify about the concerns, norms, and practices of those who define and maintain public order.[21]

This does not imply that the "true" volume of criminal behavior can be ignored. Here we part company with the revisionist critics. Surely it is important to determine whether the nature and extent of real criminal behavior (as legally defined) affect the extent of public and official concern about crime. It is equally important to know whether policies designed to control disorder affect actual behavior, or only the sense of concern. The self-reporting and victimization surveys mentioned previously provide rather direct ways of ascertaining the extent of objective criminal behavior, but they are too new and few to permit us to say with certainty whether changes in behavior are accompanied by changes in public concern and official statistics. Thus despite the desirability of having direct information about the extent of criminal behavior, we must do without such data for the cities and eras studied here. Under some circumstances, though, it may be possible to draw valid inferences, not about the actual volume of criminal behavior, but about how it changes over time.

The second question of particular interest involves how problems of public order change over time. Given our argument about the social and political reality of crime, statistics on reported crime and arrests in most contemporary societies are, in effect, the reports of the social and political system to itself about the seriousness of self-defined problems of public order. As public concern mounts, more crimes are likely to be reported; and as police concern rises, so will patrolling and arrests. Similarly, changes in the extent of official insecurity are likely to show up in changing rates of committals for trial, convictions, and—depending on the time and place—the severity of sentences. Evidently there is a circular process in which increasing concern is likely to generate higher rates of reported crime, and the reports themselves substantially influence judgments about whether policies of public order are working or in need of revision, whether officials and public institutions are competent or incompetent, and ultimately whether society at large is "healthy" or "sick."[22] Crime statistics are thus both consequence and cause of public and official concern. This may be an intensely frustrating problem for those who want to know what changing crime rates "really" mean; but for our

purposes changes in crime statistics—especially large changes—
become a telling indicator of changes in the magnitude of public
order problems and of changes in policies for dealing with them.

We have made the point that the relation between the true extent
of crime and public concern about crime is unknowable in most
present and all past circumstances. But that does not mean that
changes in the two are unrelated. It is plausible, in fact, that within
any given society an approximate interrelation exists between
changes in public concern and in criminal behavior. As particularly
threatening behavior increases in frequency, for example, concern
and official reaction are likely to increase, perhaps slowly at first,
then more rapidly than the behavior itself. Concern about crime can
grow independently of behavioral change, of course, but when this
happens increased official action will probably follow, having the
effect of "creating" more criminal behavior by legal definition and
labeling. The basic point is still valid: The extent of criminal behavior
is likely to vary over time in approximate relation to public and
official concern about criminality. Therefore the *trends* in crime
statistics are revealing about criminal behavior in ways that statistics
for one point in time cannot be. Since changes in concern and
behavior exert mutual effects only gradually, the interpretation of
year-to-year changes in crime statistics is problematic. Trends of five
to ten years' duration and longer are much more significant. Directly
they tell of changes in public and official concern; indirectly they
may permit inferences about the direction of change in criminal
behavior.

These interpretations of crime statistics assume that the data are
generated by police and courts which are mainly concerned with
controlling criminal behavior. The assumption is warranted for the
three Western cities in the study; it is not valid for Calcutta in the
twentieth century. During the last 40 years of British rule in Bengal,
and during the decades since independence in 1947, Calcutta
was swept by recurring episodes of intense political, economic, and
communal strife that posed far graver threats to public order than
ordinary crime. Under these pressures the police and courts gave less
and less attention to crime and in several periods seem to have
virtually ceased operations. The fluctuations of reported crime in
Calcutta in the twentieth century reveal much about official concern
with crime, but not in the usual way: The rulers were distracted by
larger crises that threatened their very survival. Calcutta illustrates a
general point: Crime statistics generated by effective institutions
under "normal" social conditions mean one thing, statistics generated by decaying institutions under conditions of crisis usually
mean something quite different.

CATEGORIES AND INDICATORS OF DISORDER

Whatever conceptual meaning is imputed to official data on crime and punishment, any effort to compare and contrast the data across time and among cities encounters a host of technical problems. One set of problems concerns categorization of different kinds of criminal behavior: Should it be done at all, and if so, how? A more fundamental matter is the comprehensiveness and reliability of the data available for the four cities. Whatever data are available can be compared over time only when weighted by population, which poses fresh problems related to the availability and accuracy of demographic data. Brief diagnoses of these problems follow, and our approaches to each are sketched.

Categories of Crime

Different kinds of criminal behavior inspire different degrees of concern and are differentially policed and reported; therefore they must be compared separately. The criminal codes of the four societies furnish one possible point of departure. They are in substantial agreement in their formal definitions of criminal behavior, which reflect the common cultural heritage of the three Western cities and the historical and political circumstance that Australian and Indian criminal codes descend from English common law. There are indigenous accretions and adaptations, especially in Indian law, but its basic framework remains English. There are two prohibitive barriers to employing the official categories for comparisons as given. One is their sheer number and detail. In the 1890s crime in London was reported and prosecuted under 149 specific categories organized under seven more general headings, and the criminal code of New South Wales was equally detailed. There is little if any reason to compare the relative incidence of most of the specific categories. The fine Anglo-Australian distinction between "rogue" and "notorious rogue," for example, surely makes or made no difference except to the handful of unfortunate scoundrels relegated to the latter category. And it is of some intrinsic but no comparative interest that nineteenth century New South Welshmen could be prosecuted if found "wandering with Aborigines," or that the crime returns from the London Metropolitan Police District in the early years of Queen Victoria's reign list the unique offense of "presenting a pistol at Her Majesty the Queen with intent to alarm her."

Similar and overlapping categories can always be combined for analytic purposes. The more serious problem is that categories have been repeatedly and inconsistently combined, divided, and recombined for administrative convenience in each city. New categories of offenses are defined, and old ones lapse into desuetude or are subsumed by other categories. Some categories are shuffled from one general heading to another, while the headings themselves undergo subtle and sometimes dramatic changes of scope. Generally the categories according to which crime is reported and prosecuted vary more widely within each city than among them. This tendency can be most instructive about the evolving interests and concerns of the officials who create the data, but it raises hob with systematic study of trends.[23]

Our approach has been to distinguish four general types of offenses that subsume most of the more detailed categories used in crime reports. In a few analyses all types of crime within each general category are aggregated; usually, though, comparisons are made using more specific subcategories within each. The general categories are as follows.

1. Crimes of aggression, including murder and attempts, woundings, and assault. Where official statistics permit, and they usually do, the offenses of rape, abortion, and assault in the course of robbery are excluded from this general category.

2. Crimes of acquisition, including all illegal means of acquiring money and property. White-collar crimes such as fraud and embezzlement are analyzed separately from common theft. Three different forms of theft also are distinguished in the criminal codes of the societies studied here, and in some of our analyses. In increasing order of seriousness, they are larceny, burglary, and robbery. A number of less common property offenses such as counterfeiting and receiving stolen goods are included in aggregate measures of crimes of acquisition.

3. Crimes against morality and custom include both sexual offenses and various "victimless crimes." [24] The offenses of sexual assault, deviance, and prostitution are treated as one subset of these crimes, drunkenness as another. Also under this heading we put vagrancy, gambling, and other behaviors thought to be disorderly, nonproductive, or otherwise offensive to prevailing standards of public conduct. Since the latter activities are so diverse, they are considered separately, if at all, rather than in the aggregate.

4. Crimes against public order include such instances of overt resistance to authorities as rioting, assaults on police and other officials, and prohibited political activities. Serious political offenses of this kind are rare in all the cities. In some of the cities violations of administrative regulations also are analyzed separately from offenses that are specifically political.

Several points need to be made about these general categories. First, they are not absolutely distinct, either in concept or application. Drunks resisting arrest may be found guilty of attacking police (category 4) or merely disorderly conduct (category 3), depending on the mores and procedures of the day and place. On the other hand it can be assumed that the first two general categories, crimes of aggression and acquisition, refer to quite similar kinds of objectively defined behavior in all four cities.[25] Second, some of our analyses distinguish between more and less serious offenses of each general category. Offenses that are dealt with by higher courts were and are "serious" by prevailing official definition, but those dealt with summarily can usually be assumed to be "minor." There is no particular consistency within or among cities about which offenses are treated in which way, and specific cases may be processed one way or the other depending on circumstance. We employ no "objective" definition of serious crime; rather, the measures of serious crime reflect prevailing official views about which kinds of offenses, and which offenders, are important enough to require the full and expensive attention of prosecutors, courts, and juries.[26]

Availability of Data

Before this study could begin, it was necessary to be sure that sufficient usable data on disorder could be found for the cities. Some general observations are summarized in Table I.2.1; more specific information is given in Table I.2.2. Data available for the early nineteenth century refer only or mainly to criminal cases committed to trial in the highest courts. Thus they provide an index to concern among the elites about "serious" crime, but no direct information about the extent of public concern with crime or the overall volume of official efforts to maintain order. Information on crimes known to the police and arrests begins to be reported later in the century, usually in summary fashion at first, then with increasing detail. Cases tried summarily—by magistrates, police courts, or their equivalents— were first reported at about the same time as arrests. These different kinds of data are subject to somewhat different interpretations, as suggested in Table I.2.1. When most or all data are available for the same period, as they are for more than a century in some instances, their variations can be compared over time. This kind of comparison gives information about the complex interactions among criminal behavior, public concern, and official action that could never be inferred from the analysis of the measures separately.

Most information on civil strife is found in narrative form and is not readily reduced to quantitative indicators. One exception is information on strikes, including number of incidents, participants, and working days lost. Official data on the subject have been compiled annually in the twentieth century for all Britain, though not for London separately, and for New South Wales. In our research more or less consistent information on strikes was compiled from various

Table I.2.2 The Availability of Principal Data Series on Crime and Strikes in the Four Cities[a]

Type of data	London[b]	Stockholm	Sydney[c]	Calcutta[d]
Crimes reported or known to police	1858-1974	1841-1971	1952-1970	1800-1971
Arrests	1857-1931, 1947-1974	—	1879-1893, 1914-1970	1871-1958
Accused/committed to trial	1820-1974	1841-1947	1811-1824, 1859-1971	1871-1971
Convictions for indictable crimes or higher court cases	1820-1974	1830-1951	1811-1971	1871-1971
Convictions for lesser offenses or cases disposed of summarily	1857-1913 1949-1974	1841-1951	1879-1893, 1914-1970	1920-1958
Strikes	1893-1974	1901-1970	1912-1970	1920-1958

a. These are the maximum periods for which data could be obtained for this study. Data are missing for some years in some series. Few series are precisely comparable over time because of changes in jurisdiction and procedure, scope and detail of coverage, and definition of categories of offenses.

b. Crime data are for the County of Middlesex (including the City of London), 1820-1873; and for the Metropolitan Police District (excluding the City of London) ca. 1857-1974. Strike data are for all Britain. After 1931 the statistics on higher court activities are total cases only. Data on summary drunkenness and prostitution offenses are available for longer periods than other classes of data.

c. Data for New South Wales. Statistics on convictions for lesser offenses were not used in this study.

d. Data before 1870 include fragmentary statistics for all Bengal from East India Company reports from 1800 to 1840 and data for Calcutta for eighteen years between 1840 and 1870. Data for the early 1940s are missing.

sources, mainly official ones, for Stockholm and Calcutta.

Cities have long been the seats of higher courts as well as a principal source of the courts' business, and the first modern police forces were established in response to distinctly urban problems of order. Thus one consideration that influenced our initial focus on cities, rather than on regions or entire nations, was the expectation that they would provide earlier and more reliable information on crime and public order.[27] This expectation was borne out. Quite unexpectedly, however, crime data for Calcutta, London, and Stockholm in recent decades are sparser than they were half a century ago. For Calcutta the detailed reports appear not to have been published after the late 1950s, and only summary data are published in national sources—the most useful, *Crime in India,* being restricted to official use. In London, fiscal constraints imposed by the Depression and the policies of a new commissioner of police, led to the sharp curtailment of public reporting of criminal and judicial statistics after 1931. More complete data were published beginning in 1947, but the reporting of data on trials and convictions for various offense categories has never been resumed. Such statistics are reported at the county and national level, but the Metropolitan Police District data are thereby comingled with those of several counties. Something similar happens to crime data on Stockholm beginning in the 1950s: After this time the data are less detailed than previously, and statistics on convictions have not been reported since the early 1960s. One partial explanation is that officials in both Sweden and Britain are more concerned with recording and dealing with crime on a nation-wide basis than on an urban scale.[28]

Cities and Other Jurisdictions

A deceptively difficult problem in this kind of study is matching crime and population data. Since we want to identify and diagnose changes in the relative incidence of reported crime, the raw data in official reports must be weighted by population.[29] The available data on population and crime do not always refer to the same social entity, however, and we often have had to settle for measures that refer to something other than "the city" as conventionally defined.[30] The subjects we portray statistically have been defined for us by the scope of the available data—that is, data from jurisdictions that do not necessarily or consistently coincide with the administrative or demographic boundaries of urban areas. Each city poses a somewhat different set of matching problems.

London: London has had no single administrative boundary for most of its history. Our data for crime and population prior to 1869 refer to the County of Middlesex, which at the beginning of the century included substantial rural and suburban areas but excluded the urban concentration south of the Thames. By the 1830s the demographic city had spread well beyond the boundaries of Middlesex, and the new Metropolitan Police District (MPD) reflected one administrative conception of the city's boundaries. After 1869 the data used here refer to the MPD, which has continued to expand more or less in concert with urban sprawl. The MPD notably excludes the City of London (the financial district), which historically has been separately policed, or unpoliced. The City has had a small and shrinking population during the last century, never more than two percent of the people living in the MPD.

Stockholm: The data on crime and population in Stockholm refer throughout the nineteenth and twentieth centuries to the city as administratively defined; but the administrative boundaries have changed over time and have consistently excluded many suburbs (until 1971, when the first steps were taken toward an integrated administration of the City and County of Stockholm). In 1968, for example, administrative Stockholm included only 59 percent of the population of Greater Stockholm as statistically defined; the remaining 41 percent were outside the scope of the data on crime that we use here.

Calcutta: The estimates of Calcutta's population are not particularly reliable at any time. That uncertainty compounds another imprecision: For much of the nineteenth century the crime reports referred mainly to the town of Calcutta, but the population estimates included suburbs. Moreover the judicial statistics apparently included cases from elsewhere in Bengal. Viewed in light of the limited and selective scope of Western institutions of public order in Calcutta, though, these problems fade in significance. We mentioned earlier, moreover, that in the twentieth century the exigencies of civil conflict have recurrently preoccupied the police. Crime data for Calcutta thus are mainly a function of the scope of police activities within some rather small but not constant segment of the city's enormous, sprawling population. Far from helping to quantify criminal behavior, they may not even be a good indicator of official concern—because other matters weigh so heavily that crime is of relatively little moment.[31]

Sydney: Sydney was founded in 1788, and its population is known with reasonable accuracy from that date; but the police and judicial statistics for the city as administratively defined proved far too scant for our purposes. Our solution has been to use data on crime and population for New South Wales in its entirety. Sydney is and always has been the metropole and administrative capital of the colony, later state, as well as the hub of its commercial and cultural activity; thus it is reasonable to assume that patterns of crime in New South Wales are those of Sydney writ large. Still, in demographic terms the population of metropolitan Sydney has comprised as little as 25 percent of the state's population (in the 1850s) and as much as 60 percent (in 1970).

This chapter has reviewed some implications of different conceptions of crime and strife for the comparative study of public disorder. We also have reported our views about the prospects and pitfalls of constructing comparative measures of crime, and the interpretations which can and cannot be put on them. Readers may not agree with our interpretations and solutions, but at least they know what principles guided our research and analyses.

NOTES TO CHAPTER I.2

1. Abdul Q. Lodhi and Charles Tilly, "Urbanization, Crime, and Collective Violence in 19th Century France," *American Journal of Sociology*, 79 (September 1973), 296-318. The study does not examine the more plausible possibility that crime and collective violence are correlated over time within particular cities or departments, perhaps for want of sufficient data.

2. F. Solomon et al., "Civil Rights Activity and Reduction in Crime Among Negroes," *Archives of General Psychiatry*, 12 (March 1965), 227-236.

3. William J. Chambliss, *Functional and Conflict Theories of Crime* (New York: MSS Modular Publications, 1974, Module 17), derives a Marxist theory of crime from the same premises used by Marxists to account for group conflict. Two major functionalist statements about the origins of crime and collective behavior are, respectively, Emile Durkheim, "Crime as Normal Behavior," in David Dressler, ed., *Readings in Criminology and Penology* (New York: Columbia University Press, 1972), an extract from Durkheim's *The Division of Labor in Society* (New York: Free Press, 1949); and Talcott Parsons, "Certain Primary Sources and Patterns of Aggression in the Social Structure of the Western World," in Lyman Bryson et al., eds., *Conflicts of Power in Modern Culture* (New York: Conference on Science, Philosophy, and Religion, Seventh Symposium, 1947).

4. The example is cited by E. Adamson Hoebel, "Plains Indian Law in Development: The Comanche," in Donald Cressey and David Ward, eds., *Delinquency, Crime and Social Process* (New York: Harper & Row, 1969).

5. Herbert Bloch, *Disorganization: Personal and Social* (New York: Knopf, 1952), p. 258.

6. Jerome Michael and Mortimer Adler, *Crime, Law and Social Science* (New York: Harcourt, 1933), p. 2.

7. Gwynn Nettler, *Explaining Crime* (New York: McGraw-Hill, 1974), pp. 2-5.

8. On the religious foundations of law among the Puritans and Hebrews see, respectively, George Haskins, *Law and Authority in Early Massachusetts* (New York: Macmillan, 1960) and Hyman Goldin, *Hebrew Criminal Law and Procedure* (New York: Twayne, 1952).

9. The most influential exponent of biological theories of criminality was Cesare Lombroso (1835-1909); see his *Crime: Its Causes and Remedies* (Boston: Little, Brown, 1911). His original argument that criminals are throwbacks to our primitive ancestors is still influential in Mediterranean and Latin American criminology. One contemporary manifestation of the biological approach in North America and northern Europe is the search for genetic "flaws" in

perpetrators of crimes of violence. For reviews of the biological approach, in its historical and contemporary manifestations, see Hermann Mannheim, *Comparative Criminology* (Boston: Houghton Mifflin, 1965), chs. 12 and 13, and Donald Mulvilhill and Melvin Tumin, *Crimes of Violence, Report to the National Commission on the Causes and Prevention of Violence*, vol. 12 (Washington, D.C.: Government Printing Office, 1969), ch. 7. The biological and cultural approaches are not mutually exclusive because factors of both kinds may influence criminal behavior. Our view is that the cultural and situational factors so modify the biological factors that the latter have little independent explanatory power.

10. Nettler, op. cit., p. 36. She adds the obvious qualification that the relation between criminal law and a people's moral beliefs is imprecise and changes over time.

11. This characterization of functional and conflict theories is drawn from Chambliss, op. cit.

12. There are well-established research traditions in political science and sociology for the collection and comparison of data on collective actions that are variously labeled "collective" or "political" violence, "conflict" or "instability" events. The terms are not used pejoratively but to denote sets of empirically similar occurrences. For a brief survey of this research through 1971 see T. R. Gurr, "The Calculus of Civil Conflict," *Journal of Social Issues*, 28 (No. 1, 1972). There is a parallel tradition for the comparative study of strikes; see, for example, Arthur M. Ross and George W. Hartmann, *Changing Patterns of Industrial Conflict* (New York: Wiley, 1960), and Douglas A. Hibbs, Jr., *Industrial Conflict in Advanced Industrial Societies* (Cambridge: Center for International Studies, MIT, 1974). The term "civil strife" here refers to all such occurrences, whereas elsewhere the first author has used it to refer to a somewhat less inclusive set of events; see "A Comparative Study of Civil Strife," in Hugh Davis Graham and T. R. Gurr, eds., *Violence in America: Historical and Comparative Perspectives, A Report to the National Commission on the Causes and Prevention of Violence* (New York: Praeger and Bantam Books, 1969), ch. 17.

13. There is heated academic and social debate about the labeling of such phenomena and especially about the theoretical uses and normative implications of the term "political violence." Two of the less muddled commentaries on the controversy are Terry Nardin, *Violence and the State: A Critique of Empirical Political Theory* (Beverly Hills, Calif.: Sage Professional Papers in Comparative Politics, no. 020, 1971), and Kenneth W. Grundy and Michael A. Weinstein, *The Ideologies of Violence* (Columbus: Merrill, 1974). The more neutral and comprehensive term "civil strife" is used in this study to avoid the appearance of normative judgment.

14. Contemporary studies of civil strife have revealed that the number and types of events identified vary markedly according to the journalistic source used; see Charles R. Doran et al., "A Test of Cross-National Event Reliability: Global Versus Regional Data Sources," *International Studies Quarterly*, 17 (June 1973), 175-204. The four city studies rely on a variety of historical sources, but they cannot be assumed to be absolutely comprehensive. We found virtually no references to civil strife in Calcutta during the nineteenth century, for example,

and this seems somewhat unlikely in view of its turbulent twentieth century history. Nineteenth century Stockholm, according to standard histories, was also a relatively peaceful city except for a few politically consequential riots and demonstrations. Archival research by Leif Persson and Sven Sperlings for this study, however, produced evidence of many small-scale riots and brawls between citizens and police or soldiers.

15. Daniel Bell, "The Myth of Crime Waves," in *The End of Ideology* (New York: Free Press, 1960), p. 157, cited in Herbert A. Bloch and Gilbert Geis, *Man, Crime, and Society: The Forms of Criminal Behavior* (New York: Random House, 1962), p. 164.

16. Turk, op. cit., p. 8.

17. Nettler, op. cit., ch. 4, quotation from p. 72.

18. See Bloch and Geis' useful review of evidence on "The Extent of Crime," Part 3 in *Man, Crime, and Society*. Other general discussions include Fred P. Graham, "A Contemporary History of American Crime," in Graham and Gurr, eds., *Violence in America*, ch. 13; and ch. 2, "American Criminal Statistics: An Explanation and Appraisal," in Mulvilhill and Tumin, *Crimes of Violence*, vol. 11. All these appraisals are concerned almost exclusively with crime data from North America. A general commentary on the sources, uses, and limitations of criminal statistics with special reference to Britain, is Mannheim, *Comparative Criminology*, chp. 5. The accuracy of British historical statistics on the subject has been heatedly debated. J. J. Tobias, *Crime and Industrial Society in the Nineteenth Century* (London: Batsford, 1967), categorically dismisses most nineteenth century English crime statistics. V. A. C. Gatrell and T. B. Hadden, who have made much more systematic use of those data than Tobias, conclude that they are very informative, especially about characteristics of offenders and trends in crime, in "Criminal Statistics and Their Interpretation," E. A. Wrigley, ed., *Nineteenth Century Society* (Cambridge: The University Press, 1972), pp. 336-396. The adequacy of contemporary Australian data on crime is discussed in Paul Wilson and J. Brown, *Crime and the Community* (St. Lucia: University of Queensland Press, 1973).

19. Thorsten Sellin, quoted by Fred P. Graham, "A Contemporary History."

20. Herbert A. Bloch, "Juvenile Delinquency: Myth or Threat?" *Journal of Criminal Law*, 49 (November-December, 1958), 303-309.

21. One of a class of exceptions is Turk's analysis of United States crime data with reference to what they imply about differences between the norms enforced by officials and the norms of various population groups, in ch. 5 of *Criminality and Legal Order*.

22. An important qualification is that public and elite concern about crime often increases in response, not to crime rates per se, but to the widely publicized occurrence of a few particularly dramatic acts. Our research on Sydney offered a number of examples. Moreover the importance of crime statistics evidently varies among societies. Where there are autocratic elites and repressive institutions, such data serve mainly a self-monitoring function for officials responsible for maintaining order and, as in the Soviet Union, they may never be made public. In more open societies they have more widespread impact, public and private.

23. An example is provided by the difficulties of tracing the changing incidence of murder in Stockholm over an extended period. From 1841 to 1886 reported murders are aggregated in official reports with manslaughter and attempted murder. Between 1886 and 1909 the problem is compounded by the inclusion of infanticide. After 1910 the reports distinguish among all three kinds

of offenses plus a fourth, procuring abortion. The judicial statistics on convictions, however, are aggregated quite differently. Convictions for attempted murder, murder, and manslaughter combined are reported from 1830 through 1909; convictions for infanticide and procuring abortion are separately reported until 1878, then in combination until 1912. After 1912, however, convictions for all four offenses are reported in a summary annual figure, without breakdowns. The sources are various administrative and statistical reports of the city government.

24. The concept of victimless crime makes some social sense when restricted to illegal sexual acts between consenting adults and to the use of mild narcotics and stimulants. But it is appallingly callous to apply this characterization to alcoholism, drug addiction, chronic gambling, and prostitution. The personal and social costs for most of the individuals involved are high indeed. A pressing social issue in Western societies is whether such people ought to be treated as criminals or as victims in need of help.

25. This is not to say that the magnitudes of such behaviors can therefore be compared directly, only that the offenses as legally defined and reported are similar.

26. For much of the nineteenth century there are data only on serious offenses (i.e., on those processed by the higher courts). Therefore comparisons of crime data over the very long run usually must be limited to "serious" offenses.

27. Almost all the historical studies of the subject in the United States have had an urban focus.

28. The official sources of data on crime and punishment are cited in the city studies.

29. Few of the official sources used in these studies report rates of crime (i.e., numbers of offenses per 10,000 or 100,000 population). All rates used are our calculation, which raises questions about the reliability of population estimates. At least such estimates are better than the raw data on crime because they are more easily determined, hence more accurate, and because there are no obvious reasons for error in them to be systematic (i.e., consistently higher or lower than the correct figures).

Throughout this study we follow the conventional practice of calculating rates by weighting crime data by total population, even though rates of reported crime vary widely among sex, age, and class groups. Sometimes data on the demographic characteristics of offenders are known. But such data are reported too rarely and inconsistently for us to use them for systematic comparisons over time.

30. Conventional definitions of cities refer to the concentration and spatial distribution of population. In the academic literature they are widely modified by reference to such variables as lifeways and patterns of interaction. Charles Tilly offers a good review of different approaches to the definition of communities and cities in *An Urban World* (Boston: Little, Brown, 1974), pp. 18-31.

31. Similar interpretations might conceivably be made of crime data from the other cities, especially in the nineteenth century. The difference is that in Calcutta no other interpretation is plausible.

Part II

LONDON: THE POLITICS OF

CRIME AND CONFLICT,

1800 TO THE 1970s

David Peirce
Peter N. Grabosky
Ted Robert Gurr

AUTHORS' NOTE: The first two chapters are principally the work of the first author, who also collected most of the crime statistics used in the study. The second author prepared the discussion of institutions of public order in the third and fourth chapters, incorporating materials provided by the first author. The third author is principally responsible for the discussions of crime in Chapters II.2 through II.4, the analysis of civil conflict in Chapters II.3 and II.4, and the concluding chapter. He also revised the manuscript in its entirety.

The larger study of which this is part was supported by a grant from the Center for the Study of Crime and Delinquency, National Institute of Mental Health. Portions of the first author's research were done during his tenure as a Samuel Andrew Stouffer Fellow at the Joint Center for Urban Studies of the Massachusetts Institute of Technology and Harvard University, funding provided by the Ford Foundation. The third author completed his work on the study while supported by a Common Problems Fellowship provided by the German Marshall Fund of the United States.

A number of libraries and other institutions have been exceptionally helpful to us in this work. Particularly intensive use has been made of collections at the British Museum, Harvard University, the University of Illinois, New Scotland Yard, Northwestern University, and the Radzinowicz Library at the Institute of Criminology, University of Cambridge. Her Majesty's Stationery Office has permitted us to study and cite documents at the Public Record Office.

The manuscript has benefited from helpful comments by Nigel D. Walker and David Thomas of the Institute of Criminology, though they bear no responsibility for our conclusions. Thanks also are due to Bruce H. Bank, G. Roland Peirce, Mary Elizabeth Peirce, and Rick Poore for assistance in coding data; to Anne Credicott, David Credicott, and Tina Peterson for undertaking quantitative analysis of these data; to Erika Gurr for preparing the figures; and to Margaret Guy, for typing the final manuscript.

THE DIMENSIONS OF LONDON
LIFE, 1800 TO THE 1970s

If modern London has one outstanding characteristic, it is size. By 1800 it was by virtually any definition, a metropolis rather than merely a large city. Certainly it was the largest urban area in Europe, having twice the population of Paris, its only rival. In fact, it probably contained more people than any other city in the world for most of the nineteenth century.[1] More significant than the size of its population, however, was London's preeminent position in the global polity and economy for much of our period. Until 1941 it was *the* world city; and despite the twentieth century eclipse of its previous position of dominance—an eclipse due in the main to the decline of British fortunes in world affairs—London remains a metropolis of worldwide importance.

From the time of its establishment as a major center of the Roman occupation of Britain nearly 2,000 years ago, London has continued to take advantage of its geographical position on the Thames estuary to remain a leading commercial entrepôt. And after the City of Westminster became the seat of English government during the later Middle Ages, London ceased to have any rivals among English cities. In the wake of the Black Death in the fourteenth century and the political instability of the fifteenth century London became a demographic magnet, continually augmenting its own importance—a process almost without interruption to the present day.

But London has been in recent centuries much more than a large collection of people. In a sense it can be viewed as the model for all other metropolitan areas. In no way does it conform to the pattern of Sjoberg's preindustrial city. As early as the seventeenth century London was the center of a market system much more sophisticated and complex than those existing in other Western societies. The demand for food and other essential commodities generated by the huge urban population necessitated an adequate transport system and may have been the most significant cause of the agricultural improvements that economists have regarded as a precondition to British industrialization. In contrast to most other cities of the time, London in the seventeenth and eighteenth centuries had become a dynamic force for social change.[2] The city also was a potent influence in English political and cultural life, even at this early date. It has been argued, with considerable statistical justification, that the Industrial Revolution occurred first in Britain because the preindustrial British economy was already highly developed by the mid-eighteenth century.[3] In an analogous fashion, London became the first world city not simply by virtue of its great population but because by 1800 its economic and social dynamism was internalized and self-perpetuating.

Given the size and complexity of London, which was apparent even by 1800, it would be foolhardy to attempt in one chapter a chronology of London's development in the last two centuries. Instead this chapter describes several aspects of London life that seem most relevant to a study of crime and public order: the evolving demographic, social, and economic characteristics of London society.

LONDON'S CHANGING POPULATION

London's immense size, impressive though it may be, has not been considered a virtue by all commentators. In the early nineteenth century Cobbett summed up the matter when he referred to the metropolis as a great wen. Urban planners of the twentieth century, while considerably more verbose, are hardly less disparaging and at least as pessimistic in their forecasts of urban growth and its attendant problems. At least four centuries ago there were attempts to limit metropolitan sprawl. Elizabeth I, the most resourceful of the Tudor monarchs, had been appalled when the City of London contained a mere 150,000 souls.[4] Her ministers were successful in passing legislation that prohibited immigration and new building in London. Enforcing the law was another matter, however, and the project had to be abandoned after a few years. London's growth was impervious even to the forces of disease and death, and it flourished despite a major outbreak of plague in 1665 and the Great Fire in the following year.[5] The most recent estimates of London's population growth in the seventeenth and eighteenth centuries (Table II.1.1) show a staggering rate of increase.

Although the tabulated estimates of London's growth in the

Table II.1.1 Estimated Population of London, 1600-1800

Year	Population
1600	200,000
1650	400,000
1700	575,000
1750	675,000
1800	900,000

Source: E.A. Wrigley, "A Simple Model of London's Importance in Changing English Society and Economy, 1650-1970", Past and Present, 37 (1967), 44.

Table II.1.2 London's Population, 1801-1971

Year	Middlesex	Greater London	Metropolitan Police District
1801	818,000	1,117,000	
1811	954,000	1,327,000	
1821	1,145,000	1,600,000	
1831	1,358,000	1,907,000	1,524,000
1841	1,577,000	2,239,000	2,117,000
1851	1,887,000	2,685,000	2,563,000
1861	2,206,000	3,227,000	3,119,000
1871	2,540,000	3,890,000	3,808,000
1881	2,920,000	4,770,000	4,789,000
1891	3,252,000	5,638,000	5,714,000
1901		6,586,000	6,679,000
1911		7,256,000	7,321,000
1921		7,488,000	7,462,000
1931		8,216,000	8,183,000
1941			6,282,000
1951		8,348,000	8,350,000
1961		8,183,000	8,151,000
1971		7,393,000	7,903,000

Sources: Brian Mitchell and Phyllis Deane, Abstract of British Historical Statistics (Cambridge: Cambridge University Press, 1962); Brian Mitchell and G.I. Jones, Second Abstract of British Historical Statistics (Cambridge: Cambridge University Press, 1971); Annual Reports of the Commissioner of the Metropolitan Police, published in the Parliamentary Papers and separately; and Census of England and Wales, 1891 and 1971.

precensus era are tentative, they correspond with available sources, and they reflect the general conclusions of historical demographers about the demographic revolution that antedated the Industrial Revolution. A fundamental contributor to modern history is the phenomenal increase of Europe's population that began in the early eighteenth century. Europe's population doubled in the century after 1750; in Britain the increase was still greater. By 1851 England and Wales had nearly eighteen million inhabitants, more than twice the population of 1801. The causes of this population explosion have

been hotly debated. Contrary to the conclusions of previous scholarship, it is now widely held that earlier marriages and a rising birthrate, rather than a declining death rate, and the introduction of new
elements into the diet (such as the potato), not improved medical
and public health techniques, account for much of the initial impetus
for the demographic revolution.[6]

Whatever the initial causes of the population increase, one consequence was evident: there was an extraordinary rise in the number of
people living in London. In less than two centuries (1800-1974) the
metropolitan population increased tenfold, rising at a much faster
rate than the national totals (Table II.1.2 and Figure II.1.1). The
official figures are somewhat misleading, particularly in the twentieth
century, for the metropolitan area has expanded well beyond traditional boundaries such as the Registrar General's definition of

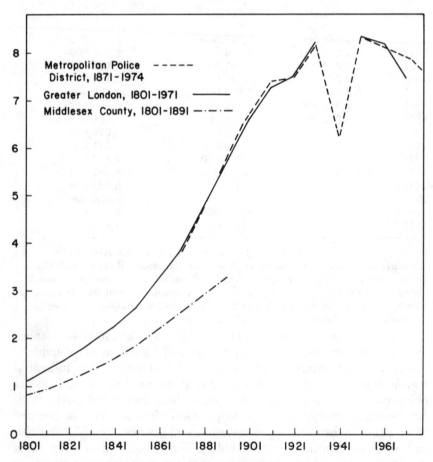

Figure II.1.1 London: Population in millions, 1801-1974

"Greater London" or the Metropolitan Police District (roughly contiguous areas). A geographer recently commented: "The Metropolitan Police District was a suitable basis for a definition of Greater London in 1901 but it was not appropriate in 1951, for it was already inadequate."[7]

Thus the decline of the growth rate in the mid-twentieth century, as revealed by the official census figures, is based on an antiquated definition of the metropolitan area. A slowdown in growth during World War I and a substantial decline in population during World War II were due to temporary wartime dislocations of population and the absence of adults in military service. It is clear, however, that London's growth rate is lower now than it was during most of the nineteenth century.[8]

Apart from sheer size, the demographic pattern of London in the last two centuries has other relevant properties. The most important is the extent of migration to the metropolis. Migration was a major factor in the city's growth during the first half of the nineteenth century, when abysmal living standards and the ravages of epidemic disease led to mortality rates that far exceeded fertility. The 1831 census shows that the death rate for children under five in Middlesex during the previous decade was 37 percent. And in 1861, 40 percent of those living in London had been born elsewhere.[9] The fact is that the demographic revolution, the huge surplus of births over deaths, was largely a rural occurrence in its initial phases, and the astonishing growth of cities in that period was due to migration from the countryside.[10] London, like other large cities, drew most of its migrants from the immediately surrounding counties in short-distance movements, but there also existed a long-distance pulling power:

> The migration into London had been affected in some measure by special migrations from all the great manufacturing and commercial centres; but the general characteristics of the movement remained the same as for the other great towns. A very great number of people had come from the extra-metropolitan parts of Middlesex and Surrey; there had also been strong migration from Kent, Essex, Hertford, and Berkshire.... The counties to the north-west ... sent a relatively small proportion of people to London; but the attractive force of the capital city was felt in every part of the United Kingdom.[11]

This migration into the metropolis was accompanied by an internal demographic movement that even in the nineteenth century could be called a suburban trend. The City of London, the ancient

center of the metropolis, was the first to feel its effects. In the early
nineteenth century the City's population had remained relatively
constant, but by the 1850s it was rapidly declining numerically as
well as proportionally, as Table II.1.3 indicates.

Table II.1.3. Population of the City of London

Year	Population
1801	128,129
1841	123,563
1881	50,569
1921	13,709

Source: *The Encyclopaedia Britannica*, 14th ed.
(New York: Encyclopaedia Britannica, 1929), Vol. 14,
p. 355.

This development in urban life did not go unnoticed by contemporaries; the Royal Commission on Municipal Corporations (1837)
noted:

> . . . an advance in the City's prosperity might render land more valuable
> for warehouses, and therefore drive out the poorer population. It is also to
> be observed that much of the importance of the City arises from its being
> the daily resort of great numbers who, as they do not actually sleep in it,
> are not strictly a part of its population; and the prevalence of this habit
> has been continually on the increase during the present century.[12]

This process has continued unabated. By the early twentieth century
most census registration districts in the central area were declining
fairly rapidly.[13] In fact, the trend to suburbanization has been so
pronounced that the standard definitions of the metropolitan area
have long ceased to reflect the demographic and economic reality of
modern London.

A second noteworthy aspect of London's population structure is
its changing ethnic composition. For most of the last 175 years the
population of London has consisted primarily of native-born English
people with relatively small admixtures of groups from elsewhere in
the British Isles or from abroad. During this period there occurred
two substantial influxes of non-English immigrants. In the mid-
nineteenth century the Irish immigrated in particularly large numbers, especially in the years after the famine. The movement has
continued in the twentieth century, though at a lower rate. The
numbers of Irish-born (Table II.1.4) underrepresent the "Irish"

Table II.1.4 The Immigrant Population of London, 1851-1971[a]

| | Residents born outside England and Wales and Scotland | | | | | |
| | Ireland | | Colonies and Commonwealth | | Foreign | |
Year	Number	%	Number	%	Number	%
1851	109,000	4.6	11,000	0.5	26,000	1.1
1861	107,000	3.8	15,000	0.5	41,000	1.5
1871	91,000	2.8	20,000	0.6	55,000	1.6
1881	80,000	2.1	27,000	0.7	60,000	1.5
1891	66,000	1.6	30,000	0.7	95,000	2.3
1901	60,000	1.3	33,000	0.7	135,000	3.0
1911	52,000	1.1	35,000	0.8	153,000	3.4
1921	52,000	1.2	42,000	0.9	146,000	3.3
1931	64,000	1.5	41,000	0.9	126,000	2.9
1951	112,000	3.3	59,000	1.8	166,000	5.0
	Ireland		Afro-Asians[b]		Europeans[c]	
	Number	%	Number	%	Number	%
1961	296,000	3.6	200,000	2.5	90,000	1.1
1971	283,000	3.8	383,000	5.1	41,000	0.5

Sources: Decennial censuses of Great Britain.

a. Percentage of the total population of the County of London, 1851-1951, and of Greater London, 1961-1971. The latter is more than twice as large as the county.

b. From India and Pakistan, West Indies, and Africa.

c. From the European-settled countries of the Commonwealth.

proportion of the population. The Irish have maintained their ethnic
identity more readily than migrants from elsewhere in the British
Isles and tended, especially in the nineteenth century, to congregate
in the poor areas of central London. As a consequence there were
and are a significant number of London-born people who regard
themselves as Irish. From the beginning the presence of the Irish
community in London was seen as a social problem; Henry Mayhew,
writing in the 1850s, was one of the first to comment on it. In
particular, the Irish have been accused repeatedly of having a greater
proclivity to crime than native-born Londoners. The historical evidence is ambiguous but the contemporary evidence is not. Studies in
the 1950s and 1960s showed that rates of arrest, conviction, and
recidivism among Irish-born men were anywhere from two to seven
times the rates for English-born men, both in London and all England and Wales. Moreover their overrepresentation was on the increase during this period. Some but by no means all of the differences could be attributed to the tendency of the Irish-born to be
younger and more often single than the English-born.[14] Since the
London Irish have been atuned to political events in Ireland, for
nearly a century they have provided activists and a base of operations
for campaigns of protest and terrorism on behalf of Irish causes.

The second wave of immigration occurred during the last generation and consisted of two main streams, one from continental
Europe—the Mediterranean countries in particular—and the other
from the former British colonies in Asia, Africa, and the West Indies.
These groups, together with the native-born Irish, have combined to
make of London a more diverse city than it has ever been in
its recorded history. In 1971 slightly less than fourteen percent of
Greater London's population was foreign-born, compared with five
percent in 1931. More exact data are given in Table II.1.4. Among
the Afro-Asians the West Indians make up the largest group, with 2.3
percent of the total population, compared with 1.9 percent for
Pakistanis and Indians and 1.1 percent for Africans. The European
immigrants, attracted by economic opportunity, have not disrupted
public order. The nonwhite immigrants, however, have been the
focus of serious social concern, and the great increase in their
absolute numbers in the last 25 years has made the issue of race
relations a vexing matter in British politics. Even in 1971, though,
they comprised just over five percent of Greater London's population and only 1.8 percent of the population of England and Wales.
The principal consequence for crime and public order has been, not
the extent of criminality among nonwhite immigrants, but the violence of racial hostility between black and white Londoners.[15]

Two other characteristics of a population said to bear on patterns
of crime are sexual imbalance and the proportional number of young

males. In Western cultures men run a higher risk than women of getting into personal and social trouble, and young, unattached men most of all. We know, for example, that many convicts in nineteenth century London prisons were young men. Thus the more numerous are young males in a population, the greater the levels of crime and deviance are likely to be; and in populations where men substantially outnumber women, there is the added element of sexual tension and interpersonal aggression among isolate males. Census data on the characteristics of London's male population are summarized in Table II.1.5. Women have consistently outnumbered men in the city since the beginning of the nineteenth century, and there are no short-term variations in sexual imbalance consequential enough to have any social impact. There are significant variations in the percentages of young males, though: our index shows distinct increases in 1821-1841, 1921-1931, and 1951-1971. The first and last of these periods had very high crime rates, as subsequent chapters show, and there appears to have been a marked increase in the late 1920s. The variations in crime rates are far greater than the variations in the proportions of young men. Yet it is entirely possible that moderate increases in the relative size of this group, by ten to twenty percent,

Table II.1.5 All Males and Young Males as Percentages of the Population of Middlesex and London, 1801-1971

Census year and coverage[a]	All Males as % of total	Males 15-29 as % of total	Index, 1971 = 100
1801 M	45.7	nd	
1811 M	45.6	nd	
1821 M	46.6	12.1	109
1831 M	46.5	13.2	119
1841 M	46.9	13.5	122
1851 IL	46.8	13.1	118
1861 IL	46.6	12.6	114
1871 IL	46.8	13.0	117
1881 IL	47.1	13.3	120
1891 IL	47.3	13.5	122
1901 IL	47.2	12.8	115
1911 IL	47.0	12.7	114
1921 IL	46.2	11.5	104
1931 IL	46.5	13.1[b]	118
1941	nd	nd	nd
1951 GL	46.7	9.1	82
1961 GL	47.7	10.1	91
1971 GL	48.0	11.1	100

Sources: Our computations from data in the decennial *Census of England and Wales*, titles and tables vary, 1801-1971

a. M = Middlesex County, IL = Inner London (the administrative county), GL = Greater London.

b. Our estimate from partial data.

may increase to a greater degree the pool of young men who cannot find legitimate social and economic niches for themselves.[16]

This cursory examination of London's demographic structure in the last two centuries confirms that London has continued to be a dynamic center for social change. The huge increase of the population alone has had enormous social consequences. In 1800 the institutions of local government, public health, and social control were ill equipped to cope with the problems created by the expanding metropolis. Urban planners of the 1970s, while perhaps perceiving the problems more realistically than their forebears, are hardly optimistic about the present or the future. Indeed, the problems are considerably more complex. Geographic mobility, in the form of suburbanization, has made rational social decisions difficult for such a large area. Ethnic diversity, particularly the immigration of non-whites, has created a climate of emotional extremism. The problems of crime and public order in London must be viewed against this varied and constantly changing demographic background.

ECONOMIC GROWTH

In the last two centuries London has differed from other British urban centers with respect to its economic configuration. The Industrial Revolution, which so radically transformed the cities of the North and Midlands, did not have such a striking physical impact on the capital. Large-scale industry and factory organization have never dominated London's economy. It is, rather, based on finance capital, trade, and skilled craftsmanship; it is and has been a service economy. During most of our period, indeed, it was not monolithic; in the nineteenth century one can hardly speak of a "metropolitan" economy, because prices and wages differed markedly from one area of London to another.[17]

London's uniqueness notwithstanding, it is virtually impossible to separate the city's economic life from that of Britain as a whole. For one thing, London has had its share of industrialization, though this has not been much investigated by economic historians. Second, by virtue of its position as market and entrepôt, London was from the beginning a major stimulus for technological innovation and British economic growth generally. London has felt as keenly as any other area the vicissitudes of the British economy in the last two centuries: its dramatic "take-off" in the late 1700s, its preeminence as "workshop of the world" by the 1850s and 1860s, its slow decline thereafter in the face of international competition, and its somewhat precipitous fall (relative to other industrialized economies) in the twentieth century context of war and economic dislocation.[18] The following discussion concentrates on London, but comments where necessary on the total British economic situation.

London's economic strength is based on its undisputed claim to be the financial and trading center of the British Isles (and, for most of the nineteenth century, of the world). The most important financial institutions—banking, insurance, investment exchanges—are centralized there. It has always been Britain's leading port. It knows few peers in the quantity and quality of its retail trade. For centuries it has had more craftsmen and skilled artisans than any other area of the country; in such specialties as fur or photographic film manufacture, it is still the only center of production.

The industrial development of the metropolis in the last two centuries is closely tied to these basic factors in its economy. In almost every type of production London is the most important manufacturing center in Britain except for such "primary" industries as agriculture, textiles, and heavy metals. London's role in the manufacturing process has been one of "finishing" products for the city's accessible market or for export. The older industries, well established by the nineteenth century, reflect this underlying economic structure. They include the production and distribution of food products, the manufacture of clothing, furniture making, and printing and allied industries. These enterprises were founded in a relatively small area in the central section around the City of London, and despite occasional efforts of entrepreneurs to move away from the center to find cheaper labor, this location is still the heart of London's industrial economy. This type of industrialization resulted in a less uniform system of labor relations and wages than existed in the large factory districts of England, though this is less true today than in the nineteenth century. Much of the production characteristic of London ordinarily has been done on a relatively small scale; many skilled artisans, for example, formerly worked at home under subcontract or "sweated" labor. Heavy industry in London during the nineteenth century was intimately connected to London's position as a major port and, until the early twentieth century, as the center for shipbuilding. The other nineteenth century industry that employed large numbers of potentially organizable workers was construction, naturally of great significance in an urban environment undergoing rapid expansion. The more skilled artisans and workers, such as bricklayers, could band together to press for higher wages, lower hours, and better working conditions.[19] In fact, strikes by members of the building industry in the 1860s were the most important episode in labor relations in the metropolis before the dock strike of 1889.

Twentieth century industrialization in London reflects marked

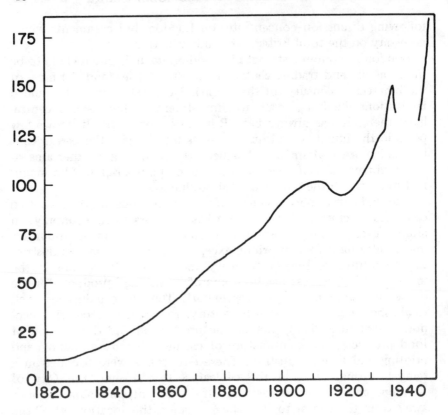

Figure II.1.2 Hoffmann's index of total industrial production in Britain, 1820-1950, 1913 = 100

demand for more sophisticated products. The new industries differ from the older ones in that they are located outside the central areas of London and require highly skilled labor—most importantly, for the design and manufacture of technical equipment and for electrical engineering. Doubtless British engineering is centered in the metropolitan area because London has always been the focal point in the country for the production of machinery, precision tools, and scientific instruments. Other recent additions to London's industrial spectrum are such major enterprises as automotive and aircraft manufacture.

This description of the variety of industrialization and the extent of technological innovation in the metropolitan economy gives a somewhat rosier picture than the facts warrant. Although it is probably true that London's economic growth over the last two centuries has been more steady than that of the country as a whole, the metropolis has been affected to a considerable extent by the inconsistent advance of the British economy in this period. There is considerable controversy over the various measurements of industrial output and national income constructed by economic historians. One of the frequently cited measurements is Walther Hoffmann's index of total industrial production (Figure II.1.2.[20]). The index shows a steady rise during the nineteenth century but relatively severe fluctuation in the twentieth. What this and similar indices fail to show is Britain's fall from primacy in the world economy. In 1800 Britain accounted for an estimated 35 percent of the world's total industrial output. Though surpassed by the United States in the 1860s, it remained the world's second major producer until World War I. By the 1960s, however, Britain was the source of well under ten percent of total industrial output. The costs of this loss of industrial primacy have included increased competition, loss of markets, the decline of many export industries, and a succession of contingent, often painful, economic adjustments whose cumulative impact on entrepreneurs and workers alike will probably prove to be as great as the impact of the Industrial Revolution itself.[21]

Coinciding with this relative decline in the British economy in the twentieth century has been the increased demand of the working class for higher wages and better working conditions. The resulting redistribution of the national income has had enormous social repercussions. In purely economic terms, the effect has been to give labor a larger share of the national wealth. This is demonstrated in the index of London artisans' real wages (money wages adjusted for cost of living) constructed by Tucker in 1935 and graphed in Figure II.1.3.[22] The index in the early nineteenth century shows the fluctuations that have been commonly documented for the economy

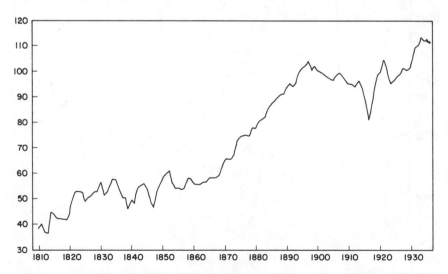

Figure II.1.3 Tucker's index of real wages of artisans in London, 1810-1935, 1900 = 100

as a whole during the period. After 1860, however, with the notable exception of the World War I years, the index of real wages rises fairly steadily, even during the Great Depression. There is no general index of real wages for London after 1935, but the money wages of various groups of craftsmen (not graphed here) show a still more pronounced upward trend.[23]

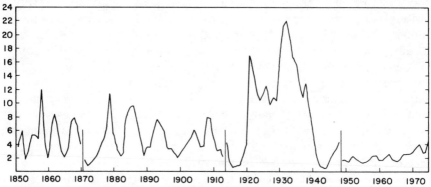

Figure II.1.4 Percentage unemployment in the United Kingdom, 1851-1912 (certain trades unions only) and 1913-1975 (all insured or registered workers)

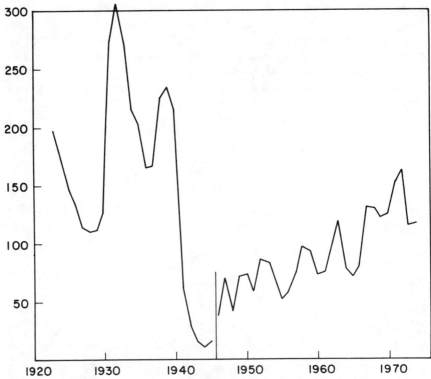

Figure II.1.5 Number of unemployed in London (1923-1948) and the southeast region (1949-1974, in thousands)

The pattern of unemployment (Figures II.1.4 and II.1.5) tells a similar story.[24] Before World War II fluctuations in unemployment follow the overall trends in the economy in both London and Great Britain as a whole. There was, of course, full employment during the war; after 1945, with the establishment of the welfare state and implementation of the employment provisions of the Beveridge Report, there continued to be nearly full employment through the mid-1960s. This was paralleled in the 1950s and early 1960s by a tremendous increase in living standards, which have declined, however, as a consequence of the current problems of the British economy. One aspect of those problems is the marked increase in unemployment since 1970 and especially in 1975-1976.[25]

A final measure of the extent of what has sometimes amounted to labor dictation of economic terms for the total society is the prevalence of strikes in the twentieth century. When negotiation has failed, and sometimes before it has been seriously attempted, labor has used the weapon of the strike to force acceptance of its demands. Figure II.1.6 shows the number of working days lost to strikes in all of Britain during the past 80 years.[26] The very high levels of strike activity between 1908 and 1926 have no subsequent parallels, but a marked relative increase is evident beginning in 1968.

Our discussion of London's economic development in the nineteenth and twentieth centuries must not omit innovations in

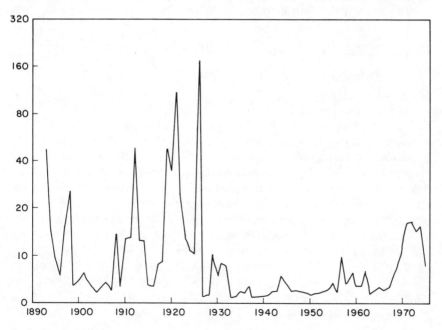

Figure II.1.6 Great Britain: Millions of working days lost in labor disputes, 1893-1975

transportation and communication, which altered the metropolis most significantly. The coming of the railroad in the early nineteenth century was responsible for much subsequent demographic expansion and suburban sprawl, while the advent of the automobile and mass transit facilities immeasurably increased population mobility. [27] In the area of communications the first major step was the introduction of the postal service, followed by the telephonic communications system.

These developments had three major consequences for crime. First, the increase in population mobility allowed the professional and semiprofessional criminals to become more dispersed throughout the metropolis; in addition, a criminal had easy access to virtually all areas of London rather than simply his own neighborhood. Second, to the detriment of the criminal's personal security, the police also gained increased mobility. At the same time better communications enabled police and penal authorities to observe more closely the activities of former convicts and suspected persons. Third, the availability of the telephone has made it easier for citizens to report offenses to the police. It is plausible to think that the "dark figure" of unreported crime, especially petty offenses against persons and property, has declined in inverse proportion to the use of the telephone. It would be difficult to measure quantitatively the impact of these factors on the committing and reporting of crime, but they should be kept in mind in considering trends in the crime rates.

THE HISTORY OF CRIME AND PUBLIC ORDER IN LONDON

The historical and sociological literature on the social, economic, and political development of London during the last two centuries is voluminous, more so than for any other city in this study. [28] But there is very little scholarly literature that treats systematically the subjects of crime and civil conflict in the urban setting. Most of the historical research on crime and deviance in Britain has treated England and Wales as a whole, and some of that research makes little use of the official data on which this study relies. [29] Specific instances of group conflict in London and elsewhere have been thoroughly documented: for example, the Chartist Movement of the 1840s, the women's suffrage movement between 1910 and 1914, and the activities of and opposition to Sir Oswald Mosley's British Union of Fascists in the 1930s. [30] But there is no single synthetic study for the nineteenth or twentieth century that has the breadth of George Rudé's small volume, *Paris and London in the Eighteenth Century: Studies in Popular Protest.* [31]

Thus to document the changing patterns of public disorder in the metropolis, we rely on specialized historical monographs and journalistic sources for civil conflict, and on governmental reports for crime. The principal official data on crime are found in the *Parliamentary Papers* and the Reports of the Commissioner of Police of the Metropolis. The former comprises the printed documents presented to Parliament in each session, including statistical returns on criminal matters beginning early in the nineteenth century. These data did not appear regularly until 1834, when the Government began compiling annual *Criminal Tables*, listing total numbers of commitments to trial and convictions for major (indictable) offenses by county. In 1856 the returns were revised and expanded to include offenses known and arrests; these reports, called *Judicial Statistics*, also contain data on prisons and prisoners. The first Report of the Commissioner was issued in 1869, and reports have appeared annually since, comprising data and information for the entire Metropolitan Police District (MPD), including statistical tables on police strength and criminal activity.[32] An additional statistical source has been the *Supplementary Judicial Statistics*, compiled and published by the Home Office since 1949 and available to scholars.

The changing scope and detail of the statistical information in these sources, rather than well-defined historical watersheds, provide the basis for dividing our analysis into three periods: 1820 to the 1870s, the 1870s to 1931, and 1932 to 1970s. For the first period the data on crime relate to the County of Middlesex (including the City of London). Naturally metropolitan London in the mid-nineteenth century included a substantially larger area, but it is impossible to determine what proportion of the cases in the adjacent Home Counties came within the jurisdiction of the metropolitan police. The two later periods employ data from the reports of the commissioner of that force and have the advantage of including virtually all the modern metropolis, except for the most recent decades, when population growth has been concentrated in the remote suburban areas. The MPD statistics were appreciably simplified and published in an abbreviated format in the years 1933 to 1945, and when more comprehensive reporting was resumed in 1946, data on arrests and convictions by type of offense were not consistently given. The break in coverage in the early 1930s, and correlated changes in the nature of police reporting, prompted the division of our analysis at this point.

The reliability of official statistics on crime is often questioned. With regard to the data for London, it seems likely that the figures for commitments to trial and convictions are reasonably accurate. Doubtless there are occasional omissions and inaccuracies, but there are fewer possibilities for errors in recording judicial proceedings than other types of criminal statistics. This is certainly not true of statistics on crimes known to the police, and arrests. Many crimes, especially sexual offenses, may not be reported to the police. Also, the police may choose not to record as a crime an act of which they have been informed—for example, a domestic quarrel leading to physical violence. A further difficulty with the police statistics is that the charge recorded may not be an accurate reflection of the crime committed (this of course is true also of the court statistics).

Even though police data do not reflect a force's information or activities with absolute fidelity, it can be asked whether they are approximately comparable over periods of time. This is a matter of prime concern for a historical study. In evaluating time series of the available statistics, two points must be kept in mind. First, there are definite breaks in the series: Not only does the categorization of crime change, but whole series of tables are dropped and new ones added. The second consideration, often cited as a reason for not accepting the validity of such statistics, is the fact that variations in the criminal law and development of police methods may have a pronounced effect on reported crime. Our tentative conclusion is that within each of the three chronological periods, the statistical trends for London are relatively accurate reflections of changing criminal activity as well as variations in the success of the authorities in dealing with crime. [33] On the other hand, it must be acknowledged that generalizations about the whole period covered by this study are much less precise and must take into account the discrepancies in reporting procedures.

A concluding word of explanation is needed about the indicators of crime used in subsequent chapters. The original sources list data according to the prevailing criminal code or classification system; these materials vary considerably over time and are in any case much too finely detailed for our purposes. For this study the data on crime have been aggregated into twenty categories of *indictable offenses*, those for which a suspected offender could be committed to trial; and nine categories of *summary offenses*, those which are dealt with summarily by magistrates. [34] Each of these 29 categories comprises groups of similar offenses, comparable over time. The analyses that follow focus principally on the indictable offenses, and not all of those. Offenses that have been relatively uncommon and of little public or official notoriety (e.g., bigamy, forgery, and blackmail) are not separately considered, though others may later choose to analyze the data we have so categorized. The categories of offenses are listed in Table II.1.6, under headings that are used for some still-more-summary comparisons.

The annual totals in each category have been divided by population estimates to provide rates per 100,000 people, which is the ratio most often used in the criminological literature. The population

*Table II.1.6. Categories of Indictable and Summary Offenses,
            Middlesex and London (MPD)*

Indictable Offenses
  Crimes against persons
      *Murder and manslaughter (excluding vehicular manslaughter)
      *Attempted murder and assaults
      Abortion
      Kidnapping and other crimes against children

  Crimes of acquisition: theft
      *Armed robbery and attempts
      *Burglary (housebreaking) and attempts
      *Auto theft
      *Larceny
      *Receiving stolen goods

  Crimes of acquisition: other
      *Fraud and embezzlement
      Forgery and couterfeiting
      Blackmail and other threats

  Crimes against sexual morality
      *Rape and attempts
      *Sexual deviance
      *Prostitution offenses (procuring, keeping bawdy houses, etc.)

  Other categories of offense
      *Public order offenses (rioting, assault on police, etc.)
      Bigamy and other crimes against the family
      Malicious offenses against property
      Miscellaneous indictable offenses
      *Total indictable offenses

Summary offenses
      *Offenses against persons
      Malicious offenses against property
      Offenses against property
      Administrative and miscellaneous offenses
      *Vagrancy
      *Drunkenness
      Motoring offenses
      *Prostitution offenses
      Total non-indictable offenses

---

*Indicators of these kinds of offenses are examined in the chapters that follow.

estimates for 1820-1870 are derived from the revised decennial totals
for Middlesex published in the Census Report of 1891.[35] The
population for years from one census to the next was estimated by
interpolation. The population figures from 1869 to 1974 are from

the reports of the Commissioner of the Metropolitan Police and also originate with the census figures (see Figure II.1.1).

These procedures have been applied to five different sets of data on public order: indictable offenses known to the police, arrests, committals to trial, convictions in judicial proceedings, and convictions by magistrates. These data are available for different time spans, as examination of data in subsequent chapters indicates. Generally we can trace the changing incidence of committals to trial and convictions for specific categories of indictable offenses in Middlesex, and later the MPD, from about 1820 to 1931; totals only are available thereafter. Some kinds of arrest data are reported from the late 1850s to 1974, but they are tabulated by indictable offense only from 1893 to 1931 and again from 1947 to 1974.[36] Some statistics on offenses known to police also are reported from the late 1850s to 1974, but until 1914 they are categorized in ways that preclude precise comparison with data on arrests or convictions or both. It is nonetheless possible to use indicators constructed from these data series to draw substantial inferences about the trends in public order and official efforts at controlling serious crime over a period of a century and a half. Where summary offenses are concerned, though, the information is more scanty. Convictions for all summary offenses are regularly reported from 1857 to 1913, along with roughly equivalent data for 1949 through 1972. Data on prostitution offenses are reported for the period from 1913 to 1931 as well. The only offense of any kind for which statistics are available throughout the history of the MPD, though, is drunkenness: These data form an unbroken series from 1831 to 1974. Such consistency may not be inappropriate, because arrests and convictions for this offense have occasioned the majority of Londoners' encounters with the police and courts throughout the period.

NOTES TO CHAPTER II.1

NOTE ON OFFICIAL BRITISH SOURCES

Acts of Parliament: The officially prescribed citations are used. An example is 2 & 3 Will. IV, c.62. This refers to the 62nd Act (c = chapter, signifying an individual act) passed by the Parliament in session during William IV's second and third (2 & 3) regnal years, which in this instance span parts of the calender years 1831 to 1833. Sometimes several successive acts are cited using the convention cc, for example cc. 27-31. A section of an act is occasionally cited, for example s.s.3 = section 3.

Command Papers: These are papers presented to Parliament by Ministers and are cited here by title, official designation (a number preceded by C., Cd., Cmd., or Cmnd., depending on the series), and year of printing.

Public Record Office (P.R.O.) Documents: These are cited using the P.R.O. designations. *H.O.* refers to the P.R.O.'s collection of Home Office documents, *Mepol.* to its collection of Metropolitan Police documents, *Pri. Com.* to Prison Commissioners documents.

1. Its population may have been surpassed by Edo (now Tokyo) in 1880, though this is uncertain. See Susan B. Hanley, "Population Trends and Economic Development in Tokugawa Japan: The Case of Bizen Province in Okayama," *Daedalus* (Spring 1968) 622-635; George Rudé, *Hanoverian London, 1714-1808* (London: Secker & Warburg, 1971), p. ix; Francis Sheppard, *London, 1808-1870: The Infernal Wen* (London: Secker & Warburg, 1971), p. xvi. In the mid-1970s United Nations data show London to be the world's eighth largest conurbation.

2. This argument is based on E. A. Wrigley, "A Simple Model of London's Importance in Changing English Society and Economy, 1650-1750," *Past and Present*, 37 (1967), 44-70.

3. See David S. Landes, *The Unbound Prometheus: Technological Change and Industrial Development in Western Europe from 1750 to the Present* (Cambridge: Cambridge University Press, 1969), pp. 12-15, 42ff; and Phyllis Deane and W. A. Cole, *British Economic Growth, 1688-1959: Trends and Structure*, 2nd ed. (Cambridge: Cambridge University Press, 1967), ch. II.

4. "The Government of London," *Westminster Review*, 105 (1876), 93.

5. S. E. Rasmusson, *London: The Unique City* (London: Jonathan Cape, 1937).

6. William L. Langer, "Europe's Initial Population Explosion," *American Historical Review*, 69 (1963-1964), 1-17, is a useful summary of the issues, and G. Kitson Clark, *The Making of Victorian England* (Cambridge: Harvard Univer-

sity Press, 1962), ch. 3, "The Increase in Population," discusses the problem from the English perspective. See also, D. V. Glass and D. E. C. Eversley, eds., *Population in History: Essays in Historical Demography* (London: Edward Arnold, 1965), a collection of the most important monographic research; E. A. Wrigley, ed., *An Introduction to English Historical Demography from the Sixteenth to the Nineteenth Century* (London: Weidenfeld & Nicolson, 1966), which contains an extensive bibliography; the issue "Historical Population Studies," *Daedalus* (Spring 1968); and E. A. Wrigley, *Population and History* (London: Weidenfeld & Nicolson, 1969).

7. T. W. Freeman, *The Conurbations of Great Britain* (Manchester: Machester University Press, 1959), pp. 66-67.

8. On the accuracy of census figures generally, see A. J. Taylor, "The Taking of the Census, 1801-1951," *British Medical Journal*, 4709 (April 7, 1951), 715-720. On London's nineteenth century population see R. Price-Williams, "The Population of London, 1801-81," *Journal of the Royal Statistical Society*, 48 (1885), 349-383.

9. Henry Jephson, *The Sanitary Evolution of London* (London: T. Fisher Unwin, 1907), p. 156.

10. See, for example, the demographic contour map in Wrigley, *Population and History*, p. 99.

11. Arthur Redford, *Labour Migration in England, 1800-1850*, 2nd ed. (Manchester: Manchester University Press, 1964), pp. 184-185.

12. *Royal Commission on Municipal Corporations*, Second Report, 1837, p. 3.

13. For a general study, see D. Friedlander and R. J. Roshier, *Internal Migration in England and Wales, 1851 to 1951* (London: Centre for Urban Studies, Report Number 6, 1966).

14. On the historical evidence see Lynn Hollen Lees, *Social Change and Social Stability Among the London Irish, 1830-1870* (unpublished dissertation, Harvard University, 1969); and her paper in Stephan Thornstrom and Richard Sennett, eds., *The Nineteenth Century City* (New Haven, Conn.: Yale University Press, 1969). Lees' views on the Irish in mid-Victorian London being objects of scorn has been contested recently by Gertrude Himmelfarb in her contribution to H. J. Dyos and Michael Wolff, eds., *The Victorian City* (London: Routledge & Kegan Paul, 1973). The contemporary evidence is reviewed by A. E. Bottoms, "Delinquency Amongst Immigrants," *Race*, 8 (No. 4, 1967), 357-383. See also John A. Jackson, *The Irish in Britain* (London: Routledge & Kegan Paul, 1963); and Jackson, "The Irish," in Centre for Urban Studies, Report Number 3, *London: Aspects of Change* (London: MacGibbon & Kee, 1964), pp. 293-308.

15. See Ruth Glass, *Newcomers* (London: Allen & Unwin, 1960). Bottoms, op. cit., reviews evidence which shows that nonwhite Commonwealth immigrants have not been substantially overrepresented among offenders, with the single exception of crimes of violence arising out of domestic disputes.

16. See H. Moller in *Comparative Studies in Society and History*, 10 (1968), 237: "Irrespective of social and economic conditions, an increase in the number of youth in any society involves an increase in socially disruptive behavior."

17. Sources for London's modern economic development include, besides the census reports and other government documents: G. L. Gomme, *London in the Reign of Victoria* (London: Blackie & Son, 1898), chs. 1-4; J. H. Clapham, "Work and Wages," in G. M. Young, ed., *Early Victorian England, 1830-1865*, 2

vols. (Oxford: Oxford University Press, 1934), Vol. I, pp. 21-35; P. G. Hall, *The Industries of London Since 1861* (London: Hutchinson, 1962); J. E. Martin, *Greater London: An Industrial Geography* (Chicago: University of Chicago Press, 1966). Geographical studies also contain much economic information: R. Clayton, ed., *The Geography of Greater London* (London: George Philip, 1964) and J. T. Coppock and Hugh C. Prince, eds., *Greater London* (London: Faber & Faber, 1964). There is a good deal of economic history in Sheppard, *London, 1808-1870.*

18. It is beyond the scope of this study to comment in more than a general way on British economic history. A recent survey, with references to the most important literature, is E. J. Hobsbawm, *Industry and Empire: The Making of Modern English Society*, Vol. II: *1750 to the Present Day* (New York: Pantheon, 1968). For international perspective, see Landes, *The Unbound Prometheus.* The statistical data are conveniently collected in Brian Mitchell and Phyllis Deane, *Abstract of British Historical Statistics* (Cambridge: Cambridge University Press, 1962) and in Brian Mitchell and H. G. Jones, *Second Abstract of British Historical Statistics* (Cambridge: Cambridge University Press, 1971).

19. See the illuminating discussion in E. J. Hobsbawm, "The Nineteenth Century London Labour Market," in Centre for Urban Affairs, Report Number 3, *London: Aspects of Change*, pp. 3-28.

20. See Walther G. Hoffman, *British Industry, 1700-1950* (Oxford: Blackwell, 1955), Table 54. The index, graphed in Figure II.1.2, includes construction and employs a double moving ten-year average.

21. On Britain's relative position in the world economy see Hobsbawn, *Industry and Empire*, esp. the figure on p. 294.

22. R. S. Tucker, "Real Wages of Artisans in London, 1729-1935," *Journal of the American Statistical Association*, 31 (March 1936), 73-84. The "artisans" are principally workers in the building trades.

23. See, for example, the indices of average weekly wage rates for bricklayers, compositors, and other London workers in *British Historical Labour Statistics 1886-1968* (London: HMSO, 1968) and later supplements, which extend from the 1850s or earlier to the 1970s.

24. Figure II.1.4 includes data from four separate series, none precisely comparable with the others. For 1851-1913 they are cumulated mainly from the records of trades unions; since relatively few workers belonged to unions maintaining such records, especially in the nineteenth century, such data provide at best a rough indicator of general unemployment. After 1913 the data were compiled for all insured workers, a much larger proportion of the workforce; after 1949 the figures are for total registered unemployed. The principal sources used are *Sixteenth Abstract of Labour Statistics* (1913); *British Labour Statistics Historical Abstract, 1886-1968*, Tables 159 and 168; and Central Statistical Office, *Monthly Digest of Statistics*, No. 354 (June 1975), Table 21.

25. Note that the data in Figure II.1.5 refer to the absolute number of unemployed; after 1945 they relate to Greater London and the southeastern counties. The upward trend through the mid-1960s is due mainly to population growth in this region.

26. From the sources listed in note 24.

27. H. J. Dyos and D. H. Aldcroft, *British Transport: An Economic Survey from the Seventeenth Century to the Twentieth* (Leicester: Leicester University Press, 1969); T. C. Barker and Michael Robbins, *A History of London Trans-*

port: Passenger Travel and the Development of the Metropolis, 2 vols. (London: Allen & Unwin, 1963), Vol. I, *The Nineteenth Century*.

28. Much of the writing on London has been the work of urban geographers or architectural historians, but there are also some major studies of the city's social development. An early example is M. Dorothy George's brilliant study of London's poor in the eighteenth century, *London Life in the Eighteenth Century* (London: Kegan Paul, 1925, reprinted with a new preface in 1965). Other contributions are to be found in Young, ed., *Early Victorian England*: J. H. Clapham, "Work and Wages," Vol. I, pp. 1-76 (section on London, 21-35); R. H. Mottram, "Town Life," Vol. I, pp. 153-223 (principally on London). A landmark collaborative history of London is now in progress, the first two volumes of which appeared in 1971: Rudé, *Hanoverian London*, and Sheppard, *London, 1808-1870*. Forthcoming is H. J. Dyos' volume on the period 1870-1914. Four invaluable surveys of London society have been conducted by contemporaries during the last century. Vivid descriptions of the life of London workers and criminals in the 1840s and 1850s by the journalist Henry Mayhew are to be found in his *London Labour and the London Poor*, 4 vols. (London, 1861-1862; reprinted London, Frank Cass, 1967); and also in Henry Mayhew and John Binny, *The Criminal Prisons of London and Scenes of Prison Life* (London, 1862; reprinted London, Frank Cass, 1968). A more systematic though prolix study dealing with late nineteenth century London, is Charles Booth, ed., *Life and Labour of the People in London*, 17 vols. (London: Macmillan, 1892-1903). During the 1930s the London School of Economics produced a sequel that surveyed metropolitan conditions during the Depression: Hubert Llewellyn Smith, ed., *The New Survey of London Life and Labour*, 9 vols. (London: School of Economics and Political Science, 1930-1935). Finally, the contemporary metropolitan scene is being analyzed in the Third London Survey by members of the University of London's Centre for Urban Studies, in Ruth Glass et al., *Third London Survey* (forthcoming). See also *London: Aspects of Change* (London: Centre for Urban Studies: Report Number 3, 1964).

29. A recent study by J. J. Tobias, *Crime and Industrial Society in the Nineteenth Century* (London: Batsford, 1967), provides a detailed examination of the literary sources but disregards the criminal statistics, on the argument that local variations in collection procedures render them valueless. This view has been criticized by many writers; see, for example, Mitchell and Jones, *Second Abstract of British Historical Statistics*, p. 198, and the reviews by Jennifer Hart in *History*, 54 (1969), 303-304; David Peirce in *American Historical Review*, 73 (1968-1969), 606-607; and Harold Perkin in *English Historical Review*, 85 (1970), 194-195. A more definitive rejoinder is provided by several excellent recent studies that make sensitive and instructive uses of official data on crime for the seventeenth through twentieth centuries. J. M. Beattie, "The Pattern of Crime in England 1660-1800," *Past and Present*, 62 (February 1974), 47-92, relies on court records. The nineteenth century national statistics are analyzed by V. A. C. Gatrell and T. B. Hadden, "Criminal Statistics and Their Interpretation," in E. A. Wrigley, ed., *Nineteenth-Century Society: Essays in the Use of Quantitative Methods for the Study of Social Data* (Cambridge: Cambridge University Press, 1972). See also K. K. Macnab, *Aspects of the History of Crime in England and Wales, 1805-1860* (unpublished thesis, University of Sussex, 1965). The national statistics for the twentieth century have been scrutinized rather thoroughly by scholars at the Institute of Criminology, University of

Cambridge; see, for example, Nigel Walker, "Crime and Penal Measures," in A. H. Halsey, ed., *Trends in British Society since 1900* (London: Macmillan, 1972), pp. 509-537; and also Nigel Walker, *Crimes, Courts and Figures: An Introduction to Criminal Statistics* (London: Penquin, 1971).

30. For citations to the relevant literature, see subsequent chapters.

31. New York: Viking, 1971. The newest contribution to the study of crime and conflict in eighteenth century, an excellent one, is Douglas Hay et al., *Albion's Fatal Tree: Crime and Society in Eighteenth Century England* (London: Allen Lane and Penguin Books, 1975).

32. For a more detailed survey see David Peirce, "Crime and Society in London, 1700-1900: A Bibliographical Survey," *Harvard Library Bulletin*, 20 (1972), 430-435. Another source for the nineteenth century are the *Criminal Returns: Metropolitan Police* (London, 1831-1892). These contain much material not included in the *Judicial Statistics* but are rather inaccessible. Complete sets are in the Library of New Scotland Yard and the Police College, Bramshill; the British Museum has only a partial collection.

33. For correspondence and memoranda on the compilation of the statistics at various periods, see *H.O.* 45/14521, 17778-177780, 19167; *Mepol* 2/469/470, 583 (P.R.O.).

34. The substantial majority of people accused of indictable offenses are in fact treated summarily, especially where larceny is concerned. The long-range trend in British police and judicial practice, documented in ch. II.3, has been to bring increasing proportions of those charged with most kinds of indictable offenses before magistrates, to save the time and expense of jury trials.

35. This report lists revised population figures from all decennial censuses, 1801-1891.

36. Arrests data by offense for 1947-1974 were located too late for use in this study.

CRIME, CONFLICT, AND
THE EVOLVING INSTITUTIONS
OF PUBLIC ORDER,
1800 TO THE 1870s

During the first two-thirds of the nineteenth century London experienced a series of remarkable socioeconomic changes reflected not only in the fluctuations of indicators of committals to trial and convictions for criminal offenses but also in the virtual remodeling of the institutions of public order in the metropolis. Viewed over the whole period, the trend in all important categories of crime is downward, though there are significant short-term variances in the opposite direction, notably in the 1830s and 1840s. The institutions dealing with crime and public order—the criminal law, the courts, the police, and the prisons—assume characteristics that foreshadow their modern form in the 1820s and 1830s.

It is difficult to relate the variations in the trends of crime or the changes in the institutions to the situation prevailing in the eighteenth century. In the first place, few of the sketchy and fragmentary statistical data for the previous period have been collected and aggregated. Second, relatively little work has been done on the problem of crime and public order in eighteenth century London. It should be emphasized, however, that the scholars who have studied that period have produced monographs of exceedingly high quality. Pride of place must go to Dorothy George, whose famous study *London Life in the Eighteenth Century* paints a picture of poverty, misery, and squalor.[1] Hogarth's *Gin Lane* is a plastic expression of George's description of the wretched conditions of urban life for the less privileged majority.

Recent scholarship has, if anything, confirmed and amplified this infelicitous view of eighteenth century London. George Rudé, operating within a Marxist framework, has analyzed many of the archival sources and reached similar conclusions.[2] A recent study of great importance is J. M. Beattie's "The Pattern of Crime in England, 1660-1800," which analyzes statistically the trends in indictments (formal charges laid against accused persons in the higher courts) in Surrey and Sussex. His graph of indictments for assault in the urban parishes of Surrey, which then comprised the parts of metropolitan London south of the Thames, is reproduced in Figure II.2.1. It provides the best statistical confirmation available of the traditional view that London in the 1730s was a violent city.[3] Even in the last decade of the eighteenth century the indictments averaged about 30 per 100,000, which is greater than the highest recorded rate for Middlesex in our nineteenth century data.[4]

The records of the House of Commons for 1817 are a statistical source of information about judicial response to crime in London during the eighteenth century. These contain statistics on persons sentenced to death and actually executed in London and Middlesex for various categories of offenses during the years 1749 to 1817. The compilers of the statistics differentiate between "years of war" and "years of peace" and remark that capital offenses seem to rise during wartime.[5] Beattie's graphs, though incomplete in many of the crucial years, seem to confirm this observation. There apparently was a rise in crime at the time of the War of the Spanish Succession

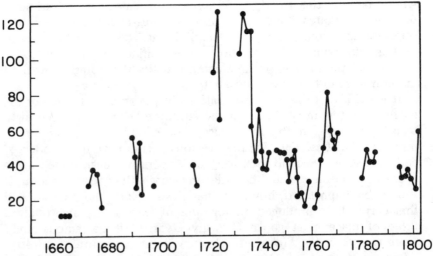

Figure II.2.1 Indictments for assault per 100,000 in the urban (London) parishes of Surrey, 1660-1800, from Beattie

(1690-1714); again, during the Seven Years War (1756-1763), though the data are hardly full; and, finally, as the Napoleonic wars got under way at the end of the century, all Beattie's graphs show a sharp upturn.

Despite the quality of scholarship produced by George, Rudé, and Beattie, there are no statistics that permit a direct comparison of eighteenth-century crime in London with that of the nineteenth. The data used in this study for the period 1820-1873 are drawn from the records of indictable committals and convictions for Middlesex, which were published in the *Parliamentary Papers* at various intervals before 1833 and annually thereafter. Middlesex was chosen for analysis because it is the most "metropolitan" of the various counties that constitute modern London, but it can hardly be claimed that the statistics reflect the situations in Essex, Surrey, and Kent (or even the metropolitan portions of those counties); through most of our period these other three counties were largely rural, though this situation was changing rapidly by 1870. Yet another feature of the statistics used here makes comparability difficult, even within the period 1820-1873: namely, the change in reporting that occurred between 1833 and 1834. The later figures are of much greater magnitude in many categories, and it is evident that the statistics for 1820-1833 did not include many indictments and convictions re- ported later. To compare, then, these Middlesex rates for the nine- teenth century directly with Beattie's data on eighteenth century "urban" Surrey is a dubious business at best. Generally, however, it appears that the short-term fluctuations of crime indicators were much greater in the earlier century and that the overall trend in offenses that attracted official attention was downward.

Turning from trends in crime and public order to a consideration of the changes in the institutions of public order, it is clear that we are dealing with a completely different situation after the mid-1830s. The criminal law was completely recodified by then, not only in the definition of offenses but also in the prescribed penalties. The Metropolitan Police was founded in 1829, and although there was popular opposition to it in the first five years, by the late 1830s the police were well on their way to becoming an established feature of London life. Similarly, there were concurrent changes in the struc- ture of the judicial system and the administration of the penal system. Most of these institutional innovations and reforms have been analyzed in the magisterial work of Leon Radzinowicz, to which the reader is referred for the wealth of detail that must be omitted here.[6] In sum, the conception and recording of crime and the institutional arrangements for maintaining public order were radically transformed during the first half of the nineteenth century.

Ultimately, of course, these changes were felt throughout Great Britain and the entire British Empire, but it is accurate enough to say that in both a legal and an applied sense they originated in London, and Londoners were the first Englishmen to be subject to a coherent, "modern" system of criminal law enforcement. The initial sections of this chapter discuss the trends in crime and conflict in London up to the early 1870s; the later sections trace the evolution of the institutions that defined and established the shape of public order. Chapters II.3 and II.4 describe the rise and decline of public order in London during the century that followed the era of reform.

TRENDS IN CRIME, 1820-1873

The indicators of crime for the 54 years 1820-1873 are constructed from annual data on committals to trial and convictions for the County of Middlesex, including the square-mile City of London. Their sources are the *Criminal Tables* (1834-1856) and *Judicial Statistics* (1856-1873) described in the preceding chapter. Only indictable offenses are included in these data; that is, those which judges and police thought serious enough to warrant trial before the higher courts. Such data are far removed from the actual incidence of criminal behavior, but statistics on crimes known to police, and arrests (which later generations believed come closer to the mark) are unavailable. What these statistics on committals and convictions register for us is the extent of serious disorder as seen through the eyes of the officials who were charged with maintaining order. The accuracy of their perceptions is inherently problematic; the experience of those brought before the courts was profoundly real.

When the indicators of total committals to trial and convictions for Middlesex are examined (Figure II.2.2) one is immediately struck by the irregular but marked decline that occurred during the half-century. Committals fell from about 270 per 100,000 in the late 1820s to about 100 in the early 1870s, while convictions declined at a somewhat lower rate, from about 180 to 75 per 100,000. Several points need to be kept in mind when trying to determine whether these declining rates are evidence of a proportional decrease in official concern about all types of indictable crime. First, larceny committals and convictions account for such a large proportion of the total that increases in less common but more serious offenses may be masked. The trends we found in specific categories show that the decline was characteristic of only some offenses.

Second, institutional factors may account for the decline. The change in reporting procedures in 1834, noted earlier, apparently inflates the rates thereafter; thus the comparable initial rates, as of

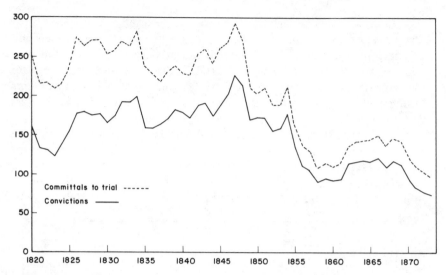

Figure II.2.2 Middlesex: Committals and convictions for all indictable offenses per 100,000, 1820-1873

the 1820s, are likely to have been still higher than those quoted previously. It also is to be noted that the ratio of convictions to committals tends to increase over the 54 years. Conceivably this was due to increasing severity in the administration of the criminal law, in which case the trend in committals would be a more accurate reflection of the declining extent of serious crime as a social problem. More likely, though, the increasing conviction ratio can be attributed to the marked improvement in policing, hence more apprehensions and committals to trial on the basis of evidence solid enough to warrant conviction. If so, the decline in convictions can be inferred to be a more accurate indicator of the trend in serious crime than might otherwise be supposed.

A third consideration is specifically political. The short-term fluctuations in committal and conviction rates, especially before 1848, parallel quite closely the ebb and flow of civil conflict (discussed in a later section), which raises the possibility that the courts used the instrumentalities of criminal law to discourage, directly or indirectly, social unrest and political protest. Insofar as this was true, it is possible to discount some of the short-term increases in committals and convictions, thereby allowing us to have more confidence in the interpretation that the underlying trend from the 1830s, if not earlier, was one of regular decline in the extent of individual crime as a social problem.

This general interpretation can be used as a working hypothesis while we examine the movement of committals and convictions for specific categories of crime. The offense generally considered most serious is, of course, murder. The variation in murder committals and convictions (Figure II.2.3) is quite irregular, as is always the case with relatively rare offenses: In the 1830s, for example, murder committals ranged from fifteen to 35 per year, with most years falling toward the lower end of the range. The trend is nonetheless downward, despite temporary upswings in the mid-1840s and mid-1860s. Committals and convictions for assault were roughly ten times as numerous as those for murder and trace a more abrupt decline. The short-term increases in murder and assault in the mid to late 1840s came during a time of economic distress and political upheaval. The reported increase in committals in the 1860s gains

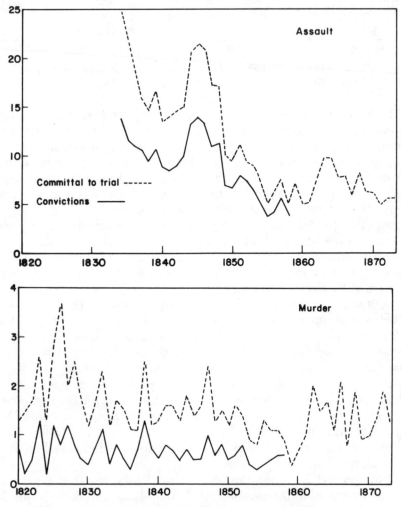

Figure II.2.3 Middlesex: Murder and assault per 100,000, 1820-1873

substance from the comments of contemporaries that violent assaults in the metropolis were on the increase. In the winter of 1862, for example, there was an outbreak of well-publicized garrotte robberies. Public insecurity over the crimes contributed to the enactment of the Garrotters Act of 1863, which prescribed corporal punishment for robberies with violence.[7] The interpretation of the high rate of committals for assault during the next five years is problematic,

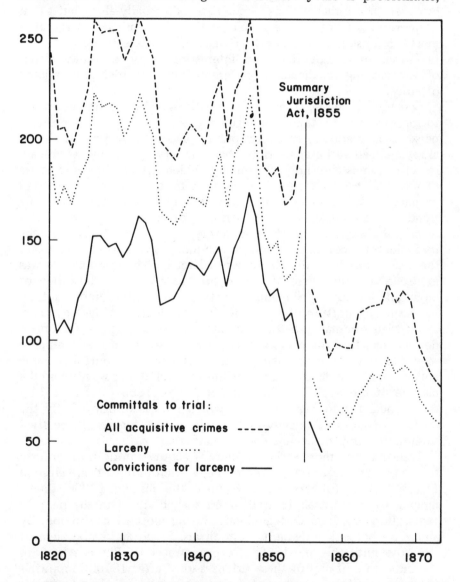

Figure II.2.4 Middlesex: Committals and convictions for all acquisitive crimes and larceny per 100,000, 1820-1873

though. Were they high because assaults remained common, or because the courts, armed with new legislation and backed by public concern, were more inclined to prosecute lesser cases to the full extent of the law?

Crimes against property apparently were far more common in London during these years than were offenses against the person. There is no need to seek special explanations for the phenomenon, however. The imbalance is characteristic of virtually all societies that keep criminal records. The simple cost-benefit explanation is that in most circumstances more is to be gained and less to be risked by theft than by assault. It is more interesting to try to find the causes of the varying incidence of different forms of theft and related offenses.

Larceny, in the legal lexicon of English-speaking countries, refers to the surreptitious taking of unguarded goods, whether from private persons or premises, shops or public places. This crime is almost always judged to be less serious than burglary, which involves breaking into homes and shops, or robbery, which entails the threat or use of force against the victim. Larceny is by far the most common of all property offenses in London during this era, as in later ones. The trend in committals and convictions for larceny (Figure II.2.4) reveals the same distinctly undulating decline we observed in the trend in total committals and convictions. It should be noted that these are rates for indictable cases of larceny. The criminal law was modified in the course of the century to adjust the definition of indictable larceny to changing monetary values. More important, an increasing proportion of nominally indictable cases of larceny came to be tried summarily before magistrates. Although these factors no doubt mean that the decline in larceny was not as great as the figure suggests, they cannot plausibly explain away all the fourfold decline between 1830 and 1873. The decline was well under way before the passage of the Summary Jurisdiction Act of 1855 (represented by the vertical bar in Figure II.2.4), which increased significantly the number of cases of larceny and simple assault that could be tried summarily. And the decline continued thereafter.

Trends in the more serious crimes of acquisition do not conform to the general pattern, however. Some relevant indicators are given in Figure II.2.5. Robbery declined until the middle 1830s, then—judging by committals to trial—more than doubled in the next 30 years. Burglary increased gradually during most of the period, by about 50 percent, judging by committals. Fraud and embezzlement also rose until the mid-1850s. No pronounced decline is evident in the indicators of any of these offenses until after 1870. Committals for receiving stolen goods (not shown separately) fell almost without

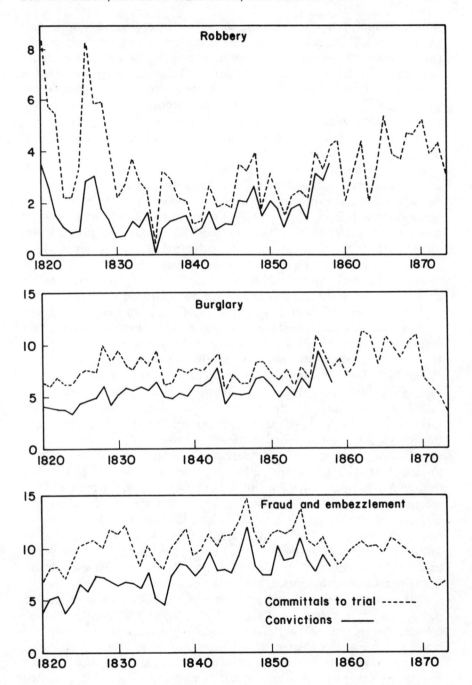

Figure II.2.5 Middlesex: Committals and convictions for serious acquisitive crimes per 100,000, 1820-1873

interruption for half a century, though, reinforcing our earlier suggestion that the principal source of stolen goods, larceny, was in social fact decreasing. Another type of acquisitive crime not shown separately on the accompanying figures is forgery, which includes the common offense of putting counterfeit coins into circulation. Forgery, unlike any other category of offense we have examined, varied cyclically. It reached its highest levels in the early 1820s, the early 1830s, and finally, when other kinds of offenses were stable or declining, in the middle 1850s.

Sexual offenses are ordinarily bracketed with murder and assault as "crimes against the person." We treat them separately here because aside from rape they signify the violation of a set of mores quite different from those relating to physical attack, and they are much more susceptible to varying legal definition and police treatment over time. The offenses so categorized are of three types (shown separately in Figure II.2.6) and all vary quite irregularly. The most numerous were offenses related to prostitution—mainly brothel-keeping. The laws seem to have been intermittently enforced, with official crackdowns in the 1840s and again in the 1860s. Cases of rape and sexual molestation of young girls were somewhat less common; in the 1830s about twenty men were committed to trial each year for such offenses and about half were convicted. Then, after 1860, London seemingly was swept by a wave of sex crimes. In fact we believe the data to be an official reflection of Victorian moral views, which in the latter half of the century led to the increasingly minute description and prohibition of what males ought not do to, or with, females of various ages. The same kind of explanation may apply to homosexual offenses among men. Committals to trial more than tripled between the late 1820s and the mid-1830s, then declined for the next three decades. Since most such offenses come to official attention through active police work, the increase probably was due to the more thorough policing that became possible after the establishment of the Metropolitan Police in 1829. Convictions remained relatively low throughout, strongly implying that the zeal of the police and the distaste of magistrates who bound over offenders to trial were not shared by jurors.

Our last category of indictable offenses consists of crimes against public order, graphed in Figure II.2.7. They are mainly rioting, assaults on police, and unlawful assembly, and of course only the most serious such offenses; lesser ones were dealt with summarily. Crimes against public order are subject to more abrupt variation than any other category of offenses and tend to be highest in years of most intense civil conflict. The peak in 1834, for example, follows the Reform Bill demonstrations of the early 1830s, one of which

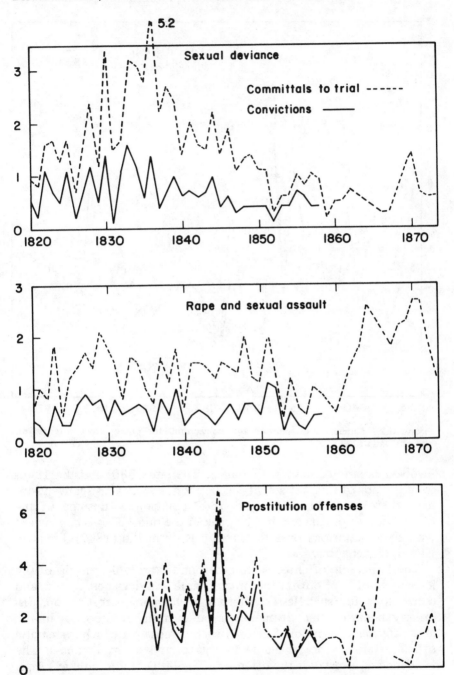

Figure II.2.6 Middlesex: Committals and convictions for sexual offenses per 100,000, 1820-1873

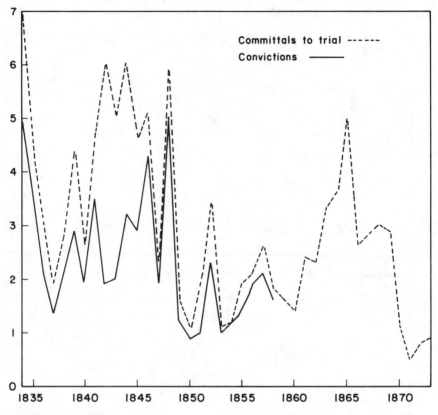

Figure II.2.7 Middlesex: Committals and convictions for public order offenses per 100,000, 1834-1873

involved a serious clash with police. The late 1830s and the 1840s were periods of Chartist activity in London, and Chartist conventions held there in 1839, 1842, and 1848 coincide with some of the highest spikes on the graph. The peak in the mid-1860s is concurrent with demonstrations over the Second Reform Bill (1867) discussed later in this chapter.

The indictable offenses examined thus far are only the tip of the iceberg of official efforts to control crime and deviance. Arrests and convictions for such lesser offenses as vagrancy, prostitution, disorderly behavior, and drunkenness far outnumber those for indictable offenses in London. The only such offense for which systematic official statistics are available in this period is drunkenness. The incidence of arrests for the offense (in the MPD, not Middlesex) from 1831 to 1873 is shown in Figure II.2.8. We note first that the rate of 2,000 arrests per 100,000 population in the early 1830s exceeds by a factor of eight the rate of committals to trial for all indictable

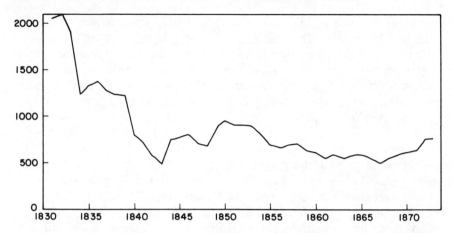

Figure II.2.8 London (MPD): Arrests for drunkenness and disorderly conduct per 100,000, 1831-1873

offenses during that period. Second, the trend thereafter is precipitously downward, several decades in advance of the decline in official action against more serious offenses. The bugbear of alternative explanations besets the interpretation of the data. Drunkenness arrests depend on active policing; thus although the data are prima facie evidence of police zeal in the 1830s, it is risky to infer from them that the problem gradually dried up as the century went on.

It is evident that official indicators of most kinds of crime for which data have survived, declined in Middlesex County during most of the five decades under review. The generalization holds true for the most common of offenses, larceny and drunkenness, and for the most threatening, murder and assault. The only significant exceptions are some types of serious property crime, which held steady or increased for most of the period. On the whole, the establishment of public order began to improve. It would seem then, that some combination of socioeconomic improvement and innovations in the institutions of social control markedly affected social behavior during these 50 years. We shall consider first some of the available data on the characteristics of offenders in London, which are suggestive on the first point. The last part of the chapter is a more detailed survey of the new policies and institutions that Londoners credited for their growing security.

CRIME AND THE QUESTION OF A "CRIMINAL CLASS"

It is hardly remarkable that the Home Office from the 1830s on began compiling and publishing statistical information about people accused of crimes and those in prisons, as well as about the frequency of crime. The decision of the government to promulgate biographical data on offenders and, after 1856, police analyses of the criminal population, was doubtless based on the nineteenth century conviction that London possessed a distinct "criminal class," a group whose members spent their time in illegal pursuits and who were responsible for most of the crimes committed in the metropolis. The concept of the "criminal class" was a new idea in the contemporary writings on crime, expressed most explicitly in the work of Henry Mayhew in the middle decades of the century. Tobias has described the gradual development of the concept with lengthy quotations from nineteenth century sources, but he does not cite the quantitative data collected to document the concept and simply remarks: "Even if the statistics were reliable, however, they would not disprove the existence of a criminal class."[8] In point of fact, the statistics do give some support to the argument for the social reality of the "criminal class." Table II.2.1 is compiled from Metropolitan Police data published from 1856 until late in the century. It summarizes the police categorization of people charged with indictable crimes for selected years from 1857 to 1873; similar returns were made of those charged with summary offenses. Not all these individuals were actually tried, and of those who were, many were not convicted. What strikes one immediately is how much the police seem to have known about the people they were arresting.

The police's information about those they arrested can be linked to their practice of keeping "houses of bad character" under regular surveillance. In 1861, a typical year, 3,160 were listed in police reports, most of them being places frequented by professional fences, thieves, and prostitutes. Nearly 14,000 "suspected persons" also were reported to be under surveillance in that year. Many were vagrants and tramps, most of the others may be assumed to have been occupants or habitues of the houses of bad character. Add to this the fact that most of the houses were concentrated in very circumscribed districts of the metropolis, and one has persuasive evidence for the existence of a group of people who lived together in known places in the rookeries and slums and engaged in criminal activities—a "criminal class." Furthermore, the existence of this class was as well known to the police as it was to such contemporary commentators as Mayhew.[9]

If a "criminal class" did exist in mid-nineteenth century London, what kinds of people composed it? Data on prisoners show that young, poor, unskilled, uneducated males in early Victorian London—as in most other times and places for which information is available—were more likely than any others to run afoul of the law. Conventional wisdom that deprived and unattached people, lacking

Table II.2.1 MPD Police Classification of Persons Charged with Indictable Offenses, Selected years 1857-1873

Year	Total Persons Charged		Class of Persons Charged (%)						
	Male	Female	Known thieves	Prostitutes	Vagrants and tramps	Suspicious characters	No known occupation	Of previous good character	Character unknown
1857	4,124	1,555	11.6	6.0	0.8	31.9	1.0	16.6	32.1
1861	3,053	919	22.9	3.9	0.7	28.3	0.7	11.5	24.4
1865	3,690	1,303	13.2	5.3	0.2	39.1	0.8	9.5	32.1
1869	4,278	1,268	16.6	4.3	0.4	36.0	1.0	12.9	28.7
1873	2,961	1,099	15.2	3.2	1.8	30.0	0.7	21.3	27.9

Source: Judicial Statistics, Parliamentary Papers, annually 1857-1873.

other opportunities, are likely to be attracted to crime, is one plausible explanation for this statistical picture. It is equally evidence that the police and courts singled out these groups for special and potentially inequitable attention. These two factors together provide a better explanation of the characteristics of the "criminal class" than either does separately.

CIVIL CONFLICT, 1800 TO THE 1870s

For modern scholars the subject of public order in London during the period 1800-1870 is part of a larger enigma. Why was there no "French Revolution" in England? Why is 1848 a relatively insignificant date in British history? How did the British people avoid the conflagrations that engulfed the Continent in the first half of the nineteenth century? The attitudes of the British political elite at the time are exemplified by Edmund Burke denouncing the French Revolution in the House of Commons in the 1790s and by the aged Duke of Wellington commanding the troops to defend London during the Chartist rally at Kennington Common in 1848. Many, perhaps most, were uncomfortably certain that violent revolution was possible, even probable. After all, Britain was hailed in 1851 as the "workshop of the world," and Karl Marx—by then a refugee in London—had proclaimed that the ultimate revolution would be achieved in the economically advanced nations. It did not happen. Why not?

Elie Halévy—an avowed admirer of British political stability in the nineteenth century, in fact an apologist for that period of seeming tranquility—saw evangelical religion and Methodism in particular as the cement that strengthened the foundations of social stability in England.[11] The Halévy thesis, which has amounted to a dogma among students of modern British history, has recently encountered significant critical opposition.[12] In fairness to Halévy, two points should be emphasized. First, his view that Methodism prevented revolution had been stressed by historians of the eighteenth century, notably Lecky[13] among English scholars. Second, no other scholar has provided a more convincing explanation of Britain's social and political stability in this period.

Halévy's successors, without disputing the thesis, have tended to emphasize other factors that may have contributed to this stability. In politics the evidence is that local interests and affiliations were paramount. Seemingly more divisive and certainly more dramatic national issues are less important in retrospect.[14] The tremendous economic growth of the nineteenth century made possible much improvement in the social and economic conditions of the common people, though there is considerable dispute over "how much" and "how soon." Another set of factors involves the leadership and certainty of purpose of the potential parties to revolutionary conflict. On the one hand, the British elite were united in their purpose of maintaining control, if not always on the specific policies by which this was to be accomplished. In the early decades of the century they were unhesitatingly ruthless in their military and judicial response to disorder. On the other hand, the working classes were fragmented and without effective leadership. In London in the eighteenth century the "mob" was aroused into violent action on several occasions, typically in response to the machinations and appeals of political figures of the middle classes.[15] By the early nineteenth century, though, it was relatively quiescent for lack of effective leadership, despite considerable suffering among the poor. Large masses of Londoners were decisive in pressing for political change in 1832 and 1867, *but* on both occasions the workers were following the lead of the middle class.[16]

The first 70 years of the nineteenth century were not without incident in London, however. The Napoleonic wars had severe economic consequences for workers in most of Britain, though probably less drastic in London than elsewhere. Tucker's indices of artisans' wages show a drop in the years 1815-1820,[17] coinciding with periodic episodes of machine-breaking and mass meetings in recently industrialized areas. One such protest meeting near Manchester in 1819 resulted in the infamous "massacre of Peterloo."[18] In the capital during this period there was a small group of revolutionary conspirators under the leadership of Dr. James Watson and Arthur Thistlewood. In December 1816, following a demonstration at Spa Fields, the conspirators marched on the City of London with the aim of seizing the Tower and the Bank of England. The crowd gave them no support and they were easily captured by the authorities. The leaders were indicted for treason, but Watson was acquitted and the charges against Thistlewood were dropped. They resumed their plotting, but by this time the government had introduced an *agent provocateur* into their circles. In February 1820 they were taken by the Bow Street Runners and Coldstream Guards at their headquarters in Cato Street, from which they had hoped to assassinate the Cabinet dining in nearby Grosvenor Square. Thistlewood and four of his associates were hanged in May. Throughout there was scarcely any popular support for the Cato Street conspirators.[19]

The return of Queen Caroline from the Continent in June 1820 was a different matter. The estranged wife of the Prince Regent, who had just succeeded as George IV, provided the people with a perfect opportunity to embarrass the unpopular monarch and the Government. For more than a year there were vast demonstrations on her behalf, carefully organized by the political leaders of the City of London who were her most ardent champions. An attempt by the Government to institute divorce proceedings in Parliament failed, and popular celebrations ensued for three days. This situation continued until the summer of 1821 when Caroline died. Even in death, however, she proved an embarrassment to the King. Her supporters determined that her funeral procession should pass through the City. The authorities naturally opposed this, but the mob blocked the procession in Kensington and forced it to turn east. In the attendant tumult several people were killed. The interesting feature of the whole episode is its political insignificance. The demonstrations in favor of Queen Caroline seem to have been simply an excuse for the London mob to rally; in practical terms nothing was accomplished.[20]

In fact, one of the principal reasons for the relative ineffectiveness of public disorder in London was that radical leaders found it extremely difficult to organize the urban masses for action. This was particularly evident during the struggle for parliamentary reform. On the accession of William IV in 1830, and with the example of the July Revolution in France, there was a great demand for reform. The populace of London, however, was curiously quiescent during the two-year controversy. The main center of the movement was Birmingham, where in January 1830 the banker Thomas Atwood founded the Birmingham Political Union, the first of the numerous unions that spearheaded the fight for reform. Unity among London's workers was prevented by the dissension between the National Union of the Working Classes, composed of radical artisans, and the National Political Union, led by Francis Place and drawing its inspiration from the Birmingham model. Only in the final crisis in May 1832 did London play a significant role, when a run on gold finally forced the King to agree to his prime minister's demand to create, if necessary, additional peers to ensure passage of the Reform Bill.[21]

Similarly, the Chartist movement of the late 1830s and 1840s received little support from the London masses, even though the Charter itself was drawn up by the London Workingmen's Association and many of the Chartist leaders were active in London's radical circles. London was the scene of the Chartist conventions in 1839 and 1842, but working men in the capital—the Spitalfields weavers, for example[22]—were not active in the movement, which was based on a much more radical set of demands for political participation than was the agitation over the Reform Bill. After 1842 Chartism would probably not have revived without the stimulus and example of the Continental revolutions in early 1848. At this point the Chartists had been preparing a "monster" petition, reportedly with six million supporting signatures, for presentation to Parliament. Meeting at a convention in early April to plan their strategy, the leaders announced a gigantic rally for April 10 on Kennington Common from which the crowd would proceed to Westminster to deliver the petition. Given such forewarning, the Government was not inactive. The Duke of Wellington was called in to command the troops, and special constables were mustered to assist the Metropolitan Police. In all, the government had at its disposal well over 100,000 men.

On April 10, 1848, the Chartist leaders arrived at the Common bearing the People's Charter and petition. Only 25,000 people had shown up for the demonstration. Police Commissioner Mayne, who was waiting to meet Feargus O'Connor, the Chartist leader, informed the latter that a peaceful meeting could be held but under no circumstances would the group be allowed to proceed to the House of Commons. The Chartists had little choice but to disperse peacefully—the turnout had been disappointing, and they were hopelessly outnumbered. When the petition was examined, it was discovered to have less than two million signatures, some of them forgeries. Chartism had come to an ignoble, indeed a farcical, end, and with it died the hope of radical change achieved by mass protest.[23]

Serious agitation for further parliamentary reform did not begin again in earnest until the 1860s, when the Reform League and a new London Workingmen's Association were founded. Several politicians had introduced bills for reform during the preceding five years, but there was no chance for such measures until the death of the Tory prime minister, Lord Palmerston, in 1865. From the spring of 1866 until the Second Reform Bill was passed a year later, the Reform League organized numerous rallies of workers to demonstrate support, the most famous meeting being held at Hyde Park on July 23, 1866. A rally two days later led to a sharp clash between some 300 reformers and 50 police in which one reformer was reported killed and 60 on both sides were injured. With this exception, there was no serious violence at any of the mass meetings, and in hindsight it may be questioned whether they had much effect on the deliberations in Parliament, by now committed to extending the franchise.[24]

In the economic sphere, no less than in the political arena, London's radicals were relatively unsuccessful in achieving broad-based support. Trades unions had been illegal, in theory at least, until the repeal of the Combination Act in 1825. Even after this point it took decades for the union movement to gain any degree of strength. The early groups, small associations of skilled artisans, were relatively ineffective. An effort to establish a national union along Owenite principles—the Grand National Consolidated Trades Union of Great

Britain and Ireland—lasted for only a few months in 1834. The most important industrial dispute of the period was in 1859-1861 when London builders went on a series of strikes. Even at this late date, however, the main issue of the struggle became that of whether the employers could prevent workers from organizing at all. Demands for better working conditions got lost in the process. The trades union movement did not emerge as a powerful force in public life until after 1870.[25]

Not all episodes of strife in London during these years had political overtones. A survey of the *Times* of London, beginning in 1840, identifies a number of other events, often involving Irish immigrants. An entry for June 30, 1841, describes a clash between police and an Irish mob in Kensington in which many immigrants were injured. Another affray on August 26, 1846, involved English and Irish workers, two of the former being killed before the police quelled the fighting. On July 12, 1853, Irish and Italian workers fought in Grays Inn Lane until constables intervened. A decade later, on September 23, 1862, the police in the same area were obliged to stop a fight between two Irish factions, and police casualties were considerable. Other examples of small-scale group conflict during this period include several clashes in spring of 1860 between church officials and parishioners resisting religious innovations at an East London church, and a fight in Islington, in November 1870, between self-appointed vigilantes and the toughs they wanted to clear off the streets.[26]

One facet of public order in early nineteenth century London deserves mention. This is the curious period of the first fifteen years of Queen Victoria's reign, when there were no less than four attempts to assassinate the young monarch. Assassination of public figures had never been a prominent feature of British life. The only prime minister so killed was Spencer Perceval in 1812. The attacks on Victoria were all the work of apparently deranged individuals, acting alone.[27] What is extraordinary about these episodes is that they occurred so frequently for a decade and then stopped completely. Many threatening letters have since been sent to the royal family and to prominent politicians, but dire results have been avoided.

In summary, the problem of controlling civil conflict in nineteenth century London was not a serious one. Political activists found it extremely difficult to organize the masses for direct action or even to enlist their support for radical causes. The occasional meetings and demonstrations were anything but violent, a marked contrast to mob action in Paris at the same period. Many factors seem to have contributed to this condition. In our view, the most immediate explanation of the low intensity of civil conflict in this era is to be found in the firm, often repressive, yet ultimately conciliatory posture of the British elite toward an urban working class which lacked both central organization and radical leadership.

INSTITUTIONS OF PUBLIC ORDER

Reforms in Criminal Law, 1800 to the 1870s

The far-reaching changes in English criminal law during the first half of the nineteenth century were not brought about in one or two sweeping legislative reenactments; rather they were achieved, like most other legal and institutional reforms in recent English history, in a series of discrete but cumulative steps. Moreover to call these changes "reforms" is to take the view of those who advocated them that they were generally beneficial to society. At the time most of these modifications were controversial and were heatedly resisted by some; and what appears in retrospect to have been an inevitable triumph of rational, liberal principles involved a protracted series of intellectual and political skirmishes between contending philosphies, political factions, and personalities, in which the reformers' victories were by no means assured.

The man most visibly responsible for the reforms effected in the 1820s was Sir Robert Peel, the greatest Tory political figure of the early nineteenth century and the prime mover of what became the Conservative Party. He was Home Secretary from 1822 to 1830, and in the following decades was twice prime minister, in 1834-1835 and 1841-1846. [28] Though Peel was not overly generous in acknowledging his debts to precursors as he pushed his reform measures through Parliament, it happens that the progressive legislation of the 1820s was the culmination of a campaign for radical change in the criminal law and its administration waged by a goodly number of intellectuals and politicians since the mid-eighteenth century.

To the modern eye criminal justice in Georgian England presents an appalling spectacle of a society in which human life was held in small regard. The application of principles of punishment was unjust and unsophisticated. Under the Hanoverians the number of capital statutes had trebled; the reformers Mackintosh and Fowell Buxton estimated that there were at least 200 offenses punishable by death at the accession of George IV in 1820. Many of the relevant statutes applied to more than one offense or variations of the same offense, and accessories were liable to the same punishment as principals. A legal system that punished with equal severity a man convicted of murder and one who consorted with gypsies would be ludicrous if the workings of such a system were not so tragic.

How did this system become established in the first place? The legislators of the eighteenth century regarded the death penalty as the method most likely to prevent crime. Often it was prescribed when it was felt that the incidence of a particular offense was increasing, regardless of the offense's seriousness. William Paley, by virtue of his tract *Principles of Moral and Political Philosophy* (1785), was the most influential apologist of existing criminal law. Like many Englishmen of his time, Paley simply regarded the threat of death as the most effective deterrent. To him there was no question of reforming the convict or providing secondary punishment for lesser offenses; nor did he think that equal sentences should be applied to those convicted for the same offense. To Paley and his English contemporaries a criminal code that operated on the principle of the sword of Damocles was both just and effective.

Such views did not prevail thoughout Enlightenment Europe. Two continental aristocrats—Montesquieu in *L'Esprit des Lois* (1748) and Cesare Beccaria in *Dei Delitti e delle Pene* (1764)—argued that punishments should reflect the gravity of the crime, and Beccaria urged the abolition of the death penalty. The latter aim was achieved in the criminal codes of Emperor Joseph II (1787) and Leopold, Grand Duke of Tuscany (1786), the liberal sons of Maria Theresa. The impact of these and other continental reforms had a decided influence on the English intellectuals and politicians who were interested in such questions, and they also gave the English system at the turn of the century the dubious distinction of being the most barbarous—in theory at least—of any major Western country.[29]

In fact, Paley's argument was not universally accepted even in England. Jeremy Bentham, the leading political and legal reformer of his age, favored the abolition of capital punishment for all offenses except murder. The goal of all punishment, in Bentham's view, was the prevention of crime; unlike Montesquieu and Beccaria, he felt that there should be variable punishments for each offence— punishment should vary according to the degree of temptation to which a criminal was subject.[30] The two other leading advocates of the reform of the criminal law in this period were William Eden and Sir Samuel Romilly. Eden's major statement on the subject was *Principles of Penal Law* (1771), which urged the abolition of capital punishment for numerous offenses and the consolidation of the whole criminal law. Romilly's first foray into the field of criminal law reform was the pamphlet *Observations . . . on Executive Justice* (1786), which argued that imprisonment should be substituted for capital punishment in many cases. His *Observations on the Criminal*

Law of England . . . (1810) criticized the haphazard administration of the criminal code.[31]

Romilly's work pushed the movement for the reform of the criminal code from a theoretical discussion of the issues to a parliamentary campaign. In 1808 Romilly succeeded in having a statute passed that repealed capital punishment for the crime of picking pockets (larceny from the person).[32] In 1811 he persuaded the legislature to replace the death penalty with transportation to Australia for the crime of stealing from bleaching-grounds; this reform was aided by petitions from the owners of such grounds requesting the change, the owners believing that prosecution would be easier and conviction more likely if the punishment were less severe.[33] His other acts, passed between 1812 and 1814, repealed capital punishment for vagrancy by soldiers and seamen, and changed the law of treason.

Despite these limited achievements, Romilly's major efforts at reform failed. In 1810 he proposed three bills that would have repealed capital punishment for shoplifting of 5 shillings or more, larceny of 40 shillings or more from dwelling-houses, and larceny of 40 shillings or more from aboard ships in navigable rivers. Even though, as Romilly pointed out, the extreme penalty was rarely imposed in these cases, the bills did not pass. He argued in vain that juries would be more willing to convict if the law were mitigated to some extent. The House of Lords, led by Eldon and Ellenborough, reiterated Paley's doctrine that a selective imposition of capital punishment was the most effective deterrent of crime.[34] Although Romilly did not live to see further reforms (he committed suicide in 1818), he deserves credit as the first of the Whig radicals to make inroads into the outmoded criminal code of Georgian England.

The mantle of reform was taken up by Sir James Mackintosh, who boasted that during his tenure as Recorder of Bombay no offenders had been executed; he was assisted by Sir Thomas Fowell Buxton, the great humanitarian noted for his role in the campaign against slavery. An indication that public opinion supported the work of the reformers came in January 1819 when the Corporation of London presented a petition to Parliament. The City fathers pointed out that many of the 200-odd offenses punishable by death, were quite minor and nonviolent. They noted the reluctance of prosecutors, juries, and judges to condemn criminals, due to the severity of the law. The failure to convict had, they believed, led to an increase in crime.[35] There were numerous petitions from other towns, as well as from grand juries and the clergy. This evidence of public support led the House of Commons to approve a proposal of Mackintosh, opposed by the Government, to appoint a select committee to investigate the criminal law.

The Select Committee of 1819 made a detailed investigation of the state of crime in the country and examined numerous witnesses, mostly from the mercantile and financial professions. They concentrated on larceny from shops and dwelling-houses, and forgery. Led by Mackintosh as chairman, the committee presented to Parliament a thorough plan for reform of the criminal law. In the first place the committee recommended the repeal of certain obsolete capital statutes including the notorious Waltham Black Act, a legislative relic of the eighteenth century that prescribed the extreme penalty for appearing armed and disguised, and also for illegal hunting and fishing. They further recommended that a second group of offenses be punished with transportation or imprisonment rather than hanging. In particular, they supported Romilly's goal of reducing the punishment for larceny in shops and dwelling-houses and on rivers. Finally, the committee urged a mitigation of punishment in cases of forgery.[36]

Mackintosh brought in several bills to implement the committee's report, but they met with little or no success. His two statutes abolishing obsolete laws and lessening the punishment for other miscellaneous offenses were drastically revised in passage[37]; the Waltham Black Act, for example, was excluded from reform. Instead of abolishing capital punishment for larceny in a shop, as the reformers wanted, Parliament passed an act restricting capital punishment to larcenies above £15 (the previous limit had been 5 shillings). [38] An attempt to reduce penalties for forgery failed. Mackintosh did succeed, however, in getting the Commons to approve a resolution early in 1822 to consider in the next session "increasing the efficacy of the Criminal Laws, by abating their undue rigour; together with measures for strengthening the Police, and for rendering the punishment of Transportation and Imprisonment more effectual for the purposes of example and reformation." In 1823 he introduced a series of resolutions to implement the recommendations of the 1819 committee, but these failed owing to the opposition of Sir Robert Peel, who had become Home Secretary in 1822. Peel, though opposed to the far-reaching aims of the Whig reformers, nevertheless agreed to bring in his own program for reform.

The Whig reformers, led by Mackintosh, had forced Peel's hand, influencing his work on the criminal code. While agreeing that there was a need to reduce capital punishment, Peel was not a determined foe of the extreme penalty. He went further than the Whigs did, however, in desiring a reform of the penal system and the establishment of an effective police for the metropolis. The Whigs, for their part, opposed a strengthened police on the grounds that it would be a danger to traditional liberties.

Peel began by persuading Parliament to pass the Gaols Act in 1823.[39] This statute provided for houses of correction in each county and some of the major urban areas, such prisons to be supported from the rates and to be inspected by justices reporting to the Home Secretary. Legislation in 1823 and 1824 permitted transported felons to be employed on public work in the colonies and remedied a few deficiencies in the Gaols Act, extending government inspection to prisons in smaller municipalities.[40]

Peel's reforms were based on the recommendations of the Select Committee of 1819, though he did not go as far as the Whig reformers on the committee had proposed. In 1823 he secured the passage of a number of reforming measures. The death penalty was abolished for larceny in shops and on board ships in navigable rivers, a reform long urged by Romilly and his followers.[41] The Waltham Black Act was finally repealed.[42] Miscellaneous crimes no longer subject to punishment by death included cutting down river banks and impersonating Greenwich Hospital pensioners.[43] In that year Peel also secured passage of an act allowing judges to refrain from pronouncing the death penalty in any cases except murder trials.[44] Peel's success as Home Secretary in getting these reforms through the House of Lords, in which Eldon had blocked all previous attempts, stands in marked contrast to the efforts of the Whig reformers who had attempted for more than a decade to force the Government on the matter. Peel's biographer claims that the bills were not passed simply because the Government was now sponsoring them; rather, he says, Peel displayed much more legislative and administrative skill, and in particular was careful to get the approval of the judges for his reforms.[45] One disgruntled politician ironically remarked that Peel was "the only reformer of the day."[46]

In the next few years Peel consolidated the laws relating to juries.[47] Then, in 1827, came the first of his major acts in consolidating the criminal law. Most of the statutes regarded as obsolete by the Select Committee of 1819 were repealed. Benefit of clergy was abolished, as was the distinction between grand and petty larceny (which meant that larceny was no longer a capital crime). The threshold value of goods stolen from a dwelling house, beyond which capital punishment was specified, was raised from 40 shillings to £5.[48] These measures constituted the greatest victory to date for the reform program. In 1828 the statutes relating to offenses against the person were consolidated.[49]

In 1830 Peel introduced a bill to consolidate the law on forgery while still retaining capital punishment for many types of this crime.

The bill met determined opposition, led by Mackintosh, in the Commons. Numerous petitions from bankers and others protesting the severity of the death penalty poured into Parliament. Mackintosh finally persuaded the lower house to remove the death penalty for all forgeries except forgery of wills. The Lords, however, revised the bill so that it conformed to Peel's wishes, and as such it became law.[50]

This was the last of Peel's measures to reform the criminal law. It had been a great achievement. Numerous obsolete statutes had been repealed, and virtually the whole of the criminal law had been consolidated into less than a dozen acts. But it was only a work of digest and consolidation. It fell short of the reformers' goals by failing to mitigate the severity of the law. And in this respect, public opinion was on the side of the reformers, not Peel. In 1831, for example, a petition to the House of Lords, signed by more than 1,000 merchants and others in the City of London who were liable to jury duty, requested Parliament to undertake further reforms.[51]

The reformers carried on their work after 1830 under the more liberal Whig ministry of Earl Grey. In 1832 an act was passed abolishing the death penalty for all coinage offenses.[52] The same year William Ewart, one of the new reformers, achieved passage of a bill that did away with capital punishment for horse, sheep, and cattle stealing and larceny from dwelling-houses.[53] A third act in this year revised the 1830 legislation on forgery so that only forging wills and certain powers of attorney remained capital offenses.[54] (It should be noted that no one was executed for forgery in England after 1830.) Parliament in 1833 made housebreaking a noncapital offense, and in the following year eliminated the death penalty for returning from transportation before the end of the sentence.[55]

After a brief return to Tory rule in 1834-1835, with Peel as prime minister, the Whigs regained power with Lord John Russell at the Home Office, and the pace of reform increased. A royal commission investigating the criminal law made its report in 1836 regarding capital punishment, and the following year Russell sponsored legislation removing the death penalty from 21 offenses, leaving only sixteen capital crimes on the books.[56] In fact, the movement for reform had been so successful that it was becoming difficult to rationalize capital punishment at all. William Ewart, who had become the leader of the reformers, began a campaign in the following decades for complete abolition. He nearly succeeded. Finally, in 1861, Parliament ended capital punishment for all crimes except murder and a few rare crimes of treason.[57] Murderers had been virtually the only criminals executed in the previous twenty years, and now the law came into conformity with practice. So the situation remained until the mid-twentieth century, when at last even the idea that murder must be punished by death began to lose ground, and the way was paved for total abolition.

Along with this breaching of the capital laws developed a curious and grim side issue. Hanging in public had long been part of the fabric of English social life. While the justification for this was the deterrence of potential offenders, in fact public executions appealed to the coarser nature of the populace. Those favoring the abolition of capital punishment wanted public executions; they feared that popular feeling would not be aroused against the practice if it were performed behind prison walls. They lost this battle, however: In 1868 an act was passed providing for executions to be carried out in prisons.[58]

The elimination of capital punishment for all offenses save murder had been a great victory for the reformers. No longer was a criminal code of Draconian severity relied on to prevent crime. Persuading juries to convict criminals who were patently guilty was not as difficult as it had been in the days when a minor offense could mean death. The victory had several important consequences for other institutions of public order. The social logic of relying on the death penalty to deter offenders was consistent with lax and spotty enforcement; it was sufficient that a few offenders be caught from time to time and publicly executed. If punishment were to fit the crime, however, more regular and consistent policing would be required. And as the law and courts came to rely on secondary punishments rather than the death penalty, it became necessary to improve and expand the prison system. The new logic of graduated punishment thus reinforced existing movements for reform of the police and prisons.

Establishing the Metropolitan Police

Like the movement for the reform of the criminal law, the impetus for the establishment of an effective, centralized police force in London dates from the mid-eighteenth century. The metropolis at that time hardly had a police "system" at all. Enforcement of the law was in the hands of local government authorities, which meant that at best the administration of justice was extremely haphazard. Outside the City of London, which had its own police force, there was no unity in local government. Each parish had had to apply to Parliament for a local improvement act, and this pattern of crazy-quilt legislation authorized local watchmen. In most metropolitan parishes these watchmen were totally ineffective in dealing with crime, and there was no cooperation among the parishes in tracking down offenders. Furthermore, the officers of the watch and the justices of the peace, who presided over the system, were notoriously venal.[59]

The first police reformers in London were the novelist Henry Fielding and his half-brother John. Henry was appointed Chief Magistrate of Westminster at Bow Street in 1748, a post which he held until his death in 1754. He received a salary of £200, thus relieving him from the need to rely on the fees that had been a source of corruption to his predecessors. In 1751 he published his pamphlet *An Enquiry into the Causes of the Late Increase of Robbers* and followed this with several other tracts on crime and vice in the metropolis. In addition, he began a journal in which he published the results of cases he had tried. He also founded a small body of "thief-takers" at Bow Street. Henry was succeeded by John, who was chief magistrate from 1754 to 1780. John continued his brother's pamphleteering work by publishing journals that circulated descriptions of criminal offenders and made Bow Street the center for information on criminals in the metropolis. With the help of a government grant he enlarged the force under his command, thus paving the way for the Bow Street Runners. While the effects of the Fielding brothers' work were not radical, at least a step had been made in the direction of establishing a regular police force to replace the old system in which householders acted as constables.[60]

The next move was an attempt by Pitt's Government in 1785 to establish a regular metropolitan police force. The bill, which applied to the City as well as the rest of London, would have ended the magistrates' jurisdiction over police officers, leaving them with only their judicial functions. There were to be three commissioners at the head of a force consisting of nine districts. The police were to be salaried, not paid by reward. At the same time the bill continued the old system of parochial constables and watchmen. Mainly owing to the opposition of the City fathers, the bill was withdrawn, and the chance for reform was lost. A similar measure, however, was put into effect in Ireland in 1786.[61]

Proposals for reform now hinged on the issue of ending the corruption of the magistracy, the so-called trading justices, which controlled the police. In 1792 Parliament passed the Middlesex Justices Act,[62] which provided for three justices of the peace at each of eight offices in the metropolis. Breaking with tradition, the justices were to be paid annual stipends and were prohibited from taking fees. Under the justices, each office had a police force consisting of not more than six constables. An important provision allowed the constables to apprehend persons suspected of criminal intent; these individuals could be then imprisoned under the Vagrant Act. The new system did much to eliminate corruption among metropolitan justices, but it did not go far in changing the police system of the metropolis. Originally a temporary measure, it was made permanent in 1812.[63]

One of the first justices appointed under the new system was Patrick Colquhoun, a former Glasgow merchant who very quickly made a name for himself as the principal voice calling for reform of the metropolitan police system. Colquhoun clearly recognized the connection between poverty and crime, and as a result of his philanthropic endeavors he has been called "the father of the soup kitchen." [64] But his chief claim to fame as a reformer is his authorship, at first anonymously, of *A Treatise on the Police of the Metropolis* (1795), which had half a dozen editions over the next decade. In it he proposed major changes in the policing of the metropolis, and he regarded his own ideas on the subject as a major innovation. He wrote: "Police in this Country may be considered as a *new Science;* the properties of which consist not in the Judicial Powers which lead to *Punishment,* and which belong to Magistrates alone; but in the Prevention and Detection of Crimes, and in those other Functions which relate to Internal Regulations for the well ordering and comfort of Civil Society." [65] Colquhoun's statement that prevention and detection of crime, rather than punishment, should be emphasized was the first expression of the modern view of the police role. He favored a great degree of centralization in the metropolitan force, commenting with approval on the French system. He proposed establishing a public prosecutor and urged that magistrates in the metropolis be given stipends. He wanted the police to be given stricter control over public houses, lodging houses, and certain tradespeople, including dairymen and other purveyors of food. Colquhoun also felt the police should have control over numerous groups of people in the potentially dangerous lower class, among whom he mentioned Jews, gypsies, servants, ballad singers, prostitutes, and dangerous convicts.[66]

To carry out his program of centralizing police in the metropolis, Colquhoun recommended the establishment of a "Central Board of Police" under the direct supervision of the Home Secretary. In addition to regulating trades and so forth, the board was to publish a *Police Gazette* and serve as a central receiving station for information about crime and criminals. This latter function was in line with Colquhoun's view that an effective police should concentrate on preventing crime rather than merely apprehending those who had committed crimes. The board was to have financial and administrative jurisdiction over the local police officers of the metropolis. Each parish was to have a force of professional police under the direction of a "high constable" in addition to the regular parochial forces, and these new officers were to be under the supervision of the central board.

The ideas Colquhoun put forward in his *Treatise* seem to have been received with public approval, except by the City of London, which was always an obstacle to movements to reform the metropolis. Colquhoun wrote four bills that would have established his system of police for the metropolis, but they were quietly dropped. [67] No further agitation for police reform occurred until 1811, when there was public hysteria after a series of shocking murders in Wapping in the East End of London. Two families, the Marrs and the Williamsons, were attacked and butchered with ripping chisel and maul. In the ensuing uproar the local watchmen were discharged and police throughout the metropolis took up the investigation. The murderer, John Williamson, was captured within a few weeks but succeeded in evading formal justice by hanging himself in his cell. There were a few calls for reform of the police, but they came to nothing. The public mood was implacably against a strengthened and centralized police force, and one writer went so far as to say: "They have an admirable police at Paris, but they pay for it dear enough. I had rather half a dozen people's throats should be cut in Ratcliffe Highway every three or four years than be subject to domiciliary visits, spies, and all the rest of Fouche's contrivances." [68]

In one not insignificant area Colquhoun's efforts bore fruit: He was responsible, together with John Harriot, for instituting the policing of the Thames and the London dockyards. The Marine Police Establishment, a private enterprise sponsored by the West Indian merchants, was founded in 1798 with 60 officers. The Thames River Act of 1800 made the system official, putting the new force under the direct control of the Home Office. The river police thus became the first professional force in the metropolis and performed outstandingly as a unit until they were made part of the new Metropolitan Police later in the century. [69]

Apart from the river police, the most professional among the various police offices in London were the Bow Street Runners, founded by the Fielding brothers. Though popular in the mideighteenth century, they have come to be regarded as the epitome of corruption and venality; perhaps this is understandable, given the contemporary system of rewards for the capture of criminals. A leading historian of the police remarks: "There is no doubt that more than one of the Bow Street policemen were actually in league with the depredators they were paid to catch, though they were generally too alert to be found out; but the confidence of the public in their thief-takers received a rude shock when Vaughan, of the Horse Patrol, was proved to have arranged a burglary for the sake of the reward that would have come to him on the conviction of the felons."[70] Despite their willingness to enrich themselves under the system of rewards for capturing offenders, the Bow Street Runners were regarded as the leading police establishment and did, to some extent, serve as a central police bureau for information about criminals in the metropolis. The force was expanded in 1805, under the direction of Sir Richard Ford, with the establishment of the Bow Street Horse Patrol. These mounted officers were stationed around the metropolis to patrol for highwaymen and other offenders. The first uniformed police in London, they owed their nickname "Robin Redbreasts" to the scarlet waistcoats they wore under the blue coats. In addition, the foot patrol was enlarged to guard the metropolitan area. Their jurisdiction was Middlesex, except for the City of London.[71]

Thus at the beginning of the nineteenth century there were some 500 professional police under the control of the Home Secretary—the Thames River Police, the Bow Street Runners, and the constables attached to the seven police magistrates' offices established in 1792. These forces were supplemented by the parochial watch numbering about 3,500 and the 1,000 watchmen in the City of London, making the grand total of police in the metropolis before the establishment of the Metropolitan Police some 5,000.[72] These forces were engaged primarily in the capture of known offenders; the role of the police as a preventive force was to come with the new officers in 1829.

The scene of activity over police reform shifted to the House of Commons after 1812; various select committees were appointed over the next decade to consider the police. Though the inadequacy of existing arrangements was recognized, no major proposals for reform issued from these committees. The Wapping murders stimulated a committee to propose in 1812 that the police be controlled by the metropolitan magistrates' offices, which had been created in 1792, but a draft bill to this effect came to nothing. Committees also met in 1816, 1817, and 1818, but little was proposed in the way of reform. In fact, the 1818 committee repeated the old argument that an effective police would be an engine of despotism: "Your Committee could imagine a system of police that might arrive at the object sought for; yet in a free country, or even in one where any unrestrained intercourse of society is admitted, such a system would of necessity be odious and repulsive, and one which no government could be able to carry into execution."[73]

With the coming of Peel to the Home Office in 1822 some advance might have been expected. A select committee that year, which the Home Secretary himself chaired, made a few minor proposals. But the idea of a more effective police was definitely rejected, and, in a classic statement, the committee reported:

It is difficult to reconcile an effective system of police, with that perfect freedom of action and exemption from interference, which are the great privileges and blessings of society in this country; and your Committee think that the forefeiture or curtailment of such advantages would be too great a sacrifice for improvements in police, or facilities in detection of crime, however desirable in themselves if abstractedly considered.[74]

A committee on criminal commitments and convictions reported in 1827 and 1828; while deploring the rise in crime, it made only slight reference to the police. Thus in 1828, on the eve of the founding of London's modern police force, the idea of a preventive police, which Colquhoun had advocated 30 years before, was still seen as a threat to traditional English liberties.[75]

The initiative for police reform now passed entirely to Sir Robert Peel, to whom belongs the credit for the establishment of the Metropolitan Police in 1829. As Chief Secretary in Ireland from 1812 to 1818, Peel had already been responsible for reforming the police in that country. During his tenure as Home Secretary in the 1820s he brought together the two disparate movements—the struggle for the reform of the criminal law and for the establishment of the police. The criminal law reformers Romilly and Mackintosh had for the most part opposed a strengthened police, seeing in it a potential instrument for government tyranny. Peel, on the other hand, felt that the amelioration of the criminal code should be accompanied by an effective police system. "It has always appeared to me," he remarked, "that the country has entirely outgrown its police institutions." [76] Accordingly, in February 1828 Peel secured the appointment of yet another select committee to inquire into increased crime in the metropolis and the subject of the police. This committee, unlike the one in 1822, was dominated by Peel's views on the police and recommended a radical reform. [77] It proposed that a police office be set up under the direct control of the Home Secretary. The office, which was to take charge of all police in the metropolis, was to be under the jurisdiction of two magistrates (later styled Commissioners of Police), thus continuing the traditional connection between justices of the peace and police. There was an important difference, however: These magistrates were to be purely executive officers and were to carry out no judicial duties. The area of the new police district had a radius of approximately eight miles around Charing Cross but specifically excluded the City of London.

The bill establishing the new police, which Peel introduced in April 1829, passed quickly through Parliament and became law.[78] The chief credit for the bill belongs to Peel, who not only possessed a Tory majority but went out of his way to secure a smooth passage of the measures. The exclusion of the City, for no logical reason (other than political expediency), nullified opposition from that quarter. It may be too that the statistical evidence Peel utilized in his speeches over the bill, evidence supported by several select committees that crime was increasing in the metropolis, convinced some members of Parliament who would otherwise have been resistant to change. What is noteworthy is that the act, while establishing the Metropolitan Police, really left all the details of the new system to the discretion of the Home Secretary. It provided that the Government, in addition to naming the two magistrates and supervising their duties, should also appoint a Receiver to handle the legal and financial business of the police. To support the new system, a police rate of 8 pence was to be levied in the metropolitan parishes affected.

Much of the success of the Metropolitan Police in its early days was due to the capable direction of its first two commissioners, Colonel Charles Rowan and Richard Mayne, who were appointed in the summer of 1829. Rowan had been a distinguished soldier in the Peninsula and Waterloo campaigns; Mayne, who was his junior, had served as a barrister on the Northern Circuit. Their first task was to organize the force and to recruit men to fill the 1,000 positions—8 superintendents, 20 inspectors, 88 sergeants, and 895 constables. The force was soon increased to 3,000 men serving in 17 divisions. After some debate, a uniform of blue greatcoat and top hat was selected. The headquarters for the police were fixed at 4 Whitehall Place, with a rear entrance on Scotland Yard, which soon gave its name to the whole building. A few of the men were recruited from the old parochial forces and the Bow Street patrols, but most of the force were inexperienced in police work. The wages for a constable were set at a guinea a week, deliberately low enough to exclude "gentlemen." In the early years there was a considerable turnover, not only because of the low wages but because many of the men were dismissed for disciplinary reasons. The police, soon nicknamed "bobbies" or "peelers," made their first appearance on the London streets on September 29, 1829. They were unarmed. The General Instructions, written by Rowan and Mayne, emphasized that the chief duty of the new police was to fulfill Colquhoun's role of a preventive police:

> It should be understood, at the outset, that the principal object to be attained is the Prevention of Crime. To this great end every effort of the Police is to be directed. The security of person and property, the preservation of the public tranquillity, and all the other objects of a Police Establishment, will thus be better effected, than by the detection and punishment of the offender, after he has succeeded in committing the crime. . . . Officers and Police Constables should endeavour to distinguish

themselves by such vigilance and activity, as may render it extremely difficult for any one to commit a crime within that portion of the town under their charge.[79]

The Metropolitan Police were not at first a popular institution. The press inveighed against the threat to liberty which the police represented. The parishes, which had been forced by the act to give up their local forces, resented in some cases the imposition of the new police rate. The magistrates appointed under the act of 1792 maintained their own constables for another ten years, and there were conflicts between them and the new police. The City of London remained outside the jurisdiction of the Metropolitan Police but its police were reformed along similar lines in 1839.[80] The police were deprived of their founder in 1830, the year Peel left the office of Home Secretary when the Tory Government fell. The crisis for the new police, however, did not come until 1833.

During the Reform Bill protests of the early 1830s the police had succeeded in maintaining order in the capital. In May 1833, in a move that may have been designed to harass the police, the more radical leaders of the National Union of the Working Classes decided to hold a large meeting at Cold Bath Fields, despite a Government ban. The Home Secretary, Melbourne, ordered the commissioners to arrest the leaders of any meeting that was held. The police, working under Rowan's immediate supervision, stopped the meeting, but one constable was stabbed to death. In the resulting inquest, the coroner's jury stated:

> We find a verdict of Justifiable Homicide on these grounds:
>   That no Riot Act was read, nor any proclamation advising the people to disperse.
>   That the Government did not take the proper precautions to prevent the meeting from assembling.
>   That the conduct of the police was ferocious, brutal and unprovoked by the people.
>   And we moreover express our anxious hope that the Government will, in future, take better precautions to prevent the recurrence of such disgraceful transactions in the Metropolis.[81]

To make matters more difficult for the police, the Home Secretary did not give full backing to the commissioners. Nevertheless, after inquiry the police were completely exonerated in the matter.[82]

Another incident in 1833 involved the activities of William Steward Popay, an overzealous sergeant in the force. While working for the police, Popay had insinuated himself into the counsels of the radicals and had, according to later evidence, been active at meetings of the National Political Union. Although one authority has seen him as "the founder and originator of the detective system,"[83] he has generally been regarded as a police spy or *agent provocateur*. There seems little question that he abused his authority, and the commissioners were criticized for not keeping rein on his activities.[84] Popay was dismissed from the force.

Despite these two troublesome incidents in 1833, the work of the police was roundly praised by a select committee that met in 1833 and 1834. The committee made a point of commending the way in which Rowan and Mayne had discharged their duties as commissioners. They reported, in conclusion:

> ... that the Metropolitan Police Force, its management, and the principles on which it is conducted deserve the confidence and support of the House. That it is well calculated to check crime, and to maintain the peace and order of the Metropolis both effectively and constitutionally. And there is satisfactory evidence of this in the fact that on no occasion since the establishment of the Metropolitan Police has the military authority been called upon to assist the civil power in repressing any disturbance....

> Your Committee, keeping in view the whole evidence now placed before The House conclude with this expression of their opinion; viz., that the Metropolitan Police Force, as respects its influence in repressing crime, and the security it has given to person and property, is one of the most valuable of modern institutions....[85]

This crisis for the Metropolitan Police, in which they were completely vindicated, left them in a strong position for the future. The hostility with which Londoners had greeted their appearance, illustrated by the use of derisive nicknames and the criticisms voiced in 1833, turned now to affection, approval, and respect for the "bobbies." The new popularity was officially recognized in 1839 when the MPD was enlarged, the Thames force was made part of the centralized police, and the metropolitan magistrates (who had been a conservative force under the leadership of Sir Frederick Roe at Bow Street) were made to relinquish their executive police functions. Lord John Russell, the Home Secretary, even threatened to bring the City under the jurisdiction of the Metropolitan Police; but this became unnecessary when the City fathers proposed to reform their police along the lines of the metropolitan model.

In 1842, after a notorious murder and several attempts on the life of Queen Victoria, the commissioners secured the acquiescence of the Home Secretary in the establishment of a nonuniformed Detective Branch consisting of two inspectors and six sergeants. This force, the forerunner of the Criminal Investigation Department, scored its first notable success in 1849 by tracking down the murderers of Patrick O'Connor. The perpetrators, a couple named Manning, were publicly hanged in front of Horsemonger Lane Gaol.

Rowan retired as commissioner in 1850. He and Mayne had worked extremely well together during the twenty-year history of the force. He was succeeded by Captain William Hay who was officially made second in command to Mayne. This partnership was not nearly as successful, and on the death of Hay in 1855 Mayne was made sole commissioner and continued to direct the force alone until he died in 1868. In his later years Mayne became extremely unpopular, as is evidence in this criticism from the *Penny Illustrated Paper:*

Sir Richard Mayne has again exhibited that capricious temper which has done so much to lower the efficiency and popularity of the force under his command and to set them upon duties that are altogether repugnant to themselves and to the public at large. That the Chief Commissioner is quite above control seems to be inferred from the fact that he never condescends either to defence or explanation. Magistrates, members of both Houses of Parliament, and, for aught we know, the chiefs of the Home Office themselves, seem to be paralyzed by his dumb authority. He treats all their questions with utter contempt, declines to discuss the question with anybody concerned, seems able to obtain all sorts of enactments for securing to himself all sorts of functions, and goes on like an irresistible fate in a blue uniform, amenable to nobody, and probably not even acquainted with popular opinion.[86]

On the whole, the Metropolitan Police acquitted themselves well during their first 40 years of service. Notwithstanding frequent carping by the press and the criticisms directed at Mayne in his final years in office, the police were well established as a London institution by the 1860s. Though the detection of crime had not been the chief objective of the force, the Detective Branch, with Charles Dickens as an earlier advocate,[87] quickly earned for itself a reputation superior to that of the old Bow Street Runners. In their main function, that of keeping order in the metropolis, the police to all appearances were successful. The indicators of serious crime declined very substantially in the 40 years after their establishment, as we have seen. It is scarcely likely that the police alone were responsible for that decline, and quite possibly their role was distinctly subsidiary to the concurrent improvement in social conditions and expansion of economic opportunities. The significant social fact is that Londoners came to believe that the Metropolitan Police were in large measure responsible for maintaining public order. It is a testament to the police and an index of popular satisfaction that no body of public opinion gave enduring voice to claims that the liberties of Londoners were lessened in the process.

The Judicial System

English judicial institutions, like the law itself, present an extremely complicated facade. As in civil suits, a criminal charge could be heard before any of several different courts. An understanding of the judicial institutions of metropolitan London is complicated because the system there differed from that in the rest of England.[88]

The most numerous judicial officers are, of course, the justices of the peace, or "magistrates." The office itself dates from the late Middle Ages and has remained an important one ever since, though its heyday was perhaps the sixteenth century, when the Tudor monarchy relied on the justices to impose its policies throughout the land. In addition to judicial duties the justices were required to perform a variety of administrative and local government tasks, and they generally have been unpaid (though the number of stipendiary magistrates has increased in recent times, especially in large cities). In criminal matters the justices had the power of summary jurisdiction over relatively minor crimes, though after 1848 this had to be exercised in petty sessions rather than by a single justice acting alone. These unpaid, so-called amateur (because they often did not have legal training) judicial officers bore much of the brunt of enforcing criminal justice. Their other important duty in criminal matters, at least until the nineteenth century, was "conserving the peace." They were in charge of the parochial constabulary until the institution of professional police forces. Even though many of these men had no background in the law, a considerable number of them made valuable contributions—in London notably the Fielding brothers and Colquhoun. The famous Bow Street Office had its origin as the residence of the "first magistrate of Westminster."[89]

Justices, acting singly or in petty sessions, were strictly limited in the types of cases they could try. Serious crimes were reserved for the quarter sessions, a quarterly court consisting of all the justices of a county, or to the assizes. (Analogous North American institutions would be county and circuit courts.) The judges at the assizes were officials of much greater stature than the justices. They were appointed by the Crown and had general commissions of *oyer* and *terminer* (to hear and determine) and gaol delivery. With the passing of the Judicature Act of 1873, cases could be appealed from magistrates' courts and quarter sessions to the Queen's Bench Division of the High Court of Justice; but until 1907 when the Court of Criminal Appeal was set up, there was rarely any recourse from the decisions of the assizes. The principal hope for those convicted was the intervention of the Home Secretary using the royal prerogative of mercy.

The assize court for the City of London and the county of Middlesex has always been the Old Bailey, the most famous of all criminal courts in English-speaking societies. The City has always maintained a great pride in its independence, and the modern Central Criminal Court there is a monument to the assertion of this spirit. For centuries, under the jurisdiction of the City's officers, the Sessions House at the Old Bailey had been the premier criminal court of the metropolis, and the adjacent prison of Newgate held individuals awaiting trial or, if convicted, execution. The court and gaol, the prison, where conditions for prisoners were notoriously bad, bulk large in the popular imagination as the scenes of numerous capital trials and public executions in the eighteenth and nineteenth centuries.

The unsavory reputation of the Old Bailey notwithstanding, its personnel and procedures were left unchanged by the Central Criminal Court Act of 1834, "An Act for establishing a new Court for the Trial of Offences committed in the Metropolis . . . for the more effective and uniform Administration of Justice. . . ." [90] Rather than establishing a new court, the act merely enlarged the jurisdiction of the old one to include parts of Essex, Kent, and Surrey, and gave its officers the right to try crimes committed on the high seas. The act of 1834 also unconditionally prohibited justices of the peace within the jurisdication of the court (an area coextensive with metropolitan London), even when they were acting in quarter sessions, from trying a multitude of serious offenses, including all capital crimes. The passage of this act underscores the fact that by 1834 the operation of the Old Bailey was regarded as satisfactory, and subsequent legislation has tended to increase rather than diminish its powers. For example, criminal cases occurring outside the court's normal jurisdiction can in exceptional circumstances be tried there by *certiorari*, and the Central Criminal Court was made a branch of the High Court the High Court of Justice by the Judicature Act of 1873.

The Penal System

The penal system of England, like the criminal code and the police, was greatly altered in the course of the early nineteenth century. The changes effected in this period, however, have not been viewed with approval by twentieth century social reformers. Albert Crew, who was hardly a wild-eyed radical, wrote in 1933:

> The prison of the nineteenth century was characterized by iron discipline, useless labour, stern repression, monotonous and insufficient diet, solitary confinement, deadly silence, physical and mental cruelty and compulsory religion. . . . A prison . . . prior to the nineteenth century was merely a place of detention; in the nineteenth century a place of punishment, and today in the twentiety century, a place of reformation.[91]

With the exception of the successful attempt to abolish capital punishment for all offenses, the criminal law and the Metropolitan Police are today basically the same institutions that have existed since the reforms of the 1820s. By contrast, the prison system is still under attack by reformers, and changes in the system have been continuous since the eighteenth century. The standard history of English prisons in the nineteenth century, the work of Sidney and Beatrice Webb, is an open assault on past and current (1922) practices. [92] Why has the penal system been an unending source of controversy? The answer appears to be threefold.

First, at no period have conditions of incarceration been pleasant, and that was emphatically true prior to the twentieth century; this situation has always been criticized by humanitarian reformers. Second, there has never been agreement (either among the elite or in English society as a whole) on what goals the prison system should accomplish: Prisons have been viewed simultaneously as places for detention, retribution, and reformation, but no one of these purposes has predominated at any given time. Third, the modern English prison system, which developed in the early nineteenth century, was established from urgent necessity rather than after rational consideration of the social purposes and effects of imprisonment. The abolition of capital punishment for all offenses except murder and the ending of transportation to the colonies left the Victorian authorities with a great number of convicts who had to be incarcerated at home. The great spate of prison building in the first half of the nineteenth century resulted in structures specifically designed for punishment and retribution; within a few decades of their construction when the goal of reformation of criminals came to be seen as desirable, these prisons were outmoded.

The eighteenth century criminal code, as previously noted, relied on capital punishment as the chief deterrent to crime. In practice transportation of those convicted to the American colonies was a frequently chosen alternative to execution in the eighteenth century, and for almost a century after the American Revolution felons were sent to Australia. [93] Prisons sometimes were relied on as places of punishment, especially for those who could not pay fines, but this did not become their primary function until after the reform of the criminal code in the 1820s. Before this time prisons served mainly as places for the detention of persons awaiting trial and dangerous persons, notably criminal lunatics. There were at this period two types of prisons: the gaol, for debtors and those to be tried, and the bridewell (or house of correction) where vagrants and beggars were put to forced labor. Theoretically, all prisons belonged to the Crown; but in practice, the local gaols and even the bridewells (supposedly under the administration of justices of the peace) were operated as private enterprises by their officials. There was no attempt to regulate these institutions by the central government. Thus it is hardly surprising that conditions were notoriously bad. A principal abuse was the imposition of fees by the gaolers on all prisoners, acquitted or not; innocent persons often were held after their trials if they could not pay the discharge fee. All entering were compelled to pay the "garnish," which provided everyone within the prison with drink. Sale of liquor was permitted within the gaols, and drunkenness was common. There was a good deal of promiscuity because in most gaols men and women were not segregated; an act of 1784 that required their separation was widely ignored. In terribly overcrowded conditions those awaiting trial and young persons often were herded together with the most depraved. But by far the worst danger of overcrowded prisons was disease. The so-called gaol fever proved lethal not only to prisoners but to officials as well; in 1750, for example, numerous officers (including the lord mayor) and jurymen at the Old Bailey perished when they were contaminated by the prisoners coming from Newgate for trial.[94]

These shocking conditions did not go unnoticed by contemporaries, but there was no real agitation for reform until the work of John Howard, who is quite properly regarded as the father of the prison reform movement. In 1773 Howard was appointed Sheriff of Bedfordshire, and, unlike his fellow sheriffs, took literally his role of overseeing the administration of the gaols. What he found in his own county appalled him, and he spent the rest of his life traveling through Great Britain and Europe studying prison conditions. His famous work *The State of the Prisons in England and Wales* first appeared in 1777 and went through several later editions. Rather than condemning prison conditions in tones of outraged morality, he presented precise statistical summaries for each gaol he visited. He argued forcefully for the abolition of fees; the ending of overcrowding and unsanitary conditions; and the institution of a model regimen of adequate diet, useful work, and religious instruction for the prisoners. His writings inspired Alexander Popham, an MP, to introduce legislation abolishing discharge fees and requiring the cleansing of gaols. Popham's two acts (passed in 1784) were not enforced, and neither were subsequent enactments, inspired by Blackstone and Eden, which proposed a national penitentiary and reform of local gaols.[95]

For nearly a quarter century after Howard's death in 1790 the prison reform movement continued feebly and met with no success. In 1816, however, Elizabeth Fry (1780-1845), a wealthy Quaker woman with considerable influence in financial and political circles, began her well-known visits to Newgate, the most infamous prison in London. With her friends she spent considerable time among the female prisoners attempting to inculcate the virtues of sobriety and cleanliness. The effects of her work on the lives of the prisoners were transient, but the efforts helped greatly to draw public attention to prisons.[96] Several parliamentary committees reported on the metropolitan prisons, and the criminal law reformers, notably Thomas Fowell Buxton, began agitating for penal reform. The first fruit of the reform movement was the passage of the Gaols Act (1823)[97] sponsored by Home Secretary Robert Peel. The act required the local justices of the peace to reform gaols along the lines of the recommendations laid down by Howard and to report regularly to the Home Secretary. This statute consolidated previous legislation on gaols, but it did not apply to all prisons, and there were no provisions for its enforcement.

The central government did not effectively enter the field of prison administration until the passage of the Prisons Act of 1835,[98] a measure sponsored by the Whig Government that was also responsible for the Factory Act, the new Poor Law, and the Municipal Corporations Act. Henceforth, teams of government inspectors—working along the lines of inspectorate investigation advocated by Bentham's disciple Edwin Chadwick—visited prisons and submitted regular reports.[99] This system of local control with government inspection endured until 1877, when all prisons were placed under the direction of the Prison Commission of the Home Office. Many former abuses (notably the old private enterprise system of gaol fees) were eliminated during this period of central inspection, but much time and effort of both the inspectors and prison administrators was expended in the controversial implementation of the "separate" system. The popularity of "separate" confinement (and such variations as the "silent" system) among the liberal prison reformers stemmed in part from a revulsion against the old overcrowding. Inspired by the experiments of the Quakers in Philadelphia in cellular isolation and the Auburn (New York) scheme of associated work but absolute silence among prisoners, the proponents of reform advocated a program in which prisoners would spend a maximum amount of time in isolation and reflection on their misdeeds. The severe regimen was to include useful labor (though in practice many were put on treadmills unconnected to other machines) and religious instruction. In its extreme form the "separate" system included masking of all prisoners (the aim of which was to prevent recognition of each other), and in Pentonville, the Middlesex convict prison where the system was most diligently applied, the pews in the chapel had dividers.[100] Apart from any humanitarian objections, the "separate" system proved unworkable: It was difficult to enforce the rigors of its discipline, and a great number of men imprisoned under these conditions became insane.[101]

In one area of the prison system—transportation of convicts—the central government had been active even in the eighteenth century, though its influence was far from salutary. After the revolt of the American colonies, criminals sentenced to transportation were held in prison hulks until shipment to Australia. The hulks, large ships anchored on the Thames, were theoretically only a stopping point for convicts; in fact, they were long-term prisons where the most degrading conditions prevailed. The Webbs condemned the hulks as the worst aspect of the British penal system: "Of all the places of confinement that British history records, the hulks were apparently the most brutalizing, the most demoralizing and the most horrible. The death rate was appalling, even for the prisons of the period."[102] For those who were sent to the penal colonies the situation was nearly as grim: Many died during the journey, especially in the early years, and an uncertain fate awaited those who arrived at their destination. In all, it is estimated that more than 150,000 people were transported to Australia.[103]

Although there was opposition within England to the system of transportation (some saw it as depriving the mother country of useful forced labor), it was abolished mainly to satisfy the colonists who opposed it. To replace transportation, Parliament in 1853 passed a Penal Servitude Act[104] that provided terms of hard labor in a convict prison. The adoption of penal servitude necessitated the building of new convict prisons or the reconstruction of existing penitentiaries.[104] The act also allowed the Home Secretary to issue a "license" to convicts who had served part of their transportation or penal servitude sentences "to be at large" during the remainder of their terms—a policy already in practice in Australia. This provision, which was generally implemented for convicted felons, marks the first appearance in England of "ticket-of-leave" men.

The idea of a national penitentiary had been expressed as early as 1778 in an unsuccessful act. The scheme was revived, however, in Jeremy Bentham's projected "panopticon," a prison in which a fantastic array of mirrors would permit constant surveillance of the inmates.[106] There was a good deal of controversy over Bentham's plan, but eventually a modified version of his design was erected on the left bank of the Thames, south of the Houses of Parliament (on the present site of the Tate Gallery) called Millbank Prison. It was opened in 1821 and during the mid-nineteenth century served, along with the hulks, as the first depot for convicts sentenced to transportation or penal servitude. Along with Pentonville, London's other convict prison, erected in 1842, it was renowned as a model of the "separate" system of prison discipline. The convict prisons housed only those convicted of serious offenses. For lesser crimes, a Londoner could expect to be imprisoned in one of the various metropolitan houses of correction—Clerkenwell, Coldbath Fields, Wandsworth, or Holloway. The most famous London prison, Newgate, was reserved for those to be tried at the Old Bailey (a few convicts receiving short sentences were detained there after trial). In addition to these institutions for criminal offenders, there were also in London prisons for debtors—King's Bench, Fleet, and Marshalsea. The sufferings of their inmates and the iniquities of their keepers have been eloquently described in the novels of Dickens. These infamous debtors' prisons were closed in the early years of Victoria's reign.[107]

The harshness of prison life in nineteenth century London can scarcely be exaggerated. The only conceivable defense of such a system (and it was voiced at the time without apology) was that imprisonment should exact retribution from the criminal. Even the advocates of prison reform among Victorians favored treatment of offenders which seems exceedingly cruel by twentieth century standards. Before 1877, when the government assumed control of all prisons, the worst abuses (gaoler's fees, drunkenness, overcrowding) were abolished or somewhat mitigated; but the concept of prison as a place of punishment, exemplified perhaps by the continuance for many decades of whipping, remained nearly unquestioned save by a few reformers. Of all areas of governmental activity aimed at coping with crime, the prison system alone continued to be a source of heated controversy.

NOTES TO CHAPTER II.2

1. George, op. cit.
2. Rudé, *Hanoverian London;* Rudé, *Paris and London in the Eighteenth Century.*
3. J. M. Beattie, "The Pattern of Crime in England, 1660-1800," *Past and Present,* 62 (February 1974), 47-95; Figure II.2.1 from p. 68.
4. The comparison is of course inexact, since we are dealing with different jurisdictions in different eras. Moreover data on committals for assault in Middlesex are available only from 1834, and the rate for that year of 27 per 100,000 is in the same range as the Surrey rates for the 1790s; see Figure II.2.2.
5. See *British Sessional Papers,* House of Commons, 1817, Vol. 16, especially the table on p. 183 entitled "London and Middlesex: Abstract of the Number of Persons who were Capitally Convicted and those who were Executed in London and Middlesex from the Year 1749 to the Year 1817. . . ." The accompanying text does not consider the alternative explanation for the observed correlation, namely, that the judiciary felt it necessary to administer justice more stringently during wartime.
6. L. Radzinowicz, *A History of the English Criminal Law and Its Administration Since 1750,* 4 vols. (London: Stevens, 1948-1968). A projected fifth volume will deal with the penal system. There is no work of comparable scope for the previous period, but a new book by E. P. Thompson provides a detailed analysis of the socioeconomic conflicts and the politics of Hanoverian England that led to the passage in 1723 of the notorious Black Act, whose horrendous penalties exemplified the harsh eighteenth century attitudes toward crime and punishment. The book is *Whigs and Hunters: The Origin of the Black Act* (London: Allen Lane and Penguin, 1975).
7. On the Garrotters Act see Gordon Rose, *The Struggle for Penal Reform* (London: Stevens, 1960), pp. 11-13, and Royal Commission on Transportation and Penal Servitude, 1863, Appendix 5, B and C.
8. Tobias, *Crime and Industrial Society,* p. 61.
9. No doubt police surveillance and the writings of journalists like Mayhew not only helped create the social belief that these people were criminals but was something of a self-fulfilling prophecy. Modern criminologists have shown how such labeling processes can affect people's self-images and subject them to public and private constraints that reinforce their deviant behavior; see, for example, the contributions in Richard L. Henshel and Robert A. Silverman, eds., *Perception in Criminology* (New York: Columbia University Press, 1975), Part III. But that is a question of how such groups originate and persist; the social fact in nineteenth century London was existence of a substantial "class" of people, known to the police in person and by residence, who made much of their living by theft, prostitution, or dealing in stolen goods.
10. Lees, *Social Change and Social Stability among the London Irish.*
11. Elie Halévy, *The Birth of Methodism in England,* translated with an introduction by Bernard Semmel (Chicago: University of Chicago Press, 1971; French original, 1906); Halévy, *History of the English People in the Nineteenth*

Century, Vol. I, *England in 1815* (London: Benn, 1949; French original, 1912), Part III.

12. E. J. Hobsbawm, *Labouring Men* (London: Weidenfeld & Nicolson, 1964); E. P. Thompson, *The Making of the English Working Class* (London: Victor Gollancz, 1963); Bernard Semmel, *The Methodist Revolution* (London: Heinemann, 1974).

13. W. E. H. Lecky, *History of England in the Eighteenth Century*, 7 vols. (London: Longmans, 1878-1890), Vol. II; see also Ronald Knox, *Enthusiasm* (Oxford: Clarendon Press, 1950) for a Catholic viewpoint.

14. Norman Gash, *Politics in the Age of Peel* (London: Longmans, 1953); H. J. Hanham, *Elections and Party Management: Politics in the Age of Gladstone and Disraeli* (London: Longmans, 1959).

15. The Gordon riots of 1780 were the most notable example of mob violence. See George, *London Life in the Eighteenth Century;* Rudé, *Hanoverian London;* Rudé, *Paris and London in the Eighteenth Century;* Lucy Sutherland, "The City of London in Eighteenth Century Politics," in Richard Pares and A. J. P. Taylor, eds., *Essays Presented to Sir Lewis Namier* (London: Macmillan, 1956).

16. Evidence and interpretation of the conditions of protest and reform in English life in this period can be found, among many other sources, in Asa Briggs, *The Age of Improvement* (New York: McKay, 1959); F. O. Darvall, *Popular Disturbances and Public Order in Regency England* (London: Oxford University Press, 1934); William L. Langer, *Political and Social Upheaval, 1832-1852* (New York: Harper & Row, 1968); Ben C. Roberts, "On the Origins and Resolution of English Working-Class Protest," in Hugh Davis Graham and Ted Robert Gurr, eds., *Violence in America: Historical and Comparative Perspectives: A Report to the National Commission on the Causes and Prevention of Violence.* (New York: Bantam Books and Praeger, 1969), ch. 7.

17. Tucker, "Real Wages," in Young, ed., *Early Victorian England*, p. 79.

18. Thompson, *Making of the English Working Class;* R. J. White, *From Waterloo to Peterloo* (London: Heinemann, 1950).

19. See John Stanhope, *The Cato Street Conspiracy* (London: Jonathan Cape, 1962).

20. See Darvall, op. cit.; Briggs, op. cit., pp. 191-192.

21. Briggs, op. cit.

22. D. J. Rowe, "Chartism and the Spitalfields Weavers," *Economic History Review*, 2nd ser., 20 (1967), 482-493.

23. General studies include Mark Hovell, *The Chartist Movement* (Manchester, 1918); G. D. H. Cole, *Chartist Portraits* (London: Macmillan, 1941); Asa Briggs, ed., *Chartist Studies* (London: Macmillan, 1959). On London, see D. J. Rowe, "The London Workingmen's Association and the 'People's Charter.' " *Past and Present*, 36 (1967), 73-86, and the debate between Rowe and I. Prothero, ibid., 38 (1967), 169-173; Rowe, "The Failure of London Chartism," *the Historical Journal*, 11 (1968), 472-487; Prothero, "Chartism in London," *Past and Present*, 44 (1969), 76-101.

24. The clash was reported in the *Times* of London. See note 26. On the bill generally, see F. B. Smith, *The Making of the Second Reform Bill* (London: Cambridge University Press, 1966); Maurice Cowling, *1867: Disraeli, Gladstone, and Revolution* (Cambridge: Cambridge University Press, 1967).

25. Sidney and Beatrice Webb, *History of Trade Unionism*, rev. ed. (London: Longmans, 1920).

26. These reports are from a systematic survey of civil conflict events reported in the *Times* by Michael Stohl of the Department of Political Science, Purdue University, who made his data collection available for this study.

27. *Mepol* 3/17. 18, 19A, 19B (P.R.O.).

28. Norman Gash, *Mr. Secretary Peel: The Life of Sir Robert Peel to 1830* (Cambridge: Harvard University Press, 1961); Norman Gash, *Sir Robert Peel: The Life of Sir Robert Peel after 1830* (Totowa, N.J.: Rowan and Littlefield, 1972).

29. Radzinowicz, *History of English Criminal Law*, Vol. I, pp. 3-40 on the extension of capital statues; Vol. I, pp. 248-259 on Paley; Vol. I, pp. 268-300 on continental thinkers and reforms. Recent studies advance the thesis that the capital statutes were ideological statements in defense of existing distributions of property and authority; see Hay et al., *Albion's Fatal Tree*, and Thompson, *Whigs and Hunters*. Some countries that abolished the death penalty retained other penalties, such as sentences to the galleys and prolonged flogging, which had the same result for most of those so sentenced.

30. Ibid., Vol. I, pp. 355-396. The chief work on Bentham and his disciples is still Eli Halévy, *The Growth of Philosophic Radicalism* (London: Faber & Gwyer, 1928; French original, 1901-1904).

31. Radzinowicz, op. cit., Vol. I, pp. 301-336.

32. 48 Geo. III, c. 129. E. O. Tuttle, *The Crusade Against Capital Punishment in Great Britain* (London: Stevens, 1961), p. 3.

33. 51 Geo. III, c. 39; 51 Geo. III, c. 41.

34. Tuttle, op. cit., pp. 4-5; Radzinowicz, op. cit., Vol. I, pp. 503-507.

35. The petition is printed in ibid., Vol. I, pp. 728-730.

36. Select Committee on Criminal Laws, 1819.

37. 1 Geo. IV, c. 115 and 1 Geo. IV, c. 116.

38. 1 Geo IV, c. 117.

39. 4 Geo. IV, c. 64.

40. 4 Geo. IV, c. 47 and 5 Geo. IV, c. 85.

41. 4 Geo. IV, c. 53.

42. 4 Geo. IV, c. 54.

43. 4 Geo. IV, c. 46.

44. 4 Geo. IV, c. 48.

45. Gash, *Mr. Secretary Peel*, pp. 329-331.

46. Quoted in Elie Halévy, *The Liberal Awakening* (New York: Barnes & Noble, 1961; French original, 1923), p. 193.

47. 6 Geo. IV, c. 50.

48. 7 & 8 Geo. IV, cc. 27-31.

49. 9 Geo. IV, c. 31.

50. 11 Geo. IV & 1 Will. IV, c. 66.

51. The petition is reprinted in Radzinowicz, op. cit., Vol. I, pp. 731-732.

52. 2 & 3 Will. IV, c. 34.

53. 2 & 3 Will. IV, c. 62.

54. 2 & 3 Will. IV, c. 123.

55. 3 & 4 Will. IV, c. 44; 4 & 5 Will. IV, c. 67.

56. 7 Will. IV and 1 Vict., cc. 84-91.

57. Radzinowicz, op. cit., Vol. IV, pp. 327-343.

58. 31 Vict., c. 24. See Radzinowicz, op. cit. Vol. 4, pp. 343-353.

59. Radzinowicz, op. cit., Vol. II. A recent survey on the police is T. A. Critchley, *A History of Police in England and Wales, 900-1966* (London:

Constable, 1967). Profitable use also has been made of an unpublished paper on the establishment of the police by Jeremy Scanlon, "Peeling the Charlies" (Cambridge, Mass., 1964).

60. Radzinowicz, op. cit., Vol. III, pp. 11-62; Charles Reith, *The Police Idea* (London: Oxford University Press, 1938), pp. 22-34.

61. Reith, op. cit., pp. 90-98.

62. 32 Geo. III, c. 53.

63. Radzinowicz, op. cit., Vol. III, pp. 126-137.

64. Douglas G. Browne, *The Rise of Scotland Yard* (London: Harrap, 1956), p. 47; David Owen, *English Philanthropy, 1660-1960* (Cambridge: Belknap Press of Harvard University Press, 1964), p. 108.

65. Patrick Colquhoun, *A Treatise on the Police of the Metropolis*, 6th ed. (London: Joseph Mawman, 1800), preface.

66. Radzinowicz, op. cit., Vol. III, pp. 258-284.

67. Ibid., Vol. III, pp. 308-311.

68. Quoted in ibid., Vol. III, p. 347.

69. 39 & 40 Geo. III, c. 87; Radzinowicz, op. cit., Vol. II, pp. 349-404.

70. W. L. Melville Lee, *A History of Police in England* (London: Methuen, 1901), p. 194.

71. Browne, op. cit., pp. 50-52; Critchley, op. cit., pp. 43-45.

72. Radzinowicz, op. cit., Vol. II, p. 533.

73. Select Committee on the Police of the Metropolis, Third Report, 1818, p. 32.

74. Select Committee on the Police of the Metropolis, 1822, p. 101.

75. An analysis of these various select committees is in Radzinowicz, op. cit., Vol. III, pp. 336-340, 354-366.

76. Quoted in Gash, *Mr. Secretary Peel*, p. 493.

77. Select Committee on the Police of the Metropolis, 1828.

78. 10 Geo. IV, c. 44.

79. Quoted in Charles Reith, *A New Study of Police History* (Edinburgh: Oliver & Boyd, 1956), pp. 135-136.

80. Radzinowicz, op. cit., Vol. IV, pp. 167-177.

81. Charles Reith, *British Police and the Democratic Ideal* (London: Oxford University Press, 1943), 139 ff, quotation 143.

82. Select Committee on Cold Bath Fields Meeting, 1833.

83. Reith, *British Police and the Democratic Ideal*, 158.

84. Select Committee on the Employment of Police as Spies, 1833.

85. Select Committee on the Police, 1834.

86. Quoted in Browne, op. cit., p. 150. On the history of the Metropolitan Police, see also J. F. Moylan, *Scotland Yard and the Metropolitan Police* (London: Putnam, 1929).

87. Philip Collins, *Dickens and Crime* (London: Macmillan, 1962).

88. For general summaries of the English judicial system see R. K. Webb, *Modern England* (New York: Dodd, Mead, 1968), pp. 614-625, and J. D. Devlin, *Criminal Courts and Procedures*, 2nd ed. (London: Butterworths, 1967).

89. Radzinowicz, op. cit., Vol. III, p. 29. There is, of course, much useful information on the subject of criminal courts throughout his work.

90. 4 & 5 Will. IV, c. 36. A useful summary of the statutes governing the operation of the court will be found in *The Corporation of London: Its Origin, Constitution, Powers and Duties* (London: Oxford University Press, 1950), pp. 69-77.

91. Albert Crew, *London Prisons of Today and Yesterday* (London: Nicholson & Watson, 1933), pp. 3-5.

92. Sidney and Beatrice Webb, *English Local Government,* Vol. VI, *English Prisons Under Local Government* (London: Frank Cass, 1963; original edition, 1922). A recent survey is R. S. E. Hinde, *The British Penal System, 1773-1950* (London: G. Duckworth, 1951).

93. Transportation to other parts of Australia continued long after the last convicts reached New South Wales in 1840, though fewer were sent in later decades. The last convict ship sailed for Western Australia in October 1867. See A. G. L. Shaw, *Convicts and the Colonies* (London: Faber & Faber, 1966), ch. 15.

94. S. and B. Webb, *English Prisons,* p. 30; R. B. Pugh, *Imprisonment in Medieval England,* (Cambridge: Cambridge University Press, 1968).

95. On John Howard, see his book, *The State of the Prisons in England and Wales* (London: W. Eyres, 1784); D. L. Howard, *John Howard: Prison Reformer* (New York: Archer House, 1963).

96. Janet Whitney, *Elizabeth Fry* (London: Batsford, 1962).

97. 4 Geo. IV, c. 64.

98. 5 & 6 Will. IV, c. 38.

99. See David Roberts, *Victorian Origins of the British Welfare State* (New Haven, Conn.: Yale University Press, 1960).

100. A picture of convicts in the Pentonville chapel is in Henry Mayhew and John Binney, *The Criminal Prisons of London* (London: Frank Cass, 1968; original edition, 1862), p. 133.

101. The standard authorities cited above all treat the subject of the "separate" system. A recent study that comes to somewhat different conclusions is U. R. Q. Henriques, "The Rise and Decline of the Separate System of Prison Discipline," *Past and Present,* 54 (1972), 61-93.

102. S. and B. Webb, op. cit., pp. 45-46.

103. Recent works on transportation are L. L. Robson, *The Convict Settlers of Australia* (Carlton: Melbourne University Press, 1965), and Shaw, *Convicts and the Colonies.* See also W. Branch Johnson, *The English Prison Hulks* (London: Johnson, 1957) and Peter N. Grabosky, *Sydney in Ferment: Crime, Dissent, and Official Reaction, 1788-1973* (Canberra: Australian National University Press, 1976).

104. 16 & 17 Vict., c. 99.

105. For an abstract of the "Powers and Duties of the Directors of Convict Prisons," see *Pri. Com.* 7/68 (P.R.O.).

106. Halévy, *Growth of Philosophic Radicalism.*

107. Mayhew and Binney, op. cit., offers a detailed description of the metropolitan prisons in the mid-nineteenth century.

CRIME, CONFLICT, AND PUBLIC ORDER
From the 1870s to the Great Depression

By the middle years of Queen Victoria's reign the more prosperous citizens of London could find much satisfaction in the conditions of metropolitan life. The visible evidence of material progress was everywhere—in the expanding net of railways that knit the city together, among the new buildings that rose on the sites of old warehouses and rookeries, in the burgeoning of municipal water, sewerage, and gas services, and even in electricity. The less tangible conditions of urban life also had improved. London still had a great many poor, but life in their neighborhoods was noticeably safer and healthier than it had been 50 years earlier; and all could potentially benefit from the many new churches, schools, Friendly societies, and charitable bodies that sought to improve the moral, mental, and material well-being of the "deserving poor." Far from least, public order had continued to improve. The decline in crimes against persons and property, which began in the 1840s, continued; and there was no serious civil conflict, either in fact or in portent. These circumstances provided few incentives to alter the institutions of public order. Such changes as were made in the criminal law, policing, court procedure, and penal treatment were for the most part extensions and refinements of the more fundamental reforms accomplished before 1850.

A perceptible change took place in the first decade of the twentieth century, not in a rising tide of economic prosperity or social progress, but in public order. Historian Standish Meacham's "sense of an impending clash,"[1] which pervaded these years, can be summarily if incompletely described as an intensification of class conflict. Militant trade unionism, which had contributed to strikes of considerable magnitude beginning in London in 1889, became particularly intense after 1907 throughout Britain and did not subside until the late 1920s. Suffragettes waged intense and often violent campaigns in London throughout the decade before World War I. Coincident with the rise in civil conflict was a temporary reversal of the decline in most indicators of crime, perhaps not by chance. This decline in public order was not enough to shake British confidence in the institutions of public order, certainly not enough to bring about wholesale innovations. Nationally there were further modifications of the criminal law, but they were scarcely sweeping. Police forces were expanded, the better to deal with protest. In the courts, change continued at the glacial pace that had characterized the latter part of the nineteenth century. Significant efforts at reform occurred only in the prison system, with the emergence of serious efforts at rehabilitation. This confidence in tested institutions seemed warranted in the decade following the war: In the mid-1920s civil conflict was muted, and the indicators of most kinds of crime were at or near the lowest levels of the whole preceding century. With the benefit of hindsight it can be said that crime was then at its lowest level in London's statistically recorded history.

TRENDS IN CRIME, 1869-1931

All Offenses

The criminal statistics for London for the 63 years 1869-1931 are more comprehensive and detailed than those for any other period, though they are neither entirely consistent nor complete. For much of the period there are simultaneous data for all aspects of police and criminal justice activity: offenses known to police, arrests, cases brought to trial, convictions before the higher courts, and convictions in summary cases. The principal indicators of crime—police activity and the courts' disposition of cases—are shown in Figures II.3.1 to II.3.3. The rates and trends in all indictable offenses for England and Wales are compared with those for London in Figure II.3.1, which gives evidence of general similarity in trends but substantial differences in short-term movements. The decrease in London during the early part of the period is more pronounced than in the country as a whole, and so is the upturn after 1927. It may occasion surprise that the rates in London after 1905 are lower

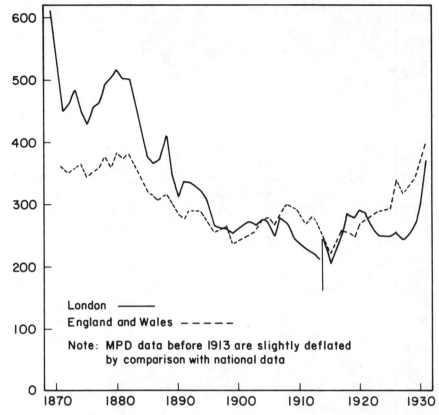

Figure II.3.1 All indictable offenses known to police per 100,000, London (MPD) and England and Wales, 1869-1931

than those for the rest of the country, but the difference cannot be taken at face value. The London police long followed the practice of recording cases in which property had disappeared without clear evidence of theft in a "Suspected Stolen Book." Such cases rarely found their way into the official crime statistics. Moreover, as the police commissioner pointed out when abolishing the system in 1932, local officers had a natural inclination to put their districts in a good light by treating as many offenses as possible as "suspected crimes." Once these offenses were included in "crimes known to police" the "crime rate" in London soared dramatically to nearly twice the national rate (cf. late 1920s data in Figure II.3.1 with those for the early 1930s in Figure II.4.1).[2]

All the indicators of the overall level of police and court activities in London (Figures II.3.2 and II.3.3) show similar trends and short-term fluctuations during the 63 years. The general trend is one of decline that reaches its lowest point, except for the war years, in

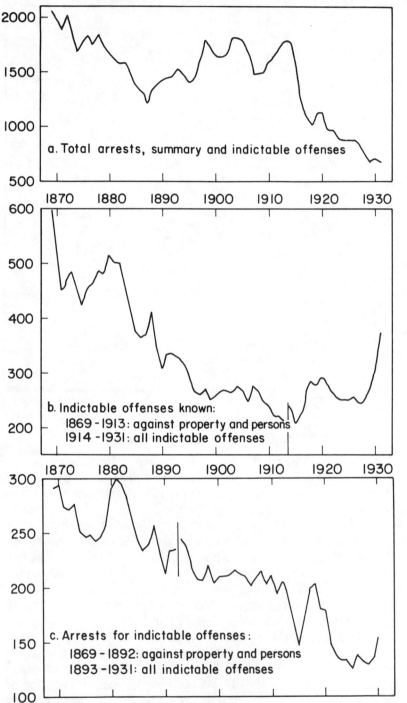

Figure II.3.2 London (MPD): Indicators of police activity per 100,000 population, 1869-1931

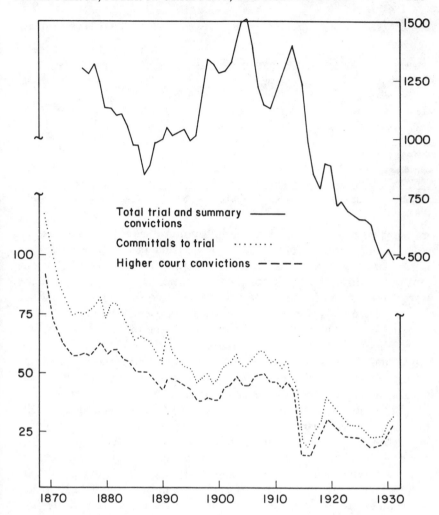

Figure II.3.3 London (MPD): Indicators of activities of the criminal justice system per 100,000 population, 1869-1931

1927-1928.[3] The rates of decline for all activities are both substantial and similar, as is evident from the comparisons in Table II.3.1. Indicators of the overall activities of the police and courts fell by eleven to twelve percent per decade, while indicators of official action against the more serious offenses declined more steeply, by fourteen percent per decade. Rates of committals to trial and subsequent convictions for serious offenses in the late 1920s were scarcely a fifth of what they had been at the beginning of the period.

The short-run variations around the long-term trend are also similar. Short-term increases in 1878-1879 and 1891-1893 coincide

Table II.3.1 Percentage Declines in Crime Indicators for London, 1869-70 to the late 1920s

Indicators	Period covered	Percentage decline, initial year = 100%	
		Total (%)	Average per decade (%)
Total arrests	1869/70 - 1929/30	66	11
Total convictions	1876/77 - 1929/30	62	12
Indictable offenses known	1869/70 - 1927/28	58[a]	10[a]
Arrests for indictable offenses	1869/70 - 1927/28	56[a]	10[a]
Committals to trial (indictable offenses)	1869/70 - 1927/28	80	14
Convictions by trial (indictable offenses)	1869/60 - 1927/28	79	14

a. Slightly underestimated because data for the initial years are less inclusive than data for the last years.

precisely with periods of high unemployment (see Figure II.1.4) and, in the second instance, serious labor conflict (see Figure II.1.6). A more enduring reversal is evident beginning in the late 1890s and continuing until shortly before the outbreak of World War I. These years were rife with economic and political conflict; and depending on one's frame of reference, the reversal could be attributed to either a corresponding increase in individual deviance or an intensification of official efforts at social control. It is worth noting that the indicators of total arrests and total convictions increase more than the indicators of indictable offenses, which is more suggestive of an increase in active policing than of an increase in official severity.

All the indicators of crime and official response decline markedly during the early years of World War I, then increase to or beyond prewar levels before beginning their final decline. The wartime dip cannot be entirely attributed to the absence of most young men on military service because the reversal sets in almost immediately, in 1916. Once again there are different explanations. One is that disillusionment with the war and the opportunities created by the absence of many police increased the incidence of criminal deviance. Another is that officials sought to increase social control during the later years of the war, lest crime impair the war effort. The indicators of trials and convictions increase much more sharply than offenses known or arrests, which gives weight to the latter interpretation.

The decline in indicators of crime before the 1920s and the increase thereafter require no special explanation but a general one that accounts for two factors: the long-term decline in virtually all indicators of crime and official response that began in the second quarter of the nineteenth century, and the reversal in that trend during the Great Depression. We consider the circumstances of the reversal in the next chapter, since only in retrospect can it be said to have been any more enduring a change than those of the previous 50 years. An interpretive question needs answering here, though: Does the long-term decline before the 1920s signify a real decline in the incidence of criminal behavior in London? We think that it does. The most telling evidence is the existence of parallel declines in all indicators of crime. If that trend does not trace an objective improvement in public order, then we must postulate a social illusion so pervasive and convincing that it lulled not only judges and magistrates but the police and the citizens into fancying that fewer crimes were occurring. A second line of argument is less direct but equally persuasive. Since this was a period of improvement in policing and the administration of justice, one would expect more rather than fewer offenses to come to official attention, especially lesser offenses and those whose detection depends on active policing. In fact, indicators of these kinds of offenses decline slightly less than those of the more serious ones—but since *both* decline, there is little doubt that a real and substantial decline in criminal behavior occurred. Gatrell and Hadden, in their analysis of English crime data for this period, made a general principle of the point:

> If... certain crime rates *decrease* over a period during which police efficiency is known to have improved, we can safely conclude that this trend reflects a movement in the actual incidence of crime rather than the effect of a purely administrative factor; if other things were equal, of course, we should normally expect rates to increase.[4]

Specific Categories of Offense

The gist of the foregoing evidence is that the total volume of criminal behavior did decline in London during these 63 years, but there were short-run fluctuations that can be as readily attributed to changing official practices as to changing criminal behavior. Now we examine the patterns of specific categories of offense to see how consistent they are with the general pattern.

Three of the accompanying graphs provide information on the varying incidence of crimes against the person. Aggregate measures appear in Figure II.3.4, including data on murder and attempted murder, manslaughter, and serious assaults (but not rape, kidnapping, or similar offenses). Convictions by the higher courts show an irregular but pronounced decline throughout the 63 years. In Figure II.3.5 the conviction rates are shown separately for murder and manslaughter (below) and attempted murder and assault (above). Both have the same downward trend, though it is more pronounced for assault than for murder. What is perhaps more important than the rate of decline is that by this period in London's history murder and manslaughter had become very rare occurrences. After 1890 they almost never exceeded 60 per year in a population of more than six million. And most of these were cases of manslaughter; murders usually were fewer than twenty per year. Not only were murders rare, almost all cases eventually culminated in arrests and trials.

The trends in known offenses against the person and in arrests (Figure II.3.4) are more difficult to assess than trends in convictions. There are data on known offenses and arrests for the entire period, but for the earlier decades the figures are not comparable with later data, nor are they as inclusive as the convictions data. The data on assaults (only some of them graphed here) show two step-level

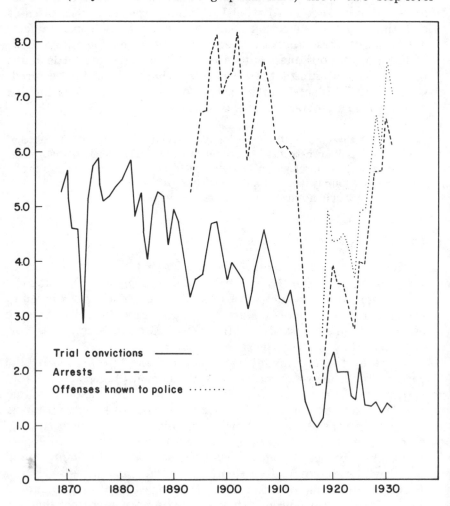

Figure II.3.4 London (MPD): Crimes against persons per 100,000, 1869-1931

increases, one in 1893-1894 when a general revision in criminal statistics was implemented,[5] the second around 1925, when under the provisions of the Criminal Justice Act of 1925, some indictable offenses previously tried before the higher courts became triable summarily. The increase in known assaults thereafter was due to a step-level increase in one specific offense, namely, the misdemeanor of malicious wounding. There was no objective increase in such offenses, but charges in many prior cases had been reduced to enable them to be tried summarily. Thus a statistical increase appeared when the provisions of the new act made it possible for the police to charge malicious woundings as indictable offenses without adding to the case load of the higher courts.[6] It also is worth noting that

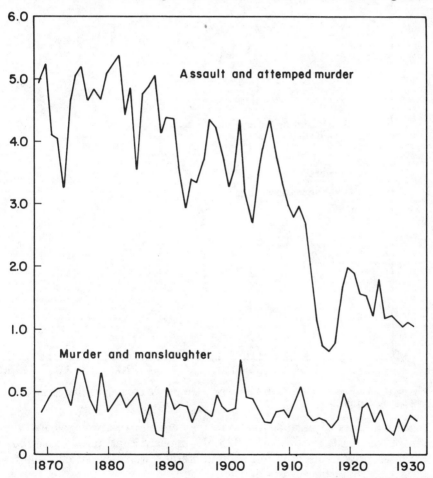

Figure II.3.5 London (MPD): Higher-court convictions for murder and assault per 100,000, 1869-1931, (scale compressed above 1.0)

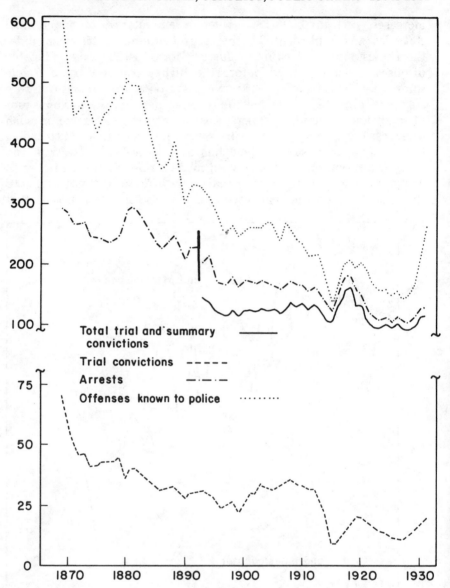

Figure II.3.6 London (MPD): All indictable thefts per 100,000, 1869-1931 (scale compressed above 100)

recorded cases of assault, like murder, were almost always cleared by arrest, at least until after 1925. It appears that the less serious offenses now being counted as "indictable" were less susceptible to detection than the more serious ones.

Less serious than any of the foregoing were the petty cases of assault and breach of peace whose incidence is shown in Figure

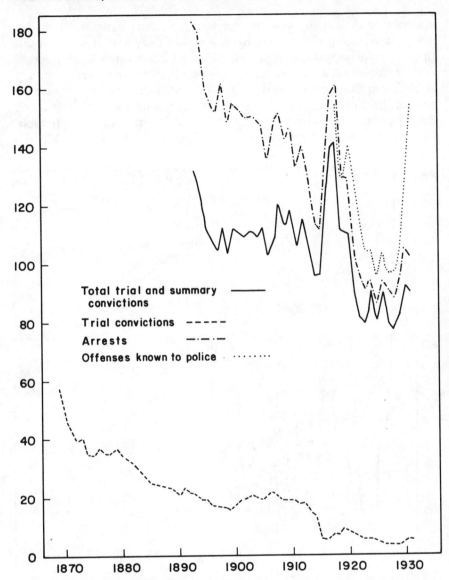

Figure II.3.7 London (MPD): Indictable larceny per 100,000, 1869-1931

II.3.14a (on p. 128). A downward trend is absolutely clear, with a 40-year decline of about 3 : 1. Convictions for these offenses were anywhere from 20 to 40 times as numerous as convictions for the more serious offenses, as can be determined from comparing the values on the vertical axes of the figures. This is one more piece of evidence that the increase in "serious" assaults considered in the previous paragraph came not from a rise in deviance or some "dark figure" of previously unreported offenses, but from a large pool of petty offenses of whose existence the police were well aware.

Thefts make up the great majority of all indictable offenses, and among the forms of theft larceny is substantially the most common. Thus we would expect the trends in all theft and in indictable larceny to parallel quite closely the trends in total offenses. Figures

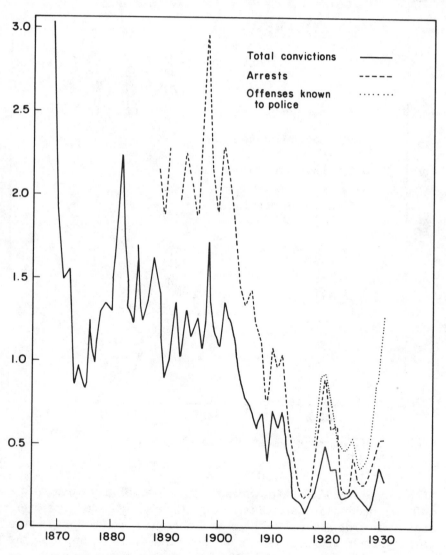

Figure II.3.8 London (MPD): Robbery per 100,000, 1869-1931

II.3.6 and II.3.7 show this to be the case. Known offenses, arrests, and convictions decline from 1869 to the late 1920s, except for temporary reversals around 1880, 1900-1910, and 1916-1920. It should be noted that the great majority of indictable larceny cases during these 60-odd years were tried by magistrates rather than before the higher courts. The values involved typically were small and rarely warranted the expense of a full trial.

Armed robbery and burglary are the less common and more serious forms of theft. Robbery was particularly rare during this period, declining from about 150 arrests per year in the 1890s to about 40 in the mid-1920s. Its incidence over time conforms to the same pattern as larceny (Figure II.3.8). Burglary, however, does not. Offenses known, arrests, committals to trial (not shown), and convictions for the offense in Figure II.3.9 all posted increases before World War I; from the 1890s on, offenses known rarely numbered less than 3,000 per year. Burglary (including housebreaking and related offenses) is a crime easily defined and recognized, and one that requires a perpetrator with rather a specific set of skills. The rising incidence of this crime was attributed by contemporaries to the existence in the metropolis of a small cadre of men who specialized in what is probably the safest and most lucrative form of common theft. The Commissioner of Police for the MPD, in his report for 1890, wrote:

> Such offenses are generally the work of professional criminals, who, after each discharge from prison, are able to commit a series of fresh offences before again falling into the hands of the police. Nor could this be prevented save by making supervision so strict and constant as would hinder such criminals for [sic.] ever obtaining employment at all.[7]

The relative success of burglars, by comparison with those who chose larceny or robbery, can be seen by contrasting the ratio of offenses known to arrests for the three crimes: The ratios for larceny and robbery are nearly 1 : 1 during the fourteen years for which data are available, while the ratio for burglary is on the order of 4 : 1. And many burglars scored far more than four times before being arrested, if indeed they ever were. In a case tried early in 1891, a gang called the City Road burglars were convicted of 86 separate cases of burglary and housebreaking and were believed by police to have been responsible for other cases as well.[8]

The rising rate of burglary during a period when most other offenses were on the decline was the occasion for considerable comment in police reports. The commissioner's report for 1908 offered three reasons:

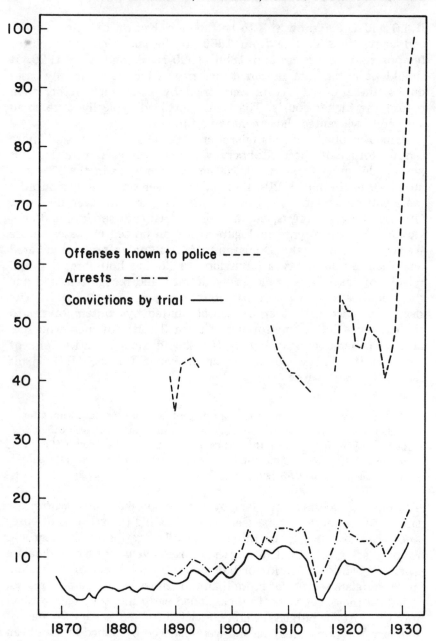

Figure II.3.9 London (MPD): Burglary per 100,000, 1869-1931

(1) The rapid and cheap transit by tube and motor omnibus, which enables a professional housebreaker to live an orderly life in one part of London, and commit his offences in another where he is quite unknown; (2) the spread of insurance against burglary, which seems to make the householder neglectful of simple precautions for the safety of his property; and (3) the growing use of ornamental leaded panes of glass in hall doors, which can be displaced by the afternoon housebreaker sufficiently to admit his fingers to the latch. . . .[9]

Still other factors are mentioned in the commissioner's report for 1920 in an attempt to account for a fresh rash of burglaries. He pointed out that most of the offenses were committed in temporarily empty dwellings in suburban areas, where the increased cost of living had prevented many householders from employing servants. More warehouses and shops were being victimized by night because poorly secured, a condition he attributed to "the high cost of labour and protective material and the comparatively low cost of insurance. . . ." Finally, he cited the "unsettlement produced by demobilisation coupled lately with extensive unemployment."[10] The general interpretation is plausible enough: Burglary was on the increase mainly

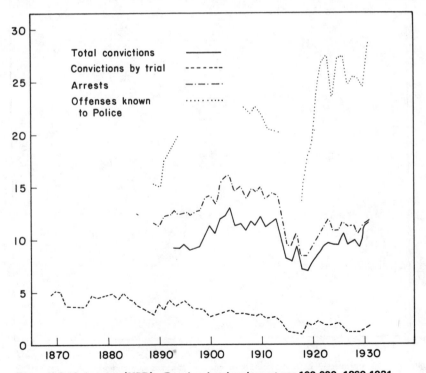

Figure II.3.10 London (MPD): Fraud and embezzlement per 100,000, 1869-1931

because of increased opportunity. The one point that warrants skepticism is the hopeful assertion of one commissioner that "as a matter of fact the criminals seldom ultimately escape, though only a small proportion of their crimes are usually brought home to them."[11]

Fraud and embezzlement make up the last category of crimes against property to be examined separately here. Convictions by trial show an irregular 3 : 1 decline between 1870 and 1927-1928 (Figure II.3.10). As with larcenies, a substantial proportion of offenders were dealt with summarily; arrests and total convictions trace much the same pattern as do larceny and total theft. Known offenses, though, rise very sharply immediately after World War I and continue upward into the early 1930s.

Indictable sex crimes were relatively uncommon between 1864 and 1931. Our aggregate measures of their incidence (Figure II.3.11)

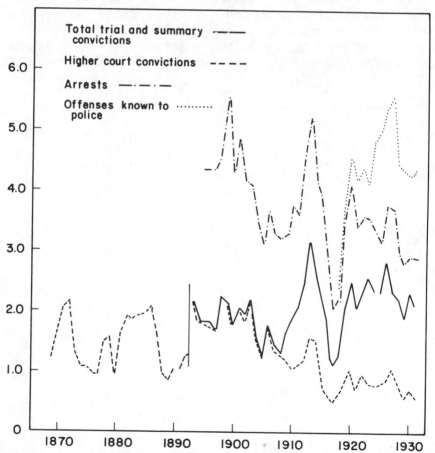

Figure II.3.11 London (MPD): Indictable offenses of sexual assault, deviance, and prostitution per 100,000, 1869-1931

suggest that both arrests and higher court convictions declined after 1893. (The step change in convictions in 1893 is due to the addition of indecent assaults on females to the category.) The aggregate measures combine statistics on three rather different kinds of offense: rape and attempted rape, including the "defilement" of girls under sixteen, unnatural offenses and attempts (i.e., homosexual acts), and indictable offenses related to prostitution, especially procuring and keeping bawdy houses. Except possibly for rape, these offenses depend more on active policing for their detection than on citizens' complaints; thus at least some of their variation reflects changing official emphases. We know, for example, that there was official concern about prostitution and stepped-up police enforcement during the 1880s (see the discussion of criminal law later in this chapter). When offenses of all three types are examined separately, prostitution offenses prove to have declined most sharply, almost to zero by the 1920s. Serious sexual assaults also declined markedly, judging by the conviction ratios in Figure II.3.12, whereas serious homosexual offenses increased considerably after 1910. (Figure II.3.12 differs from Figure II.3.11 by excluding convictions for the more numerous but less serious offenses of indecent assault on females and indecency with males.) One is tempted to interpret these contradictory trends as evidence of declining official concern about heterosexual deviance and an increase in efforts to control homo-

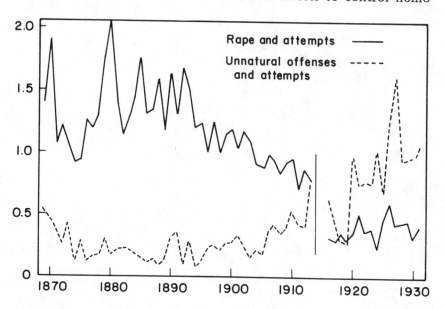

Figure II.3.12 London (MPD): Serious sexual offences known to police per 100,000, 1869-1931

sexual behavior. One feature almost surely reflects a real behavioral change, though: the sharp decline of almost all indicators during the war years. Unlike the common trend in crime indicators for these years, sex offenses remained low throughout the war, surely because most of the male population at risk was otherwise occupied.

Offenses against public order are the least common of all the general categories we have examined. The absolute numbers of offenses known, arrests, and convictions are given in Figure II.3.13 for the last century. These crimes consist mainly of assaults on policemen and rioting, and consequently they have much more explicit political content than any other measure of individual crime. The general pattern shows them to be particularly numerous in the 1870s and 1880s, and again between 1910 and 1920. They exhibit pronounced spikes in 1869, 1882, 1888, 1891, 1912, 1914, and 1925, some but not all of which coincide with particular protests and clashes with police.

Thus far the discussion has centered on indictable offenses, those which are theoretically subject to trial before the higher courts. The less serious summary offenses were far more common than indictable

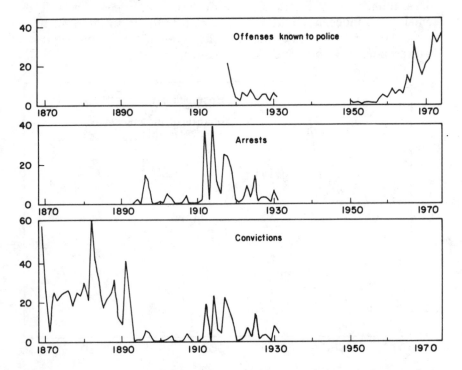

Figure II.3.13 London (MPD): Indictable public order offenses, absolute numbers, 1869-1974

ones in London during this period (as in all others). In the first decade of the twentieth century, for example, arrests for indictable offenses averaged about 210 per 100,000 population per year, while the comparable ratio for summary offenses was 1,430, nearly seven times as great. Because of the practice of trying most indictable offenses before magistrates, an even greater proportion of convictions was meted out by the magistrates' courts. In the same decade there were about 1,300 convictions per 100,000 per year in these courts, compared with fewer than 50 per 100,000 in the quarter session and assize courts. Some data on convictions for summary offenses are plotted in Figure II.3.14. The declining incidence of petty assaults in Figure II.3.14a has already been discussed. Here we examine the trends in convictions for three other common offenses.

The one offense for which Londoners were most likely to be arrested, and convicted, was drunkenness (Figure II.3.14b). The incidence of convictions triples between the 1880s and 1913, an increase accounting for most of the upward surge in total convictions shown above in Figure II.3.3. After the war the rate was much lower and diminishing. The incidence of convictions for the other summary offenses shown, vagrancy and prostitution, was also quite irregular. Before the twentieth century, vagrancy laws in Europe were traditionally a means of controlling a surplus population of the unemployed and unemployable.[12] The fluctuations in the London data are not visibly correlated with economic conditions, however, nor with the changing intensity of social and political tension. The variance in prostitution offenses lacks any obvious socioeconomic explanation, though it may be that the declining trend during the last two decades of this period was partly attributable to the expanding job market for women.

The simplest way of accounting for the trends in vagrancy and prostitution, and in drunkenness as well, is to attribute them to changes in official concern generally and policing in particular. All three are social offenses in which arrests depend on active policing, and all three trace a very similar pattern between 1894 and 1913: a sharp upward trend interrupted temporarily around 1907-1908. The similarity suggests that all were part of a concerted effort to achieve a more "orderly" city by discouraging garden-variety nuisances. Such a policy, if it was that, would be an understandable extension of a Victorian moralism that had already achieved such successes in reducing the nastier forms of social decay. An alternative or supplementary explanation is that the trends trace part of an official response to rising class tensions, but it is unlikely that the police and magistrates perceived drunks, beggars, or soliciting whores as threats

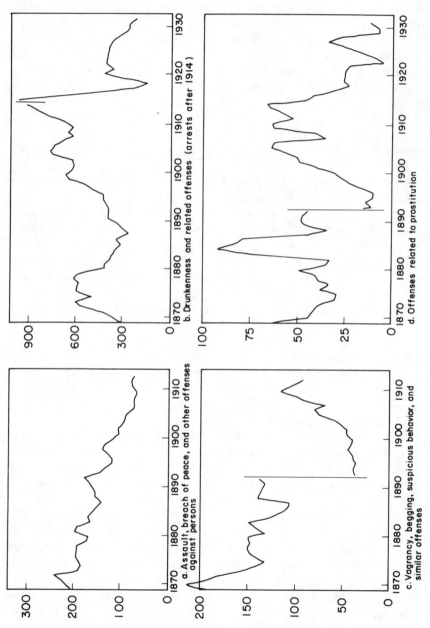

Figure II.3.14 London (MPD): Persons convicted for various summary (petty) offenses per 100,000, 1869-1931

to the establishment. One possibility that can be ruled out immediately is increased police strength per se; the MPD force varied little in proportional size from the 1880s until 1910. Thus convincing explanations of the trends in these offenses require more detailed historical analysis than can be attempted here.

Some of the sharp variations in the offenses named have specific official explanations. Police commissioners acknowledged that the decline in arrests for drunkenness during World War I was probably due to temporary lack of police manpower, for example. More intriguing is the decline in convictions for prostitution offenses after 1922, which is attributable to a temporary change in police and magistrates' practices. Arrests for these offenses were mainly for "soliciting," and only the evidence of the arresting officer was offered at trials. Police judgments were sometimes in error, and after much press criticism of one false arrest in Hyde Park in 1921, some magistrates said that they would no longer convict on unsubstantiated police testimony. The temporary result was a sharp drop in arrests, from 2,504 in 1921 to 538 in 1923.[13]

CIVIL CONFLICT FROM THE 1870s TO THE GREAT DEPRESSION

In the decades after 1870 the characteristics of civil strife in London and the objects of protest movements underwent a change. The episodes of collective action in the first two-thirds of the century differed from eighteenth century events principally because they were better led (which is not to say well or consistently led) and were usually directed toward specific goals. This latter aspect of early nineteenth century protest in London is illustrated by the political aims of collective protest: The largest and most significant mass movements were directed toward parliamentary reform and achievement of the Chartist demands. It could be argued that the real bases of these agitations were social and economic grievances. But it cannot be denied that the stated goals were nearly always political.

After 1870 collective protest broadened from specifically political agitation to other areas, notably trades union action to gain higher wages and better working conditions. The lack of interest in political matters is shown by the relative indifference to the passing of the Third Reform Act in 1884, a measure that brought nearly total manhood suffrage. The subsequent popular agitation for women's suffrage, though obviously political in its goals, was never as broadly based a movement as those that preceded the Reform Acts of 1832 and 1867. Irish protest and violence, an ever-present factor in modern British politics, though also nominally political, was much colored by resentment over ethnicity and class discrimination, and by the demand for Irish independence.

In short, the most important and persistent movement of popular protest in this period was the "new unionism" of the late nineteenth century.[14] Unlike the earlier phases of union activity, the labor groups at this point were characterized by much stronger organization and better leadership. The principal issues were the economic betterment of workers and improvements in industrial relations. There were, of course, political goals that found expression in the creation of the Labour Party. But this third party was very distinctly a minority until the 1920s, when the Liberals suffered sudden death.

The New Unionism

One of the chief distinctions between the new unionism and the old lay in the socioeconomic makeup of union membership. Previously unions had been combinations of skilled craftsmen; from the late 1880s they began to include all workers in an industry regardless of occupational status. A second difference, as noted, was in union leadership. The new leaders were dedicated men of more experience and talent than most of their predessors. Often they had been active in the older unions of skilled workers and brought with them abilities to help organize the unskilled. In addition to their expertise, many were by this time dedicated socialists, a fact which was to influence not only the development of the trades unions but British political life generally.

Many of the leaders of the new unionism were involved in the episode known as "Bloody Sunday." A meeting of the Social Democratic Federation scheduled for Sunday, November 13, 1887, was banned by the Commissioner of the Metropolitan Police, Sir Charles Warren. However, the socialists, who had been accustomed to holding meetings in Trafalgar Square and resented the commissioner's new policy of arbitrarily allowing or prohibiting the events, decided to challenge the edict by meeting anyway. The result was a massive confrontation between police and people; there were several deaths, many injuries, and much (probably justified) popular resentment against Warren.[15] Rallies of unemployed, which had been frequent occurrences since October, continued on into December, with no further violence of consequence.

What is more remarkable is that the major episode of labor unrest of the period—the London dock strike of 1889—was relatively peaceful. In London dockers were essentially a large force of casual laborers, occasionally employed for 4 or 5 pence an hour. They were famous for being among the poorest members of London's unskilled working force, at a time of rising prosperity for many other workers. In mid-August 1889 a group of casual dockers approached Ben Tillett, a man of unimpressive background who had been a labor organizer for several years, and persuaded him to formulate their demands and lead them. With Tillett they decided on a guaranteed wage of sixpence per hour with overtime at 8 pence and a minimum employment of four hours a day. The strike, which began August 14, was nonviolent. The dockers daily marched through the streets and soon won public sympathy for their claims. Cardinal Manning and the Lord Mayor intervened as negotiators, and within a month the employers acceded to the laborers' demands.

The significance of the dockers' success was immense. For the first time a group of unskilled workers had organized and achieved their goals without serious disruption or the threat of violence. Thus the strike gave impetus to the unionist movement; the dockers' union itself soon numbered 30,000 members, and other unskilled workers throughout London began to unite. Another important result of the dock strike was the successful marriage of the old union leadership with the new; Tom Mann and John Burns, skilled workers and experienced unionists, had joined forces and shared their experience with Tillett and his casual laborers.[16] In the future trades unions were to be a more forceful element in British life.

"Bloody Sunday" and the dock strike of 1889 were only the most visible manifestations of chronic conflict arising out of the demands of London's workers. In February 1886, for example, a rally of Social Democrats in Trafalgar Square had turned into a riot in which upper-class homes were looted and people in carriages were attacked. Precisely a year later a similar event also resulted in extensive property damage, and in 1891, four years after Bloody Sunday, the socialists held another series of public meetings, some of which were roughly dispersed by police. After the turn of the century Trafalgar Square and Hyde Park continued to be used as rallying points by the Social Democratic Federation and other groups of workers; such meetings were especially numerous between 1905 and 1909, a period of substantial unemployment and declining wages. Scuffles with the police and occasional arrests punctuated these rallies, but none reached riot proportions.[17]

The Suffragettes

If working-class men, represented in the new unionism, were rarely violent in their methods, the same could not be said of some of the women who began to agitate for the vote at the beginning of the new century. In fact, the women's suffrage movement is a watershed in the history of English political reform. On the one hand it was the final phase in a centuries old struggle for the extension of political rights to ever-larger segments of the British population. At the beginning of the nineteenth century those rights were restricted largely to the nobility, the gentry, and men of the upper middle class. The Reform Act of 1884 enfranchised almost all men, however, and the suffrage movement brought the process to its logical conclusion, securing women's rights to vote and sit in Parliament. On the other hand the suffragette faction of the movement was the first protest group in recent British history to advocate and make consistent use of violence for the achievement of goals. The rhetoric of violence and its calculated use for symbolic effect, so familiar in protest movements in Western societies in the last few decades, follow a pattern cut in London in the decade before World War I.

The quest for women's suffrage had nineteenth century origins but was never taken seriously by more than a handful of British politicians. The agitational phase of the movement can be dated from 1905, when Christabel Pankhurst and Annie Kenney were sentenced to prison after interrupting a speech by Sir Edward Grey in Manchester. The organization they represented, the Women's Social and Political Union, had been founded in Manchester two years earlier by Christabel's mother, Emmeline Pankhurst. In the decade prior to World War I, scarcely any Liberal politician, representing as he did the political party in power, was immune from demonstration and derision by advocates of women's suffrage during public appearances. (Some of the Liberals, notably Grey and Lloyd George, were powerful proponents of women's suffrage, though the most helpful supporters were socialists like Keir Hardie.)

In the first five years the suffragettes aroused a good deal of popular support, and a number of bills giving the vote to women were introduced in Parliament. The Government withheld its support on each occasion, however, dooming them to failure. Thus in 1911 the more militant faction of the movement took a decidedly violent turn at the instigation of Christabel Pankhurst. Initially their tactics included mass marches and confrontations with the police, who at first were somewhat at a loss to deal with the situation. Under intensified pressure, they adopted harsher tactics and broke a good many heads when women resisted arrest. Once in court the suffragettes refused to pay their fines and were sent to prison, where many went on hunger strikes and were forcibly fed by prison authorities. Most of the militants and many of the rank-and-file suffragettes were of the upper middle class, and their sufferings at the hands of the authorities had the hoped-for effect of winning them considerable public sympathy—but failed to elicit political concession. An escalating campaign of attacks on public and private property followed, involving extensive use of arson and bombs, and on one memorable occasion in 1912 the breaking of hundreds of windows on London's more fashionable thoroughfares. A few dramatic physical attacks were made on political figures too, by women armed with whips, hatchets, and even pistols. More by chance than design, no serious injuries were inflicted. The overtly violent phase of the suffragette movement led to a substantial diminution of popular support. Politicians seem to have been increasingly disposed to give women the vote, but the Government refused to give the impression of conceding to pressure.

At the outbreak of war in 1914 the suffragettes immediately abandoned their campaign, and within weeks the Pankhursts were calling on women to support the war effort, which they did in great measure. In 1918 the Government introduced a bill to enfranchise women over 30 who had the requisite property qualifications, and it passed with virtually no dissent.[18] A few years later the last legislative step toward equal suffrage for women was taken. One view is that success was due not to the Pankhursts and their cohorts, but to the tremendous contribution British women had made during the war. Lord Brockway wrote that it was "the service of women in the war effort which won them the vote. . . ."[19] But it is clear that the suffragettes and their more peaceful sisters in the National Union of Women's Suffrage Societies together were responsible for making credible a reform that to most men in 1905 was unthinkable. It is also likely that political leaders in 1918 wished to forestall any resumption of suffragette activities once the war was over. Nevertheless the suffragettes and their followers believed that their campaign had been instrumental in securing women's political rights. It is a moot question whether a disavowal of disruptive tactics would have led to a prompter response.

Immigrants, Anarchists, and Others

Militant workers and the women's suffrage movement were the most sustained and consequential sources of civil conflict in London from the 1880s to 1914, but they were by no means the only ones. The Irish continued to be a threat to public order. Immigrant Irish workers often were involved in punch-ups with their neighbors and the police during the 1880s and 1890s, and the 1880s were a time of agitation over home rule for Ireland. There were bombings in London and clashes between political supporters of different positions on the issue. The issue was to emerge again with a vengeance during World War I.[20]

London throughout this era was a haven for political refugees from continental countries, representing the entire political spectrum. Some found in Britain not only refuge but fertile ground for political activity, and the momentous "Battle of Sidney Street" involved a group of Russian emigres, allegedly anarchists. The murder of three London policemen in December 1910 was attributed to the group, which was soon traced to a house in East London. At the direction of Winston Churchill, then Home Secretary, they were besieged by a large force of police, firemen, and soldiers. Despite heavy gunfire and the use of field artillery, the gang held out until fire destroyed the house. A large arsenal was found in the ruins but no trace of the leader, one "Peter the Painter." The use of armed police, soldiers, and artillery in the city became the subject of heated controversy. So was the presence of political emigres, who for some time thereafter were subject to increased surveillance and were suspected by police and public alike of being the perpetrators of unsolved crimes.[21]

London during the prewar decades offers other instances of riot and protest that were not manifestations of enduring socioeconomic or political disputes. A few examples: The Salvation Army was a militant body in its early years and in the late 1880s was involved in skirmishes with the police. In 1904, in the East End, Orthodox Jews battled socialist Jews over religious issues. And in July 1908 Hyde Park was the setting for a gathering of some 60,000 people protesting a Government bill aimed at more stringent licensing of the retail liquor trade. It is scarcely surprising that a city with seven million inhabitants, at the hub of a thriving commercial and political empire, bursting with new social and political ideas, should have had such diverse kinds of strife and protest.

The Impact of World War I

Although crime and civil conflict of all types declined during the first years of war, the years immediately preceding the conflict were turbulent ones. Not only the women, but the unions and the Irish had resorted to violent and disruptive tactics. Most labor unrest had taken place outside London, but in May 1913 the London dockers again went on strike with Ben Tillett praying, "O God, strike Lord Devonport dead" (Lord Devonport was the head of the Port of London Authority).[22] This time Tillett was less successful than in 1889; God and Devonport both proved intractable, and the outcome was the end of militant unionism for the time being.

The chief effect of World War I on British society was a mobilization of people and resources to a degree that had not been seen since the Napoleonic wars. It was, of course, the first war in which mass media were fully employed, and government propaganda against the "Boche" was highly effective.[23] More to the point, however, was the reorganization of the society and economy that occurred during wartime. An example germane to our study is the decision of Home Office officials, early in the war, to collect and publish criminal statistics in less detail than had been used before 1914.

Civil disobedience was another problem, and Bertrand Russell was imprisoned for his pacifist stand.[24] His position was unusual, for most "forward-thinking" people supported the war aims and effort. Not only the intellectuals, but labor leaders as well, abandoned their internationalist postures: The international European labor movement split on nationalist lines in August 1914. The war was required, as well as the Russian Revolution, before a new worldwide Marxist movement could be fostered.

It has been suggested that World War I unleashed extraordinary forces in British society. Old methods of social organization and control proved not only outmoded but ineffective.[25] A striking instance of that change directly relevant to this study is, in fact, a strike by large numbers of the London police themselves in 1918-1919, an act that before the war would have been almost unthinkable. The data we examined show that the London police succeeded in controlling the upsurge in crime during the unsettled years immediately after the war, but failed to stop the slow, irregular increase that began again in the late 1920s, even before the Great Depression.

Postwar Labor Conflict

One of the legacies of the war was a persistently high rate of unemployment. In 1919-1920 it exceeded fifteen percent in Britain as a whole, and though it declined somewhat thereafter, it hovered throughout the decade around the ten percent mark, a figure that was more than twice the average level of unemployment between 1900 and 1914 (Figure II.1.4). Economic adversity at first spurred a great deal of strike activity, especially from 1919 through 1922 (Figure II.1.6). Some of the protest in London was violent. On May 27, 1919, a large number of demobilized soldiers marched on the House of Commons to ask for jobs, and a fight at the police barricades left many on both sides injured. The next year, on October 19, a group of unemployed workers marched toward government offices on Downing Street and there clashed with police. Windows of government buildings were smashed and some 50 serious injuries reported.

The persistence of unsettled economic conditions set the stage for the General Strike of 1926. British labor had flirted with the Bolsheviks, [26] but the trades unions were actually unprepared for the events that took place. The precipitating incident was a strike by the miners, always an underprivileged group in the British economy. The miners persuaded the General Council of the Trades Union Congress to call a general strike on May 3, 1926, but the action lasted for a mere eight days, the council yielding to the Government in a humiliating fashion. [27] There was no serious disorder connected with the strike in London, but the authorities were prepared for all contingencies. The Special Constabulary, an honorary force in existence since wartime, was expanded from 12,000 to more than 60,000 members. At the same time a Civil Constabulary Reserve was established, a paid civilian force organized with military assistance but placed at the disposal of the Metropolitan Police. The early collapse of the strike meant that little use was made of either group. [28]

There followed a good deal of argument about whether the strike had been a legal action; but the result was a crushing defeat for the labor movement. It was not to recover as a political force until 1945 when the second Labour Government implemented decades of planning by laying the foundations of the modern British welfare state.

THE INSTITUTIONS OF PUBLIC ORDER, 1870-1930

Criminal Law

English criminal law changed relatively little during 1870-1930 by comparison with the wholesale reforms of the early nineteenth century, yet there was a discernible trend toward the increasing regulation of human activities. Enactments that broadened or contracted the boundaries of defined criminality were infrequent, but those that were implemented were of some consequence.

Among the more significant modifications to the criminal law during the period were those concerned with unions and their activities. The Trades Union Act of 1871 expressly legitimized unions and limited their members' criminal liability to acts considered criminal in themselves. The Conspiracy and Protection of Property Act of 1875, however, was aimed at the suppression of industrial protest and made the offenses of intimidation, watching, besetting, and hiding tools punishable on summary conviction by a fine of £20 or three months' imprisonment. [29] The legal status of picketing was obscured by this act and became an issue of paramount public concern in the aftermath of the Taff Vale decision in 1901, which held trades unions liable for civil damages resulting from work stoppages. Fortunately for organized labor, the restraints imposed by this decision were not to endure. The elections of 1905 resulted in a massive swing to the Liberals, and the Trade Disputes Act of 1906 defined peaceful picketing as lawful and exempted trades unions from all liability for the torts of their officers.[30] The trades union movement was no longer at an untenable disadvantage.

Reaction by the Conservative Government to the General Strike of 1926 was predictable. The Trade Disputes Act of 1927 prohibited any strike (a) that had "any object other than or in addition to the furtherance of a trade dispute within the trade or industry in which the strikers are engaged" or (b) was "designed or calculated to coerce the Government either directly or by inflicting hardship upon the community." It also prohibited unions from exacting from workers compulsory contributions to the organizations' political funds.[31] The Labour opposition was incensed by these provisions, despite their essentially symbolic nature. Following Labour's return to power in 1929, an attempt was made to repeal the offensive sections; it failed because neither the Government nor the act's dedicated opponents were strong enough to prevail. Moreover, general strikes, or the threat thereof, were among the least of the problems facing Britons of any social class in 1930.

Another manifestation of the authorities' reliance on the instrumentality of criminal law to control dissent was the Police Act of 1919, which was passed in reaction to the London police strike. One of its objectives was to dissuade future efforts at raising the consciousness of constables: Men who caused or who attempted to cause disaffection among the members of any police force were liable to a maximum of two years' hard labor.[32]

Among the most celebrated of British criminal policies were the various measures directed at the regulation of sexual activity. Victorian morality, which was indeed repressive, was clearly reflected in the criminal law of the day. Ironically, the same morality that held illicit sex to be so reprehensible served to generate considerable demand for and supply of the service in question.[33] Moreover, economic opportunities were so limited that many young women had the unhappy choice of a life of prostitution or one of abject poverty. But authorities remained preoccupied with symptoms; girls of a tender age were walking the streets, and whether for reasons of aesthetics, concern for the less fortunate, or the energetic campaigning of Mrs. George Butler and the Ladies' National Association, members of Parliament were troubled.[34] The result was the Criminal Law Amendment Act of 1885, directed at every currently known form of prostitution, procuring, and brothel-keeping. By defining its terms more broadly, the act effectively closed the loopholes in previous statutes that had permitted prostitution to flourish openly.

Although the effect of this act was to drive the trade underground rather than to suppress it, condemnation of unrestrained sexuality was relentless. The Indecent Advertisements Act of 1889 threatened public purveyors of indecent advertising copy with a fine of 40 shillings or a month's imprisonment. Included in the definition of "indecent" were references to syphilis, nervous debility, or any other complaint relating to sexual intercourse. [35] One form of sexual behavior long considered deviant but yet to be defined as criminal was incest. Historically incest was an ecclesiastical offense, but few cases came to the attention of the Church of England's moribund ecclesiastical courts. A number of attempts to pass legislation on the subject, attributed in part to pressures from the Church, culminated in the Punishment of Incest Act of 1908. This act created a number of offenses for which both males and females over the age of consent were liable. [36] Otherwise, official attention to illicit sex continued in the form of increased penalties and more precisely articulated definitions. The Criminal Law (Amendment) Act of 1912 made certain convictions for male prostitution and procuring females punishable by whipping. The Criminal Law (Amendment) Act of 1922 updated the common law offense of "keeping a bawdy house" by extending criminal liability to lessors, lessees, and agents. [37]

This was also a period of growing humanitarian concern about the well-being of children, born and unborn. One legal manifestation was the passage of a series of enactments banning cruelty to children. Other acts were aimed at controlling infanticide and baby farming. The 1870s saw the enactment of the Infant Life Protection Act of 1872 and the Births and Deaths Registration Act of 1874, which specified a number of requirements designed to curtail the unrestrained traffic in and neglect of infants. Among the offenses made punishable under the latter enactment were failure to notify authorities of a birth within 42 days, unauthorized burial of a stillborn child, burying a deceased infant as if it had been stillborn, and falsifying birth or death certificates. [38] Destruction of the fetus rather than the living infant became the prevalent way of dealing with unwanted pregnancies during the early twentieth century. Restrictions on terminations of pregnancy remained rigid, and the penalty of life imprisonment prescribed in the Offences Against the Person Act of 1861 remained in force. Only in 1929 did the Infant Life (Preservation) Act permit terminations of pregnancy, and then only to preserve the life of the mother. Meanwhile, judges became ever more reluctant to pronounce the death sentence on women found guilty of infanticide. In the latter decades of the nineteenth century it became the Home Secretary's practice to reprieve all mothers so charged, and efforts were made as early as 1872 to amend the law of homicide accordingly. But it was not until 1922 that the lesser offences of infanticide and child destruction were formally added to the criminal law.[39]

Advances in explosives technology and the perceived threat of insurrectionary activity prompted enactment of the Explosives Act of 1875 and the Explosive Substances Act of 1883. The former statute added to existing provisions of the Malicious Damage Act of 1861 by regulating the manufacture, sale, storage, and transport of explosive substances, and imposing a fine of £100 per day for the unauthorized manufacture of gunpowder. The latter enactment increased penalties for the manufacture and possession of explosive materials for use in unlawful purposes to fourteen years' penal servitude. [40] The increased availability of captured German firearms after the Armistice moved authorities to introduce the Firearms Act of 1920. The manufacture and sale of firearms and ammunition was thereby limited to individuals duly registered, and a license from the police was required for possession of a weapon. Thus the new offense of using or carrying an unlicensed gun was created.[41]

The early decades of the twentieth century also saw the imposition of controls over narcotic substances. Most important of these was the Dangerous Drugs Act of 1920, which virtually prohibited the private use of such drugs and their importation, manufacture, or sale. Indeed, one section of the act outlawed the sale or possession of some kinds of smoking utensils. Three years later the act was amended to criminalize aiding and abetting, soliciting and inciting, and attempting to commit the offenses in question.[42]

A number of measures directed at the suppression of Irish nationalist activity were enacted during the period, but since these were not directly relevant to crime and public order in London, they are not dealt with here.[43] In any event, the heightened concern for national security during the World War I era was reflected in legislative enactments. Laws defining sedition and treason had long since reached their full development, but certain matters relating to espionage remained relatively undefined. The Official Secrets Acts of 1911 and 1920 and the Defence of the Realm (Consolidation) Act of 1914 provided detailed descriptions and penalties for espionage and related crimes, and empowered the king in council to issue regulations for securing public safety.[44]

One last area in which new offenses were defined was official corruption, which was the subject of Prevention of Corruption Acts passed in 1889, 1906, and 1916. Otherwise, there was little substantive change in the British criminal law between 1870 and 1930. The Perjury Act of 1911, the Forgery Act of 1913, and the Larceny Act of 1916 all served to consolidate existing law relating to these respective offenses. A number of archaic crimes remained "on the books" and were subject to occasional enforcement. An unfortunate gentleman named Gott who distributed antireligious literature while bearing a sign marked "God and Gott" was successfully prosecuted for blasphemy in 1922.[45]

The Metropolitan Police

The size of the Metropolitan Police Force kept abreast of the growth in London's population during the last three decades of the nineteenth century; throughout the period, force levels tended to fluctuate around a figure of 25 policemen per 10,000 inhabitants. A slight expansion occurred in 1882-1884 in response to the heightened concern over increases in theft, but by the turn of the century the proportional strength of the force had returned to its normal level. The intensification of suffragette protest and industrial unrest in the second decade of the new century, however, coincided with the most significant expansion of the force in recent history. Between 1908 and 1915 the authorized strength of the force was increased by about 4,100 men, though part of the increase has a prosaic explanation: 1,600 men were added to make it possible for all officers to have a weekly rest day, rather than one per fortnight, as previously (see below).[46] By the start of World War I, the absolute size of the force exceeded 22,000, as shown in Figure II.3.15; the

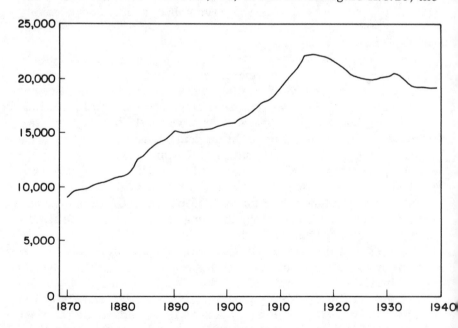

Figure II.3.15 London: Manpower of the metropolitan police force, 1870-1939

number of policemen per 10,000 inhabitants had increased by a third over the previous decade. Following this peak, the size of the force declined in both absolute and proportional terms over the next two decades. This diminution in manpower continued without interruption, despite the significant periods of industrial conflict that marked the 1920s.

There was little change in the structure and style of the Metropolitan Police during the last half of the nineteenth century. Moreover, wages were low, working conditions austere, and improvements gradual and grudging. W. S. Gilbert was quite close to the mark with the refrain "A policeman's lot is not a happy one." Constables were compensated at the level of unskilled agricultural workers, whose existence in Britain at the time was anything but comfortable. To earn their subsistence wages, members of the Metropolitan force worked a seven-day week. They were granted one free day each fortnight and an annual seven-day holiday without pay.[47]

Some constables suffered in silence, but others were more inclined to activism. A small strike was called in London in 1872 over the right to organize for purposes of collective bargaining. Although it was suppressed with little effort (the leaders were imprisoned), it heralded two more significant expressions of policemen's discontent—the strikes of 1890 and the series of stoppages in 1918-1919. The events following World War I were by far the most serious. London was bereft of police for a number of hours, and in the aftermath some 1,000 men were dismissed for misconduct. There were, however, no serious disorders comparable to those which occurred under similar circumstances in Liverpool.

Despite the dismissal of large numbers of officers as a result of the various work stoppages, the London protests in particular spurred reforms in working conditions. The Police Act of 1890 guaranteed a pension scheme after 25 years of service, or after 15 years in case of medical disability. Policemen were accorded the right to vote in parliamentary elections from 1887, and in municipal elections from 1893. Annual leave was increased at the turn of the century, and a six-day work week was instituted in 1910. In the tense early months of 1919 the Government responded to the walkout with a substantial pay increase and appointed a committee under Lord Desborough to review working conditions and the issues of police wages. The committee's report had lasting national implications. It recommended further centralization of British police forces, standardization of remuneration and conditions of service, and the establishment of a quasi-public organization, insulated from trades union influence, for the future representation of policemen's interests.[48] The Police Act of 1919 implemented the major recommendations of the Desborough committee and formalized the compromise imposed on dissident officers. While the lot of the London policeman was discernibly happier in the 1920s than at any time previous, his prospects for further protest were severely curtailed.

Given the relative austerity of life on a policeman's salary in the years before 1920, it is hardly surprising that some members of the Metropolitan force were tempted to augment their income by illicit means. Indeed, three of the four chief inspectors in the Detective Branch were convicted for corrupt practices in 1877.[49] This scandal prompted an administrative reorganization and the establishment of a Criminal Investigation Department. While the establishment of the new CID in the late 1870s enabled detectives on the Metropolitan force to escape the pejorative nickname given their previous office (the Defective Department), their activities were by no means immune from criticism. The notorious Jack the Ripper was never identified, much less apprehended. And, at least in the imagination of the public, the CID was consistently outdone by a contemporary fictional competitor named Holmes.

The resurgence of Irish nationalist activism in 1884 brought about the establishment of the "Special Irish Branch" of the CID, charged with the suppression of Fenian terrorist activity. The Irish proved to have no monopoly on terrorism, however, and the organization was renamed "Special Branch" to signify its broadened concern with the Spanish, Armenian, Italian, and Russian anarchists who were active in London toward the end of Queen Victoria's reign.

Although the Metropolitan force was considerably burdened with the tasks of controlling street crime during the late 1880s, they received periodic instructions from the Home Secretary directing their attention to prostitution. Toward the end of 1888, orders to crack down on brothel-keeping in the East End were said to be futile by the Commissioner of Police himself. Official attention to brothels, he contended, would only bring about increased street solicitation, and he estimated the number of women working the district at about 1,200. The commissioner maintained that "in driving the brothel keepers away from certain neighbourhoods much would be done to demoralize London generally. It is impossible to stop the supply where the demand exists."[50]

The public image of the Metropolitan force varied significantly during the first three decades of the twentieth century. New accusations of bribery and heavy-handedness surrounding police attention to prostitutes and street bookmakers prompted the appointment of a royal commission in 1906. The commission reported that occasional misconduct had taken place but was by no means widespread. The commissioners concluded that complaints were few in number relative to the size of the Metropolitan force.[51]

Throughout the period, the Metropolitan force continued to be called to perform peripheral functions. While less preoccupied than their rural counterparts with swine and cattle licenses and with the supervision of sheep dipping, police in London were nevertheless required to attend to the regulation of weights and measures, the licensing of vehicles and public houses, and the like. Another area of police activity from 1854 to 1891 was the abatement of smoke nuisances, and summonses issued in this regard were the subject of many pages and tables in the reports of the Commissioner of Police during the 1870s and 1880s. During World War I police responsibilities were expanded to include alien registration, enforcement of the blackout, and the coordination of air raid warning activities— tasks made the more difficult because many officers were seconded to military service.[52]

Police conduct during the General Strike of 1926 served greatly to enhance the force's image. Their ability to avoid antagonizing significant segments of the public during a period of extreme political and social tension is indeed noteworthy. But the task of enforcing (or attempting to enforce) an archaic and comprehensive body of criminal law sometimes detracted from their public image. CID personnel were charged with enforcing hours of sales at London nightclubs during the 1920s and predictable problems involving bribery soon arose.[53] Another royal commission was appointed in 1929, this time to investigate an allegation of interrogative malpractice. The inquiry, however, was not limited to the case at hand. The commissioners' report argued that the mission and image of the police were significantly impaired by the unwieldy task with which they were charged.

> Many complaints which have reached us have proved, on investigation, to be in effect directed not against the police themselves but against the laws which the police are called upon to enforce. . . . In our view, the attempt to enforce obsolete laws, or laws manifestly out of harmony with public opinion, will always be liable to expose the police to temptations and to react upon their morale and efficiency.[54]

Otherwise the early years of the new century marked a period of significant innovation in criminalistics. The techniques of fingerprinting developed by Bertillon and Galton were introduced at Scotland Yard before the turn of the century, and were soon improved. A systematic classification using *modus operandi* was begun in 1909; in the following year the Thames division of the Metropolitan force began replacing rowboats with motorized craft. Elsewhere on the force, horsedrawn vehicles were giving way to motor cars; a "flying squad" of mobile plainclothesmen was established in 1919. Four years later, a primitive wireless communications system was introduced. The era of modern police technology had begun.[55] Neither in this period nor later has police modernization in London extended to weapons, though. Like the first "bobbies," the Metropolitan Police continued to be "armed" only with a stick, now carried concealed in a trouser leg. On rare occasions officers on especially dangerous assignments were and are authorized to carry firearms, but more often than not they have declined the opportunity.

The Courts and Criminal Procedure

Changes in the structure and procedure of criminal courts between 1870 and 1930 appear to have had one primary goal—increased efficiency in the processing of cases. Although some steps were taken to protect and enhance the rights of the accused, notably during Liberal and Labour regimes, concern for the quick disposition of cases remained paramount.

Continuing a trend set by the Criminal Justice Act of 1855, the number of indictable offenses that could be tried summarily was significantly expanded by legislation enacted in 1879, 1899, and 1925. Legally this option was at the discretion of the accused, but he or she was provided with a number of incentives to choose it, especially since maximum punishment on summary conviction was limited to six months' imprisonment and/or a fine of £100. This disposition of cases, while not the result of explicit bargaining, was often equivalent to a negotiated plea of guilty. Defendants who sacrificed the somewhat greater possibility of acquittal attending a trial by jury gained a speedier disposition of their case and a lighter sentence. The institutionalization of such streamlined dispositions even extended to the police decision to arrest and charge; in lieu of being charged with housebreaking (an offense triable only on indictment), suspects were often charged with theft (triable on indictment or summarily). Depending on the strength of evidence against him, the understanding that the accused would seek the speedier and more lenient alternative was implicit.[56]

The net effect of these procedures was that by 1930 roughly 85 percent of all persons accused of indictable offenses were tried summarily. Not all categories of offense were equally affected, though. Murder and manslaughter, armed robbery, and offenses against public order were virtually always tried by the higher courts. The growing reliance on summary justice for other types of offense between the 1890s and 1931 is documented graphically in Figure II.3.16. Larceny and fraud usually were tried summarily throughout the period, sex offenses and assault increasingly so. By 1930 only burglary, among the offenses shown, was regularly tried before the higher courts, no doubt because of the professional character of most

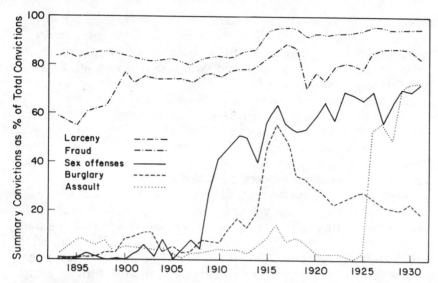

Figure II.3.16 London (MPD): The trend toward summary disposition of indictable offenses, 1893-1931

of the offenders described earlier in this chapter. Note too that there was a distinct increase in reliance on summary justice during the war years, probably due to wartime constraints on judicial resources.

The growing reliance on summary justice, a manifestation perhaps of official self-interest, was early implemented and readily expanded. The object of protecting the innocent from errors of judicial judgment, which spurred reformers' attempts to establish provisions for appeal in criminal cases, proved more difficult to put into effect. Not only did it imply the fallibility of judges, it ran contrary to the trend toward increased efficiency. The Judicature Act of 1873 established a Court of Appeal for civil matters, but it created no criminal counterpart. The Court of Crown Cases Reversed, established in 1848, heard an average of eight appeals annually from all of Britain on matters of law, and the alternative of the royal prerogative of mercy was available, but these cumbersome mechanisms were infrequently used. The structural asymmetry in the British judiciary was not prolonged for any want of proposals for reform; indeed, the idea for a criminal appeals court had been entertained in Parliament no less than 28 times in the 70 years before 1907. In that year, the Liberal Campbell-Bannerman Government, prompted by continuing repercussions over a gross miscarriage of justice in the case of Adolf Beck, some years earlier, produced the Criminal Appeal Act of 1907.[57]

The new Court of Criminal Appeal entertained appeals on questions of fact and law and was empowered to quash convictions and reduce or increase sentences. It could not, however, order a new trial. During the period 1907-1930 the court heard approximately 90 appeals each year from an annual average of 500 applications. By 1930 roughly 30 convictions had been quashed and 30 sentences varied each year since 1907.[58]

The only other significant modification in the structure of the British courts during the period occurred pursuant to the Children Act of 1908. That statute provided for the establishment of special juvenile courts for accused offenders under the age of sixteen. Perhaps more significant were the institutional provisions for the treatment of juvenile offenders, discussed below.

The discretion of sentencing judges and magistrates was broadened around the turn of the century, particularly with regard to the disposition of first offenders. Courts were empowered by the Summary Jurisdiction Act of 1879 and by the First Offenders Act of 1887 to discharge convicted persons on payment of security, a process called "binding over." Such practices were further institutionalized by the Probation of Offenders Act of 1907, which gave statutory effect to supervised probation as an alternative to imprisonment.

One of the more significant reforms in the area of criminal procedure was introduced by the Criminal Justice Administration Act of 1914. In addition to broadening conditions of eligibility for probation, the act compelled courts to allow additional time in which to make payment for individuals who had been fined. Although liberty remained conditional on one's personal wealth, the number of individuals admitted to prison in default of payment of fines declined a full 50 percent after the act was implemented.[59]

Measures designed to protect the rights of the defendant in criminal cases were rare in the 1870-1930 period. The Criminal Evidence Act of 1898 enabled defendants to give evidence in their own behalf. Although freedom from compulsory self-incrimination was of course preserved, the act made the services of defense counsel harder to do without. Legal advice, however, was unavailable to most indigent defendants, and proposals were put forth in 1903 to provide counsel to indigent defendants at public expense. The Poor Prisoners Defence Act of 1903 was unfortunately but a shadow of the legislation initially introduced. The services provided were limited to trials on indictment, and defendants were required to disclose their defense to establish eligibility for the services. Thus the vast majority of defendants were not eligible for publicly provided counsel, and those who enjoyed the "right" were faced with disadvantages that did not burden their more affluent counterparts.[60]

Dissatisfaction with inadequate measures to protect defendants' interests led to the introduction in 1919 of a Bill to Establish the Office of Public Defender. It failed of passage, and in response to the petitions of various religious and social service organizations protesting gross inequalities in the administration of justice, the Government appointed a Committee on Legal Aid and the Poor in 1925. The committee's report was essentially an apology for the status quo. It rejected the idea of establishing an Office of Public Defender and recommended only marginal changes to existing policy. Although the Poor Prisoners' Defence Act of 1930 extended provisions for representation of the indigent to courts of summary jurisdiction, and abolished mandatory disclosure of defense, the legislation had little impact. Only a handful of the thousands of indigent defendants received representation, for the discretionary provisions were not implemented assiduously by the magistracy.

One major step in the development of the rights of defendants was an increasing reliance on insanity as a defense. The principles enunciated in *R.* v. *McNaughton* (1843) represented a major liberal advance in determining criminal responsibility. Although the case was decided prior to 1870, the McNaughton rules had their most significant impact in the late nineteenth and twentieth centuries. Always a controversial matter, both theoretically and when applied in practice (usually capital cases), the utilization of insanity as a defense has been a product of changing conceptions of mental illness as well as legislation and actual court cases.[61]

The Prisons and Punishment

The last three decades of the nineteenth century saw some significant changes in the British prisons system. Transportation was rarely used after 1853 and discontinued in 1867; capital punishment was rarely imposed. Prisons had become the first, last, and only resort for serious offenders.

British prisons in the 1860s were governed by local authorities, and there were thus no national standards of prison management. A Select Committee of the House of Lords on Prison Discipline, appointed in 1863, criticized numerous deficiencies that attended local administration. In some jurisdictions the crank and treadwheel were still in use, and the dormitory accommodations permitted free association of inmates—a situation regarded with increasing disfavor. The Prison Act of 1865 mandated certain uniform staffing requirements and paved the way for the centralization of British prisons in 1877.[62]

The Prisons Act of 1877 brought the management of prisons under the jurisdiction of the Home Office and created the Prison

Commission, a body of five members appointed by and responsible to the Home Secretary. The first chairman of the Prison Commission was Sir Edmund Du Cane, a former Royal Engineer with extensive experience in the supervision of convict labor in western Australia. Standardization was the hallmark of his term as chairman, and the treatment of convicts in his system was as austere as it was uniform. The separate (i.e., solitary) system was strictly enforced, and prisoners were forbidden to communicate. Prison food was intentionally meager and plain, the labor stultifying, the sleeping surfaces hard. Du Cane's prisons were managed under the principles of deterrence and retribution within the general imperative of economy. The paramilitary staff structure was retained, and former servicemen were welcomed as warders.

Conditions of employment for prison staff were far from comfortable. Committees of inquiry were appointed in 1882 and again in 1891 in response to staff demands for more favorable wages, working hours, and promotion opportunities. Some improvements were achieved, but the issue of prison staff was eclipsed in the mid-1890s by larger questions of prison policy.[63] Increasing public criticism of crowded prisons in London, and the publication of critical articles by the Reverend W. D. Morrison, an assistant chaplain in the prison service, prompted the most celebrated investigation in the history of the British prisons system. A committee chaired by Herbert John Gladstone, MP, was appointed in 1894 and instructed to examine prison accommodation, labor, discipline, visits and communications with prisoners, and the treatment of young offenders.

The evidence assembled by the Gladstone committee constituted a grim indictment of the Du Cane administration. Public sentiment increasingly favored a new goal for the prisons system— rehabilitation. Reform of the offender, and the individualized treatment required to that end, stood in conflict with the operating principles of Du Cane's department. Moreover, the harshness of prison conditions at the time was found to have as a by-product considerable human wreckage. Prisoners subject to the separate system not infrequently went mad, and a Salvation Army colonel who had assisted many convicts immediately after their release from prison testified, ". . . we find a greater number of them incapable of pursuing an ordinary occupation. They are mentally weak and wasted, requiring careful treatment for months."[64]

The numerous recommendations of the Gladstone committee were keyed to the general principles of individualized treatment and rehabilitation. Formally, the committee proposed that the status of the principles be elevated to that of deterrence. The report called for the abolition of the treadwheel and crank, the introduction of a more varied diet, and the extension of privileges to receive visits from friends and relatives. In addition, the committee proposed that a system of classification be implemented, suggesting the desirability of protecting younger offenders from more hardened criminals.[65]

As it happened, Sir Edmund Du Cane had reached retirement age and chose to step down when the Gladstone report was promulgated. His successor, Evelyn John Ruggles-Brise, was a career civil servant who had served on the Prison Commission since 1892. Ruggles-Brise found himself assuming the chairmanship at the beginning of a new era of British penal practice, and he was confronted with the dilemma of reconciling the essentially conflicting goals of deterrence and rehabilitation. The first significant step in this direction was taken in the Prison Act of 1898, which reduced the use of corporal punishment for prison disciplinary offenses and established a simple classification system. "Convicts" (those under sentence for periods in excess of three years) constituted one category. "Prisoners" were divided into three groups, with political prisoners, and offenders with no serious prior record being segreated from the remainder of the inmates.

Other provisions in the 1898 act broadened the rule-making power of Prison Commissioners, permitting a more fluid formulation and implementation of policy without the necessity of submitting each minor change for parliamentary ratification. The turn of the century brought structural innovations introduced by law. The initial movement away from incarceration began with the aforementioned First Offenders Act of 1887 and Probation of Offenders Act of 1907. Liberal governments during the period 1906-1913 introduced a range of policies designed to reduce the number of individuals imprisoned;[66] the results of this program are dramatically apparent in Figure II.3.17. Between 1905 and 1918 receptions declined from 200,000 to 25,000 per year and the daily average population from 21,000 to less than 10,000, mainly because of the more lenient provisions for the payment of fines mentioned above.[67]

Pursuant to one of the major themes of the Gladstone report, Ruggles-Brise began in 1902 to experiment with a new type of institution, initially termed "penal reformatory." Males between the ages of 16 and 21 were selected from prisons around the country and brought to the old convict prison at Fort Borstal, where they were given special treatment that included physical training, instruction in academic subjects, and "useful" labor. The program proved successful to the authorities and was institutionalized by Part I of the Prevention of Crime Act of 1908. Facilities for juvenile offenders were thereafter called borstals. Part II of the act provided for a somewhat harsher penal measure—preventive detention. Courts were

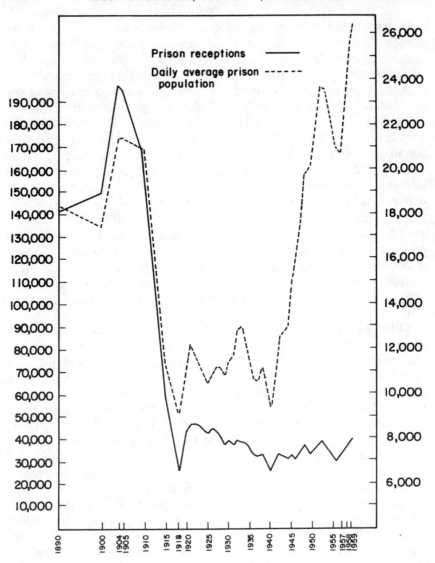

Figure II.3.17 Great Britain: Annual prison receptions and daily average population, 1890-1959

empowered to award two sentences to offenders defined as habitual criminals: one for the offense in question, the other for an additional period of five to ten years.[68]

Although somewhat more benign from the perspective of those who had been imprisoned under Du Cane, the Ruggles-Brise administration could hardly be regarded as permissive. Short haircuts, uniforms marked with broad arrows, and the requirement that inmates turn to face the wall upon the approach of a prison official were still the rule until after World War I.

Public criticism of prison administration under Ruggles-Brise was also vocal; the Penal Reform League was founded in 1907, joining the Howard Association in the vanguard of the movement for reform. No less a man of letters than John Galsworthy was starkly critical in his play *Justice* (1910), which presented the plight of a prisoner devastated by separate confinement at Dartmoor. In 1921 the Penal Reform League merged with the Howard Association to make up the Howard League for Penal Reform. That year also marked the retirement of Ruggles-Brise, but public pressure to reduce the harshness of prison conditions continued. In 1922 a review of British prisons by Stephen Hobhouse and A. Fenner Brockway, two conscientious objectors who had been imprisoned during the war, renewed the call for rehabilitation as the paramount aim of penal policy. [69] Thus a number of antiquated policies were abolished in the years before 1930. Visiting privileges were significantly expanded, arrows were removed from prisoners' uniforms, and haircut regulations were relaxed. It should be noted, however, that nearly a quarter-century had elapsed since the appearance of the Gladstone Report.

The death penalty remained in use from 1870 to 1930, although the new century saw an increasing number of reprieves. Opposition to capital punishment was never strong enough to bring about outright abolition, and most policy initiatives were directed not at repeal of the penalty but at reducing the range of circumstances under which it could be imposed. There were, for example, six futile attempts during the period 1866-1881 to create certain categories of noncapital murder. The aforementioned Infanticide Act of 1922, however, succeeded in this regard. Among the provisions of the Children Act of 1908 was the abolition of the death penalty for individuals under sixteen years of age. Abolitionist support was strongest in the ranks of the Labour Party, but the Labour governments that came to power in the 1920s were too weak to prevail on such a controversial issue. A select committee appointed by the MacDonald Government in 1929 rather cautiously recommended a five-year experimental moratorium on executions, but the Government soon fell, and humanitarian sentiment was eclipsed by the economic concerns of the Depression. [70]

Symbolic of the new beginnings in British prison administration during this era was the closing of outmoded penal facilities. The most notable example in London was the destruction of Newgate Gaol in 1902. [71] For centuries this institution had been a physical monument to English inhumanity toward those accused of crime. It would have been difficult to see it without visualizing the procession to Tyburn or the executions that took place at the prison itself. On the spot where Newgate had stood was erected the new building of the Central Criminal Court, the Old Bailey. Atop the great dome is a golden statue representing Justice with her scales. The figure is blindfolded, perhaps less to ensure impartiality than to avoid viewing the scene of so much human misery.

NOTES TO CHAPTER II.3

1. Standish Meacham, " 'The Sense of an Impending Clash': English Working Class Unrest before the First World War," *American Historical Review*, 77 (December 1972), 1343-1364.

2. In addition to the data from the annual Report of the Commissioner of Police of the Metropolis, which appear in the *Parliamentary Papers*, this section uses data from the retrospective tables that appear in the appendices of the separately published editions of that report. These tables, most of them unfortunately dropped after 1914, provide data on various categories of offenses known and arrests for periods up to 30 years. The "Suspected Stolen Book" is discussed in the Report of the Commissioner . . . 1932, pp. 16-17.

3. Not all the indicators are precisely comparable over time: vertical bars are used in these and subsequent figures to interrupt the trend lines at points when changes were introduced in the categorization and reporting of data. In Figure II.3.2b, for example, there is a break at 1913 because the reports of the Commissioner of Police before that date listed total known felonies against property and principal offenses against the person but did not list other indictable offenses, which can be estimated from other information to have been about 10 percent of the total; hence the pre-1914 data are deflated by about that proportion. The same is true for arrests for indictable offenses before 1892, in Figure II.3.2c.

4. Gatrell and Hadden, "Criminal Statistics," in Wrigley, ed., *Nineteenth Century Society*, p. 361.

5. See Select Committee to Revise the Criminal Portion of the Judicial Statistics, 1895. The changes are summarily reviewed (along with commentaries on earlier changes) by Gatrell and Hadden, in Wrigley, ed., op. cit., pp. 345-346.

6. Report of the Commissioner . . . 1926, pp. 15-16, confirms this interpretation. There are many other instances of changes in the scope and recording of official data, but few extended explanations are offered here. Changes that might otherwise affect the interpretation of variations in the crime data are mentioned briefly and are symbolized, where appropriate, by vertical bars on the figures; see note 3.

7. Report of the Commissioner . . . 1890, p. 5.

8. Report of the Commissioner . . . 1891, p. 5. The reports for this period include detailed tables categorizing the location of burglaries, the time of their occurrence, the precise method of entry, value of goods taken, etc.

9. Report of the Commissioner . . . 1908, pp. 7-8.

10. Report of the Commissioner . . . 1920, p. 8.

11. Report of the Commissioner . . . 1891, p. 5.

12. On the socioeconomic bases of vagrancy laws see Georg Rusche and Otto Kirchheimer, *Punishment and Social Structure* (New York: Columbia University Press, 1939), chs. 2 and 3. On English vagrancy laws see William J. Chambliss, "A Sociological Analysis of the Law of Vagrancy," *Social Problems*, 12 (Summer 1964), 67-77.

13. Fluctuations in the policing of drunkenness are discussed in Report of the Commissioner . . . 1920, p. 4. The Hyde Park case and its consequences are

the object of acerbic comments in the reports for 1922 (p. 9) and 1923 (pp. 20-21).

14. See Henry Pelling, *A History of British Trade Unionism*, 2nd ed. (London: Macmillan, 1972).

15. R. C. K. Ensor, *England, 1870-1914*, Vol. 14 in G. N. Clark, ed., *Oxford History of England* (Oxford: Clarendon Press, 1936), pp. 180-181. A view more favorable to Commissioner Warren is Browne, *Rise of Scotland Yard op. cit.*, pp. 203-205.

16. See Pelling, op. cit., pp. 94-97. Primary sources include Benjamin Tillett, *Memories and Reflexions* (London: John Long, 1931) and H. L. Smith and V. Nash, *The Story of the Dockers' Strike* (London: T. Fisher Unwin, 1889).

17. This paragraph's chronicle of working-class protest, and similar events listed below, are from Michael Stohl's unpublished survey of conflict events reported in the *Times;* see note 26 in ch. II.2.

18. The literature on the suffragette movement is large. A good recent study is Constance Rover's *Women's Suffrage and Party Politics in Britain, 1866-1914* (London: Routledge & Kegan Paul, 1967). See also Roger Fulford, *Votes for Women: The Story of a Struggle* (London: Faber & Faber, 1957); Harold Priestley, *Voice of Protest: A History of Civil Unrest in Great Britain* (London: Leslie Frewin, 1968), pp. 242-265; Marian Ramelson, *The Petticoat Rebellion: A Century of Struggle for Women's Rights* (London: Lawrence & Wishart, 1967). Emmeline Pankhurst and her two daughters Christabel and Sylvia published books detailing their roles in the movement. For the police perspective on the suffragettes, see *H.O.* 3/1016; Mepol 2/1145 (P.R.O.).

19. Fenner Brockway, preface to Rover, op. cit., p. 5.

20. For a number of references to the Irish question see W. G. Carlton Hall, *Political Crime: A Critical Essay on the Law and Its Administration in Cases of a Certain Type* (London: Allen & Unwin, 1923).

21. H. J. Hoeveler, "Die Schlacht von London," *Braunschweiger Kriminalstatistik*, Vol. 15 (1961), pp. 59-62, 92-94; abstracted in *Excerpta Criminologica*, Vol. 1 (1961), pp. 429-430.

22. Pelling, op. cit., p. 137.

23. Phillip Knightley, *The First Casualty: The War Correspondent as Hero, Propagandist, and Myth Maker* (London: Andre Deutsch, 1975), ch. 5, provides a detailed account of the extraordinary extent to which the Government used both legal means and informal pressure to control the reporting of the war by the British (i.e., the London) press. He suggests that if the truth had become known to the British public, support for the war effort would have evaporated.

24. Bertrand Russell, *The Autobiography of Bertrand Russell, 1914-1944* (Boston: Little, Brown, 1968), ch. 1.

25. Arthur Marwick, *The Deluge: British Society and the First World War* (London: The Bodley Head, 1965).

26. Stephan R. Graubard, *British Labor and the Russian Revolution* (Cambridge: Harvard University Press, 1956).

27. Pelling, op. cit., pp. 173-180.

28. Report of the Commissioner . . . 1927, p. 7.

29. 38 & 39 Vict., c. 86.

30. 6 Edw. VII, c. 47.

31. See R. Y. Hedges and A. Winterbottom, *A Legal History of Trade Unionism* (London: Longmans, 1930).

32. 9 & 10 Geo. V, c. 46.

33. See Kellow Chesney, *The Victorian Underworld* (Harmondsworth: Penguin Books, 1972), pp. 372-374.

34. Report of the House of Lords Committee on the Law Relating to the Protection of Young Girls, 1881-1882.

35. 52 & 53 Vict., c. 18, s.5. Although venereal disease constituted a substantial health problem, the act was also directed at contraceptives and abortifacients.

36. 8 Edw. VII, c. 45; S. Kirson Weinberg, *Incest Behavior* (New York: Citadel Press, 1955), pp. 22-26.

37. 2 & 3 Geo. V, c. 20; 12 & 13 Geo. V, c. 56, s.3(c).

38. 37 & 38 Vict., c. 88.

39. Infanticide Act, 1922 (12 & 13 Geo. V, c. 11); Infant Life (Preservation) Act, 1929 (19 & 20 Geo. V, c. 34, s.2(2)). For a brief history of the law and judicial practice regarding infanticide cases, see Nigel D. Walker, *Crime and Insanity in England*, Vol. I: *The Historical Perspective* (Edinburgh: Edinburgh University Press, 1968), ch. 7.

40. 38 & 39 Vict., c. 17; 46 & 47 Vict., c. 3.

41. 10 & 11 Geo. V, c. 43.

42. 7 & 8 Geo. V, c. 46; Dangerous Drugs and Poisons (Amendment) Act, 1923 (13 & 14 Geo. V, c. 5).

43. See Hall, *Political Crime*, on the Irish question and relevant statutes.

44. 1 & 2 Geo. V, c. 28; 10 & 11 Geo. V, c. 75; for a discussion of these various enactments, see Hall, op. cit.

45. 1922, 16 Cr. App. Rep. 87. It should be noted that the offense of blasphemy was limited to scandalous ridicule of the Christian religion; mockery of other religions was quite legal.

46. Report of the Commissioner . . . 1911, p. 4.

47. Critchley, *A History of Police in England and Wales*, p. 152.

48. Reports of the Committee on the Police Service, Cmd. 574 and Cmd. 874, 1920.

49. Critchley, op. cit., p. 161.

50. Quoted in Browne, op. cit., p. 207.

51. Royal Commission upon the Duties of the Metropolitan Police, Cd. 4156, 1908.

52. J. P. Martin and Gail Wilson, *The Police: A Study in Manpower* (London: Heinemann, 1969), pp. 26-37.

53. Sir Ronald Howe, *The Story of Scotland Yard* (London: A. Barker, 1965), pp. 117-128.

54. Royal Commission on Police Powers and Procedure, Cmd. 3297, 1929, pars. 16-17.

55. Douglas G. Browne and Alan S. H. Brock, *Fingerprints: Fifty Years of Scientific Crime Detection* (London: Harrap, 1953).

56. R. M. Jackson, *The Machinery of Justice in England*, 5th ed. (Cambridge: Cambridge University Press, 1967), pp. 112-113.

57. Beck was twice wrongly convicted of fraud through false identifications. See Brian Abel-Smith and Robert Stevens, *Lawyers and the Courts* (London: Heinemann, 1967), pp. 99-100.

58. Caleb P. Patterson, *The Administration of Justice in Great Britain* (Austin: University of Texas Press, 1936), pp. 167-170.

59. Cicely M. Craven, "The Trend of Criminal Legislation," in Leon Radzino-wicz, ed., *Penal Reform in England* (London: Macmillan, 1946), pp. 23, 27; Home Office, Report of the Commissioners of Prisons for the Year 1959, pp. 7-10.

60. Abel-Smith and Stevens, op. cit., pp. 150-164.

61. See Nigel D. Walker, op. cit. On the treatment of the criminally insane, see Kathleen Jones, *Lunacy, Law, and Conscience, 1744-1845: The Social History of the Care of the Insane* (London: Routledge & Kegan Paul, 1955); Kathleen Jones, *Mental Health and Social Policy, 1845-1959* (London: Routledge & Kegan Paul, 1960).

62. See S. and B. Webb, *English Prisons.*

63. J. E. Thomas, *The English Prison Officer Since 1850* (London: Routledge & Kegan Paul, 1972), ch. 5.

64. Quoted in Anthony Babington, *The English Bastille* (London: Macdonald, 1971), p. 233.

65. Report from the Departmental Committee on Prisons, C. 7702, 1895. See also J. E. Hall Williams, *The English Penal System in Transition* (London: Butterworths, 1970). Du Cane's philosophy on prisons is expressed in his book, *The Punishment and Prevention of Crime* (London: Macmillan, 1885).

66. The legislation in question included the Children Act of 1908, the Prevention of Crime Act of 1908, the Mental Deficiency and Lunacy Act of 1913, and the Criminal Justice Administration Act of 1914. See Gordon Rose, *The Struggle for Penal Reform: The Howard League and its Predecessors* (London: Stevens, 1961), chs. 5-7.

67. The graph is from the Home Office, Report of the Commissioners of Prisons for the Year 1959, p. 10.

68. Borstal and preventive detention practices are discussed in the Annual Report of the Commissioners of Prisons, 1909. Two other sources on this period are Evelyn Ruggles-Brise, *The English Prison System* (London: Macmillan, 1921) and Lionel W. Fox, *The English Prison and Borstal Systems* (London: Routledge & Kegan Paul, 1952).

69. Stephen Hobhouse and A. Fenner Brockway, *English Prisons Today* (London: Longmans, 1922).

70. Report from the Select Committee on Capital Punishment (London: HMSO, 1931).

71. See William Eden Hooper, *The Central Criminal Court of London; Being a Survey of the History of the Court and Newgate, and the Fleet and other Gaols. . . .* (London: Eyre & Spottiswood, 1909).

CRIME, CONFLICT, AND PUBLIC ORDER
From the Great Depression to the 1970s

The years since the Great Depression represent more than four decades of almost unremitting crisis for Britain, hence for London as well. At the depth of the Depression, in 1931-1932, more than twenty percent of the British labor force was unemployed; in London 300,000 men in a population of eight million were out of work. The national unemployment rate never dropped below ten percent until the onset of World War II in 1939. Britain was nominally a victor in that conflict, but the indirect costs were incalculable. The country emerged from the war with an antiquated industrial establishment ill-suited to postwar domestic and export production, lacking the capital and, it is often said, the entrepreneurial spirit and skills to rebuild. The postwar Labour Government, committed as it was to massive social programs and the redistribution of income, provided little encouragement or incentive to overcome these conditions.

The postwar decade was one of austerity for almost all Britons, its principal redeeming feature being that jobs of some sort and social services were available for virtually everyone. This period also saw the loss of empire. Between 1946 and 1963 almost every significant colonial territory of the Crown gained independence. It is a tribute to Britain's leaders that they recognized the inevitable and accommodated the forces of nationalism rather than offering military resistance. Thus they retained at least some of the economic advantages of empire, but they lost irretrievably their guaranteed markets for British goods, safe havens for investment capital, and, less visibly but equally important, posts in colonial administration and business for men who found opportunities limited at home. There was something of a resurgence of the British economy in the 1950s and 1960s, but its fragility under new conditions became painfully evident in the 1970s under the crippling combination of the energy crisis, labor conflict, and double-digit inflation. Britain suffered more and longer from these conditions than almost any other country in Europe, and it is easy to place part of the blame on political ineptitude and administrative mismanagement by a government that by 1976 was consuming slightly more than 60 percent of the gross national product.[1]

One cannot prove that economic dislocation and social change lead inevitably to public disorder, but the inferential evidence is certainly strong. Almost all indicators of crime and official effort at controlling it increase throughout these 40-odd years, and at an accelerating rate. The increase is characteristic of all Britain and greater in London than elsewhere. By the mid-1970s the recorded rates of common crime surpassed their highest nineteenth century levels. London also was the stage for rallies and protests over innumerable political and social issues during this era, yet rarely were they disruptive. Beginning in the 1960s, however, protest turned increasingly malevolent, then deadly. What changed least in these decades of crisis and decay were the institutions of public order. Modifications in the criminal law were relatively modest. The London police incorporated the technological improvements of other Western police forces, but neither their numbers nor style of policing changed in any substantial way. The only significant innovations of the period were the abolition of capital punishment and an acceleration of judicial and penal policies that provided alternatives to conventional imprisonment.

TRENDS IN CRIME, 1932-1974

If official statistics have any validity, the late 1920s were the most orderly in London's statistically documented history. Just when and how the reversal of a century-long improving trend in public order began is obscured by changes and lacunae in reporting between 1925 and 1932. Thereafter, every indicator traces an upward curve. The magnitude of the increase is evident in Figure II.4.1, which shows the rate of indictable offenses known to police for London and for all England and Wales, using conventional scaling. It is evident that the increase occurred in two discontinuous waves. Known offenses almost doubled between the early 1930s and 1946, then subsided;

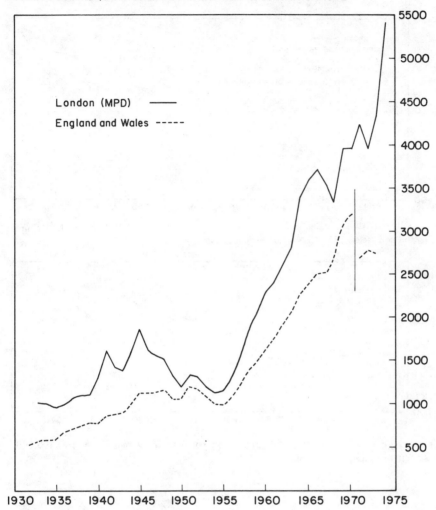

Figure II.4.1 Indictable offenses known to police in London (MPD) and England and Wales per 100,000, 1932-1974

after 1955 the upward trend resumed with a vengeance, interrupted by a temporary abatement in the late 1960s.[2]

Every aggregate indicator of crime in London, including offenses known, arrests, and convictions, reveals the same upward trend. These indicators are geometrically scaled in Figures II.4.2 to II.4.4 to facilitate visual comparison. From 1932-1933 to the 1970s indictable offenses known to police increased by 390 percent, total arrests by 300 percent, convictions by magistrates by 290 percent, and convictions by the higher courts by more than 500 percent. (These figures represent less than half, sometimes no more than a quarter of

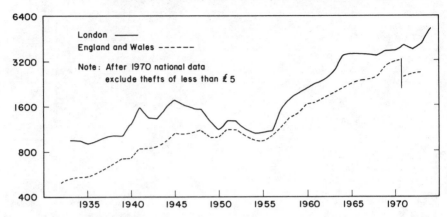

Figure II.4.2 All indictable offenses known to police per 100,000, London (MPD) and England and Wales, 1931-1974 (geometrically scaled)

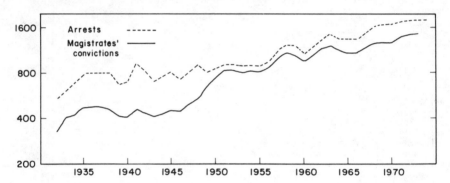

Figure II.4.3 London (MPD): All arrests and convictions by magistrates per 100,000, 1932-1974 (geometrically scaled)

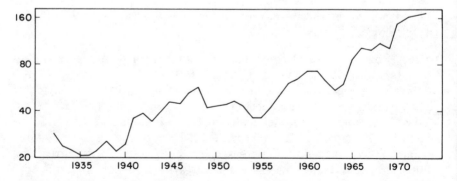

Figure II.4.4 London (MPD): Convictions by higher courts per 100,000, 1932-1973 (geometrically scaled)

all court cases and convictions. The remainder, including most traffic cases, were initiated by police summons rather than arrest.) Not all the indicators peak and decline after the war, though: Arrests remained roughly constant; convictions by magistrates increased. Evidently there was increased police attention to petty offenses during these years at the same time that more serious offenses declined.

In the previous chapter we suggested that the similarity of trends in different measures of crime and official behavior was evidence that such trends reflected, with varying degrees of distortion, an underlying social reality. The same interpretation seems to apply to the aggregate measures just examined; a look at trends in specific categories of offenses reinforces this conclusion, because virtually every category of serious offense shows the same trends. At this point our analysis is hampered by a lack of data for all except property offenses for the 1930s and early 1940s, and because data on offenses known to police are the only ones readily available. But there is no reason to think that statistics on arrests or convictions for each category of offense over the 40-odd years would lead to significantly different conclusions.

Some statistical comparisons of different categories of indictable offenses are given in Table II.4.1 for selected years from 1935 to 1974. Absolute numbers of offenses are shown to give the reader a better sense of the growing magnitude of London's problems of public order. None of the increase in absolute offenses can be attributed to population growth because the MPD's highest population during this period was 8.70 million in 1938; the postwar population never exceeded 8.42 million and by 1974 was down to 7.65 million. The trends in specific categories are considered in the following paragraphs; here some general observations are in order.

The three kinds of property crime in Table II.4.1 all correspond to the general pattern already described; that is, they rose, then declined temporarily in the late 1940s. Crimes against the person (murder and assault, sexual offenses) did not; they remained relatively low until the 1950s. The preponderance of property offenses also is evident from the table. Of the 400,000 indictable offenses in 1974, only 3 percent were crimes against the person. Among the property crimes, the distribution is 1 percent robbery, 22 percent burglary, and 74 percent others, mainly larceny from dwellings, cars, and shops.

Also included in Table II.4.1 is the proportion of cases cleared up, a statistic regularly reported by the police after 1934 and reflecting the number of cases in which arrests were made or summonses issued. It is not the same as the ratio of arrests, or convictions, to

Table II.4.1 Types of Offenses Reported and Cleared Up in London, 1935-1974[a]

Type of offense	1935	1945	1955	1960	1965	1970	1974
Murder, assaults, woundings, etc.							
Number of cases	854[b]	972	1,251	2,703	4,264	7,204	9,585[c]
Proportion cleared up	nd	.73	.83	.77	.73	.71	.67
Robbery and assault with intent to rob							
Number of cases	89	354	237	763	1,609	2,369	3,151
Proportion cleared up	.54[d]	.41	.59	.32	.26	.34	.29
Burglary from shops and dwellings							
Number of cases	11,572	22,955	14,312	33,509	48,812	74,908	88,163
Proportion cleared up	.20	.21	.25	.19	.17	.17	.17
All other indictable offenses against property[e]							
Number of cases	68,764	128,954	75,623	146,336	216,604	227,938	295,287
Proportion cleared up	.29	.21	.30	.24	.20	.30	.29
Sexual offenses[f]							
Number of cases	825[b]	1,107	1,706	1,975	2,111	3,144	2,990[c]
Proportion cleared up	nd	.74	.80	.75	.69	.73	.70

Sources: Reports of the Commissioner of Police of the Metropolis for the years shown, except data for 1935, 1938, and 1945 are principally from the Report for 1946. Also see Home Office Supplementary Judicial Statistics.

a. Offenses cleared up are those in which the police arrest a suspected offender. Multiple offenses admitted by a single defendant are counted as cleared up; apparently the clearance rate is not adjusted downward in those cases where a suspect is found innocent.

b. Data for 1938.

c. 1974 data for these categories are not precisely comparable with previous years' data.

d. Average clearance rate for 1934-1938.

e. Including larceny, receiving, and fraud; in 1974 forgery also is included.

f. Including bigamy and some unclassified offenses against persons.

offenses known, since offenders often admit to multiple offenses. Crimes against the person are cleared with commendable frequency, property offenses much less often; for burglary the rate is about one in six. Changes in clearance rates over time provide a measure of police efficiency in the face of escalating crime, and it is evident that for most of the offenses shown, the more numerous the cases, the lower the clearance rate. Clearances tend to decline after 1955 for robbery, burglary, and offenses against the person; the temporary improvement that is evident between 1965 and 1970 is attributed in police reports to intensification of police effort. Undoubtedly there were official pressures to improve the rate. The commissioner's report for 1965 observes that although at least ten other cities in the country had higher rates of recorded crime, the clearance rate in the metropolis was the lowest in the country.[3]

For more exact comparisons of the trends in indictable offenses we can refer to Figures II.4.5 to II.4.8. Known murders and serious assaults are plotted in Figure II.4.5; note that different numerical scales and ratios are used for each. Murder and manslaughter (including a few cases of infanticide) were at their lowest recorded rate around 1950; between then and 1974 they increased by about 400

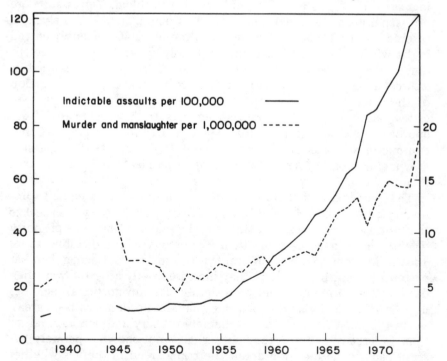

Figure II.4.5 London (MPD): Murder per million and indictable assault per 100,000, known to police, 1938, 1945-1974

percent. In absolute numbers, the police reported 18 murders and 22 cases of manslaughter in 1950 in London compared with 127 murders and 15 cases of manslaughter in 1974, in a slightly smaller population. The homicide rate in 1974 was about 19 per million; one must go back to the 1870s to find comparable rates, and even these were attributable to the use of a more inclusive definition of manslaughter. Despite the increase in homicides, the London police continued to be remarkably successful in solving them. Throughout the postwar years they regularly reported that 90 percent or more homicides were cleared by arrest.

Murder in London remains a comparatively uncommon crime; not so indictable woundings and assaults, which increased from less than 1,000 per year in the late 1940s to nearly 10,000 per year in the early 1970s. There is no evidence to support the hypothesis that some of this increase has been due to the treatment of increasing numbers of minor cases as indictable. The increase shown in Figure II.4.5 is continuous, without the step changes in assault in the mid-1920s caused by the classification of minor offenses as indictable. Nor do the reports of the Commissioner of Police make reference to any recording change. On the contrary, they comment on the increase in assaults as a real and growing problem. Yet assaults are not separately discussed until 1950, when a detailed analysis is offered. Of 1,011 cases of malicious wounding, 40 percent occurred in brawls or fights, 19 percent in family quarrels, and 7 percent during the course of arrest, with most of the others classified as "miscellaneous."[4] The report for 1972 remarks that "the proportion of these incidents which are of a domestic nature or involve associates rather than total strangers appears to have decreased from approximately a half in 1960 to about a third in 1972."[5] Other comments and specific offenses described for the 1970s suggest a growing number of group attacks by juveniles "for motives other than robbery."

The increase in indictable crimes of acquisition is equally pronounced (Figures II.4.6 and II.4.7). The pattern is nearly identical to that for total offenses, and this is to be expected because property offenses have made up more than 90 percent of all indictable crimes known in London. The different forms of theft trace a familiar pattern: Except for burglary, they increase briefly after the war, then decline; thereafter all rapidly accelerate. The proportional increases in each (Figure II.4.7) demonstrate that the upsurge has been greatest in the most serious offenses, namely robbery and burglary, rather than in larceny or fraud (or "autocrime," not shown separately). A significant social question about the rising trend in theft is whether its direct impact is felt more by private individuals or by institutions, businesses in particular. The question cannot be answered from the available data for robbery, since many of the victims in the MPD have been employees conveying money or goods. For burglary, we can make direct comparisons of housebreaking offenses as a proportion of all break-ins. For 1935 the figure is 52 percent; for 1945, 34 percent; for 1955, 45 percent; for 1965, 49 percent; and for 1974, 57 percent. Comparable and exact estimates cannot be made for larceny, but detailed data for 1955 and 1965 show that 75 percent of cases involve personal property.[6] Another indication of the prevalence of personal over commercial victimization is that shoplifting is never more than a tenth of total larcenies during the period under review.

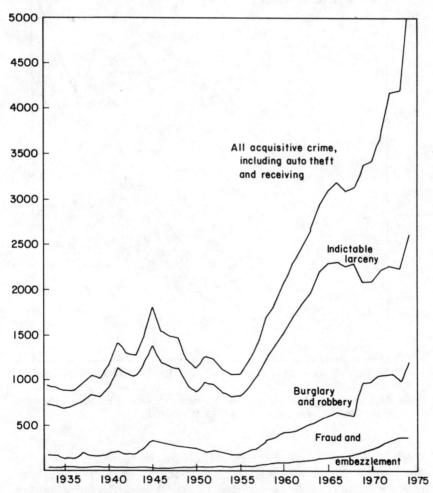

Figure II.4.6 London (MPD): Indictable crimes of acquisition known to police per 100,000, 1933-1974

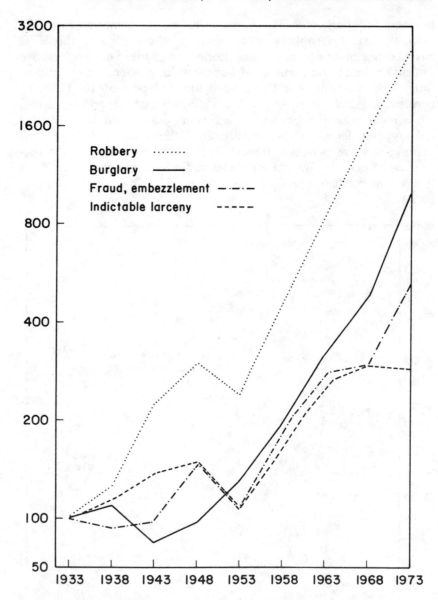

Figure II.4.7 London (MPD): Proportional increases in crimes of acquisition known to police per 100,000, at 5-year intervals 1933-1973, 1933 = 100

A popular sociological interpretation of the recorded increase in the various forms of theft is that citizens began *reporting* large numbers of previously unreported thefts. It is difficult to identify incentives that might have caused such a change in London during the last 25 years, and it is unlikely that in London in the early 1950s there "really" were 80,000 to 90,000 burglaries (the 1974 level), but people chose to report to the police only 12,000 or 14,000. Phones by which to report offenses to the police have been within walking distance of most Londoners throughout this period, and constables patrolling on foot have long been a feature of neighborhood life. Police clearance rates for burglary and larceny have been relatively low and declining during the period, providing less, not more incentive to report. The late 1950s and the 1960s were times of growing prosperity, from which it follows that the perceived seriousness of a £20 theft also declined. In short, one would expect proportionally fewer thefts to be reported to police during this period. This may explain why reports of the most serious kinds of theft have increased at greater rates than larceny during the past 25 years. If we assume that the increase reflects an underlying behavioral reality, people afflicted by a rising tide of theft are rather likely to report major losses, if only for insurance purposes, whereas they are more disposed to resign themselves to petty thievery.

Evidence and logic suggest that the somewhat distorted picture furnished by the recorded increase in theft in London during the last 25 years is the reverse of what is often argued. Theft probably has increased *more* than the official statistics show.[7]

The London police during the last four decades have not sought esoteric explanations for the apparent rise in theft: They have been as convinced as the victims that they were dealing with a real phenomenon. Reports of the commissioners often attempt to account for the rise and occasional decline in theft. Their general thrust is to credit public policies for temporary declines and to blame increases on social and economic forces. In 1934 Commissioner Trenchard summarized a discussion of the contradictory effects of economic conditions on property crime: "Although improved economic conditions may tend to bring crime figures down, the extent of crime must always vary with the extent of opportunity for crime, and the steady development of the Metropolitan Area cannot fail to produce an ever widening sphere of opportunity."[8] Two different themes are evident in discussions of opportunity. One was the proliferation of stealable property, both private and commercial; the other was the failure of owners to take measures to secure their homes, autos, and shops. Commissioner Game, Trenchard's successor, cited the primary importance of unemployment among youth as a cause of crime and added that this was a view widely held by officers.[9]

Later reports seldom gave much attention to economic factors per se and focused instead on social factors, a discussion to which

Commissioner Game contributed the banal observation that "the acquisitive instinct is becoming stronger than the urge to honesty."[10] In the 1961 report Commissioner Simpson emphasized "imitative encouragement" by the press and television, saying that "the daily presentation in dramatic form of violent and other crime, and anti-social behaviour, in a contemporary setting contributes largely to increased criminal activity."[11] Eight years later Commissioner Waldron attributed soaring theft to "our permissive society, the lack of parental influence on young people and the lowering of moral values."[12]

On the credit side of the ledger, for the police at least, was the improvement in public order in the late 1940s and early 1950s. Commissioner Scott's 1949 report singled out the Criminal Justice Act of 1948, which created new sentences of corrective training and preventive detention:

> There is no doubt that its implications have been fully appreciated by the criminal community. When habitual criminals are found on arrest to be in possession of copies of an Act of Parliament it is a safe assumption that their study of the new criminal law is dictated by something more than an academic interest, and indeed it is reported that in some cases housebreakers have disposed of the tools of their trade. . . . Experience will show whether . . . contrary to what has so often been said, it is in fact possible to make men honest by Act of Parliament.[13]

The report for 1954, by Commissioner Nott-Bower, casts a broader net:

> The improvement in supplies of goods of all kinds helps to make crime less profitable and therefore less attractive: and there can be little doubt that there is less incentive towards the commission of crime when the country is enjoying a period of relative prosperity and full employment. One would like to feel too that there has been some tightening up of moral standards. . . . Nevertheless, I think it can be justly claimed that a most important factor has been the success achieved by the police both in their preventive and detective activities. . . .[14]

Nott-Bower's prognosis was soon to be proved wrong, however, and the reports of the next twenty years provide few occasions for self-congratulation.

The changing incidence of sexual assaults and deviance is shown in Figure II.4.8; both offenses increase irregularly, but the latter (consisting mainly of buggery and indecency between males) much less so. Indictable prostitution offenses, included in the total, have been rare; they include procuring and keeping bawdy houses.[15] There are intrinsic general grounds for questioning the validity of data on sexual offenses. Homosexual acts usually come to police attention as a result of active policing rather than citizens' reports, whereas the reporting of rape and indecent assaults on women is inhibited by victims' fears of notoriety. Rape is undoubtedly the most serious of these offenses. Numbers actually reported in the MPD increased from 10 in 1938 to 22 in 1950, 66 in 1960, 141 in 1970, and 156 in 1974. The increase parallels so closely that of other offenses against the person that a real increase is the best explanation, not a growing willingness to report. The interpretation of homosexual deviance is made especially difficult in London by the passage of the Sexual Offences Act of 1967, which decriminalized virtually all private

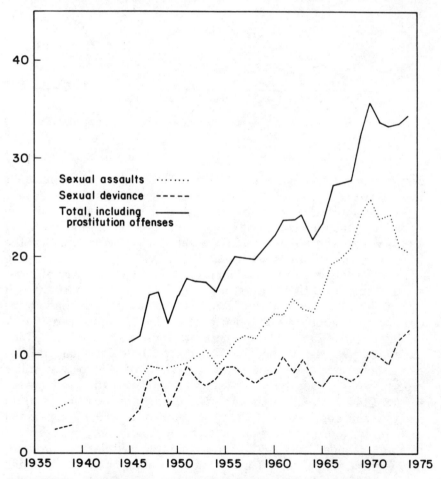

Figure II.4.8 London (MPD): Indictable offenses of sexual assault, deviance, and prostitution known to police per 100,000, 1938, 1945-1972

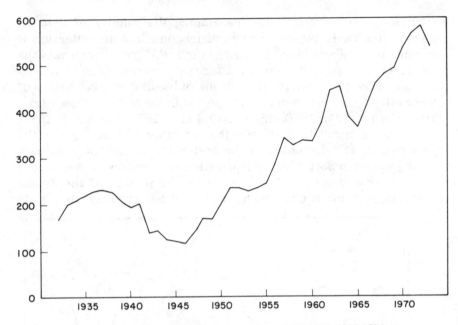

Figure II.4.9 London (MPD): Arrests for Drunkenness per 100,000, 1931-1974

sexual acts between consenting adults. The act was passed pursuant to the recommendations of the Wolfenden committee a decade earlier (discussed later in this chapter), and it may be that the essentially stable incidence of homosexual offenses in the 1950s and 1960s was due to police inattention. But that leaves unexplained the increase in known offenses after 1960.

Finally we have partial data on the incidence of summary offenses which came to official attention, graphed in Figures II.4.9 and II.4.10. The most common occasion for arrest during the period was drunkenness, about 40,000 per year by 1970, exclusive of drunk driving arrests. The trend was similar to those we have examined for indictable offenses: an increase during the 1930s, a wartime decline, and a 500 percent increase thereafter. None of the postwar police reports contains any commentary on the reasons for the increase. Figure II.4.10 reveals little variation during the postwar years in petty assault and breach of the peace, unlike the general increase in more serious forms of assault. Vagrancy is the only category of offense examined thus far that shows a prolonged decline; proceedings (equivalent to arrests) were few in absolute numbers, declining by the 1960s to 400 a year or less. Prostitution offenses, principally for soliciting, were several times as numerous. The apparent increase in the early 1960s can be attributed to a campaign to clean up the

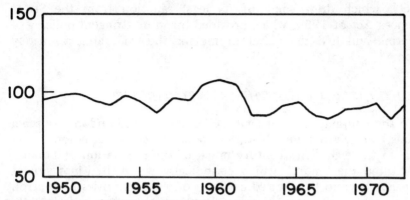

a. Assault, breach of peace, and other offenses against persons

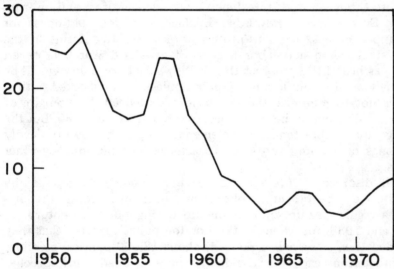

b. Vagrancy, begging, suspicious behavior, and similar offenses

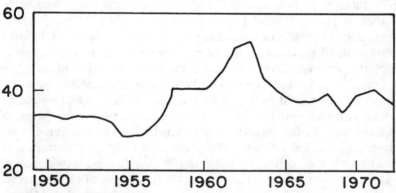

c. Offenses related to prostitution

Figure II.4.10 London (MPD): Persons proceeded against for various summary (petty) offenses per 100,000, 1949-1972

streets, which drew some of its legal sanction from the Street Offences Act of 1959, which provided for more stringent policing of soliciting and had the effect of moving the trade almost entirely indoors.[16]

CIVIL CONFLICT FROM THE 1930s TO THE 1970s

To the contemporary observer, civil conflict in London may seem serious, but viewed in a historical perspective the situation is less grim. In the eighteenth century much of the population of London constituted the "mob," which periodically was incited into violent rampages beyond the limited capacity of the authorities to control. In the nineteenth century, especially during the period 1815-1848, the elite often felt itself threatened by the danger of revolution from below. Even as late as Edwardian England, the "good old days" for the upper classes, popular protest took disruptive forms in the feminist rebellion and labor unrest. Since World War I, however, there has been little prospect that British society or polity would be rent by violent revolution, nor London pillaged in unchecked rioting. This is not to minimize the seriousness, or indeed the strength, of collective disorder in the recent past, particularly since 1960. But the only genuinely threatening new element has been the onset of deadly bombings by factions too small to achieve their purposes by other means.

Civil disorder in London can be understood only against the backdrop of the peaceful political and economic protest that has been a regular feature of London life throughout this century. In 1937 and 1938, for example, the London police reported that they attended (i.e., observed or policed) about 12,000 political meetings and processions each year. Evidently these included many speeches and indoor meetings with small attendance. In each year from 1970 to 1974 there were between 400 and 500 consequential demonstrations that required special police arrangements. Every conceivable domestic and international issue has provided an occasion for demonstrations and, often as not, counterdemonstrations: unemployment, fascism, the Spanish Civil War, the Italian invasion of Ethiopia, the Suez Canal dispute, rent increases, lack of wage increases, nuclear disarmament, apartheid in South Africa, the Vietnam war, control of nonwhite immigration, Irish civil rights, Black Power, civil wars in Bangladesh and Biafra, government control of student union funds, Palestinian rights, the invasion of Cyprus, the right to abortion, and no small number of others. Some activists have fancied long-distance processions, others preferred marching on the House of Commons to lobby MPs en masse; still others favored petitions delivered to foreign embassies or to 10 Downing Street. Rallies have been the perennial favorite, though, large ones at Hyde Park or Trafalgar Square, smaller ones wherever a few hundred supporters could gather. The thing to be kept in mind is that not one in fifty of these events has involved serious disorder. Our commentary on civil conflict is concerned less with the vast majority of peaceful and legal protests than with the handful of actions and campaigns that led, deliberately or by miscalculation, to serious breaches of public order.[17]

Labor Unrest

With the failure of the General Strike in 1926, British trades unions entered a relatively moribund period. The Labour Party, under Ramsay MacDonald in the 1930s, seemed almost hostile to the rights and needs of the working class. Moreover, the harsh economic conditions of the Depression years prevented union leaders from pressing for more than the most elementary demands. By the mid-1930s, however, this situation began to change. There are numerous ways of measuring the extent of unionized labor's discontent. To

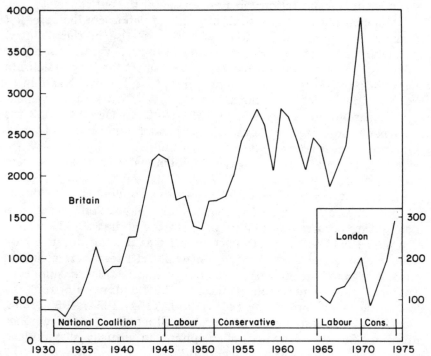

Figure II.4.11 Numbers of work stoppages and governing parties in Britain, 1930-1971, and London, 1965-1974

take one index, the number of work stoppages increased substantially in this period. In the early 1930s they averaged about 400 per year in the country as a whole, but in the second half of the decade they were never less than 800 a year (Figure II.4.11).[18] This may not be the most accurate measure of the phenomenon, for 1926 (the year of the general strike) saw more workers involved in stoppages and more working days lost than any other year in this century.[19] But in terms of government relations with unions, and the efforts of politicians or bureaucrats to mediate in labor-management negotiations, the rise in the number of cases to be handled is most significant.

It can be readily observed from Figure II.4.11 that labor has had a profound impact on British politics in the recent period. During epochs of Labour Party control—the late 1940s and the mid- and late 1960s—the number of stoppages declined sharply. In periods of Conservative rule, however, stoppages rose constantly. The result, particularly in the 1960s and 1970s, has been the ability of organized labor to determine which political party shall maintain power. The implications of course are enormous. Though strikes are not illegal, a stoppage in a major industry—especially any dealing with power resources or transportation—creates a crisis for the entire society.

The economic and political impacts of labor conflict are felt as much or more in London as anywhere else in the country. But labor conflict has rarely posed a direct threat to public order in London, not during the years since the Depression. In the 1930s the only serious labor conflict in London was due to the activities of the National Unemployed Workers Movement and similar groups, especially in 1931-1932. In October 1932 the movement organized a large hunger march on London to protest the Government's decision to impose a means test for people on relief, and a week of demonstrations and violent clashes ensued.

Almost every year except 1939-1945 the London Trades Council has organized a May Day rally, traditionally held at Trafalgar Square, but fighting occurred only in 1950 when the affair was held in spite of a police ban. In the years since World War II labor disputes have often required police protection, especially at sites where picketing was in progress and on the occasion of demonstrations in support of strikers. There were serious strikes on the London waterfront, by dockworkers and others, in 1949, 1950, 1951, 1954, 1957, 1958, and 1961. Some lasted a month or more; all required extensive police attention. But the recurring police epitaph to virtually all these and other strikes is: "No disorder occurred."

Strikes increased in frequency in London during the late 1960s and early 1970s, as is evident in Figure II.4.11. Most were small in scale and without incident, but participants in others showed a new militancy and willingness to go beyond conventional strike action. The Industrial Relations Bill, introduced by a Conservative Government in 1970 to control the rash of strikes through compulsory arbitration, inspired massive opposition by the Trades Union Congress (TUC). In February 1971 the TUC mobilized more than 100,000 members for a coordinated series of rallies and demonstrations, by far the largest seen in London for many years. Similar activities on a smaller scale continued into 1972, a year of extensive industrial unrest, including the national miners' strike, which lasted for seven weeks in January and February. New and potentially disruptive tactics were employed in London, including the use of mass picketing and squads of "flying pickets" to interrupt fuel deliveries throughout the metropolis. The next year saw many industrial disputes centering on the Government's incomes policy, and another TUC march. The new tactics of labor protest were, in short, more disruptive than the conventional ones, but they stopped short of violence and rarely necessitated arrests. Their purposes were essentially political, and it is likely that the police response, like that of the Government, was dictated as much by political as economic considerations.

Other signs of economic conflict in London during the postwar decades have been squatters' and tenants' movements. Such actions have always been very localized and have not had the public attention of strikes and political processions, but their recurrence is evidence of smoldering resentment about the housing issue. Police reports refer to them immediately after World War II and again, in increasingly organized forms, in 1960, 1963, 1969, and 1974.

Political Protest and the Rise of Civil Disobedience

In the upsurge of political rallies and demonstrations in prewar London the most strident voices were those of the British Union of Fascists (BUF) and their opponents. The BUF, led by Sir Oswald Mosley, began as a conventional political movement inspired by Mussolini's example in Italy and supported by Britons disaffected by major parties that had proved unable to cope with the Depression. They held several large and innumerable small rallies in London each year from 1933 to 1938. The activities of the BUF attracted even larger numbers of counterdemonstrations. One by the United Jewish Protest Committee in 1933 was said by police to have had 20,000 to 30,000 participants. In 1936 the BUF adopted a policy of active "Jew-baiting" whose words inspired some members to depredatory deeds. The principal result, though, was increasingly violent retaliation by opposing groups. Thereafter every BUF rally became a potential and often an actual occasion for brawls. In 1937 the Commissioner of Police reported that of 11,804 meetings and processions that had to be policed, more than 7,000 were fascist or antifascist. The onset of World War II in 1938 put an effective end to the BUF's public activities. An attempt by Mosley to resuscitate the movement in the early 1960s attracted more derision and counter-demonstrators than support.[19]

A century ago Ralph Waldo Emerson commented on the passion displayed by the British in all aspects of public affairs: "They have a wonderful heat in the pursuit of a public aim."[20] Londoners in those days, however, were excited by questions of domestic politics. After World War II collective action usually focused on issues over which even the British authorities had little or no control. For the first decade after the war, in fact, there were few demonstrations of any kind in London, partly because the Commissioner of Police imposed an almost continuous series of bans from 1948 to 1951. Demonstrations later in the 1950s were sometimes large but almost always orderly. In 1955 a major protest against the rearmament of Germany was held at the House of Commons, and the following year saw numerous demonstrations in response to the invasion of the Suez Canal and the Hungarian Revolution. In 1957 the National Association of Tenants and Residents organized two large demonstrations against the Rent Bill then before Parliament.

The major protest movements of the postwar era began with the "Ban the Bomb" movement, led by Lord Russell who, though well advanced in age, provided charisma and encouraged a large following.[21] From small beginnings in 1957, the movement guided by the Committee for Nuclear Disarmament (CND) carried out rallies and marches in London and environs for more than a decade. By 1960 they could muster 20,000 and more for marches to Trafalgar Square. Such meetings had little effect, though. It was irrelevant whether they influenced the foreign policies of the Conservative administration of Harold Macmillan, since by this time the British had lost what little nuclear independence they possessed. In the eyes of the world the protest appeared meaningless in light of Britain's decline in power to the second rank, or worse, while marches on the United States and Soviet embassies to protest nuclear testing had no visible impact whatsoever. Habits of protest die hard, though, and in 1970 one reads of a thin remnant of 700 protesters carrying out the now-traditional Easter march.

Irrelevancy was only one of the liabilities of the Ban the Bomb movement. Another was the emergence of newer and more immediate issues that attracted the energies of the foot-soldiers of protest. Foremost among these was the support given by the British government to American intervention in Vietnam, which was the object of innumerable demonstrations and rallies from 1965 through the early 1970s. At their height, in October 1968, the war protesters could produce 30,000 for a single demonstration.[22] This was by no means the only international issue to draw fire during these years. Groups opposing apartheid in South Africa were less numerous but just as active, and their cause has proved to be a more enduring one.

The protest movements of the 1960s and early 1970s found most of their recruits among the young and undoubtedly reflected the international revolt of college and university students in that era. In England as elsewhere, the leaders of the protests and many of their supporters were the educated children of the Establishment: Many were also involved in actions protesting university policies and curricula. The London demonstrators had no success in enlisting workers' support, however, and hence were unable to effect political change. Even large-scale marches by London and national student organizations in 1971-1972 to protest government reorganization of student union finances had little political impact.[23]

Most of the protesters of this era were peaceful in intent. It is rather inconsistent, after all, to promote pacifism by violent means. Moreover the London police employed crowd control techniques that did not rely on force and required a remarkable restraint on the part of constables subject to verbal abuse and physical buffetings. Commissioner Waldron described police policies toward demonstrations in his report for 1971:

> No demonstration has been prevented from taking place; in most demonstrations there is excellent co-operation between police and public; and all demonstrations have been controlled without the setting up of riot squads or the use of special equipment such as water-cannon or tear gas. All training has been directed to methods of containment which are appropriate to a civilian force. The work has demanded tolerance, patience and self-discipline and often courage of a high order. . . .[24]

Neither the accounts of the press nor of independent observers give any reason to doubt that the London police were uniformly disciplined and nonviolent in their behavior.

The Rise of Political Violence

Police tactics of restraint were frustrating to a militant minority of protesters who actively sought confrontation and disruption. Such a minority existed in the British youth movement just as in student populations in most other Western countries. One of the indicators of their activity, as well as a general index of the intensity of protest in London, is the number of demonstrators arrested by police. Such data are reported with some regularity in the police reports after 1950 and have been compiled and graphed in Figure II.4.12.[25] The very high numbers in 1962-1964 represent the activities of the "Committee of 100," a group opposed to all manifestations of militarism, who advocated mass civil disobedience as a means of overwhelming police and administrative machinery. They staged large demonstrations, five in 1961 alone, in which they blocked traffic and disobeyed police orders. The nature of the police response is evident in the arrest figures, and the committee found it increasingly difficult to gain support for their tactics. In the late 1960s—1968 seems to have been a watershed year—small groups of militants began to try to turn hitherto peaceful demonstrations into violent confrontations. The relatively high level of arrests thereafter is a mark of their success.

The London police could cope with violent confrontation, partly because most of the protesters wished to avoid it as much as the police. The more ominous threat to public order in London since

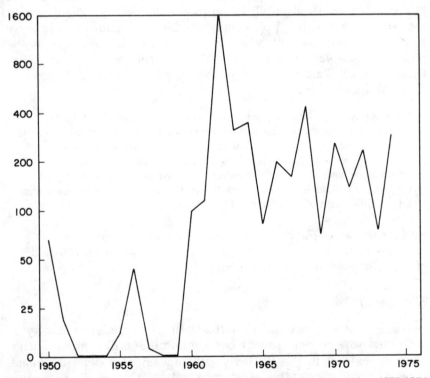

Figure II.4.12 London (MPD): Arrests in political demonstrations and clashes, 1950-1974 (geometrically scaled)

1969 has been bombings. Political bombings are not new in London. Some earlier incidents were mentioned in the previous chapter. At the onset of World War II the Irish Republican Army (IRA) carried out a short-lived campaign of bombings, perpetuating about 60 in London in 1939. Then in 1968 a clandestine group of revolutionaries calling themselves the "Angry Brigade" exploded a series of bombs at the homes of officials and, in 1971, in the Post Office Tower and at an army drill hall in London. There were no injuries in these blasts, but four Brigade members were sentenced to long prison terms.

A much more extensive and deadly campaign of bombings was begun by the Provisional branch of the IRA in 1973, in an effort to "bring the war home to Britain" and force the withdrawal of British troops from Northern Ireland. At first they used mainly letter and incendiary bombs, then massive car bombs. In 1974 there were 139 bombing incidents and the targets included Westminster Hall and the Tower of London; four people were killed and a number of others maimed. In 1975 the campaign was continued in the city, with bombings directed at fashionable restaurants, and the death toll was considerably greater. By 1976 the most intensive security precautions were in force in public and many private establishments throughout the city, yet bombings and attempts continued, and so did the British presence in Northern Ireland. One nasty side effect of the campaign was a pervasive sense of insecurity among Londoners; another was the increase in anonymous bomb threats, 8,000 of which were telephoned to police in 1974 alone.[26]

Ethnic Conflict

One other serious problem of public order in post-World War II London has been the reaction of native borns to the immigrants from the former colonies. The influx of large numbers of people from the West Indies, the subcontinent of India, and Africa has inevitably created problems of social and economic adjustment. These immigrants are no more than five percent of the present population proportion of London, far smaller a proportion than the black populations of most major American cities. The situation has been exacerbated, however, by the outspoken expression of racial prejudice. Such feelings were omnipresent in British dealings with their overseas subjects but were rarely expressed in the British Isles until large-scale immigration had begun. In August and September 1958 there was considerable rioting and harassment by white Londoners against the immigrant population of the Notting Hill district. Gang attacks on nonwhites became common enough to label "Paki-bashing." Youths of West Indian origin have become particularly resentful of white hostility. In the south London borough of Lambeth, which has a particularly large concentration of black residents (more than 30 percent in its two central wards), there were serious attacks on white policemen by crowds of black youths in 1973, 1975, and again in 1976.

The situation has been one that even the Labour governments, supposedly reformist in all matters, have been unable to deal with, except by passing restrictive legislation; one might even say especially the Labour governments, since much of the resentment against the immigrants has come from the working class.[27] The upper and middle classes have also revealed prejudice, however. From their ranks has emerged a potent backlash movement, spearheaded by the outspoken Enoch Powell.[28] This cause, like many others, has provided the occasion for protest marches in London. Four hundred members of the Immigration Control Association marched on 10 Downing Street in July 1968 and were challenged violently by 500 marchers from the Movement for Colonial Freedom. In the 1970s, despite or perhaps because of the onset of economic crisis, ethnic tension has continued to increase. Despite extremists' talk of expulsion, immigration continues but at a much reduced rate. Its cessation might make it possible for processes of social accommodation to take effect.

INSTITUTIONS OF PUBLIC ORDER, 1930 TO THE 1970s

The Criminal Law

In the years since 1930 Parliament has added to the criminal law on a number of occasions. Old acts have been consolidated and modernized, some new offenses created, and some old ones eliminated. Some of the acts have been inconsequential; others have had considerable social and political significance. Their net effect has been to increase legal restrictions on individual liberty, though most of the liberties infringed are ones few Britons are likely to wish to indulge. There has also been one major step toward relaxation of prohibitions on sexual activity between consenting adults.

Mass protest among the unemployed and the increasingly strident and militant activities of Mosley's British Union of Fascists prompted enactment of the Public Order Act of 1936.[29] The act reasserted numerous prohibitions on public protest activity already in force under an array of existing statutes: The use of threatening, abusive, or insulting words in a public place, for example, had long been illegal. New provisions explicitly prohibited the organizing, training, and equipping of quasi-military organizations, as well as the possession of offensive weapons at public meetings and processions. The act's prohibition of the wearing in public of uniforms signifying association with political organizations obviously was aimed at the BUF. The act also gave commissioners of police powers to impose three-month bans on all political processions or, short of that, to prescribe their routes. Both provisions were used in London on a number of occasions in subsequent years.

The threat of domestic unrest, however, was soon eclipsed by the reality of international conflict. The Emergency Powers (Defence) Act of 1939 granted virtually unlimited powers to issue regulations in furtherance of the war effort. The ukases that followed embodied restrictions on the flying of carrier pigeons, on the carrying of cameras in certain strategic locations, and on certain forms of public expression, primarily involving criticism of Britain's war policies.

One of the more noteworthy extensions of the criminal law during the period occurred in the area of firearms regulation. The Firearms Act of 1937, in addition to regulating the sale and transfer of firearms in general, prohibited the possession of automatic and gas weapons. Whereas these provisions may have been inspired partly by the perceived threat of paramilitary groups, postwar legislation was explicitly directed at individual perpetrators of violent crimes. The Prevention of Crime Act of 1953 forbade the carrying of offensive weapons without lawful authority or reasonable excuse. There were more than 200 convictions under the act (which applied to cutting instruments as well as to firearms) in the MPD during the first two years of its implementation. The Firearms Act of 1965 provided for a maximum of five years' imprisonment for those convicted of carrying firearms in public.

Further expansion of the criminal law was obviously stimulated by the racial antagonism that became increasingly intense during the early 1960s. The Race Relations Act of 1965 was designed to facilitate the integration of nonwhite immigrants into British society and created the offense of incitement to racial hatred. Maximum penalties under the act were two years' imprisonment and a fine of £1,000.[30] In London the first eleven persons against whom proceedings were reported under the act were, ironically enough, nonwhite supporters of the Black Power movement.[31]

Although most forms of common crime had long since been described in great statutory detail, refinements of criminal definitions have occurred on occasion. Drastic increases in rates of property crime prompted Parliament to enact the Theft Act of 1968, a general consolidation of existing statutes governing the various crimes of acquisition. The act also created the new category of offense of "aggravated burglary"—burglary committed while in possession of a firearm. The offense carried a maximum sentence of life imprisonment. One of the most recent additions to the criminal law is the Prevention of Terrorism (Temporary Provisions) Act of 1974, passed in the aftermath of IRA bombings in Birmingham and London. It provided extended powers of arrest and detention of suspected terrorists.[32]

There were also an assortment of behaviors decriminalized since the 1930s. During the Depression years the Vagrancy Act of 1935 modified the century-old Vagrancy Act of 1824 by removing the criminal penalties against sleeping out without visible means of sustenance. Under the old act the accused was ordinarily freed if he had a shilling or two in his pocket; under the new one, it had to be proved that he had refused an offer of shelter. The extension of free shelter facilities made the latter alternative a real one. In the MPD, at any rate, begging was much more common an offense during the 1930s than sleeping out.[33] Another retrenchment of the boundaries of criminal deviance was made by the Suicide Act of 1961, which removed the threat of criminal penalties against those who failed in attempted suicide.

Without question the most significant reforms of the substantive criminal law during the twentieth century related to consensual sexual activity. A reforming impulse had been stimulated both by the writings of criminologists and the less restrained life-style during World War II and the postwar years—mores underscored by the statistical studies of Americans conducted by Kinsey and his colleagues. In 1954 the Home Office appointed a committee chaired by Sir John Wolfenden to make recommendations on those parts of the criminal code relating to homosexuality and prostitution. It has been said that a private motive behind the appointment of the committee was the dismay of some members of the government and Parliament at being solicited by prostitutes of both sexes while on their way home from evening sessions of the House of Commons.

The committee, after much deliberation and the resignation of two members, published its report in 1957.[34] There was considerable disagreement among the witnesses before the committee, but its recommendations, reached with reservations by some members, were straightforward enough. The committee proposed that Parliament pass legislation abolishing as a crime homosexual activities between adult males in private. While prostitution itself had never been regarded as a criminal act, related aspects (procuring, brothel-keeping, and so forth) had been. For these offenses related to prostitution the committee found itself at odds over what should be done. Half the members wrote reservations to the recommendations, reflecting no doubt the ambivalent attitude of society toward these questions. The report caused something of a furor at the time, though after twenty years it seems to be an outmoded statement about sexual conduct in a civilized society.[35]

If the committee's recommendations on the subject of prostitution were so encumbered with reservations as to be extremely vague, the recommendations regarding homosexuality were clear enough. (It should be noted that the criminal code covered only homosexual acts between males; female homosexual acts have never been defined as criminal.) Because of the reluctance of the legislature to face the issue, however, it was ten years until Parliament passed the Sexual Offenses Act of 1967. This measure condoned sexual acts of virtually any kind between adults in private. For the first time since the 1820s, behavior legally regarded as a major (i.e., indictable) offense was exempted from criminal prosecution. Behavior related to prostitution, on the other hand, remained criminalized. Indeed, the Street Offenses Act of 1959 raised penalties for street solicitation and dropped the requirement for proof of annoyance as ground for conviction. The law had an obvious initial impact on street walking, as overt soliciting soon became rare.

Another significant retrenchment of criminal law was accomplished in 1967; it concerned illegal terminations of pregnancy. Public attitudes toward abortion had changed gradually in the decades after 1930. In accordance with the provisions of the Infant Life (Preservation) Act of 1929, preservation of the mother's life was the only recognized ground for a legal abortion. Nonetheless resort to illegal terminations was widespread, particularly during the Depression years. Because of the extremely low visibility of the behavior in question, prosecutions were infrequent—never more than 100 throughout Britain in any given year. In keeping with changing social views in other Western countries, such rigid de jure prohibitions met with increasing disfavor. An Abortion Law Reform Association was founded in 1936, and two years later further relaxation of prohibitions resulted from the Bourne case, which involved a London gynecologist who admitted performing an abortion on the fourteen-year-old victim of a rape by two soldiers. Bourne was acquitted after the trial judge instructed the jurors to undertake a broad interpretation of what was meant by "the woman's life."

Nevertheless, considerable stigma continued to attach to those who performed and those who underwent abortions. Illicit activities thrived, sanitary considerations often were neglected, and the handful of annual prosecutions provided some upright citizens with symbolic satisfaction. Despite the Thalidomide tragedies and the examples of liberalized statutes in Japan and numerous Eastern European nations, Parliament continued to resist legislative reform.

With medical and reform interests aligned against organized religious groups, the former prevailed in the liberalized atmosphere of the late 1960s. The Abortion Act of 1967 permitted termination of pregnancy at the discretion of two registered medical practitioners.[36]

Decriminalization in 1967 was not limited to moral offenses. One year earlier the Law Commission had recommended that a number of archaic provisions be stricken from the criminal law, and part of the Criminal Law Act of 1967 was devoted to this task.[37] Thus the Brawling Act of 1553, the Sedition Act of 1661, and the Blasphemy Act of 1697 were all repealed. Doubtless many were relieved to learn that they no longer ran the risk of arrest for "being out and about when decent folk are abed"—the offense at common law known as "night walking." The crimes of challenging to fight, eavesdropping, and being a common scold were similarly abolished.

By no means, however, was the British criminal law of the early 1970s brought into full correspondence with contemporary thought and prevailing behavior. Public intoxication, for example, remained a crime rather than an occasion for treatment and continued to be prosecuted energetically (Figure II.4.9). In 1969 it became an offense to tattoo anyone under eighteen years of age for nonmedical reasons. And numerous prohibitions of yesteryear remained formally in effect, albeit in desuetude. The Tumultuous Petitioning Act of 1661 still held that no person shall

> repair to His Majesty or both or either Houses of Parliament, upon pretence of presenting or delivering any petition . . . accompanied with excessive number of people, nor at any one time with above the number of ten persons, upon pain of incurring a penalty not exceeding one hundred pounds, and three months imprisonment for every offence. . . .[38]

There were hundreds of occasions between 1930 and 1975 on which this act could have been applied.

The Metropolitan Police

For most of the last three decades the Metropolitan Police have been underpaid, understrength, and overworked. No doubt the conditions are causally related. The decline in the manpower of the force that began in the aftermath of World War I was to last three decades. The largest drop in manpower occurred during and immediately following World War I and continued through 1946, when there were fewer than 13,000 uniformed police in London, a full 30 percent less than in 1930. Manpower levels increased beginning in 1947, and the number of uniformed officers reached 17,625 at the end of 1974.

The changing strength of the uniformed force is shown in Figure II.4.13. The most significant growth, though, has been the expansion of the CID. This branch has nearly trebled in the decades since the war, including a major expansion after 1963 to deal with the soaring rate of serious crime. By 1974 the CID had nearly 3,500 members. Policewomen in London also became more numerous during this period, although the 726 women police in 1974 were less than three percent of the total force. Backing up the regular police establishment is a large civil staff that in 1974 numbered nearly 16,000— mostly administrative and clerical posts, along with some traffic wardens and school crossing guards.[39]

Although the salary increases and other benefits awarded as a result of the Desborough Report (1919)[40] had made policing a relatively attractive vocational alternative to the average Londoner between the wars, these advantages were not to endure. Postwar inflation and rising industrial wages eroded the relative attractiveness of police work, and recruitment became the most serious internal problem of the force. The MPD's actual uniformed strength has varied from 12 to 30 percent below its authorized strength since 1945. Figure II.4.14 shows graphically the extent to which the force has been undermanned since 1943. In the 1930s the force was never

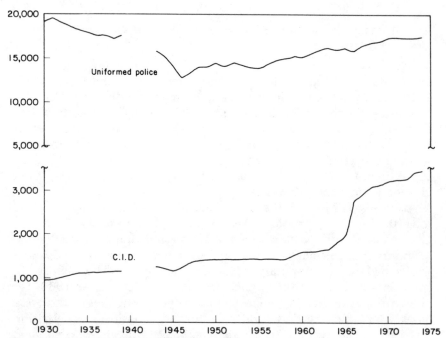

Figure II.4.13 London (MPD): Effective strength of the uniformed police and the criminal investigation department, 1930-1974

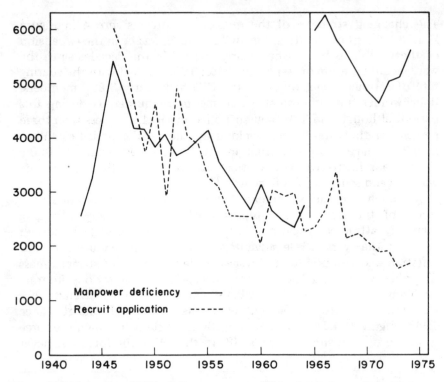

Figure II.4.14 London (MPD): Police manpower deficiencies and recruit applications, 1943-1974

understrength by more than 900 men, and usually much less; since 1945 it has never been closer than 2,300 men to authorized strength. The abrupt increase after 1965 is due to a step increase in established strength. The figure also includes postwar data on the number of would-be recruits who were sufficiently interested in a police career to take the preliminary examination. The persistent decline in the latter figure indicates that although most Londoners like their "bobbies," fewer and fewer want to join them.

Attempts to improve the policeman's lot have not been enough to solve the recruiting problem. Annual leave was increased in 1946 and 1948 and the work week reduced in 1955 (to 44 hours) and 1964 (to 42 hours). Wage increases won by policemen during the 1950s and 1960s had some temporary effects on recruiting: The increase in applicants and reduction in the shortage of officers after 1960 was due to a substantial pay increase in that year. But these gains were quickly diluted by inflation. Meanwhile, considerable attrition occurred in the ranks of the more experienced officers, who resigned in significant numbers to take positions in the private sector or in other domestic police forces. Such premature retirement of experienced personnel was regularly cited by commissioners in the years following World War II as one of the most pressing problems facing the Metropolitan force.

Activities of the police became ever more specialized in the era of modern law enforcement. As London's population of motor vehicles increased, the direction of traffic occupied increasing amounts of police energies. By 1935 one out of every six uniformed members of the Metropolitan Police was engaged in traffic work on a daily basis.[41] It was not, however, until 1960 that civilian traffic wardens were taken on.

The burdens of having to enforce a comprehensive criminal law, in addition to performing numerous functions unrelated to conventional law enforcement, continued to weigh heavily on the police. With the outbreak of war in 1939, they had to assume still further responsibilities. In addition to enforcing the Defence Regulations, as noted earlier, members of the Metropolitan force were assigned intensive sentry and patrol duties to guard against sabotage. Moreover, the assorted civil defense services (including rescue and evacuation functions, which they performed during the years of intermittent air attacks from 1940 to 1945) were as demanding as they were heroic. It was perhaps some consolation to members of the beleaguered force that many potential criminals were overseas in uniform and that petrol rationing reduced the burdens of traffic control.

Extraneous duties continued to pose such serious problems during the postwar period that a Home Office committee recommended in 1953 that police be excused from their duties under the Weights and Measures and Food and Drug Acts. Other responsibilities of which the police were relieved included an array of licensing and inspection duties under the Pet Animals Act of 1951, the Shops Act of 1950, and the various Pharmacy and Poisons Acts.[42] One would imagine that these extraneous duties, under conditions of chronic manpower shortage, would have precluded attention to all but the most serious forms of criminality. Nevertheless, a former head of the CID boasted that the Obscene Publications Squad seized nearly 400,000 items in 1963, "the greater part being obscene paper-backed novels imported from the U.S.A."[43] Moreover, arrests for public drunkenness in the metropolis increased, surpassing 40,000 per year by the early 1970s.

As postwar increases in crime and road traffic added to the strain on police resources, there was growing concern over the efficiency and accountability of the various forces throughout Britain. One incident involving an assault by a member of the Metropolitan Police and the subsequent failure to implement disciplinary proceedings prompted the appointment of a royal commission in 1960. The commission's terms of reference were exceptionally broad, ranging from disciplinary proceedings to salary matters to the question of nationalizing British police forces. The commission's report, promulgated in 1962, recognized the advantages that nationalization could bring but suggested that preservation of local autonomy was preferable.[44] The Police Act of 1964 implemented most of the commission's recommendations: Operational control of police remained decentralized, with the Metropolitan Police still directly responsible to the Home Secretary. The act did mandate a certain amount of nationwide administrative standardization, however. The powers of the Home Office were expanded to allow it to direct interforce cooperation, and the Home Secretary was authorized to head the investigation of complaints against members of any local force.

An internal measure of the disciplinary problems faced by the Metropolitan Police is the number of men and women who have had to be dismissed, or required to resign, for misconduct. These numbers have been faithfully reported by police commissioners since the 1860s. Five-year averages are given in Table II.4.2 for the past 55 years, with representative figures for early periods. It can be seen that from the point of view of the police the problem has been relatively minor in recent years, far less serious than it was in the nineteenth century, or even the 1920s. Much of the improvement no doubt can be attributed to higher recruiting standards and the expanded use of training and probationary periods for new constables.

Table II.4.2 Dismissals from the Metropolitan Police Force for Misconduct, Five-Year Totals

Years	Total dismissals	Dismissals as % of uniformed force
1866-1870	1,987	22.17
1886-1890	907	6.36
1901-1905	516	3.12
1921-1925	331	1.69
1926-1930	266	1.39
1931-1935	176	0.94
1936-1940	109	0.63
1941-1945	65	0.41
1946-1950	59	0.42
1951-1955	84	0.58
1956-1960	81	0.53
1961-1965	98	0.60
1966-1970	63	0.37
1971-1974	97	0.55

Source: Reports of the Commissioner of Police for the Metropolis, various years, tables titled "Removals from the Force," our calculation of totals and percentages.

The public image of the Metropolitan Police, although certainly more favorable than that of their counterparts in most other Western societies, was somewhat tarnished in the 1960s. In addition to the incident that led to the appointment of the royal commission in 1960, proceedings were brought in 1963 against a detective sergeant and three police constables for a variety of offenses, including fabricating evidence, perjury, and assault. The sergeant was adjudged insane, which did not improve the police image, and further official inquiries were carried out.[45] The renaissance of collective protest during the 1960s also increased friction between the police and public, especially youths. There is little question that the Metropolitan Police continue to enjoy considerable public support, yet the number of formal complaints lodged against them is growing (Table II.4.3). The most common cause of complaints (perhaps a fifth of the total) has been the incivility of officers toward the public. Complaints of police brutality, bribery, and mistaken arrest also have been fairly common. The commissioner is required by the Police Act of 1964 to investigate each such complaint; as the results in the table indicate, less than a tenth have been substantiated, leading to some kind of disciplinary action. Another indication of public and official concern was the establishment in 1972 of the special A.10 Branch of the Metropolitan Police to investigate the most serious complaints against policemen. The branch subsequently uncovered the most serious case of corruption ever found among the Metropolitan Police.

Table II.4.3 Formal Complaints Against the Metropolitan Police and Their Outcome, 1963-1974[a]

Year	Number of complainants	Substantiated complaints (%)
1963	1,614	8.6
1964	1,870	10.3
1965	2,460	9.6
1966	2,412	9.7
1967	2,639	8.3
1968	2,924	6.9
1969	3,296	7.7
1970	3,509	5.8
1971	3,165	6.9
1972	3,922	6.1
1973	3,940	7.0
1974	4,155	6.0

Source: Reports of the Commissioner of Police of the Metropolis, 1964-1974.
a. Complainants often brought charges against several officers. The figures are based on individuals making complaints, not the number of complainees.

Early in 1976 twelve high-ranking officers, including former heads of the Murder Squad, the Obscene Publications Squad, and the Flying Squad were charged with having accepted bribes from pornographers for as long as fifteen years.

Among the more significant changes in the structure of the Metropolitan Police were those implemented in response to the increase in terrorist activity in the early 1970s. Following an attempted airline hijacking in September 1970 a number of constables were assigned to assist in the inspection of baggage at Heathrow Airport. They thus augmented the existing airport security force, the British Airports Authority Constabulary. In 1974 the Metropolitan Police assumed primary responsibility for the policing of Heathrow. The vulnerability of foreign diplomatic personnel to kidnapping and assassination led to the establishment in 1974 of a Diplomatic Protection Group within the Metropolitan force. In addition to the special detachment of assigned officers and mobile patrols, a number of particularly vulnerable diplomatic establishments were fitted with emergency communications equipment. The hand of the police vis-a-vis terrorists in general was strengthened in 1974 with the enactment of the Prevention of Terrorism (Temporary Provisions) Act, already mentioned. Despite these and such other innovations as the augmentation of the CID and the Bomb Squad, terrorists bombings in London continued at an alarming rate.[46]

The Courts and Criminal Procedure

Expeditious processing of cases continued to be the primary object of most modifications in criminal procedure. The expansion of summary jurisdiction, which was so significant during the early decades of the century, continued. Indeed, the increase in rates of arrest that began in the 1950s made such procedural streamlining almost imperative. The Criminal Justice Administration Act of 1962 extended still further the offenses that could be tried summarily, subject to the consent of the accused. By 1965 close to 90 percent of all indictable offenses were in fact tried summarily. Although defendants who accepted prosecution proposals that they be tried summarily thus waived their right to a jury trial, it has been suggested that they gained some advantage in return. Until the mid-1960s the requirements for jury service, whether de facto or de jure, tended to limit membership on juries to representatives of the middle and upper classes, individuals often not able to identify or sympathize with the average working-class defendant.[47] Magistrates, though drawn almost exclusively from the same classes, could be said to have a degree of tolerance, based on extended acquaintance with the kinds of offenders appearing before them. Since 1965 the situation has changed somewhat; an act passed in that year governing the valuation of dwellings brought almost all householders within the limits of jury eligibility and has greatly increased working-class jurors.

The processing of more serious cases was streamlined in 1933 with the abolition of grand juries. Offenders concerned are thus sent to trial as soon as the justice's preliminary inquiry is completed.

The year 1948 saw changes in criminal procedure affecting diverse classes of offenders. Among its less significant reforms, the Criminal Justice Act of 1948 abolished the anachronistic privilege of peerage, and incumbents of the House of Lords were no longer triable only by members of that body for treason or felony.[48] The act, however, had a more important bearing on less eminent defendants. It served both to expand and to contract the sentencing latitude of courts, for the purpose of reducing reliance on custodial punishment. The act extended power to impose a fine in lieu of imprisonment on convicted felons; previously this option had applied only to the sentencing of misdemeanants. Another provision reduced the courts' discretion by stipulating that courts of summary jurisdiction might not impose imprisonment on a person under seventeen years of age, nor courts of assize or quarter sessions on those under fifteen.

Changes in the appellate process during the period were also noteworthy. The Criminal Appeal Act of 1964 authorized the Court of Criminal Appeal to grant new trials following the overturning of a conviction. Previously an appellant whose conviction had been quashed could not be tried again on the same charges. Structurally, the Court of Criminal Appeal was integrated with the civil appellate court in 1966, becoming the Criminal Division of the Court of Appeal.

Still other changes in criminal procedure implemented during the decades after 1930 sustained trends established in earlier years. The Money Payments (Justices Procedure) Act of 1935 required consideration of the defendant's financial status prior to the imposition of a fine; the act's implementation was followed by a 45 percent drop in persons admitted to prison in default of payment.

Increasing burdens on the criminal justice system prompted enactment of the Criminal Justice Administration Act of 1962, which created a number of new judgeships. Two years later a reorganization of local government and the creation of Greater London as an administrative and political entity was followed by a restructuring of the criminal courts in the metropolis. Greater London was divided into five commission areas, each the functional equivalent of counties elsewhere in Britain. Thus each area had its own set of justices and its own quarter sessions. The Central Criminal Court, "Old

Bailey," served as the quarter sessions court for Inner London, and as the assize court for the entire metropolitan area.

Concern for streamlining the process of disposition and reducing pressures on the prisons system was reaffirmed by the Criminal Justice Act of 1967. The act allowed the acceptance of majority verdicts in jury trials after juries had deliberated for two hours without arriving at a consensus. The legislation scarcely revolutionized criminal procedure, however, since only seven percent of jury verdicts in the first fifteen months of its operation reflected anything less than unanimity.[49] Otherwise the act required that defendants who appeared before magistrates' courts on offenses carrying a maximum of six months' imprisonment be released on bail, and suspended sentences were to be awarded defendants convicted of such charges.

The position of the less affluent defendant in the British criminal justice system improved in the decades after 1930. The Summary Jurisdiction (Appeals) Act of 1933 abolished security for costs and made provisions for free legal aid, thus facilitating appeals of magistrates' decisions to quarter sessions. Schemes for representation of the indigent were, however, far from perfect. The systems in operation under provisions of the Legal Aid and Advice Act of 1949 and the Legal Aid Acts of 1964 and 1974 provided for the reimbursement of private counsel for services rendered to clients who satisfied a means test. Whether through the defendants' inertia or the conservatism of court authorities, actual provision of legal aid remained beyond the reach of most. In the early 1970s it was estimated that 95 percent of all defendants were not represented at the time of their first appearance in magistrates' courts, and unrepresented guilty pleas constituted a large number of dispositions.[50]

The Prisons and Punishment

Diversification and expansion both characterized British prisons in the decades after 1930, the latter in direct response to the unprecedented overcrowding which occurred in the years after World War II (Figure II.3.17). The most significant developments during the 1930s were the expansion of borstal facilities and the establishment of open borstals. Much of the success of these innovations must be attributed to Alexander Paterson, a prison commissioner who sought to model borstals more after English public schools than adult prisons. By the end of the decade, the first open facility for adult offenders had also been established.[51]

The 1930s were not entirely tranquil, however. Increasing discontent among the inmates at Dartmoor erupted in a riot in January

1932. The prisoners controlled the inside of the prison for a number of hours, but the revolt was contained and eventually suppressed by armed police. There was remarkably little bloodshed and no fatalities. Nevertheless the uprising foreshadowed the problems of security and unrest that were to plague prison administrators in later years.

The Criminal Justice Act of 1948 introduced a number of changes to correctional practice—some merely symbolic, others of greater substance. The archaic terms "penal servitude" and "criminal lunatic" were dropped from the official lexicon, but the realities of confinement symbolized by these labels remained the same. The act contributed to the evolving differentiation of the British prisons system by providing for detention centers as alternatives to normal facilities for offenders between the ages of 14 and 21. Provisions for preventive detention were also modified, and certain offenders over 30 who had suffered four separate convictions were liable to an extra five to fourteen years in custody.

By 1948 conditions of crowding in His Majesty's prisons were visibly worsening and energetic plans for expansion were begun. The daily average prison population had increased from 10,000 to over 20,000 in less than a decade, and more than 2,000 prisoners were being kept three to a cell. Expansion programs were unfortunately outstripped by the "productivity" of the nation's criminal courts, however, and the number of prisoners kept three to a cell tripled during the following decade. By 1974 new construction and changing sentencing policies had reduced the number somewhat.

In addition to problems of overcrowding, one of the more pressing concerns of prison authorities in the years after World War II was that of security. The dramatic escape of one George Blake from Wormwood Scrubs prompted the appointment of a commission of inquiry under Earl Mountbatten in 1966. The commission concluded that there was no genuinely secure prison in Britain, although the report commended existing plans for a new installation at Albany on the Isle of Wight.[52] After the report appeared, more than £2 million was spent in enhancing the security apparatus of British prisons; dogs, alarm hardware, and perimeter patrols were all deployed. In accordance with the recommendations of the Mountbatten Commission, prisoners were reclassified according to their degree of security risk. Not surprisingly, such a significant investment in security considerations made the inmate's lot all the less pleasant, and numerous instances of collective unrest occurred during the early 1970s. None, however, was of the magnitude of the 1932 Dartmoor mutiny.

One significant alteration in the administrative structure of the prison system was accomplished in 1963. The Prison Commission was abolished and replaced by a Prisons Department within the Home Office. The change was intended to facilitate an integrated penal policy and also to enable career prison officers to rise to the very top of their administrative hierarchy. In fact it has proved to be a controversial and not wholly successful reform. A high rate of turnover among senior officials has contributed to a lack of coherent policy, and virtually none of the directors under the new system has been a career prison officer.

By the early 1970s the British prison system had expanded markedly. An average of more than 36,000 persons were in custody in 1973. The size of the staff reached 15,000, a threefold increase over the previous two decades. The number of institutions totaled 111, nearly double that of 1950. Annual expenditures exceeded £50 million, more than eight times the total during the years following World War II. One of the most striking features of the British prison system was its diversity. There were both open and closed facilities for almost every category of prisoner: young males, young females, women, and men. There were, in addition, special security centers, special facilities for life prisoners and for short- and long-term recidivists, psychiatric centers, and a number of other institutions. More than 17,000 acres was under cultivation by prisoners.

The task of building new prisons was inhibited somewhat by shortages of construction materials and by governmental measures to reduce capital expenditures during a period of rampant inflation. The chronic crowding that characterized British prisons by the early 1970s quite naturally generated considerable interest in noncustodial alternatives. The trend was particularly evident in the Criminal Justice Act of 1972, which essentially says that sentences of imprisonment are to be awarded only as a last resort. It enjoins the courts from imprisoning a defendant who has not been in prison before, unless convinced that no other measures are appropriate, and empowers courts to defer sentences for a period of up to six months, with an eye to suspending them altogether. The act also provides for an experimental program of community service orders as an alternative to imprisonment. Offenders are sentenced to perform various community service tasks in addition to their work or educational activity. The penalty can be regarded as a fine not of money but of leisure, and it is minimally disruptive to an individual's family or work life.[53]

A question invariably asked about more lenient judicial and penal policies is whether they lead to recidivism or rehabilitation. The London police reports for 1950 through 1971 include information that bears indirectly on this question in the form of data on whether persons arrested for indictable offenses had previous police records—a concept not defined in the reports but presumably referring to prior arrests. Between 28 and 40 percent of all those arrested had "records," and the high point is in the early 1950s when arrests were relatively few. People under 21 were less likely to have records, but not much less, and the range of variation is still narrower. Persons arrested for burglary, an offense the reports repeatedly attributed to professionals, included a predictably high number of repeaters, from 37 to 52 percent. Generally, burglars and youthful offenders were least likely to have previous records in the early 1960s. There is no evidence in these data, except possibly an upturn in 1970-1971, to implicate increased leniency as a cause of recidivism. What the data suggest, rather, is that London's new "criminal class" throughout the postwar period included a preponderance of one-shot (or once-caught) young thieves who were not very likely to pass through the courts again.[54]

The debate over capital punishment was renewed in the years after World War II, with Quakers, members of the Howard League, and Labour MPs among the more articulate proponents of abolition. The House of Lords succeeded in eliminating from the Criminal Justice Act of 1948 an abolition clause that had passed through Commons by a very narrow margin. Following this defeat Prime Minister Attlee appointed a royal commission, which after four years of deliberation recommended retention of the death penalty.[55] Public opinion polls showed that throughout this period only a minority of British adults favored abolition. The proportion was increasing, however, apparently under the influence of several well-publicized and notorious cases.

In one complicated case a man was convicted and executed for a murder that had been committed, it was later learned, by someone else. Then, in 1955, an attractive young woman named Ruth Ellis pled guilty to the murder of her lover. The Home Secretary failed to intervene, despite the apparently suicidal motive for her plea, and she was the last woman to be executed in England. The attitude of the Government was thoroughly denounced by demonstrators and in the popular press.

The Royal Commission on Capital Punishment of 1949-1953 had recommended some reforms, specifically the abolition of death sentences for many types of murder. The House of Commons, by this period, already had a majority in favor of complete abolition of the penalty. As a result of the predisposition of the MPs and public anger over recent executions, the Homicide Act of 1957 was passed. This provided for a moratorium on executions for all but the most aggravated cases of homicide and treason. In 1965 Parliament passed the Murder Act, which eliminated the death penalty for all murders; only certain forms of treason could be so punished, and executions were effectively abolished. Calls for the reinstitution of the death penalty were heard in some quarters in the aftermath of terrorist attacks in the early 1970s, but there appeared to be insufficient support in Parliament for such a change in policy.[56]

Corporal punishment, which had a long tradition in British history, was laid to rest with somewhat less fanfare. Whipping fell into increasing disuse during the twentieth century and was abolished as a form of punishment for criminal offenses by the Criminal Justice Act of 1948. Corporal punishment had long been abolished in borstals and had never been allowed in detention centers, but it continued to be used as a punishment for prison disciplinary infractions until abandoned by administrative decision of the Home Secretary in 1963. The Criminal Justice Act of 1967 formally ratified the end, for the time being, of the long and agonizing history of physical punishment in English penal institutions.

NOTES TO CHAPTER II.4

1. For a thorough, fully documented, but uncritical set of studies of twentieth century Britain see A. H. Halsey, ed., *Trends in British Society since 1900*. Less academic but more incisive is Anthony Sampson, *New Anatomy of Britain* (London: Hodder & Stoughton, 1971). A critical evaluation of the economy is Robert Bacon and Walter Eltis, *Britain's Economic Problem: Too Few Producers* (London: Macmillan, 1976). On the high and rising level of public spending see the Labour Government's White Paper, Public Expenditure to 1979-80, Cmnd. 6393, 1976.

2. A study of the patterns of crime in England and Wales in the twentieth century that relies largely on official statistics is F. H. McClintock and N. Howard Avison, *Crime in England and Wales* (London: Heinemann, 1968). A recent journalistic survey is Clive Borrell and Brian Cashinella, *Crime in Britain Today* (London: Routledge & Kegan Paul, 1975).

3. Report of the Commissioner of Police of the Metropolis for the Year 1965, p. 7.

4. Report of the Commissioner . . . 1950, p. 45.

5. Report of the Commissioner . . . 1972, p. 45.

6. Assuming that auto theft, theft from vehicles, and thefts from dwellings, offices, and persons are principally of personal property, and that thefts from shops, warehouses, telephone boxes, etc., are principally of commercial or public property. See Reports of the Commissioner . . . 1955, pp. 47-51, and 1965, pp. 52-58.

7. A general discussion on the uses and limitations of criminal statistics, with special reference to Britain, is Hermann Mannheim, *Comparative Criminology* (Boston: Houghton Mifflin, 1965), ch. 5. A critical view of the process by which official statistics are generated, emphasizing their unreliability as a guide to social behavior, is Stephen Box, *Deviance, Reality and Society* (London: Holt, Rinehart & Winston, 1971), ch. 6. A commentary on their usefulness for criminological studies that take a Marxist approach, as indicators of the class basis of criminal justice systems in capitalist societies, is Ian Taylor, Paul Walton, and Jock Young, "Critical Criminology in Britain: Review and Prospects," in their edited volume *Critical Criminology* (London: Routledge & Kegan Paul, 1975). The assessment which most closely parallels ours, on most points, is Nigel D. Walker, *Crimes, Courts and Figures: An Introduction to Criminal Statistics* (London: Penguin, 1971). Victimization surveys, in which a sample of residents are asked what crimes they have suffered, would resolve some of the questions about the validity of official data on crime in London. Such a survey was conducted in the early 1970s by Richard Sparks, Hazel Genn, and David Dodd, but its results had not been published at this writing.

8. Report of the Commissioner . . . 1934, p. 19.

9. Report of the Commissioner . . . 1937, p. 10.

10. Ibid., 6.

11. Report of the Commissioner . . . 1961, p. 10.

12. Report of the Commissioner . . . 1969, p. 8.

13. Report of the Commissioner . . . 1949, p. 8.

14. Report of the Commissioner . . . 1954, p. 7.

15. The sexual offenses in Figure II.4.8 are less inclusive than the data on sexual offenses in Table II.4.1; the latter include incest, bigamy, and some other uncommon sex crimes as well.

16. Report of the Commissioner . . . 1960, p. 11.

17. Most of the examples of protest and data on numbers of events given above, and in subsequent paragraphs, are from narrative commentaries in the Reports of the Commissioner of Police for 1930 through 1974, except 1940-1942, for which we could not obtain reports. Reports before 1955 contain less detailed information than later ones.

18. Data on strikes in Britain are from *British Historical Labour Statistics* and later supplements. Data on strikes in London are listed annually in the police commissioner's reports beginning in 1965.

19. In addition to the police commissioner's reports for the 1930s see Robert Benewick's study of the fascist movement, *Political Violence and Public Order: A Study of British Fascism* (London: Allen Lane and Penguin, 1969).

20. In *English Traits*, Howard Mumford Jones, ed. (Cambridge.: Belknap Press of Harvard University Press, 1966; originally published in 1856), p. 58.

21. Bertrand Russell, *The Autobiography of Bertrand Russell, 1944-1969* (New York: Simon & Schuster, 1969), passim.

22. Estimates of numbers of participants in various marches in this section are from the reports of the police commissioner and are often considerably lower than estimates announced by organizers or published in the press.

23. There is an extensive literature on the international student movement, though relatively little of it deals with Britain. For a fictionalized account of student activism against military policies, see C. P. Snow, *Last Things* (London: Macmillan, 1970).

24. Report of the Commissioner . . . 1971, p. 11.

25. The data for 1950 to 1971 are compiled from narrative accounts of particular events in the reports of the police commissioner, and while they include arrests in all major events it is impossible to determine whether arrests in all minor events are included. Complete tabulations for 1972-1974 are given in the Report of the Commissioner . . . 1974, pp. 111-118, including detailed information on the kinds of charges brought and the disposition of cases in some specific events.

26. A review of recent terrorist acts in Britain appears in Lester A. Sobel, ed., *Political Terrorism* (New York: Facts on File, 1975), pp. 216-218. Also see the Report of the Commissioner . . . 1974, pp. 20-21.

27. See Glass, *Newcomers;* on the problem generally, see Monica Charlot, *Naissance d'un problème raciale: Minorités de couleur en Grande-Bretagne* (Paris: Librairie Armand Colin, 1972). A study of trade union attitudes on the racial question is Monty Meth, *Brothers to All Men?* (London: Runnymede Industrial Unit, 1972).

28. V. S. Anand and F. A. Ridley, *The Enigma of Enoch Powell: An Essay in Political Realism* (London: Medusa Press, 1969); Tom Stacey, *Immigration and Enoch Powell* (London: Tom Stacey, Ltd., 1970).

29. For a discussion of this and other statutes relating to public order offenses, see Ian Brownlie, *The Law Relating to Public Order* (London: Butterworths, 1968).

30. D. G. T. Williams, "Racial Incitement and Public Order," *Criminal Law Review* (June 1966), pp. 320-327.

31. Report of the Commissioner . . . 1967, p. 17.

32. Report of the Commissioner . . . 1974, p. 21.

33. Report of the Commissioner . . . 1935, p. 61.

34. Report of the Committee on Homosexual Offences and Prostitution (Cmnd. 247), 1957.

35. For a psychoanalyst's views on the Wolfenden Report see Charles Berg, *Fear, Punishment, Anxiety, and the Wolfenden Report* (London: Allen & Unwin, 1959).

36. For a discussion of abortion in law and practice, see Anthony Hordern, *Legal Abortion: The English Experience* (Oxford: Pergamon Press, 1971).

37. See Great Britain, Law Commission Report Number 3, *Proposals to Abolish Certain Ancient Criminal Offences*, 1966.

38. 13 Chas. II c. 5 (1661). See Brownlie, op. cit.

39. Detailed data on the effective strength of the Metropolitan Police, its several branches and supporting staffs, vacancies, and recruitment are to be found in the annual Reports of the Commissioner. The data graphed in the accompanying figures are from this source.

40. See Chapter II.3.

41. Martin and Wilson, *The Police*, p. 62.

42. Home Office, Report of the Committee on Police Extraneous Duties, 1953.

43. Howe, *Story of Scotland Yard*, p. 148.

44. Home Office, Report of the Royal Commission on Police, 1962.

45. Report of the Commissioner . . . 1964, pp. 14-15.

46. For the best public accounts of terrorist and counterterrorist activities see the annual Reports of the Commissioner of Police and coverage in the *Times* and the *Economist*.

47. R. M. Jackson, "Jury Trial To-day," in L. Radzinowicz and J. W. C. Turner, eds., *The Modern Approach to Criminal Law* (Cambridge Studies in Criminal Science No. 4, London: Macmillan, 1945).

48. Although rarely exercised, the privilege of peerage was not unused. One lord was tried by his peers for vehicular manslaughter in 1936.

49. Barbara Wootton, "The Changing Face of British Criminal Justice," in Norval Morris and Mark Perlman, eds., *Law and Crime: Essays in Honor of Sir John Barry* (New York: Gordon & Breach, 1972), p. 106.

50. Justice, *The Unrepresented Defendant in Magistrates' Courts* (London: Stevens, 1971). For a discussion of legal aid in general, see Abel-Smith and Stevens, *Lawyers and the Courts*, chs. 6 and 12.

51. For a discussion of Paterson's influence, see J. E. Thomas, *The English Prison Officer*, ch. 8.

52. Home Office, Report of the Inquiry into Prison Escapes and Security, 1966.

53. Robert Thoresby, "The Criminal Justice Act 1972," *Modern Law Review*, 26 (July 1973), pp. 417-423.

54. The validity of these data are open to question, since police are more likely to zero in on known offenders than others when making arrests. Thus we can assume that the data understate the "amateur" proportion of offenders. It would be interesting to know why the reporting of these statistics was given up without explanation in 1972.

55. Report of the Royal Commission on Capital Punishment, Cmnd. 8932, 1953. In fairness to the commission, its terms of reference precluded a recommendation of abolition. Three decades earlier a select committee of the House of Commons had made the opposite recommendation, that capital punishment be abolished for a five-year trial period, but no such legislation was passed. Select Committee on Capital Punishment, 1930, p. 98.

56. On the history of attempts to eliminate capital punishment in Britain see James B. Cristoph, *Capital Punishment and British Politics* (Chicago: University of Chicago Press, 1962) and Tuttle, *The Crusade Against Capital Punishment.*

SOME CONCLUSIONS ON THE RISE AND DECLINE OF PUBLIC ORDER IN LONDON

London was chosen for comparative study because we sought a clearer understanding of two kinds of issues. We accepted at the outset the commonplace historical assumption that during the course of the nineteenth century the metropolis became a safer and more civil place in which to live. One purpose was to document the ways in which the city's problems of public order had in fact changed over time, in magnitude and in character. The second objective was to identify the public policies and institutions that were associated with the improvement of public order in the nineteenth and early twentieth centuries, and with its apparent decline in recent years. Considerable evidence on both issues has been surveyed in the preceding chapters and is reviewed briefly here. The more fundamental question posed by the evidence is one of social causality. For we must conclude with the paradox that the institutions and circumstances that seemed so efficacious in the establishment of order in the 1800s have had little restraining effect on resurgent disorder in the third quarter of the present century.

PUBLIC ORDER

The Reversing Trend in Crime, 1820 to the 1970s

Official data on crime for London show that most offenses against persons and property declined during the latter half of the nineteenth century and remained at a relatively low level into the 1920s.

Coincident with the Depression they began to increase, subsiding after World War II, then skyrocketing after 1950, so that by 1975 they appeared to have reached or exceeded the levels that prevailed in the 1830s and 1840s. We have considered at some length the manifold questions of interpretation that arise when dealing with official data on crime. The impact of particular changes in policing, recording, and judicial policies have been examined to see whether they can account for the recorded changes. Some short-term increases and decreases in London's crime rates are artifacts of procedural change, but the long-run trends cannot be so explained.

Three levels of meaning can be imputed to trends in indicators of crime: First, that they reflect variations in the extent of official efforts at control; second, that they signify degrees of citizens' concern about victimization; or third, that they represent changes in criminal behavior. There can be no doubt that the reversing trend describes with some accuracy a century-long decline in the magnitude of official attempts to control crime, and a shorter-run increase. The same trends are found in all measures of official activity: data on arrests, on committals to trial, and on convictions. We are almost as confident that during the last century Londoners' experience of common crime has followed the same pattern: The incidence of crimes known to police, of the kinds that depend mainly on citizens' reports, trace the same curve. Since the statistical manifestations of citizens' concern and official actions are generally similar, we can be reasonably sure that the volume of threatening social behavior also changed in this fashion over time. It may not have changed to the same degree, either up or down, as the indicators, nor always with the same short-term variations, but change it did. In the 1830s and 1840s there was much more thievery and assault in London than there was in the 1920s, perhaps five times as much relative to population, while in the 1970s the incidence of indictable crimes is some five times the recorded level of 50 years ago and rising fast.

Not all kinds of crime changed to the same degree, nor did all follow the same trend. The reversing curve is a reasonably accurate characterization of the changes in crimes that are of most concern to ordinary people: murder, rape, armed robbery, assault, fraud, and larceny, to name them in ascending order of frequency. The one signal exception is burglary, whose incidence held steady or increased while the others declined. There are also a good many offenses whose detection depends mainly on active policing, among them drunkenness and disorderly conduct, vagrancy, prostitution, and homosexual behavior. None of these offenses shows a distinct reversing trend. They vary more irregularly, in ways that often can be attributed to known changes in the law or in enforcement policies. Only drunkenness, among these so-called victimless crimes, shows a pronounced increase since the 1950s.

Although the data on crime surveyed here cover a century and a half, they do not extend as far back in time as we would like. A study by Beattie, cited in Chapter II.2 (note 3), provides information from court records on the incidence of personal and property crime from 1660 to 1800, not for London per se but for its southern environs.[1] In another study we have mentioned several times, Gatrell and Hadden examined the data on crime for all England and Wales from 1805 to 1892.[2] If London was characterized by the same patterns evident in these two studies, we can conclude that the years from 1820 to 1850 mark the crest of a wave of disorder that began in the aftermath of the Napoleonic wars. Thus records of the eighteenth century yield evidence of another great wave of crime, or at least of judicial activity designed to control crime, which crested in the 1730s. In this longer perspective, then, the nineteenth century decline in concern about crime in London probably was no more unique than the current increase. We are not dealing with an unprecedented phenomenon but a recurring one that may be susceptible to general explanation. At this point, though, we are concerned principally to document the phenomenon, not to provide a satisfying explanation.

Trends in Civil Conflict, 1800 to the 1970s

When one looks across the last two centuries of London's history it is clear that public disorder and collective protest have changed greatly, but not in ways that can be said to constitute a cyclical or reversing pattern. The changes have been a good deal more complex in the manifestations of conflict, in the goals of the participants in protest activities, and in the organization and leadership of the dissidents.

Through the first half of the nineteenth century, popular protest in London resembled that of the eighteenth century. While the "mob" in its classical form no longer existed, there were still episodes of fairly aimless rampaging, such as those that accompanied the return of Queen Caroline in 1820. The significant change was that the masses could be mobilized for political goals. Sometimes their objectives were advanced, the Reform Acts of 1832 and 1867 being the principal examples; at other times, notably in the case of Chartism, mass action was a failure. The crux of the difference is that the political elite responded to pressures and demands of the middle classes, regardless of whether those demands were supported by the working classes; when the proletariat sought independently to express their demands, whether for political enfranchisement or the right to organize "combinations," the response was harsh and unbending.

After 1870 collective protest assumed new forms, was directed toward different goals, and generally had the advantage of better leadership. It also could claim fresh successes. The London dock strike of 1889, with its attendant processions and rallies, was a clear victory for unskilled labor. It gave encouragement to, though it did not inaugurate, a disposition of London's workers to resort regularly to strikes and to take to the streets in the pursuit of economic objectives. Despite recurrent displays of such behavior, rarely in the last 85 years has any violence or serious disruption resulted from labor protest in London. The costs and gains have been mainly economic, visible not in police or court records but in wage indices and inflation rates.

Physical disruption has been a calculated tactic not of labor but of political movements, including the suffragette movement from 1906 to 1914 and Mosley's British Union of Fascists during the 1930s. The first group sought confrontations with the police; the second gained publicity by egging its antagonists into combat. The former scored political successes; the latter was an utter failure. Both contributed to an alternative style for collective protest that has had many imitators in London, especially since 1960.

Group protests over international issues became increasingly frequent in London during the 1950s, resuming a practice evident in the 1930s. Most of the demonstrations followed the orderly tradition established by the labor marchers of the late nineteenth century, but as the 1960s wore on an increasing proportion entailed the calculated use of force. Militant student revolutionaries were at the core of this violent protest, but by the mid-1970s most of them apparently had retired to less visible activities. Though street protest continued to be fairly common, it almost always took a more orderly course.

In the 1970s the most serious problem of public order in London was the threat of bombings, some by would-be revolutionaries, most by IRA terrorists. These actions were also in an old London tradition, one that can be traced at least as far back as the activities of exiled continental revolutionaries and advocates of Irish independence in the decades before World War I. The contemporary terrorists have proved more deadly, however, and violence by Irish partisans in London will end only when a settlement is effected in Northern Ireland.

Disruptive political demonstrations seem to have gone temporarily out of fashion. The enduring forms of civil conflict in London are less visible but of greater portent for the society. London's growing population of nonwhites, for example, have been the focus of sporadic outbursts of violence for years. The rapid expansion of the city's population of southern Europeans may create similar tensions. Probably most serious is conflict between organized labor and everyone else over the control and distribution of an economic "pie" that is no longer expanding and may in fact be shrinking. It is a conflict that affects all British society, of course, but directly or indirectly it has enormous impact in London. The immediate outlook for a metropolitan London free of violent manifestations of conflict now seems better than it did a decade ago. But the long-range forecast for social harmony is bleak.

CHANGES IN ELITE VIEWS AND EVOLUTION OF THE INSTITUTIONS OF PUBLIC ORDER

There have been manifold changes over the last two centuries in how the British elite have perceived public order in London.[3] Until 1850 they viewed the urban masses as dangerous and potentially revolutionary. With the decline in crime and the more visible evidences of hostility toward the ruling classes during the ensuing century their attitudes changed considerably. Revolution was no longer thought to be a possibility, and the common people were regarded with greater tolerance, if not respect. Urban crime was seen as a social problem that was being adequately controlled by the authorities and institutions of public order. One might expect this confidence to have been shaken by the resurgence of urban crime and civil strife during the past several decades. If so, there has been remarkably little effort to reform institutions or to add substantially to the resources devoted to existing ones. Crime control has not been made a major issue by either of the major parties. There are no influential groups of intellectuals or reformers advocating programmatic change. Only the practitioners, speaking through the Police Federation and the Police Superintendents' Association of England and Wales, have been vocally concerned about the decline of public order.

In some ways elite opinions have been reflected in the innovations made in the laws relating to social control. But this has been by no means a consistent phenomenon; in other words, variations in the volume of crime and strife and changes in elite views about these problems have not always preceded legal change. The reform of the criminal code in the early nineteenth century, for example, was carried through during a period of great disorder when many members of the ruling class were actively opposed to any redefinition of criminal behavior or mitigation of the punishments meted out to persons convicted. Even though the recodification of the 1820s simply reflected the reality of the times, that no one was being prosecuted for many of the old offenses and that many parts of the criminal code were in fact dead letters, there was nonetheless strenuous opposition to the reform movement in Parliament and among members of the judiciary. In recent decades there were two major thrusts of national reform in the criminal law: the abolition of capital punishment and the redrafting of the law relating to sexual offenses. Both were almost entirely irrelevant to London's principal contemporary problems of public order, namely, the rising incidence of theft and assault and the appearance of disruptive political protest.

During most of the period there has been a substantial measure of agreement among the elite on the structure and operation of the police and judicial institutions. After the initial controversy over the establishment of the Metropolitan Police, the "bobbies" became an integral part of London life. On the other hand, contemporary attitudes toward this supposed lynch-pin of public order are remarkably ambivalent. Intellectuals and the London press are highly critical of the police, not because they have failed to stem the tide of rising crime, but because of their alleged authoritarianism and infringements of citizens' rights. And never in the past 30 years has the pay of the London police been raised enough to attract qualified recruits in sufficient numbers to close the gap between the authorized and the actual strength of the force. No such ambivalence is or has been evident in attitudes toward the judicial system. There has always been a considerable degree of consensus among the elite about the slowly evolving structure and procedures of the judicial system. As we have seen, the changes that have been accomplished have expanded defendants' rights and improved the courts' efficiency, the former being more subject to controversy than the latter.

For two centuries, however, the penal system has provoked criticism and dissension within the governing classes, principally because there has never been agreement on what goals are desirable for the penal system. Today, in fact, the range of opinion is as great as it ever has been. Some advocate a return to corporal punishment, including the whip and public executions. Others argue that imprisonment itself is as outmoded as the pillory, the scaffold, or transportation. The majority opinion is to be found somewhere between these two extremes, among those who favor rehabilitation for individuals who might benefit from it and long-term incarceration of others for the protection of society. For most of the British prison population it is a distinction without a difference, because limited resources preclude substantial programs of rehabilitation and also make it too costly to fill scarce prison cells with permanent occupants. Despite such constraints, perhaps in some degree because of them, there appears to be considerable scope now for experimentation in penal practices and their alternatives.

A puzzle raised by this discussion needs to be made explicit. High levels of public disorder in early nineteenth century London, and all Britain, were a spur to comprehensive reform in criminal law, in city policing, in sentencing, and in penal practices. Why has no comparable sense of crisis or spirit of reform been evident in the last quarter-century? It may be that the British pride in the efficacy and adaptability of their political institutions has inhibited thoughts of further innovation. Perhaps the unbounded enthusiasm and belief in progress characteristic of the early industrial age were prerequisites to sweeping institutional change. Or perhaps Britain has been paralyzed into inaction by the trauma of loss of empire and economic decline. But these explanations are too glib and general to be convincing. One other more specific factor can be suggested. It is that disorder poses less threat to contemporary elites than it did to the ruling class of 150 years ago.

In the first half of the nineteenth century the governing elite feared revolution from below. Their potential allies, the rising commercial classes, were threatened by theft and assault from which there was little public or private protection. Contemporary disorder has posed no threat of comparable magnitude, not to the more privileged segments of British society. Talk of revolution has been bombastic; the principal casualties have been the long-suffering ranks of bobbies, turning back abusive demonstrators. The more powerful and prosperous Londoners live in relatively "safe" parts of the city or its suburbs. Material goods are plentiful, and anyway the more prosperous people are protected by insurance. Commercial establishments, which can pass the costs on to consumers as a kind of hidden tax, are also insured. The victims of assault and theft who have little or no recourse are members of the working class. As long as they are the principal victims, there is little incentive for the Cabinet, the senior civil service, the academic experts and critics, or the press to improve the quality of public order. Of course the argument is only a hypothesis.

ON THE SOCIAL FOUNDATIONS OF PUBLIC ORDER

Also inhibiting the establishment of concerted efforts to improve public order in London is the lack of agreement among politicians, administrators, and experts on what kinds of policies and socio-

Table II.5.1 Some Correlates of Short-Term Fluctuations in
Indictable Crimes, Middlesex County, 1820-1873[a]

Type of crime	Beta coefficients			R^{2}[b]	D-W[c]
	Population % change	Real wages	Industrial production		
Serious crimes of aggression[d]	−.07	.06	−.29*	.05	2.05
Serious crimes of acquisition[e]	.04	−.09	−.27*	.07	1.85
Burglary	.04	.05	−.05	.01	2.17
Larceny	.04	−.25*	.02	.08	1.86
Fraud	.02	−.19	−.31**	.12**	2.05
Total indictable offenses	.02	−.24*	−.07	.09	1.85

  * Significant at the .10 level.
** Significant at the .01 level.
a. The crime data are population-weighted indicators of committals to trial for indictable offenses. The crime data and the economic indicators were detrended by removing the linear component. To correct for high autocorrelation in the residuals, a computer program for generalized least squares (Gridmax) was used.
b. The R^2 is corrected for sample size and number of independent variables.
c. Durbin-Watson statistic.
d. Murder, manslaughter, indictable assault, and similar offenses.
e. Robbery, burglary, larceny, receiving, fraud, and similar offenses.

economic conditions are conducive to that end. There are reasons for thinking that the nineteenth century reforms, which have been given so much credit for the reduction of crime in Victorian London, and all Britain, were not solely or primarily responsible. Leon Radzinowicz made the point well when he said, two decades ago: "The potentiality of criminal legislation and penal system combined, for influencing the phenomenon of crime, has been greatly exaggerated in all countries."[4] Recent developments confirm that opinion. The institutions of public order that worked so well in the late nineteenth and early twentieth centuries have not visibly deteriorated. If anything they have improved, whether one applies conventional standards of administrative efficiency or of liberal reform. The Metropolitan Police are better equipped, more obedient to their superiors, and more civil to the public than their nineteenth century predecessors. The courts' efficiency has been improved, the rights of defendants have been expanded, though not always adequately ensured. Those adjudged guilty can be dealt with in a great variety of ways, some of which provide the means as well as incentives to stay clear of trouble in the future.

But neither its long-established efficiency nor the humanitarian elements in the modern criminal justice system of Britain have halted the rise in disorder since 1950. The reason surely is that the extent of criminal behavior, like the magnitude and character of civil conflict, depends as much as or more on the constellation of fundamental social and economic forces than it does on the specific institutions and policies of public order. Since so much of crime in London has always been property crime, one can suppose that economic factors are central. But two contrary hypotheses apply: one, that property crime increases as a function of want; the other, that it increases as a function of the growing availability of material goods to be stolen. Our analyses of crime and economic data for London show that both have had validity.

We have made a preliminary test of the economic hypotheses by correlating indicators of indictable crime with several measures of economic stress and well-being, adding also a measure of population growth. Three analyses were made: one for Middlesex for the years 1820 to 1873, using data on committals to trial; a second for the MPD using data on indictable offenses known to police, 1869 to 1931; and a third, also for the MPD, using the post-1933 data on indictable offenses known to police. Measures of six different categories of crime were used for each period, as shown in Tables II.5.1 through II.5.3. The crime indicators were detrended to avoid inflating the regression coefficients; the detrended data represent the annual fluctuations of crime rates around the linear trend. The tables report the results of multiple regression analyses in which economic and population variables, listed across the top of each table, are used simultaneously to predict to variations in crime. The figures shown are beta coefficients, which indicate the relative importance of each explanatory variable.

The results can be summarized briefly. First, the rate of population growth is never a significant correlate of any type of crime, although in the most recent period it seems to be having some impact on crimes against the person, which increased in years when population growth was particularly high, decreased when it was low. The more interesting results are obtained using the economic variables. In the period 1820-1873, both property offenses and crimes against the person tended to be lower when industrial production and real wages were high—and vice versa. Not much of the variation in crime is so explained (the corrected R^2 values are very low), but the results are consistent with the "want" theory of property crime, which apparently applies to crimes against the person also. In the second period, 1869-1931, there is a dramatic reversal of relationships. When industrial production was high, rates of all types of crime except fraud were significantly higher. The same was true, though to a lesser

Table II.5.2 Some Correlates of Short-term Fluctuations in Indictable Crimes, London (MPD), 1869-1931[a]

Type of crime	Beta coefficients				R^2[b]	D-W[c]
	Population % change	Real wages	Industrial production	Unemploy-ment		
Serious crimes of aggression[d]	.11	.19	.43**	.10	.12*	2.12
Serious crimes of acquisition[e]	.17	.23	.39**	.11	.07	1.85
Burglary	.07	.24*	.67**	.09	.14*	2.09
Larceny	−.10	.26*	.54**	−.01	.10*	1.70
Fraud	−.01	.04	.10	.24	.04	2.02
Total indictable offenses	−.07	.30*	.82**	.06	.09*	1.20

* Significant at the .10 level.
** Significant at the .01 level.

a. The crime data are population-weighted indicators of known principle plus indictable offenses. The crime data and the economic indicators were detrended by removing the linear component. To correct for high autocorrelation in the residuals, a computer program for generalized least squares (Gridmax) was used.

b. The R^2 is corrected for sample size and number of independent variables.

c. Durbin-Watson statistic.

d. Murder, manslaughter, indictable assault, and similar offenses.

e. Robbery, burglary, larceny, receiving, fraud, and similar offenses.

Table II.5.3 Some Correlates of Short-term Fluctuations in
Indictable Crimes, London (MPD), 1933-1972[a]

| Type of crime | Beta coefficients | | | D-W[b] |
	Population % change	Money wages	Unemployment	
Serious crimes of aggression[c]	.21	.29*	.03	2.10
Serious crimes of acquisition[d]	−.02	.18	.01	1.91
Burglary	−.02	.15	.02	1.92
Larceny	−.07	.22	−.32*	1.41
Fraud	−.05	.09	.18	.65
Total indictable offenses	−.15	.26	−.20	1.70

* Significant at the .10 level.

a. The crime data are population-weighted indicators of known indictable offenses. They were detrended by removing the linear component. To correct for high autocorrelation in the residuals, a computer program for generalized least squares (Gridmax) was used.

b. Durbin-Watson statistic.

c. Murder, manslaughter, indictable assault, and similar offenses. These data are for 1945-1972.

d. Robbery, burglary, larceny, receiving, fraud, and similar offenses.

extent, when real wages were high. There were only slight and insignificant relationships between high unemployment and short-term increases in crime. The same pattern holds for the most recent period as well, when most types of crime tended to increase as wages increased. It also is evident that larceny was significantly lower when unemployment was high—a finding that is consistent with data examined in Chapter II.4 showing that larceny rates were much lower in the Great Depression than they were in the full-employment decades of the 1950s and 1960s. The results of these analyses for the last century, in short, are all consistent with the "opportunity" hypothesis, and for the most recent period they positively contradict the deprivation explanation of property crime.[5]

One interpretation of these findings is that a reversal in social causality occurred in London in the late nineteenth or early twentieth century. More likely, though, we are faced with evidence of two different socioeconomic processes. In times of want, the people most affected steal out of necessity. In the economic slumps of nineteenth century, so many people were pushed so close to the margin of survival that the gains of theft frequently outweighted the attendant risks. The other process is one of increased opportunity coupled with increased resentment by the young and the poor of others' affluence. When many are poor and few are rich, it is probably easier to accept one's own poverty and more difficult to alleviate it by theft than when one is in a shrinking minority of the poor. And this process is no doubt reinforced by the perception that "everybody gets away with it," where "everybody" comprises not only one's larcenous friends but all the laborers and clerks who are believed to nick from their employers' stock. There is, in short, an erosion of the "respect for property" that was such an important element in Victorian moralism, and the rising rate of property crime probably documents its progress better than any other social indicator.

The second hypothesis—it remains that—by no means explains all the resurgence of common crime in contemporary London. In a statistical sense only some variation is explained by economic factors, whereas the explanation just suggested depends substantively not on structural economic factors per se but on the more problematic way in which people perceive and respond to their absolute and relative levels of material well-being. The root of the problem of economic crime is to be found in the very ethos of materialism. One does not have to agree with radical criminologists in Britain to recognize the accuracy of their contention that "a society which is predicated on the unequal right to the accumulation of property *gives rise* to the legal and illegal desire to accumulate property as rapidly as possible."[6] What has changed over time is the social balance among desire, opportunity, and risk that determines whether legal or illegal means are taken to the desired end.

It also should be evident that this kind of socioeconomic explanation for property crime does not directly account for the historical decline and contemporary increase in assault, rape, murder, and similar crimes. The statistical analyses show that serious crimes of aggression have been affected in the same anomalous ways by want and prosperity throughout the past 150 years. The pattern cannot be explained by imputing economic motives to assault, because assaults with intent to rob are not included in these data. So we are left with the social fact that in recent decades "respect for persons," as well as "respect for property" has declined as material prosperity has increased. This suggests in turn that some explanations that are not specifically economic must be sought. That task requires evidence and theory about changing social values and norms far exceeding the scope of this case study.

We are not suggesting that the institutional innovations of the nineteenth century were only accidentally connected with the century of improvement in public order that followed their establish-ment. We do believe that they were effective insofar as they rein-forced existing social and economic tendencies. But that does not imply that the same institutional arrangements can be counted on to maintain or to reestablish social order now. A substantial reduction of contemporary crime probably would require either an improve-ment in the social and economic malaise from which Britain suffers, a fundamental restructuring of the institutions of public order, or quite possibly both. Any such changes are likely to depend on political decisions taken at the national level, and they will involve all Britain, not just London. Thus far there has been little disposition by most political figures or experts to treat rising crime as a crisis worthy of programmatic attention. This may not be an altogether unreasonable response since the contemporary sources of crime are so manifold and ill-understood that there is no certainty about the effects of any new departures for good or bad. Meanwhile the majority of Britons, and Londoners, presumably will continue to accept the fear and fact of crime stoically, as one more tax on their social and material well-being.

NOTES TO CHAPTER II.5

1. See Figure II.2.1.
2. Gatrell and Hadden, in Wrigley, ed., *Nineteenth Century Society*, Part 2.
3. The term "elite" and its synonym "ruling class" are used here in a nonperjorative sense to refer to the groups that have exerted most influence on governmental policies. Their composition has broadened markedly during the last 150 years and now includes not only the leading figures of the two major parties but all those whose views they solicit and respond to on matters of public policy, including industrialists, trades union leaders, senior civil servants, many experts and intellectuals, and some of the media.
4. "Changing Attitudes Towards Crime and the Devices Used to Combat It," lecture delivered to the Royal Institute of Great Britain, February 28, 1958.
5. Also see David Peirce, "Urban Economics and Crime: London, 1800-1975," paper read to the American Historical Association, December 28-30, 1975, Atlanta.
6. Taylor, Walton, and Young, *Critical Criminology*, p. 34.

Part III

STOCKHOLM: THE POLITICS OF

CRIME AND CONFLICT,

1750 TO THE 1970s

Peter N. Grabosky
Leif Persson
Sven Sperlings

AUTHORS' NOTE: This part makes substantial use of background papers prepared by and data gathered by Sven Sperlings and Leif Persson, and by graduate students at the University of Stockholm working under their guidance. Specific papers and contributors are cited in the notes. We also draw on background research by Eve Harris, Karsten Åström, and David Peirce, and data analyses carried out by Tina Peterson. Comments and suggestions on a draft version were provided by Leif Lenke, Hanns von Hofer, and Ingemar Rexed.

THE DEVELOPMENT OF
STOCKHOLM

BEFORE 1850

    Although Stockholm's emergence as a major European city is a relatively recent phenomenon, its founding as a fortress and trade center dates to the mid-thirteenth century. Situated on an archipelago between the Baltic Sea and Lake Mälaren, it was a place of no little strategic significance; by 1250 a fortress had been constructed on an island at the narrows where the Royal Palace presently stands. The name Stockholm is said to derive from *stockar* (logs), which were sunk around the *holm* (island), to strengthen its defense.[1] Birger Jarl, the king's chief minister, who is generally regarded as the founder of Stockholm, made further contributions to the town's commercial development. Jarl entered a trade agreement with the merchants of Lübeck, granting the latter freedom from customs charges, and this soon ensured Stockholm's status as the main commercial center and principal fortress in Sweden. Among the town's major exports were pine pitch, flour, butter, and iron products from the mines situated in the Mälaren uplands; products imported included German beer, wine, cloth, and spices (primarily salt) for use in preserving meat. Although early fourteenth century Stockholm was a less than cosmopolitan place, German influence was visible. Many of the oldest buildings were constructed by foreign workmen after the continental style.[2]

    During the early years the town's population growth and spatial expansion were negligible. By the beginning of the sixteenth century, some 250 years after its founding, Stockholm's population was about 6,000. Like most urban places of the time, the town was walled; it was, moreover, situated on an island. In 1581 a visiting Italian nobleman referred to it as a primitive country town; the population had only reached 8,000.[3]

The first period of rapid population increase occurred during Sweden's rise to European prominence in the seventeenth century. The number of inhabitants rose to more than 50,000 by 1680. Subsequently the rate of population growth was much more gradual. As is illustrated in Figure III.1.1, the number of inhabitants actually declined on two occasions, at the beginning of both the eighteenth and nineteenth centuries. By 1850 the population was slightly in excess of 90,000. Swedish society remained overwhelmingly rural, and not until the mid-1800s did the urban population of Sweden exceed ten percent of the national total. The growth in Stockholm's population was more attributable to natural increase than to urban drift.

The town's geopolitical centrality became even more significant during Sweden's ascendancy as a great power in the mid-seventeenth century. The expansion of copper and iron mining at the beginning of the century, also a period of unprecedented agricultural productivity, supported a standard of living that for the average Swede was not surpassed for more than two centuries. When Sweden emerged victorious from the Thirty Years War, Stockholm was the center of an empire consisting of Finland, the Baltic states, and parts of northern Germany. The city's importance was strategic as well as

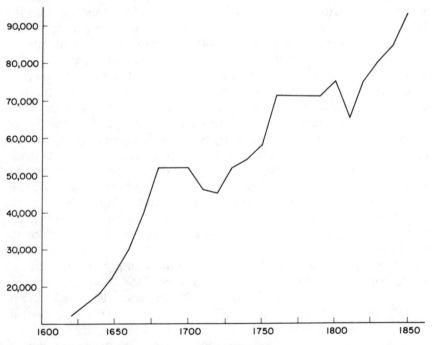

Figure III.1.1 Stockholm's population growth, 1620-1850

administrative. The shipyards of Stockholm built and equipped the Swedish fleet, and government factories produced various kinds of war materiel.

The eighteenth and early nineteenth centuries saw continued expansion of commercial and administrative activity in Stockholm, but growth in the manufacturing sector was inhibited by the delay in the development of steam power, attributable to lack of capital and prohibitive transportation costs. The most dramatic period of industrial and urban growth in Stockholm did not begin until the 1850s.

The social composition of Stockholm's population did not change drastically in the century after 1750, although the size of the middle class did expand somewhat. Between 1800 and 1850 the number of civil servants and proprietors grew from just over one-fifth to slightly more than one-fourth of the population. Some 70 percent of the population were laborers or domestic servants. The most affluent group was, of course, the nobility; it comprised no more than three percent of the population. Available census data reveal a proportional overrepresentation of women in Stockholm at the beginning of the nineteenth century, and this phenomenon has characterized the city for most of its recent history. The age structure of Stockholm's population remained relatively stable during the period. The largest group, individuals between the ages of 20 and 34, expanded slightly during the early nineteenth century, when they comprised roughly one-third of the city's population.

Initially the growth of the city was inhibited by an unhappy fact of life in early Stockholm—the threat of foreign invasion. Throughout the fourteenth and fifteenth centuries Danish rulers periodically attempted to seize Sweden. They were successful on occasion, although resistance by the Swedes was generally stiff. Stockholm itself was beseiged numerous times and was under Danish rule more than once during the early sixteenth century. The last period of foreign conquest, which began in 1520, was particularly sanguinary. The Danish King Kristian II attempted to crush Swedish resistance in that year by beheading 82 leading citizens in what came to be known as the Stockholm bloodbath. In 1523, however, Gustav Vasa led a rebellion that freed the country from the Danes; he reinstated the Swedish monarchy and reigned as king for 37 years. Stockholm was officially designated as the capital of Sweden during his reign, in 1536.

Although records are scanty, and there are no statistics on crime and civil strife, it appears that Stockholm's early years were far from tranquil. Responsibility for watch and ward was borne by the general public during peacetime prior to 1590. In that year a formal watch was appointed whose members were eventually nicknamed "sausages." The significance of this appellation remains unclear, but it probably was not complimentary, because the streets of Stockholm were regarded as notably unsafe by night far into the seventeenth century.[4]

The increase in population during the 1600s necessitated certain administrative adjustments. An office of the Governor of Stockholm was created in 1636, and its incumbent was invested with considerable authority over such matters as taxes, town planning, and the town guard. Not surprisingly, it was during this period that the first significant physical expansion of the town took place. Admiral Claes Fleming, the first Governor of Stockholm, presided over the first attempt at city planning in Swedish history. The wall surrounding the island, which formed the original nucleus of the city, was torn down in 1640 and a street pattern was laid out in Norrmalm, the part of the mainland to the immediate north. By fortune and foresight, the plan satisfactorily accommodated Stockholm's growth for the following two centuries.

Among the effects of the Thirty Years War were the arousal of a substantial appetite for news and the kindling of a nationalistic spirit. The establishment of the first Swedish newspaper in 1645 was directed at the first of these inclinations; the weekly was edited by the chief postmaster in Stockholm and is published today as *Post-och Inrikestidningar*. Concern for the Swedish national identity was reflected in the founding of the College of Antiquities in 1667. Such preoccupation with the cultural heritage was understandable given the prevailing patriotic mood.

By 1700 town life had become complex enough to warrant the imposition of a number of administrative controls. Ordinances enacted during the period were said to regulate everything from the sale of bread to the dress of loose women.[5] Certain phenomena, however, were beyond the control of municipal officials. An epidemic of bubonic plague took the lives of nearly 18,000 Stockholmers during the six months following its outbreak in August 1710. Despite long-standing requirements concerning the composition of building materials, fires appear to have been a consistent threat throughout the eighteenth century. In 1723, a particularly bad year, three large fires occurred during April and May; fires also devastated the Klara district in 1751 and Södermalm, the southern mainland part of the town, in 1759 and 1773.

The urban problems of the 1700s were compounded by Sweden's decline as a major European power. The taxes necessary to maintain a large military force placed a severe burden on the Swedish peasantry; desperate officials opted to debase the currency, and prices doubled in the decade following 1755. The discomforts arising from 100 percent inflation were hardly alleviated during the Pomeranian War (1756-1763), when thousands of breadwinners were abroad with their regiments, thus unable to contribute to the support of their families.[6]

The last three decades of the eighteenth century were eventful ones in Stockholm and must be regarded as among the most turbulent in the city's modern history. Competition for power between the king and the nobility had been a chronic characteristic of Swedish political history, and struggles during this period were particularly intense. Shortly after Gustavus III succeeded his father in 1771 he consolidated his position with a bloodless coup, carried out with support from the garrison of Stockholm. The constitution of 1772, which the new king presented to the Estates (nobility; clergy; burghers; and peasantry), left no doubt who would be the most influential actor in Swedish politics. Further augmentation of monarchial privilege occurred in 1789 in the form of the Act of Union and Security, which served to intensify the nobles' antagonism. Although the king had implemented a number of reforms, thus retaining the support of the clergy and peasantry, the antipathy of the nobles was too intense. On March 16, 1792, a former Guards officer, who had been hired by the nobles and bore a personal grudge against Gustavus III, mortally wounded the king during a masked ball at the Stockholm Opera House.

Quite predictably, the intrigue among Swedish political elites along with the occasional periods of war and economic hardship served to engender substantial civil disorder during the Gustavian era. Such activity could hardly have been inhibited by the enormous quantities of aquavit that was being consumed by Stockholmers. It has been estimated that the number of taverns in Stockholm at the end of the century exceeded 700.[7] Interestingly enough, the period is as well remembered for its architectural excellence.

In 1796 Gustavus IV ascended the throne, assuming power from his uncle, the regent, who had managed affairs since the assassination of Gustavus III. The new king was not an astute ruler: his foreign and domestic policies continued to burden his subjects with inflation, war, and economic stagnation. Moreover, the king had little use for collective decision making, and thus did little to cultivate favor among members of the nobility. Once again the monarch's inability to govern provoked an uprising; Gustavus IV was arrested by dissident troops in 1809 and spent the rest of his life in exile.

Public health problems remained burdensome; tuberculosis was the largest cause of adult deaths, while children perished most often from smallpox. Smallpox and cholera epidemics in 1774, 1783, and 1799, and exceptionally poor harvests during the periods 1761-1764,

1780-1783, and 1798-1800, served to inhibit population growth in Stockholm and in the nation at large.[8]

At the beginning of the nineteenth century, the greatest problems facing Stockholmers continued to be those of public health and sanitation. Sanitary conditions during the first decade of the century can best be described as hideous, and some 35 percent of all children died before their first birthday. These rates declined somewhat in subsequent years, but remained at 25 percent as late as 1880. Despite the migration of some people from rural areas, the city's population declined from 75,000 to 65,000 during the period 1800-1810. The situation was aggravated by the severe casualties sustained by Swedes abroad during the war years of 1808-1809. Subsequent urban growth was slow until it began to escalate around midcentury. Epidemics continued to impede the increase; there were 3,500 deaths from cholera in 1834.[9]

Political developments during the period included elements of reform and repression. The Constitution Act of 1809 established the foundation for the development of the modern Swedish political system, although it left great powers in the hands of the king and provided no opportunity for legitimate political participation by individuals lacking wealth or property. There were, however, unprecedented guarantees of freedom of the press, speech, and worship, and the office of *Justitieombudsman* was created to protect private individuals from abuses of power by public servants. These guarantees were not always realized, however. King Charles John (1818-1844) was one monarch who felt particularly threatened by criticism, and he presided over the enactment of the *Indragningsmakt*, a censorship law that enabled the government to seize any publication deemed to be contrary to the national interest. This and other measures designed to discourage dissent (including the use of a secret police) appeared at times to have been counterproductive. Members of an emerging liberal middle class were not content to remain silent, and the liberal newspaper *Aftonbladet*, founded in 1830, was in the vanguard of criticism. Moreover, great restrictions on freedom of religion were in effect until the latter part of the century. Such an issue, however, afforded little basis for social conflict because of the absence of any religious minority groups of significant size.

Conflicts between liberals and conservatives were manifest not only in the press and in the Riksdag but on the streets of Stockholm as well. Political riots of particular intensity occurred in 1838 and 1848, and although repression was harsh, the ineluctable emergence of the middle classes heralded the reforms that were implemented later in the century. Trade and landholding restrictions had already been relaxed, and in 1842 a system of compulsory education was introduced. Every parish was required to establish an elementary school, and attendance was mandatory until a certain level of proficiency was attained.

Oscar I (1844-1859) was in no small way responsible for many of these innovative policies. Considerably more liberal than were his predecessors, Oscar had published a significant treatise on penal reform while crown prince.[10] Soon after he assumed the throne he presided over the repeal of the *Indragningsmakt*, which had already fallen into disuse. In 1845 the inheritance rights of rural women were broadened to conform with those of their urban counterparts. Two years later a poor law was passed that required towns to care for their indigent residents. Oscar's reign also saw further educational reforms and the implementation of many of the prison policies advocated in the crown prince's treatise. Despite these innovations the franchise remained severely limited, and the only avenue of political expression open to the working classes of Stockholm was street protest.

Organized political activity by Stockholm's workers did not begin until much later in the century, but the foundation for this mobilization was established in the 1830s in the form of the temperance movement. Copious consumption of alcohol has a long tradition in Sweden,[11] and attempts to regulate distillation and drinking have been recurring themes in Stockholm's history. Although the early temperance movement was closely linked to organized religion and did not serve to raise class consciousness among the workers of Stockholm, it set an organizational precedent for later temperance movements, which enjoyed increasing working-class support and indeed introduced many working-class politicians of the early twentieth century to organized political activity.[12]

THE INDUSTRIAL REVOLUTION IN STOCKHOLM, 1850-1930

The second half of the nineteenth century marked a drastic departure from previous trends in Stockholm's history. In addition to experiencing a sharp increase in population, the city underwent significant industrial growth. The expansion of the sawmill industry in the north of Sweden created new markets for Stockholm's products. The agricultural areas around the capital experienced a boom during the Crimean War (1853-1856) when grain exports increased significantly. Manufacturing activity in Stockholm had also become more diversified. The advent of steam power facilitated the growth of the machine industry, and although there was stagnation in the textile industry, the retail trade, transportation, and service sectors remained generally healthy. Moreover, the aforementioned increases in population created a strong demand for housing construction. The beginning of the twentieth century brought further expansion and diversification of Stockholm's industrial base. Food, chemicals, machine production, and printing enterprises were among the most prominent.[13]

The era of industrialization in Stockholm was interrupted frequently by periods of economic contraction. A crisis of foreign credit, combined with a series of poor harvests, contributed to a significant downturn in the late 1860s. The building industry suffered setbacks at the end of the 1870s and 1880s, and the latter cycle lasted into the early 1890s before beginning its upswing. The year 1909 was the occasion for yet another recession, but the most difficult years were still to come.

The outbreak of World War I brought severe hardship to Sweden; the disruption of international trade was followed by a diminution of

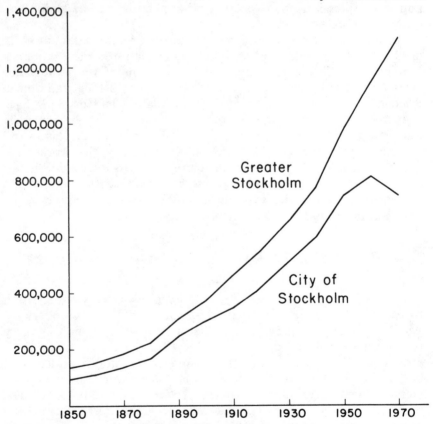

Figure III.1.2 Stockholm's population growth, 1850-1970

export earnings and severe shortages of the commodities that were normally imported. Sweden, of course, maintained its century-old policy of neutrality, despite significant losses of her merchant fleet. A severe economic contraction, no doubt aggravated by the absence of war production and by the presence at home of the entire labor force, was accompanied by rampant inflation and by the first significant decline in the real wages of industrial workers since the late 1860s. These unhappy circumstances were to have substantial political repercussions, as noted below.

In 1850, after 600 years of existence, Stockholm's population was still less than 100,000. The latter half of the nineteenth century was a period of massive population growth, and the city's population had tripled by 1900 (see Figure III.1.2). These developments, moreover, occurred despite persistent problems of public health, two periods of severe economic contraction, and the emigration of thousands of urban and rural Swedes to the United States. The basis for this growth is readily discernible; fertility rates for both urban and rural populations were high and remained so throughout the century. Infant mortality and crude death rates, although consistently much higher in Stockholm than elsewhere in Sweden, declined steadily. Migratory movement (both domestic and overseas) tended to originate in rural areas, and the loss of Stockholmers who chose to leave Sweden was more than offset by the influx from the farms. Not the least significant factor was the new tradition of Swedish aloofness from international hostilities.

The early years of the current century saw a continuation of the dramatic increase in the population of Stockholm, despite the persistence of emigration to the United States. Although more than 11,000 Stockholmers left Sweden during the years 1900-1909, the population of the city proper increased fourteen percent during the decade. Even more significant was Stockholm's emergence as a metropolitan area; the population of the inner suburban area doubled during the period and approached 50,000 in 1910.

The age and sex distribution of Stockholm's population remained fairly stable throughout the nineteenth century (Table III.1.1). Females comprised a majority of all age groups except, during the period 1820-1860, for individuals in their thirties. The greatest imbalance between the sexes occurred among individuals over 50. Significant changes, however, were visible in Sweden's occupational structure. As Table III.1.2 indicates, the years after 1850 were accompanied by an increase in the proportion of the economically productive population involved in industry, and by a decline in the traditional dominance of agriculture. The Swedish middle class also expanded during this period, as is further illustrated by Figure

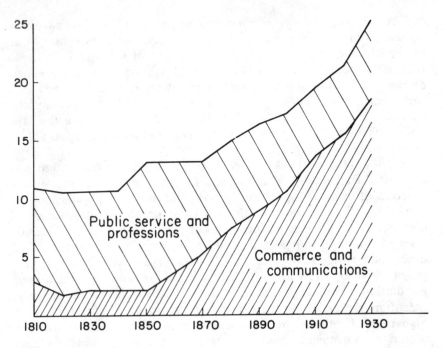

Figure III.1.3 Growth of Sweden's middle classes, 1810-1930, as a percent of economically-productive population

III.1.3. These changes were not without important political implications.

One consequence of the late nineteenth century building boom was an increasing residential segregation of social classes. The rich residential diversity described by Strindberg in his autobiographical novel *Tjanstekvinnans son* gave way to concentrations of working-class tenements and large, elegant apartment houses. During this period planners had also proposed the construction of grand boulevards after the fashion of Paris and Vienna, but plans were curtailed; Sveavagen, one of the widest of the proposed avenues, was narrowed from 60 to about 30 meters.

The mid-1800s saw an important extension of municipal services in Stockholm. The first gas works began operation in 1853, permitting better illumination of city streets. Municipally organized sanitation and water systems were introduced in 1861, and sidewalks were installed. In 1871 construction of Central Station was completed, providing a major transportation link, and steam-propelled ferries greatly facilitated transportation among islands of the archipelago. By the turn of the century, population increase on the periphery of the central city outstripped that of the inner core. The development of Sundbyberg on the northern railway route began in the late

Table III.1.1 Age and Sex Distribution of the Population, 1800-1970

Year	Male (%)	Under 15 (%)	20-30 (%)	Over 60 (%)
1800	45.5	22.7	19.7	9.4
1820	46.4	21.4	22.9	7.8
1840	45.9	22.8	24.5	5.9
1860	45.8	22.4	23.4	5.9
1880	44.7	23.1	22.7	6.6
1900	45.7	23.7	21.9	8.2
1920	44.7	20.1	20.7	10.1
1940	44.9	13.8	19.5	11.9
1960	46.8	19.0	12.3	17.2
1970	46.9	14.6	16.9	23.5

Source: Gösta Ahlberg, Stockholms Befolkningsutveckling efter 1850 (Stockholm: Almquist & Wiksells, 1958); Folkräkningen den 1 november 1960, Del. I.; Folk- och bostadsräkningen 1970, Del. I.

1870s, marking the first significant example of suburban development. A number of impressive city landmarks were constructed during the period, among them the National Museum, the new Opera House, and the Academy of Arts.

The growth of industry and transportation did not make for an idyllic urban existence, however. Numerous economic contractions

Table III.1.2 Distribution of Economically Productive Population of Sweden by Main Occupational Groups, 1810-1930

Year	Percentage of Population				
	Agriculture and subsidiary occupations	Industry and handicrafts	Commerce and communications	Public service, professions, and so on	Total (%)
1810	82.4	6.7	2.8	8.1	100.0
1820	82.6	7.0	1.7	8.7	100.0
1830	82.1	7.4	2.1	8.4	100.0
1840	80.9	8.5	2.2	8.4	100.0
1850	77.9	9.1	2.0	11.0	100.0
1870	72.4	14.6	5.2	7.8	100.0
1880	67.9	17.4	7.3	7.4	100.0
1890	62.1	21.7	8.7	7.5	100.0
1900	55.1	27.8	10.4	6.7	100.0
1910	48.8	32.0	13.4	5.8	100.0
1920	44.0	35.0	15.2	5.8	100.0
1930	39.4	35.7	18.2	6.7	100.0

Source: Dorothy Swaine Thomas, Social and Economic Aspects of Swedish Population Movements, 1750-1933 (New York: Macmillan, 1941), p. 93.

Table III.1.3 Population of Stockholm and Environs, 1800-1970

Year	City proper	Inner suburbs	Outer suburbs	Greater Stockholm
1800	75,517	—	—	—
1810	65,474	—	—	—
1820	75,569	—	—	—
1830	80,621	—	—	—
1840	84,161	—	—	—
1850	93,070	7,550	27,850	132,000
1860	112,391	8,150	28,900	153,350
1870	136,016	9,000	31,200	180,050
1880	168,775	11,900	34,250	221,600
1890	246,454	13,050	34,750	302,500
1900	300,624	23,200	35,600	371,850
1910	342,343	48,550	41,500	461,950
1920	419,440	71,750	44,600	543,750
1930	502,213	96,200	46,287	654,549
1940	590,503	118,850	48,607	769,049
1950	744,143	179,252	60,554	983,949
1960	808,603	251,720	82,416	1,142,739
1970	746,560	361,832	195,241	1,303,633

Source: Statistisk Årsbok för Stockholms Stad, 1904-1970. Gösta Ahlberg, *Stockholms Befolkningsutveckling efter 1850* (Stockholm: Almqvist & Wiksell, 1958), p. 157. *Folk-och bostadsräkningen 1970,* Del 1. Befolkning i kommuner och forsamlingar m.m. (Stockholm: Statistiska Centralbyrån, 1972).

have been mentioned, and some five percent of the city's population was served by the city's primitive welfare system in 1885. Conditions were sufficiently unpleasant to motivate more than 21,000 Stockholmers to leave the city for the United States between 1881 and 1893.[14] For those fortunate enough to find work, wages were low and hours were long. Although prohibitions on child labor in certain industries date to the late 1840s, employers were often able to minimize wage costs by employing inmates of prisons and workhouses at "bargain" rates.

In addition to its population growth, Stockholm continued to expand spatially. The suburb of Brannkyrka was incorporated in 1913, and Bromma was annexed three years later. Of symbolic significance was the enhancement of the city's international reputation by virtue of its hosting the Olympic games of 1912. City officials, while unable to forecast future growth trends with precision, were far from shortsighted. They began to purchase open land on the city's outskirts, thus setting a precedent that greatly facilitated the task of regional planners in years to come. In 1904 the city acquired some 2,000 hectares, an area exceeding that of Stockholm itself at the time. In 1912 the city acquired Farsta, then an agricultural property; acquisitions in 1927 and 1931 later constituted the site of the satellite suburb of Vällingby. The patterns of peripheral urban growth are suggested in Table III.1.3. Building activity changed the face of the city during the period, as the first skyscrapers and a number of smaller office buildings were constructed. New public buildings included the Council Hall, the Municipal Hall, the House of Parliament, the Stadium, and the Museum of Natural History.

The parliamentary reforms of the mid-nineteenth century reflected the emerging political influence of a middle class but were hardly democratic in thrust.[15] The old Riksdag, which was based on the four Estates, was replaced by a bicameral legislature; members of the upper chamber were indirectly elected by city and county councils, and members of the lower house were directly elected. Membership in both houses was limited to individuals with substantial incomes or property holdings, and the franchise was extended to males over 21 who possessed assets sufficient for election to the lower house. Members of the hereditary nobility dominated the upper house, whereas the most influential members of the lower chamber were conservative rural landowners and urban merchants and industrialists.

Ironically, this new legislature was less sympathetic to the interests of urban wage earners than its predecessor had been: Members sought to maintain, if not increase, existing inequalities in the distribution of wealth, and the 75 percent of the adult male population that could not vote had no voice in policy matters. Illustrative of the reactionary nature of the new Riksdag was the poor relief "reform" of 1871, which deprived recipients of the right to appeal adverse decisions of local authorities—a privilege that had been accorded them 24 years earlier. The political atmosphere represented by these developments did little to discourage the mass emigration mentioned previously.

Significant extension of the franchise was a natural consequence of the growth and mobilization of an industrial working class, but the voice of labor was barely audible by the end of the nineteenth century. The first significant industrial dispute occurred in the northern timber region at Sundsvall in 1879, where the strikers were soundly suppressed with armed force. Meanwhile the first meeting of socialists took place at Stockholm in 1881, a socialist organization was formed in 1884, and a newspaper, *Socialdemokraten*, was founded in the following year. Hjalmar Branting, who eventually became the first socialist prime minister, was among the founders of the Swedish Social Democratic Workers party in 1889; he was elected to the lower house in 1897. Indicative of the political status of socialists was a law enacted in 1899 that defined picketing, peaceful or otherwise, as a crime punishable by two years' imprisonment.

The years 1900 to 1920 constitute one of the most crucial periods in Swedish political history. At the outset, the suffrage system was among the most restrictive of any nation with an ostensibly representative constitution. In 1908 only 9.4 percent of the population was entitled to vote, but in the short period of thirteen years universal adult franchise was achieved. This relatively peaceful yet rapid evolution was to have profound effects on the future development of Swedish society.

Although the real wages of Swedish industrial workers had increased by more than 50 percent between 1870 and the turn of the century, the life of the worker was by no means comfortable. Moreover, most of the wealth that had been generated during the boom years of the late nineteenth century had been retained by employers and entrepreneurs. It was estimated in 1908 that 55 percent of the total wealth of the nation was held by 1.5 percent of the population, and 25 percent of the country's private property was said to be controlled by 0.1 percent of all property owners.[16] Thus it was hardly surprising that the expansion of an urban industrial workforce was accompanied by growing discontent.

The increasing unionization of Swedish workers could not be suppressed, and, in recognition of this, the Swedish Employers Confederation was established in 1902. Four years later a public agency for the purpose of mediating labor-management disputes was introduced. These developments served to legitimize rather than weaken the labor movement. At the same time, despite its growth, the movement was still too small and insufficiently cohesive to constitute an independent political force, especially in light of the aforementioned franchise restrictions. From the point of view of the handful of Social Democrats in the Riksdag at the turn of the century, the only course of action was to join in coalition with liberal Riksdagsmen and seek small-scale reforms and extension of the franchise.

However, some members of the Swedish working class were impatient with the intransigence of government and management. Scores of strikes were called during the period 1901-1908 for improvement of wages, working conditions, and in some cases, extension of the franchise. There was a general strike over wages and conditions in 1909, but since less than a third of Swedish workers were employed in industry, and many of the workplaces were situated in remote or rural areas, the strike was broken. Although union membership declined immediately after the strike ended, the event apparently served an important communicative function; conservatives noted that current trends in Swedish industrial development, combined with democratization in other Western societies, made continued suppression of Swedish workers an untenable strategy. The insecurity of the elite was heightened by contemporary events in Russia. Bowing to what they perceived as the inevitable, conservatives chose to accede to demands for incremental reform and to seek compromise rather than to force violent conflict.[17] The Riksdag, which had already adopted universal male suffrage in elections to the lower chamber, enacted an old-age pensions scheme in 1913. Further reforms were to follow.

THE RECENT HISTORY OF STOCKHOLM, 1930-1974

The onset of the Depression in 1930 was accompanied by substantial economic distress in Stockholm. In addition to unemployment, a decrease in wages and working hours in 1932 brought about a significant decline in the purchasing power of industrial workers. The Social Democrats returned to power in the fall of that year and began to implement some of the most innovative policies of social intervention yet seen anywhere. Thousands of unemployed workers participated in public works projects, and more than 100,000 workers were so employed in 1934. Government subsidies were available for housing construction in urban areas, and a system of voluntary unemployment insurance was introduced in 1934. The birthrate in Sweden had fallen consistently since the turn of the century, and to ease the financial burdens of childrearing the government began granting pre- and postnatal benefits to mothers in 1937, and it instituted a program of subsidized school lunches. These and other social programs, including a national dental health plan in 1938, attracted worldwide attention to Sweden. The Swedish system was viewed by many as an attractive compromise between socialism and laissez-faire capitalism; Marquis Childs referred to it as "the middle way."[18]

Sweden again declared neutrality in World War II, but European nations by that time had become so interdependent that Sweden, too, had burdens to bear. Once again, the disruption of international trade had a dislocating effect on the Swedish economy, necessitating the imposition of price and rent controls and the rationing of food. But Sweden suffered none of the massive devastation experienced by the belligerent nations in Europe; postwar recovery was swift and impressive. Social Democratic governments continued to develop and expand their programs of social insurance, and compulsory health insurance was begun in 1956. At the same time industry continued

Table III.1.4 Distribution of Labor Force in Stockholm by
Occupational Groups, 1860-1970

	Percentage of labor force					
Year	Industry and handicrafts	Communi-cations	Trade	Official services	Other	Total (%)
1860	48.4	4.6	15.4	23.0	8.6	100.0
1870	44.0	5.5	13.0	22.3	15.2	100.0
1880	47.7	5.8	15.3	17.1	14.1	100.0
1890	46.1	6.3	16.5	15.5	15.6	100.0
1900	45.1	8.6	18.7	14.9	12.7	100.0
1910	44.4	9.7	26.2	14.6	5.1	100.0
1920	45.6	9.6	25.6	14.1	5.1	100.0
1930	41.9	11.0	29.2	15.5	2.4	100.0
1940	41.7	10.5	32.2	14.7	0.9	100.0
1950	36.6	10.6	31.3	20.0	1.5	100.0
1960 (est.)	37.8	9.3	30.6	21.3	1.0	100.0
1970 (est.)	25.8	9.4	32.2	31.5	1.1	100.0

Source: Gösta Ahlberg, Stockholms Befolkningsutveckling efter 1850 (Stockholm: Almquist & Wiksells, 1958), p. 129; Folk-och bostadsräkningen, 1970.

to thrive, and unemployment was all but eliminated. Sweden had become, and was to remain, one of the most affluent nations in the world.

Before World War II, manufacturing industries, particularly in metal, paper, printing, and food, constituted the largest single source of employment for Stockholmers; wholesale and retail trade occupations comprised the next largest category. Domestic service, which was the second largest source of employment during the early nineteenth century, had nearly disappeared. In subsequent years the expansion of the public sector produced a noticeable change in Stockholm's occupational structure. By 1970 nearly a third of Stockholm's working population were civil servants (see Table III.1.4).

The years after 1945 saw the emergence of Stockholm as a major metropolitan area. The population of the city proper reached 800,000 in 1960, but diminished thereafter as increasing numbers of Stockholmers chose to settle in the outer suburbs. The population of the suburban area doubled in the decade prior to 1970 and soon surpassed 200,000. By 1970 more than 1.3 million Swedes (16 percent of the nation's population) inhabited the greater Stockholm area; it has been estimated that these figures will remain stable. After centuries as a predominantly rural nation, Sweden had become urbanized (Table III.1.5).

The sex structure of Stockholm's population is still slightly imbalanced; women continue to constitute a majority, particularly

Table III.1.5 Patterns of Urbanization, 1882-1960

Year	Population in cities larger than 100,000 (%)	Population in cities Larger than 25,000 (%)
1882	4	7
1900	8	11
1930	14	22[a]
1960	22	41[a]
1970	28	—

Source: Adapted from A. S. Banks, Cross-Polity Time Series Data (Cambridge: MIT Press, 1971); Statistisk Årsbok för Sverige.
a. Larger than 20,000.

among persons over 60 years of age. The low birthrates during the Depression years and since 1950 are reflected in a relatively large proportion of the population in their twenties and over 45. The population retains an overwhelming racial and ethnic homogeneity; nearly half the aliens who reside in the city are from other Scandinavian countries, and there exist no "ghettoized minorities."[19]

Although there was a slight centrifugal movement of workplaces in conjunction with the spatial expansion of the city during our century, almost three-fourths of all Stockholmers work in the central business district. Jobs lost to Stockholm by virtue of the movement of industry to outlying areas have been more than compensated for by an expansion of the civil service and of retail trade.

Among the more impressive aspects of Stockholm's twentieth century history has been the widely heralded progress in planning and development. As already noted, the foresight of city officials was apparent as early as 1640; this tradition continues to the present. Perhaps the most significant innovations may be seen in the satellite suburbs that have been developed since 1950.[20] The first of these new towns, the Vällingby group, was constructed to the northwest of the city center in the early 1950s. Consisting of attractive apartment complexes, with nearby retail stores, schools, and parks, the new communities lie within easy commuting distance of the central city. Subsequent residential developments were established at Farsta, south of the city, in the late 1950s and on a larger scale at Skarholmen, to the southwest, in the early 1960s. Other satellite developments were completed at Tensta and Norra Jarva, north of the city center, in the late 1960s and early 1970s, respectively. Access to the central business district was facilitated by the construction of the Tunnelbana, a high-speed public transportation system that was begun in 1945; it radiates outward from the heart of the city to the planned communities. By the early 1970s it comprised the world's tenth largest subway network. Development toward the northeast was inhibited by the state's reluctance to part with its holdings in that area, but the city had acquired more than 200 square miles of land outside of the city limits by 1970.

Considerable progress was also made in the area of urban renewal, although not without some protest from merchants and environmentalists. A partial reconstruction of the Norrmalm business district, just north of the old city island, has included not only the construction of modern office blocks, but also a system of tunnels to accommodate motor traffic with minimal congestion. Also among recent projects in the inner city area were the restoration and improvement of Gamla Stan, the old town on the city island, and the preservation of Ostra Mariaberget, an eighteenth century neighborhood at Södermalm, south of the city center.

A more recent innovation has occurred in the area of governmental structure. As the expanding city became more inextricably linked with the surrounding municipalities, it became apparent that the existing fragmentation of governmental authority inhibited future planning. Thus there was created in 1971 the Greater Stockholm County Council, with responsibilities for regional planning, hospitals, medical and dental care, secondary education, legal aid, day-care centers, homes for the aged and physically handicapped, and transportation, among other services.[21] By the early 1970s it seemed apparent that the quality of life in urban Stockholm, already surpassing that of most of the world's cities, was likely to remain at an impressively high level.

NOTES TO CHAPTER III.1

Note: These abbreviations are used in the following references:
AK   *Andra Kammaren* (Second Chamber)
RProt *Riksdag Protokoll* (Riksdag proceedings)
SOU   *Statens offentliga utredningar* (State official report)
SFS   *Svensk Författningssamling* (Collected Swedish Statutes)

1. W. William-Olsson, *Stockholm: Structure and Development* (Uppsala: Almqvist & Wiksell, 1960), p. 9. The development of Stockholm was to some degree hastened by the earlier sacking of a nearby commercial center, Sigtuna, by Estonian pirates. See Nils Ahnlund, *Stockholms Historia före Gustav Vasa* (Stockholm: P. A. Norstedt & Söner, 1953), p. 31. For an alternative legend on the original of the city's name, see K. W. Gullers and Steig Trenter, *The Old Town of Stockholm* (Stockholm: P. A. Norstedt & Söner, 1953), p. 7.

2. Gullers and Trenter, op. cit., p. 8. The commercial significance of early Stockholm is reviewed in Ingrid Hammarström, *Stockholm i Svensk Ekonomi 1850-1924* (Stockholm, Almqvist & Wiksell, 1970), pp. 3-4.

3. Gullers and Trenter, op. cit., p. 21.

4. Ibid., p. 67.

5. Burnett Anderson, *Stockholm: Capital and Crossroads* (Stockholm: The Swedish Institute, 1953), p. 79.

6. Nils Wester, *Kungl. Politi-och Brandkommissionen, Studier Rörande Stockholms Stads Polisväsen under 1700-talet* (Stockholm: P. A. Norstedt & Söner, 1946), pp. 140, 204.

7. Gustaf Utterström, *Jordbrukets Arbetare, Levnadsvillkor och Arbetsliv på Landsbygden från Frihetstiden till Mitten av 1800-talet* (Stockholm: Tidens Forlag, 1957), p. 24.

8. Crude death rates and infant mortality rates were about half again as high for Swedish urban areas as for rural areas until late in the nineteenth century. See Dorothy Swaine Thomas, *Social and Economic Aspects of Swedish Population Movements, 1750-1933* (New York: Macmillan, 1941), p. 24.

9. Anderson, op. cit., p. 82.

10. Oscar I, *On Punishments and Prisons* (Transl. Alfred May; London: Smith, Elder & Co., 1842).

11. Kettil Bruun, *Alkohol i Norden* (Stockholm: Albert Bonniers, 1973), p. 24; Eli F. Heckscher, *Svenskt Arbete och Liv* (Stockholm: Aldus, 1968), pp. 25-26.

12. Sven Lundquist, "Nykterhetsrörelsen," *Den Svenska Historien*, Del 9 (Stockholm: Albert Bonniers, 1969), p. 165.

13. Hammarström, op. cit., pp. 211ff; pp. 353ff.

14. *Berättelse angaende Stockholms Kommunalförvaltning jämte statiska uppgifter*, 1881-1893.

15. For an excellent study of the development of democracy in Sweden, see Dankwart A. Rustow, *The Politics of Compromise* (Princeton, N.J.: Princeton University Press, 1956); also Douglas V. Verney, *Parliamentary Reform in Sweden, 1866-1921* (Oxford: Oxford University Press, 1957). A concise over-

view appears in D. A. Rustow, "Sweden's Transition to Democracy: Some Notes Toward a Genetic Theory," *Scandinavian Political Studies*, 6 (1971), 9-26.

16. Kurt Samuelsson, *From Great Power to Welfare State* (London: Allen & Unwin, 1968), p. 201.

17. Timothy A. Tilton, "The Social Origins of Liberal Democracy: The Swedish Case," *American Political Science Review*, 68 (June 1974), 561-571.

18. Marquis Childs, *Sweden: The Middle Way* (New Haven, Conn.: Yale University Press, 1936).

19. Some of the newer suburbs, such as Tensta, have a relatively high percentage of foreign residents (approximately 40 percent). By the end of 1973, non-Scandinavian aliens comprised less than four percent of the city's resident population, however.

20. Among the best accounts in English of Swedish urban planning are Ella Odmann and Gun-Britt Dahlberg, *Urbanization in Sweden* (Stockholm: Government Publishing House, 1970); Ann Louise Strong, *Planned Urban Environments* (Baltimore: Johns Hopkins University Press, 1971), pp. 5-64; Stockholm Stadsbyggnadskontor, *Stockholm: Urban Environment* (Stockholm: Almqvist & Wiksell, 1972); and Hjalmar Mehr, "Stockholm," in William A. Robson and D. E. Regan, Eds., *Great Cities of the World: Their Government, Politics, and Planning* (Beverly Hills, Calif.: Sage Publications, 1972), pp. 875-901. These new towns are not without their critics, though. It has been claimed that the satellite communities, many of which are inhabited by low-income tenants, serve to reinforce patterns of class segregation, increase anonymity, and conceal social problems.

21. Thomas J. Anton, *Governing Greater Stockholm: A Study of Policy Development and System Change* (Berkeley: University of California Press, 1975).

CRIME, CONFLICT, AND PUBLIC ORDER, 1750-1850

PATTERNS OF CRIME AND CONFLICT

The study of crime and civil disturbance during Stockholm's earlier years is made difficult by the scarcity of statistics and by the paucity of narrative accounts. The earliest available crime statistics, which refer to persons sentenced for drunkenness, appear irregularly from 1814 and continuously from 1825. Statistics on persons sentenced for all categories of theft are available from 1830. Data concerning crimes of violence against the general public and against public officials begin to appear in the mid-1840s. Fragmentary narrative accounts of riots and civil disorders are available for most of the century from 1750 to 1850.

The data reflect relatively high levels of crime in comparison with subsequent years; series of drunkenness and theft rates are also marked by considerable fluctuation, as Figures III.2.1 and III.2.2 indicate. Although the series show no consistent relationship with each other or with measures of economic well-being (Figure III.2.3), some interesting patterns are evident. There is a rough inverse relationship between the two series: theft rates were high during the period 1838-1843 and in 1846, when drunkenness rates were correspondingly low. Drunkenness rates, on the other hand, were high during 1833-1834, 1843-1844, and in 1850, which are troughs in the theft series. Although relationships are imperfect, economic factors seem to have had some influence on the trends in question. Drunkenness rates tended to be high in years following good or improved harvests, reflecting increases in the supply of and the demand for grain spirits;[1] rates of theft tended to rise during times of relative

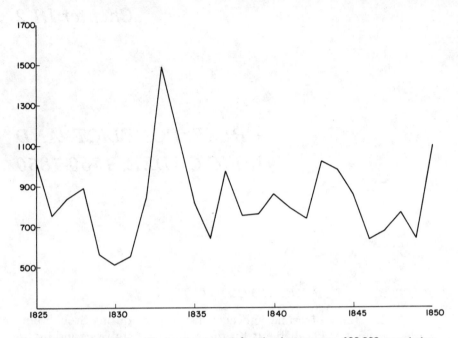

Figure III.2.1 Stockholm: Persons sentenced for drunkenness per 100,000 population, 1825-1850

Figure III.2.2 Stockholm: Persons sentenced for all categories of theft per 100,000 population, 1830-1850

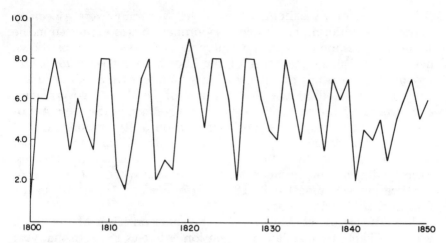

Figure III.2.3 Sweden: Harvest index, 1800-1850

austerity. The latter relationship is less pronounced, however, since the entire period under observation was one of chronic unemployment in Stockholm.[2] The rise in rates of theft also may have been partly attributable to an increase in the proportion of the population between the ages of 15 and 30 during the 1830s.

Narrative accounts of criminality during the century are scanty, but they suggest that authorities were preoccupied with questions of vagrancy throughout the period. Widespread begging was the focus of a parliamentary committee investigation as early as 1731.[3] A workhouse was established to the south of the city island in 1773, and another was opened at Norrmalm in 1797. The former institution, built to house 150 inmates, was crammed with as many as 800 on more than one occasion.[4] Prosecutions for vagrancy constituted some 45 percent of the cases reported by the Police Chamber in 1819, and in the late 1830s approximately one-third of the inmates of the major prisons in Sweden were serving time for various crimes of indolence.[5] Though a detailed description of the demographic background of offenders during the period is precluded by the scarcity of data, two characteristics are strikingly apparent. The typical criminal in the years before 1850 was poor and male. Most prison inmates were without education, and women comprised at most fifteen percent of the total.

Illicit distilling was also the subject of official concern during the late eighteenth and early nineteenth centuries. The state sought to monopolize distilling for purposes of maximizing revenues beginning in 1776, but home distilling had become a social institution. Despite energetic attempts to prosecute offenders, home production and attendant smuggling operations continued.[6]

The elites of Stockholm and Sweden generally were especially sensitive to criticism, and when disapprobation was expressed in the street they responded with considerable repressive force, as shown below. Criticism in the pages of the liberal newspaper *Aftonbladet* provoked censorship, despite written guarantees of freedom of the press incorporated in the Constitution of 1809. The government, empowered by the paradoxically named Freedom of the Press Act of 1812, sought to stop the paper's publication on the grounds that it constituted a danger to public security. The editor of the paper solved the problem by publishing the paper after each official confiscation with a new number after its name. When the power of confiscation was repealed in 1844, *Aftonbladet 21* was still in the vanguard of liberal opinion.[7]

The offense of lèse-majesté (i.e., personal criticism of the king), was punishable by mandatory execution as late as 1832. In that year the conviction of Anders Lindeberg, an associate of the editor of *Aftonbladet*, provided the occasion for one of the more embarrassing situations in Swedish history. Charles XIV, who had been the target of Lindeberg's published attacks, thought capital punishment a bit too severe in this case and commuted the sentence to three years' imprisonment. Lindeberg, however, demanded the punishment that had been formally prescribed, thus compelling the king to proclaim amnesty for all political prisoners. At the time, Lindeberg was the only individual in the country in that particular category.[8]

The struggles for political power between monarchs and the nobility had a profound influence on the development of the Swedish political system and a secondary effect on activities in the streets of Stockholm. Gustavus III consolidated his power in the two bloodless coups of 1772 and 1789, but he was assassinated in 1792 as related earlier. The members of the military who were stationed in the capital appeared generally supportive of the king, and there had been no armed resistance to his establishment of absolute rule. Following the assassination there was a tightening of surveillance at the gates of the city and an increase in patrol activity, but no visible violence.

In 1809 military officers were instrumental in deposing Gustavus IV. His fall from power and the subsequent adoption of the Constitution precipitated no immediate disorder, but conflict over his successor proved to be bloody.

Most of the collective disorders that occurred in Stockholm during the late eighteenth and early nineteenth centuries cannot be traced to factors of economic adversity. Some disturbances, particularly small ones, appear to have been more directly attributable to the chronic unemployment of the period. During the Pomeranian War (1756-1763) there were numerous incidents of street fighting and plundering around the market areas of the city when farmers arrived from surrounding areas with their commodities.[9] The most severe periods of economic hardship were occasions for food riots elsewhere in Sweden, but none occurred in Stockholm.

Labor-management conflict was rare during the period, and only one strike has been documented. In 1824 two iron carriers sought to induce their colleagues to stop work following a cut in pay. The two were arrested and a hundred of their fellow workers marched to the police station in protest. Following the arrest of four more, the men returned to work. There were no further strikes until the industrial workforce became much larger and economic conditions improved.

The incidents of civil strife that did take place in the capital during the period reflect two clear trends: The conflicts appear to have become increasingly violent, and they were more explicitly directed against the prevailing autocracy. Two disorders arising during the war with Russia in 1788 had a distinctly prowar orientation. In August 1788 a crowd of a few hundred artisans and tradespeople threatened a group of military officers who had resigned from the Swedish army in protest against the war policies of Gustavus III. The so-called traitors were protected from the angry mob by the police.[10] Support for the war was by no means limited to the middle classes. In 1790 after the sea battle at Svensksund in which Sweden, despite substantial losses, claimed victory, there was a rather raucous celebration in the streets of Stockholm; participants' enthusiasm was heightened by the free flow of corn brandy. Support for the war was by no means universal, however, and a number of antiwar protests also occurred during the period. According to police historian Nils Staf, war-related demonstrations were without precedent in Stockholm's history.[11]

During the closing years of the eighteenth century, public hostility toward the police force and town guard was manifest in two separate collective disturbances. Early in 1793, following an apparent assault on two civilians by two officers of the guard, a large crowd assembled, led by a bookkeeper, Niklas Ebel. The police were unsuccessful in dispersing the crowd, a task accomplished only by a charge by a troop of dragoons. The event has since been known as "Ebel's Riot."[12] Six years later the police commissioner was the target of stones thrown by members of a crowd during a celebration at Södermalm on the king's birthday. The participants, who reportedly had been drinking aquavit, were ultimately driven off by troops.[13]

The growth of a middle class in the early nineteenth century (Figure III.1.3) created in the capital political tensions that were soon to have violent manifestations. Following the overthrow of Gustavus IV in 1809, the uncle of the deposed monarch became king; he was childless, and a young Danish prince was named heir apparent. In May 1810 the successor to the throne died after suffering an apparent heart attack while participating in military exercises; it was rumored that the prince had been poisoned by nobles sympathetic with the exiled king. During the prince's funeral procession through central Stockholm, Count Axel von Fersen, a nobleman of strong Gustavian sympathies who was suspected of complicity in the death of the prince, became the target of verbal threats from the assembled mourners. To many members of the crowd von Fersen symbolized the continued exclusion of the middle class from positions of political influence. The passions of von Fersen's antagonists escalated, and the count was pulled from his carriage but managed to escape twice from his attackers. While many troops and city guardsmen stood by in relative passivity, the count was taken from the headquarters of the guard and beaten to death. Rioting continued for a few hours afterward until troops were ordered to fire on the rioters. Eight persons died, and about 50 soldiers were injured. It has been noted that participants in the Fersen riot were not primarily journeymen and workers. Indeed, there appears to have been an overrepresentation of artisans, civil servants, and military personnel.[14]

Following the Fersen riot, the streets of Stockholm were free from significant collective disorder until 1838. In March of that year a man named Crusenstolpe was sentenced to three years imprisonment for lèse-majesté. According to accounts of the trial, a substantial tumult broke out in the courtroom when the sentence was pronounced. When the convicted man was to be taken to the fort of Vaxholm outside Stockholm, a crowd of 2,000 to 3,000 people gathered at Södermalmstorg. A series of clashes with troops resulted in two deaths and numerous injuries, and disturbances occurred in other parts of the city during succeeding days. As was the case in the earlier Fersen riot, participants in the Crusenstolpe disorders were artisans, merchants, and other members of the new middle class who continued to chafe under the authorities' intolerance of dissent and resistance to political reform.[15]

The year 1848 was a tumultuous one in Europe, and there were more than a few traces of radical protest activity in Stockholm. The residence of August von Hartmansdorff, the conservative leader, was the scene of a riot that spring, and disturbances continued for a period of a few days. Consequences were severe: An estimated 30 fatalities and numerous injuries were reported. Unlike the riots earlier in the century, the events of 1848 appear to have attracted as participants a substantial number of workers, who sought the introduction of universal suffrage and the abolition of the monarchy. The traditional middle-class liberal element was also present but less inclined to express long-standing grievances in the streets.[16]

THE RULERS AND THE LAW

Swedish criminal law evolved over the centuries from a system of private vengeance to a code that proscribed certain behaviors and specified appropriate punishments for each category. The centralization and unification of Swedish law dates to the fourteenth century. The dominant principle of the early Swedish criminal law was the *lex talionis*; as in most societies of the period, the law was detailed and severe. During the reign of Gustavus Adolphus (1611-1632), the killing of a stag or swan was punishable by death, the practice of witchcraft by burning.

The criminal law in effect in 1750 derived from a recodification in 1734, which reflected the Swedish elite's new faith in the principle of deterrence. The primary purpose of the criminal law was to attach to behaviors defined as criminal penalties of sufficient severity that potential violators would be intimidated and unwilling to risk the prescribed punishments. The 68 offenses punishable by death under the code of 1734 ranged from premeditated murder, unwarranted criticism of the king and the royal family, blasphemy, and sorcery to an entire series of acquisitive crimes with and without violence. Execution took the form of hanging or beheading, or, in the case of female offenders, burning. Certain individuals were also broken on the wheel and exhibited publicly; in other cases, the right hand was cut off prior to execution.

Other punishments meted out during the late eighteenth century included flogging, imprisonment with hard labor or on a diet of bread and water, the loss of civil rights (imposed primarily on those convicted of fraud), the payment of fines, and public display in or outside a church.[17]

As was the case in other European societies at the time, Swedish elites began to evince more humanitarian inclinations. The primary inspiration was provided by the French Enlightenment. In 1779 a number of offenses were dropped from the list of capital crimes, among them sorcery, bigamy, larceny from a church, and larceny by third- and fourth-time repeaters. Gustavus III had abolished the use of torture in 1772 and had proposed the abolition of capital punishment for all offenses except parricide and treason. There was considerable resistance to this reform from the Riksdag, however, and it was not implemented.

A commission was appointed in 1809 to recodify the criminal law, and drafts were submitted to the Estates in 1815 and 1832. A new commission submitted its drafts in 1839 and 1844. Each of these proposals met with criticism from the nobility and clergy, the more conservative elements of the Riksdag, and only piecemeal reforms were implemented during the period.

Among the more noteworthy changes in the criminal law during the first half of the nineteenth century were those directed at the large number of unemployed persons in Stockholm. Ordinances requiring military service or forced labor for beggars and those without other means of support were enacted in 1802 and 1804. Full implementation of these policies proved impossible because public facilities could not accommodate all such persons. Revised legislation in 1819 required forced labor only of former convicts without lawful means of support and of other individuals who were viewed as constituting an explicit public nuisance. Compulsory military service was no longer imposed. In 1833 indefinite sentences of public labor were imposed on individuals unable to prove a means of subsistence or to post a cash bond. Prison facilities were employed to house indigents, who were not treated differently from those who had been imprisoned for "conventional" crimes. Thirteen years later, in 1846, such treatment was limited to those who had previously been convicted of a crime or had previously performed public labor. The duration of their detention was limited to two to four years. Throughout the period it appears that authorities were as incapable of controlling the indigent population as they were unwilling to take steps to alleviate conditions of poverty. The situation was aggravated by the general reluctance of employers to hire former convicts.[18]

Prostitution appears to have been common in Stockholm during the early nineteenth century. Despite official proscriptions on brothel keeping, an offense punishable by a maximum of three years' forced labor, most of the inns and public houses in Stockholm offered more to their patrons than strong drink. Official reaction to these practices appears to have taken the form of regulation. In 1838 the police force applied the delicate label of "coffee tavern" to a number of establishments and accorded them special supervision. An increase in the incidence of venereal disease during the 1840s, however, generated demands for further control of prostitution. In 1847, a special office was established to which prostitutes were required to report twice weekly for examinations, and 174 women were officially registered there during that year.[19] Further regulatory policies were implemented in the years after 1850.

INSTITUTIONS OF PUBLIC ORDER

The Police

The task of policing Stockholm during the early years of the city's history fell to a number of organizations.[20] The city guard, organized in 1594, was under the command of a *stadsmajor* and was

equipped and paid by the burghers. The guard's primary responsibility was to patrol the streets and guard the town gates. In 1729 a
fire guard was established to prevent the spread of fires in the city.
Its members patrolled the streets of Stockholm each night and were
also available to perform law enforcement functions. The operations
of both these forces were inhibited because members lived throughout the city rather than in central locations, thus were difficult to
mobilize in emergencies.

In addition to the fire and city guards, a garrison usually consisting
of two regiments and a naval squadron was stationed in the city.
Members of the garrison had secondary responsibilities for law
enforcement and patrolled between the various locations in the city
where their barracks were situated. The mid-eighteenth century saw
the establishment of a small city police force, whose members were
primarily responsible for the apprehension and prosecution of
offenders. In the early years of its existence the police force had no
patrol duties. In 1797 Stockholm was divided into police districts to
facilitate public communication with the force. Around this time the
wages of policemen were increased, but many segments of the public
remained strongly dissatisfied with police services. Policemen continued to be recruited from working-class backgrounds and had the
reputation of being a rather rough lot.

Records of personnel strength of the various organizations are
imperfect and do not reflect temporary changes in size. There were
in 1812 approximately 200 men attached to the garrison, 200 serving
with the fire guard, 100 with the city guard, and 88 in the police
force. This constituted a relatively high level of law enforcement
manpower for a city whose population only reached 80,000 in 1830.
Nevertheless, in the early 1830s an apparent increase in the incidence
of thefts and burglaries moved the merchants of Stockholm to
request more intensive patrolling of the city. The night patrols were
augmented, and the new members were paid in cash and, occasionally, with liquor. Complaints were also directed at the inadequacy of the city guard, whose members bore the additional
responsibility of guarding prisoners, and at the fire guard, whose
effectiveness had been lessened by low recruiting standards. In 1833
the latter two forces were combined to form the Military Corps of
the City of Stockholm (Stockholms stads militarcorps, which was
quartered in barracks and placed under the direct command of the
Governor of Stockholm. The force numbered 144 in addition to its
officers.

Following the Crusenstolpe riots of 1838, intensive patrols were
organized in the city; according to reports in the press, military
pickets seemed omnipresent. Groups as small as eight or ten persons

were dispersed by police or by garrison troops, and arrests were numerous.[21] Such intensive surveillance did nothing to lessen the chronic public antagonism toward agents of law enforcement and order maintenance. In the following year three police stations were opened in the city, and policies were implemented that were designed to improve police-community relations. Addresses of policemen were made public, and members of the force were directed to establish residence in the district to which they were assigned. Relations still appear to have been less than cordial, however, for in 1840, after repeated requests, policemen were authorized to purchase and carry a short sword. Although rates of theft appeared to decline after 1846, public insecurity remained high and dissatisfaction with police services persisted. Reports by the Governor of Stockholm for the years 1843-1847 reflected particular displeasure with the night patrols conducted by the Military Corps, and at the behest of the royal government, the governor began to explore the possibilities of further police reforms.[22]

Plans laid in the aftermath of the 1848 riots for a reorganization of the Stockholm police were implemented in 1850. Stockholm's new police force was awarded primary responsibility for law enforcement and order maintenance in the city. The Military Corps of the City of Stockholm was reduced in size, and its responsibilities were limited to those of fire fighting. The troops of the garrison were charged with protecting the areas surrounding the city and also served as a reserve force in the event of severe public disturbances.

The organizational structure of the new force was uncomplicated. The city was divided into ten tracts, roughly congruent with the geographical boundaries of Stockholm's clerical congregations. Each tract, under the management of a police superintendent, was divided into two chief constable districts (overkonstapelsdistrikt), and each of these was in turn divided into four patrol districts. Each of the 80 districts was patrolled nightly in two shifts, two constables to a shift. The patrol organization was under the direct control of the Governor of Stockholm. The 390 men who comprised the new force were equipped with uniforms, whereas previously a silver badge had been the only identifying symbol. Wages were also increased, and weapons (short swords by night, batons by day) were provided at public expense. The reforms were financed by means of an increase in the cost of licenses to sell or serve liquor in the city. The 1850 reorganization appears to have been well received. Governors' reports from the years following the reform stated the desirability of further increasing police salaries but made no adverse references to police performance per se.

The Administration of Justice

The Swedish judicial system, which had been reorganized following enactment of the 1734 code, was further modified prior to 1850. The lowest level of the judiciary in Stockholm was the police court, where petty offenses such as drunkenness and minor assault were tried by the governor, later by the police commissioner. More serious offenses were under the jurisdiction of the *Kämnersratten* and the *Rådhustratten*. The latter, a municipal court of second instance, became the main trial court following the abolition of the Kämnersratten in 1850. The *Svea Hovrätt*, an intermediate court of appeals for the Stockholm region, was established in 1614 by Gustavus Adolphus. It had both criminal and civil jurisdiction. The court of last resort, founded in 1784, was the High Court of Justice *(Högsta Domstolen)*, and this body assumed powers of review previously held by the king.

Under the provisions of the 1734 code, the majority of crimes were punishable by fine or by capital or corporal punishment. The prisons that existed during the eighteenth century were clearly indicative of the morality and economic interests of Sweden's elite. The distaste with which these individuals viewed indolence in general has been mentioned, and penal institutions served the purpose of organizing efficiently a pool of inexpensive labor. Indeed, eighteenth century workhouses were managed by local manufacturers under the administrative control of the department of commerce.[23] There were, moreover, canals to be dug and fortifications to be constructed throughout the kingdom.

Conditions in Swedish prisons at the end of the eighteenth century were scarcely less grim than in those abroad, and very little thought had been given to their improvement prior to the visit to Stockholm in 1781 of John Howard, the British penal reformer.[24] Appalling sanitary conditions in the *spinnhus* (workhouse) at Stockholm gave rise to an official investigation in the early 1790s. Calls for reform by the Governor of Stockholm, Rear Admiral Modée, and by the chairman of the national board of health, Dr. David von Schulzenheim, led to a royal decree that established minimum standards of sanitation and humane treatment in 1798. A number of prominent figures, including Georg Adlersparre, Carl af Forselles, and Erik Gustav Geijer, advocated further improvements to the nation's prisons, but it took the crime wave of the 1830s and the energetic activities of a member of the royal family to bring about a significant change in policy.[25]

Meanwhile reliance on imprisonment as a treatment was steadily increasing. As Sweden became less belligerent, fewer men were required for military service. Population increases led to an unprecedented surplus of labor, and penal institutions began to serve the primary function of warehouses to isolate and discipline those who threatened the status quo.[26]

The first significant impetus for the reform of the Swedish criminal justice system occurred in 1840, when Crown Prince Oscar published *On Punishments and Prisons*, a call for the restructuring of the national penal system. The tone of Oscar's introductory chapter, dealing with matters of crime and punishment in general, was far more progressive than was the thinking of his contemporaries in the Swedish upper class. The fundamental premise of Oscar's work was hardly revolutionary. In his view, the criminal justice system existed to preserve the stability of the state and to protect the lives and property of its inhabitants. However he believed these ends were best served by the implementation of social policies outside the purview of the criminal justice system itself. Among the reforms proposed by the prince were the promotion of true religion, general enlightenment, and greater economic well-being.[27] It was no coincidence that a national system of compulsory education was established in 1842, and shortly after Oscar's succession to the throne in 1844 the state lottery was abolished.

Oscar's orientation toward the purpose of punishment marked a significant departure from the prevailing themes of deterrence and revenge. Indeed, he strongly endorsed the rehabilitative inclinations of the law reform committee of 1832 and quoted the following passage on corporal punishment from its report:

> ... this debasing punishment crushes those dispositions for improvement founded in human nature, brings him to despair, or makes him a sworn enemy to that state, whose laws have placed him in so degrading a position, that the hope or possibility of raising himself from it has been cut off, all means of obtaining a living and regaining the respect and confidence of his fellow creatures being to him closed.[28]

Oscar's recommendations for the abolition of capital punishment were based primarily on the inadequacies of this penalty as a deterrent. He did, however, make one argument based on personal self-interest. With regard to the matter of commuting sentences of death, he suggested:

> This question is difficult to decide, and requires a length of time and degree of activity, which, by the abolition of capital punishments, might be spared for the advancement of other subjects, important to the welfare of the state. In order fully to understand the importance of this remark, it would be necessary to imagine one's self in the Monarch's place; and to consider how great a portion of his time must be taken up, when an

average of 61 cases of capital punishment are brought forward yearly in Sweden, consequently more than one every week; for the nature of these cases prevents their being compared with usual administrative questions.[29]

The Swedish prison system was not really a system at all at the time of publication of Oscar's treatise. Aside from the workhouses constructed to accommodate the destitute, there were no prisons established solely to house criminal offenders. Military and municipal buildings had basement custodial facilities, and small lockups were maintained in some towns. The prisons served simply as warehouses; conditions were typically austere, and authorities were more concerned with keeping the prisoners in custody than with their well-being. When prisoners were called on to perform occasional labor outside these facilities, they were closely guarded by armed troops.

Administration of Swedish prisons was decentralized; some facilities were under the supervision of the naval forces, others under that of the army, and some came under municipal administration. Although proposals for centralization had been voiced by von Schulzenheim as early as 1799 and by a national commission in 1832, coordinated management of prisons was not instituted until 1859. There were, moreover, no provisions for the rehabilitation of former prisoners, who had difficulty in securing employment following their release.[30]

The years prior to 1850 were marked by a gradual mitigation of the severity of punishment. Condemned men were no longer broken on the wheel after 1835, and cadavers were not publicly exhibited after 1841. Maiming and burning at the stake were also formally

Table III.2.1 Sweden: Average Annual Number
of Executions, 1750-1850

Year	Number
1751-1760	36.2
1761-1770	26.3
1771-1780	14.1
1781-1790	6.2
1791-1800	6.0
1801-1810	7.0
1811-1820	9.6
1821-1830	11.0
1831-1835	15.4
1836-1840	11.6
1841-1845	7.0
1846-1850	4.4

Source: Statistisk Årsbok för Sverige, 1940, p. 283.

abolished in 1841.[31] Reliance on capital punishment diminished during the period 1750-1850, although between 1821 and 1840 there was some increase in the annual number of executions, as Table III.2.1 illustrates. Despite this trend away from the use of fatal force, the rate of executions per capita in Sweden during the years 1838-1839 was second only to that of Spain among European nations for which data were available.[32]

Prince Oscar's discussion of contemporary correctional practices and proposals for reform was a detailed document. Inspired by the thought of John Howard and other reformers in Europe and America, Oscar recommended the introduction of vocational and religious training, the segregation of vagrants from those convicted of other crimes, and the establishment of prison facilities throughout the kingdom to minimize the logistical problems involved in transporting prisoners long distances. The latter proposal reflected an emerging notion of community-based corrections, and the prince wrote disapprovingly of "the moving of the prisoners from that neighborhood to which they are afterwards to return."[33]

One of the prince's more progressive proposals was the establishment of citizens' aftercare societies on the model of those founded in Philadelphia, London, and Dusseldorf. From Oscar's perspective, the maintenance of a community was in large part the responsibility of that community's members. He asserted that the prisoner's

> return to evil must be prevented by his being able to obtain honest employment. Here is an extensive field for communal and private exertion.... After the law has executed the punishment, and the state has taken care of the inward improvement, it is the business of the citizen to offer a helping hand to the individual restored to freedom.[34]

Almost immediately following the publication of Oscar's work, the Riksdag appropriated a very large sum to begin implementing the proposed reforms. The use of irons as a means of restraining prisoners was discontinued in 1845, and by midcentury construction or renovation was completed on the central prisons at Stockholm, Göteborg, and Malmö. Ten smaller departmental facilities were also established, three of them situated in Stockholm. The period at midcentury was to mark the high point of Swedish authorities' reliance on imprisonment as a means of social control.

THE CONSEQUENCES OF POLICIES OF PUBLIC ORDER

The impact of the public order policies implemented before 1850 remains unclear, but certain recurring patterns can be noticed.

Attempts to suppress dissent and to continue the exclusion of the middle and lower classes from an active role in the political process became less successful as these groups became larger and more aware of their deprivation. The use of force succeeded in quelling specific disturbances but appears to have further inflamed the passions that initially gave rise to the disorders.

The full impact of the police and prison reforms of the late 1840s did not become visible until the latter half of the century. It appears, however, that the intransigence of conservative elements in the Riksdag with regard to criminal law and penal reform had little effect on those with criminal inclinations. The limited statistical evidence available suggests that criminality was more responsive to economic fluctuation than to crime control policies per se. The influence of socioeconomic conditions on patterns of criminality was again apparent during the period of dramatic urban growth and industrialization in the years after 1850.

NOTES TO CHAPTER III.2

1. The relationship of drunkenness and economic conditions was noted by the Governor of Stockholm in the late 1820s. He suggested that a decrease in the number of convictions after 1825 was due "to nothing else but the rising price and lesser supply of liquor in its turn due to the bad harvest of 1826." *Kongl. Maj:ts Öfverstathållare i Stockholm stad till Kongl. Maj:t år 1828 afgifne Femårsberättelse* (Stockholm, 1829), p. 25.

2. Rune Hedman, "Massan vid Fersenska upploppet," *Historisk Tidskrift* (1969), p. 9.

3. Wester, op. cit., p. 204.

4. Sven Sperlings, "Dihlströmska Inrättningen 1886" (Opubl. trebetygsuppsats, Historiska Institutionen, Stockholms Universitet, 1968), p. 4; Joseph Müller, *Fattigvården i Stockholm från äldre till nyare tid jämte beskrivning af Stockholms stads arbetsinrättning* (Stockholm: Iduns Tryckeriaktiebolag 1906), p. 319.

5. Our term for such offenses as vagrancy, begging, and vagabondage. See Gustaf Fridolf Almquist, *Résumé Historique de la Réforme Pénitentiare en Suède depuis le Commencement du XIX Siècle* (Stockholm: P. A. Norstedt & Söner, 1885), p. 8.

6. During the poor harvest years of 1798 and 1799 prohibitions were imposed on distilling in general. Reduced supply of raw materials was probably a more effective impediment to home distilling than any form of governmental intervention. See Sten Carlsson and Jerker Rosen, *Svensk Historia* (Stockholm: Svenska Bokforlaget, 1964), Vol. II, pp. 212, 393; and Karl Key-Åberg, *Stockholms Utskänkningsbolag dess organisation och tjugofemåriga verksamhet* (Stockholm: P. A. Norstedt & Söner, 1902), p. 12.

7. Ture Nerman, *Crusenstolpes kravaller* (Stockholm: Saxon & Lindström, 1938), p. 22ff.

8. Stewart Oakley, *A Short History of Sweden* (New York: Praeger, 1966), p. 189.

9. Wester, op. cit., p. 109.

10. Nils Staf, *Polisväsendet i Stockholm 1776-1850* (Stockholm: H. Geber, 1950), p. 133.

11. Ibid., p. 167.

12. Ibid., p. 215.

13. Ibid., p. 287.

14. Hedman, op. cit., pp. 21-22, 39.

15. Nerman, op. cit.

16. Staf, op. cit., p. 456; Knut Bäckström, *Götrek och manifestet* (Stockholm: Gidlund, 1972), p. 20; Oakley, op. cit., p. 189.

17. Almquist, op. cit., pp. 2-3. See also Michael Brush, "The Swedish Penal Code of 1965," *Duke Law Journal*, 67: 1 (1968), 67-93. For a concise history of Swedish criminal law, see Per-Edwin Wallén, *Svensk strafrätts historia*, 2 vols. (Stockholm: Almqvist & Wiksell, 1973).

18. Almquist, op. cit., pp. 67-68, 25.

19. Gunilla Johanssen, "Prostitution in Stockholm During the Latter Part of the 19th Century" (unpublished manuscript, University of Stockholm, 1974), pp. 1-3.

20. For a history of the Stockholm police before 1850, see Staf, op. cit.

21. Nerman, op. cit.

22. *Kongl. Maj:ts Öfverstathållare i Stockholm stad till Kongl. Maj:t åren 1843-47 afgifne Femårsberättelse* (Stockholm, 1848), pp. 24-25.

23. Annika Snare, "Prisons in Sweden: A Historical Analysis of Penal Practice." Paper presented to the Second Conference of the European Group on Deviance and Social Control, University of Essex, 1974, p. 2. For a brief history of Swedish prisons, see Torsten Erikssen, *Kriminalvård: Idéer och Experiment* (Stockholm: P. A. Norsted & Söner, 1967), pp. 205-326.

24. Siegfrid Wieselgren, *Sveriges fängelser och fångvärd från äldre tider til våra dagar. Ett bidrag till svensk kulturhistoria* (Stockholm: P. A. Norsted & Söner, 1895), pp. 291-294.

25. B. J. Hovde, *The Scandinavian Countries, 1720-1865* (Boston: Chapman & Grimes, 1943), Vol. II, pp. 609-703.

26. Snare, op. cit., p. 4. It is also possible to view changes in penal practice in light of larger social trends. The period around 1850 was one of significant institutional development in general; other institutions of social control (i.e., law enforcement and education) were also subject to reorganization and expansion. See Hanns von Hofer, "Die Entwicklung der Freiheitsstrafe in Schweden," *Kriminologisches Journal* (forthcoming).

27. Oscar I, op. cit., pp. 7, 28.

28. Ibid., pp. 23-24.

29. Ibid., p. 12.

30. Almquist, op. cit., pp. 4-7.

31. Almquist, op. cit., pp. 13-14.

32. Almquist, *La Suède: Ses Progrès Sociaux et Ses Institutions Pénitentiares* (Stockholm: P. A. Norstedt & Söner, 1879), p. 24.

33. Oscar, op. cit., p. 116.

34. Ibid., pp. 145-146.

CRIME, CONFLICT, AND PUBLIC ORDER, 1850-1930

PATTERNS OF CRIME AND CONFLICT

Although rates of violent crime showed a long-term decline during the years after 1850, trends in other forms of disorder followed a much less consistent pattern. Some types of criminal behavior, such as fraud and embezzlement, increased over the long run. Others, including collective disorder, were subject to considerable fluctuation.

Criminal statistics for Stockholm during the late nineteenth and early twentieth centuries have been compiled with some regularity.[1] Certain inconsistencies in accounting procedures (some resulting from the criminal law reform in 1865, others from changes in administrative practices during the period) preclude precise comparison over time of rates for some offenses. These problems prove particularly burdensome with regard to various kinds of homicide.

Reported infanticides, for example, were recorded separately in returns prior to 1887. Beginning in that year, they were included among murders and manslaughters. Arrests and convictions for infanticide were accorded separate listing until 1879, at which time they were subsumed under the category "procuring abortion." This accounting procedure remained in effect until 1913, when arrests and convictions for procuring abortion were incorporated in statistics for the offense of murder.

Such inconsistencies in compilation may tell us something about the evolving values of government officials, but they make it difficult to render any generalizations about long-term trends in the incidence of abortion, infanticide, or murder. Indeed, this would be virtually impossible were it not for a striking property of the data available for each of the three categories: Their rates, whether singly or in combination, were very low throughout the period. For example, from the time returns were first published in the 1830s, the annual number of reported murders in Stockholm exceeded ten on only four occasions, all during the period 1890-1909, when the category included infanticide. The incidence of reported abortion was negligible until after the turn of the century, and, although there was some increase in totals after that time, the yearly average number of abortions known to the police was only 10.9 during the decade of the 1920s.

Statistics on abortion and infanticide, however, were notoriously deceptive. High rates of illegitimate birth and general conditions of economic austerity contributed to what was known as baby farming *(änglamakeri).*[2] The practice appears to have been prevalent around the turn of the century. Few people who offered to care for foster children in return for a fee were altruistically motivated. Many youngsters died from neglect, but such deaths were not easy to identify in an era of high infant mortality.[3] Those who survived were often put to work, and the laws of the day were more protective of the rights of foster parents than of children in their charge. Indeed, the term "foster children industry" was common at the time.[4]

Although abortion and infanticide were offenses that could be concealed from the authorities with little difficulty, the murder of an

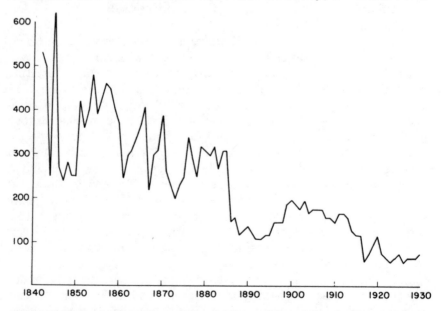

Figure III.3.1 Stockholm: Persons sentenced for assault and breach of the peace per 100,000 population, 1842-1930

adult was much more visible. The extremely low incidence of this form of behavior is remarkable, given the dramatic increase in the population of Stockholm during 1850 to 1930 (from 93,000 to more than 500,000 inhabitants). This was a period of rapid industrialization, marked by some relatively severe economic contractions. The reluctance of Stockholmers to use fatal force remained distinct from their propensities toward less drastic forms of violence. Rates of conviction for assault and breach of the peace (Figure III.3.1) were high during the mid-nineteenth century (roughly 300 per 100,000 inhabitants) but declined to below 100 by 1930.

During the 1890s substantial concern about unsafe streets was voiced in the city's newspapers. Primary blame for this condition was placed on young male gang members known as "hooligans." The gangs were named after the areas of the city in which their members resided (e.g., Katarinaligan, Atlasligan, and Surbrunnsligan). Despite the establishment in 1898 of a committee to investigate the phenomenon, hooliganism appears to have involved little more than an occasional clash between rival gangs.

Rates of theft posted a long-term decline during the period but showed some significant fluctuations (Figure III.3.2). The late 1860s,

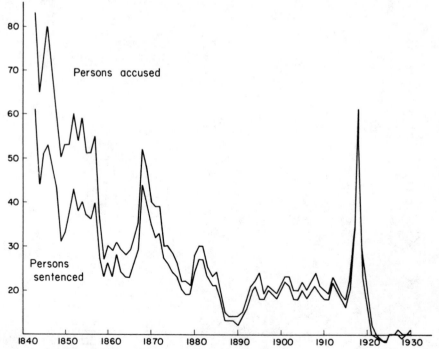

Figure III.3.2 Stockholm: Persons accused and sentenced, all categories of theft, per 100,000 population, 1843-1930

the early 1880s and 1890s, and, most strikingly, the World War I years saw sharp increases in rates of theft. Fraud and embezzlement, on the other hand, showed a consistent long-term increase, punctuated by short-term peaks in 1892, 1906, 1918, and 1930 (Figure III.3.3).

Dramatic increases in rates of conviction for drunkenness before the peak years of 1860, 1877, 1908, and 1919 were followed by similarly sharp declines, and the rates of 1930 were roughly comparable to those of the mid-nineteenth century (Figure III.3.4). One striking aspect of the drunkenness figures is their magnitude; in the peak years between 1875 and 1915 it was not unusual for 3.5 to 4.5 percent of the population to be convicted. The number of individuals convicted of the offense was doubtless less because of chronic recidivism. Authorities appear to have been especially attentive to disorderly conduct during the last quarter of the nineteenth century and in the first quarter of the twentieth, but rates otherwise look stable.

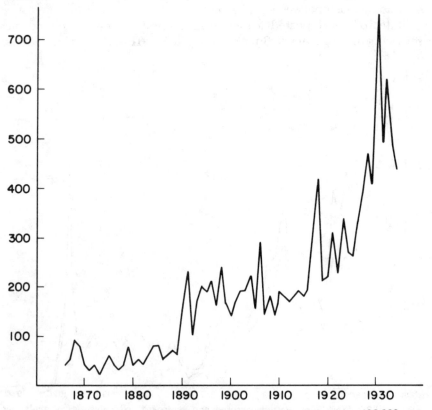

Figure III.3.3 Stockholm: Reported cases of fraud and embezzlement per 100,000 population, 1866-1934

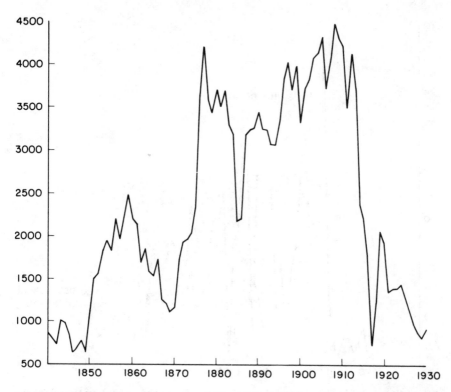

Figure III.3.4 Stockholm: Persons sentenced for drunkenness per 100,000 population, 1840-1930

Certain forms of consensual sexual activity apparently met with increasing official tolerance by the 1860s. There were approximately 30 convictions for fornication per year in the city during the years 1845-1854, but within a decade the total was negligible. Convictions for adultery, which numbered from 11 to 22 per year at midcentury, also virtually disappeared. The absence of a substantial change in the traditionally high rate of illegitimate births suggests the futility of official proscription. Data on nonconsensual violations of sexual mores (Figure III.3.5) reveal no clear trends. Rates of conviction for minor indecencies fluctuate drastically between 1870 and 1930 but begin and end the period at a rather low level. Gross sexual offenses, which include child molesting, show a very slight upward trend marked by considerable fluctuation.

The influence of economic conditions on rates of crime is again most apparent with regard to theft and drunkenness. Sharp upward movements in reported theft begin in 1866, 1880, 1891, and 1916. Each of these years either accompanied or followed immediately a period of economic adversity (Figure III.3.6). Indeed, the sharpest increase in rates of theft (1915-1918) occurred during a period that

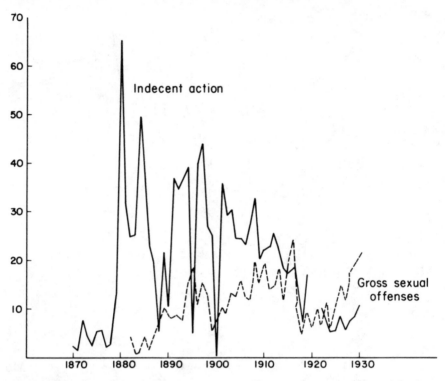

Figure III.3.5 Stockholm: Reported gross sexual offenses and persons sentenced for indecent action per 100,000, 1870-1930

has since come to be known as the "hunger years." The only noteworthy exception to this pattern took the form of a continued decrease in rates of theft during the economic downturn beginning in the mid-1880s. As the contraction persisted, however, an increase in theft convictions became evident. Sharp declines in theft rates occurred in the boom years of the late 1850s, the 1870s, and the years following World War I. These boom years were the occasion for typical increases in rates of conviction for drunkenness, which in turn dropped off in the 1860s, to a lesser extent during the mid-1880s, and in the World War I period.[5]

Rates of reported fraud and embezzlement—acquisitive crimes of the "white-collar" variety—followed a general upward trend that became quite pronounced after 1910. This series appears to have been less responsive to cycles of boom and depression than was the conventional theft series, despite discernible upswings in the early 1890s and during the war period. Rates of other offenses seem to have been influenced by noneconomic factors. The relationship between acquisitive criminality and economic conditions may also have been affected by changing tendencies to report such crimes. Since losses sustained during periods of economic adversity tend to be felt all the more sharply, victims may have reported them with more regularity than during relatively good times. Such a conjecture, however, is not subject to test.

Available data on the social and demographic backgrounds of offenders reveal some remarkable consistencies.[6] The typical

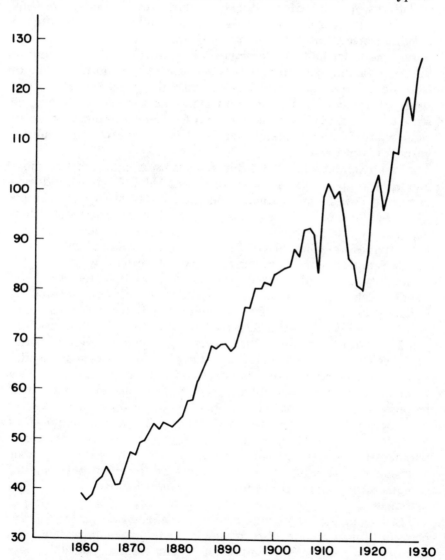

Figure III.3.6 Sweden: Index of real wages of workers in mining and manufacturing, 1860-1930

offender during the period was a poor unmarried male between the ages of 21 and 30. Females represented from six to twelve percent of the general criminal population, and from ten to twenty percent of those convicted of theft. Moreover, there appear to have been no significant changes in these proportions during the period. The clientele of the criminal justice system remained overwhelmingly working class.

Patterns of civil strife in Stockholm during the decades from 1850 to 1930 reflect the shifting tides of political and industrial conflict in Swedish society, at least up to the time of World War I. Clashes during the latter half of the nineteenth century usually arose out of the long-standing antagonism between the public and the police or troops quartered in the city. Subsequently they tended to stem from issues of franchise restriction and labor-management tension. Civil strife focused explicitly on conditions of extreme economic adversity were relatively unusual and were visible only during the "hunger years" of World War I.

A rare example of violence directed against members of a religious minority group was the anti-Semitic riot of 1852. A 45-year-old wine merchant, Lewi Lamm, attracted widespread attention by marrying his 17-year-old niece. During a two-day period there were periodic gatherings outside Lamm's house and in front of a neighboring synagogue, but activities were limited to the breaking of windows and the shouting of anti-Semitic slogans. Police arrested sixteen participants.[7]

Hostility toward the police of Stockholm was heightened in 1864 during a demonstration in favor of Swedish intervention on behalf of Denmark in her war with Prussia. Following a number of clashes, a crowd of about 1,000 was dispersed with the use of a water cannon, and 139 arrests were made.[8] The event precipitated severe criticism of Police Commissioner Wallenberg. Early the following year a leaflet was published depicting the commissioner as a statue with water hose in hand, surrounded by four pigs in police caps and armed with batons. Authorities reacted to this less-than-subtle metaphor by confiscating 1,025 copies of the lampoon.[9] There followed a series of protests that included the stoning of three police offices (where a number of windows were smashed) by groups comprised primarily of journeymen and workers. No fatalities were recorded, but some 62 demonstrators were convicted and awarded stiff fines or jail sentences.[10]

The unveiling of the statue of Karl XII at Kungsträgården was the occasion for a minor disturbance in 1868. An enterprising contractor, who had received permission to construct a grandstand near the site of the unveiling ceremonies, intended to charge an admission fee to as many spectators as he could accommodate. A number of individuals sought to destroy the platform in protest against what they perceived as greedy opportunism, and 36 arrests resulted.[11]

The 1870s were marked by disturbances involving troops stationed in the city, many of whom spent their leisure time in the numerous taverns located in the vicinity of the barracks. The soldiers were regarded as a rough and rowdy lot and were not infrequently arrested for their excesses. One such arrest in a public bar at Djurgården in August 1872 aroused both soldiers and members of the general public to the extent that a sizable crowd assembled outside of the police office, demanding the release of the arrested soldier. The protesters managed to break into the station, and the guardsman was able to escape. The riot was free of fatalities, although twelve policemen were injured.[12] The year 1875 saw three more large disturbances involving soldiers, one occasioned by an assignment of extra drill, the others resulting from fisticuffs between soldiers and civilians in Berzelii Park. Each of these events was characterized by police arrests and by demands from an assembled crowd for the release of those apprehended. In all, 47 arrests and one fatality resulted.[13]

One of the more violent disorders in the history of Stockholm occurred in September 1885, when a crowd of thousands assembled in front of the Grand Hotel to hear a free concert by the popular singer Kristina Nilson. There were few police on hand, and they were unable to control the crowd. As the audience began to move away from the hotel at the end of the performance, new crowds approached. Many people had been misinformed about the time of the concert and were just arriving. Confusion turned into panic: Nineteen people were trampled to death, and 100 were injured. The chief of police, who happened to be in the singer's hotel room at the time but took no action during the emergency, was censured for negligence.[14]

The phenomenon of collective public reaction to an arrest was common during the last quarter of the nineteenth century and was largely attributable to the unsavory reputation of the police during those years. Constables tended to be poorly educated and were known to drink while on duty. Rates of convictions for disorderly conduct and for forcible resistance to officials—charges generally made against participants in street disturbances—are further illustrative of events during the period (Figures III.3.7 and III.3.8). Disorderly conduct rates rose sharply from about 1865 to a peak in 1881, tending to decline thereafter. Rates of offenses against public authorities had declined from the high levels recorded during the 1840s but then began a gradual increase that lasted until the early years of the twentieth century.

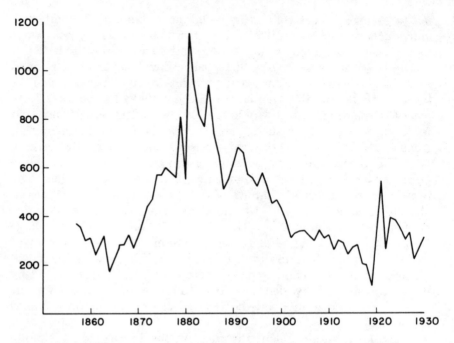

Figure III.3.7 Stockholm: Persons sentenced for disorderly conduct per 100,000 population, 1857-1930

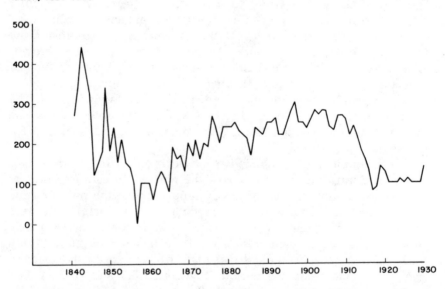

Figure III.3.8 Stockholm: Persons sentenced for violence or threats against officials, forcible resistance to officials, and other offenses against public authorities per 100,000 population, 1841-1930

The visible discontent among members of Stockholm's working class in the turbulent year of 1848 had never really abated. The parliamentary reforms of 1866 were relatively hollow, and the substantial increase in the city's population after 1860 swelled the ranks of the dissidents. An incident of industrial sabotage at Nybroviken in 1867 was illustrative of the tensions arising from industrialization, and 35 strikes occurred in the city between 1852 and 1879. It was not until the growth of the trade union movement in the 1890s, however, that significant industrial disturbances took place.[15]

Previously most of the strikes had been undertaken by skilled laborers; the work stoppages were of relatively short duration and were nonviolent. The 1890s, however, brought increased participation in strike activity by unskilled workers. There was also growing reliance by employers on strike-breakers, who received police protection, heightening traditional antagonism toward the police. Two strikes during the first decade of the twentieth century resulted in clashes with police. The tram workers' strike in 1900 at one point inspired a demonstration of some 6,000 strikers and sympathizers. The garbage collectors' strike in the spring of 1905 led to disturbances that were suppressed by two squadrons of cavalry. Although neither event resulted in fatalities, the latter produced 30 arrests and numerous injuries.

The general strike of 1909 followed a series of lockouts by Swedish employers, and despite the participation in the walkout of some 40,000 workers in Stockholm, there was no violence.[16] Indeed, leaders of the strike took great pains to prevent any outbreaks. The strike is generally regarded by historians as a setback for organized labor. The Social Democratic party was experiencing internal conflict. Its membership had begun to decline before the strike was called, and the erosion continued after the action petered out. A minor extension of the franchise was implemented during the period, but Sweden had to experience one more period of severe economic contraction and working-class mobilization before the gains of organized labor became visible.

Meanwhile, protest demonstrations over issues of political reform and economic relief had become stormier. One such meeting at Stortorget in February 1892 was attended by about 4,000 people; 27 participants were arrested, but no violence was reported.[17] Ten years later a franchise march from Lilljans to the People's Palace was the occasion for clashes between police and demonstrators, and some were prosecuted. Conservative spokesmen contended that participants were primarily drawn from the ranks of idle teenagers and "loose people," but evidence suggests that the most active protesters were workmen.[18]

Debate over continuing Sweden's tradition of neutrality resumed after the outbreak of World War I, and a number of demonstrations pro and con were held in the capital. One demonstration for neutrality led by the Social Democratic leader, Hjalmar Branting, attracted 100,000 peaceful participants. Sweden remained neutral during the war, only to suffer a severe depression resulting from the disruption of international trade. Soaring inflation was accompanied by food shortages, and suspicions of hoarding were rampant. Workers made forays into the countryside to "take inventories," and protests in the city were frequent. The only recorded instance of a food riot in Stockholm, the so-called potato riot, occurred in May 1917. A merchant was discovered to have been withholding some potatoes from sale, and a group of angry women prevailed on him to put his stock on the market. Two thousand people soon gathered, and when the inventory was exhausted, the crowd's anger was transferred to the police. Mounted police dispersed the crowd, and twenty persons were arrested.

The conservative government's unwillingness to restrain profiteering during the food shortages, combined with its apparent breach of neutrality during the Luxburg affair, led to a Liberal-Social Democratic coalition government following the elections of 1917.[19] Conservatives in Sweden concluded from events in Russia that continued resistance to reform would be fraught with great risk; they regarded the extension of democracy as the lesser of two evils. Aside from protests on behalf of leftists in the Finnish civil war and minor disturbances surrounding a strike at a building site in 1930, the streets of Stockholm were peaceful after the introduction of universal franchise in 1921. Dissident citizens had finally won the right to express their grievances through elected representatives.

THE RULERS AND THE LAW

Swedish penal law underwent significant change after 1850; with few exceptions, the modifications tended to involve lessening of the severity of official sanctions rather than broadening or narrowing the boundaries of defined criminality. One sign of diminishing severity was decreasing reliance on capital punishment. Numerous offenses were removed from the category of capital crimes in the 1850s and made punishable by life imprisonment; among them were robbery and counterfeiting in 1855, infanticide in 1858, and manslaughter in 1861. The 1865 recodification of the criminal law summarized these piecemeal reforms and made execution discretionary for all capital offenses except homicide committed by a prisoner at hard labor. In fact, even this provision had its discretionary components, since sentences could be commuted to life imprisonment under extenuating circumstances, and the power of royal pardon was retained. Soon capital punishment was all but abandoned in Sweden; only fifteen executions took place after 1865. The Riksdag came within one vote of abolishing the penalty in 1867, a noteworthy division for such a conservative body. The last execution in Sweden occurred in 1908, and the death penalty was formally abolished in 1921.

One significant characteristic of the 1865 recodification was the degree of attention devoted to potential aggravating or mitigating circumstances surrounding most noncapital offenses. The code provided for considerable latitude in sentencing and at the time of its implementation was regarded as one of the most progressive criminal codes in Europe.[20]

During the latter half of the nineteenth century, authorities in Sweden implemented a number of policies designed to regulate undesirable collective behavior. The heightening of industrial conflict toward the end of the century precipitated a series of modifications to the criminal law designed to suppress strikes and to discourage other forms of public protest.[21] One of the more significant measures, known as the "muzzle law" *(Munkorgslagen)*, was enacted in 1889. In response to oblique references to violent revolution in the Social Democratic press, the law extended the offense of incitement to crime to include public order offenses. The law was generally used to harass Social Democratic leaders; Hjalmar Branting himself was convicted in 1895 and sentenced to three months' imprisonment, although the High Court reduced his sentence to a fine in the following year.[22] A more severe measure was the so-called Åkarp Amendment of 1899, which prohibited attempts, either by threat or by violence, to induce anyone to participate in an on-the-job work stoppage. Such actions were made punishable by imprisonment with hard labor. Riksdag debate on the Åkarp Amendment was unusually heated, for the provision concerning criminalization of intent per se was inconsistent with contemporary legal practice. Such harsh regulations reflected the hostility with which Swedish conservatives viewed labor agitators, and the following remarks by a clergyman in the Riksdag are further illustrative: "If this will constitute a burden for the strike leaders and their front men, so be it, for such people should be regarded as no different from noxious animals."[23] Although the Åkarp Amendment and the "muzzle law" remained in effect until the late 1930s, they were not much invoked after the arrival of universal franchise in 1921.

In addition, officials sought to deal with some kinds of deviant behavior by means of administrative machinery outside the criminal justice system. The authorities were preoccupied with vagrancy during much of the nineteenth century, not because of any chronic labor shortage but owing to the persistent unemployment of the period. Large numbers of "drifters" were thought to constitute a potential threat to public order, and official attentiveness to this problem remained strong throughout the early years of Stockholm's rapid urban growth. Authorities made a partial distinction between actual criminals and potential criminals and chose to treat vagrancy as a civil matter. The institutions established to this end, however, were quasi-penal. The Vagrancy Act of 1885 empowered county boards to determine whether individuals wandered about "in idleness without seeking work" or threatened "public safety, order, and morals." Those unhappy souls who were judged to violate the act were liable to internment in agricultural colonies for a maximum of three years.[24] The new vagrancy law was heralded by some as "not a little advance in justice and humanity," but it appeared to others as a mere juggling of political symbols. The law's ambiguous wording constituted an implicit threat to the emerging socialist movement.[25] The rise in Liberal and Social Democratic influence during the first decades of the new century was accompanied by a sharp diminution in the application of the law, as Table III.3.1 illustrates. It was eventually replaced by systems of unemployment insurance and sociomedical treatment of chronic alcoholics.[26]

The system of police regulation of prostitution that began in 1838 was expanded in 1859 with the establishment of the *Prostitutionsbyrån*. This special agency within the police force was responsible for maintaining a registry of prostitutes, and for enforcing certain standards of behavior. Registrants were prohibited from appearing in public after 11 p.m., from enticing prospective clients

Table III.3.1 Sweden: Average Yearly Apprehensions
for Vagrancy, 1876-1930

Year	Number
1876-1880	7,173
1881-1885	5,884
1886-1890	2,491
1891-1895	2,009
1896-1900	2,187
1901-1905	2,562
1906-1910	2,332
1911-1915	1,999
1916-1920	965
1921-1925	891
1926-1930	726

Source: Statistisk Årsbok för Sverige, 1940, p. 283.

through the window or with shouts, and from wearing sensational clothing. Violations of these regulations were punishable by fine or by forced labor for one year.[27] The *Reglementeringssystemet*, as it was called, functioned imperfectly. Clandestine prostitution flourished, whether through brothels, street solicitation, or establishments falsely designated as "cigar shops" and "shooting galleries." Continued high rates of venereal disease prompted officials to consider alternatives to police regulation, and in the early years of the current century an official commission recommended their abolition. In 1918 these recommendations were implemented, and a venereal disease control program was established, based on free clinics and compulsory registration of VD cases. Professional prostitutes became subject to the provisions of the Vagrancy Act, thus were formally exempt from criminal proceedings, although liable to internment on the pronouncement of civil authorities. Feminist groups protested that application of the Vagrancy Act to prostitutes but not to their clients constituted a form of sex discrimination, but the act was already falling into desuetude. By 1930 it was applied only in exceptional cases, and a policy of official tolerance prevailed.[28]

Public concern with juvenile rowdiness around the turn of the century brought about significant modification of the criminal law with regard to youthful offenders. In accordance with legislation enacted in 1902, children under fifteen who were found to have committed a criminal offense were subject to the supervision of a child welfare board empowered to place delinquents under supervision or, where deemed appropriate, to order a child's confinement in a juvenile institution. Offenders between the ages of 15 and 21 were subject to the general provisions of the criminal law but could be sentenced to correctional education in special facilities for up to four years.[29] Paradoxically, this term was quite often in excess of the sentence an adult offender might draw for a comparable offense.

Official attempts to reduce the rate of alcohol consumption were conditioned by an array of widely divergent values held by varied interests. Authorities were concerned with the physical and social well-being of the citizenry and were also attentive to what appeared to be a distinct relationship between drinking and crime. Not the least of the official aims was the augmentation of government revenue. With the coming of industrialization, employers voiced increasing concern over the adverse effects of alcohol consumption on employee productivity.[30] The temperance movement had its base in the liberal and working-class segments of society and indeed became one of the great popular movements in Swedish history. Its concerns lay primarily with the health and well-being of the general public.

The convergent aims of such diverse groups made for increasing efforts at regulating consumption. Beginning with a renewed prohibition on household distilling in 1855, the latter part of the nineteenth century was a time of such policies as the reduction in the number of retail licenses and the introduction of a retail liquor monopoly.[31] Total prohibition was in effect briefly during the 1909 general strike, and a system of rationing was introduced in 1914. The issue of prohibition was put before the public in a referendum in 1922, but it failed of passage. Although the foregoing policies were accompanied by attempts at circumvention in the form of illicit distilling and smuggling, rates of consumption appear to have remained stable in the years following World War I and were considerably lower than they had been during the closing years of the nineteenth century.[32]

The phenomenon of chronic alcoholism became the target of governmental activity during the early 1900s, and although the resulting policies lay beyond the purview of the criminal law, they were distinctly quasi-penal. The focus of concern was not on the chronic alcoholic per se but on those who were in a state of manifest physical debilitation or were regarded as a burden on or nuisance to family or society. Internment of such individuals became compulsory in 1913, following the lines of the existing procedures for the internment of vagrants, which largely dropped from use. Indeed, many who had been interned under the Vagrancy Act were themselves addicted to alcohol; the Inebriety Act improved on the existing system by providing internees with specialized rehabilitation programs. In a manner similar to that of the vagrancy program internship, proceedings were initiated by a local temperance board. The internship could last four years for offenders alleged to be dangerous.[33]

Despite the diminishing severity of penal sanctions in general, authorities saw fit to impose strong restrictions on the few individuals thought to be dangerous or incorrigible. Chronic recidivists, offenders deemed mentally defective, and those regarded as not responsive to rehabilitation were liable to indefinite detention under the provisions of the Habitual Criminals and Abnormal Offenders Acts of 1927. Sixty-six individuals were sentenced under these statutes between 1927 and 1929, mainly for crimes against property.[34]

INSTITUTIONS OF PUBLIC ORDER

The Police

Police activity in Stockholm after the reorganization of 1850 was increasingly diversified. A detective force consisting of four constables under the supervision of a district attorney was established in 1853. Their responsibilities lay in the citywide surveillance of suspected criminals. The group was given the formal designation of detective department *(detectivavdelningen)* in 1864. The special unit created in 1859 for the purpose of regulating prostitution has been mentioned. In 1876 the Central Department, a special unit responsible for the training of recruits, was established. The formal program included training in departmental regulations, civil and criminal law, fencing and military drill, and the operation of a telephone switchboard. A year-long apprenticeship included patrol work, and recruits were officially designated constables following satisfactory completion of a qualifying examination. Additional responsibilities of the Central Department consisted of traffic control and order maintenance. The department also included a detachment of mounted police.

In 1885 a special group known as the *ordonnansavdelningen* was formed and undertook responsibilities that were without precedent in the civil strata of Stockholm. Comprised of six constables and one police superintendent, the group was primarily involved in welfare work with the families of arrested persons. In addition, the constables served as orderlies for police officials.

A riot squad, formally constituted within the Central Department in 1887, was provided with a wagon and a sleigh to enhance its mobility. Throughout the period garrison troops and reserve constables were available for temporary crowd control assignments.

By the turn of the century members of the police force had grown increasingly dissatisfied over the lack of employment security and educational opportunities. Members of the force could be fired summarily if their superiors deemed their performance unsuitable, and this was a particular grievance. A union was organized in 1903 but failed to bring about an immediate improvement of working conditions. Although the City of Stockholm established a school for policemen in 1917, further reforms had to await the enactment of legislation at the national level in 1925, when standards for salary, retirement pensions, and vacations were established, as well as a program of insurance in case of death or accident in the line of duty. The state assumed control of the school previously established by the city and also instituted organizational changes permitting the deployment of police across district boundaries in certain extraordinary situations. These steps were the first taken in the direction of a national reorganization of police forces, a policy implemented in 1965.

Meanwhile, the differentiation of police activity continued. A central bureau for fingerprints established in 1907 provided criminalogical services for police departments throughout Sweden during the period 1920-1939. In 1917 the detective force was removed from the operational control of the district attorney's office and renamed the Criminal Investigation Division. Three years later a special unit consisting of sixteen men was formed in response to the increased activity in illegal distilling. A harbor police unit, equipped with motorboat, was also created in that year for the purpose of reducing smuggling operations.

Changes in the size and structure of the Stockholm police are reflected in Table III.3.2 and Figure III.3.9. The growth of the force

Table III.3.2 Stockholm Police Force, Size and Organization, 1850-1924

Year	Detective Department CID	Prostitution Department	Orderly Department	Central Department	Harbor Department	District Patrols
1850	—	—	—	—	—	390
1853	4	—	—	—	—	406
1907	68	12	17	121	—	477
1915	73	12	17	182	—	559
1918	102	12	17	148	—	569
1922	119	—	38	190	15	619
1924	124	—	39	195	15	610

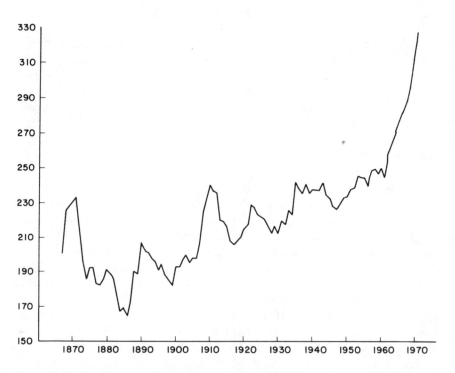

Figure III.3.9 Stockholm: Police manpower levels per 100,000 population, 1867-1970

kept abreast of the city's population increase with the exception of the last three decades of the nineteenth century. Changes in the pattern of growth appear to have been governed primarily by budgetary considerations, although the significant augmentation of 1900-1910 can be largely explained by the political tensions of the time.

The Administration of Justice

A number of significant innovations were introduced in a judicial system whose fundamental structure remained little changed from what it had been in 1850. Traditionally, petty offenses committed in Stockholm were tried before the police court, with the Governor of Stockholm acting as the presiding judge. In the mid-nineteenth century, as the administrative affairs of the growing city became increasingly time-consuming, the governor delegated his judicial responsibilities to the chief of police, who thus found himself performing the roles of chief law enforcement officer, prosecutor, and judge. To lighten the burdens on the chief, a special judgeship was created for the police court in 1864.

The movement away from mandatory sentences, first apparent in the provisions of the law concerning capital punishment, was extended to lesser offenses after the turn of the century. The introduction of the suspended sentence, inspired by similar modification of the British judicial process, took place in 1906. Applicable initially to prisoners awarded sentences of up to three months' hard labor or six months' simple imprisonment, its provisions were extended to six months and one year, respectively, in 1918. Suspensions were conditional on good behavior during a period of probation supervised by an officer of the court and were subject to revocation. There was increasing reliance on probation during the 1920s, when the recidivism rate among probationers was about ten percent.[35]

Following a precedent set in Göteborg, the City of Stockholm in 1884 retained and paid a lawyer to assist the needy with legal problems. The services of one person were soon found to be inadequate, and a full-time bureau was established in 1913. Six years later the Riksdag passed the Free Legal Proceedings Act, designed to assist indigent and low-income citizens in bearing the costs of both civil and criminal cases. Discretion regarding determination of need was conferred on the court, and judges were empowered to waive court costs, appoint a public attorney, or authorize reimbursement for privately retained counsel. Although most of those who benefited from the statute were litigants in civil cases, a number of criminal defendants were accorded representation.[36]

Despite the impressive response to the recommendations of Crown Prince Oscar, Swedish prisons were not without their shortcomings. In the early 1850s about one prisoner in five suffered from scurvy. Inmates at Långholmen in Stockholm were allowed to consume aquavit, and on one December day in 1853 a group of dissatisfied and intoxicated prisoners began a riot. Although the riot was finally suppressed by a detachment of troops and a group of volunteers from a nearby factory, considerable damage occurred and a number of prisoners' rolls and documents were burned.

In 1859 the central board established in 1825 for the administration of workhouses became the *Fångvårdsstyrelsen*, or National Prisons Board, the central authority for all prisons in Sweden. Shortly thereafter, a program was introduced that involved the hiring of prison labor by private manufacturers. Such arrangements, reminiscent of eighteenth century workhouse policies, endured for a number of decades; prisoners from Långholmen worked at the Stockholms Yllefabriks AB from 1867 to 1896. The major benefits of these programs seem to have fallen to the employers, who were thereby able to undercut an already glutted labor market.[37]

Meanwhile, the ambitious program of construction that had begun in midcentury continued. Thirty-four regional prisons were constructed by 1864, and renovations were completed on the central prisons during the 1870s. Although custodial conditions were still quite grim by twentieth century standards, Sweden had become a recognized leader in penal reform, and Stockholm was selected as the site of the International Penitentiary Congress of 1878. The trend toward small, specialized facilities continued throughout the period, with prisoners classified and assigned to facilities according to age, length and type of sentence, mental capacity, and prospects for rehabilitation. Prisoners could also be transferred to minimum-security institutions as they demonstrated cooperativeness and responsibility. By the 1880s prisoners were receiving a small salary for their labor and had access to general instruction and religious training. In 1885 Swedish prison libraries contained 36,000 volumes.[38]

Throughout the period a general reduction in the length of prison sentences took place. Fewer and fewer life sentences were awarded after 1850, and hundreds of life sentences were reduced by royal order, as Table III.3.3 indicates. This practice was formalized by the Conditional Release Act of 1906, which authorized the granting of parole to any prisoner who had served two-thirds of his sentence. By 1931 more than 1,500 prisoners had been formally paroled, and only three were noted as having violated the conditions of their release.[39] Authorities came to rely much more heavily on parole in subsequent years.

Table III.3.3 Sweden: Prisoners Serving Life Sentences, 1851-1930

Years	Average number of life sentences awarded	Average number of prisoners serving life terms
1851-1855	137	1,501
1856-1860	81	1,403
1861-1865	89	1,195
1866-1870	54	967
1871-1875	43	687
1876-1880	25	505
1881-1885	16	361
1886-1890	16	262
1891-1895	9	207
1896-1900	8	161
1901-1905	4	119
1906-1910	4	81
1911-1915	1	61
1916-1920	2	46
1921-1925	3	36
1926-1930	3	29

Source: Statistisk Årsbok för Sverige, 1940, p.283

One of the most influential discussions of correctional practice during the period was that of Knut Olivecrona, a distinguished jurist.[40] Although some of his criticisms were quite reactionary (he contended that prisoners were overfed and should not be paid), others were progressive. Olivecrona recommended that younger prisoners and juveniles be accorded specialized treatment apart from conventional criminals, and this reform was soon implemented. Perhaps Olivecrona's most significant contribution lay in his criticism of the deprivation of civic rights. Offenders serving time for crimes against property were prohibited from voting, holding public office, or engaging in commerce for five to ten years after their release from prison. The provisions concerning voting and holding office made little difference under the rigid franchise restrictions of the period, but limitations on commercial activity severely impeded readjustment during the early years of freedom. Although Olivecrona's criticisms were echoed by Liberal leader S. A. Hedin and by the chaplain at Långholmen Prison, deprivation of civic rights continued until the 1930s.[41]

THE CONSEQUENCES OF POLICIES OF PUBLIC ORDER

It appears that criminality and civil strife were more responsive to cyclical changes in the economy and to fundamental alterations in the political structure than they were to reforms in the criminal justice system. Riots (and thefts) tended to occur during periods of economic austerity, particularly before the introduction of universal franchise. The increase in white-collar criminality seems to have been largely a function of expanding opportunities—the number of white-collar jobs in Stockholm grew considerably during the period. Apparently the influence of rapid urban growth was rather slight, the dislocations of rapid urbanization being reflected primarily in increased rates of disorderly conduct, drunkenness, and vagrancy-type offenses.

Throughout the period there was a decrease in the tendency to resort to violence by state and citizen alike. Diminishing reliance on capital punishment was accompanied by declining rates of assault and a consistently low rate of homicide. It is impossible to specify the causes of these trends, but one may speculate that the growth of humanitarian thought was facilitated by the unusual homogeneity of the society. Perhaps the individual and the government followed each other's example.

Changes in the size and structure of the police force appear to have had little impact on the incidence of disorder. Public mistrust endured long after steps toward professionalization were taken in 1876. Moreover, the years of greatest growth in the size of the force (1910-1912) were followed by a drastic increase in theft.[42]

NOTES TO CHAPTER III.3

1. Criminal statistics for years before 1866 may be found in *Bidrag till Sveriges officiella statistik—Ser. B Rättsväsendet*. For the period 1866-1905, see *Berättelse angående Stockholms Kommunalförvaltning;* for 1906 and subsequent years, see *Statistisk Årsbok för Stockholms Stad.*

2. See Sven Ulric Palme, *Samhället och barnen på änglamakerskornas tid* (Fataburen: Nordiska museets och Skansens årsbok, 1971).

3. As late as 1905 a woman in Stockholm was accused of having taken in seventeen foster children at the same time, and of these seven had already perished. Apart from general neglect, the woman had given the children opium. See Ann-Charlotte Pergament, "Anteckningar om de utomäktenskapliga barnens rättsliga ställning i Sverige före 1917 års lagstiftningsverk" (Trebetygsuppsats, Historiska Institutet, Stockholms Universitet, 1970), p. 16.

4. Ibid., p. 23.

5. The decrease in rates of conviction for drunkenness during the mid-1880s was also attributable to relaxed enforcement practices. Police for a time were escorting drunks home rather than to the police chamber. It should also be noted that boom times in Stockholm during the late nineteenth century saw unusually large numbers of single men arriving from rural areas to take seasonal construction jobs.

6. Irregular data on the sex, age, and occupational backgrounds of offenders at various stages of disposition may be found in *Statistisk Årsbok för Stockholms Stad.*

7. Annika Christiansson, Christer Damm, and Torsten Heinberg, "Upplopp, Strejker, och Demonstrationer i Stockholm Åren 1800-1970" (Kriminalvetenskapliga Institutet, Stockholms Universitet, 1974), pp. 23-24.

8. Jane Cederquist, "Upplopp i Stockholm, 1860-1900" (Historiska Institutet, Stockholms Universitet, 1971), p. 14.

9. Ibid., p. 20.

10. Ibid., p. 31.

11. Christiansson et al., op. cit., pp. 25-26.

12. Ibid., p. 25.

13. Ibid., p. 44. See also *Rådhusrättens protokoll 1875*, avd. 6, nr. 214.

14. Christiansson et al., op. cit., p. 27.

15. Forty-four trade unions were founded in Stockholm during the years 1885-1889. Jane Cederquist, "Strike Behaviour Among Different Strata Within the Working Class in Stockholm, 1870-1910" (Unpublished paper, University of Stockholm, n.d.), p. 22.

16. For a general discussion of the strike see Bernt Schiller, *Storstrejken 1909: Förhistoria och orsaker* (Göteborg: Akademiförlaget, 1967).

17. Cederquist, "Upplopp i Stockholm," p. 23.

18. Ibid., p. 49; Jane Helin, En rösträttsdemonstration i Stockholm år 1902," in *Fran Medeltid till dataålder; festskrift till Sven Ulrik Palme* (Uddevalla: Rabén & Sjögren 1972), pp. 115-116.

19. The Luxburg affair involved the use of the Swedish diplomatic cable by Germany. For a discussion of the tensions of the time and their influence on reform, see Tilton, "Social Origins of Liberal Democracy."

20. Raoul de la Grasserie, *Les Codes Suédois de 1734* (Paris: A. Pedone, 1895), pp. LV-LVII.

21. The period 1887-1890 was marked by legislation empowering authorities to arrest public speakers and to disperse gatherings without any disruption having occurred. See de la Grasserie, op. cit., pp. 137-144; and Per Eklund, *Rätten i Klasskampen* (Stockholm: Tidensforlag, 1974).

22. Eklund, op. cit. p. 328. Branting's speech contained a vague allusion to mutiny in the event of a Swedish invasion of Norway.

23. AK 1899:9:29 (Transl. Karsten Åström). See also Eklund, op. cit., p. 101ff.

24. Olof Kinberg, "Criminal Policy in Sweden During the Last Fifty Years," *Journal of Criminal Law and Criminology*, 24 (1933), 314-135.

25. *Fattigvård och folkförsäkring*, andra serien 7 hft, p. 1; Leif Kihlberg, *Folktribunen Adolf Hedin* (Stockholm: Albert Bonniers, 1972).

26. Hardy Göransson, "Treatment of Criminals and Other Asocial Individuals," *Annals of the American Academy of Political and Social Science*, 197 (May 1939), 132.

27. Johanssen, "Prostitution in Stockholm," p. 3.

28. Kinberg, op. cit., p. 312; S. Hellerstrom and M. Tottie, "Venereal Diseases in Sweden: 1813-1962," *Acta Demato-Venereologica*, 43: 3 (1963), 199-202.

29. Göransson, op. cit., pp. 128-130.

30. *Beredningsutskottets utlåtande och memorial* 1864-1867; 1865-1876-1877.

31. *Beredningsutskottets utlåtande och memorial 1864-1867; Utskänknings-bolagets protokoll, SSA;* Halfdan Bengtsson, "The Temperance Movement and Temperance Legislation in Sweden," *Annals of the American Academy of Political and Social Science*, 197 (May 1938), 134-153.

32. Rates of arrest for drunkenness, liquor consumption, and incidence of chronic alcoholism in Stockholm all decreased during the period 1900-1930. See Olov Kinberg, "Temperance Legislation in Sweden," *Annals of the American Academy of Political and Social Science*, 163, (September 1932), 210-211.

33. Kinberg, "Criminal Policy in Sweden," pp. 313-315.

34. Ibid., pp. 320-330.

35. Ibid., p. 317.

36. Lloyd K. Garrison, "Legal Service for Low Income Groups in Sweden," *American Bar Association Journal*, 26 (March 1940), 215-220; 26, (April 1940), pp. 293-297.

37. Gunnar Rudstedt, *Långholmen, Spinnhusset och fängelset under två sekel* (Lund: Carl Bloms, 1972), pp. 140-141.

38. G. F. Almquist, *Résumé Historique*, p. 46. Many of these books were religious tracts, which, if at all read by the inmates, were generally not very entertaining.

39. Kinberg, "Criminal Policy in Sweden," p. 318.

40. Knut Olivecrona, *Om orsakerna till återfall i brott och om medlen att minska dessa orsakers skadliga verkningar* (Stockholm: P. A. Norstedt & Söner, 1872).

41. Sven Sperlings, "Kriminalitetsutvecklingen i Stockholm 1840-1964," (unpublished manuscript, Institute of Criminology, University of Stockholm, 1973), p. 55; *Social Tidskrift*, 1907, no. 4, p. 167.
42. While such an increase could be interpreted as reflecting greater police efficiency, it appears to have reflected real changes in the rate of criminal behavior per se.

CRIME, CONFLICT, AND PUBLIC ORDER, 1931-1970s

PATTERNS OF CRIME AND CONFLICT

Patterns of criminality in Stockholm since 1930 demonstrate some rather striking trends. These may be assessed with some certainty up to 1965, when the reorganization of police and the recodification of the criminal law was accompanied by changes in accounting procedures.[1] The most significant trends are the dramatic increases in rates of acquisitive crime, which began in the 1940s. Rates of theft were low and relatively stable until 1938, but by 1942 they surpassed the rates that had been reached during the "crime wave" of World War I (Figure III.4.1). After a brief decline in 1950, the rates continued sharply upward; the increase from 1930 to 1970 was approximately sevenfold. Rates of robberies and reported fraud and embezzlement showed a similar rise (Figures III.4.2 and III.4.3). A gradual upswing in the white-collar crimes was punctuated by peaks in 1930 and 1951, then rates rose to unprecedented levels throughout the 1950s, interrupted only by a brief drop in 1969.

It is important to recognize that these increases were visible within numerous specific categories of theft—from robbery to shoplifting— and also at various states of the dispositional process—from reporting to conviction. Thus the chances that these trends represent solely a statistical artifact, not a real increase in rates of crime, are slim.

Violent crime also posted an increase during the period, but a less drastic one. Rates of reported assault and battery remained low and relatively stable until 1952, when they began an irregular upward movement(Figure III.4.4). Homicide rates remained strikingly low, although an aggregate index of murder, attempted murder, and

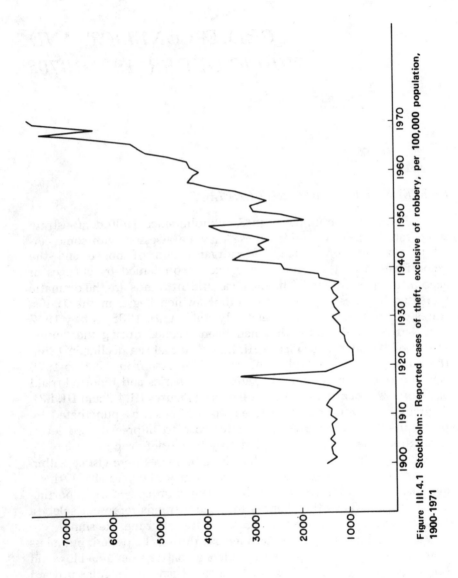

Figure III.4.1 Stockholm: Reported cases of theft, exclusive of robbery, per 100,000 population, 1900-1971

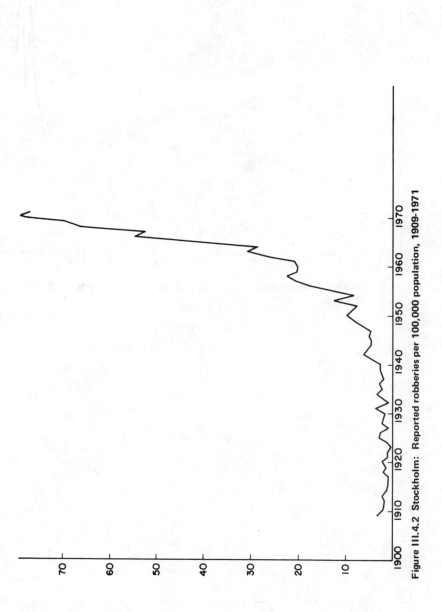

Figure III.4.2 Stockholm: Reported robberies per 100,000 population, 1909-1971

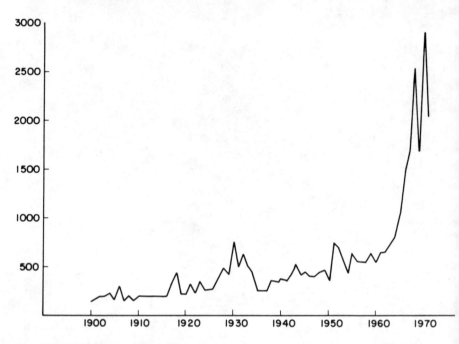

Figure III.4.3 Stockholm: Reported cases of fraud and embezzlement per 100,000 population, 1900-1971

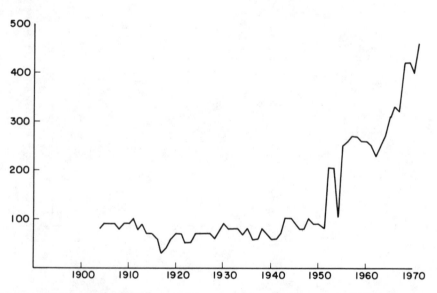

Figure III.4.4 Stockholm: Reported cases of assault and battery per 100,000 population, 1904-1971

manslaughter offenses rose during the 1950s and 1960s before dropping off to (normal) low levels by the end of the decade (Figure III.4.5). The latter fluctuations did not reflect any real changes in the incidence of serious violence, however; they instead resulted from inconsistencies in the use of the label "attempted murder" to refer to more serious assaults.[2]

One major increase observed during the period was the significant jump in rates of conviction for drunkenness that followed the abolition of liquor rationing in 1955 (Figure III.4.6).[3] Drunkenness constituted the largest source of arrests for nontraffic offenses during the period 1955-1965 and prompted authorities to consider alternatives to rigorous enforcement of the applicable law.

Statistics on the incidence of criminal abortion suffer from problems of reportability and inclusion with other crimes. In general, they reflect sporadic enforcement of abortion laws, the increased

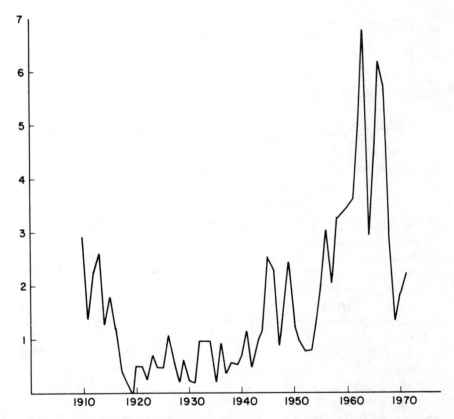

Figure III.4.5 Stockholm: Reported cases of murder, attempted murder, and manslaughter per 100,000 population, 1910-1971

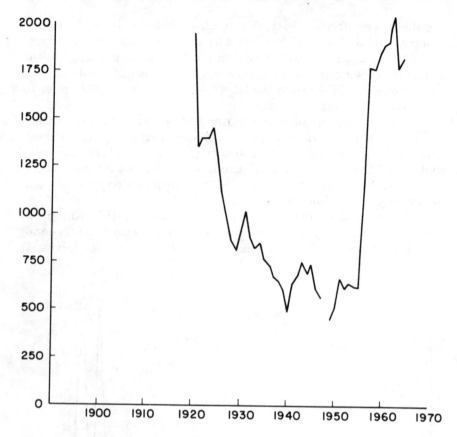

Figure III.4.6 Stockholm: Convictions for drunkenness per 100,000 population, 1920-1971

effectiveness of contraceptive methods, and the gradual relaxation of definitions of criminal abortion in the late 1960s. The most intensive enforcement efforts took place in 1934, when a professional abortionist was discovered, and during the late 1940s (Figure III.4.7). Debate on the issue of criminal abortions became intense in the early 1970s, as de jure prohibitions remained in force despite growing public opposition to their application.

The reported incidence of "crimes inflicting damage," primarily vandalism against public and private property, manifested a trend similar to that of acquisitive crime. Rates remained low until 1948, then began a sharp upward movement that continued through the early 1970s (Figure III.4.8). Rates of reported rape posted an irregular increase, but this offense remained relatively rare. The incidence of convictions for indecent public behavior remained low

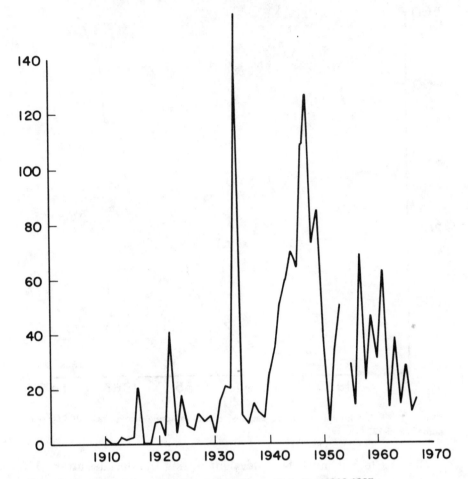

Figure III.4.7 Stockholm: Illegal abortions known to the police, 1910-1967

throughout this period (see Figure III.4.9), probably because of some combination of an actual decline in morally offensive behavior and more official toleration.

Some abuse of amphetamines was noted in Sweden during the period 1938-1960. Drug use did not appear to have posed significant problems for officials until the mid-1960s, however, when the traffic in cannabis and harder drugs began to increase in Stockholm and the larger cities, spreading to rural areas of the country as well. Increasing demand for illicit drugs led to considerable smuggling activity and produced a crackdown on offenders. Beginning in 1967 there were 641 arrests made in Sweden, and the total increased to more than 2,900 in 1969.[4]

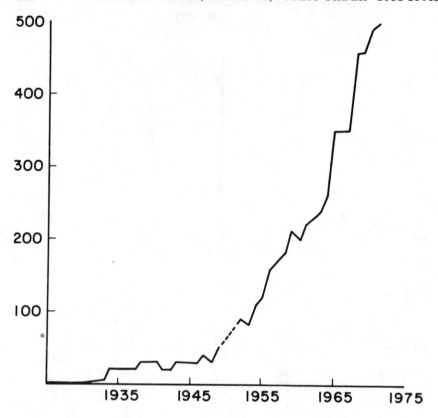

Figure III.4.8 Stockholm: Reported cases of crimes inflicting damage per 100,000 population, 1925-1971

Civil strife was much less prevalent during the decades after 1930 than before. The granting of universal franchise and the continued dominance of Social Democratic governments served to relieve much of the discontent that had been expressed in the streets of Stockholm during earlier years. With few exceptions, the riots that did occur were free of explicit ideological content. Street fights among groups of young males during March 1948 attracted large numbers of onlookers, but these disturbances came to an end without serious incident when mounted police dispersed a crowd of about 5,000 following a fracas at Södermalm. Three years later a similar series of "street" fights occurred in Berzelii Park. Damages or injuries apparently were not significant, but suppression of the disturbances was inhibited by lack of police manpower.

New Year's Eve 1956-1957 was the occasion for one of the larger riots in Stockholm's recent history. A few windows were smashed and one car was overturned, but most of the participants' animosity

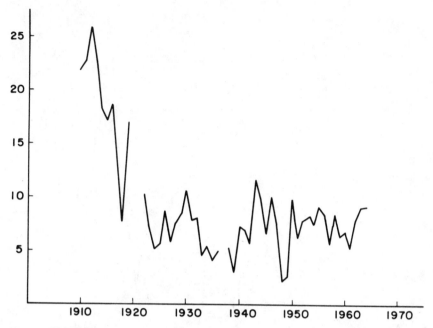

Figure III.4.9 Stockholm: Convictions for indecent action per 100,000 population, 1910-1964

appears to have been directed at the police.[5] A brawl between groups of youths at Hötorget in 1965 had similar overtones. One policeman was injured and a police car overturned. Twenty-five arrests resulted. Although small-scale clashes occurred in subsequent years, there were no serious or lasting consequences. The principal manifestation of these and subsequent disorders is the high incidence of offenses involving violence or threats against officials (mainly the police) in the 1950s and 1960s, evident in Figure III.4.10.

The growing American involvement in Indochina inspired a number of demonstrations in Stockholm during the late 1960s; these were not directed at domestic authorities, however, and typically were limited to an occasional smashing of windows at the U.S. Trade Center and the burning of the American flag. Forty protesters were arrested during one demonstration in 1966. By 1969 Swedish authorities had themselves become outspokenly critical of United States foreign policy and treated the demonstrations with considerable restraint.

In the spring of 1971 a series of protests arose over the impending removal of a stand of elm trees to facilitate construction of a new subway station. The protests were largely nonviolent, although demonstrators were sometimes singled out for attack by unsympathetic motorcycle gang members. City officials relented, having

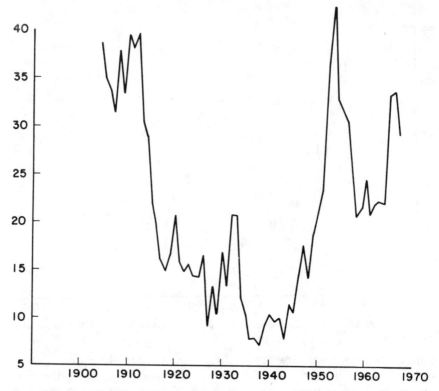

Figure III.4.10 Stockholm: Reported offenses involving violence or threats against officials per 100,000 population, 1904-1967

decided that construction could proceed without removing the trees.[6]

The economic correlates of crime rates in Stockholm after 1930 reflect a sharp departure from the patterns visible in previous eras. The most severe economic contraction of the period, the Depression of the 1930s, was not accompanied by an increase in rates of theft, as might be expected. These rates remained low and stable until 1938, by which time the rate of unemployment in Sweden had fallen to below 10 percent for the first time in nearly a decade. Rates of drunkenness were low during the Depression, but the downward trend had begun during the relatively comfortable decade of the 1920s and appears to have been more profoundly influenced by the system of rationing then in force. Only the incidence of illegal abortions appears to have increased during the period of economic hardship.

It is strikingly obvious that the dramatic increases in theft and the more gradual increases in rates of violent crime began during a period of economic recovery and continued during times of unparalleled prosperity. Ironically, Stockholm's most recent crime wave occurred as expanding municipal and national services raised levels of well-being to a degree that would be viewed by much of the world's population as idyllic.

These developments, which might at first be puzzling, are open to a number of plausible explanations. Most obvious are the factors that reflect the relationship of the city to the metropolitan area as a whole. Although the population of the city proper declined during the 1960s, that of the Stockholm region continued to grow. The increased mobility of metropolitan Stockholmers facilitated travel into the city for such diverse activities as work, recreation, shopping, and crime. Furthermore, increases in rates of crime were partially attributable to a decline in the base population from which the rates were calculated. In addition, the police reorganization of 1965 was accompanied by changes in accounting procedures. Official returns before 1965 tended to understate the incidence of certain minor offenses. Following the reorganization, official records reflected more accurately the volume of offenses known to the police.

These artifactual amplifications account for only a portion of the observed increases, however; other factors must be considered. First among these is the possibility that criminality may vary with opportunity. The tenfold increase in the number of automobiles registered in Sweden between 1950 and 1971 could hardly have discouraged auto theft, which showed a fivefold increase during the same period. Similarly, the display of retail merchandise became more open and products themselves more abundant than at any previous time. Sharply rising rates of fraud and embezzlement may be largely explained by the appearance and increasing use of such negotiable instruments as checks and credit cards. The rates themselves were significantly amplified by the practice of counting each illegal transaction as a separate offense.

Rates of assault appear also to have been influenced by the expansion of opportunity; members of the first postwar generation were reaching the age at which aggressiveness is often expressed with the fists. The relative size of this age cohort accounted for proportionately more prospective adversaries. Moreover, inhibitions of aggressive behavior were unquestionably lowered by the increase in the consumption of alcohol during the late 1960s and early 1970s. Rates of assault and rates of alcohol consumption during the period showed a strong positive relationship.[7]

The demographic characteristics of offenders were subject to little change during the period, although two departures from previous patterns were evident. An estimated 25 percent of petty thefts in the

1960s were attributed to very youthful offenders—those below the age of fifteen. The age of those convicted of assault also appears to have dropped slightly from previous years; individuals between the ages of fifteen and seventeen are noticeably overrepresented, followed closely by those between the ages of eighteen and twenty.[8] In addition, foreign nationals—particularly Finns and Yugoslavs—committed more than a proportionate share of theft and assault. Otherwise the typical offender of the early 1970s conformed to a more traditional mold; single males from low-income groups continued to dominate the clientele of the criminal justice system. This class differential is also apparent, although to a lesser extent, among those convicted of drunken driving. The improvement in the status of women in Swedish society during the twentieth century has produced no wave of female criminality. Rates of crime by females have increased, to be sure, but not as much as rates of male criminality: Females constitute a smaller proportion of all offenders than they did as "second-class citizens."[9]

The consistent relationship between socioeconomic status and criminality over the course of Stockholm's history seems to clash with conventional notions of an emerging socialist society. Income inequalities remain, however, and Swedish workers tend to be well aware of and generally dissatisfied with these differences.[10] It is therefore premature to describe Sweden as a classless society, and the socioeconomic correlates of criminality will likely persist as long as such inequalities are perceived.

THE RULERS AND THE LAW

Piecemeal modification of Swedish criminal law has occurred periodically since 1930, and these changes were summarized in the revised criminal code that became effective in 1965. In addition to the criminal code, a number of other statutes define behaviors punishable by fine or imprisonment. The most important concern drunken driving and various narcotics offenses; others cover such diverse behavior as unfair commercial activity (1931), violations of fish and game regulations (1938, 1950), and tax evasion (1971). The penal code was itself expanded in 1971 to proscribe seizure of aircraft and interference with aircraft operations.

Intemperance on the highway was viewed with intense concern by Swedish authorities as far back as the 1930s. Indeed, a group of nineteen temperance-minded Riksdagsmen from five different parties advocated the imprisonment of convicted drunken drivers in 1923. The temperance motorists' association (MHF) was founded in 1932 and has consistently pressed for stronger sanctions against drinking drivers.[11] Legislation in 1934 prescribed mandatory prison sentences for routine drunk driving offenses, and amendments in 1941 made driving with a blood alcohol concentration of 0.08 percent or more a criminal offense per se. The offense carried a heavy fine, and offenders with concentrations of 0.15 percent or more were subject to imprisonment. New legislation enacted in 1957 broadened the scope of existing statutes by lowering the minimum liability level from 0.08 to 0.05 percent. Recidivism was met with progressively more stringent punishment, including longer prison terms and loss of license. Provisions of the civil law were also modified to discourage driving while intoxicated. Convicted drunken drivers who were involved in traffic accidents were required to reimburse insurance companies for successful damage claims.

In the years after World War II a number of statutes were enacted that in effect created new criminal offenses, albeit relatively minor ones. A requirement as of 1947 that employers deduct tax payments from payrolls resulted in nearly 30,000 prosecutions (nationwide) for delinquency by 1961; the vast majority of offenders were assessed small fines. The application of drunken driving sanctions was extended to operators of mopeds (motor-powered bicycles) in 1952, and more than 1,000 intoxicated moped drivers were prosecuted during the following eight years. A national health insurance scheme introduced in 1955 was accompanied by a few cases of fraud, and some 536 convictions were obtained by 1961.

To the surprise of some officials, the relaxation of administrative regulations concerning liquor rationing had a counterproductive effect. It was assumed that the abolition of rationing in 1955 would eliminate the demand for the services of small-scale bootleggers. Ironically, bootleggers seem to have capitalized on the abolition to increase their own supplies. Although official statistics no doubt reflect variations in enforcement practices, arrests for illegal sales were more numerous after 1955 than before.[12]

The difficulties experienced by Swedish authorities in controlling criminality during recent years have produced a wide range of policies. Whereas some forms of behavior, such as narcotics use and drunken driving, have been viewed with particular concern and have been subject to increased penalties, some rather surprising proposals have been suggested for other crimes. In 1971 an official commission report on petty thefts recognized the limited utility of the penal sanction and the relative unimportance of small-scale pilfering. In the midst of the "crime wave," the commission recommended that penalties for small-scale shoplifting and pilfering be reduced and that merchants warn first offenders rather than report their crimes to the police. A year later an official amendment to police regulations explicitly discouraged police from prosecuting shoplifting offenses where the value of goods stolen did not exceed 20 kronor.[13]

Swedish authorities responded to the increase in abuse of amphetamines in the late 1930s with incremental attempts at control. Prescription requirements were imposed on a number of drugs in 1938, and the formal designation of certain substances as narcotics was broadened in 1944 and in 1959. Significant increases in the use of illicit drugs during the late 1960s elicited great concern from members of the medical and welfare professions, the general public, and the police. The head of the Swedish national police attributed much of the increase in rates of theft and assault to drug use.[14] The narcotics penal law that took effect in 1968 specified three distinct categories of offense: misdemeanors, felonies, and gross felonies. The growing alarm of officials over the unabated traffic in drugs was reflected in the 1969 legislation that increased the maximum penalty for drug offenses to six years' imprisonment. This maximum was raised to ten years in 1972. Few offenses in the Swedish penal code carried punishments this severe; ten years was the maximum penalty prescribed for robbery with aggravated violence.

In contrast to trends in certain other Western societies, there existed in Sweden no significant group of individuals who advocated the decriminalization of drug offenses. Differences of opinion were limited to matters concerning treatment of offenders—health officials favored more emphasis on therapy and rehabilitation, and law enforcement officials remained committed to a policy of more severe penal sanctions. Legislators, police, and welfare officials alike were able to capitalize on public anxiety over drug use. The police in particular received significant increases in appropriations, and the government was able to preempt conservative criticism by increasing the severity of penalties.

While official actions aimed at regulating alcohol and drug consumption were creating new crimes and criminals, offenses against sexual morality were the objects of substantial decriminalization. Consensual sexual activity has met with increasing tolerance in Sweden throughout the twentieth century, partly because of the absence of extremist religious elements in Swedish society, and also because rights of privacy are highly respected. Laws on fornication had fallen into disuse long before their formal abrogation in 1918, and criminal proceedings against adulterers were discontinued in 1937. Homosexual behavior between consenting adults was decriminalized after 1944.[15]

An example of more gradual decriminalization may be seen in the evolution of laws on abortion. As late as the 1930s, abortion per se was a criminal offense, although the practice was tolerated in the (few) cases of endangerment to the woman's life or health if pregnancy were not halted. During the Depression period, up to 70 fatalities per year in Sweden were attributed to criminal abortions; the increase in abortions, as noted earlier, was also reflected in police statistics. These events prompted the appointment of a royal commission, whose proposals for cautious reform of existing law were implemented in 1939. From that time, abortions could legally be performed on women who were insane, imbecilic, or the victims of rape or incest, in addition to those whose physical well-being was believed to be in jeopardy. The increase in illegal abortions in the years following World War II was accompanied by further narrowing of defined criminality. In 1946 liability to prosecution of the woman herself was limited to cases involving aggravating circumstances. In the same year abortions were permitted when attending social circumstances might contribute to the impairment of a woman's physical or mental powers. In 1963 the definition of criminal abortion was further narrowed, and the operation became permissible when the risk of fetal injury or deformity was apparent. This policy was an obvious outgrowth of the Thalidomide controversy of the early 1960s. In each of these situations, determinations of eligibility were made by the National Board of Health and Welfare, by two attending physicians, or by one physician in cases of emergency.

According to the penal code, Swedes are liable to prosecution under Swedish law for offenses they commit in foreign jurisdictions. In 1965 a number of Swedish women were threatened with prosecution for having obtained abortions in Poland, but a substantial public outcry contributed to officials' decisions not to prosecute. Renewed debate on the abortion issue brought about the appointment of another royal commission in 1965, and the number of officially approved abortions increased fivefold in the next seven years.[16] The commission's report, published in 1971, did not explicitly recommend the introduction of abortion on demand, but it seemed to endorse the existing de facto liberalization.[17] Public debate on the issue continued, with feminist and medical associations proposing further relaxation of the laws, while religious and conservative groups remained in opposition. The law that took effect in January 1975 authorized qualified physicians to terminate pregnancies on request during the first trimester; the gradual evolution from capital offense to accepted practice was concluded.[18]

The 1965 penal code was subject to amendments in the years following its implementation. The most significant contractions of the boundaries of defined criminality occurred in the areas of public protest. In 1965 prohibitions against strikes by public servants were abolished. Authorities had become even more tolerant of public dissent by 1970, and, although provisions of the code concerning incitement to rebellion remained in force, a new amendment provided for immunity in petty cases. In addition, sections of the code proscribing insults to Swedish or foreign national symbols were repealed. Protest demonstrations thus came to be regarded as legitimate forms of political expression.

Developments after 1965 were not confined to decriminalization, however. A 1970 amendment to the penal code expanded prohibitions on expressions of disrespect for an ethnic group, and a new offense, unlawful discrimination, was created. The modification proscribed discrimination on grounds of race, skin color, national or ethnic origin, or religious creed in the course of commerce or public assembly.[19]

INSTITUTIONS OF PUBLIC ORDER

The Police

Changes in the organization of the Stockholm police force were of a relatively minor nature in the years prior to the nationalization of Swedish police in 1965. Following the 1932 demonstration at Ådalen in the north of Sweden, where troops fired on striking workers and killed five, the national government financed a small augmentation of the forces in Stockholm and in other municipalities. These nationally financed forces constituted a mobile auxiliary force for use in future labor disturbances.

The size of the Stockholm force increased steadily during the period, keeping roughly abreast of the city's population increase. A significant augmentation begun in the early 1960s, apparently in response to the rise in crime rates, was continued after the national reorganization. The manpower of the harbor patrol was temporarily increased to more than 100 during World War II, then reduced to its normal size (fewer than ten) during the later 1940s. In 1951 a wage dispute precipitated the resignation of large numbers of policemen, and there were more than 300 vacancies in the force between July and November. The force was temporarily bolstered with special constables from other police districts and returned to its normal strength soon thereafter. Police believed, however, that the temporary shortage of personnel contributed to the Berzelii Park disturbances of that year.[20] Of considerable significance was the growth of a private security industry in Sweden. By the early 1970s there were more private policemen in Stockholm than city officers. Some police functions, such as the guarding of foreign embassies, were undertaken by a private firm on government contract.

The nationalization of the Swedish police forces had its roots in the aforementioned policies of 1925 and 1932, but the major impetus for reform arose from large-scale social changes. By 1964 Sweden's population of 7.7 million was served by 554 separate police districts. As the nation was undergoing a period of rapid urbanization, the rural hinterlands remained sparsely populated, and more than 70 percent of the existing districts were manned by fewer than ten policemen. Such extreme decentralization inhibited both the specialization of police activity and the coordination necessary to conduct large-scale operations. The advent of the automobile had greatly increased the mobility of criminals, thus demanding new styles of investigation and law enforcement. In a period marked by rapidly increasing crime rates and chronically high rates of traffic fatalities, authorities saw no alternatives to centralization.

At the top of the new organizational structure was the National Police Board, consisting of a commissioner, a deputy commissioner, and five members appointed by the government. Administrative boards were established at the county level under the authority of a county police commissioner. Each county was in turn divided into police districts, headed by a chief constable. The reorganization reduced the number of districts in Sweden to 118. Under the provisions of the national reorganization, the National Police Board assumed responsibility for training, recruitment, and collective bargaining, and for such varied central functions as the operation of data processing and forensic laboratory facilities. Responsibility for prosecutorial and related functions was removed from the realm of police activity and placed with newly created national public prosecutors' and bailiffs' offices.[21]

The new police organization in Stockholm consisted of five separate departments, with responsibilities for administration, personnel, patrol operations, investigation, and traffic control. Following the 1965 reform there were thirteen separate districts within Stockholm; further centralization implemented in 1971 reduced these to seven.

Official concern with drugs and related offenses produced an energetic response by police and customs officials during the late 1960s. The increased number of arrests after 1967 was noted earlier; in addition, more than one-fourth of the criminal investigation personnel in the police force was assigned to drug-related work by 1970. There is little question that control of drugs had become an issue of highest priority for Swedish officials.[22]

The image of the policeman in Stockholm appears to have improved markedly during the twentieth century. In the 1960s recuitment standards (both physical and educational) were high, and there was an abundance of applicants for available vacancies on the force, both before and after reorganization. Wages and working conditions improved significantly, and the salary of a young constable was roughly commensurate with that of a secondary school teacher. Opportunities for professional advancement were numerous, as academic and professional educational programs were established and expanded.[23]

Public attitudes toward the police were favorable in the early 1970s. Although the absence of earlier studies precludes comparison over time, a nationwide survey conducted in 1973 revealed that nearly 80 percent of the Swedish public "rather liked" the police and would prefer to see more policemen on patrol. There appeared to be some dissatisfaction with the existing emphasis on patrolling by car; respondents indicated that positive communication with the police would be enhanced by more foot patrols. Those who experienced personal contact with the police tended to report positive orientations. Attitudes were somewhat less favorable among Stockholmers, especially those between the ages of 15 and 24. Even this group was generally favorable, however.[24] Memories of the disturbances of the mid-1950s were fading, and the antagonisms that were manifest during the previous century have had no recent counterpart.

The Administration of Justice

In 1942 the Swedish judicial system underwent major structural change. Previously, courts of first instance in Stockholm other than the police court consisted of eight sections, some with jurisdiction over certain types of civil cases, others with combined civil and criminal jurisdiction. The 1942 Code of Judicial Procedure created three specialized criminal courts with jurisdictions dependent on the severity of penalties to be awarded. The police court, which processed only the most minor offenses punishable by fine, was retained. The first of the new courts, with jurisdiction over more severe offenses punishable by fine, was presided over by a single judge. A three-judge panel tried offenders liable to a maximum of two years' imprisonment, and a judge and seven to nine lay judges had jurisdiction over more severe cases. Judicial procedure was also modified in the context of these reforms. Judges played a less active role in examining defendants; the prosecutor's responsibilities were thus expanded, and criminal proceedings became more adversarial.[25]

The increased volume of parking and traffic violations in Sweden provided further impetus for a streamlining of judicial procedure. The code presented offenders with the opportunity to accept the summary imposition of a fine in lieu of standing trial. In subsequent years the provisions of this innovation, common to most "automotive" societies, were extended to such minor offenses as drunkenness and shoplifting. Offenders retained the right to a court trial, however. The new procedures appear to have met with considerable success from the standpoint of the government, since a committee was appointed in 1968 to explore further extensions in simple criminal cases. In 1970 these summary fine procedures were made applicable to all offenses punishable by fine and, at the discretion of the prosecutor, to a few selected offenses punishable by a maximum of six months' imprisonment.[26]

In keeping with the trend toward individualizing treatment approaches, the discretionary powers of public prosecutors were broadened considerably during the period. The 1942 code contained general provisions for remission of prosecution, and extensions of discretion with regard to specific categories of offenders were granted by the Temperance Act of 1954, the Child Welfare Act of 1960, and the Law with Special Provisions Concerning Juvenile Offenders of 1964. The nationwide total of remissions under each of these statutes exceeded 21,000 in 1970. Increased concern for the individual offender was further reflected in the 1964 Law on Personal Case Study in Criminal Proceedings, a statute establishing detailed requirements for presentence investigations. Although the structure of courts of first instance has since remained unchanged, there has been an increase in the use of full-panel proceedings. This development has resulted from the practice of summarily imposing fines to dispose of lesser offenses and from the rise in the incidence of serious crimes triable by a full panel. Appeals to intermediate courts of appeals and to the High Court of Justice are very infrequent, and judgments of lower courts are usually affirmed.[27]

By the late 1960s it was apparent that existing provisions for legal aid had become inadequate. Disproportionate burdens were borne by middle-income defendants, and there was no access to legal aid for individuals involved in proceedings before administrative boards. In 1972 the Ministry of Justice proposed a comprehensive system of legal aid in criminal, civil, and administrative matters, based on the individual's ability to pay. Clients whose annual income was below a defined "basic amount" (20,000 kronor or $4,100 in 1972) were to obtain services free of charge, while those with incomes up to 58,500 kronor ($12,000) were required to pay an increasing proportion of the cost. Individuals whose incomes exceeded the latter figure paid the full cost of services. Participating attorneys were drawn from both the private bar and the civil service.[28]

Without question, the most significant changes in the recent history of the Swedish criminal justice system have occurred in the area of corrections. Diversification and amelioration of prison conditions have occurred consistently since 1930, and there has been increased reliance on noncustodial treatment methods. Authorities came to view criminality as a product of adverse social circumstances, not the result of some innate individual shortcoming. The successful reintegration of the offender into society emerged as the primary goal, and the intentional infliction of suffering on the convicted criminal became an antiquated correctional strategy. Moreover, the emphasis on rehabilitation continued to predominate throughout the crime wave of the 1960s and 1970s. Only narcotics and drunken driving offenses appear to have occasioned an emphasis on deterrence; the dramatic increases in rates of theft and other offenses has not provoked significant changes in penal practice.

As recently as the early 1930s, more than 10,000 individuals in Sweden were sentenced to prison every year for nonpayment of fines. The Social Democratic governments in power after 1932 implemented policies designed to alleviate these conditions by reducing the inequities inherent in the penal law. Fines were levied proportional to the offender's income, and a system of payment by installments was introduced. By the end of the 1930s fines were converted to imprisonment only if the offender was regarded as unduly negligent or intransigent. The annual number of such prison admissions was reduced to well under 1,000 by the end of the decade and continued to decline in subsequent years (Figure III.4.11).[29]

Among the other innovations introduced during the 1930s was the granting of furloughs to prisoners when there was death or illness in

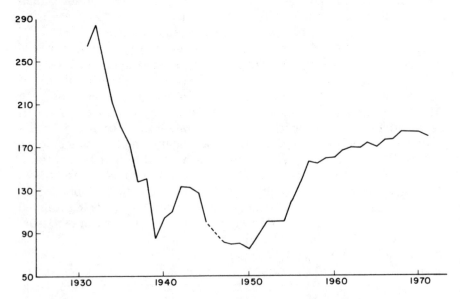

Figure III.4.11 Sweden: Prison receptions per 100,000 population, 1931-1971

the family. The first furlough was awarded in 1938, and eligibility provisions were extended in 1945. A work release program, permitting prisoners to work for private employers during the day and to return to prison after working hours, was introduced in 1937. The program was refined during the 1940s and its clientele limited to those prisoners who were nearing the end of their sentences. Although subject to some abuses, the program was regarded as quite effective in facilitating the transition from imprisonment to private life.

Despite the gradual improvement in prison conditions (corporal punishment for disciplinary infractions was abolished in 1925, and hard sleeping surfaces in 1934), the prison system was subject to occasional criticism. In 1939 allegations by Else Kleen that inmates at Långholmen had been assaulted by guards were pronounced unfounded following an official investigation, and the complainant was sentenced to two months' imprisonment for defamation. A book to which she had written a preface was ordered confiscated by the High Court of Justice, prompting the resignation of Olov Kinberg, an outspoken advocate of penal reform who was then head of the Institute of Forensic Psychiatry at Långholmen. These events attracted considerable attention to Swedish correctional practice, and some of the more successful policies of previous years were soon expanded.[30]

A new probation law took effect in 1944, permitting judges to suspend sentences of up to one year at hard labor and two years of simple imprisonment.[31] The parole system was expanded in 1945, and conditional release made obligatory when a prisoner had served five-sixths of his sentence. The Prisons Board assumed full responsibility for the parole system, and by the time a new penal code was enacted in 1965, more than 70 percent of the board's clientele was noninstitutional.[32]

The humanitarian basis of the Swedish corrections system was reaffirmed in the 1965 penal code; the statute contains a stipulation that prisoners be treated with consideration for their human dignity. The increasing emphasis on noncustodial treatment was symbolized by the change in the national administration's name from *Fångvårdsstyrelsen* (National Prisons Board) to *Kriminalvårdsstyrelsen* (National Correctional Administration). The trend toward shorter sentences that had begun in the nineteenth century continued. As of January 1971 there were only fourteen prisoners serving life sentences in all Sweden, and 90 percent of all sentences awarded were for terms less than one year. Prisoners in custody enjoyed privileges with few precedents outside Sweden. About 10,000 furloughs were granted to inmates annually, and holiday prisons were established where a small number of long-term prisoners were able to spend a month each year with their families in special villages with minimal supervision. Minimum-security facilities were expanded to include prisons where inmates could live with their families and retain private employment.[33] These innovations, in addition to the establishment of conjugal visiting privileges in more conventional institutions, are regarded as having significantly inhibited the incidence of homosexual activity among inmates.[34]

Innovations also occurred in the areas of community-based corrections and aftercare. Throughout Sweden there exist some 12,000 volunteer supervisors of parolees and probationers, but there remain discernible barriers to postprison employment. By the mid-1970s the noninstitutional proportion of the Correctional Administration's clientele had increased to more than 80 percent. Of the approximately 4,000 prisoners in custody, slightly more than half were in closed institutions, the others in minimum-security and youth facilities.

Despite the numerous reforms of the past few decades, there remained an undercurrent of unrest among inmates. The vast majority perceived their treatment as unjust, and drug use in prisons increased during the late 1960s. Work activity within custodial facilities became the target of increasing antagonism, and resentment has increased over the low wages paid to inmates. Protests occurred in 1968 and in subsequent years, and a minor incident in 1972 involved the taking of a hostage. Recent research has also revealed that institutional treatment constitutes a barrier to rehabilitation; recidivism was still chronic in the early 1970s. It thus appeared that custodial treatment would be imposed only as a last resort, and authorities would continue to rely on community-based noncustodial alternatives.[35]

This direction was confirmed in 1971 by an official report that recommended individualized treatment for all convicted offenders and noncustodial or open facilities for all but the most dangerous. The increase in rates of crime and the persisting problems of recidivism and escape were viewed by the authorities with continued calm, and any frustrations that exist among correctional officials do not seem destined to be directed at inmates. Further recommendations included the granting of more frequent furloughs, increased inmate participation in decision making, and the expansion of educational and recreational facilities. The report also proposed that work by inmates no longer be compulsory and that remuneration of inmates be made commensurate with performance.[36]

The 1971 report was received unfavorably in many quarters, however. Custodial officials were predictably unenthusiastic about inmate participation in decision making, and the National Association of Prison Inmates (FFCO), founded in 1971, petitioned for further extension of prisoners' rights and privileges. One of the more influential progressive organizations, the National Association for the Humanization of Corrections (KRUM), was established in 1966; KRUM members petitioned for the extension of inmates' rights and were outspoken in their calls for the abolition of prisons. This public pressure, combined with the report of a second commission even more committed to noncustodial alternatives than was its predecessor, had a significant impact. Subsequent statements from the Ministry of Justice revealed that a substantial reduction of the prison population had become a primary goal.[37]

Amendments to the penal code in 1974 made ambiguous "guarantees" of prisoners' rights; in effect, the so-called rights continued to be privileges subject to discretionary extension and withdrawal.[38] Nevertheless, the direction of Swedish correctional practice remained clear. Official commitment to and public pressure for noncustodial alternatives appeared unlikely to reverse.

THE CONSEQUENCES OF POLICIES OF PUBLIC ORDER

The numerous innovations in crime control strategy implemented in Sweden since 1930 appear to have had no immediate impact on crime per se, but the long-term consequences of these policies remain to be assessed. The reorganization and augmentation of police forces occurred during a period of rising crime rates, and despite an apparent improvement in police-community relations, the rate of acquisitive crime seems to follow an upward curve. The impact of the severe penalties imposed on intoxicated motorists has also been problematic; recent research has indicated that trends in traffic fatalities were not affected by the increases in penalties imposed in 1934, 1941, or 1957.[39] The incidence of criminal abortion appears to have been less responsive to energetic law enforcement than to the development of contraceptive technology.

It might be argued that the increase in various forms of criminality is attributable to insufficient punishment, yet provisions for the indefinite internment of recidivists continue to be implemented. Recidivism is no more a problem in Sweden than it is in more punitively oriented societies. Much of the petty crime in Stockholm is committed by juveniles, on the other hand, suggesting that authorities will continue to rely on institutions outside the criminal justice system for many policy alternatives.

NOTES TO CHAPTER III.4

1. Data on offenses reported, offenses cleared, and convictions in the city of Stockholm appear annually in the *Statistik Årsbok för Stockholms Stad.*

2. Coroners' reports reflect no fluctuation in the homicide rate. Most homicides were typical "crimes of passion," and attacks by "unknown assailants" very rare.

3. Trends in rates of reported offenses involving violence or threats against officials (Figure III.4.10) are roughly similar to those of drunkenness, although of much lower magnitude. They are largely explicable in terms of drunks resisting arrest.

4. Carl Persson and O. Jornander, "The Drug Problem in Sweden," *International Criminal Police Review,* 24: 232 (1969), 235-241; Esbjorn Esbjornson, "The Drug Problem in Sweden: The Results of the 1969 Campaign," *International Criminal Police Review,* 25: 241 (1970), 251-256; Leonard Goldberg, "Drug Abuse in Sweden," *Bulletin on Narcotics,* 20:1 (January-March, 1968), 1-31 (Part I); 20:2 (April-June, 1968), 9-36 (Part II).

5. SOU 1959:37 passim.

6. These events were reported in *Dagens Nyheter,* March-May, 1971, and are summarized in Thomas J. Anton, *Governing Greater Stockholm* (Berkeley: University of California Press, 1975), pp. 204-206.

7. Leif Persson, "Till fället gör tjuven?" *Nordisk Tidsskrift för Kriminalvidenskab,* 1975; and Leif Lenke, "Våldsbrott och Alkohol: En Studie av Misshandelsbrottens Utveckling" (Kriminalvetenskapliga Institutet, Stockholms Universitet, 1975).

8. SOU 1971:10; Lenke, op. cit.

9. Although many have written of equality between the sexes in Sweden, such claims are often inflated. Salaries remain unequal, and women constituted only 20 percent of the total Riksdag membership as of 1974. Their representation in local government and industrial management is even weaker.

10. Redistribution of income in the decades after World War II has been very gradual. The most affluent 10 percent of the Swedish population received 34.2 percent of all income in 1951; this total had only been reduced to 32.1 percent by 1968. See SOU 1970:71. For a study of Swedish workers' perceptions of the class structure, see Richard Scase, "Images of Inequality in Sweden and Britain," *Human Relations,* 28: 3 (April 1975), 261-278.

11. Although the majority of the 1923 coalition were Liberals, the coalition included four Social Democrats, one Conservative, two Farmers, and one Communist (Motion AK 1923: 262). Public membership has declined in recent years, but temperance interests are strongly represented in the Riksdag; as of 1975, 26 Riksdagsmen were themselves members of the MHF. For discussions of the politics of Swedish road safety, see Hans Klette, *Rattfylleribrottet* (Akademisk Avhandling: Lunds Universitet, 1970), and H. Laurence Ross, "The Scandinavian Myth: The Effectiveness of Drinking and Driving Legislation in Sweden and Norway," *The Journal of Legal Studies,* IV:2 (June 1975), 285-310.

12. K. Lithner, "Changing Society and New Types of Crime," *Nordisk Tidsskrift for Kriminalvidenskab,* 52:1 (1964), 18-38. The totals cited by Lith-

ner apply to Sweden as a whole. Continued demand for the services of bootleggers was attributable to the closing hours of retail distributors.

13. For the commission report, see SOU 1971:10. For the amendment to
Section 14 of police regulations, see SFS 1972:25. Although the decriminalization of public drunkenness was proposed by an official commission in 1968, no
such policy had been implemented by the mid-1970s. Official explanations cited
the prohibitive cost of establishing detoxification centers, while reaffirming
commitment to eventual decriminalization (RProt 1972:103, pp. 96ff).

14. Persson and Jornander, op. cit., p. 237.

15. See Brush, "Swedish Penal Code of 1965," and Sten Rudholm, "Swedish
Legislation and Practice Concerning Sexual Offences," *English Studies in
Criminal Science*, Vol. 9 (1957), 445-464.

16. Birgitta Linner, *Sex and Society in Sweden* (New York: Random House,
1967), ch. 8; H. Sjövall, "Abortion and Contraception in Sweden, 1870-1970,"
Zeitschrift für Rechtsmedizin, 70:4 (1972), 107-209; R. Lindelius, "Abortlag-
stiftningen och dess tillämpning," *Läkartidningen*, 67:47 (1970), 5509-5519. In
addition to the liberalized interpretation of abortion laws, the introduction of
oral contraceptives has contributed to a decline in the demand for illegal
abortions. See H. Sjövall, "De demografiska effekterna av födelsekontroll och
legal abort," *Läkartidningen*, 67:45 (1970), 5261-5272; and G. Geijerstam,
"Legala aborter och preventiv födelsekontroll i Sverige under perioden
1968-1972," *Läkartidningen*, 70:32 (1973), 2766-2770.

17. SOU 1971:58. The report advocated the retention of required certifica-
tion by a national board and recommended further state investment in various
policies designed to lighten the burdens of child-rearing. These included the
extension of maternity/paternity leaves from six months to one year and an
expansion of the children's allowance and day-care facilities.

18. Abortions performed by persons lacking appropriate medical certifica-
tion are still punishable by fine or imprisonment; requests for abortion after the
first trimester must be approved by a hospital board, and after eighteen weeks
by the National Social Board (SFS 1974:595). For an overview of organized
interests and their positions on the issue see SOU 1972:39.

19. This provision was enacted in response to the UN Convention on the
Elimination of All Forms of Racial Discrimination. See Lennart Geijer (introduction) in Thorsten Sellin (Transl.), *The Penal Code of Sweden* (South Hackensack, N.J.: Rothman, 1972), ch. 16, Sections 5, 7-10.

20. *Svenska Dagbladets Årsbok*, 1951, p. 51.

21. "Sweden's New Police Organisation," *International Criminal Police Review*, 23:219 (1968), 159-169.

22. Esbjornson, op. cit., p. 251.

23. E. Michael Salzer, "Swedish Police Training Stresses Education," *Police
Chief*, 34 (August 1967), 48-50.

24. Curt Falkenstam, "Opinions About Police in Sweden," *Police Chief*, 40
(September 1973), 34-36; "What the Swedish People Think of Their Police,"
International Criminal Police Review 29 (May 1974), 132-133. See also the
report of the multipartisan parliamentary crime commission, Justitiedepart-
mentet, Ds Ju 1973:5.

25. For an overview of the Swedish judicial system at the time of reform, see
Eric Burtin, *Les Tribunaux et la Procédure en Justice du Royaume de Suède*
(Paris: Rousseau, 1948).

26. These included shoplifting and minor fraud offenses. In 1974 the committee recommended a further extension of these provisions to all offenses punishable by a maximum of six months' imprisonment, again subject to prosecutorial discretion (SOU 1974:27).

27. Alvar Nelson, *Responses to Crime: An Introduction to Swedish Criminal Law and Procedure* (South Hackensack, N.J.: Rothman, 1972), pp. 74-78.

28. Ulf K. Nordenson, "The Proposed Swedish Systems of Free Legal Assistance and of Compensation to Victims of Crime, *Zeitschrift für Rechtsmedizin*, 70:2 (1972), 103-108.

29. Rudstedt, op. cit., p. 205.

30. Ibid., p. 203.

31. Judges were empowered to suspend a sentence per se, as well as to suspend the execution of a sentence.

32. Thorsten Sellin, *Recent Penal Legislation in Sweden* (Stockholm: P. A. Norstedt & Söner, 1947); on the 1965 Penal Code, see Thorsten Sellin (Transl.) *The Penal Code of Sweden* (Stockholm: Ministry of Justice, 1965), introduction by Ivar Strahl; Brush, op. cit.

33. Gunnar Marnell, "Comparative Correctional Systems: United States and Sweden," *Criminal Law Bulletin*, 8:9 (1972) 748-760. It should be noted that holiday and family prisons are not in widespread use; those that do exist can accommodate only a few offenders.

34. Ulla Bondeson, *Fången i Fångsamhället* (Stockholm: P. A. Norstedt & Söner, 1974), p. 592. There also exists a general disdain for sexual deviance among Swedish prison inmates.

35. Ibid., pp. 591-606.

36. SOU 1971:74, pp. 16-25.

37. It is significant that proposals for the continued de-emphasis of custodial treatment were also directed at the ten percent of the average daily prison population convicted of drunken driving (SOU 1970:61, p. 370). This extension had not been implemented at the time of this writing, however.

Public pressure played a significant part in the government's abandonment of plans to expand maximum security prison facilities. For a discussion of KRUM and its influence on official policy, see Thomas Mathiesen, *The Politics of Abolition*, Scandinavian Studies in Criminology, Vol. 4 (Oslo: Universitetsforlaget, 1974), and Gunnar Marnell, "Penal Reform: A Swedish Viewpoint," *Howard Journal of Penology and Crime Prevention*, 16:1 (1974), 8. For a statement of official policy vis à vis the future custodial treatment, see Justitie-departementet, Informationssekreterare, 1975-01-31 (address by Minister of Justice, Lennart Geijer). For the 1972 report on correctional policy, see SOU 1972:64. A secondary but not insignificant motive for reducing the size of the prison population is the high cost of custodial treatment.

38. This new legislation also extended the opportunity for extramural activity for all but the most dangerous prisoners (SFS 1974:203). Again, a major impetus for noncustodial treatment has been the rather high monetary cost of maintaining a prisoner in custody.

39. H. Laurence Ross, "Does the Threat of Jail Deter Scandinavia's Drinking Drivers?" *Traffic Safety*, January 1975, 10-13; "The Scandinavian Myth . . ." op. cit. January 1975 saw the implementation of a number of pilot programs designed to enhance deterrent effects by increasing the risk of detection and conviction. The programs generally involved expansion of authority to initiate breath and blood tests (SFS 1974:829).

CRIME, CONFLICT, AND PUBLIC ORDER
Some Conclusions

EXPLAINING TRENDS IN CRIME

One of the most significant characteristics of the history of crime in Stockholm has been the distinct curvilinear pattern in rates of acquisitive crime. The nineteenth and early twentieth centuries witnessed a long-term decline in rates of theft, although the trend was punctuated by significant increases during periods of economic contraction. This trend, however, lasted only until the fourth decade of the twentieth century, when a dramatic reversal occurred. Since then rates have increased continuously, apparently uninfluenced by minor economic fluctuations in what has been an era of high and rising prosperity.

Few would insist that property crime, much less crime in general, can be viewed as a monolithic phenomenon, universally subject to the influence of specific and consistent causes. The periods of economic deprivation that ostensibly caused short-term increases during the nineteenth century have had no counterparts during the years since World War II. Improvements in the health and well-being of the average Stockholmer have been consistent since the late 1800s at least. One is thus moved to seek explanations in the social, political, and economic conditions accompanying each of these trends.

One of the more enticing explanations has been mentioned briefly—the hypothesized relationship between criminality and opportunity. The increase in the number and variety of consumer goods available during the most recent decades of the twentieth century has been unprecedented. It is quite possible that the increasing affluence of Swedish society stimulated temptation. Also supportive of this "opportunity" explanation are the data presented in Figure III.3.3, which show that the long-term increase in fraud and embezzlement began during the last decade of the nineteenth century, well before long-term rates of theft had "bottomed out." It was during this era that the economic system became so well developed that the significant incidence of such offenses could occur.

Other plausible explanations of these paradoxical patterns lie in larger social changes. Despite the massive drift to the city during the second half of the nineteenth century, Stockholm was a place in which residents could build an identification with their community. The construction booms of the period created socially segregated housing facilities, thus more homogeneous neighborhoods.[1] These developments of neighborhood solidarity may have been eclipsed in subsequent years by continuing urban growth, however. As the city's population continued to grow and become mobile, urban life may have slowly transformed into one characterized by rootlessness and anonymity.

Rates of assault manifested curvilinear patterns similar to those of theft, but somewhat less pronounced. Since these figures also appear to have been influenced by a number of different factors at various periods in Stockholm's history, a closer inspection of the periods of decline and increase is warranted. The long-term decline during the nineteenth century can be attributed partly to the improvement of social and economic conditions during the period, but the sharper decrease that began in 1880 may have been produced by two unrelated factors. The growth of the temperance movement, combined with the reduction in the number of public bars in the city, altered the patterns of liquor consumption and may have served to reduce the incidence of drunken brawling. On the other hand, the mobilization of the working class during the period could have produced a shift in the shape and direction of conflict. Aggressiveness that previously had taken the form of fights among members of the working class came to be expressed as interclass conflict. Although some of these energies were no doubt diverted to the nonviolent ends of political organization, a discernible increase in the rate of violent offenses against public authorities occurred in the later 1800s (Figure III.3.8). This sharpening of class conflict was no doubt facilitated by trends in housing segregation and community development noted earlier.[2]

The proposed relationships between economic deprivation, opportunity, and rates of acquisitive crime can be tested empirically. We selected indicators of economic hardship and opportunity to be correlated with various measures of acquisitive crime and carried out two sets of analyses: one for the period before 1914, another for the period after 1925. We chose these points of demarcation because of data availability and also because the World War I period is often regarded by historians as a turning point in Western social and economic development. Only some of the relations discussed previously could be tested in this way, though. We lack, for example, precise ways of measuring community cohesion. The indicators included in the analyses are listed in Table III.5.1. After a number of preliminary analyses, the most suitable indicators were selected and detrended for a final set of multiple regression analyses; the results are reported in Tables III.5.2 and III.5.3. The coefficients signify the

Table III.5.1 Indicators of the Determinants of Crime[a]

(Data Are Annual Figures for the City of Stockholm, Unless Otherwise Noted)

Indicators used in pre-1914 analyses

Mortality	Deaths per 1,000 inhabitants
Real wages	Sweden: annual change in real wages (%)
Population growth	Annual change in number of inhabitants (%)
Alcohol consumption	Aquavit consumption (liters per inhabitant)
Manufactured products	Sweden: value of manufactured products (millions) of kronor) controlled for cost of living

Indicators used in post-1925 analyses[b]

Manufactured products	Sweden: value of manufactured products (millions) of kronor) controlled for cost of living
Welfare/unemployment	Mean standard scores for Sweden: trade unionists unemployed (all Sweden %) and welfare recipients per 1,000 inhabitants (Stockholm)
Real wages	Sweden: annual change in real wages (%)
Population growth	Annual change in number of inhabitants (%)
Alcohol consumption	Sweden: total alcohol consumption (liters per inhabitant)

a. Measures of police manpower also were used in initial analyses and proved to have strong positive relationships with changes in crime rates. Time-lagged analyses showed that police manpower changed mainly in response to changing crime rates rather than vice versa, the police measures were excluded from the final regression analyses.

b. Mortality rates were excluded from the post-1925 analyses because they showed very little annual variation. In the earlier period they varied considerably from year to year and were noticably higher during years of economic hardship.

relative importance of each independent variable as a determinant of the several crime measures.

The results of the analysis of acquisitive crime from the 1860s through 1913 (the years for which we have complete data) show that theft tended to be high during hard times. In particular, years of unusually high mortality and low real wages saw higher than average reports, trials, and convictions for theft. The "opportunity" hypothesis is not consistently supported, though. When productivity was relatively high, as measured by the value of manufactured products, reported thefts were significantly lower than at other times, whereas trials and convictions were slightly (not significantly) higher. All

Table IV.5.2 *Stockholm: Determinants of Acquisitive Crime (Standardized Regression Coefficients)*

Early period	Theft convictions, 1862-1913	Theft trials, 1862-1913	Reported theft, 1866-1913
Mortality	.73***	.72***	.27
Real wages	−.15	−.13	−.17
Population growth	.06	.06	.10
Manufactured products	.21	.15	−.43*
R^2	.38	.40	.49
Durbin-Watson statistic	.64	.59	1.02

Recent period	Theft convictions, 1925-1963	Reported theft, 1925-1969	Reported fraud, 1925-1969	Reported robbery, 1925-1969
Real wages	.09	.03	−.04	.04
Welfare unemployment	.07	.04	−.01	.02
Population growth	.10	.03	.44*	.37
Manufactured products	.87***	.89***	.30	.57**
R^2	.86	.82	.51	.78
Durbin-Watson statistic	.69	.70	.66	.40

* Significant at the .05 level.
** Significant at the .01 level.
*** Significant at the .001 level.

three, and especially reported theft, would have to be positive to support the "opportunity" explanation.

The determinants of theft during the later period, from 1925 to the 1960s, are distinctly different. The influence of material abundance is strikingly evident: The value of manufactured products is by far the strongest determinant of theft reports and convictions and reported robbery, and the second-strongest determinant of reported fraud. There is no relationship whatsoever between declining real wages and rising acquisitive crime. Moreover, a composite indicator of unemployment and welfare assistance has no relation to theft, robbery, or fraud. Thus in the twentieth century aggregate measures

Table III.5.3 Stockholm: Determinants of Violent Crime
(Standardized Regression Coefficients)

Early period 1879-1907	Homicide trials	Homicide convictions	Assault trials	Assault convictions
Mortality	.19	.16	.08	−.14
Real wages	−.32	−.30	−.10	−.11
Population growth	−.03	.01	−.04	.01
Alcohol consumption	.37	.39	.86***	.97***
R^2	.38	.36	.85	.76
Durbin-Watson statistic	1.95	1.88	.91	1.11

Recent period	Reported homicides, 1926-1969	Reported serious assaults, 1926-1969	Minor assault trials, 1926-1947
Real wages	−.05	−.09	.28
Welfare/ unemployment	−.08	.05	.20
Population growth	.68***	.44***	−.48*
Alcohol consumption	.01	.50***	.20
R^2	.47	.81	.31
Durbin-Watson statistic	1.17	.91	.78

   * Significant at the .05 level.
  ** Significant at the .01 level.
*** Significant at the .001 level.

of "hardship" have no bearing on the incidence of economic crime, and the results instead support the opportunity hypothesis.

Similar analyses of the correlates of violent crime are reported in Table III.5.3. During the late nineteenth and early twentieth centuries, incidence of violent crime was high during periods of austerity, and especially during periods of high alcohol consumption. Rates of assault in particular appear to be almost entirely a function of alcohol consumption. In the later period, from 1926 to the 1960s, the evidence is more ambiguous but economic austerity and alcohol consumption both appear to be among the significant causes of assault. Rapid population growth also appears to be implicated as an important contributing factor to homicide and serious assault, but not to minor assault.

The results of the analyses just reviewed suggest that, in Stockholm, crimes of violence and acquisition have had somewhat different social origins. Measures of social disorganization—high alcohol consumption, rapid population growth, and to a lesser degree economic hardship—all have been associated with high levels of interpersonal violence. Theft, on the other hand, has been much more responsive to changes in economic conditions. Before 1914 theft increased during years of economic slump but was not much affected by prosperity; since the 1920s the opposite pattern holds, with theft increasing hand in hand with rising prosperity, hence opportunity. It is important to qualify these results by pointing out that they do not directly "explain" either the long-term nineteenth century decline in both kinds of offense or their post-1940 increases. Since we used techniques that removed the effects of long-term trends, the results signify the short-term impact of changing social and economic conditions on annual changes in crime rates. The findings are only tentative because the linear, additive models tested here no doubt oversimplify the processes by which crime is generated and because the measures of the determinants of crime are partial and indirect. Yet despite these limitations, the equations account for a considerable proportion of the variance in most of the crime rates, as indicated by R^2 values which average well over .50. The results thus lend considerable credibility to the interpretations suggested here and in the preceding chapters.

The increase in crimes against the person during the 1950s has a number of possible explanations, some related to the nineteenth century trends and others virtually unique. The abolition of liquor rationing in 1955 and the introduction of medium strength (3.6 percent) beer a decade later could not have had an inhibiting effect on aggressive behavior. The increase in Stockholm's Finnish population also appears to have been a factor; Finnish aliens were significantly overrepresented in Swedish prisons during the 1960s. The aforementioned decline in neighborhood solidarity, combined with the absence of overt class conflict, may have contributed to a return to the kind of aggressive behavior that characterized the mid-1800s.

There remains yet another plausible explanation for the apparent increase in aggressive criminality—that of statistical artifact. The effect of changing distribution of the metropolitan population and police recording practices on crime rates in general has been noted. Although it would be unrealistic to contend that there has been no increase whatsoever in the rate of assault, the increase that has been recorded could have been amplified by a greater willingness of Stockholmers to report this type of offense. Thus the diminished public tolerance for aggressive crime may have contributed to the success of the police in identifying such behavior.

No doubt some individuals in Sweden and in other corners of the world would attribute the increases in rates of crime in Stockholm to the developing leniency of Swedish authorities during the twentieth century. There can be little question that, except for drug offenders and drunken drivers, contemporary Swedish criminals are treated more benignly than they have been at any time in Swedish history; the possibility that penal sanctions are not severe enough to constitute sufficient deterrent to potential transgressors is a matter of fundamental importance.

Whether one chooses to refer to contemporary correctional strategy as a coddling of criminals or as humanitarian treatment grounded in respect for individual dignity, it should be noted that mitigation of punishment has been a characteristic of Swedish correctional practice for two centuries. Neither the diminishing reliance on physical punishments throughout the nineteenth century nor the evolution of noncustodial treatment during the early twentieth century was accompanied by consistent increases in crime. Thus the link between contemporary "correctional permissiveness" and high rates of crime is questionable. Moreover, many Swedish authorities informed by evaluative research remain convinced that custodial treatment has limited rehabilitative or deterrent utility. Indeed, there is Swedish evidence to support the common contention that offenders imprisoned for conventional crimes are further socialized into a subculture of criminality.[3]

A review of fragmentary statistical returns suggests that rates of recidivism during the 1960s were lower than those of the late 1800s.[4] As long as the fundamental goal of Swedish criminal justice remains the reintegration of the offender in society, custodial facilities will continue to accommodate only those members of society viewed as most dangerous or incorrigible.

TRENDS IN CIVIL STRIFE

The pattern of political violence and civil strife during Stockholm's history has been one of considerable variety. The period of tension between monarchy and nobility during the decades around 1800 can be regarded as the least stable era in modern Swedish political history. Elite factions not uncommonly relied on the threat or use of force to preserve or enhance their influence. The constitution of 1809 provided a framework within which power could be transferred without violence. Although the subsequent transition to parliamentary democracy was slow by European standards, there were no assassinations after 1792 and no coups after 1809.

Civil strife in the years since 1750 has had a number of themes. In general, there has been a decline in the use of violence by authorities and citizenry alike. Most of the riots occurred during the last six decades of the nineteenth century, whereas protest demonstrations were most prevalent during the rise of the labor movement (1880-1930) and after 1965. During the first half of the nineteenth century civil disturbances involving members of the working class arose initially from antagonism toward the police and town guard. Although the workers' displeasure with agencies of law enforcement was quite obvious, the resulting disturbances had no specific ideological content. Disorders whose principal protagonists were middle class, on the other hand, were more explicitly political. The most significant riots during the early nineteenth century were caused specifically by authorities' resistance to demands for political reform and attempts to suppress criticism. The first articulate expression of working-class grievance occurred in 1848, and it heralded seven decades of political and industrial protest. From the mid-1800s until the introduction of the universal franchise in 1921, participants in collective disturbances and protest demonstrations were drawn almost exclusively from working classes.

Violent suppression of collective protest characterized the period up to 1850; the 30 fatalities that resulted from the disturbances in 1848 marked the most sanguinary episode. Official restraint was discernible in subsequent conflicts, no doubt partly because the leaders of the emerging labor movement lacked a tradition of violence. The most notable exception occurred during the bloody suppression of the protests at Adalen in the north of Sweden in 1932. Otherwise, the impetus for civil strife was largely eliminated following the establishment of parliamentary democracy.

Collective disturbances in the decades after World War II were varied and tended to be smaller and much less turbulent than were events of the previous century. Initially they reflected what might be described as undirected rowdiness, reminiscent of working-class disorders in the early 1800s. More recent activities once again reflected explicit policy goals of participants. At no time during recent history has the legitimacy of the political system been violently challenged, however.

EVOLVING POLICIES OF PUBLIC ORDER

Swedish criminal law has not evolved through consistent expansion or contraction of defined criminality; rather, there has been a perceptible adjustment to changes in the composition of elites and their values. The most significant examples of decriminalization have occurred in the areas of consensual sexual activity, and to a lesser extent in the areas of industrial and political protest. The creation of new criminal offenses first appeared in response to mobilization of the working class during the late nineteenth century. Subsequent expansion of the criminal law was inspired by the unfavorable social consequences that accompanied the invention of the automobile and the arrival of international air travel.

The philosophical basis of the 1865 code reflected the thinking of the classical school of criminology; punishments were to be awarded in proportion to the severity of the offense. The modern code retains a classical basis but has been profoundly influenced by positivist criminological thought. The numerous provisions for individualized disposition are illustrative. Contemporary criminal law thus represents a compromise between societal groups having divergent orientations to the offender. Each offense carries a prescribed range of penalties, reflecting diverse values that might be applied. Individuals whose goals are rehabilitative are satisfied by alternatives that range from suspension of prosecution to the indefinite internment of chronic recidivists.

The development of police organizations in Stockholm has followed a pattern not uncommon to most Western societies. From the initial deployment of a town guard, bolstered by garrison troops for controlling large-scale disorders, law enforcement institutions evolved to a modern, professional, national police force. Early agencies of social control were criticized for their inefficiency and poor conduct and were subject to periodic reorganization and augmentation during periods of public insecurity. The trend toward centralization of the force and specialization of its components was an inevitable consequence of technological change. Inspired by the increasing urbanization of Swedish society, nationalization was facilitated by developments in transportation and communications.

Correctional practice in Sweden followed an evolutionary path consistent with contemporary forms of social and economic organization. Physical punishments began to fall into disuse during the mid-eighteenth century as humanitarian values became more widespread. At the same time, those who saw no intrinsic worth in the offender as a human being came to recognize the potential value of his labor. Thus authorities placed increasing emphasis on imprisonment with labor as a treatment method.

By the middle 1800s there was a surplus rather than a scarcity of labor. Swedish elites continued to rely on incarceration, however, as a means of isolating the members of society who seemed most threatening. By the end of the nineteenth century, custodial treatment had become more rehabilitative in purpose, if not in effect. Increasing attention was paid to the inmate's education, religious and secular. There followed during the twentieth century a move away from imprisonment both as a deterrent and as a vehicle of rehabilitation.

Experimentation with such noncustodial alternatives as probation and parole led to expansion of and greater reliance on these practices; custodial facilities that remained tended to be small and specialized, oriented almost exclusively toward the resocialization of offenders into Swedish society. There were a few noteworthy deviations from the pattern, however. Behaviors viewed by authorities as particularly troublesome or socially undesirable were punished by measures as severe as those employed in other advanced industrial societies. Drug offenders were dealt with harshly by Swedish standards, although the penalties to which they were subject were more benign than those imposed in other jurisdictions.[5] Drunken driving offenses, however, were treated with severity unmatched except by other Scandinavian societies.

A distinctive feature of Swedish correctional practice was the use of institutions outside the criminal justice system to cope with behaviors dealt with elsewhere by courts and prisons. These trends were first visible in the administrative control of vagrancy during the later nineteenth century, although the measures employed were quite coercive by modern standards. At the beginning of the twentieth century the establishment of juvenile welfare boards removed a considerable amount of criminal behavior from the jurisdiction of the criminal justice system. The temperance boards, by assuming responsibilities for chronic alcoholics, had a similar effect.

Although the trends described were partly influenced by independent social and political forces, they were subject to substantial interaction. Increases in crime and strife were followed with some regularity by reform and augmentation of police forces, but only rarely by increases in the severity of sanctions. The emergence of behaviors regarded by contemporary authorities as particularly threatening (labor protest, drunken driving, and drug use) elicited an expansion of the criminal law. On the other hand certain offenses that came to be regarded as less harmful (e.g., consensual sexual activity) have been subject to administrative control or outright decriminalization.

The one trend that appears to have been little influenced by short-term changes in crime and strife was that of correctional practice. Whereas crime waves over the past two centuries may have slowed the pace of change on occasion, at no time did the authorities abandon efforts at ameliorative innovation. Swedish officials remained committed to rehabilitative treatment despite sharp increases in the rates of many offenses in the decades after 1930. The custodial population remained small (Table III.5.4), even though the intake of the criminal justice system increased dramatically.

Table III.5.4 Sweden: Average Annual Number of Prisoners in Custody on December 31: 1837-1970

Years	Annual Average	Rate per 100,000 inhabitants
1837-1840	4,884	157.4
1841-1845	5,818	179.5
1846-1850	5,809	170.6
1851-1855	5,884	164.6
1856-1860	5,042	134.5
1861-1865	4,947	123.1
1866-1870	6,089	146.0
1871-1875	4,929	114.7
1876-1880	4,560	100.9
1881-1885	4,178	90.5
1886-1890	3,986	83.9
1891-1895	3,389	69.9
1896-1900	3,172	62.8
1901-1905	3,132	59.9
1906-1910	2,992	54.0
1911-1915	2,976	52.8
1916-1920	3,158	54.2
1921-1925	2,228	37.2
1926-1930	2,502	41.0
1931-1935	2,428	39.1
1936-1940	1,991	31.6
1941-1945	2,785	42.9
1946-1950	2,244	32.6
1951-1955	3,056	42.5
1956-1960	4,357	58.6
1961-1965	4,990	65.3
1966-1970	4,898	61.3

Source: Statistisk Årsbok för Sverige.

Moreover, official commitment to the policy of reducing this population further was vigorously reaffirmed. Such a commitment was reinforced by the existence of a strong antiprison lobby, the absence of a procustodial counterpart, and the increasing costs of imprisonment. Few public officials sought to manipulate public concern about crime or to advocate increased reliance on liberty-depriving sanctions, except in cases involving drugs and drunken driving. Finally, authorities have viewed with considerable respect findings of social scientists demonstrating that imprisonment itself has a significant criminogenic effect.

The impetus for various innovations in crime control policies over the course of Stockholm's history may be discerned with little difficulty, but the effects of these policies on the behaviors at which they were aimed has been less clear. Attempts to suppress some activities that accompanied the emergence of large-scale social movements succeeded only in "postponing the inevitable." The experiences of working-class mobilization and the abortion reform movement are illustrative. Other strategies appear to have been successful, but only in part. Attempts to control the distribution of alcohol had some ameliorative effect on the incidence of chronic alcoholism, while stimulating a substantial illicit trade in liquor. Drunken driving has by no means been eradicated.

Crimes against persons and property seem to be more subject to the influence of larger social forces than to criminal justice policy. The augmentation and professionalization of the police force was an inevitable consequence of increases in crime but appears to have had no permanent effect on the incidence of criminal behavior.

By the mid-1970s Swedish officials had begun to devote increasing attention to questions of general prevention and less to matters of offender treatment. Thus the price of alcoholic beverages was periodically increased, and proposals placing greater emphasis on the certainty of identifying and convicting drunken drivers were entertained.[6] Although these and similar themes may be indicative of a fundamental change in Swedish crime control policy, no explicit redirection of outlook had been expressed at the time of this writing.

Despite the progressive image of the Swedish criminal justice system, some critics maintain that the potential for harsh repression of social undesirables is quite real. In addition to the escalation of penalties for drug offenses, extremely strict antiterrorist measures were enacted in 1973. Directed primarily at Croatian and Palestinian organizations, the law empowered police to tap phones, open mail, and search the dwelling places of foreigners suspected of terrorism. The law also provided for summary deportation.[7]

Prospects for the future of public order in Stockholm can be assessed only with difficulty, for certain important factors defy prediction. The social and cultural homogeneity of the population, combined with the absence of severe economic inequalities, would appear to preclude the emergence of intense intergroup conflict. Violence, whether interpersonal or collective, has little basis in modern Swedish culture, and future immigration programs are likely to be engineered with considerable care. Moreover, an impressive example has been set by a national government that has neither waged war for a century and a half nor conducted an execution in more than six decades. Sweden, however, does not exist outside the global economic system, and the advent of adversity in a society so accustomed to affluence could easily rekindle aggressive inclinations.

The future of acquisitive criminality is even less certain. Propensities to theft, if in fact stimulated by an era of affluence, are unlikely to subside in the event of future economic contraction. Indeed, under such circumstances they are quite likely to intensify. Whether the temptations of petty pilfering and vandalism will be attractive to succeeding generations of Swedish children remains to be seen. Meanwhile we can speculate that if acquisitive tendencies weaken, it will not be because of the imposition of draconian measures of social control. If respect for public and private property is not inculcated by family, school, or community, it is unlikely to be acquired at all, and Swedes will have to tolerate the consequences, as many affluent Stockholmers and officials already seem prepared to do.

NOTES TO CHAPTER III.5

1. The absence of wealthy residents in close proximity to those less affluent is further supportive of the "opportunity" hypothesis.

2. See Sven Sperlings, "Crimes of Violence in Stockholm During the Last Years of the 19th Century" (Unpublished paper, Institute of Criminology, University of Stockholm, 1974).

3. Bondeson, *Fången i Fångsamhället*, pp. 581-608

4. G. F. Almquist, *La Suède*, pp. 122-147; *Sveriges Officiella Statistik, Kriminalvården* (1960-1970), passim.

5. Cf. the Swedish maximum of ten years' imprisonment with the life sentences imposed in certain American jurisdictions.

6. Ch. III.4, note 39. The idea of general deterrence is by no means new to Swedish crime control policy. Rather, authorities appear to be contemplating a greater investment in preoffense intervention than was the case in the treatment-oriented past.

7. SFS 1973:162. The Yugoslav ambassador to Sweden was assassinated by Croatian nationalists in 1971.

Part IV

SYDNEY: THE POLITICS OF CRIME AND CONFLICT, 1788 TO THE 1970s

Peter N. Grabosky

AUTHOR'S NOTE: This is an abridged version of a book by Peter N. Grabosky entitled Sydney in Ferment: Crime, Dissent, and Official Reaction, 1788-1973, *published in 1976 by Australian National University Press.*

GROWTH OF THE CITY

THE FOUNDING: 1788-1809

The history of public order in Sydney begins in London, for it was there that the original direction of Sydney's history was mapped. During the late eighteenth century a substantial increase in crime in London and elsewhere had aroused the anxieties and antagonisms of the dominant segments of British society.[1] Prisons were packed to overcrowding, and the loss of the American colonies, to which thousands of convicts had previously been transported, aggravated the situation. The House of Commons, having decided in 1784 to renew transportation, called on the Home Office to select a site. Among the alternative locations considered were Canada, the West Indies, and the west coast of Africa. Based on the recommendation of Captain Cook, who had explored the site in 1770, the Home Secretary, Lord Sydney, selected Botany Bay on the east coast of what Cook had named New South Wales.[2]

Arthur Phillip, a retired naval officer, was chosen to found the colony; he and his fleet set sail from England in May 1787 and arrived at Botany Bay in January 1788. Since the Botany Bay area was swampy and lacked fresh water, Phillip set out northward in an effort to locate a better setting. A short distance up the coast he passed between two massive heads and into an immense protected harbor. Phillip ultimately selected a small cove at the mouth of a freshwater stream, where the bulk of his 700 convicts and 200 marines began landing on January 26, 1788. He chose to call it Sydney Cove, in honor of the Home Secretary.

More than 6,000 convicts had landed at Sydney by the end of the eighteenth century; most were lower-class Englishmen who had been convicted of burglary, larceny, or other offenses against property.[3] A number of Irish convicts were also transported for similar property offenses or for crimes of protest against British rule.

Sydney in its embryonic state could hardly be described as a city; it was a military encampment in a beautiful but very wild natural setting. The climate was unpredictable, the soil not particularly fertile. The convicts, most of whom were originally from towns and cities, were largely ignorant of agricultural technique and went about their work with an understandable lack of enthusiasm. Members of the marine detachment undertook nonmilitary tasks with extreme reluctance. In July 1788 Phillip wrote to London requesting that migration to the colony by free settlers be encouraged,[4] and the combination of social and environmental factors had brought about near-famine conditions by 1790.

A firm economic foundation was established by 1800. In addition to what Sean Glynn has termed an "invisible export commodity," jail services,[5] timber from the mainland and from Norfolk Island provided materials for construction in the colony and became its first major "visible" export. Even more significant was the contribution of the enterprising John Macarthur, whose early experiments with sheep breeding were to lead to the emergence of the wool industry. To encourage agricultural productivity, the early governors granted land generously. A system of assigning convicts as servants to free settlers and officers was institutionalized in 1804, but even before that time convict labor could be obtained at minimal expense. Meanwhile, enterprising officers of the New South Wales Corps (a unit specially recruited for service in the colony, which replaced the marine detachment in 1792) were able to monopolize imports to the colony, thus amassing considerable wealth.

Although invested with almost absolute authority, the early governors of New South Wales were somewhat less than omnipotent. Home Secretaries, ever intent on minimizing the expense of the new colony, determined the number and frequency of convict arrivals and imposed numerous budgetary constraints. Members of the military establishment, which gradually evolved into a commercial establishment, were able to protect their interests even in the face of the governor's opposition.

Aside from attacks on and by the aboriginal population, the principal problems of public order in the early years centered on controlling the convict population. By far the most prevalent serious crimes were the various forms of theft, which according to incomplete records accounted for three out of every four serious crimes. Less than fifteen percent involved violence against the person, and only five percent constituted transgressions of sexual morality.[6]

Indeed, sexual behavior in the settlement was relatively unrestrained, limited mainly by the dearth of women. The most common form of disorderly behavior during the early days was drunkenness. A staggering volume of spirits was imported legitimately, much more was smuggled in or illicitly distilled, and by the beginning of the nineteenth century heavy drinking had become a colonial institution.[7] Officers of the New South Wales Corps were able to monopolize the liquor trade, and in 1808 a group of them overthrew Governor Bligh because his efforts to stem the flow were overly energetic. The only other serious challenge to the government came in 1804, when it became necessary to suppress a rebellion attempted by about 300 Irish convicts, many of them transported for nationalist activity.[8]

1810-1829

The town of Sydney underwent impressive social and architectural changes during the administration of Governor Macquarie (1810-1821). Colonial society had inherited British class distinctions, and these inclinations were reinforced by the colony's unique status as a penal settlement. Convicts, of course, comprised the lowest social stratum. They were present in New South Wales to suffer for their transgressions, to redeem themselves if possible, and to provide cheap labor. The growing number of emancipists (those who had served their terms of sentence or who had been pardoned) were also regarded by the free population as inferior. They could, however, enjoy economic freedom if not social equality. Macquarie attempted to bestow dignity on the emancipists, a number of whom had

Table IV.1.1 Selected Demographic Aspects of New South Wales
               Population, 1788-1850

Year	Population	% Male	% Convict
1788	1,035	78.5	69.2
1796	4,100	72.0	58.2
1800	5,217	72.4	29.9
1805	6,950	68.9	22.4
1810	10,096	65.5	—
1815	13,116	65.3	—
1820	28,024	70.0	38.8
1826	38,890	76.6	41.9
1830	44,588	76.0	41.7
1835	71,304	72.9	38.3
1840	127,468	67.1	30.1
1845	187,918	60.5	9.0

Sources: Historical Records of Australia; New South Wales Colonial Secretary, Returns of the Colony.

become successful entrepreneurs and farmers. Ironically, his attempts served to harden the biases of more than a few "respectable" members of New South Wales society, arousing further class antagonisms. Meanwhile the first sizable generations of native-born New South Welshmen were growing up, thus complicating the class distinctions. In 1820 Sydney's population had reached 8,000; convicts made up approximately 30 percent of this total and former convicts approximately 25 percent. Table IV.1.1 gives data for the entire colony, 1788-1850.

The establishment of the Legislative Council in 1824 constituted a noteworthy change in the colony's political structure. Although the body acted only in an advisory capacity, it reflected the growing influence of the agricultural and commercial elite and heralded a departure from the prevailing autocratic structure of military rule. An ambitious program of public works was carried out during Macquarie's term, despite pressures from the home government to limit colonial expenditure. Under the direction of Macquarie and the architect Francis Greenway, a former convict, roads and buildings were constructed which gave the town a much more respectable and less haphazard physical shape.

By 1820 Sydney was no longer a town in support of a penal settlement; the penal settlement existed in support of a town that had an increasingly diverse economy. Sydney was the capital and administrative center of a small but growing colony. Whaling and sealing activities were expanding in the South Pacific, and Sydney was situated conveniently proximate to trade routes. Exports of wool exceeded 100,000 pounds in 1820, and the grazing industry was on the threshold of explosive growth. Despite the uncertainties of drought and flood, agricultural productivity was impressive.

The disproportionate number of men in Sydney's population, a fact of life since the founding of the colony, persisted throughout the period. Indeed, males in the population of New South Wales increased from 65 percent in 1810 to 75 percent in 1830, largely because of Britain's increasing reliance on New South Wales as a penal colony in the aftermath of the Napoleonic wars. The imbalance between the sexes was even greater among the convicts: Throughout the 1820s more than 90 percent of the convict population of New South Wales was male.

The economy of the colony was sound during most of the period from 1810 to 1830, but deprivation was not entirely absent. A Benevolent Society, established in 1813, was able to identify 150 destitute people in the town, the majority infirm with age or chronically ill.[9] In the late 1820s a prolonged drought brought about the colony's first economic contraction in the nineteenth century. Although not as severe or as widespread as the depressions to come, it temporarily ended the boom of the two previous decades.

Crimes against property continued to be common. Most notorious and colorful among such offenses was bushranging, a type of highway robbery usually carried out by escaped convicts, armed and mounted. Public order policies were extremely punitive, probably to the point that violent acts by the authorities exceeded all other manifestations of physical violence. Hangings in the colony reached a record yearly high of 52 in 1829, and floggings were administered by the thousands. Capital punishment was generally meted out to those convicted of burglary, robbery, murder, and rape, and male convicts were flogged for a host of lesser offenses from neglect of work to insubordination.[10]

1830-1850

During the years from 1830 to 1850 Australia "rode the sheep's back." Wool ruled Sydney's economy and employment structure to a greater extent than in any other period; transport, export, and supporting services had long surpassed jailkeeping as primary occupations. The port had become a busy one—100 vessels were registered in Sydney in 1834. As in many seaports, Sydney had its unsavory waterfront area, the Rocks. Situated on rocky terrain just west of Sydney Cove, the Rocks area was Sydney's first slum; it was celebrated throughout most of the century for its grog shops, gambling dens, and brothels.

The 1830s and 1840s also were years of exploration and rural settlement. The vast hinterland attracted increasing numbers of settlers, and new trends in convict management called for the dispersion of convicts throughout rural areas, with the result that by 1840 only 25 percent of the population of New South Wales resided in Sydney. Land policies increasingly favored large holders, however, and the trend reversed. Table IV.1.2 shows that Sydney's population has continued to grow at the expense of the rest of New South Wales for 130 years.[11]

Transportation to New South Wales continued at the rate of more than 3,000 per year during the period 1830-1838,[12] but although the convict population was at its largest, it was dispersed; Sydney was no longer an urban jail. Indeed, efforts from within the colony to dispel the image were intensive. In 1831 the government began sponsoring assisted passage for free immigrants, and more than 130,000 had arrived in New South Wales by 1859. Because of this influx of free migrants, the percentage of convicts in the total population decreased: By 1840 fewer than three New South Welshmen in ten were convicts. Assisted passage for free immigrants also reduced the necessity to rely on convict labor, and free New South Welshmen came to regard transportation as increasingly burdensome; it detracted from pride and security. Few were disappointed, then, when the home government decided to end transportation to New South Wales in 1840.

Sydney was incorporated as a city in 1842. Its population, plus that of its new eastern, southern, and western suburbs, was close to 40,000, and gas lighting had been introduced in 1841. As the decade ended, the *Sydney Morning Herald* called attention to the crying need for sewers.[13] Visitors were struck with the "Englishness" of the

Table IV.1.2 *Estimated Proportion of New South Wales Population Residing in Sydney Metropolitan Area, Selected Years 1810-1970*

Year	Estimated Population	Estimated percentage[a] resident in Sydney
1810	10,096	70
1820	29,665	27
1825	38,313	29
1833	62,112	26
1841	145,303	25
1851[b]	197,265	27
1856	288,361	24
1860[c]	348,546	27
1870	497,992	27
1881	777,025	31
1891	1,153,170	35
1901	1,375,455	36
1911[d]	1,699,376	39
1921[e]	2,131,690	42
1931	2,566,314	47
1941	2,813,056	47
1954	3,462,313	54
1961	3,917,013	56
1970	4,563,252	60

Sources: Historical Records of Australia; New South Wales Colonial Secretary, *Returns of the Colony; New South Wales Statistical Register; Official Year Book of New South Wales.*

[a] Figures prior to 1841 refer specifically to Sydney Town. Subsequent figures refer to metropolitan area; boundaries of the metropolitan area expanded periodically throughout twentieth century.

[b] Victoria separated from New South Wales in 1851.

[c] Queensland separated in 1895.

[d] Australian Capital Territory separated in 1911.

[e] Jervis Bay Area separated in 1916.

city and, aside from the climate, found it reminiscent of Brighton or Plymouth.

By the end of the 1830s commerce in the colony had expanded rapidly. Investment from abroad was plentiful, enabling subsidy of assisted migration. In turn, the availability of labor encouraged further investment. The optimism of the late 1830s was, however, short-lived. Rampant speculation and easy extension of credit were checked by a contraction of the money market in 1840. Drought conditions drastically curtailed agricultural and pastoral productivity. By 1843 a drop in wool prices and a general financial crisis brought the rich to bankruptcy and the poor to destitution. Indeed, wool prices had declined so much that large flocks could no longer be supported, and sheep were boiled down by the thousand for tallow.

Politically, however, 1843 could be regarded as a year of progress. Elections to the Legislative Council were held for the first time, although franchise was limited. While the governor remained the paramount figure, the stage was set for the creation of the Legislative Assembly and the attainment of responsible government on the bicameral parliamentary model in 1856.

The incidence of most kinds of crime appeared to decrease sharply during these decades, despite flurries of private and public concern about absconding convicts, deserting seamen, and the Cabbage Tree Hat Mob of young male Sydneysiders, who gained notoriety by insulting or otherwise harassing the "respectable" people of the city. The tradition of intemperance remained strong, though. Governor Gipps wrote in 1840 that "drunkenness, the fruitful parent of every species of crime, is still the prevailing vice of the Colony."[14] The most dramatic changes were in the policies followed by authorities. In the 1840s, after the cessation of transportation, hangings averaged fewer than eight per year compared with an average of more than 28 annually in the 1830s. And with the end of the convict era, flogging quickly fell into disuse.

1851-1870

Sydney's population exceeded 50,000 in 1850, the year of the incorporation of the University of Sydney. The university was to become a source of great civic pride, symbolic of the city's progress since the uncomfortable days of the convict era. Meanwhile the announcement of the discovery of gold in central New South Wales in 1851 had both a sudden impact and a lasting influence on the city. The pace of everyday activity quickened perceptibly; many native Sydneysiders left their homes and employment and headed west in search of the big strike. As stories of easily acquired fortunes reached the world, thousands of adventurers made their way to Australia, passing through Sydney en route to the gold fields. Another consequence of the attraction of the gold fields was a substantial labor shortage in the metropolitan area. Wages reached unprecedented levels, and the general level of affluence was in clear contrast with the hard times of a decade earlier. Families without breadwinners were destitute, however, because of rampant inflation.

By the early 1860s the boom had ended; the condition of the working classes in Sydney was sufficiently deprived to warrant a governmental inquiry in 1861. The select committee's report revealed widespread unemployment, squalid housing conditions, and streets "infested" with vagrant or neglected children. Noting the high death rates among adult and child populations alike, the report referred to a "gradual process of human slaughter that is silently going on."[15] The committee's report, with recommendations for improvements in health and housing and for employment on public works, was rejected by the Legislative Assembly. On the positive side, the Education Act of 1867 provided for compulsory primary education in New South Wales. Its enactment was timely, for as men returned from the gold fields in the late 1850s and began establishing families, the birthrate rose considerably.

Population growth, stimulated by the gold rush, was strong and steady. Close to 54,000 people inhabited Sydney and its suburbs in 1851, but the total grew to 96,000 a decade later and to 137,000 by 1871. The population of rural New South Wales increased, but Sydney's rate of increase was proportionally greater. The sex structure of Sydney's population also changed significantly during the gold rush years. Men were actually underrepresented in the city during the late 1850s.[16] Although the statistical masculinity of the colony's population decreased only gradually throughout the century, the population of the Sydney metropolitan area remained relatively balanced.

The general pattern of Sydney's urban growth had become apparent by 1870 and differed in two respects from urbanization in most other Western societies. Whereas the development of European cities has been largely attributable to industrialization and migration from rural areas, Sydney grew in advance of both industrial activity and rural settlement. Aside from the late 1850s and early 1860s, during the drift back to the city from the gold fields, Sydney's population increase during the nineteenth century was due almost entirely to overseas migration and natural increase. The other striking characteristic of urbanization in New South Wales has been the overwhelming concentration of its population in the capital city. This imbalance in population distribution between the metropolis and a vast, empty hinterland is typical of Australian urban development. Glynn has offered some eminently plausible explanations for this demographic dominance.[17] In the early days of settlement, access to the hinterland was somewhat limited; it was not until 1814 that a path across the Blue Mountains was found. The dominance and capital-intensive nature of the grazing industry in the first half of the nineteenth century also militated against widespread rural settlement. This tendency was reinforced by land policies later in the century that favored large holdings. In addition, most of the migrants to New South Wales had been urban dwellers before their arrival; they found Sydney a familiar setting, more attractive than the bush, and chose to remain in the city. These inclinations were reinforced as Sydney grew, providing a greater range of employment, educational, and cultural opportunities, which increasingly outweighed those of the hinterland.

Low rates of arrests and convictions for crime, and the lack of manifest public anxiety about public order, suggest that the 1850s and 1860s in Sydney were characterized by the civility and security that contemporary observers reported in London. Drunkenness, prostitution, and juvenile rowdiness gave occasional but not persistent grounds for concern. There were only minor episodes of group violence, including a New Year's Eve riot in 1850, a protest-turned-riot by unemployed workers a decade later, and numerous attacks on Chinese at Lambing Flat, some distance from Sydney, in the warm months of 1860-1861.

1871-1900

Unprecedented construction and metropolitan expansion characterized the last 30 years of the nineteenth century in Sydney. During the 1870s the advent of horse-drawn trams and omnibuses and improved ferry services permitted much suburban development, and the population of the suburbs surpassed that of the city for the first time. Steam-powered trams soon began to replace the horse-drawn vehicles, and by the turn of the century there were close to 100 miles of tramways in the metropolitan area.

The 1880s were prosperous times in Sydney. While thousands of narrow, two-story terraced houses were erected in such inner suburbs as Woolloomooloo, Glebe, and Paddington, general prosperity and new transport facilities encouraged a further building boom in such newly subdivided areas as Alexandria and Brighton to the south and St. Leonards across the harbor to the north. E. C. Fry states that 600 builders and 100 architects were active in Sydney in 1888.[18] In that year the population of the expanding metropolis was just under 350,000.

Primary production continued to dominate the New South Wales economy, yet construction and light industry had increased markedly. Factory employment in the metropolitan area reached 26,000 by 1888, almost double the total of a decade earlier.[19]

Despite the unprecedented affluence enjoyed by so many in Sydney, more than a few experienced privation. Streets in the poorer neighborhoods of the metropolitan area were dirty and neglected; houses were cramped, badly ventilated, and poorly lit. James, writing in the late 1870s, spoke of common lodging houses accommodating more than 70 people in six small rooms.[20] Parks and recreation areas were noticeably few. The dedication of Centennial Park in 1888 helped alleviate the problem somewhat, but its location favored residents of the eastern suburbs.

Tied as it was to the fiscal fortunes of Europe, the economy of New South Wales was exceedingly vulnerable to fluctuations abroad. In 1892 a crisis in international finance moved overseas investors to turn away from Australia; the flow of capital that had sustained the boom years before 1890 thus disappeared. In addition, the rapid expansion in housing construction and suburban subdivision resulted in an oversupply of houses and a collapse of the market, further aggravating economic difficulties.

Antagonism toward nonwhite races had been present in the colony since the founding. Anti-Chinese sentiment was particularly strong within the working class, whose members feared that unrestricted Chinese immigration would result in an invasion of coolie labor; there was sporadic public protest calling for Chinese exclusion. With the enactment by the New South Wales Parliament of the Chinese Restriction and Regulation Act of 1888, migration and naturalization of Chinese virtually ceased.

Although there was very little opposition to the exclusion of Chinese, a much graver source of political and social strain was the emergence of industrial conflict. As commerce and industry thrived in the colony during the 1870s and 1880s, so too did the trade union movement. While labor-management relations were characterized by cordiality unparalleled in Europe or America, workers became increasingly aware of the powers inherent in organization and of the improvements in working conditions that could be gained by trade union action.

To judge by public outcry and police action, the 1880s were disorderly times despite the prosperity. Arrests for drunkenness increased markedly each year. Public outrage was strikingly vocal over "larrikinism," the expression used to describe a range of youthful activity from loitering and use of insulting language to occasional attacks on police. The 3,500 Chinese of Sydney were widely suspected of gambling, opium smoking, and traffic in white slavery.[21] Two famous rape trials, the Mount Rennie and Büttner cases, were accorded widespread press coverage and provoked heated public debate. It is easy enough in retrospect to diagnose Sydney's social concerns in this decade as a manifestation of a more demanding Victorian morality, rather than as an episode of social disintegration. The same cannot be said of the Great Strike of 1890, which mobilized 10,000 strikers and sympathizers in the largest collective protest in Sydney's history to that time. Far from being illusory, the strike began a chronic labor-management struggle that erupted periodically in Sydney during the following 60 years, with profound effects on politics and public order.

1901-1920

Sydney began the twentieth century with an outbreak of bubonic plague. The epidemic, in March 1900, claimed 112 lives and provided the incentive for a small but historic urban renewal project in the rat-infested area of the Rocks closest to Darling Harbour.[22] In January 1901 Sydney was the scene of ceremonies celebrating the establishment of the Commonwealth of Australia. In 1908 Jack Johnson's rise to the World's Heavyweight Championship at Rushcutters' Bay further enhanced Sydney's international reputation. By this time, the population of the metropolitan area was 560,000 and increasing steadily; the period 1901-1911 saw an increase of 30 percent, and the figure for the following decade was 40 percent. In racial and ethnic terms, Sydney's population remained overwhelmingly white and of British or Irish heritage.

Further progress in transportation included the establishment of the first electric tram service, introduced on George Street in 1900, and the founding of the Sydney Harbour Trust. The latter agency, charged with the administration of the port of Sydney, oversaw a reconstruction of the waterfront that was to affirm Sydney's stature as one of the world's foremost seaports.

Although a number of factories were operating in the metropolitan area, most workers were employed in service occupations, administration, distribution, transportation, and communications. Primary production continued to be the backbone of the economy.

Meanwhile, the Australian labor movement had shifted its strategy from industrial to political action. Extension of the franchise and payment of salaries to officeholders had enabled trade union officials to seek and win seats in the Legislative Assembly. The Labor Party was able to wield considerable influence in the Assembly by the turn of the century. Legislation for the improvement and regulation of working conditions in New South Wales factories dated to 1896, an old-age pension scheme was enacted in 1900, and an invalid pension was established in 1908.[23] The first Labor Government was installed in Sydney in 1910.

Despite its physical distance from the scene of hostilities, Australia was greatly affected by World War I. Thousands of Sydneysiders died in combat; debate over the issue of conscription was heated, and protest demonstrations were frequent. The war had an impact on Sydney's industrial structure as well. With transportation to and from Europe severely restricted, import capabilities were limited. Living costs and unemployment rose together, and the frustrations of Sydney's workers increased accordingly. Forced under these circumstances to strive for a greater level of self-sufficiency, Australians set to work bolstering their industrial establishment. Industrial development in Alexandria and Waterloo, at the southern fringe of the city of Sydney and close to railway facilities, was accompanied by a population increase in the near eastern suburbs.

Despite the wartime setting, industrial tensions continued to flare periodically; the general strike of 1917 and lesser strikes two years later showed that the cleavages between labor and management remained sharp. Times were hard for a good many workers in the years following the armistice, too. According to D. W. Rawson, unemployment in the city reached fourteen percent in 1921.[24] Two years later V. G. Childe referred to the "distress and actual starvation" of some Sydney workers, apparently unmatched since the depression of the 1890s.[25] The inner suburbs of Camperdown, Glebe, Surry Hills, Redfern, and Woolloomooloo had become congested, their old and poorly constructed residences deteriorating. As the economy readjusted to the dislocations brought about by the war, the 1920s became years of significant building activity. Slum clearance and new construction reached a peak in 1924, when a contract was awarded an English firm to construct a bridge across the harbor, a long-overdue project first suggested over a century before by the architect Greenway.

Sydney before 1910 seems to have achieved public order. The incidence of virtually every type of crime continued to decline from levels already low in 1900, but all changed as war approached. Arrests for serious crimes against persons and property increased markedly, beginning in 1912. In February 1916 hundreds of soldiers from training camps looted and caroused in downtown Sydney; later that year a series of fires in Sydney stores were attributed to the Industrial Workers of the World (IWW), precipitating a vigorous campaign to suppress political dissent. Two years of apparent domestic tranquility followed, but the armistice that marked the end of violence in Europe was followed by a sharp increase in the incidence of reported crime in New South Wales. Statistics on homicide and assault show a distinct rise, though not as great as the increase in acquisitive crimes between 1918 and 1920.

1921-1940

By the mid-1920s in Sydney, technological advances were such that new horizons of urban development had emerged. The electrification of the suburban railways served further to increase the suburbanite's mobility; in addition, the extension in 1932 of the underground railway to the centrally located Wynyard Station greatly facilitated access to the central city. Even more significant was the opening in 1932 of the Harbour Bridge, which served as a spur to northward urban expansion.

Sydney's urban growth was stalled throughout the 1930s, however, by the Depression. European investment in Australia ceased almost completely. This drastic decline, combined with plummeting wool prices, was followed by an increase in the rate of unemployment; at the height of the Depression in 1932, nearly one of three workers was idle. Evictions became increasingly numerous, first from homes, then from city parks, and thousands of homeless people began to occupy open land on the fringe of the metropolitan area.[26] Recovery from the Depression was slow; overseas investment and migration resumed and expanded very gradually. By the end of the decade, however, Australia was once again at war, and survival had become a military rather than an economic problem.

The incidence of most kinds of crime declined in the early 1920s to something like the levels in the first decade of the century, but there was an apparent increase toward the end of the decade. As motor cars became more numerous, so did cases of auto theft. Gangs of razor slashers competed for the lucrative local trade in cocaine during the late 1920s, until the Depression dried up the demand. Strikes, and confrontations among strikers, nonunion laborers, and police, were frequent as the Depression worsened. The growing ranks of unemployed workers held frequent meetings and demonstrations, too; depending on time, place, or sponsorship, these gatherings were often disrupted by the police or by a militaristic right-wing group called the New Guard. The Depression also provided the occasion for small-scale dole riots over the distribution of public assistance, and eviction riots.

1941-1955

World War II, in addition to marking a definitive end to the Depression, also ended the Australian's geographical and psychological isolation in a disconcerting manner. The bombing of Darwin in February 1942 and the sinking of a Japanese midget submarine in Sydney Harbour four months later were severe jolts to a people for whom previous wars had been distant affairs. With the war's end, activities in the Sydney metropolitan area turned to the tasks of demobilization. Returning servicemen were provided with housing and educational subsidies, and most quickly found employment in a rapidly expanding postwar economy. Stimulated by unprecedented overseas demand for Australian primary products and by the momentum of wartime manufacturing, Sydney experienced economic growth even greater than that of the boom years of the 1880s. Even the paralyzing coal strike of 1949, which contributed to the fall of the federal Labor Government, did little more than force a temporary pause in Sydney's economic growth.

The end of the war brought new waves of immigrants to Australia, at least half of them of non-British origin. Australia's readiness to receive refugees constituted a marked departure from previous immigration policy; assisted migrants from Central and Eastern Europe were to make a lasting contribution to a culture that had previously been isolated and homogeneous. Already Australia's most cosmopolitan city, Sydney attracted its share of new Australians. The metropolitan area's population grew impressively, passing 1.5 million in 1948. Thousands of older dwellings in the city proper and inner suburbs were regarded as substandard, and pressures of demand brought about increasing subdivision of the metropolitan fringe, thus making way for the suburban sprawl that characterizes the metropolitan area today.

Unlike the years after World War I, there was little apparent change in the pattern of serious crime after 1945. There were substantial short-term fluctuations in arrests for prostitution and after-hours grog selling, a function of variation in police enforcement. The rate of arrests for drunkenness, however, more than doubled over a five-year period, then began a gradual decline. There also were a handful of incidents of collective protest, some evolving out of labor disputes and others focusing on Cold War issues.[27]

1956-1973

The face of Sydney changed in the 1960s to an extent unparalleled in the twentieth century. The period could be described as "the decade of the developer." An unprecedented level of commercial affluence was reflected in the towering office blocks that rose both in the central business district and across the harbor in North Sydney. For the vast majority of Sydneysiders whose income no longer permits the luxury of harborside living, suburban development provides living space. Middle-income and working-class suburbs, consisting largely of detached bungalows roofed in red tile, now extend twenty miles to the southwest toward Bankstown and Liverpool. Middle- and upper-class suburbs reach north to Hornsby, and east to the ocean on both sides of the harbor.

The population of the Sydney metropolitan area increased by twenty percent from 1960 to 1970 and reached three million by the mid-1970s. A striking though temporary demographic change has been the coming of age of the postwar baby crop: young males aged 18 to 24 increased by 58 percent during the decade ending in 1969. Sydney continued to grow more rapidly than other urban and country areas of the state, with six of ten New South Welshmen residing in the city by 1970. Part of the increase is due to the wave of immigration that began after the war and continues to add to the city's ethnic diversity. Those of Anglo-Saxon or Celtic heritage still comprise the vast majority of the city's people, but small neighborhoods of Greek, Italian, and Yugoslav migrants and their offspring may be found on the fringe of the city proper and in the inner ring of suburbs. By 1966, 13.3 percent of Sydney's inhabitants were non-British European migrants.[28] In addition to attracting the bulk of the overseas migrants to New South Wales, Sydney also draws people from the country areas of the state. R. J. Lawrence attributes one-sixth of Sydney's recent growth to rural-urban movement.[29]

Spurred by a mineral boom, industrial development, and a substantial increase in exports, the standard of living has risen markedly in New South Wales over the past two decades. Aside from a slight recession in 1960, when unemployment reached four percent, jobs have been available for almost everyone during the period. Sydney factory employment increased to more than 400,000 by 1968. Although a worker's wages remain relatively low in comparison to those of an American counterpart, the average resident of Sydney enjoys a level of material comfort greater than it has been at any time in the past. Moreover, Australian living standards compare quite favorably with those of other Western industrial societies.

There exist no precise figures on the distribution of income in Sydney, yet few residents experience either great wealth or dire poverty. Those who suffer most are the small number of aborigines in Sydney (about 10,000), the aged and chronically ill, and large families of unskilled and semiskilled industrial laborers.

The citizens and authorities of New South Wales continue their long-standing habit of directing occasional bursts of self-righteousness against common moral offenses. Prostitution and illegal betting on horse racing were the object of such attention during the 1960s; the latter problem was "solved" with the establishment in 1965 of institutionalized off-track betting under state control. Illegal abortions and "pack rape" attracted special attention in 1970 and after. Of greater public concern, however, were the more numerous and familiar categories of offenses against persons and property; beginning in 1963, police reports reflect dramatic increases in the rates of burglary, larceny, assault and robbery, and armed robbery. Similar trends were noted in other Western cities, and, in Sydney as elsewhere, there is little to suggest that they are mainly an artifact of better policing or reporting systems; rather, they seem to reflect real and substantial changes in behavior.

There also has been a recrudescence of collective protest in Sydney, a form of activity that had been absent since the late 1940s. The decision of the Menzies Government in 1965 to commit Australian troops to the American operations in Vietnam engendered widespread opposition, especially among university students. Thousands of young Australians participated in protest demonstrations and marches between 1965 and 1972, and though Sydney protests were generally nonviolent, acts of civil disobedience and arrests were not infrequent. Growing sympathy for the cause of racial equality, and a visit by the South African rugby team to Australia in 1971, have provided occasions for new rounds of demonstrations.

NOTES TO CHAPTER IV. 1

General Note: These abbreviations are used in references throughout this section: HRA = *Historical Records of Australia;* M.L. = Mitchell Library, Sydney; BT = Bigge Commission Transcripts.

1. A. G. L. Shaw, *Convicts and the Colonies* (London: Faber & Faber,
1966); M. D. George, *London Life in the XVIIIth Century* (New York: Harper &
Row, 1964).
2. It appears that geopolitical and strategic considerations also influenced
Lord Sydney's choice. For a fuller discussion, see Geoffrey Blainey, *The
Tyranny of Distance* (Malbourne: Sun Books, 1966).
3. L. L. Robson, *The Convict Settlers of Australia* (Melbourne: Melbourne
University Press, 1965).
4. Phillip to Nepean, July 9, 1788, *Historical Records of Australia*, Ser. I,
Vol. 7, p. 54.
5. Sean Glynn, *Urbanisation in Australian History, 1788-, 900* (Melbourne:
Thomas Nelson Ltd., 1970).
6. N.S.W. Court of Criminal Jurisdiction, *Minutes of Evidence.* Archives of
New South Wales, 1147 A & B.
7. Walter S. Campbell, "The Use and Abuse of Stimulants in the Early Days
of Settlement in N.S.W.," *Royal Australian Historical Society, Journal and
Proceedings*, 18 (1932), 95.
8. C. M. H. Clark, *A History of Australia*, Vol. I (Parkville: Melbourne
University Press, 1962), pp. 171-173.
9. Alan Birch and David S. Macmillan, eds., *The Sydney Scene: 1788-1960*
(Parkville: Melbourne University Press, 1962), pp. 45-46.
10. Annual returns of executions during the nineteenth century may be
found in New South Wales Colonial Secretary, *Returns of the Colony*
1824-1856, and New South Wales *Statistical Register*, 1857-1900.
11. Discussion of rural-urban population distribution is complicated somewhat by alterations to the boundaries of both New South Wales and the
metropolitan area. For example, when part of southeastern New South Wales
became the Colony of Victoria in 1851, Sydney's statistical dominance increased
markedly. Similar distortion has resulted from the incorporation of municipalities into the metropolitan area at various times in the twentieth century.
Despite these artifactual amplifications, Sydney's overshadowing of the hinterlands has been very real and quite substantial.
12. R. B. Madgwick, *Immigration into Eastern Australia, 1788-1851*
(Sydney: Sydney University Press, 1937); A. A. Hayden, "N.S.W. Immigration
Policy, 1856-1900," *Transactions of the American Philosophical Society*, 61,
(1971), 5.
13. *Sydney Morning Herald*, November 6, 1850.
14. George Gipps, "Report on the General State of the Colony, 1840,"
Mitchell Library MSS. A1226, p. 132.

15. N.S.W. Legislative Assembly, *Report from the Select Committee on the Condition of the Working Classes of the Metropolis* (Sydney: Government Printer, 1861), p. 9.

16. New South Wales, Colonial Secretary, *Returns of the Colony, 1857.* Archives of New South Wales, 4/290, p. 506.

17. Glynn, op. cit., pp. 10-41.

18. E. C. Fry, "Growth of an Australian Metropolis," in R. S. Parker and P. N. Troy, eds., *The Politics of Urban Growth* (Canberra: Australian National University Press, 1972), p. 12.

19. New South Wales, *Statistical Register, 1888* (Sydney: Government Printer, 1889), p. 166.

20. John Stanley James, *The Vagabond Papers* (Melbourne: Melbourne University Press, 1969), p. 47.

21. N.S.W. Parliament, Report of the Royal Commission on Chinese Gambling (Sydney: Government Printer, 1892); *A Century of Journalism: The Sydney Morning Herald 1831-1931* (Sydney: John Fairfax and Sons, 1931), p. 325.

22. W. M. Hughes, *Crusts and Crusades* (Sydney: Angus and Robertson, 1947), p. 175.

23. Robin Gollan, *Radical and Working Class Politics: A Study of Eastern Australia, 1850-1910* (Melbourne: Melbourne University Press, 1960), pp. 158-161.

24. D. W. Rawson, "Political Violence in Australia," *Dissent,* no. 22 (Autumn 1968), 23.

25. V. G. Childe, *How Labour Governs* (London: Labour Publishing Co., 1923), p. 184.

26. The best general picture of the Depression era is provided in L. J. Louis and Ian Turner, eds., *The Depression of the 1930s* (North Melbourne: Cassel Australia, 1968).

27 See, for example, Alastair Davidson, *The Communist Party of Australia* (Stanford: Hoover Institution Press, 1969), pp. 107-114.

28. *Official Year Book of New South Wales, 1971* (Sydney: V. C. N. Blight, Government Printer, 1972), p. 265.

29. R. J. Lawrence, "Social Welfare and Urban Growth" in Parker and Troy, eds., op. cit., p. 101.

THE FOUNDING AND ERA OF TRANSPORTATION, 1788-1840

PATTERNS OF CRIME AND CONFLICT, 1788-1840

Disorderly behavior became a fact of life in Sydney only days after the British flag was unfurled over the settlement. On February 6, 1788, the convict women, who had remained on board the ships pending the construction of suitable shelter ashore, disembarked. An extra ration of rum was issued, and the first evening of "debauchery and riot" in recorded Australian history took place.[1] More serious offenses soon followed; there were at least eleven trials for theft and three for assault during the first year of the settlement. Property offenses remained the most prevalent form of serious crime from the early years of the colony until the end of transportation in 1840. In the earliest decades, food and clothing were most often taken, and occasionally such luxury items as wine, tobacco, or soap. Assault and homicide were much less prevalent, but by the mid-1790s at least one or two rapes and homicides appear to have been committed each year.

The Home Government began sending Irish convicts to New South Wales in 1791. Many were transported for conventional offenses against persons and property, but others were sent out for crimes of protest. As their shared awareness of ill treatment at the hands of the Anglo-Saxon heightened, the Irish convicts became even more intent on obtaining revenge if not liberty. An alleged conspiracy of Irish convicts in 1800 moved the authorities to flog five suspects with 1,000 lashes each, and twelve others with up to 500 lashes. In March 1804 an Irish convict named William Johnston gathered more than 300 of his compatriots and began a march on Sydney from the outer settlement of Castle Hill. On learning of the convicts' activity,

Governor King proclaimed the equivalent of martial law and dispatched a platoon of 27 regular troops to engage the insurgents. In rather quick order, the two leaders of the Irish group were captured, nine others were shot dead, and the remainder were put to flight. Forty or so of the more deeply involved survivors were ultimately captured; eight were hanged, nine were given floggings of up to 500 lashes, and others were transported to the Coal River Penal Settlement.[2]

For want of female companionship or other recreational diversions, Sydney's early residents indulged quite freely in drink. The practice of compensating convict laborers in rum for extra work was informal at first, but it became institutionalized, and consumption of spirits reached awesome proportions. A.G.L. Shaw relates that in 1801 the adult population of New South Wales consumed the annual equivalent of eight gallons of spirits per person. The demand for spirits was exploited by a group of officers of the New South Wales Corps, who monopolized imports and charged greatly inflated prices; they soon earned the nickname "Rum Corps" for their regiment.[3] Attempts to limit the consumption of spirits were less than successful. Governor King undertook to reduce the volume of spirits imported into the colony, but his aims were largely thwarted by an increase in smuggling and illicit distillation.

The traffic in spirits also provided a background for the only coup d'état in Australian history. William Bligh, who had commanded the *Bounty* at the time of the mutiny in 1799, assumed the governorship of New South Wales in 1806. The same abrasive, temperamental nature and authoritarian leanings that had inflamed the mutineers were soon visible in Sydney. Undertaking with predictable zeal the struggles against the vested interests of the colony that had frustrated his predecessors, Bligh was soon given the nickname Caligula. His tantrums and barrages of insult were frequent occurrences and, in a colony as small and remote as New South Wales, were bound to elicit reaction. When members of the military and economic elite expressed public discontent with the direction of the colony, Bligh moved to charge the officers with sedition. On January 26, 1808, when Bligh ordered the cancellation of a traditional ceremony and celebration commemorating the founding of the colony, a group of officers of the New South Wales Corps placed him under house arrest. The celebration took place as scheduled; Bligh's unpopularity was such that only his daughter and his secretary sided with him.[4]

When Lachlan Macquarie assumed the governorship of New South Wales in 1810, Sydney Town was relatively free of serious crime. As Table IV.2.1 indicates, property crime continued to be the most prevalent form of serious disorder in the colony. Homicides and

serious assaults were apparently rare, rape and sodomy were almost
never reported. A sharp increase in the apparent rate of theft toward
the end of the decade marked the first "crime wave" of the nineteenth century in Sydney. In addition to serious thefts, the incidence
of lesser offenses (punishable summarily by magistrates) appears to
have doubled between 1819 and 1820—perhaps reflecting the imposition of more rigorous standards of public order (Table IV.2.2).
Among the minor offenses in question were some that applied only
to convicts—attempts to escape, absence without leave, insolence,
and unlawful sale of clothing. Other forms of behavior more generally applicable included disorderly conduct, intoxication, and riot.[5]

Much of the deviant behavior of the day was attributable one way
or another to the demand for spirits. Another form of disorder
involved the perverse exploitation of the few aboriginals who chose
to remain in the vicinity of Sydney. Occasionally a group of colonists

*Table IV.2.1 Supreme Court, Committals per 1,000 Inhabitants,
Selected Offenses, New South Wales, 1811-1821*

Year	Murder and serious assault	Serious crime against sexual morality	Serious property crimes
1811	.90	.00	3.00
1812	.73	.00	2.45
1813	.67	.17	4.58
1814	.92	.08	3.42
1815	n.a.	n.a.	n.a.
1816	.44	.00	1.94
1817	.83	.06	5.22
1818	.55	.14	4.86
1819	.38	.08	2.80
1820	.36	.07	5.86
1821	.30	.03	6.17

Source: New South Wales Colonial Secretary, *Returns of the Colony*

*Table IV.2.2 Unspecified General Offenses Committed in the Sydney
Area, 1817-1820*

Year	Total
1817	380
1818	575
1819	665
1820	1,369

Source: Appendix to Bigge Commission Report (Mitchell Library, Vol. 130)

got two natives slightly drunk and encouraged them to fight each other with knives or spears. The outcomes of such episodes were predictably barbarous.[6]

Although 1822 was an atypically busy year in the courts of New South Wales, the early 1820s otherwise showed little change in rates of committals (Table IV.2.3). The discontinuity in 1822, according to Governor Brisbane, was attributable to the judge advocate's having held circuit in Van Diemen's Land to clear up a backlog of cases there. There was in the late 1820s a noteworthy statistical increase in serious property crimes but without similar trends in either homicide or serious assault. Then from 1830 through 1840 the incidence of serious thefts declined to a tenth of its initial level, as indexed by Supreme Court convictions (see Figure IV.2.1).

Many distinctive features of criminality in New South Wales are not apparent in statistical summaries. In the 1820s a particularly colorful form of criminal deviance emerged. From time to time some of the less docile convicts made their escape, acquired firearms and horses, and headed for the bush, gaining their subsequent livelihood from attacks on settlers and travelers in rural areas. "Bushrangers," as they were called, had become so active by 1825 that the Legislative Council passed a unanimous resolution urging "prompt and decisive measures" to suppress "the daring Robbers who have formed themselves into Bandittis in these parts of the Colony."[7]

As settlers penetrated more deeply into the hinterland of New South Wales, conflict with aboriginals became increasingly common. Recent interpretations view aboriginal hostility as guerrilla-type resistance to European encroachment. In any event, aboriginal attacks on settlers or livestock often precipitated punitive expeditions, and the reciprocally increasing hostility resulted in a great deal of bloodshed, much of which has been neglected by historians. The massacre of

Table IV.2.3 Courts of Criminal Jurisdiction, Committals per 1,000
Population, Selected Offenses in New South Wales,
1819-1824

Year	Total committals: all offenses	Murder	Burglary	Assault	Highway robbery
1819	2.49	.50	.35	.35	.69
1820	3.64	.32	.82	.32	.79
1821	4.31	.20	.57	.24	1.42
1822	6.27	.34	1.21	.57	1.55
1823	5.00	.26	.65	n.a.	.78
1824	2.99	.48	.62	.08	.25

Source: New South Wales Colonial Secretary, Returns of the Colony.

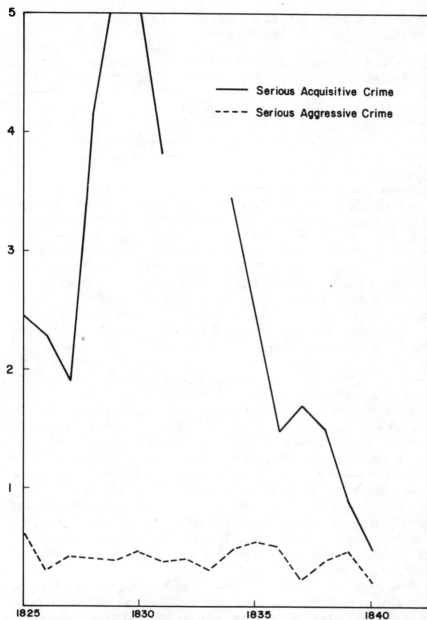

Figure IV.2.1 New South Wales: Supreme court convictions per 1000 inhabitants, crimes against persons and property, 1825-1840

almost 60 aboriginals by a group of volunteer Mounted Police near Myall Creek in 1838 did not result in a trial, since attempts to obtain evidence were unsuccessful. Later in the year, at the same location, the murder of 28 natives by a group of white station hands resulted in the conviction and execution at Sydney of seven of the offenders.[8]

DEMOGRAPHIC AND ECONOMIC CONDITIONS
OF PUBLIC ORDER, 1788-1840

Patterns of crime and conflict in the colony's first 50 years were influenced in a very direct way by the changing characteristics of the population. There was also one substantial episode of increased criminality concurrent with economic adversity.

The social structure of New South Wales during the early years of settlement was, in a word, imbalanced. Three-quarters of the original colonists were lower-class Englishmen, mostly males, who happened also to be convicted criminals. It is difficult to imagine a population more disposed to deviance as conventionally defined and more likely to be treated by authorities as offenders. There were relatively few women among those who landed with the First Fleet; approximately 180 female convicts and 30 wives were among the party, which numbered slightly more than 1,000. The early pattern of population growth in New South Wales was erratic and largely a function of convict arrivals. The number of convicts in the population remained around 2,000 for most of the colony's first two decades, while the military and administrative establishment grew steadily. The influx of Irish convicts that began in 1791 also had a profound effect on public order in the colony. By the end of 1800, there were more than 1,000 Irishmen in the colony, more than twenty percent of the total population. Their resentment of British dominance was predictable, as was their rebelliousness.

Changes in policy occurring after 1820 had altered significantly the proportion of convicts in the colony by 1840. Despite an increase in the number of arriving transported convicts, the introduction of assisted passage for free settlers in 1831 partially redressed the demographic imbalance. In 1841 Sydney's population was only 58 percent male, and convict residents numbered only 10 percent.[9] It is worth noting that the substantial increase in male and convict population between 1817 and 1821 was not followed by a major increase in rates of criminality, but the decline of these proportions in the 1830s coincided with decreases in most of our indicators of criminality.

The economic privations of the colony's early years undoubtedly provided compelling motivation for thefts of foodstuffs, but theft also appears to have been common in the years of relative prosperity that began in the 1790s. At the end of the 1820s, though, New South Welshmen experienced a period of serious economic adversity. A drought set in during 1827 and lasted until the end of the decade. Crop failures were common, and property was seized and sold. These were also the years of a very substantial increase in serious theft, noted previously. By the early 1830s, however, productivity in the wool industry increased, wool prices rose, and the colony began a decade of economic expansion. And with that expansion, property crimes declined precipitously. Since we have only data on high court committals and convictions for this period, though, we cannot say with certainty how much of this rise and decline was a function of a real increase in theft and how much reflected an increase in the seriousness with which authorities regarded economic crime.

PUBLIC OPINION AND POLITICAL INTERESTS, 1788-1840

Contemporary Opinion

Speculation on the causes of criminal deviance during the first years of settlement involved a simple argument. Thefts occurred because crime had been a way of life for most of the colonists. Indeed, their very presence in New South Wales was directly attributable to those inclinations. Deviant tendencies were aggravated, moreover, by the near-famine conditions which prevailed in 1790 and 1792. Governor Phillip, in commenting on the theft of 30 percent of the colony's corn harvest, provided a blunt diagnosis:

> From the time the corn began to ripen to the time it was housed, the convicts were pressed by hunger, and great quantities were stolen and concealed in the woods; several convicts died from feeding on it in its crude state, when carrying the grain to the public granary. But in speaking of these people, it is but just to observe that I can recollect very few crimes during the last three years but what have been committed to procure the necessaries of life.[10]

As the population became more diverse, opinion on the causes of criminal deviance tended to focus on the size and distribution of the convict population. The fall in the apparent rate of property crime from 1818 to 1819 was generally regarded as due to the opening of a convict barracks in Sydney during the latter year.[11] Convicts previously had not been provided with accommodations and consequently were forced to seek out and pay for their own lodging. The decline proved to be quite temporary, however, as rates increased in 1820 and 1821. John T. Bigge, who was undertaking an exhaustive examination of the colony and its administration, attributed the 1820 increase to the recent growth in the size of the convict population and to greater vigilance by the police force.[12] In addition, Bigge blamed a good deal of the disorderly behavior of the day on the scarcity of women.[13]

The voluminous testimony gathered by Bigge during his inquiry revealed some divergence of opinion within the colony on the causes of the apparent increase in acquisitive crime during 1820. John Blaxland, one of the early free settlers in New South Wales, suggested that the courts and the governor had become too lenient and that the greater severity of punishments awarded in previous years had acted as a more successful deterrent.[14] Blaxland's brother Gregory viewed matters differently, suggesting that apparent increases in theft were generally attributable to the existence of greater opportunity. Without doubt, there were more people to be robbed and more cattle to be stolen than at any previous time in the history of New South Wales.[15] Another more "liberal" view was expressed in 1824 by Governor Brisbane, who wrote:

> it is a remarkable fact . . . that every murder or diabolical crime which has been committed in the Colony since my arrival has been perpetrated by Roman Catholics, and this I ascribe entirely to their barbarous ignorance, and total want of education, the invariable companions of Bigotry and cruelty, as well as the Parent of crime. . . .[16]

His recommendation was that more priests be sent for the spiritual instruction of the group identified.

Most contemporary speculation on the causes of crime during the 1820s and 1830s assumed the existence of a criminal class, and almost universally the convicts were regarded as prone to criminal deviance by definition. Official references to an increase in robbery with violence in the spring of 1826 include the attempts of Captain F. N. Rossi, First Police Magistrate in Sydney, to explain the disorder. Rossi argued that such crimes were the work of large numbers of former convicts, now free by expiration of sentence, who had come to Sydney to obtain certificates of freedom. According to Rossi, these men encountered their "old associates and confederates" and tended to lapse into their old ways.[17]

Preoccupation with the deviant inclinations of the convict classes was to endure well past the cessation of transportation to New South Wales. John Macarthur, a wealthy free pastoralist who wanted to maintain a rigid class distinction in the colony, claimed that

> of the cases brought before juries in the Criminal Courts, a very small portion are from the class either of Emigrants or Natives of the Colony— nearly the whole mass of crime being committed either by convicts, or by those who have been in that condition.[18]

The size and visibility of the convict population tended to inhibit further contemplation on the etiological aspects of crime. There were those, however, who viewed the harsh treatment experienced by some convicts not as a deterrent, but rather as conducive to anti-social behavior, and Governor Bourke maintained in 1834:

> Severity carried beyond a certain point, especially towards men of violent
> or turbulent feelings will only tend to inflame their indisposition to labor
> into more dangerous acts of desperation and revenge and the history of
> this Colony during periods in which greater severity was occasionally
> exercised has fully borne out the truth of this observation.[19]

Finally, a few suggested that disorder might have been attributable
to inefficiency in the existing law enforcement apparatus. Captain
Rossi cited a difficulty that was to inhibit police activity in New
South Wales for another 30 years: "The want of an effective inter-
course and connection between the police of Sydney and that of the
Districts in the Interior."[20]

The Rulers and the Law

In general, members of the first elite in New South Wales shared
the common view that crime was a natural impulse of the convict
classes, an impulse that was intensified by conditions of material
scarcity. Impelled by this belief, officials of the colony sought first
to control deviance by limiting opportunities—thus they attempted
to restrict freedom of association, the distribution of spirits, and
access to weapons.

The second line of attack was the issuance of increasingly detailed
regulations of virtually every sphere of human behavior. Punitive
measures of great severity were a last resort. Such policies were not
followed consistently, however; they varied considerably, especially
in the early years, according to the personalities and preferences of
successive governors.

Under the provisions of their respective commissions, the first
governors of New South Wales were invested with considerable
authority. They were to enforce the existing laws of the realm;
beyond that the governors were military commanders empowered to
rule by decree.[21] During the colony's perilous first years the crime
regarded by Governor Phillip with greatest gravity was theft. In the
abstract, such behavior violated the sanctity of property. Under the
particularly austere conditions of New South Wales, theft of foodstuffs quite visibly jeopardized the existence of the whole population. Because theft was covered extensively in the existing criminal
law, Phillip had only to issue General Orders that established curfews
and forbade convicts to exchange their possessions or clothing for
money, spirits, or tobacco.

Stirrings on the part of the recently arrived Irish convicts aroused
Phillip's successor, Governor John Hunter. A man with little fond-
ness for the Irish, Hunter viewed the insolence of the Irish convicts as
troublesome and their cohesiveness and class consciousness as threat-

ening.[22] He responded to rumors of a conspiracy with brutal punishment and a spate of regulations for the more effective control of convicts. In 1795, for example, Hunter ordered convicts to carry passes on their person. Such policies were continued by Governor King, who in April 1802 proclaimed the production or concealment of pikes to be an offense punishable by execution. In May 1806, a few months before his departure from the colony. King issued two General Orders limiting freedom of assembly; the more stringent of the two created the offense of being at large without authorization.[23]

A substantial change in policies toward the convict population was foreshadowed by the arrival of Governor Lachlan Macquarie, who landed in Sydney with his own 73rd Regiment, assuming the governorship on January 1, 1810. He placed considerable value on discipline and obedience and, like many commanders, resented criticism or opposition. Unlike those who preceded him, however, Macquarie brought to Sydney a certain evangelistic zeal and sense of moral rectitude consistent with his Scottish heritage.

Shortly after assuming office, Macquarie reduced the number of licensed public houses and created the offense of selling spirits during divine services. He was offended by the rather loose practice of cohabitation that was prevalent and expressed support for the institution of marriage, which he recommended to all eligible parties. He also defined indecent profanation of the Sabbath as a crime and made Sunday church attendance mandatory for all convicts.[24]

Despite Macquarie's reputation for tolerance and fairness and concern for rehabilitation (see below), there remained glaring asymmetries in the New South Wales criminal justice system. The Select Committee on Transportation (1812) noted that among the cases tried before the Court of Criminal Jurisdiction in 1810, "a person charged with shooting at and wounding a native, was tried simply for an assault, whilst another who had committed a similar offence against a European, was tried on the same day for life."[25]

Minor offenses committed by convicts were punishable by flogging, whereas free settlers were usually fined for their transgressions. Absence from work or insolence to an overseer could bring a convict 50 lashes, but free men convicted for minor assaults were fined one or two pounds. Two sentences from the Bench at Windsor in 1819 provide an interesting view of the convict's legal status. One free settler was fined £10 for harboring a runaway, while another convicted of striking a convict in government service was awarded a fine of a shilling.[26]

Macquarie's sympathy for the emancipists in the colony irritated many free settlers. Prominent citizens complained bitterly of the privileges Macquarie bestowed on the emancipist class. Their complaints were also directed at London, where the authorities, concerned over the expense of the colony and its effectiveness in deterring British criminal deviance, commissioned a thorough investigation of New South Wales and its administration. The Bigge Commission Report, published in three parts during 1822 and 1823, constituted a general repudiation of Macquarie's policies. Whereas Macquarie regarded New South Wales as a colony to be developed, Bigge and Secretary of State for War and the Colonies Bathurst were more concerned with the suppression of postwar disorders in London and sought a much greater emphasis on the retributive and deterrent functions of the colony. Macquarie, always sensitive to criticism, resigned in 1821 and returned to England. The rehabilitative themes for which he has since been celebrated were a long time in re-emerging.

Macquarie's successor, Sir Thomas Brisbane, was an aloof and pious individual, less interested in the exercise of political power than in the science of astronomy. The direction of his governorship was thus largely provided by the authorities in London, who responded to the recommendations of the Bigge Commission with calls for the exercise of more stringent discipline over the convicts. In particular, Brisbane was charged with expanding the system of convict assignment, the procedure by which convicts were given out as servants and laborers to members of the public.

With the appointment of Lieutenant General Ralph Darling to the governorship in December 1825, the colony of New South Wales entered what was perhaps its most punitive phase. To a greater extent than his immediate predecessors, Darling valued discipline, obedience, and organization. When criticism of his severity began to appear in the Sydney press, Darling introduced legislation to define press criticism of the colonial government as a crime, imposed taxes on newspapers, and provided for the registration and regulation of publishing activities. Darling undertook the prosecution of some of his more vocal critics, and relationships between him and the public deteriorated still further.

Later in Darling's administration, in 1828, the law relating to property offenses was revised, but only in the form of an adoption verbatim of existing British law. The importance contemporary elites accorded the protection of property can be seen from the breadth and severity of the law's provisions. Punishable by hanging were robbery from the person, stealing from a church, burglary, housebreaking, stealing horses, cows, or sheep, and obtaining money by threatening to accuse a party of an infamous crime. Dozens of other clauses, pertaining to particular types of unlawful appropriation, from thefts of vegetables to thefts from oyster beds, were included in

the act; noncapital sentences usually involved secondary transportation to the penal settlements at Norfolk Island or Coal
River, or imprisonment with hard labor. Other kinds of larceny
were punishable by transportation for a maximum of seven years,
or by imprisonment for two years with hard labor or in solitary
confinement.[27]

Another special concern of the New South Wales elite was an
assured supply of obedient labor. The shortage of workers was a
chronic problem and was especially burdensome before assisted
migration began in 1831. To minimize any economic inconvenience
that might result from diminished productivity of the nonconvict
labor force, Darling turned to masters and servants legislation of the
traditional British type. "An Act for the better Regulation of Servants, Labourers, and Work People" (1828) made the offenses of
neglecting to work, refusing to work, or absenting oneself from work
punishable by a maximum of six months' imprisonment, and for-
feiture of all wages and pay. Servants destroying or losing any
property entrusted to them could be required to pay double damages
or to serve a maximum of six months in prison.[28] A few years later
the persisting labor shortage and the elite's long-standing distaste for
indolence led to the passage of "An Act for the prevention of
Vagrancy, and for the punishment of Idle and Disorderly Persons,
Rogues and Vagabonds, and Incorrigible Rogues, in the Colony of
New South Wales," (1835).[29] This act introduced an entirely new
range of offenses from alms gathering by false pretense to one
uniquely antipodean, that of lodging or wandering in company with
aborigines. The act delineated categories that were to endure for well
over a century in New South Wales law. Individuals thrice convicted
of drunkenness within a year, or persons without visible lawful
means of support, were classed as "idle and disorderly persons,"
subject to a maximum of three months' hard labor. Second
offenders, persons betting or exposing themselves in public, and
individuals loitering with intent to commit a felony were considered
"rogues and vagabonds" and could receive a maximum sentence of six
months' hard labor. A second conviction as "rogue and vagabond" led
the offender to be classed as an "incorrigible rogue," liable to punishment of hard labor, whipping, and one year's imprisonment.

The increasing size and spatial dispersion of the convict population
posed substantial problems for the maintenance of order, for the
escape of an assigned convict constituted not only an economic loss
but, given the attractions of bushranging, a potential physical threat
as well. A measure enacted during 1830 in response to bushranging
and housebreaking greatly expanded police powers of search and
detention of suspected criminals and promised the speedy execution

of those convicted of robbery or housebreaking.[30] The "Bushranging Act," as it was popularly called, empowered any free person to apprehend any stranger on suspicion of being a convict illegally at large, placing the burden of proof of identity on the accused.

It is quite evident that three conditions valued highly by the elite—control of the convict population, the security of property, and the availability of docile, inexpensive labor—underlay much of the rule-making and legislative activity of the first 50 years. These values also influenced other institutions of public order, to which we now turn.

INSTITUTIONS OF PUBLIC ORDER AND THEIR EFFECTS, 1788-1840

The Police

The first law enforcement organization in Australia was exceedingly modest. In August 1789 Governor Phillip appointed twelve convicts of respectable behavior as a night watch to guard the public stores. Although the military establishment could have performed certain law enforcement functions, its members were reluctant to undertake any responsibilities other than the defense of the colony. The one significant occasion for military involvement in the maintenance of domestic order, the suppression of the Irish convicts' rebellion, was an isolated event.

By 1810 the population of Sydney had grown so large that the existing system of night patrols was deemed inadequate. Macquarie established the first formal police force in that year and appointed D'Arcy Wentworth as Principal Superintendent. The town was divided into five districts, each having a watch house, one district constable, and six petty constables attached to it. District constables were paid £10 per year and provided with food and clothing; petty constables were supplied with food and clothing but received no other compensation. Each constable on patrol carried a cutlass and a rattle, the forerunner of the police whistle. A special responsibility of the constable was to apprehend suspected persons found at large in the town after 9 p.m. The first constables included both free men and emancipists, and their conduct was generally regarded as satisfactory.[31]

By the mid-1820s the Sydney Town Police had begun to face problems of increasing severity. In the face of continuing pressures from London to minimize expenditures, it was chronically shorthanded. Hazel King relates that Sydney patrolmen worked through

the night in six-hour shifts and spent a good part of each day
performing such administrative duties as serving warrants and attending court.[32] Pay was painfully low, and recruitment of responsible
candidates for the force was difficult. During an eighteen-month
period in 1825-1826, there were 25 resignations and 57 dismissals for
misconduct from a force whose average strength was 50.[33]

Captain F. N. Rossi, appointed Principal Superintendent of Police
in New South Wales in 1825, made frequent requests for more
manpower and better remuneration, but without success. The
Sydney Police Act of 1833 complicated matters still further by
creating additional responsibilities unrelated to conventional law
enforcement. In the absence of any municipal institutions, the
Sydney police became involved in such activities as public health,
pollution control, and the licensing of dogs, carts, and boats.[34]
Colonel H. C. Wilson replaced Rossi in 1833, and although the
calibre of recruits improved somewhat under his administration,
Wilson like Rossi was personally burdened with both administrative
and judicial responsibilities. Moreover, the hours of duty for patrolmen were extemely taxing: Constables patrolled in alternate two-
hour shifts two nights out of every three.[35]

In 1835, meanwhile, a decision was reached in London that had a
substantial impact on law enforcement in New South Wales. Beginning in that year the Home Government placed the entire burden of
colonial police expenditures on the New South Wales treasury.
Neither the governor nor the members of the Legislative Council
could prevail on the Home Government to reverse its decision, but
they did what they could to minimize the burden on the treasury in
Sydney. New South Wales had become a relatively orderly place in
1839, and in that year a select committee on police and gaols
recommended a reduction in the size of the Sydney constabulary
from 114 to 80.[36]

Judicial and Penal Institutions

The judicial structure of early New South Wales would have been
appropriate for a military prison; the senior judicial office, that of
judge advocate, was occupied by military officers without training in
the law. The Court of Criminal Jurisdiction was in fact a court
martial, its members drawn from the commissioned officers of the
colony.

Penal practices employed during the first years in New South
Wales ranged from the brutal to the benign. Capital and corporal
punishments were awarded generously, the latter particularly so.
Returns from the original Court of Criminal Jurisdiction[37] reveal the

severity of the sentences. A laborer convicted in 1789 of stealing a pound of tobacco was given 500 lashes; the following year a man convicted of stealing three pounds of potatoes was sentenced to receive 2,000. Appropriation of more valuable items, and offenses in general that were committed in a dwelling house, were punishable by hanging. Death sentences, however, were often commuted to transportation for seven- or fourteen-year periods at Norfolk Island or Coal River. Here offenders were subjected to the most austere conditions of hard labor, under iron (often literally) discipline.

In contrast to the harsh disincentives to crime were the rewards that might be extended to convicts for industrious obedience. Beginning in 1790 governors were authorized to grant to well-behaved convicts pardons that were unconditional or conditional on the individual remaining in the colony. Shortly thereafter, during the administration of Governor King, passes, or "tickets of leave" were issued, which excused a convict from his assigned labor and permitted him to earn an independent livelihood. According to A.G.L. Shaw, motives other than rehabilitation often underlay the granting of tickets of leave. To minimize the strain on the public stores, tickets were granted to any convict with the capability of self-support, regardless of behavioral merit.[38]

Significant institutional changes during the 1820s and 1830s marked the beginning of a departure from military rule. The Legislative Council, created in 1824, represented the first structural departure from gubernatorial autocracy. Although the Council was an appointed body having only limited advisory powers, it provided a foundation for future constitutional development and collective decision making. The evolution of the legal process during the period was of equal significance. A population limited to convicts, soldiers, and administrators might be served well by a system of courts martial, but as the number of free settlers increased, pressures mounted to institute trials by jury. But the Home Government, extremely reluctant to introduce such policies in what was still a prison, postponed any alterations until 1833. At that point, defendants were able to choose between a civil jury trial and a court martial.

The transition from courts martial to the system of civil juries appears to have taken place without difficulty. Chief Justice Forbes noted in 1836, after the policy of optional jury trial had been in effect for three years, that rates of conviction of jury trials were no lower than those of courts martial. Indeed, he concluded that the introduction of trial by jury in New South Wales had been long overdue.[39] But it was not until 1839, a half-century after the colony's founding, that military juries were abolished.

This institutional trend notwithstanding, the convict population of the colony increased to a record high during the 1830s. Richard Bourke, who took office in 1832, is regarded by some historians as one of the more humanitarian of the early governors, but he achieved the reputation in spite of continued pressures from the Home Government to use severe measures of control. In August 1832 Bourke saw to the repeal of the harsh acts Darling had passed to discipline the convict population and replaced them with measures of significantly reduced severity.[40] Most important were the restrictions he placed on magistrates' powers of awarding corporal punishment. Humanitarianism in 1832 had its harsh side, however, for even under Bourke's reforms, insubordination, abusive language, or neglect of work were punishable by 50 lashes.[41] Despite Bourke's reputation for humaneness, available data reflect no significant decreases in either the volume or the severity of physical punishment administered during his term as governor. During the middle 1830s the equivalent of one convict in every four was flogged, although many were punished more than once in a given year. The number of hangings tended to fluctuate from year to year. At no time during Bourke's tenure did the number of executions reach the record of 52 set in 1829, yet 1834 and 1835 were among the busiest ever for New South Wales hangmen.

A number of approaches to the treatment of deviance were employed during the 1820s and 1830s in New South Wales, and all were severe, inexpensive, or both. Offenders convicted of serious crimes in New South Wales courts were often transported to one of the colony's main penal establishments: Port Macquarie, Moreton Bay, or Norfolk Island. These places, notorious for their brutality, existed not to reform the offender but to maximize the individual's suffering for his transgressions and to instill dread in potential miscreants. Labor was extremely arduous, disciplinary infractions were punished by brutal flogging, and general conditions were such that death rates were extraordinarily high.

Since secondary transportation was relatively costly and unproductive, a number of alternatives were devised to exploit convict labor more efficiently. Lesser offenders, for example, were often sentenced to labor on a treadmill, a punishment that some observers at the time regarded as more effective than flogging. An investigatory committee reported that during a four and one-half month period at the end of 1824, no less than 657,315 pounds of wheat and 32,960 pounds of bran were ground at one mill.[42]

There were, however, many more criminals in New South Wales than were needed to grind the amount of grain available, and in 1826 Governor Darling established chain gangs to work on public works projects. More than 5,000 convicts, almost one in five of those transported to the colony during the decade, worked on the roads at one time or another during the period 1826-1836. Shaw describes how the prisoners were locked up at night in "prisoners' boxes," small containers mounted on wheels. To maximize productivity of the road gangs, flogging was freely employed during the day.[43]

The chronic shortage of free labor during the 1830s led to the increasing reliance on "assignment" of convicts as servants to private citizens. In addition to facilitating economic development in rural areas, the dispersal of convicts throughout the colony was regarded as conducive to rehabilitation. The greatest drawback of assignment as a penal strategy was its ultimate arbitrariness. Whereas some convicts were assigned to humane masters, others fell into the hands of sadists. Authorities agreed that for some, assignment could only be regarded as a reward, but for those less fortunate, the severity of treatment came close to exceeding the heinousness of their transgression. The arbitrariness and lack of uniformity inherent in the system of convict assignment moved authorities in London to reject it in favor of a return to gang labor.

Effects

The various crime control strategies adopted by the early governors were not without their shortcomings. Despite the savage brutality of the punishments awarded those convicted of robbing from the public stores, the thefts continued. Some hungry convicts may have been deterred by the threat of lash or scaffold, but others obviously were not. Moreover, as successful harvests generated an abundance of provisions, thieves turned from necessities to "luxury" items. In addition, the settlement's embryonic police force varied in terms of effectiveness. While Phillip proudly related a diminution in the incidence of robbery following the establishment of the night watch,[44] Hunter reported six years later that some of his sentinels were involved in thefts from public stores.[45] Attempts to limit the supply of spirits in the colony were also unsuccessful. The political power wielded by members of the New South Wales Corps between 1792 and 1809 was sufficient to preclude effective restriction of smuggling and the illicit distribution of spirits. We see here another of the earlier attempts in New South Wales to enforce a law opposed by a large number of citizens; the theme recurs frequently in the following pages.

Between 1810 and 1821 the ends of Governor Macquarie and of the Home Office were thwarted, mainly because they were fundamentally incompatible. Officials in London wanted to make New

South Wales a place that Britons and Irishmen of deviant inclinations would hold in utmost dread. Macquarie, on the other hand, sought to develop the colony in a much wider social and economic context. Indeed, the governor's rehabilitative strategies of convict management may have succeeded in making life in Sydney more pleasant for a transgressor than was his previous existence in London. As convicts began to land in New South Wales in increasing numbers toward the end of the decade, neither Macquarie's humaneness nor his new police force were successful in limiting crime. Criminals in Britain do not appear to have been deterred by the threat of transportation to Sydney, and their arrival in the antipodes strained severely the system of treatments that had been developed for a much smaller convict population.

In the 1830s the Bushranging Act (1830) was followed by an apparent diminution in the incidence of serious theft, which helped persuade authorities that the act had functioned as an effective deterrent. Governor Bourke, while regarding the legislation as somewhat repressive, was convinced by the unanimous opinion of the Legislative Council that the statute had been successful in restoring order.[46] Two years later, when Bourke reluctantly renewed the act a second time, he suggested that feelings of security were substantially reinforced by its continued operation. Evidence that the act may have served as much a symbolic as a strategic function may be gleaned from the statement of a police official that few if any apprehensions or convictions took place under the act anywhere in the colony.[47] It is worth noting that the years 1828 and 1829 were accompanied by severe economic contraction, and economic recovery coincided with the diminution of bushranging. This is neither the first nor the last instance in which we find New South Wales authorities attributing a decline in crime to their public order policies when the same result can be explained with equal plausibility by reference to socioeconomic change.

NOTES TO CHAPTER IV.2

1. Clark, op. cit., p. 88.

2. Humphrey McQueen, "Convicts and Rebels," *Labour History*, no. 15 (November 1968), 8.

3. A. G. L. Shaw, "Aspects of N.S.W., 1788-, 810," *Journal of the Royal Australian Historical Society* 57, pt. 2 (June 1971), 103-104.

4. Evatt has shown that Bligh did have some sympathizers among the free settlers of the colony. Their lack of overt support for the deposed governor thus may have been attributable to tolerance of the insurgents combined with fears of reprisal. H. V. Evatt, *Rum Rebellion* (Sydney: Angus and Robertson, 1938).

5. John T. Bigge, *Report of the Commissioner of Inquiry into the State of the Colony of New South Wales* (London: 1823), Irish University Press Series of British Parliamentary Papers, *Colonies: Australia, I*, p. 98.

6. Clark, op. cit., p. 317.

7. N.S.W. Legislative Council, 6 September, 1825. Mitchell Library MSS, A1267, Vol. X, pp. 224-225.

8. C. D. Rowley, *The Destruction of Aboriginal Society* (Harmondsworth: Penquin Books, 1972), pp. 17, 37-38.

9. New South Wales Colonial Secretary, *Returns of the Colony, 1841* (Archives of New South Wales, 4/290), pp. 257-258.

10. Phillip to Dundas, 3 October 1792, HRA I, 1, pp. 373-374.

11. Bigge Commission, Minutes of Evidence, M.L. BT Box 2, p. 567.

12. Bigge, Report . . ., p. 99.

13. Ibid., p. 106.

14. Bigge Commission, Minutes of Evidence, M.L. BT Box 7, p. 2138.

15. Ibid., p. 2142.

16. Brisbane to Bathurst, 28 October, 1824, Mitchell Library MSS, A1267, pt. 4, pp. 25-26.

17. F. N. Rossi, First Police Magistrate, Report of 7 October, 1826. Mitchell Library MSS, A1197, pp. 516-518.

18. John Macarthur, "Petition to His Majesty and to the House of Commons," 9 February, 1837. Mitchell Library MSS, A234, p. 98.

19. Bourke to Stanley, 15 January 1834, Mitchell Library MSS, A1267, pt. 5, p. 588.

20. Rossi, op. cit.

21. A. C. V. Melbourne, *Early Constitutional Development in Australia*, 2d ed. (St. Lucia: University of Queensland Press, 1963), pp. 6-28.

22. Indeed, Hunter referred to Irish convicts as "liars and perjurers" and recommended that they be sent to Africa. HRA I, 3, p. 175; p. 348.

23. McQueen, op. cit., pp. 5-6.

24. Clark, op. cit., pp. 265-269.

25. Great Britain, Parliament, Select Committee on Transportation to New South Wales, First Report with Minutes of Evidence and Appendix (London: 1812), Irish University Press Series of British Parliamentary Papers, *Transportation, I*, p. 8.

26. Bigge Commission, Minutes of Evidence, M.L. BT Box 12, pp. 190-229.

27. Geo. IV 1 (26 March, 1828).

28. Geo. IV 9 (17 July, 1828).

29. 6 Will. IV 6 (25 August, 1835).

30. 11 Geo. IV 10 (21 April, 1830).

31. Bigge Commission, Minutes of Evidence, M.L. BT Box 2, p. 560.

32. Hazel King, "Some Aspects of Police Administration in N.S.W., 1825-1851," *Journal of the Royal Australian Historical Society*, 42: 5 (December 1956), 217.

33. Rossi, op. cit., p. 527.

34. King, op. cit., p. 218. In addition, see the testimony of Colonel H. C. Wilson in N.S.W. Legislative Council, *Minutes of Evidence Taken Before the Select Committee on Police* (Sydney: Government Printer, 1835), p. 36.

35. Ibid., p. 35.

36. N.S.W. Legislative Council, Report of the Committee on Police and Gaols (Sydney: T. Trood, 1839), p. 25.

37. Note 6, Ch. IV.1.

38. Shaw, *Convicts and the Colonies*, p. 73.

39. Forbes to Glenelg, 12 April, 1836, Mitchell Library MSS, A741, pp. 120-122.

40. 3 Will. IV 3 (1 October, 1832).

41. Hazel King, "The Humanitarian Leanings of Governor Bourke," *Historical Studies*, 10:37 (November 1961), p. 27.

42. N.S.W. Legislative Council, "Extracts from the Report of the Committee on the Subject of Tread-Wheel Labour" (Sydney: 1825), p. 348.

43. Shaw, *Convicts and the Colonies*, p. 215.

44. Phillip to Sydney, 12 February, 1790, HRA I, 1, p. 144.

45. Hunter to Portland, 12 November 1796, HRA I, 1, p. 676.

46. Bourke to Goderich, 22 March, 1832, Mitchell Library MSS, A1210, p. 379.

47. N.S.W. Legislative Council, "Report of the Select Committee on the Bushranging Bill, July 2, 1834," in N.S.W. Legislative Council, *Votes and Proceedings*, 1835, p. 7. A contradictory interpretation suggests that numerous arrests were made under the act and that these apprehensions were often quite arbitrary. See Alexander Harris, *Settlers and Convicts; or Recollections of Sixteen Years' Labour in the Australian Backwoods, by an Emigrant Mechanic*, 2d ed. (Melbourne: Melbourne University Press, 1964), pp. 81-83.

THE VICTORIAN ERA, 1841-1900

PATTERNS OF CRIME AND CONFLICT, 1841-1900

Sydney had become a noticeably orderly place by 1840. As Governor Gipps wrote in 1841, "In Sydney, the security of property is perhaps as great, and public decency as well preserved, as in most seaport towns in England."[1] This situation was soon to change, however. Sydney's population exceeded 40,000 in 1844, yet the city was still relatively small, and murders produced more than a little alarm. Two particularly well-publicized homicides in 1843 and 1844 were committed during a period also marked by an apparent increase in burglary. Public pressure brought about the appointment of a select committee to investigate the insecurity of life and property in Sydney; the committee concluded that although crime in the aggregate appeared not to have increased, a greater than usual proportion of aggravated offenses had been committed. Arrest data for 1841-1844 (Table IV.3.1) tend to reflect this interpretation; apprehensions for burglary, robbery, and assault showed yearly increases, whereas those for drunkenness and willful exposure (presumably urination in public) decreased.

For the first time since the uprising of the Irish convicts, Sydney was the scene of occasional collective disorder, none of which had serious political consequences. It may best be described as general rowdiness and mischief-making with overtones of class antagonism. Sydney's first delinquent gang, the Cabbage Tree Hat Mob, appeared in the 1840s and attracted considerable attention for their harassment of upper-class Sydneysiders. The group's activities were generally limited to the delivery of insulting or offensive remarks to wealthier passers-by, and the occasional knocking off of the symbol of high status, the tall black hat.[2]

Table IV.3.1 Free Persons Taken into Custody for Selected Offenses
in New South Wales, 1841-1844

Offense	1841	1842	1843	1844 (January 1-May 31)
Murder	15	1	11	6
Rape	8	8	3	—
Common assault	276	363	413	182
Burglary	10	13	29	⎰ 110
Robbery	61	106	139	⎱
Theft and larceny	611	701	665	249
Forgery	11	38	14	10
Disorderly prostitutes	265	420	274	106
Disorderly character	731	262	227	214
Drunkenness	7710	4240	3289	866
Exposure of the person	252	109	86	21

Source: N.S.W. Legislative Council, Report of the Select Committee on the Insecurity of Life and Property, Sydney: 1844.

The first elections in Sydney took place in 1843 in a rather raucous setting: candidates distributed free drink to potential supporters, and drunken mobs spilled through the streets, fighting with political opponents. At least one polling booth was smashed, injuries were numerous, and one person was killed. The New Year's Eve riot of 1850 involved young males whose energies were focused almost entirely on the destruction of property; editorials in the *Sydney Morning Herald* referred to the participants as "frolicsome" or "giddy."[3] Small-scale delinquency continued into the 1850s, but public concern over the insulting language of teenage boys was soon eclipsed by the rush for gold.

As recovery from the Depression became the boom of the gold rush, attentions of many New South Welshmen turned once again to drink—or at least police attention returned to those who had been drinking. Drunkenness arrests increased so sharply during the early 1850s that a select committee on intemperance was appointed by the Legislative Council. The committee concluded that whereas drunkenness had increased, there was no corresponding increase in other crime.[4] Thus despite the frantic pace of the gold rush, Sydney had become, in terms of crime, a relatively tranquil place. Indeed, the period at midcentury witnessed the beginning of what was to be a very long-term decline in the rates of most serious offenses. During the 1860s and 1870s criminality attracted little attention. Although the attempted assassination of the visiting Duke of Edinburgh by an alleged Fenian in 1868 aroused fears of Irish conspiratorial activity, these proved to be unfounded. By 1880, however, deviant behavior once again had become a public issue.

The last two decades of the nineteenth century in Sydney were rich years historically, marked by an intriguing juxtaposition of themes antique and modern. Antipathy toward Orientals was growing throughout New South Wales, and public demonstration in support of their exclusion were not uncommon. Protest against the attempted debarkation in Sydney of a group of Chinese in 1888 was followed by legislation restricting further immigration. The act constituted a significant step in the development of the White Australia Policy.[5]

Given the strict Victorian standards of sexual morality that had become accepted by 1880, the disproportionate attention accorded sexual deviance was to have been expected. Apparently in 1882-1886 unusual official attention was directed at sex offenses, as Figure IV.3.1 indicates. Arrests for rape and attempted rape declined after the peak year of 1886, but lesser sexual offenses other than indecent exposure reached a high in 1892. Indecent exposure cases reached a peak in the mid-1880s, probably because of two parallel changes—the increase in arrests for drunkenness or changing standards of bathing attire.

One of the most famous criminal trials in Sydney's history, the Mount Rennie case, took place in 1886.[6] The charge was rape, a capital offense at the time, and the case involved the trial of twelve teenage boys for the alleged gang rape of a girl in Moore Park. The "outrage" was generally received with vocal indignation, but when nine of the twelve defendants were sentenced to be hanged, a considerable debate arose.[7] Four of the boys were finally executed, and debate over capital punishment continued until the end of the century.

Arrests were widely employed as means of social control in the early 1880s. Although there were more than 75 arrests per 1,000 population in 1881, the annual rate has averaged under 45 during the twentieth century, and in no year has it exceeded 50. Then as now, the offense of drunkenness provided the greatest source of arrests. Apprehensions for drunkenness and vagrancy offenses showed a decrease in the late and mid-1880s, respectively, whereas gambling arrests increased in the early 1890s. Rates of arrest for crimes against persons and property remained relatively low and stable throughout the period.

Another form of public disorder that received much attention in Sydney during the closing years of the nineteenth century was referred to as larrikinism. Although the expression "larrikin" was applied very loosely to young males with delinquent inclinations,

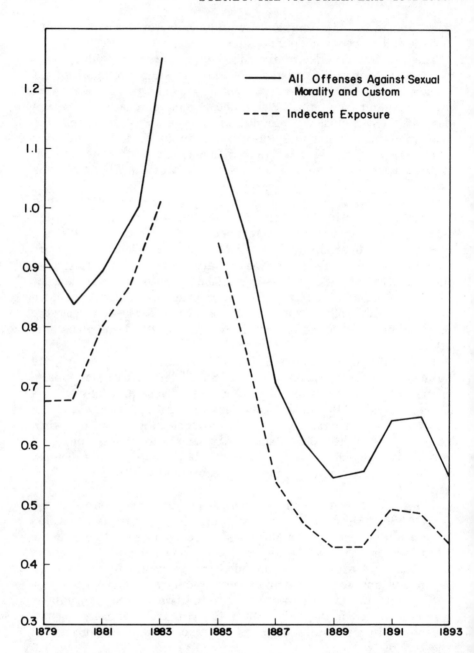

Figure IV.3.1 New South Wales: Arrests per 1000 population, indecent exposure and all offenses against sexual morality and custom, 1879-1893

larrikins were, more strictly speaking, members of street gangs or "pushes" whose diverse activities included the wearing of extravagant clothing (high-heeled boots, bell-bottom trousers, and brightly colored scarves), loitering on street corners, and making suggestive remarks to passers-by. Since larrikins, like their predecessors in the 1840s, were drawn from Sydney's working class, their general comportment and behavior tended to offend the sensibilities of some. More dangerous manifestations of larrikinism included pitched battles between rival "pushes" and, in some cases, assaults on pedestrians and policemen.[8]

A more significant historical phenomenon than larrikinism, and one without precedent in Sydney, was that of large-scale labor protest. Large strikes occurred in New South Wales during 1885, 1886, 1888, and 1890. The 1890 action, by shearers and maritime workers, was unprecedented in Australian history. Picketing and occasional harassment of nonunion labor led to the appointment of special constables and to the deployment of colonial artillery. At one point during the strike, 10,000 sympathizers paraded through the streets of Sydney in a column a mile and a half long. After three months, the use of nonunion labor defeated the strikers.

DEMOGRAPHIC AND ECONOMIC CONDITIONS OF PUBLIC ORDER, 1841-1900

Accompanying the relative decline in the incidence of serious crime were larger social changes. The racial and ethnic dimensions of Sydney's population remained overwhelmingly white and British, but Sydney's demographic structure began to take on a new shape in the 1840s; the 1851 census revealed a pattern considerably different from those of the past (Table IV.3.2). The convict population was

Table IV.3.2 Selected Population Statistics, Sydney Police District, 1841-1851

Year	Total population	Total male population	Males aged 21-45, % of total population	Unmarried males, % of total male population	Males, % of total population
1841	35,507	20,733	33%	71%	58%
1846	49,630	27,015	26%	66%	54%
1851	58,993	30,031	20%	66%	51%

Source: N.S.W. Census Returns

now negligible, and the imbalance between the sexes had disappeared. One out of every three males was married, and the number of males between the ages of 21 and 45 had declined to only 20 percent of the total population. Despite continuing migration from England and Ireland, almost two-thirds of all New South Welshmen counted in the 1891 census were Australian born, and only 6.6 percent were of Irish birth. The Britishness of the population was overwhelming: By the turn of the century more than 95 percent of the population of New South Wales was born either in Australia or in the United Kingdom; 70 percent were Protestant, a fourth Roman Catholic.

Arrest records for the period reveal a number of interesting patterns. Perhaps most striking is that the vast majority of those arrested were immigrants (Table IV.3.3). Irish-born offenders in

Table IV.3.3 Percentage Apprehended Who Were Born Outside Australasia, New South Wales, 1885-1893

	Persons born outside Australasia	
Year	% of total N.S.W. population	% of persons apprehended
1881	27.8	—
1885		67.7
1886		66.7
1887		63.6
1888		61.3
1889		59.0
1890		59.3
1891	23.9	58.5
1892		56.6
1893		54.3

Source: Statistical Registers of New South Wales.

Table IV.3.4 Percentage of Irish-Born Arrested for Selected Offense Categories, New South Wales, 1891 and 1901

	% Irish-born arrested				
Year	% Irish born, total N.S.W. population	Offenses against the person	Offenses against property with violence	Offenses against property without violence	Forgery and offenses against the currency	Offenses against good order
1891	6.6	13.9	13.0	10.1	13.0	23.4
1901	4.4	6.8	4.1	6.7	3.4	16.3

Source: Statistical Registers of New South Wales.

particular were overrepresented in most arrest categories, especially those of offenses against the person and against good order (Tables IV.3.3 and IV.3.4). In what seems to be a universal Western pattern, males between the ages of 25 and 30 were overrepresented among those apprehended in the 1890s.

Economic fluctuation in mid-nineteenth century New South Wales was extreme. Speculation in land and livestock led to unrealistically high prices, and the impact of overseas economic contractions brought about numerous bankruptcies and widespread unemployment in Sydney. The summer of 1843 marked the worst of the Depression period, but recovery was slow. Exports increased haltingly for the remainder of the decade, and it was not until the discovery of gold in 1851 that boom times reappeared. Relationships between the level of prosperity and short-term fluctuations in the incidence of crime during the 1840s and 1850s reveal interesting patterns. Rates of arrest for drunkenness tended to fall off during the period of economic contraction and to increase sharply during the gold rush years. This general relationship has persisted in New South Wales to the present.

After a slight contraction at the end of the gold rush, the economy of New South Wales experienced a boom that endured until the end of the 1880s. But the following decade was accompanied by the most significant period of economic adversity to confront Sydney in a half-century. An international financial crisis that began late in 1890 resulted in substantial withdrawals of investments from Australian houses of finance. A number of banks in Sydney folded, land values and commodity prices fell drastically, and unemployment rose. For those fortunate enough to remain employed, the level of real wages dropped ten percent. Aside from the predictable diminution in the rate of arrests for drunkenness, the Depression appears to have had no immediate effect on the incidence of disorder. The collective protests that did occur during the period preceded the worst of the Depression years and were more the result of increasing working-class consciousness than of economic adversity.

PUBLIC OPINION AND POLITICAL INTERESTS, 1841-1900

Contemporary Opinion

The Report of the Select Committee on the Insecurity of Life and Property (1844) suggested a number of causes for the increase in crime during the early 1840s, and foremost was the economic contraction. For the more fortunate, wages were low; the unemployed enjoyed none at all. Such conditions of deprivation, following so soon after the boom of the late 1830s, were seen as having aroused acquisitive tendencies.[9] The report also suggested that certain demographic considerations underlay the increase in criminal deviance. A number of former inmates of the penal settlement at Norfolk Island, their sentences having expired, had recently arrived in Sydney and were automatically regarded as unsavory characters. The concentration of prisoners in Sydney that followed the abolition of convict assignment in 1841 was perceived as conducive to disorder as well; in particular, the committee criticized the lax supervision of the convict barracks at Hyde Park. The inefficiency of the police force, a seemingly perennial theme in New South Wales, was yet another factor cited in the report. Although the size of the Sydney force had been substantially reduced since the 1830s, the committee's criticism was primarily directed at the decentralized structure of police organization.[10] By the late 1840s, when Sydney had returned to a more orderly state, the *Sydney Morning Herald* attributed the tranquility of the times to a decline in the convict population.[11]

Contemporary views on the causes of crime during the last decades of the nineteenth century were plentiful and diverse. Larrikinism evoked more etiological speculation than any other deviant phenomena and remained a topic for discussion over a period of at least twenty years. Many viewed larrikinism as a product of affluence. In 1881 the *Bulletin* claimed

> Our larrikins are as much the outcome of the prosperity of the laboring classes as of anything else. . . . The peculiar prominence they attain is clearly attributable to the comparative ease with which they, as compared with the same class in the old world, can acquire the means for indulgence and for idleness.[12]

The themes of parental neglect and lack of religious training in public schools were popular throughout the 1880s. An especially wide-ranging discussion of larrikinism was offered in 1897 by a prison administrator, Frederick Neitenstein. In addition to citing defective home life and parental neglect, Neitenstein suggested that the absence of recreational opportunity led youth in Sydney to seek less socially acceptable diversions. He also blamed the unsavory literature, dancing halls, and gaming establishments present in the city. Neitenstein believed that the public's perception of larrikinism was greatly influenced by the news media. The widespread press coverage accorded the "pushes," he claimed, may have stimulated some emulative behavior; in any event, the attentions of the press seemed to encourage a kind of taxonomic carelessness, and many employed the term "larrikinism" to designate any street disturbance. Moreover, media amplifications of these kinds of deviance may also have served to raise public insecurity to a level unjustified by empirical reality.[13] Despite the popularity during the period of a song entitled "Afraid to go Home in the Dark," Neitenstein maintained that Sydney's streets were relatively safe.

The argument that drunkenness contributed to the increase in many forms of crime appeared again and again. During testimony before the Intoxicating Drink Inquiry Commission in 1887, the Inspector-General of Police estimated that three-fourths of all crime was directly attributable to drink,[14] and a former Chaplain at Berrima Gaol attributed 90 percent of crime "directly or indirectly" to excessive use of intoxicants.[15] These estimates undoubtedly were inflated by the prevailing practice of zealously prosecuting drunkenness per se as an offense.

Mental disorder also was held to contribute to criminal deviance; the theme of innate criminality had long been a popular one in New South Wales, and personality disturbances were still regarded as more or less spontaneous phenomena. In 1886 Harold Stephen argued that "Criminals, for the most part, are mad to a certain extent; their moral sense is so degraded from their birth upwards, that they are not sane on the point of morality......"[16]

Despite the popularity of explanations based on notions of inherent badness, some observers suggested that criminal deviance had social bases. In the 1880s it became widely accepted that prison life, far from reforming the offender, corrupted him still further. The Comptroller-General of Prisons himself maintained in 1882 that "there can be no question but that plural cellular occupation is the hot bed of crime extension, and that many a man is corrupted, and many a crime planned during the long hours of the night in associated cells."[17]

Two other suspected causes of criminal deviance, urbanization and economic deprivation, received slight attention during the period. As Sydney's population growth continued to outstrip that of the rural hinterland, one early advocate of decentralization argued that "the evil of gambling which we see about us comes from the rotten condition of society. It is the consequence of the wretched system which draws thousands into the cities."[18] In 1893 the Inspector-General of Police suggested that economic adversity tended to stimulate property crime. He argued that many thefts arose as a result of "undoubted distress from lack of employment."[19] A cursory review of contemporary debates and commentary, however, reveals no further references to these factors.

The Rulers and the Law

Chronic labor shortages have traditionally accompanied periods of affluence in New South Wales. This phenomenon was of particular significance in shaping elite attitudes toward deviance during the mid-nineteenth century. Workers who refused to complete the terms of their engagements or who absented themselves from work were regarded not only as sinful souls but as threats to the economic well-being of their employers. Masters and Servants legislation had been a part of English law since at least 1349,[20] and the 1840 amendment to the 1828 New South Wales Act reaffirmed the gravity with which the shirking of work responsibilities was regarded.[21]

Sydney's position as a busy seaport in an affluent colony had a further effect on the supply of labor. Seamen whose ships called at Port Jackson were greatly tempted by the wages to be earned ashore, and desertion and insubordination were quite prevalent. Masters of vessels whose crews were so inclined complained of a great delay and inconvenience and prevailed on the Legislative Council to take appropriate action. The resulting Water Police Act (1843) provided for an expansion of the Water Police and imposed the penalty of up to three months' hard labor for desertion or insubordination.[22]

As economic conditions deteriorated during the early 1840s and increasing numbers of hitherto respectable citizens suffered the embarrassment of bankruptcy, indebtedness became a somewhat less disgraceful condition than it had been in previous years. The treatment generally accorded this form of deviance was arrest and imprisonment, and, as the threat of such sanctions became more immediate, Governor Gipps pronounced them "oppressive" and "unnecessary." In 1843, the worst of the depression years, the punishment of imprisonment for debt was legally abolished.[23]

By the end of the convict era the spirit of humane reformism then current in Britain had reached New South Wales and was reflected in a very visible trend away from physical punishment. Table IV.3.5 suggests that hangings were much less frequent following the cessa-

Table IV.3.5 Number of Executions in New South Wales, 1825-1859

Years	Capital convictions	Executions	Executions % of capital convictions
1825-1829	437	139	32%
1830-1834	718	169	24%
1835-1839	494	119	24%
1840-1844	131	55	42%
1845-1849	48	19	40%
1850-1854	38	19	50%
1855-1859	47	17	36%

Source: N.S.W. Colonial Secretary, Returns of the Colony.

tion of transportation. Moreover, corporal punishment, which had been administered liberally as recently as the late 1830s, was all but discontinued.

The changes in public opinion that accompanied the decreasing reliance on hanging as a treatment for deviance covered many themes. The *Atlas*, a liberal newspaper published in Sydney during the 1840s, opposed capital punishment mainly on empirical grounds and articulated arguments that were to be voiced by opponents of hanging in New South Wales for the following 110 years. One dominant editorial theme was that hanging was not a successful deterrent. Indeed, execution could act as a stimulus to emulation and actually served in part to provoke the taking of human life.[24] In addition, under certain circumstances of interacting homicidal and suicidal impulses, the threat of capital punishment might even encourage desperate acts.[25] The claim that public execution tended to reinforce the depravity of lower-class spectators,[26] hardly a novel theme, was also voiced in editorials. The *Atlas*, however, was more concerned with the unintended consequences of capital punishment for the criminal justice system.

> Need we remind Sir Charles FitzRoy, that in every chapter of our criminal code where public opinion has pronounced the punishment to be too severe, the law has become obsolete, and fallen into disuse before the legislature has repealed it? And that when the severity of punishment has been properly relaxed, magistrates have always been more ready to commit, prosecutors to persevere, and juries to convict![27]

Thus the orientations of the New South Wales elite toward the disorders of the period tended to reflect the humanitarian movement. The severity of penal sanctions was generally mitigated, and, aside from the creation of offenses involving the desertion of seamen, there were no significant expansions of the criminal law. It was appropriate that these developments coincided with the end of the convict era in New South Wales.

Toward the end of the nineteenth century in New South Wales, the power of the pastoralists was eclipsed by that of the urban middle class. Commercial and professional interests, overwhelmingly Protestant, rose to prominence in Parliament; their orientations toward deviant behavior were strongly grounded in the climate of Victorian morality.

Elite preoccupation with sex was the most striking theme of the period. Sexuality was an undeniable part of human existence in Sydney, and although parliamentarians could not legislate it away, they did their best to regulate and repress it. Sexual deviance and other forms of deviant behavior with sexual overtones were viewed

with special indignation, as reflected by certain penalties prescribed
in the Criminal Law Amendment Act of 1883. Both forcible rape
and carnal knowledge of a female under ten years of age were
punishable by death; the severity of these penalties seems to have
had no parallel elsewhere in the British empire at the time, except in
Tasmania. The "abominable crime of buggery" was punishable by a
maximum term of life imprisonment. In addition, offenders convicted of attempted rape, various offenses related to carnal knowledge, indecent assault, and willful exposure were subject to both
whipping and imprisonment. Another manifestation of these attitudes was the moral outrage precipitated by the alleged Mount
Rennie rape in 1886, cited earlier.

So great was the desire of some to protect Australian womanhood
that a Seduction Punishment Bill was introduced in the New South
Wales Legislative Assembly in 1887. The bill proposed not only to
make seduction a criminal offense, punishable by up to two years'
hard labor, but also to define as criminal any attempt to have illicit
connection with a girl of "previously chaste character." It failed of
passage, but the following year an Abolition of Whipping Bill was
defeated in the Assembly by the members who viewed corporal
punishment as a necessary instrument of retribution for sexual
offenders. In 1892 defenders of virtue introduced a Vice Suppression
Bill that proposed, among other things, to raise the age of consent
from sixteen to seventeen and to create the offense of securing
females for the purpose of prostitution. This bill, however, contained
such drastic provisions of, police search and other deprivations of
legal rights that it, too, failed of enactment.

The closing years of the nineteenth century formed the high point
of prohibitionist activity in New South Wales. Anglicans dominated
the temperance movement, energetically calling attention to the
wave of drunkenness that was apparently engulfing Sydney. The
commission of inquiry that reported in 1887 on matters related to
intoxication found, however, that the rate of consumption of beer,
wine, and spirits had decreased substantially over the past decade and
was not very different from rates in the other Australian colonies.
Instead, the commission recommended a different definition of the
social problem:

> Our laws have started with the assumption that drunkenness is a crime,
> and have treated it accordingly; and now, after many years of experience,
> we find that our efforts at repression have failed in the most disastrous
> manner. We have not succeeded in producing any amelioration in the
> habits of the habitual drunkard, and our gaol treatment, though it had
> admittedly been instrumental in prolonging the drunkard's life, has yet
> done nothing to help or to induce him to reform. Another method now

remains to be tried. We may cease to regard the habitual drunkard as a mere criminal to be punished by fine and imprisonment, and inquire whether something may not be accomplished by treating him as one who suffers from a disease which is, to some extent, analogous to temporary or intermittent derangement of mind.[28]

Despite this recommendation, drunkenness continued to be regarded as a crime. Prohibitionists were successful only in bringing about a reduction in the number of licensed public houses in the city and in maintaining Sunday closing regulations.

Gambling, a traditional Sydney pastime, was also distasteful to the authorities, although it failed to evoke as indignant a response as did deviant sexual behavior. In 1891 the issue of gambling precipitated an inquiry about a broad range of deviant behavior. Accusations that members of Sydney's Chinese population were involved in gambling, opium smoking, and white slave traffic aroused public indignation and brought about the appointment of a royal commission. The racism that pervaded late nineteenth century Australian society manifested itself throughout the hearings. Nonetheless the commission concluded that whereas some Chinese did operate gambling establishments and a few did smoke opium, allegations of white slavery were unfounded.[29]

Reaction in Parliament to the prevalence of child neglect and "baby farming" brought about significant redefinitional legislation in 1892. The Children's Protection Act, inspired by contemporary legislation in Britain and Victoria, provided that all adoptions be registered and that all infant deaths be reported within 24 hours and be subjected to inquest. Penal clauses in the act provided for a fine of £50 or twelve months' imprisonment for persons found guilty of abusing or neglecting children.

Larrikinism evoked official reaction according to the relative gravity of particular acts of delinquency. Boisterous behavior or loitering were viewed as simple annoyances, but insulting language directed at female pedestrians was a more serious offense. Assaults on members of the public or on policemen were accompanied by calls for corporal punishment. The Disorderly Conduct Suppression Bill, introduced in the Legislative Assembly during 1892, proposed to increase the fine and jail term for the existing offense of "riotous behavior" and prescribed penalties of whipping in certain cases of assault. Its provisions were largely redundant; ample provision for corporal punishment existed in the decade-old Criminal Law Amendment Act.

While public antipathy toward many forms of deviant behavior increased, a countertrend toward less punitiveness also developed.

The election of Labor representatives to the Legislative Assembly—36 of them in 1891—was accompanied by a movement to abolish capital and corporal punishment. Legislative attempts failed, but reformers in New South Wales were able to effect other fundamental changes in criminal procedures and penalties.

The Criminal Law and Evidence Amendment Act of 1891[30] enabled a defendant charged with an indictable offense to give evidence on his own behalf. The First Offenders Probation Act of 1894[31] constituted one of the major reforms of the period. Stimulated by crowded prison conditions and the growing realization that imprisonment often had only the worst influence on the offender, the act allowed judges to order a period of probation in lieu of a prison sentence for a first offender. The enactment of this legislation marked the first significant use of noncustodial treatment since the convict era. In addition to providing for the enactment of these reforms, the populist and working-class bloc in the Legislative Assembly was successful in helping stifle a spate of potentially repressive proposals such as the Vice Suppression and Disorderly Conduct Suppression bills.

The last decades of the nineteenth century thus saw substantial divergence in articulated attitudes toward deviant behavior. The defenders of middle-class morality stood in contrast to the more "common" citizens who sought to avoid further curtailment of individual freedom. Predictably, the legislative struggles between the two groups resulted in measures both of repression and of reform.

INSTITUTIONS OF PUBLIC ORDER AND THEIR EFFECTS, 1841-1900

The Police

In 1840 police services in New South Wales could still be described in two words: fragmented and uncoordinated. There were six separate police forces in the colony in the years prior to 1851; the City Police and the Water Police covered Sydney, and the hinterland was patrolled by the Mounted Police, the Border Police, the Native Police, and the Rural Constabulary. Moreover, procedures for information exchange among the various forces were lacking, and joint action was further inhibited by interdepartmental jealousies.

Although centralization of police services had been recommended as early as 1820 by Bigge and by subsequent committees in 1835 and 1839, the reorganization of police in New South Wales had always been impeded by fiscal constraint or by insufficient public demand.

The relatively tranquil years preceding 1842 led many to believe that existing police appropriations were unnecessarily generous, and both appropriations and the force level were cut back markedly. In 1843 and 1844 the Sydney Police Force was partially funded at the municipal level, and the Sydney Corporation was no less willing to curtail expenditures than were the governor and Legislative Council. Hazel King reveals that between 1839 and 1844 the size of the Sydney Police Force was reduced by well over one-third and reached a low of 95 in the latter year.[32] When events in 1844 illustrated the inadequacies of existing financing, full responsibility for police appropriations was again placed with the Legislative Council.

Problems of administrative structure and fiscal rigidity were not the only factors detracting from the efficiency of law enforcement in New South Wales; crises of leadership continued throughout the 1840s. Three consecutive chiefs of police in Sydney were dismissed for alleged indiscretions—in 1839, 1848, and 1849; by midcentury the quality of the Sydney Police Force was at its lowest. Working conditions were so adverse that free men were reluctant to join the force, and many policemen continued to be drawn from the ranks of ticket-of-leave holders. The scandals visible in the higher levels of the force had their counterparts among the rank and file. C.G.N. Lockhart described Sydney's constables as "such confirmed drunkards that they could not be trusted out of surveillance," suggesting that many of them were "infirm old men," or "petty tyrants with itching palms."[33]

Another committee, appointed in the aftermath of the 1850 New Year's Eve riot, found similar faults and made similar recommendations. The Police Regulation Act of 1850 provided for the appointment of an Inspector-General of Police, who was supposed to coordinate various law enforcement functions, but the measure was disallowed by the Home Government on a technicality. The advent of the gold rush, concern for attaining responsible government, and the rapid succession of cabinets during the period caused the Legislative Council to postpone further action.

It was not until 1862, after a new outbreak of bushranging again illustrated the need for centralized law enforcement machinery, that definitive action was undertaken. The Police Regulation Act established the essential structure of the New South Wales Police Force that has endured to the present. Under the 1862 act the colony was split into police divisions; for example, existing law enforcement personnel in Sydney were incorporated into the Metropolitan Division. Each division was under the responsibility of a superintendent, who was in turn responsible to the Inspector-General, John McLerie.

By the end of the nineteenth century the New South Wales Police Force had assumed a wide range of responsibilities, many quite unrelated to the conventional tasks of law enforcement. In addition to licensing public houses and supervising the increasing volume of vehicular traffic in the metropolis, the police had been assigned duties ranging from the control of truancy to the administration of the Diseased Animals and Meat Act to dogcatching. Inspectors-general complained consistently that the assumption of these extraneous responsibilities detracted from the overall efficiency of the force, but with notable lack of success; by the turn of the century police had been given the duties of investigating applications for old-age pensions, compiling electoral lists of newly enfranchised women, and inspecting shearing sheds. Other socioeconomic phenomena imposed further responsibilities on the police. As industrial strife increased, the normal strength of the force was regarded as insufficient, and steps were undertaken for temporary augmentation of the force by appointing special constables and temporarily reassigning colonial defense forces. In 1892 industrial difficulties at Broken Hill, in the southwestern part of the colony, necessitated the temporary transfer of 221 officers from the Metropolitan District.

Acts of violence against police in Sydney appeared to increase in the late 1880s, and considerable debate arose over the desirability of providing members of the force with firearms.[34] Although the inspector-general himself was quoted in 1889 as opposing the routine arming of the police,[55] events militated in favor of a change in policy. Violence against police continued unabated, and, following a skirmish between police and three armed burglars in 1894, police on duty were equipped with pistols.

Meanwhile allegations that policemen tended to employ unwarranted force were heard from time to time in Parliament.[36] It appears, however, that in general, the police exercised relative self-restraint. Perhaps the greatest opportunity for police heavy handedness arose during the 1890 strike, yet this event produced but a handful of arrests and injuries.

Penal Institutions

The cessation of transportation to New South Wales coincided with what was perhaps the most significant experiment in penal practice in Australian history: Captain Alexander Maconochie's activity on Norfolk Island.[37] Maconochie, a naval officer who served as secretary to the lieutenant governor of Van Diemen's Land in the late 1830s, believed that rehabilitation should be the ultimate goal of punishment. Whereas most of his contemporaries subscribed to the view that the offender should suffer, Maconochie maintained that the purpose of treatment was the restoration of the offender to functioning membership in society. The operation of the convict system in Van Diemen's Land was regarded by Maconochie as degrading to both the prisoners and their keepers. He recommended the introduction of alternative treatment approaches based on rewards as incentives to cooperative behavior.

Maconochie's writings had stirred the interest of officials in London, and he was appointed Commandant of the Norfolk Island Penal Settlement in 1840. During his tenure on Norfolk Island Maconochie experimented with an array of unprecedented policies. The most significant of these was the "mark system," under which prisoners were awarded points or marks for good conduct. Disciplinary offenses were punished by fines expressed in marks, and often a given prisoner's tally would determine not only the range of privileges accorded him, but also the duration of his sentence. Maconochie's efforts to approximate normal social conditions on Norfolk Island led him to establish situations of group cooperation permitting members of a group to share responsibility for one another's behavior, gaining or losing marks accordingly. Official reaction to Maconochie's experimentation, however, was unfavorable. In New South Wales, where the tradition of harsh treatment was a half-century old, his policies were greeted with ridicule or anger. The Home Government, while willing to underwrite experimentation with Maconochie's correctional strategies, was reluctant to implement them. Authorities in London refused to amend prison regulations to permit the mark system to become fully operational. Disturbed at the expense of the project, and concerned that the deterrent and retributive dimensions of punishment were being neglected at Norfolk Island, the Colonial Secretary, Lord Derby, recalled Maconochie in 1843.

Maconochie's brief period of attempted reform occurred during a time of major structural change in New South Wales penal practice. The rapid influx of free migrants to the colony helped alleviate the labor shortage; this, combined with the general desire to transcend the heritage of "convictism," moved the authorities to discontinue the assignment of convicts and to rely instead first on their employment on public works projects and later on their simple incarceration. The decision of the Home Government to discontinue the transportation to Norfolk Island of offenders convicted in New South Wales moved Governor Gipps to establish a prison at Cockatoo Island in Sydney Harbour and to construct a prison at Darlinghurst.

With the exception of a variation on the mark system implemented between 1851 and 1858, New South Wales prisons in the 1850s were quite unlike what Maconochie might have envisioned.

When it came to the attention of the authorities in 1858 that, under
the modified mark system, a person convicted of manslaughter could
earn his freedom in three years and three months, this arrangement
was also abolished. Inmates of the prison on Cockatoo Island, denied
this incentive to good behavior, responded with resistance and
insubordination. Conditions in the prison grew so disorderly that a
select committee was appointed in 1861; its report provided the first
thorough review of penal practices in New South Wales since the
cessation of transportation. It criticized the calibre of the prison
warders, the nutritional and working conditions in the prison, and
the prevalence of homosexual practices among prisoners. The committee's recommendations were numerous, and in some cases surprisingly innovative. They urged that more commodious living areas
be provided, that sewage facilities be constructed, and that prisoners
be given the opportunity to attend divine services regularly. The
committee also proposed the reintroduction of the mark system and
the extension of educational opportunity to inmates. The report
further suggested that prisoners be given productive employment
with remuneration to minimize the difficulties of readjustment on
discharge.[38]

Attitudes among the elite of the colony toward the committee's
recommendations were mixed, for the view that the prisoner's lot
should remain an uncomfortable one was still prevalent. In practice
there were a few ameliorations of prison conditions. A modified
mark system was reinstituted, and haircut regulations were relaxed.
Another reform of the period involved the classification and segregation of different types of offenders, with variable treatments administered according to the nature and severity of the offense.[39] Otherwise the prison system of New South Wales remained essentially
unchanged from the convict era to the end of the nineteenth
century. The primary concerns of prison administrators during the
1870s were the productivity and profitability of prison labor. The
comptroller-general of prisons emphasized labor matters in each of
his annual reports, complaining that prisoners convicted of drunkenness returned again and again for short sentences, a treatment that
proved to be neither productive nor rehabilitative.

Since imprisonment remained the dominant treatment during the
1880s and 1890s, prisons in New South Wales became increasingly
crowded. To an extent unsurpassed before or since, prisons served as
warehouses for drunkards, vagrants, the aged and infirm, and
lunatics, in addition to the more conventional clientele. The peak
years of 1884-1886 saw the annual totals of prison receptions exceed
20,000 and 22 of every 1,000 New South Welshmen were admitted
to prison in each of these years.

Despite an occasional reference to rehabilitative aims by prison administrators, retribution and deterrence continued to serve as foundations of correctional policy. Comptroller-General Maclean, sensitive to public suspicions that prison conditions were insufficiently harsh, revealed that prisoners under sentence of less than a year were provided with four ounces of meat twice weekly and suggested "This cannot be considered a temptation to prison life by members of a meat-eating community."[40] Three years later Maclean had to increase the rations of short-sentenced prisoners to maintain their strength.[41] The reaction of prisoners to such conditions was predictable. Breaches of discipline were frequent, and prisoners at the new facility at Bathurst rioted for several days in November 1889. George Miller succeeded Maclean as Comptroller-General of Prisons in 1890 and called for conditions that in many respects were even more austere, such as the reintroduction of corporal punishment and the bread-and-water diet. Despite Miller's requests, the New South Wales government remained unwilling to introduce corporal punishment for offenses related to larrikinism, but they provided him in 1893 with sufficient latitude to effect major restrictions in prison diet and living conditions. In 1894, with the government's authorization, he reinstituted the use of the gag, a mechanical device inserted in prisoners' mouths to prevent them from speaking, to check what he termed "blasphemous and frequently vile and filthy language."[42] Intensive criticism from opposition members moved the government to withdraw this authority in the following year, however.

Frederick W. Neitenstein became Comptroller-General of Prisons in June 1896 and presided over a significant restructuring of the New South Wales prisons system. Unlike his predecessors, Neitenstein was as concerned with reform as with deterrence or retribution. Steadfastly opposed to the existing functions of prisons as warehouses for the castoffs of society, he refined classification procedures and attempted to treat individuals rather than offenses. Neitenstein was aware of overseas developments in penal practice, and during his term as comptroller-general he presented numerous policy recommendations to the ministers of justice under whom he served. Some of these suggestions were never acted on (e.g., that of treating drunkenness as a medical rather than as a criminal matter), but many significant changes were introduced during Neitenstein's term or shortly thereafter. Library and sanitary facilities were greatly expanded, eligibility for remission of sentence in cases of good behavior was broadened considerably, dark cells were abolished, and provisions for solitary confinement were limited. The steady decline in the number of prison admissions that began in 1894 permitted the allotment of a separate cell to each prisoner by the turn of the century. Cells were lighted in the, evening, and the opportunity for physical exercise was increased. Just prior to discharge prisoners were accorded more privileges and increased visiting rights, and efforts were made to aid them in securing employment. Pay and working conditions of Prisons Department personnel were also improved significantly.[43]

In keeping with the trend toward noncustodial correction that began with the First Offenders Probation Act, the Justices Fines Act of 1899 provided for partial remission of sentences when offenders imprisoned in default of payment of fines were able to pay a portion

Table IV.3.6 *Prisoners Liberated Under the Provisions of the First Offenders Probation Act and Subsequent Statutes in New South Wales, 1895-1907*

Year	Persons liberated	Prison receptions per 1,000 population
1895	184	14.8
1896	62	13.4
1897	78	11.4
1898	145	11.4
1899	153	10.7
1900	120	10.5
1901	179	10.4
1902	241	10.2
1903	232	10.6
1904	385	9.7
1905	371	9.0
1906	219	8.0
1907	325	7.5

Source: *New South Wales Statistical Registers.*

Table.IV.3.7 *Remission of Sentence by Part Payment of Fines in New South Wales, 1902-1909*

Year	Persons imprisoned in default of payment of fines	Prisoners released after paying portion of fines	Days remitted by part payment of fines
1902	8,062	1,008	20,179
1903	8,379	1,081	20,198
1904	7,681	1,287	22,035
1905	7,347	1,247	22,389
1906	6,853	1,327	14,100
1907	6,635	1,510	28,379
1908	7,158	1,538	29,147
1909	6,471	1,435	29,773

Source: *New South Wales Statistical Registers.*

of the sum in question. Thousands of man-years of imprisonment were spared by these measures, as Tables IV.3.6 and IV.3.7 indicate.

At least one effect of Neitenstein's reforms was readily visible. Reported breaches of prison discipline decreased 40 percent from 1897 to 1901.[44] Neitenstein's tenure marked a fundamental change in New South Wales correctional practice. The rehabilitative orientations to deviance that had lain dormant since the days of Maconochie were revived and came to constitute the ideal (if not always realized) direction of New South Wales penal institutions in the twentieth century.

Effects

The impact of official response to the disorder of the 1840s defies complete assessment, for during the period larger structural changes were evident and significant. By 1842 wages had fallen, unemployment was increasing, and the temptations to leave one's work or to desert one's ship had largely disappeared. Thus economic conditions had all but obviated the need for Masters and Servants laws and legislation regulating seamen.[45] Changing patterns of conventional criminality appear also to have been influenced by economic fluctuation. The crime wave of the early 1840s seemed to decline as economic conditions improved later in the decade, and the incidence of criminal deviance had begun to subside even before assertive official action had been taken; the Select Committee on the Insecurity of Life and Property (1844) served a largely symbolic function. As a gesture in response to public pressure, the appointment of the committee gave the impression that the government was acting assertively.[46]

The centralization of New South Wales police forces in 1862 was widely regarded as a worthwhile innovation that was 40 years overdue. There was little doubt that the facilities of communication available to the reorganized force were in no small part responsible for the success in suppressing the bushranging of the 1860s.

The marked decline in rates of criminality that occurred in New South Wales during the mid-nineteenth century was influenced by a number of factors. Since the major innovations in law enforcement and correctional policy were not implemented until the downward trend was well underway, and since judicial processes do not appear to have been altered in a manner that would produce an artifactual decline in committal and conviction rates, the diminution of disorder seems to have been more attributable to larger socioeconomic changes than to policies of public order. The end of the convict era was accompanied by a significant change in the demographic structure of the colony. The proportion of females and free persons in the colony increased; these groups were of course less inclined to engage in behavior defined by contemporary authorities as criminal. Moreover, the second half of the nineteenth century witnessed an increase in economic well-being that was characteristic of most Western societies. Though austere by today's standards, material conditions in Sydney improved significantly during the period of economic expansion after 1850.

The apparent decline of larrikinism in Sydney in the late 1890s provides a specific illustration of the ambiguous relation between official policies, socioeconomic change, and change in deviant behavior. Certainly the decline of larrikinism attracted less public attention than did its rise. There also were apparent misconceptions about the effectiveness of the treatments aimed at its suppression. Retrospective interpretations such as those of Brodsky[47] and the authors of editorials and letters in the *Sydney Morning Herald* [48] have been based on the contention that larrikinism was effectively suppressed by the application of corporal punishment. Existing records provide little support for these claims, however. Because the expression larrikinism was employed in reference to behaviors as varied as insulting language and assault, any blanket assertions are risky. It is quite evident that by the mid-1890s floggings for infractions of prison discipline were infrequent, and sentences of flogging for criminal offenses were very rare. Police records reveal that at least twice in 1893 and once in 1895 floggings were administered in cases of wanton assault.[49] Comptrollers-general of prisons explicitly

Table IV.3.8   Arrests for Selected Offenses Related to Larrikinism in Police District 4, Sydney, January-June, 1891-1900

Year	Riotous behavior	Assault on police	Common assault	Obscene or indecent language	Injury to property	Total
1891	33	17	32	47	14	143
1892	31	20	36	60	23	170
1893	39	13	30	47	16	145
1894	46	11	19	51	14	141
1895	47	12	37	53	7	156
1896	30	10	31	52	12	135
1897	36	8	49	29	12	134
1898	45	13	35	31	7	131
1899	31	8	35	35	12	121
1900	16	10	42	41	10	119

Source: N.S.W. Legislative Assembly, "Police Reports Respecting Disturbances Between the Military and a Certain Section of the Public known as 'Pushes,'" 1900, p.5.

recommended from 1890 to 1892 that whippings be administered to youthful minor offenders, but they appear to have accepted the treatment of restricted rations as an adequate substitute.[50] Whatever punishments were awarded to the youthful delinquents of the day, the data in Table IV.3.8 suggest that there was but a slight diminution in the incidence of "larrikin-type offenses" during the decade, at least in the particular district of Sydney the police had designated a "high-crime area."

Larrikinism in general seems to have been less influenced by official policy than by larger social change. Although no significant change in the colony's age and sex structure exists to explain any decline, Maclachlan suggested a number of causes for the gradual disappearance of larrikinism, including the introduction of free and compulsory education and increased access by members of the working class to organized recreational facilities.[51] It might also be suggested that, by the turn of the century, the New South Wales public had grown accustomed to and more tolerant of youthful exuberance.

NOTES TO CHAPTER IV.3

1. Gipps, op. cit., p. 133.
2. G. C. Mundy, *Our Antipodes: or, Residence and Rambles in the Australasian Colonies*, 3d ed. (London: Richard Bentley, 1855), p. 17.
3. *Sydney Morning Herald*, January 12, 1850, p. 2; January 23, 1850, p. 2.
4. N.S.W. Legislative Council, Report from the Select Committee on Intemperance (Sydney: Government Printer, 1854).
5. For an overview of this aspect of Australian history, see Myra Willard, *History of the White Australia Policy to 1920* (Melbourne: Melbourne University Press, 1923).
6. This trial and the equally notorious Büttner case of 1889 are discussed in Frank Clune, *Scandals of Sydney Town* (Sydney: Angus and Robertson, 1957).
7. *Bulletin* (Sydney) extraordinary, December 26, 1886, pp. 2-3.
8. The phenomenon of larrikinism has been accorded considerable attention; literary treatments range from sophisticated analysis to blatant polemic. See N. S. Maclachlan, "Larrikinism in Australia" (unpublished thesis, University of Melbourne); Ambrose Pratt, " 'Push' Larrikinism in Australia," *Blackwood's Magazine*, 1029 (July 1901), 27-40; "Ajax" (pseud.), "Larrikinism," *Sydney Quarterly Magazine*, I:2 (January 1844), 207-215; Nat Gould, *Town and Bush* (London: George Routledge and Sons, 1896); *Bulletin* (Sydney), June 18, 1881; June 17, 1882; *Sydney Morning Herald*, June 26, 1893.
9. Report from the Select Committee on the Insecurity of Life and Property (1844), p. 2.
10. Ibid., p. 5.
11. *Sydney Morning Herald*, January 3, 1847.
12. "The Larrikin Residuum," in C. M. H. Clark, ed., *Select Documents in Australian History, 1851-1900* (Sydney: Angus and Robertson, 1955), p. 687.
13. N.S.W. Department of Prisons, *Annual Report for the Year 1896* (Sydney: Government Printer, 1897), pp. 63-64.
14. Ibid., p. 33.
15. Ibid., p. 31.
16. New South Wales *Parliamentary Debates*, 1st ser., Vol. 22, August 27, 1886, p. 4385. (Harold Stephen, MLA).
17. N.S.W. Department of Prisons, *Annual Report for the Year 1882* (Sydney: Government Printer, 1883), p. 2.
18. New South Wales *Parliamentary Debates*, 1st ser., Vol. 51, May 26, 1891, p. 228. (John Haynes, MLA).
19. N.S.W. Department of Police, *Annual Report for the Year 1893* (Sydney: Government Printer, 1894), p. 3.
20. The first Statute of Laborers was enacted in 1349 because of a labor shortage following the Black Death. See T. F. T. Plucknett, *A Concise History of the Common Law*, 5th ed. (London: Butterworths, 1956), p. 32.
21. Masters and Servants (Amendment) Act 4 Vict. 23 (20 October, 1840).
22. An Act for the further and better Regulation and Government of Seamen within the Colony of New South Wales and its Dependencies and for establishing a Water Police 4 Vict. 17 (1840).

23. Gipps to Stanley, 7 October, 1843, Mitchell Library MSS, A1232, pp. 39-53.

24. *Atlas*, December 7, 1844, p. 16.

25. *Atlas*, February 11, 1845, pp. 124-125.

26. *Atlas*, February 22, 1845, p. 146.

27. *Atlas*, March 13, 1847, p. 122.

28. N.S.W. Legislative Assembly, *Report of the Intoxicating Drink Inquiry Commission* (Sydney: Charles Potter, Government Printer, 1887), p. 43.

29. N.S.W. Parliament, *Report of the Royal Commission on Chinese Gambling* (Sydney: Government Printer, 1892), p. 21.

30. 55 Vict. 5 (1891).

31. 57 Vict. 23 (1894).

32. King, "Some Aspects of Police Administration in N.S.W., 1825-1851," p. 221.

33. C. G. N. Lockhart, "Sketch of a Proposed System of Police for the Colony of N.S.W.," (1850) Archives of New South Wales, 2/674.15, p. 6.

34. New South Wales, *Parliamentary Debates*, 1st ser., Vol. 60, October 5, 1892, p. 945.

35. New South Wales, *Parliamentary Debates*, 1st ser., Vol. 39, June 25, 1889, p. 2439.

36. New South Wales, *Parliamentary Debates*, 1st ser., Vol. 40, July 31, 1889, p. 3590; 1st ser., Vol. 42, October 9, 1889, p. 6168.

37. For the best review of Maconochie's life and work, see John Barry, *Alexander Maconochie of Norfolk Island* (Melbourne: Oxford University Press, 1958).

38. N.S.W. Legislative Assembly, Report of the Select Committee on Public Prisons in Sydney and Cumberland (Sydney: Government Printer, 1861), p. 6.

39. These regulations were established in 1867 under the provisions of the "Act for the further Regulation of Gaols, Prisons, and Houses of Correction in the Colony of N.S.W. and its Dependencies, and for other purposes relating thereto," (4 Vict. 29, 26 December, 1840) euphemistically known as the "Prisons Regulation Act."

40. N.S.W. Department of Prisons, *Annual Report for the Year 1885* (Sydney: Government Printer, 1886), p. 2.

41. N.S.W. Department of Prisons, *Annual Report for the Year 1888* (Sydney: Government Printer, 1889), p. 2.

42. N.S.W. Department of Prisons, *Annual Report for the Year 1894* (Sydney: Government Printer, 1895), p. 2.

43. John R. Lee, "Modern Methods of Prison Reform," Mitchell Library MSS, B688.

44. N.S.W. Department of Prisons, *Annual Report for the Year 1901* (Sydney: Government Printer, 1902), p. 6.

45. Mitchell Library MSS, A1233, pp. 69-70.

46. *Sydney Morning Herald*, October 2, 1844, p. 3.

47. Isadore Brodsky, *Sydney Looks Back* (Sydney: Angus and Robertson, 1957).

48. *Sydney Morning Herald*, June 28, 1933, p. 2; August 15, 1946, p. 2.

49. N.S.W. Legislative Assembly, "Police Reports Respecting Disturbances Between the Military and a Certain Section of the Public Known as 'Pushes' " (Sydney: William Applegate Gullick, Government Printer, 1900), p. 5.

50. N.S.W. Department of Prisons, *Annual Report for the Year 1890* (Sydney: Government Printer, 1891), p. 2; *Annual Report for the Year 1891* (Sydney: Government Printer, 1892), p. 2; *Annual Report for the Year 1892* (Sydney: Government Printer, 1893), p. 2; *Annual Report for the Year 1893* (Sydney: Government Printer, 1894), p. 2; *Annual Report for the Year 1894* (Sydney: Government Printer, 1895), p. 2; *Annual Report for the Year 1895* (Sydney: Government Printer, 1896), p. 2; N.S.W. Legislative Assembly, *Correspondence Respecting the Reintroduction of the Use of the Gag in the Gaols of the Colony* (Sydney: Charles Potter, Government Printer, 1895), p. 2; N.S.W. Legislative Assembly, *Minutes, Reports, and Circulars Respecting the Treatment of Seventh Class Prisoners* (Sydney: Charles Potter, Government Printer, 1895).

51. Maclachlan, op. cit.

Chapter IV.4

CRIME, CONFLICT, AND
PUBLIC ORDER, 1901-1939

PATTERNS OF CRIME AND CONFLICT, 1901-1939

    The general decline in levels of crime that began in the closing years of the nineteenth century continued unabated until shortly before the outbreak of World War I. Available statistics suggest that the first decade of the twentieth century was a period of tranquility in Sydney that has not been matched before or since. While rates of crimes against persons remained relatively low and stable through the end of the 1930s, patterns of serious theft revealed sharp increases in the aftermath of World War I and in the late 1920s. Rates of robbery with violence rose sharply in the years before and after the war. Rates of property crime in general tended to remain relatively high throughout the Depression (Table IV.4.1), though not nearly so high as they were to become later. The police appeared to pay quite close attention to gambling during most of the period 1930-1935, and significant increases in arrest rates during various years suggest that periodic crackdowns were undertaken. Prostitution and related offenses received similarly close attention in 1916-1917, 1922-1923, and 1928, before arrest rates dropped sharply during the Depression.

    The most interesting pattern in arrest rates during the period involves fluctuations in arrests for drunkenness and related offenses. Here the rates tend to vary quite closely with the business cycle, rising during the 1920s, dropping off at the beginning of the Depression, reaching a low point during 1931-1932, and increasing during the following years of economic recovery. These changes may have been attributable in part to elasticity in the public's effective demand for intoxicants and to the greater preoccupation of the police with other forms of behavior during periods of economic hardship. Arrest data are given in Figures IV.4.1 and IV.4.2 and in Table IV.4.1.

With the exception of opium smoking by some members of the Chinese population, the use of drugs other than alcohol was historically very rare in Sydney.[1] This situation changed, however, in the late 1920s with the emergence of a thriving traffic in cocaine. The potential for profits stimulated considerable competition, and the conflicts that developed between competing entrepreneurs were relatively violent by Sydney standards. Originally the pistol was widely used, but following enactment of licensing legislation in 1927 this weapon was replaced by the razor. By 1928 the "razor gangs" were receiving widespread newspaper coverage and had captured the public's attention. Public alarm was generally unjustified, however, since razor weapons were used almost exclusively by and among those directly involved in the drug trade, prostitution, or other illicit enterprises.[2]

The most dramatic incidents of civil strife during the period consisted of a series of clashes and protests over diverse issues. Most of these events were limited in scope and duration but were not without political impact. The outbreak of World War I precipitated a wave of nationalism in Australia; the renaissance of reverence for Motherland and Empire was reflected in the rush to enlist for combat service and in the crowds gathered in the streets singing "God Save the King." Despite the broad consensus, a few Sydneysiders viewed military service without enthusiasm. A branch of the Industrial Workers of the World had been established in Sydney during 1907,

Table IV.4.1 Selected Offense Categories, Arrest Rates per 1,000 Population, New South Wales, 1925-1936

Year	Aggressive Crime	Acquisitive Crime	Drunken- ness	Prosti- tution	Gambling	Vagrancy
1925	1.30	3.65	13.23	.73	.54	.56
1926	1.41	4.06	13.46	.99	.74	.65
1927	1.35	4.20	13.58	.86	.73	.73
1928	1.31	4.68	14.35	1.25	.94	.79
1929	1.27	5.43	13.43	.94	.82	.73
1930	1.17	6.40	10.27	.52	1.13	.71
1931	1.13	6.67	8.26	.31	1.48	.64
1932	1.22	6.48	8.42	.29	1.42	.53
1933	1.01	7.10	9.85	.29	1.76	.53
1934	.99	6.45	10.20	.43	1.87	.55
1935	1.05	6.99	10.71	.36	2.02	.58
1936	.99	6.33	11.71	.33	1.99	.51

Source: N.S.W. Police Department, Annual Reports.

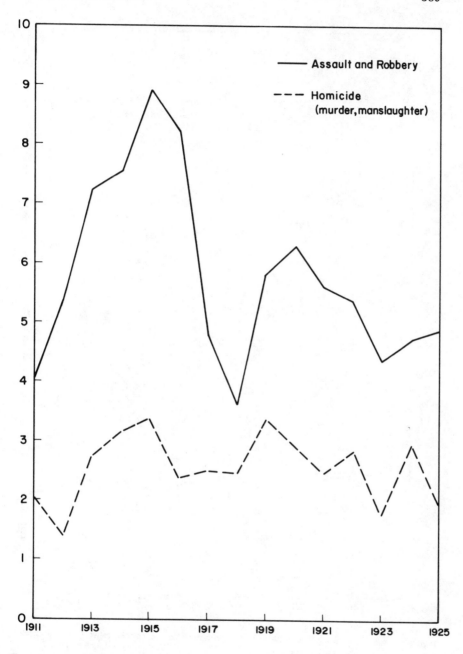

Figure IV.4.1 New South Wales: Arrests for homicide and assaults and robbery per 1000 population, 1911-1925

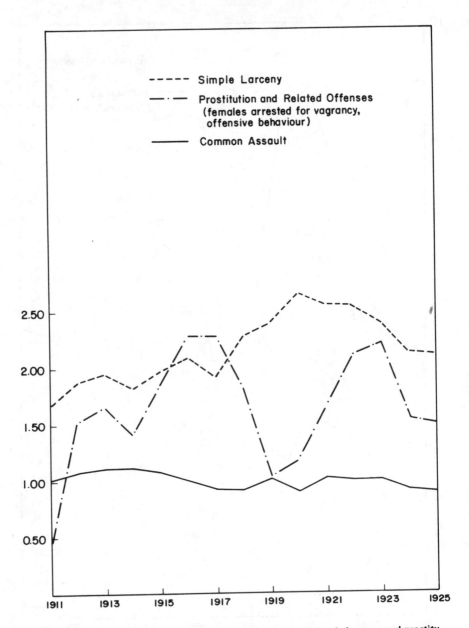

Figure IV.4.2 New South Wales: Arrests for common assault, simple larceny, and prostitution and related offenses per 1000 population

and its members stood in the vanguard of antiwar activity. This prompted police raids on IWW premises and arrests of its more vocal members on charges ranging from riotous behavior to conduct prejudicial to recruiting. As the war continued and Allied losses mounted, the federal Prime Minister W. M. Hughes advocated conscription for overseas service to provide replacements sorely needed at the front. IWW criticism grew in intensity, and, after a series of fires had occurred in Sydney department stores and warehouses during the winter of 1916, twelve of the "Wobblies" were arrested on charges of treason and arson.[3]

The year 1916 was a particularly troubled one in Sydney; it began with one of the more unusual riots in the city's history. Pressures to maintain the supply of recruits for the war effort were great, and training camps in Australia were uncomfortable and overcrowded. Conditions at one base near Liverpool were among the most austere; in February a large number of soldiers reacted to an increase in drill by walking out of camp and storming a hotel in Liverpool. Having appropriated and consumed the publican's supply of beer and spirits, a number of the troops began brawling among themselves and with the police, while others made their way to the railway station and boarded trains for Sydney. Noisy, drunken soldiers arrived at Central Railway Station in train after train and marched through the city overturning fruit carts and smashing windows. Meanwhile a group of about 500 soldiers was confronted by an armed military picket at the station; several shots were fired, killing one rioter and wounding six others. Activity on the streets of the city was disorganized and consisted primarily of small groups of soldiers wandering around the city, drinking and looting well into the night. In addition to the casualties at Central Station, four policemen were injured and 60 rioters were arrested. The Commonwealth responded to the disturbance by ordering the six o'clock closing of hotels under the War Precautions Act, and no further incidents of this kind occurred.[4]

Wartime economic conditions provided another source of tension; wages were fixed during the later war years, while prices rose and industrial discontent heightened accordingly. Although the IWW enjoyed only minimal support in the New South Wales labor movement, their advocacy of work slowdowns became attractive to many Sydney workingmen. A general strike occurred in 1917, reinforcing the authorities' enmity toward the IWW. Arrests of the movement's remaining active membership soon followed and by the end of 1917, some 80 Wobblies were in prison.[5] Official responses to the 1917 strikes included the recruitment of strikebreakers from country areas, and with economic conditions austere, the strikers soon capitulated.

Class antagonisms flared again in Sydney during 1929 when large-scale industrial disturbances arose in both the timber and coal industries. In February timber workers struck against an arbitration award that reduced wages and rescinded previous improvements in working conditions, and proprietors of the coal mines in northern New South Wales sought to reduce wages by initiating a lockout of some 10,000 miners. Protest marches and picketing were prevalent both in Sydney and in the north, and toward the end of the year police opened fire on a group of miners at Rothbury, wounding seven and killing one.[6]

The use of nonunion labor under police protection dealt a harsh blow to both the miners and the timber workers. By the end of 1929 the Depression had arrived, unemployment was increasing, and workers in both industries had no choice but to return to work on terms dictated by management. The onset of the Depression replaced industrial unrest with tensions of a different kind. As unemployment increased, large numbers of jobless workers took to the streets in protest; others joined them, and efforts of police to disperse the gatherings were often intense, though no fatalities occurred.[7]

Although the eviction riots that broke out during the worst of the Depression years were not widespread, they constituted a high water mark of tension between police and public. Thousands of impoverished tenants left their homes and established camps around the metropolitan area, but others were reluctant to move. In a few of the more extreme situations, attempts by police to execute eviction orders grew into pitched battles with resisting tenants and attracted large numbers of spectators generally unsympathetic to the police. These events often resulted in injuries to both sides and in the arrest of the resisters. One such riot in Newtown in June 1931 produced nineteen arrests; seventeen arrests were made following a similar incident a month later in suburban Bankstown.[8]

DEMOGRAPHIC AND ECONOMIC CONDITIONS OF PUBLIC ORDER, 1901-1939

Although the population of the Sydney metropolitan area reached one million in 1926, there were no significant changes in rate of growth during the first four decades of the twentieth century that appear to have had any significant effect on public order. Annual increases were steady but not sharp, and the rate of growth slowed considerably during the 1930s. Population density remained relatively low during the period, decreasing slightly in some inner suburban neighborhoods as a result of metropolitan expansion. The arrival of a few non-British European migrants during the 1920s made but a small dent in an overwhelmingly homogeneous society. According to the 1933 census, Italian-born residents of Sydney totaled slightly more than 3,000; the Italian community received disproportionate

Table IV.4.2 Percentage of Trade Unionists Unemployed in
New South Wales, 1920-1942

Year	%
1920	6.9
1922	11.4
1924	12.6
1925	11.0
1928	11.3
1929	11.5
1930	21.7
1931	30.8
1932	32.5
1933	28.9
1934	24.7
1935	20.6
1936	15.4
1938	9.9
1939	11.0
1940	11.0
1941	4.7
1942	1.8

Source: Commonwealth Year Books.

attention, however, because of the activities of the "Camorra,"
reputedly an Italo-Australian criminal gang.[9]

Economic conditions during the first four decades of the century
were subject to drastic change. There was a period of growth and
expansion prior to World War I, but the hostilities of 1914 brought
about a reduction in exports and strains in the domestic economy.
The 1920s were again years of expansion, which ended rather
abruptly with the global economic crisis and the Depression of the
1930s. As estimated unemployment rates in Sydney rose from about
11 percent in 1928 to about 33 percent in 1932 (Table IV.4.2),
industrial protest was replaced by political protest. Material deprivation was widespread, and thousands were without means of support—
a condition unprecedented in scope, if not in intensity, in the history
of New South Wales. As was the case in most Western societies,
recov   slow; it was fully accomplished only at the onset of
Worl(

PUBLIC OPINION AND POLITICAL INTERESTS, 1901-1939

The Rulers and the Law

During the years of relative tranquility that preceded World War I,
political elites in New South Wales were generally preoccupied with

matters other than public order. This orientation changed, however, as political protest grew more visible. Elite attitudes toward political dissent were particularly hostile during the war years; criticism of government policy was viewed at best as unpatriotic, and more commonly as seditious. The IWW was perceived by both federal and state governments as the most threatening movement of the time. Not only did the Wobblies' outspoken attacks focus on parliamentary democracy and racial purity, they were also directed at institutions, from conventional trade unionism to the monarchy to the war effort, each of which was loyally embraced by a large segment of society. Australia's distance from the front lines may have contributed to the need of elites from both major parties to project the image of a closer threat, and the IWW served as a convenient scapegoat.

> It was held responsible for the strike wave, for the defeat of the politicians by the industrialists within the Labor Party; most heinous of all, it was anti-conscription, anti-war, anti-British, pro-German—or so respectable opinion said.[10]

Legislative activity reflected these inclinations quite accurately; a number of new offenses were created, and police were afforded generous procedural liberties. The Commonwealth War Precautions Act of 1914-1915, a typical example of sweeping wartime legislation, greatly expanded powers of search and seizure. It provided in addition for the detention and relocation of resident aliens, at the discretion of the government. The Commonwealth Crimes Act of 1914 broadened the definition of treason to include assistance in any form to any public enemy; the offense was punishable by death.

Following the IWW arson trial, at which all twelve defendants were convicted of sedition and conspiracy, the Hughes Government acted swiftly against the organization as a whole. In December 1916 a Commonwealth Unlawful Associations Bill was introduced and quickly enacted. The act declared the IWW to be an unlawful association and defined membership in the organization as criminal behavior punishable by six months' imprisonment. In the aftermath of the passage of the act, IWW activity continued under the label of "Workers Defence and Release Committees." The act, however, was amended in July 1917, and the Governor General was empowered to declare associations unlawful, thus obviating the need for future definitional amendments. The amendment was passed despite opposition and was followed by the arrest of the movement's entire active membership.

Political elites in New South Wales have never appreciated dissent, and their reaction to it during the war years was predictable. Antipathy to criticism was quickly translated into numerous provisions limiting political freedom, and these remained in effect and continued to be implemented long after the armistice. The most enduring legacy of the war period, however, was the division of public and political opinion about public order along class and party lines—a division that was intensified with the onset of the Depression. The nature of the division is apparent in the virtually antithetical policies of Labor and Nationalist Parties toward crime and public unrest.

Members of the Labor Party tended to view crime generally as a byproduct of a malfunctioning social system, thus advocated widespread structural change combined with a rehabilitative treatment of the offender. For example, arguments from the Labor benches stressed the inequitable distribution of wealth; a prominent Labor spokesman, H. V. Evatt, maintained during a 1925 debate on capital punishment that "much serious crime is due to poverty, to disease, and to insufficient provision for the health and wellbeing of the community."[11]

With the economic contraction in 1929, Labor members continued to emphasize distributive themes.

> With regard to starvation and misery, there has been more crime during the present Government's regime than at any other period, and this is brought about by the economic conditions. When men become desperate they are driven to crime to try to get food and shelter for their children.[12]

Legislative developments during the period of Labor government from June 1925 to October 1927 reflected these inclinations. The Pistol License Act of 1927, which required the licensing of handguns, and the Police Offences (Amendment) Drugs Act of 1927, regulating the distribution of narcotics by physicians and pharmacists, were the most significant redefinitions of the period. An attempt to legislate the abolition of capital punishment was unsuccessful, and the traditional Labor policy of commuting the sentences of those convicted of capital crimes was continued.

Members of the National Party, in power from October 1927 to November 1930, held quite different views. They reacted to crime with anger and moral indignation; intent on maintaining the docility and availability of the workforce, they regarded industrial protest as a dire economic threat. Foremost among their assumptions was the belief that primary responsibility for deviant behavior lay with the individual—an attitude that contrasted starkly with the structural approach taken by Labor members. As one Nationalist offered, somewhat tautologically, "Criminals exist because they are criminals; they exist because their inner vision is warped and because they are of criminal instincts."[13] Thus the Nationalists saw their task as one of suppressing the individual's deviant inclinations and protecting the existing socioeconomic environment. Nationalist views of crime included a more explicitly political theme as well. During debates they frequently accused the Labor members of unwarranted sympathy with criminals.

> Hon. gentlemen opposite are altogether too softhearted in regard to persons who commit crimes, and it is that sort of sympathy which encourages them in crime. They say, "We have always got a good backer in the Labour Party, which will stand behind us."[14]

The response of the Bavin Government to events in 1928 and 1929 involved the most significant broadening of the New South Wales criminal law in the twentieth century and aroused the wrath of the Labor opposition. The Crimes (Amendment) Act of 1929 constituted the first of a series of extensions of the criminal law. Possession of a razor at or immediately before the time of arrest on any charge became an offense punishable by six months' imprisonment. Opposition members had little sympathy for razor slashers, but they were strongly opposed to the act's provisions for whipping as a penalty for malicious wounding with a razor. In another clause, shoplifting offenses by females were removed from the coverage of the First Offenders (Women) Act of 1919, which provided for closed hearings in cases of minor first offenses by women. This provision did not involve a broadening of definition but, rather, an attempt to deter shoplifting by according public exposure to apprehended offenders.

The Crimes (Intimidation and Molestation) Act passed later in 1929 and inspired by British legislation two years earlier, was enacted in the shadow of the 1929 timber workers' strike. The act was specifically intended to suppress collective protest by striking workers and to ensure continued access of strikebreakers to their places of employment. In particular, the government sought to define mass picketing as criminal, for reasons indicated by the following remarks of Premier Bavin during debate on the bill:

> It will be readily understood that with the massing of 500 or 1,000 men around the gate of any working premises where a volunteer labourer wished to offer his services, it is not necessary for them to exercise any form of violence or to make any threats; the mere fact of their massing there and watching a man, even without deliberately insulting him or doing anything for which a policeman could arrest them, is sufficient intimidation to prevent any ordinary man from presenting himself for work.[15]

At another point he referred to mass picketing as "a form of tyranny that has hardly ever been equalled in the history of the world."[16] Members of the Labor opposition were predictably incensed at what they perceived as blatant legislative bias. Labor criticisms were to no avail, however, and the legislation was enacted soon thereafter.

The Intimidation and Molestation Act as finally passed also contained modifications of criminal procedure. In July 1929 seven union leaders were arrested in Sydney on charges of conspiracy to unlawfully molest, intimidate, and assault nonunionists. The offenses in question were subject to trial before a jury, and for want of sufficient evidence the prosecution was unable to obtain a conviction. To assure future convictions on similar charges, the government had the act provide for the relevant offenses to be tried summarily rather than before a jury.

The moral side of the Nationalists' concerns was manifest in the Vagrancy (Amendment) Act of 1929, which was directed at Sydney prostitutes and razor gangs and created the offense of consorting with reputed criminals. Thus for merely associating with people of "bad character" an individual was subject to six months' imprisonment. The bill as originally introduced included a provision that arrest on charges of being "idle and disorderly" constituted prima facie evidence of guilt, but this rather drastic clause was struck in committee.

INSTITUTIONS OF PUBLIC ORDER AND THEIR EFFECTS, 1901-1939

The Police

The per capita size of the New South Wales Police Force had reached an unprecedented high in 1904 but declined sharply during the following peaceful decade. Manpower resources were severely strained during World War I, largely because of an increase in resignations from the force and the department's assumption of numerous additional administrative responsibilities.[17] Although the police were relieved of responsibility for regulation and supervision of Weights and Measures in 1916, they continued to perform a vast array of extraneous taks. Administration of state liquor laws had always involved the allocation of considerable resources for licensing and inspection, and motor vehicle registration became increasingly burdensome as more people came to own automobiles. The general strike of 1917 further increased the burdens on the already undermanned police force; the protection of strikebreakers necessitated substantial redeployment of large numbers of officers. With existing manpower resources strained to the limit, the force was augmented, following the precedent of 1890, with the appointment of 521 special constables drawn from the public service at large and from the Prisons Department.[18]

The growth of political protest during the war years was accompanied by yet another noteworthy expansion in the role of the New South Wales police. Political espionage and surveillance activity were undertaken for the first time on a significant scale, and unlike the more routine administrative responsibilities these were approached with apparent enthusiasm. At the outbreak of the war, liaison was established between the New South Wales Police Department and Commonwealth military intelligence officials for the purpose of apprehending and interning enemy aliens. Soon thereafter, subversion experts in the New South Wales Force infiltrated the IWW and collected substantial quantities of information on its membership and activities. Even after the effective suppression of the IWW, surveillance of leftist activity in Sydney continued. Plainclothes police recorded hundreds of pages of summaries of speeches and meetings held in the Sydney Domain during 1918 and 1919 and, in some cases even reported on meetings held under the auspices of the opposition Labor Party.[19] Moreover, historians are in general agreement that a large part of the evidence used to convict the twelve Wobblie arson conspirators was the product of police fabrication.[20] Although police activity in New South Wales had never been free of implicit political undertones, events of World War I established a precedent. Here for the first time the New South Wales police performed an explicitly political function; they were actively engaged in the suppression of dissent, often by means of highly doubtful legal propriety.

A major change in Australian police organization took place in 1917 after circumstances of considerable embarrassment to Prime Minister Hughes. The prime minister's arguments in support of his proposed conscription policies met with a decidely cool reception in Queensland, and while addressing a crowd at Warwick, Hughes was the target of a well-aimed egg. The local police sergeant refused to arrest the culprit, however, and the premier of Queensland, an outspoken opponent of conscription, viewed the affair with amused tolerance. To lessen the possibility of similar occurrences in the future, Hughes established the Commonwealth Police Force shortly afterward.[21]

A number of minor changes in the structure of the New South Wales Police Department were implemented during the 1920s and 1930s, most of them involving expansion of police functions. A Drug Bureau was established in 1926 for the purpose of restraining the traffic in cocaine and other narcotic substances;[22] in 1934 the Police Offences Amendment (Drugs) Act removed the burden of administering the law relating to dangerous drugs from the Pharmacy Board and placed it with the police.[23] A Consorting Squad was organized in 1929 for the more efficient surveillance and apprehension of "reputed" criminals under the Vagrancy (Amendment) Act.[24] In 1930 another special squad was established and given the responsibility of suppressing illegal betting and sly grog selling.[25] Meanwhile renewed attention to dissident activity was reflected in the establishment of a mobile squad, a plainclothes group that vigorously harassed and dispersed political meetings and demonstrations.[26] The Criminal Investigation Branch underwent reorganization in 1929, based on the structure of the Liverpool (England) police, and expanded in 1931. The reorganizations were designed to streamline allocation of investigative responsibility and to prevent overlapping inquiry.[27]

The most exceptional development of the period, though, was the rise of a paramilitary organization called the New Guard, which arrogated to itself a number of police functions. In October 1930, as economic conditions worsened and street protest by the unemployed grew more prevalent, the colorful and outspoken J. T. Lang formed a Labor government. He was perceived by many in professional and mercantile occupations as the herald of socialism. To protect private enterprise and the empire from Lang, the unemployed, and communism, a group of middle-class veterans of World War I organized a private domestic security force in Sydney which they styled the New Guard. It probably was modeled on similar organizations established in European countries during the Depression, but it had no parallels in the history of New South Wales.[28] The movement was very largely based on class and age—the membership was drawn almost exclusively from the suburban middle-class males born between 1885 and 1900. The founder of the New Guard, Eric Campbell, described the goals of the movement in his memoirs:

> Our objective, as I saw it was twofold: first to preserve law and order and maintain services in case of civil strife breaking out as a direct result of the economic crisis, and second, to foil any attempt, constitutional or unconstitutional, by the government to foist socialization upon the people.[29]

New Guard activity in Sydney involved the extensive surveillance of leftist activity. On numerous occasions, members of the Guard harassed and disrupted communist meetings, occasionally with the tolerance of the police. In addition, members of the movement devised elaborate plans to take over and maintain gas, electric, water, and sewage services in the event of industrial unrest. An offer of New Guard volunteer labor during a 1931 maritime strike was declined by shipping executives. In December 1931 police estimated the membership of the New Guard in the metropolitan area at 36,000; the movement, however, was short-lived. With Lang's fall from power in May 1932, it had become evident that the threat of a socialist revolution, if ever real, had subsided. Campbell left Sydney on a tour of Europe, and when he returned the organization had all but dissolved.

The Judicial Structure

A number of alterations were made in New South Wales criminal procedure during the early part of the twentieth century, tending generally to reflect the spirit of progressive reform that characterized those years. In keeping with contemporary trends, a system of childrens' courts was established by the Neglected Children and Juvenile Offenders Act of 1905. Juveniles charged with murder or rape retained the right to trial by jury, but the act provided that lesser offenders be given a private hearing before a magistrate, with the right of appeal to quarter sessions courts. The Poor Prisoners Defence Act of 1907 marked a significant extension of legal assistance. Previously it had been the practice of the state to support the defense in capital cases when the defendant was indigent; the 1907 act extended eligibility to all cases involving indictable offenses, at the discretion of the presiding judge. An amendment intended to create an office of public defender was rejected, however, because too many members feared that the office would tend to encourage incompetence and nepotism.

A significant modification of the judicial structure of New South Wales had been introduced by the Criminal Appeal Act of 1912. The act established a court of criminal appeal, empowered to hear appeals against improper convictions and requests for review of sentence generally. Whereas opposition members tended to view the act as a threat to the ministerial monopoly of the prerogative of mercy, the government saw it as a worthwhile reform, following the constitution of a similar court in England in 1907. The New South Wales act in theory broadened the avenues of redress for convicted offenders, but the appeals court was generally reluctant to quash convictions or to vary sentences. In the decade 1915-1924, for example, there were only 527 appeals on behalf of 12,968 persons tried before the higher courts, and in only 108 instances were convictions quashed, new trials granted, or sentences changed. The New South Wales judiciary underwent no other significant modifications before World War II.

Penal Policies and Institutions

Throughout the late nineteenth century authorities in New South Wales were troubled about recidivism; prison officials advocated lengthened or cumulative sentences for those thought to be habitually criminal. Under the Habitual Criminals Act of 1905, certain recidivists could be detained "during His Majesty's pleasure," or, in other words, awarded indeterminate sentences. This type of treatment had been suggested in the mid-nineteenth century by Captain Maconochie as a means of giving the offender an incentive for reform. Whatever its purpose or impact, however, the act was not extensively used; during the first twenty years the act was in force, only 106 offenders in New South Wales were declared habitual criminals. The reluctance of the courts to award indeterminate sentences reflected the deeply entrenched belief that the primary purpose of imprisonment was not rehabilitation but punishment, for a fixed and calculable term, proportionate to the wickedness of the offense. This sentiment is still widely held in the judiciary and magistracy of New South Wales.

Imprisonment remained the dominant treatment during the first two decades of the new century, and, although the gradual amelioration of custodial conditions that began at the turn of the century continued, prison life remained uncomfortable at best. Vance Marshall, a radical activist who served a term for his protest activities, reported an unpleasant experience with coarse uniforms, unlighted cells, and beating administered by prison warders.[30] An important innovation was the establishment of two minimum-security facilities, an afforestation camp in 1913 and a prison farm in 1914. These were among the first facilities to be established as a result of Comptroller-General Neitenstein's plans for diversification. Such facilities not only served a productive function, but were also thought to provide a much healthier social atmosphere for less dangerous offenders, and many more were established in the 1920s and 1930s.

Nevertheless, certain correctional anachronisms were still very much a part of the New South Wales criminal justice system. The use of leg irons to restrain prisoners in transit was not discontinued until 1917.[31] Despite the continued pleadings of comptrollers-general for at least two decades, well over two-thirds of those entering prison in 1919 were sentenced in default of payment of fines.[32] Although floggings had not been formally administered in New South Wales since the turn of the century, provisions for corporal punishment remained in force and were even broadened in 1929 by the Crimes (Amendment) Act.

If imprisonment remained the dominant response to crime throughout the period, alternative treatment approaches were advocated with increasing frequency in the 1920s. In general, Labor Party members were inclined toward reformative treatment, while Nationalists emphasized deterrence and retribution. These distinctions were clearly evident during debate on the Capital Punishment Abolition Bill, introduced in 1925. Nationalists opposed abolition, arguing that capital punishment gave expression to a "healthy feeling of anger"[33] and accusing the Labor members of sentimentality. Nationalists also adhered consistently to the view that the threat of severe physical punishment was effective as a deterrent.

> It is commonly known that the average criminal is a coward. The man who is criminally inclined is also a coward by instinct, and if he sees the penalty of death facing him he will think a thousand times before committing the crime of murder, therefore it must act as a deterrent.[34]

Labor members, citing empirical evidence from the United States and Queensland, suggested that capital punishment was no better a deterrent than imprisonment. Moreover, they argued that the possibility of execution rendered it more difficult to obtain convictions in capital cases, pointing out as well that execution was final, thus irremediable in case of error.

Effects

Public policy seems to have had little lasting impact on the incidence of criminal deviance during the era of the Great War. The energetic suppression of the IWW may have inhibited the expression of political dissent, but proposals to institute conscription for overseas service were rejected in two referenda and then abandoned. In addition, the Australian Communist Party was founded in Sydney in 1920. If nothing else, official policy during the period succeeded in reinforcing public mistrust of the police force.[35]

The precise effects of various authoritative approaches to the treatment of crime are impossible to assess, but certain patterns of impact are discernible. The Pistol Licensing Act of 1927 did appear to restrain the use of handguns, but an alternative and equally threatening (if not always equally fatal) weapon, the razor, was adopted by those who persisted in arming themselves.

Of the various measures intended to suppress razor gang activity, the Vagrancy (Amendment) Act of 1929 was heralded by the authorities as most successful. The Commissioner of Police claimed in 1930 that "no other Act of Parliament had been of such assistance for years in ridding the city and streets of undesirables."[36] The Chief Commissioner in Victoria announced that numerous disreputable characters had begun to arrive in Melbourne from Sydney, and the Chief Secretary of New South Wales asserted that the effects of the act exceeded his expectations.[37] More arrests for consorting were made in Sydney during January and February 1930, and razor gang activity became less prevalent. Economic conditions, however, also appear to have had an appreciable effect on gang activity. As the Depression grew in severity, the traffic in cocaine that had provided the basis for considerable gang hostility decreased somewhat. Thus the decline of the razor gangs may have been as much attributable to the business cycle as to energetic prosecution under the Consorting Act.

Similarly, the occurrence of industrial stife may have been even more susceptible to economic fluctuation. Strikes in New South Wales tend to be both less frequent and less successful during periods of economic contraction, and gains to be won by means of industrial protest vary inversely with the unemployment rate. The impact of such legislation as the Crimes (Intimidation and Molestation) Act of 1929 on the incidence of picketing and other forms of industrial protest thus was largely masked by systemic change.

Street demonstrations by unemployed workers and eviction riots were likewise responsive to Depression conditions. Such events occurred only during the worst periods of economic contraction and diminished as conditions improved. Although activities of the police and the New Guard appeared to have some suppressive impact, their primary effect was the further erosion of respect by the working-class public for law enforcement officials.[38]

Excursus: Two Cases of Redefinition of Criminality

The late 1930s and early 1940s provide two instances of strenuous official attempts to expand the operative definition of criminal deviance in New South Wales. The objects of these attentions were bettors in the first instance and Communist Party members in the other.

By the mid-1930s Australia had begun to recover from the Depression, and New South Welshmen began once again to indulge their appetite for gambling. The state lottery established in 1932 by the Lang Government had been warmly received, but wagering on horse races remained an extremely popular practice. The act of placing a wager with an off-course local bookmaker, known as "starting price (or SP) betting" remained a crime, and by 1935 police turned their attention to the practice with increasing zeal. The superintendent of the Metropolitan Police District estimated in 1935 that 75 percent of the public did not object to the practice of SP betting, and it was not surprising that public reaction varied directly with the intensity of police prosecution. The police made numerous arrests, and members of Parliament began to raise objections; a royal commission was soon appointed. The commission's report affirmed what had long been obvious to the average resident of Sydney: Illegal betting was widespread, "in spite of the inhibitions of the law which is apparently powerless to stop it."[39]

The report did not question the wisdom of defining SP betting as a crime, but it raised serious questions about police practices. Among the activities undertaken by the police in the enforcement of betting laws were the deployment of undercover agents, the unlawful entry of private residences, and the presentation of false evidence in criminal proceedings. Referring particularly to the use of police agents, the commission concluded that

> The odd conviction that may be obtained as a result of their services is greatly outweighed by the disadvantages consequent upon their employment. They are spies and informers, and their use creates distrust in the minds of the public. It was abundantly clear from cases heard before the Commission that their evidence, generally speaking, is entirely untrustworthy.[40]

In any event, the police relaxed their vigilance somewhat in the aftermath of the commission's report, and arrests for gambling offenses decreased somewhat in the late 1930s.

To suppress political dissent during the 1920s and 1930s, the federal government had armed itself with an array of provisions of such sweeping generality that they could easily have been construed to proscribe even the mildest criticism. Under the 1926 Amendment to the Commonwealth Crimes Act, for example, any group could be declared unlawful for promoting ill will between classes, or for advocating or encouraging the overthrow by force or violence of "the established government of any civilized country."[41] Such acts were the basis for the prosecution of communist activity in Sydney, but official practices became quite erratic after the outbreak of World War II. The Australian Communist Party, responding with dogged loyalty to policy directions from Moscow, denounced the Allied cause after the signing of the Nazi-Soviet pact in April 1940. The Commonwealth government reacted by placing a ban on Communist Party literature in May; in the following month the party was declared an unlawful association under existing National Security (Subversive Associations) regulations. Attempts at suppressing communist activity included frequent police raids in Sydney,[42] but there appears to have been no lasting repressive effect. The movement went underground, meetings continued, and membership increased. With the German invasion of the Soviet Union in June 1941, the ACP reversed its policy and came out heavily in support of the war effort. The Commonwealth government continued to define the party as an unlawful association, but enforcement efforts decreased. By October the "illegal" communist press enjoyed a weekly nation-wide circulation of 50,000.[43] By the end of the year the party had been redefined as a lawful association, and party members were spared official harassment until after the war.

NOTES TO CHAPTER IV. 4

1. The extent to which patent cough medicines were used indiscriminately during the early years of the present century has not been determined.

2. *Sydney Morning Herald*, January 7, 1928, p. 16.

3. The definitive work on the alleged arsonists is Ian Turner's *Sydney's Burning*, rev. ed. (Sydney: Alpha Books, 1969).

4. *Sydney Morning Herald*, February 15, 1916, p. 9; February 16, 1916, p. 14; February 18, 1916, p. 7.

5. P. J. Rushton, "The Revolutionary Ideology of the Industrial Workers of the World in Australia," *Historical Studies*, 15: 59 (October 1972), 445.

6. The Rothbury shooting was an event of considerable historical significance; it was the most severe repression of labor protest in twentieth century New South Wales.

7. D. W. Rawson, "Political Violence in Australia," pt. 2, *Dissent*, no. 23 (Spring 1969) 35-38.

8. *Sydney Morning Herald*, June 20, 1931, p. 6; July 3, 1931, p. 6; July 9, 1931, p. 6; July 10, 1931, p. 7.

9. *Sydney Morning Herald*, December 24, 1930, p. 9.

10. Ian Turner, *Industrial Labour and Politics* (Canberra: Australian National University Press, 1965), p. 122.

11. *New South Wales Parliamentary Debates*, September 3, 1925, p. 574.

12. *New South Wales Parliamentary Debates*, September 18, 1929, p. 87. (P. M. McGirr, MLC).

13. *New South Wales Parliamentary Debates*, September 3, 1925, p. 579. (Mr. Kay, MLA).

14. *New South Wales Parliamentary Debates*, February 26, 1929, p. 3203. (John T. Ness, MLA).

15. *New South Wales Parliamentary Debates*, September 26, 1929, p. 383.

16. *New South Wales Parliamentary Debates*, September 26, 1929, p. 382.

17. N.S.W. Police Department *Annual Report for the Year 1916* (Sydney: Government Printer, 1917), p. 6.

18. N.S.W. Police Department *Annual Report for the Year 1917* (Sydney: Government Printer, 1918), p. 6.

19. "Police Reports on Political Meetings Held in Sydney Domain," Archives of New South Wales, 7/5589; 7/5594.

20. Turner, *Sydney's Burning*, pp. 204-211; Patrick O'Farrell "The Trial of the Sydney Twelve" *Quadrant* 16:75 (January-February, 1972), 52-67.

21. Brian Fitzpatrick, *The Australian Commonwealth* (Melbourne: F. W. Cheshire, 1956), pp. 238-243.

22. N.S.W. Police Department, *Annual Report for the Year 1926* (Sydney: Alfred James Kent, Government Printer, 1927), p. 3.

23. N.S.W. Police Department, *Annual Report for the Year 1934* (Sydney: Government Printer, 1935), p. 2.

24. N.S.W. Police Department, *Annual Report for the Year 1929* (Sydney: Alfred James Kent, Government Printer, 1930), p. 5.

25. N.S.W. Police Department, *Annual Report for the Year 1931* (Sydney: Government Printer, 1932), p. 5.

26. Fitzpatrick, op. cit., p. 127.

27. N.S.W. Police Department, *Annual Report for the Year 1929*, p. 5.

28. For a view of the New Guard through the eyes of its leader, see Eric Campbell, *The Rallying Point* (Melbourne: Melbourne University Press, 1965); for a more academic discussion, see Phyllis Mitchell, "Australian Patriots: A Study of the New Guard," *Australian Economic History Review*, 9:2 (September 1969), 156-178. An official interpretation of the movement may be found in N.S.W. Police Department, "Inquiries Relative to the New Guard Movement and Its Objects," *New South Wales Parliamentary Papers*, 1931-1932, Vol. 5, p. 1057.

29. E. Campbell, op. cit., p. 72.

30. Vance Marshall, *The World of the Living Dead* and *Jail from Within* (Sydney: Wentworth Press, 1969).

31. N.S.W. Department of Prisons, *Annual Report for the Year 1917* (Sydney: Government Printer, 1918), p. 7.

32. N.S.W. Department of Prisons, *Annual Report for the Year 1919* (Sydney: Government Printer, 1920), p. 55.

33. *New South Wales Parliamentary Debates*, September 3, 1925, p. 638. (Mr. Bavin, MLA).

34. Ibid., pp. 619-620. (Mr. Arkins, MLA).

35. O'Farrell, op. cit., p. 67.

36. *Sydney Morning Herald*, March 6, 1930, p. 11.

37. *Sydney Morning Herald*, January 9, 1930, p. 12.

38. Some sense of this erosion may be obtained from a set of documents entitled "Protests by Various Organizations Against Treatment of Demonstrations by Unemployed, 1933-1934," Archives of New South Wales, 7815. The role of the New Guard in the suppression of protest is discussed by Mitchell, op. cit., p. 168, E. Campbell, op. cit., p. 69, and Rawson, op. cit., p. 36. Rawson also discusses direct police activity against protesters.

39. N.S.W. Legislative Assembly, Report of the Royal Commission of Inquiry into Allegations Against the Police in Connection with the Suppression of Illicit Betting (Sydney: David Harold Paisley, Government Printer, 1936), p. 117.

40. Ibid., pp. 118-1, 9.

41. Crimes (Amendment) Act, 1926 (Commonwealth) Sec. 30A(a.).

42. Davidson, *The Communist Party of Australia*, p. 81.

43. Ibid., p. 82.

CRIME, CONFLICT, AND PUBLIC ORDER, 1940-1970s

PATTERNS OF CRIME AND CONFLICT, 1940-1973

The outbreak of World War II had little impact on the apparent incidence of most forms of crime. As might be expected during a period of mobilization and troop movements, rates of arrests for prostitution and common assault rose markedly. Otherwise, the beginning of a long-term increase in rates of property crime was the most noticeable change in existing trends.

As Table IV.5.1 indicates the end of the war brought little discontinuity in the nature of criminal deviance in Sydney, unlike the upsurge of some kinds of crime following World War I. The scarcity of consumer goods that had been accompanied by widespread black marketing during the war years diminished considerably. Police expressed concern at increases in armed violence and aggressive crime in general, but arrest data reveal remarkable stability in rates for most serious offenses. The Vice Squad was slightly more attentive to gambling and sly grog selling in Sydney during 1944 and 1945, but eased off in subsequent years. By far the most striking development in postwar Sydney was the massive increase in arrests for drunkenness. Huge annual increases occurred between 1945 and 1948, to the extent that drunkenness offenders constituted well over half the total input to the New South Wales criminal justice system at the end of the decade (Table IV.5.2).

The 1950s witnessed a sharp increase in rates of theft and a moderate upward drift in the rate of sex offenses. Despite references to an "age of lawlessness,"[1] however, the most recent fifteen-year period in Sydney's history has not been marked by a uniform

Table IV.5.1 Arrests per 1,000 Inhabitants for Selected Offenses in New South Wales, 1943-1951

Year	Homicide	Serious assault	Assault and robbery	Breaking and entering	Simple larceny
1943	.020	.086	.044	1.400	3.075
1944	.028	.095	.042	1.330	2.709
1945	.029	.089	.038	1.413	2.797
1946	.030	.100	.044	1.379	2.586
1947	.025	.093	.034	1.182	2.721
1948	.033	.106	.036	.833	2.516
1949	.028	.106	.036	.916	2.459
1950	.029	.090	.021	.787	2.456
1951	.038	.096	.032	.683	2.678

Source: New South Wales Police Department, Annual Reports.

Table IV.5.2 Arrests for Drunkenness and Related Offenses[a] in New South Wales, 1943-1951

Year	Arrests	Rate per 1,000 population	Drunkenness arrests, % of total arrests for offenses other than traffic violations
1943	34,956	12.2	31.9
1944	34,620	11.9	34.1
1945	43,624	14.9	37.4
1946	62,430	21.1	44.3
1947	67,580	22.5	47.7
1948	82,981	27.2	55.0
1949	78,485	24.9	52.9
1950	78,840	24.3	53.2
1951	83,349	25.1	54.4

[a]Drunkenness, drunkenness with disorderly conduct, and Inebriates Act Violations.
Source: New South Wales Police Department Annual Reports.

increase in all kinds of criminally deviant behavior. Tables IV.5.3 and IV.5.4 are illustrative: Homicide rates remained relatively stable, declining slightly at the end of the decade. Rates of serious assault increased approximately 50 percent between 1965 and 1970, steadily at first, with a pause in 1969, and a marked rise in 1970. By far the most striking trend in criminal deviance during Sydney's recent history has been the increase in property crime. Beginning in 1963, rates of burglary, larceny, armed robbery, and robbery with assault showed sharp annual increases. Between 1963 and 1970 rates of reported larceny and breaking and entering increased more than 100 percent and the rate of reported assault and robbery increased

Table IV.5.3 Offenses Known to the Police per 100,000 Population, Selected Offenses New South Wales, 1960-1970

Year	Homicides[a]	Serious assault[b]	Rape and attempts	Armed robbery	Assault and robbery	Breaking and entering	Larceny	Embezzlement	False pretences
1960	4.0	11.5	2.1	.6	4.5	204.8	393.8	10.5	86.2
1961	4.0	11.6	2.3	.6	4.8	206.8	410.9	15.4	88.7
1962	3.9	12.3	2.1	.5	4.5	203.3	383.3	14.2	94.4
1963	3.9	11.0	3.0	.3	3.4	228.6	384.6	21.3	104.0
1964	4.7	14.0	3.3	.6	4.2	239.9	388.3	21.0	100.3
1965	5.1	12.4	2.9	1.1	5.4	298.2	430.7	22.7	90.2
1966	3.9	13.2	2.8	1.8	6.0	315.0	437.6	20.4	87.6
1967	3.9	14.0	3.9	1.9	6.6	315.3	507.5	13.9	82.2
1968	4.4	15.1	4.7	2.3	9.6	439.2	625.4	18.9	81.9
1969	3.6	15.0	4.8	5.1	11.0	484.8	636.6	14.9	89.6
1970	3.2	18.5	4.4	4.0	13.9	618.3	831.4	15.9	101.8

a. Murder and manslaughter.
b. Attempted murder and actual bodily harm.
Source: New South Wales Police Department, Annual Reports.

Table IV.5.4 Arrests for Drunkenness and Related Offenses[a]
in New South Wales, 1960-1970

Year	Arrests	Rate per 1,000 population	Drunkenness arrests, % of total arrests for offenses other than traffic violations
1960	69,455	17.9	39.1
1961	68,710	17.4	36.4
1962	69,463	17.3	36.6
1963	66,647	16.4	34.2
1964	62,523	15.1	31.4
1965	64,039	15.2	32.4
1966	56,942	13.4	30.1
1967	56,235	13.0	29.7
1968	58,758	13.2	30.7
1969	60,405	13.3	30.6
1970	59,682	12.9	31.6

[a]Drunkenness, drunkenness with disorderly conduct, Inebriates Act violations.
Source: New South Wales Police Department Annual Reports.

300 percent. The rate of reported armed robberies increased sixteen-fold from 1963 to 1969 before dropping off slightly in 1970. Continuing an upward trend that began in the late 1950s, the rate of "Rape and attempts" known to the police rose by 100 percent during the 1960s. Media response to these drastic increases in assault, rape, and property crime were predictable. Headlines in Sydney's evening papers, the Sun and Mirror, frequently referred bluntly to the behavior in question, and the public sense of insecurity increased accordingly. Particular attention was focused on the apparent increase in the incidence of group rape, referred to locally as "pack rape."

In a lower key there has also been much public concern about crimes against morality and custom. Arrests for drunkenness have remained the single most common offense in New South Wales but have declined in both absolute and proportional terms. Prostitution and homosexuality have attracted a good deal more attention, albeit sporadically. In the 1960s, Paul Wilson has estimated, some 15,000 men availed themselves of the services of prostitutes in Sydney each week.[2] As has been true for most of the city's history, though, the enforcement of laws that forbid soliciting, the keeping of brothels, and other related behaviors appears to have been very irregular. Arrest records (Table IV.5.5) show an increase in the mid-1960s, followed by a sharp decline at the end of the decade. These data are more revealing about variations in police activity than about the extent of prostitution.[3]

Table IV.5.5 Prostitution and Related Offenses[a] in New South Wales, 1960-1970

Year	Arrests	Arrest per 1,000 population
1960	7,002	1.81
1961	7,169	1.81
1962	8,037	2.00
1963	13,580	3.33
1964	15,436	3.73
1965	13,561	3.22
1966	12,880	3.04
1967	8,946	2.07
1968	3,441	.78
1969	2,411	.53
1970	3,632	.71

a. Prostitution, suffer; prostitution, male person living on; soliciting by known prostitute; offensive behavior (female); vagrancy (female), Vagrancy Act offenses (female).
Source: New South Wales Police Department, Annual Reports.

In the late 1960s, the New South Wales Police became more vigilant with respect to male homosexuality. Certain members of the Vice Squad undertook an intensive surveillance of public lavatories in Sydney, and arrests for a number of offenses involving deviant sexual behavior posted a significant increase. The energetic activity of the "Indecency Squad," as the detail was informally named, met with rather unfavorable public response, however, and its members were reassigned at the end of 1969.[4] There also was a flurry of police activity in 1970 aimed at abortionists, who hitherto had performed thousands of abortions in Sydney each year with little official interference.[5] The immediate occasion for the change in police policies was public concern over disclosures by Bertram Wainer, a Melbourne physician, that members of the police force in neighboring Victoria had received numerous payments from abortionists.

Group protest and confrontations with authorities in Sydney were confined mainly to the years immediately after World War II and to the late 1960s and early 1970s. The issues, however, were quite different. The ideological conflicts of the 1920s and 1930s lay dormant during the period of active combat but revived at the onset of the Cold War. Industrial protest reappeared in 1947 and reached a peak during the coal strike two years later. The first episode occurred during a strike of wharf laborers in Sydney during March 1947, which prompted a public meeting on the Domain for the purpose of recruiting volunteer labor. The meeting was disrupted by a group of about 100 Communist waterside workers, and nineteen were arrested on charges of assault, indecent language, and offensive behavior.[6] Four months later a group of students from the University of Sydney assembled outside the offices of the Dutch Consul-General on Margaret Street in protest against Dutch colonial policy in the East Indies. The students were joined by a small number of wharf laborers and soon thereafter by a contingent of policemen, some in plainclothes and others in uniform. The police, members of a mobile unit called the "21 Squad," dispersed the assembly with force and attacked a number of demonstrators.[7]

The strike by New South Wales coal miners in 1949 was the largest and most significant industrial conflict in twenty years. The miners refused to submit to arbitration their strike over wages, hours, and working conditions, posing a threat to the New South Wales economy generally. Workers in many industries were laid off, numerous services were curtailed, and the supply of beer diminished drastically. The Commonwealth and state Labor governments were forced by circumstances into increasingly militant postures; a National Emergency (Coal Strike) Act was passed in Canberra, the Sydney headquarters of the Australian Communist Party was raided, and a number of union officials were arrested.[8] As the strike wore on, it became increasingly evident that a crisis was at hand for whatever conscious revolutionary movement existed in New South Wales. The energetic prosecution of trade union militants, however, combined with the deployment of Commonwealth troops to the coal fields to take over mining operations, brought about the defeat of the strike. Moreover, the economic impact of the strike was so great that public sympathy for the miners eroded rapidly. Anticommunist and antistriker sympathy grew, and the eventual defeat of the strike met with general approval.

Minor demonstrations occurred in the year following the coal strike. Sydney radicals protested the UN operations in Korea (which involved a contingent of Australian troops) and the development of nuclear weaponry, but only a handful of arrests resulted, and the demonstrations were free of violence.[9]

There was virtually no overt group conflict in Sydney during the 1950s and early 1960s, and when such behavior reappeared the issues were explicitly political, in contrast to the industrial protest that had been a major source of turmoil in Sydney since the 1890s. Conscription laws were reactivated in 1965, and Australian troops were deployed in Vietnam shortly thereafter. These events occasioned numerous rallies and marches in Sydney, most of them student-based and highly organized. Two or three major protests, with more than 1,000 participants, were staged each year from 1965 to 1972, and smaller scale demonstrations occurred more frequently, inspired by events in the war or by visits to Sydney of prominent public figures associated with war or conscription policies.[10] The largest protests took place in 1970 in the aftermath of the invasion of Cambodia by American and South Vietnamese forces.[11] Protest activity generally involved marches from the University of Sydney through the city, ending in a rally at central city locations such as the steps of Town Hall, Martin Place, or Chifley Square. Protest directed specifically at conscription sometimes involved "sit-in" style occupations of Commonwealth offices.[12]

By international standards the Sydney protest activities were non-violent; the only protest-related fatality occurred when a Common-wealth police officer died of a heart attack while carrying sit-in protesters from an office building.[13] Injuries were infrequent, and numbers of arrests varied substantially from one demonstration to the next, largely dependent on mutual expectations and hostilities between participants and police. The Moratorium march in September 1970 provoked one of the stronger official reactions in recent memory; arrests totaled 200, and relations between police and demonstrators were unusually strained.[14] A further 187 arrests were made during an antiwar demonstration in May 1971.[15]

During the 1950s and 1960s young Australians also had become increasingly dissatisfied with the Commonwealth Liberal Govern-ment's continued tacit approval of South African apartheid policy. Small protests occurred early in 1971, and the occasion for larger demonstrations arose during an Australian tour by a South African rugby team in July of that year. Attempts to disrupt the matches in Sydney were met with massive deployments of police; 220 arrests were made during a one-week period, almost two-thirds of them during a match at the Sydney Cricket Ground on July 10.[16] As in the case of antiwar protest, the Sydney antiapartheid demonstrations resulted in relatively few injuries.

DEMOGRAPHIC AND ECONOMIC CONDITIONS OF PUBLIC ORDER, 1940-1973

Despite substantial demographic and economic change during the postwar period, there is no prima facie connection between these factors and changes in the pattern of criminal behavior. One of the more striking demographic developments in the history of New South Wales, the influx of large numbers of immigrants from Eastern and Southern Europe, began in the late 1940s. Commonwealth officials, recalling the high rates of criminality among migrants in the nineteenth century, were apprehensive at first, but recent research by Ronald Francis has shown that immigrants generally are underrepresented among the New South Wales prison population, with the exception of Yugoslavs, who seem to be more likely to commit crimes of violence, and New Zealanders.[17]

Paul Ward has revealed that conviction rates for Yugoslav-born offenders tend not to vary across categories of offense, and that Yugoslavs are also overrepresented among those convicted of property crime.[18] He suggests that reluctance on the part of the former Commonwealth Liberal Government to deport offenders to a communist nation has increased the opportunity for recidivism. Offenses by New Zealanders may be explained by the great freedom of movement between New Zealand and New South Wales. Since passage to Australia is relatively inexpensive and passports are not required for entry, New Zealanders with tendencies toward deviance may be tempted to leave their small and homogeneous society for the greater diversity and anonymity of a large metropolis. At the very least, large numbers of young New Zealanders who visit Australia on working holidays expand the age cohort of potential delinquents.

Although criminality among migrant groups remains relatively low, the possibility that immigration indirectly influences the incidence of criminal deviance is very real. In general, increasing cultural heterogeneity can hardly be expected to widen acceptance of the behavioral standards of the New South Wales elite, which are largely derived from the Victorian era. Moreover, Australian-born sons and grandsons of southern and eastern European migrants are disproportionately found in lower income groups and have thus far achieved very little social or economic mobility. Criminal statistics do not reflect ethnicity, however, and the full effect of Sydney's increasing ethnic heterogeneity has yet to be assessed.

Another possibly relevant demographic factor is urban growth per se. The total population of the Sydney metropolitan area grew by approximately twenty percent during the decade of the 1960s, a numerical increase of more than half a million. The size of Sydney's population and the spatial expanse of the metropolitan area may have enhanced one's ability to achieve anonymity, making apprehension of offenders more difficult. However it is doubtful that these factors alone have contributed more than a slight amount to the drastic increases in assault and property crimes since 1963.

A breakdown of general population growth trends presents a more informative picture. The number of 18 to 24 year old males in New South Wales increased by 58 percent from 1959 to 1969. Since the beginning of the present century, males in this age range have been identified as the most crime prone group in New South Wales. It has thus been suggested by the New South Wales Bureau of Crime Statistics and Research that the recent "crime wave" may be partly explained in terms of the growth of this high-risk population.[19] Recent research by Paul Ward, which reveals a rather stable rate of convictions for 18 to 24 year olds, further supports the hypothesis.[20] Moreover, rates of offenses that tend less to be associated with young males, such as homicide and embezzlement, have shown no apparent trend in recent years.

Economic factors do not have any obvious or simple relation to crime in Sydney in the past 30 years. The entire postwar era has been virtually free of economic dislocation. Aside from a slight recession in the early 1960s, the economy has expanded steadily, and unemployment has been extremely low. The soaring rate of crimes of acquisition during this period of unparalleled material prosperity has thus encouraged alternatives to the traditional hypotheses that theft is a product of poverty or of general economic adversity. First among these is what might be called the "relative deprivation" hypothesis. Although very few Sydneysiders are denied the basic necessities of food, clothing, and shelter, many have become increasingly aware of the greater prosperity of other segments of the population. This greater visibility of material things, amplified by widespread media advertising, may simultaneously entice and frustrate those who lack the means to buy. Such persons may then turn to illegal means of acquisition.

Closely related to the theme of relative deprivation and temptation is that of increasing opportunity.[21] There are, quite simply, more objects to steal in Sydney today than at any time in the past. Automobiles, television sets, and other attractive items exist in unprecedented quantity, while retailers continue to display their merchandise as openly as ever before. Evidence that the majority of burglaries in Sydney occur in the affluent eastern and northern suburbs, whereas the majority of apprehended burglars live elsewhere, lends some weight to this contention.[22]

The hypothesis of increased opportunity might also explain increases in rates of offenses against the person. It has been suggested by Paul Ward that the postwar "baby boom" has produced not only more potential criminals but more potential victims as well. In Sydney today there are more young women to rape and more young men with whom to fight than ever before.[23]

PUBLIC OPINION AND POLITICAL INTERESTS, 1940-1973

Contemporary Opinion

Despite the lack of any apparent increase in serious crime in the 1940s, explanations of wartime and postwar criminal deviance were abundant. Commissioner of Police William J. MacKay attributed violent crime to "a certain moral looseness" characteristic of wartime, and to the disruption of normal family relationships. MacKay also offered the traditional explanation of police manpower shortage.[24] There were other postwar apologia offered by the police, many of them familiar. The demobilization brought back to Sydney thousands of young men who were no longer subject to the rigors of military discipline, and many faced an uncertain future. With the reduction in rationing at the end of the war, the demand for black market consumer goods fell off quickly. According to police spokesmen, the black market had provided an easy source of large sums of "safe" money for entrepreneurs; many of these individuals had been involved in the more common forms of property crime before the war and were apparently returning to those practices.[25]

Attempts to explain the marked increases in some categories of crime in the 1960s have varied widely in terms both of substantive thrust and scientific rigor. One noteworthy change in perspectives is the growing view of deviant behavior as a social product. Whereas some observers as recently as the late 1940s viewed deviance as a phenomenon stemming from innate causes, most contemporary opinion focuses on the environmental etiology of crime. Rather than addressing themselves to particular kinds of criminality, interpreters today suggest factors that have, they contend, encouraged deviance in general. Perhaps their best-known argument attributes the recent increase in crime to an atmosphere of permissiveness. These observers suggest, in a manner strikingly reminiscent of opinion in the 1880s, that an increase in personal freedom, combined with a decline in educational and family discipline, have served to loosen the restraints that hitherto contained deviant behavior. Universal peacetime military service, it is said somewhat nostalgically,

> had the effect of making most young men conscious participants in the surging nationalism, militarism, and imperial loyalty of those days.
>
> Combined with strong, even tyrannical classroom and parental discipline, as well as a still-harsh economic system, young people were shown clearly and forcibly where the older generation said their obligations lay.[26]

Another popular explanation for the recent increase in crime, particularly with government and police spokesmen, is the theme of insufficient deterrence. In the simplest terms, crime has increased because police are too few in number and punishments insufficiently severe. The strength of the New South Wales force, a major issue in the 1965 state election, remains a perennial topic of discussion. The notion that criminals are coddled has been familiar in Sydney since at least 1800. Members of the Liberal Government, in office from 1965 to 1976, often argued in behalf of the need for longer sentences. Spokesmen for the police also have consistently advocated an increase in the severity of criminal sanctions.

As the increase in rates of acquisitive crime continued unabated throughout the mid-1960s, greater attention was focused on the public's relative ignorance of crime prevention methods. The police force in particular was outspoken in its advocacy of a more protective posture on the part of banks and commercial establishments. Insurance companies began to encourage homeowners to install improved alarm and locking mechanisms, and automobile owners were warned against leaving their vehicles unlocked. Thus to a certain extent the absence of sufficient public precaution was regarded as having contributed to the increase in crime.

The official concern that arose in 1969 over the pack rape issue was accompanied by extensive discussion of social conditions. Among the suggested roots of pack rape was the drabness of industrial life.

> In considering the problem of pack rape, we must face up to the unpleasant fact that our form of society takes very little heed of the young unskilled workers and provides few outlets for the development of their personalities, which are often repressed by industrial conditions becoming more and more dehumanized.[27]

The Select Committee on Violent Sex Crimes (1969) proposed numerous correlates of the pack rape phenomenon, not least of which was family instability. Suggesting that many offenders had come from homes in which divorce, drinking, and gambling were a way of life, the committee concluded that socialization processes had been distorted and traditional values had not been inculcated.[28] It seems reasonable to infer that similar interpretations would also apply to more conventional kinds of crime.

One necessarily speculative explanation for the apparent increase in certain types of crime involves differential reportability. It had been generally accepted in the United States that only a fraction of crimes committed ever come to the attention of the police. Recent research in Australia suggests the existence there of a similar situation.[29] Such findings raise problematic questions about changes over time in the reportability of certain offenses. A woman in 1890, for example, may have been reluctant to report having been raped, fearing the stigma attached to such victimization at that time. Her present-day counterpart may be much less hesitant, however. Similarly, the percentage of assaults known to the police may have increased as a result of changing social values and a diminishing tolerance for interpersonal violence. Although these suggestions are plausible and are held by some Australian academic experts, they are not subject to direct empirical confirmation.

The Rulers and the Law

Considerable difference of opinion continues to exist within New South Wales society on matters of criminal law and crime control strategy; as has been the case throughout the twentieth century, disagreements are generally based on party lines.

Toward the end of the 1940s, as the Cold War began to dominate Australian political life and as protest activity became more visible, the theme of the Communist menace was heard with increasing prevalence. Although the Australian Labor Party controlled both federal and state Parliaments during the postwar years, the major direction of political debate was forced by the federal opposition leader R. G. Menzies. An arch-conservative with deep reverence for British royalty and civilization, Menzies had developed strong antagonism toward the Soviet Union and toward the Australian Communist Party in the 1930s. Like Churchill, whom he admired greatly, Menzies perceived an increasing threat to British civilization from communism, whether international or domestic, and saw an imminent danger of war with the Soviet Union. Quite aware that the theme could be exploited in domestic politics, he proceeded to make the symbol of Red menace the keystone of Australian political discourse; this convention was maintained throughout the 1950s and 1960s. The Labor Party was thus forced to act defensively; just as the *Sydney Morning Herald* referred to the 1949 coal strike as "part of the Russian Cold War," [30] Labor blamed the strike on the Communist Party of Australia.[31]

During the 1949 election campaign in the aftermath of the coal strike, Menzies pledged to proscribe the Communist Party if his recently formed Liberal Party were elected. His campaign was successful, and in April 1950 he introduced in federal Parliament the Communist Party Dissolution Bill. Reminiscent of the unlawful associations legislation of World War I, the bill declared the Communist Party an unlawful association, disqualified its members from holding public or trade union office, and provided for a five-year prison sentence for continued participation in party activities. Although the bill was enacted in October 1950, it was disallowed as unconstitutional by the High Court of Australia the following March. However Menzies was strongly committed to the policy and he called for new elections to both houses of Parliament and campaigned again

on a pledge to amend the federal constitution by submitting the issue
to a referendum. After Menzies was returned to power and the new
Parliament enacted enabling legislation, the issue was submitted to
the Australian people in the referendum of September 1951. Despite
Menzies' energetic efforts, the issue was defeated by a narrow
margin, and membership in the Communist Party has remained
beyond the boundaries of crime as officially defined.

Most postwar debate over criminal law, and most revisions in the
criminal statutes, have concerned individual crime rather than
political activity. The debate over capital punishment was a major
issue in the 1950s. Because there had been relatively little crime in
1955, the fourteenth consecutive year of Labor dominance in state
politics, the introduction of legislation to abolish capital punishment
was timely. Although no executions had taken place during Labor's
years in power, there was sincere desire to make a definitive legislative break with the hanging heritage in New South Wales. Debate on
the issue covered familiar ground. Those opposed to abolition
regarded hanging as an effective deterrent, or as punishment well
deserved by transgressors who were "animals in human form." Those
favoring abolition suggested that hanging was barbaric, did not act as
a deterrent, and made convictions in capital cases very difficult to
obtain. [32] Since the mid-1950s were relatively tranquil years, the
abolitionists were able to prevail over their opponents with little
difficulty. The relevant provisions of the Crimes (Amendment) Act
of 1955 abolished capital punishment for all offenses save treason
and piracy.

The Liberals returned to power at the state level in 1965, however,
and one of the themes stressed by Robin Askin, when leader of the
Liberal opposition, was the ineffectiveness of the Labor Government
in reducing crime. The Liberal response was not to reimpose the
death penalty or expand the definition of criminality but rather to
increase the penalties for many types of criminal behavior. For
example, the Crimes (Amendment) Act of 1966 increased the
penalty for armed robbery from fourteen to twenty years imprisonment, and the Police Offences, Vagrancy, and Crimes (Amendment)
Act of 1967 increased fines for lesser assaults. Fines for a whole
range of summary offenses were increased by the Summary Offences
Act of 1970.

Another and much more complex issue of debate has concerned
the seriousness of various kinds of crime and deviance, and the
related question of decriminalization of some of them. There is
virtual unanimity about the serious threat posed by such offenses
against persons and property as homicide, rape, the various types of
assault, and traditional crimes of acquisition. Other offenses, par-

ticularly the so-called victimless crimes, are viewed more diversely. Those who advocate the "decriminalization" of such offenses as abortion, homosexual behavior, and public drunkenness are still in a minority, [33] yet there is obviously less consensus about the "wrongfulness" of these behaviors than there is regarding such acts as murder and armed robbery. Moreover, considerable difference of opinion exists as to how strenuously laws regarding environmental offenses and other forms of "corporate crime" should be enforced. Protest is believed as more or less legitimate depending on the issue and on the ideological concurrence of the public. The state Liberal Government regarded political protest with uncomfortable tolerance at best, and more often with hostile indignation. Political dissent, when expressed in terms of injury to persons or property, is opposed by the vast majority of society.

Certain interrelated attitudes of the political elite of New South Wales and of society generally, however, sustain the present definitional boundaries of criminal behavior. First, the striking racial and ethnic homogeneity of Australian society has been a dominant cultural characteristic since the original settlement. Anglo-Saxon Protestant values have been questioned periodically, but only from political and industrial radicals. Even these challenges were directed primarily at the distribution of wealth, leaving mores of sexual behavior largely untouched. Over the past fifteen years, unprecedented innovations in transport and communication have exposed New South Welshmen to a vast range of external influences. Sydney is no longer an isolated place but a cosmopolitan city, where a rich diversity of attitudes are expressed and inclinations exercised. There exists nevertheless within New South Wales society generally and among members of the Liberal party in particular a kind of cultural monism that is reflected in the following statement by a Liberal member of the New South Wales Legislative Assembly.

A shared morality is the cement of society. A recognized morality is as necessary to society's existence as a recognized government.

Accordingly, that recognized morality is entitled to protection, and to the support of the law for such protection. In short, it is permissible for any society to take the steps needed to preserve its own existence as an organized society. Immorality—even sexual immorality in private—may like treason be something that ultimately jeopardizes a society's continued existence. [34]

This perceived threat to dominant cultural values is complemented and reinforced by a tendency to perceive the many forms of deviant behavior en bloc. Each is subjectively linked to others in a manner unjustified by empirical reality. Thus behaviors as diverse as pack rape, cannabis smoking, and political protest are regarded alike as products of permissiveness; blanket rejection of deviance in general is reinforced. The following statement by another Liberal member of the New South Wales Legislative Assembly is illustrative:

> The fact is that our society, after devoting enormous sums for education and other social services, has produced a generation whose vocal leaders throw scorn at everything we thought was precious.

> On the one hand we have such reprehensible conduct as vandalism, robbery, assault, mass rape, and drug addiction, while on the other the organisation of sit-ins, demonstrations, and even riots. Honesty, virtue, dignity and the rule of law are in the discard.[35]

One consequence of the prevalence of such views is to decrease the possibilities for selective decriminalization.

Given the relative homogeneity of elite views on what constitutes criminal deviance, there never has been a comprehensive redefinition of the New South Wales criminal law; piecemeal amendment has been rare, even in the postwar period of substantial social change. One of the few examples of decriminalization in recent years occurred during the closing years of the Labor regime, when, in response to the recommendations of a royal commission, a state-operated off-track betting system, the Totalisator Agency Board, was established. It was estimated that close to 30 percent of the population in the Sydney metropolitan area engaged in illegal betting,[36] and the Police Commissioner of New South Wales testified before the commission that the existing law was unenforceable.[37] These observations, combined with the Labor Government's relative receptiveness to social change, the long tradition of horse racing in New South Wales, and public tolerance for SP betting, made the task of redefinition much easier.

A more abrupt instance of decriminalizing redefinition occurred in the aftermath of the 1972 federal elections, which saw the Australian Labor Party return to power after 23 years in opposition. The ALP had consistently opposed the Liberal Government's war and conscription policies, and included in the 1972 party platform was a pledge to abolish national service and to cease prosecution of the offenders who had resisted. Shortly after he was asked to form a government, Prime Minister Whitlam announced the abolition of conscription, the release from custody of the seven conscientious objectors who had been imprisoned under the previous government, and the cessation of further arrests and prosecutions for resistance.

The decision constituted one of the more sudden reversals of policy in recent Australian history.

Other pressures to narrow the scope of the criminal law in New South Wales have arisen from many segments of the society in recent years, but the advocates of particular redefinitions thus far have lacked the political means to overcome intractable opposition from government. One example is recent advocacy of decriminalization of public drunkenness. In March 1973 a symposium was held in Sydney at which social welfare specialists, sociologists, and criminologists suggested that drunkenness be treated as a medicosocial problem rather than as a criminal offense. They advocated that temporary accommodation, counseling, and rehabilitation services be made available to derelict alcoholics as an alternative to arrest and fine or imprisonment. Government and police in New South Wales, however, argued that existing procedures maximized protection of both individual and society.[38]

Advocates of legalized abortion are perhaps the best organized of any reform interest in New South Wales. In addition to the New South Wales Abortion Law Reform Association, groups as diverse as the General Assembly of the Presbyterian Church and the New South Wales Humanist Society have called for the liberalization of existing statutes. Newly influential women's rights and environmental protection groups have also widened the scope of support for redefinition.[39] Their activity has been reinforced by the aforementioned scandal in Victoria, by the enactment of liberal statutes in the United Kingdom (1967) and South Australia (1969), and by the 1973 decision of the United States Supreme Court which allowed abortion on demand during the first trimester of pregnancy. Opposition to redefinition rests in the Roman Catholic community and in the government's general intolerance of sexual freedom. The older theme of "populate or perish" serves but a small residual role, and present opposition to reform has a moral rather than a racial or economic basis.

Meanwhile, a trial court decision in 1971 has had a significant impact on the question of abortion in New South Wales; juries are now instructed that they may take social factors into account in determining the necessity of a termination of pregnancy.[40] Although statutes dealing with abortion remain unchanged, by late 1973 many general practitioners in Sydney were performing the operation on a routine basis.[41]

There has been very little broadening of the New South Wales criminal law in recent years, the law itself being sufficiently general to encompass most forms of deviant behavior. Exceptions have been few and relatively insignificant. Kidnapping and obtaining credit by fraud were first defined as criminal offenses by the Crimes (Amendment) Act of 1961, and a number of offenses relating to aircraft were created by the Crimes (Amendment) Act of 1967. The Vagrancy, Disorderly Houses, and Other Acts (Amendment) Act of 1968 created the offense of being on premises habitually used by prostitutes and specifically prohibited the use of massage parlors for purposes of prostitution, thus facilitating police access to such establishments. The Summary Offences Act of 1970 created the offense of loitering for the purpose of prostitution in or near a public place. Subsequent attempts to broaden the definition of criminal deviance have been limited largely to what might be termed "rhetorical modernization." The Summary Offences Act of 1970 and the Commonwealth Public Order (Protection of Persons and Property) Act of 1971 both contained provisions directed specifically at sit-in protests. These definitions complemented existing statutes dealing with unlawful assembly and interfering with public officials. The Summary Offences Act repealed a whole range of archaic categories of offenses but used broadly defined and occasionally vague terms as substitutes. Thus such rustic expressions as "rogue and vagabond" and "incorrigible rogue" were replaced by the offense of "having no visible means of support." Similarly, "obscene," "indecent," "profane," "threatening," "abusive," or "insulting" language was redefined as "unseemly." The basic purpose of the 1970 and 1971 acts, however, was not to criminalize new areas of behavior. Freedom of assembly and procession in Sydney had been and remains contingent on the approval of the commissioner of police. The legislation was intended instead to modernize and generalize the existing definitions, to enhance deterrent effect by increasing penalties, and to symbolize governmental response to and express moral indignation over the apparent increase in small-scale deviant behavior.

INSTITUTIONS OF PUBLIC ORDER AND THEIR EFFECTS, 1940-1973

The Police

Although a number of small-scale innovations have been introduced in recent years, the fundamental structure of the New South Wales Police Department has remained essentially unchanged. Power within the force is still centralized in the office of the commissioner, who is directly responsible to the premier. Antiquated and rigid height, weight, and vision requirements and low salaries have inhibited recruitment efforts, and members of the force continue to be drawn largely from conservative, working-class backgrounds. Their exposure to divergent values is minimal, and resistance to structural innovation in the department remains strong.

The immediate postwar years were particularly difficult ones for the police; a large number of constables, dissatisfied with having to put in a six-day week for £6 6s. (less than thirty dollars), resigned from the force. In 1946 the turnover was approximately eight percent, and in his 1946 report, the commissioner admitted that the personnel shortage necessitated shortening the training of recruits.[42] In the following year wages were increased, a five-day week was adopted, and the minimum age for recruits was reduced from 21 to 19 years. These innovations were accompanied by the appointment of an additional 508 members to the force. Even in the early 1970s promotions below officer rank were based mainly on seniority, but the principle of basing advancement to middle and higher ranks on merit and achievement was firmly established. Many higher ranking officers also have begun to avail themselves of increasing opportunities for professional education. In-service training programs have been expanded, and special courses in criminology and law are offered by the University of Sydney.

Throughout its history the New South Wales Police Department has had two major objectives: To prevent crime and apprehend suspected perpetrators. The incidence of reported crime increased in recent years, though, and both police and government viewed the rise not as an adverse reflection on police efficacy but as a justification for an increase in the size of the force. Thus the most visible change in the force in recent years has been in its size. Table IV.5.6 shows that the increase has been substantial in relative as well as absolute

*Table IV.5.6 Growth of the Police Force in New South Wales,
        1960-1970*

Year	Size of force	Annual increase, %	Police per 1,000 citizens
1960	5,130	2.35	1.32
1961	5,309	3.49	1.34
1962	5,416	2.02	1.35
1963	5,560	2.66	1.36
1964	5,700	2.52	1.38
1965	5,885	2.02	1.40
1966	6,276	6.64	1.48
1967	6,607	5.27	1.52
1968	6,914	4.65	1.56
1969	7,066	2.20	1.56
1970	7,144	1.10	1.54

Source: New South Wales Police Department, Annual Reports.

terms, and that the most substantial increase followed immediately the return to power of the Liberal party.

Another noteworthy development in the New South Wales police system during the 1960s was a considerable increase in private security forces. As proprietors of banks, department stores, and other large commercial establishments in Sydney began to suffer from the wave of offenses against property in mid-decade, they developed or augmented in-house security arrangements. In addition, there arose in Sydney a private security industry consisting not only of patrols and watchmen but of armored car and cash-carrying services as well. By the early 1970s the industry had grown rapidly in terms of both labor-intensive services and electronic alarm and surveillance systems. The New South Wales police welcomed the advent of the security industry, regarding it not as a threat or an implied criticism of their effectiveness, but as proper and long overdue precautionary activity by the public. The only difficulty posed by private security services for the official police has been that many experienced officers are resigning the public force for the higher wages available in the private sector.

Given the interactive constraints of broadly defined criminal deviance and finite police manpower, the general pattern of police activity in Sydney has remained relatively unchanged in recent years. Response to deviant behavior tends to vary according to the gravity attributed to the offense in question. Homicide, the more serious assault cases, armed robbery, and other "serious" crimes of acquisition receive rather intensive and uniform attention. Smaller scale property offenses are so numerous that they elicit little reaction other than renewed calls for greater precautions by the public. Political protest tends to attract a sizable police presence, maintained with general restraint, although occasional mass arrests and physical heavy-handedness have been noted. Offenses such as abortion, prostitution, and homosexual behavior, because of widespread practice, general invisibility, and low physical and material threat, are subject to more sporadic official response. The suppression of these activities has very low priority, especially in light of the increase in "serious" crime. The occasional crackdown that generally follows media amplification of public announcements by legislators, clergymen, or citizen groups serves little more than a symbolic function. Drunkenness, on the other hand, receives much attention because of its prevalence and ease of detection. The cost in terms of fiscal and human resources of such dedicated enforcement remains quite high, [43] but it appears to be a sacrifice both police and political elites are willing to make.

The presence of corrupt practices within the New South Wales Police Department itself, a recurring theme in the history of the force, has reemerged in recent years. Although no situation of the magnitude of the abortion scandal in Victoria has occurred, allegations of bribery and of extortion are not infrequent. The suggestion that members of the Vice Squad are personally active in brothel keeping has been voiced from time to time, and a number of officers have been dismissed for the unauthorized disclosure of information to private insurance investigators. Excessive use of physical force by New South Wales officers seems to occur less frequently than in the past, and killings by police, though not unknown, are extremely rare.[44] However investigative proceedings of such behavior are undertaken within the department and away from public view, and it is impossible to determine the extent to which criminal actions within the police force are tolerated or prosecuted.[45]

The New South Wales Police Department also has come under sharp criticism for some of its crime reporting procedures. A longstanding practice in the force has been the keeping of "Paddy's book," a record of purse snatchings, bicycle thefts, and other smallscale offenses that do not appear in official crime totals. The introduction of a computerized information retrieval system in 1970 was accompanied by a change in data recording practices, and as a result large numbers of previously undisclosed offenses came to the attention of high-ranking members of the department. Realizing that even partial disclosure of these data would reveal the informality of previous reporting practices and result in substantially higher crime totals, the commissioner withheld any such references from his 1970 annual report. Shortly thereafter, a detective-sergeant who had been working with the new information system made public the shortcomings of previous official reports in an unauthorized announcement that caused considerable embarrassment to the government and to the commissioner of police. A widely publicized attempt was made to have Detective-Sergeant Arantz committed to a psychiatric institution, and when this failed the officer was dismissed from the force for unauthorized disclosure of confidential information. The Arantz affair stimulated intense criticism from members of the Labor opposition[46] and was only one of a number of circumstances reinforcing the coolness that has traditionally characterized public attitudes toward the police in Sydney. In the 1940s the lack of support for the police was manifest in the widespread feeling that members of the force were going about their duties in certain matters with a bit too much zeal; the intensity with which drunkenness was prosecuted had a markedly unfavorable impact. Even the *Sydney Morning Herald*, hardly sympathetic to leftist causes, reacted with consternation when members of the 21 Squad forcibly broke up the Margaret Street demonstration of July 1947. Sternly critical of police "basher tactics" a *Herald* editorial concluded "The police have come very badly out of the whole affair in Margaret Street. The impression left is that they provoked rather than prevented the more serious aspects of the disturbance."[47] Further complaints concerning police behavior were heard from the Legislative Assembly. Not only were the Consorting and Vice Squads alleged to have harassed innocent people, but arrests for drunkenness were believed to be indiscriminate.

In addition to providing the theme of electoral discourse, the Cold War served to stimulate institutional innovation. In 1949, the federal Labor Government established the Australian Security Intelligence Organization, intended to defend the Commonwealth against espionage, sabotage, and subversive activity. Thus ASIO relieved the police forces of New South Wales and other states of some of the burdens of political espionage that had adversely affected their public images during most of the previous 40 years.

Hostility toward the police has nonetheless increased in recent years. Chappell and Wilson revealed that Sydneysiders had grown markedly less supportive of the police during the period 1967-1970.[48] Although this change in attitude was partially attributable to spillover from the abortion scandal in Victoria, a number of equally plausible explanations can be offered. The vagueness and generality of summary offenses legislation in New South Wales preclude all but the most selective enforcement. An individual's arrest, whether for unseemly language or for a motoring offense, appears often to be arbitrary, and, at worst, simply biased. Antipathy toward the police tends to be greater among younger people, suggesting that police comportment during recent situations of collective protest may have had the effect of eroding public support somewhat. Chappell and Wilson have also noted the possibility that the class background and training of police in New South Wales tend to insulate members of the force from nonprofessional contact with the general citizenry, further contributing to polarization.[49]

The Judicial Processes

The maldistribution of legal services remains one of the more persistent and severe sources of bias in the New South Wales criminal justice system. The Public Defenders Act of 1969 extended the potential scope of legal aid for indigent defendants to committal proceedings, but there still exists no right to counsel for most recidivists. Guilty pleas were being offered in 85 percent of all higher court cases in the early 1970s, reflecting widespread plea bargaining. In addition, legal aid for the indigent is generally unavailable at the level of petty sessions, where the overwhelming majority of criminal cases are heard.[50] Studies have yet to be undertaken at other stages of the criminal process in New South Wales, but some evidence suggests, not surprisingly, that the absence of representation tends to work toward the disadvantage of the defendant in courts of petty sessions. A preliminary report by the New South Wales Bureau of Crime Statistics and Research (1973) reveals that first offenders represented by counsel before the lower courts tended to receive significantly more favorable treatment than did individuals without representation.[51] These distinctions remained significantly visible across such diverse categories of offense as larceny, driving, and summary offense cases, tending to confirm the suspicion that favorable treatment before the law is often purchasable.[52]

The most impressive of recent developments in the distribution of legal assistance was the founding of the Aboriginal Legal Service, a nongovernmental organization established in 1970. Inspired originally by heavy-handed police conduct in the neighborhood of Redfern, which has a large population of aboriginals, a group of young, articulate aborigines contacted a number of Sydney lawyers, with the intention of bringing charges against the police. From these early meetings, there emerged an organization that provides aborigines in Sydney with legal assistance on civil and criminal matters. Financed by a Commonwealth grant and private donations, the service has its own legal and paralegal staff and also relies on a panel of Sydney barristers and solicitors who have volunteered their services without fee. In addition to the favorable impact of the service on the position of aborigines in court, relations between the police and the aboriginal community became considerably less strained.[53]

Penal Institutions

Although members of the Howard Prison Reform League claimed during the late 1940s that the prisons of New South Wales were among the best in the world,[54] there was no dearth of criticism from other quarters.[55] The Department of Prisons underwent a number of changes during the postwar years, principally by adopting innovations that had been previously instituted overseas. A classification committee was established at Long Bay, permitting the more systematic assignment of prisoners to the different facilities and training programs. A consulting psychiatrist and a full-time psychologist were appointed to the department, clothing issues were improved, and educational opportunities for prisoners were broadened. In addition, the first steps were taken in 1951 to institutionalize a system of parole. As a necessary corollary of the initial appointment of a parole board, 1951 also saw the establishment of the Adult Probation

Service, under which officers were to supervise the conduct of offenders released under the new scheme.

The issue of corporal punishment, a treatment still permitted (if not practiced) under the Crimes Act, reemerged briefly in 1946 after a number of violent crimes reached the public's attention. In effect, the rate of violent crime appears to have increased only slightly, as Table IV.5.3 indicates. Nevertheless, a Sydney judge threatened to award sentences of flogging for offenders convicted of violent crime, and the *Sydney Morning Herald* agreed that such a deterrent might be the only suitable corrective.[56] The subsequent debate blew over quickly, however, and corporal punishment remained a dormant, although legally permissible method of dealing with offenders.

The increasing numbers of offenders entering the criminal justice system in the 1960s placed considerable pressure on the physical resources of the department (renamed the Department of Corrective Services in 1970). One significant consequence has been increased reliance on noncustodial correctional alternatives, as Table IV.5.7 indicates. In recent years it has become the practice to grant probation to first offenders for all but the most serious offenses. With the enactment of the Parole of Prisoners Act of 1966, the Parol Board was invested with decisional autonomy. Parole services have been greatly expanded, and the yearly number of prisoners granted conditional release has almost tripled. Two other recent innovations, periodic detention and work release, represent further movement in the direction of noncustodial, community-based treatment. Periodic detention prisoners serve their sentence over a series of weekends, at a minimum-security facility at the Long Bay complex in Sydney. Begun in 1971, the periodic detention program has involved only a

Table IV.5.7 Trends in Custodial and Noncustodial Correction in New South Wales, 1965-1971

Year	Daily average prison population	Prisoners released on probation	Prisoners in custody at end of year	Prisoners released on parole and license
1964-1965		n.a.	2,957	338
1965-1966	3,369	n.a.	3,140	325
1966-1967	3,504	n.a.	3,334	324
1967-1968	3,642	n.a.	3,292	631
1968-1969	3,685	1,828	3,345	659
1969-1970	3,823	2,149	3,351	719
1970-1971	3,953	2,119	3,493	935

Sources: Official Year Book of New South Wales, N.S.W. Department of Corrective Services, Annual Reports; New South Wales Prison Statistics.

very small number of prisoners and is still a pilot program. It does reflect, however, a growing interest in treatment approaches that permit an offender to maintain more normal familial and social relationships. Under the work release program, established in 1969, selected prisoners are assisted in securing employment outside of prison but remain in custody during nonworking hours.

The work release and periodic detention schemes remain relatively insignificant, however, in that each program accommodates only 30 to 40 prisoners at a time. Within the custodial setting the trend toward diversification has also continued. The individual who is awarded a custodial sentence may be assigned by the classification committee to one of an entire range of installations, from maximum-security prisons to minimum-security work camps and farms. To a great extent, however, prisons in New South Wales continue to serve as rather austere warehouses for social undesirables. The barriers to maintenance of self-esteem and healthy social relationships imposed by such a setting are recognized by the New South Wales government. The Minister of Justice remarked in 1971

> We want prisoners to be "normal" to which end we place them in an abnormal environment, unlike anything else on the outside, in daily contact with fellow inmates, many of them abnormal by any definition. Even the best managed institution is an abnormal environment for human beings and no way yet devised has overcome that handicap. Take away from a man his freedom, his right to make decisions, his opportunity for sexual and family life, and you deprive him of three of the most precious things in life. The longer his sentence, the more likely a prisoner is to be corrupted by the institutional climate.[57]

There remains in New South Wales society, however, a persistent attachment to the themes of deterrence and retribution which, combined with the common desire to forget about those in prison, lessen the likelihood of major structural change in the near future.

Effects

Because of the low validity of New South Wales crime statistics in relation to most kinds of offenses, the effects of recent public action on the extent of crime in Sydney are difficult to assess. It is virtually impossible to determine how much the incidence of criminal behavior has been influenced by the various treatment approaches, and the following impressions must be regarded as speculative. The severity of sanctions may have a deterrent effect in some circumstances, but it is readily apparent that armed robberies and assaults were committed with even greater frequency after penalties were increased in 1966 and 1967. Similarly, thousands of antiwar and antiapartheid demonstrators took to the streets in 1971 despite recent summary offenses legislation and the authorities' increased reliance on arrest in situations of collective protest. Nor has the substantial increase in the size of the New South Wales Police Department over the past decade had any apparent effect on the incidence of crime. Stable patterns of such offenses as homicide and drunkenness appear to be unchanged, and visible upward trends in the rate of assaults and acquisitive crime were largely undisturbed. Sporadic police attention to prostitution, gambling, abortion, and homosexual offenses seems to have produced short-term repressive effects, but the inelasticity of these behaviors precludes any lasting control. As was suggested earlier, periodic crackdowns serve a largely symbolic function and provide at best for the quarantining and de facto licensing of the behaviors in question.

NOTES TO CHAPTER IV.5

1. *New South Wales Parliamentary Debates*, November 18, 1970, p. 7958 (Anne Press, MLC).

2. Paul Wilson, *The Sexual Dilemma* (St. Lucia: University of Queensland Press, 1971), p. 67.

3. Plausible alternative explanations for the post-1967 decline in rates of arrest for prostitution abound. The following, suggested by Paul Ward, should be regarded as neither exhaustive nor mutually exclusive: (a) The Vice Squad may have relaxed its activity in return for bribe payments. (b) The prostitution "industry" may have become less centralized; increasing use of one-girl "shift" houses and "massage parlors" at the expense of large-scale brothels may have reduced the ratio of arrests per raid. (c) Prostitutes may have been subject to less frequent arrests but to increased fines on conviction. In other words, the police and magistracy may have adopted a more efficient system of de facto licensing. (d) Police may have reacted to the policy of one Sydney magistrate who is reputed to have refused to convict alleged prostitutes on charges of offensive behavior, demanding that they be charged with the more serious offense of soliciting. (e) There may have been less prostitution.

4. It is rumored that the real reason for the cessation of the squad's activity was pressure brought to bear because of the embarrassing arrest of some unidentified person with significant political influence. This interpretation is unsubstantiated but nevertheless is not altogether implausible.

5. Estimates of the number of abortions performed in Australia each year range between 20,000 and 120,000, with the average of plausible estimates at about 75,000. If unlawful terminations were distributed across urban places in proportion to population size, about 15,000 such offenses would be committed in the Sydney metropolitan area annually. For further discussions of national estimates, see Wilson, op. cit., pp. 15-17.

6. *Sydney Morning Herald*, March 20, 1974, p. 1; *Tribune* (Sydney) March 21, 1947, p. 1.

7. *Sydney Morning Herald*, July 25, 1947, p. 1; August 30, 1947, p. 5; September 18, 1947, p. 2.

8. *Sydney Morning Herald*, July 9, 1949, p. 1.

9. *Sydney Morning Herald*, July 5, 1950, p. 3; August 31, 1950, p. 1.

10. *Sydney Morning Herald*, July 3, 1968, p. 1.

11. *Sydney Morning Herald*, May 9, 1970, p. 1.

12. *Sydney Morning Herald*, June 26, 1968, p. 1; April 12, 1969, p. 1.

13. *Sydney Morning Herald*, June 26, 1968, p. 1.

14. *Sydney Morning Herald*, September 19, 1970, p. 1.

15. *Sydney Morning Herald*, May 22, 1971, p. 3.

16. *Sydney Morning Herald*, July 12, 1971, p. 3; Stewart Harris, *Political Football: The Springbok Tour of Australia, 1971* (Melbourne: Gold Star Publications, 1972).

17. Ronald Francis, "Migration and Crime in Australia" in Duncan Chappell and Paul Wilson, eds. *The Australian Criminal Justice System* (Sydney: Butterworth & Co., 1972), pp. 201-224; "Migrant Imprisonment Rates in N.S.W. Since

Federation," *Australian and New Zealand Journal of Criminology*, 5:4 (1972), 206-219.

18. Paul Ward, *An Analysis of Higher Court Statistics, 1968-1971* (Sydney: The University of Sydney Institute of Criminology, 1972).

19. Informal communication, N.S.W. Bureau of Crime Statistics and Research, November 1972.

20. Paul Ward, op. cit.

21. Paul Ward and Greg Woods, *Law and Order in Australia* (Sydney: Angus and Robertson, 1972), pp. 168-169.

22. *The Australian*, November 25, 1972, p. 13d.

23. Personal communication, March 1974.

24. *Sydney Morning Herald*, May 23, 1946, p. 4.

25. *Sydney Morning Herald*, January 31, 1945, p. 2.

26. Michael Cannon, "Violence: The Australian Heritage" (Part II), *National Times Magazine*, March 12, 1973, p. 29.

27. *New South Wales Parliamentary Debates*, November 13, 1969, p. 2006. (Edna S. Roper, MLC).

28. N.S.W. Legislative Council, *Report from the Select Committee on Violent Sex Crimes* (Sydney: Government Printer, 1969), pp. xvi-xvii.

29. Paul Wilson and J. Brown, *Crime and the Community* (St. Lucia: University of Queensland Press, 1973); N.S.W. Bureau of Crime Statistics and Research, Statistical Report 12: Unreported Crime (Sydney: N.S.W. Bureau of Crime Statistics and Research, 1974).

30. *Sydney Morning Herald*, July 18, 1949, p. 4.

31. Leicester Webb, *Communism and Democracy in Australia* (Melbourne: F. W. Cheshire, 1954), p. 13.

32. *New South Wales Parliamentary Debates*, March 23, 1955, p. 3250 et seq.

33. Recent evidence suggests that public tolerance of some of these behaviors has increased substantially in recent years. See Chappell and Paul Wilson, eds. op. cit., p. 158; See also Wilson and Brown, op. cit.

34. *New South Wales Parliamentary Debates*, November 17, 1970, p. 7899 (J. A. Cameron, MLA).

35. *Sydney Morning Herald*, April 22, 1969, p. 2. (E. D. Darby, MLA).

36. N.S.W. Parliament, Report of the Royal Commission of Inquiry into Off the Course Betting in N.S.W. (Sydney: V. C. N. Blight, Government Printer, 1963), p. 17.

37. Ibid., pp. 25-26.

38. Remarks before a Forum of the Council of Social Service of New South Wales, by J. C. Maddison, N.S.W. Minister of Justice, and R. H. Lucas, Superintendent in Charge, Police Prosecuting Branch, N.S.W. Police Department, Sydney, March 23, 1973.

39. Wilson, op. cit., p. 138.

40. R. V. Wald and Wall (1971) 3 Dist. Court Rep. (N.S.W.) 25. Decision by Judge Levine.

41. Personal communication, G. D. Woods, March 6, 1974.

42. N.S.W. Police Department, *Annual Report for the Year 1946* (Sydney: Government Printer, 1947), p. 3.

43. The N.S.W. Bureau of Crime Statistics and Research estimates that the annual cost of processing Sydney and inner suburban drunks through the criminal justice system at A$122,000. See N.S.W. Bureau of Crime Statistics and

Research, Statistical Report 7: *City Drunks: A Possible New Direction* (Sydney: N.S.W. Bureau of Crime Statistics and Research, February 1973).

44. Richard W. Harding, *Police Killings in Australia* (Harmondsworth: Penguin Books, 1970).

45. The justification usually advanced in favor of intradepartmental investigation is that under such procedures police being questioned cannot refuse to answer, on pain of immediate dismissal. Senior members of the force argue that if investigation were conducted by some kind of public tribunal, it would be necessary to extend the normal right against self-incrimination to the officers under scrutiny, with the consequent likelihood that neither proof of offense nor dismissal would be possible. The validity of this argument is debatable.

46. Interview with Philip Arantz, December 4, 1972.

47. *Sydney Morning Herald*, September 18, 1947, p. 2.

48. Chappell and Wilson, eds., op. cit., pp. 321-322. Greg Woods regards a significant proportion of public attitude toward the police as elastic, tending to vary between poles of support and opposition. Such an interpretation can only be confirmed through further survey research, however. Personal communication, March 6, 1974.

49. Chappell and Wilson, eds., op. cit., p. 322.

50. The order of priorities for the distribution of legal aid for indigent defendants is as follows: first offenders, frequent recidivists, and occasional recidivists facing serious charges. Personal communication, G. D. Woods, March 6, 1974. Only one-third of the defendants appearing before courts of petty sessions in 1972 were represented by counsel. N.S.W. Bureau of Crime Statistics and Research, Statistical Report 11: *Petty Sessions 1972* (Sydney: N.S.W. Bureau of Crime Statistics and Research, November, 1973), p. 4.

51. N.S.W. Bureau of Crime Statistics and Research, "Legal Representation and Outcome" (Sydney: N.S.W. Bureau of Crime Statistics and Research, 1972).

52. Purchasability refers in the New South Wales context to the distribution of legal services, not to judicial corruption.

53. J. H. Wootten, "The Aboriginal Legal Service, Report to Annual General Meeting," 30 August, 1971; Greg Woods speculates that the Legal Service, by making aborigines in Sydney more aware of their rights, has increased tensions between the police and aboriginal community. He states that the police tend to resent the service to a considerable extent. Personal communication, March 6, 1974.

54. Howard Prison Reform League, *Minute Book*, 14 December, 1945, pp. 181-182.

55. Frank Snow, Ed., *Forgotten Men* (Sydney: Prison Reform Council of New South Wales, 1947).

56. *Sydney Morning Herald*, July 20, 1946, p. 2.

57. J. C. Maddison, address delivered at the Sixth Biennial Conference of the Australian Crime Prevention, and After-Care Council, Canberra, 1971.

CONCLUSION
Trends in Crime, Conflict, and
Policies of Public Order

Precise measurement of the changing incidence of crime in the history of Sydney is precluded by factors of two kinds. Because of the administrative structure of New South Wales, relevant data have ordinarily been compiled for the colony or state as a whole, and useful statistics applicable only to the city or metropolitan area are extremely rare. A second, more universal difficulty inheres in the low validity of the different measures of criminality that have been employed at various times during the past two centuries in New South Wales. At no time can the researcher find an ideographic portrait of criminal behavior in all its luxuriant diversity. Rather, an image is initially created by sociolegal definitions of criminality, then processed through the many filters of the New South Wales criminal justice system: imperfect detection, selective enforcement, partial reporting, selective prosecution. The amount of distortion introduced by these filters is and always will be problematical.

The most consistently available indicators of criminality during the nineteenth century are returns of convictions at the highest level of the colony's judicial process, the Supreme Court. With the exception of a 30-year period at midcentury, these high court conviction data are complemented by returns of committals for trial in the same courts.[1] Beginning in 1859 returns of committals (cases brought to trial) and convictions in the courts of quarter sessions, the middle level of the colony's judicial structure, are available and permit an aggregation of statistics of the higher criminal courts. From 1893

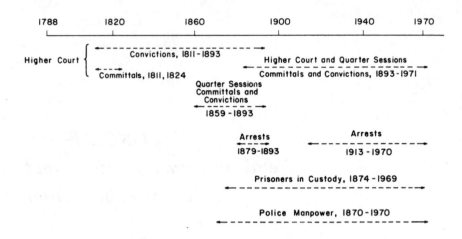

Figure IV.6.1 Availability of data on crime and institutions of public order in New South Wales, 1788-1971

until the present, quarter sessions and high court returns of committals and convictions are based on distinct persons, rather than offenses. These statistics are published in aggregated form, combining quarter sessions and high court cases.

As in virtually all judicial systems, cases that reach the higher levels of the New South Wales system are relatively few; throughout the history of New South Wales, most cases entering the criminal justice system and all less serious cases have been dealt with at the level of petty sessions. Unfortunately, information on less serious offenses is not available for years prior to 1879. Arrest data by offense have been compiled and published for years between 1879 and 1893 and from 1913 to the present. They thus permit a mapping, albeit an imperfect one, of police activity, as well as a portrayal of changes over time in the incidence of lesser offenses. Figure IV.6.1 describes the data available for mapping long-term trends in criminal deviance.

HISTORICAL TRENDS

Long-term trends in criminality, civil strife, and official response in New South Wales may be easily described if not precisely portrayed; Figures IV.6.2 through IV.6.13 are illustrative. The rate of crimes against the person ("aggressive crime") appears to have fallen sharply following the cessation of transportation in 1840 (Figure IV.6.3), diminishing gradually throughout the twentieth century despite slight upturns in the late 1910s, 1940s, and 1960s (Figures

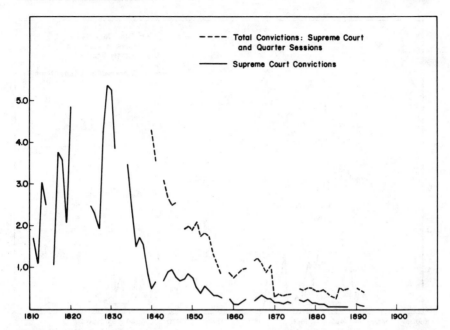

Figure IV.6.2 New South Wales: Convictions per 1000 population, serious acquisitive crime, 1811-1892

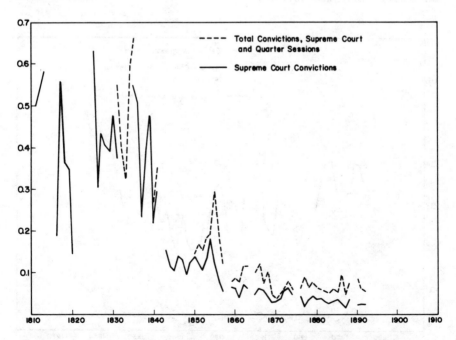

Figure IV.6.3 New South Wales: Convictions per 1000 population, serious aggressive crime, 1811-1892

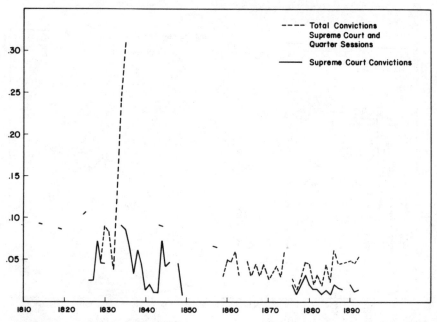

Figure IV.6.4 New South Wales: Convictions per 1000 population, serious crimes against sexual morality and custom, 1814-1892

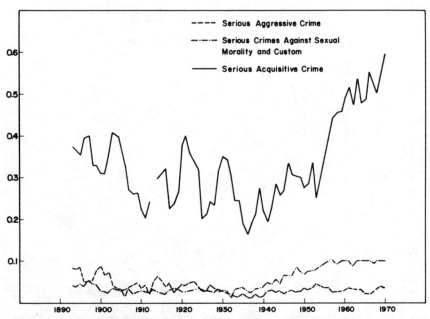

Figure IV.6.5 New South Wales: Higher court convictions per 1000 population, selected offense categories, 1893-1970

IV.6.5 and IV.6.6). The changing pattern of acquisitive crime is roughly similar to that of offenses against the person. After a sharp decline from the high rates of the early nineteenth century (Figure IV.6.2), the decline throughout most of the present century has been gradual, with the exception of upturns at the end of World War I and at the beginning of the Depression in 1930. Throughout most of the 1960s, however, acquisitive crimes appeared to increase sharply, with present rates roughly comparable to those of the late 1880s (Figures IV.6.5 and IV.6.7).

Trends in serious crime against sexual morality and custom describe a more complicated pattern. Although the reported incidence of these offenses was very low during the first years of settlement, rates increased during the 1820s and 1830s, then manifested the drop typical of most New South Wales rates during the mid-nineteenth century. After an upturn in the late 1880s, the rates declined again, rising briefly during the late 1920s, falling once again, and rising in 1970 to a level that was roughly comparable to that of 1880 (Figures IV.6.4, IV.6.5, and IV.6.6). The data on arrests for offenses other than traffic violations follow the first four phases just mentioned but post a general decline beginning in the mid-1960s.

One of the more striking aspects of the New South Wales criminal justice system has been the watchfulness of the authorities with

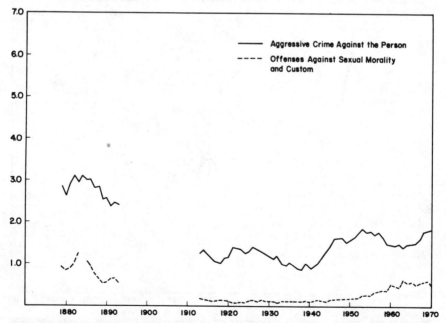

Figure IV.6.6 New South Wales: Arrests for crimes of aggression and offenses against sexual morality and custom per 1000 population, 1879-1970

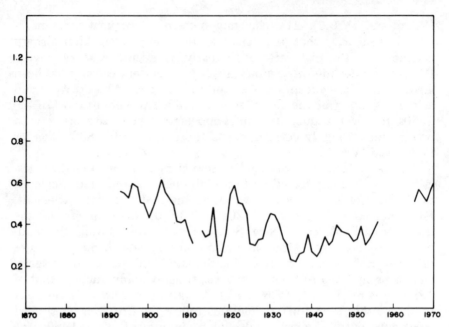

Figure IV.6.7 New South Wales: High court and quarter sessions, committals per 1000 population, serious crimes of acquisition, 1893-1970

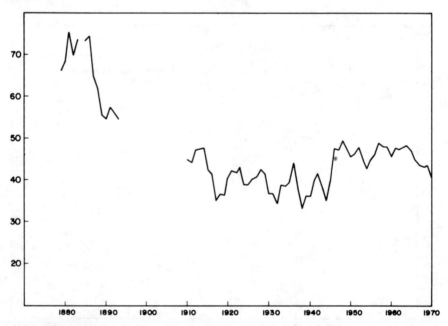

Figure IV.6.8 New South Wales: Offenses other than traffic violations, arrests per 1000 population, 1879-1970

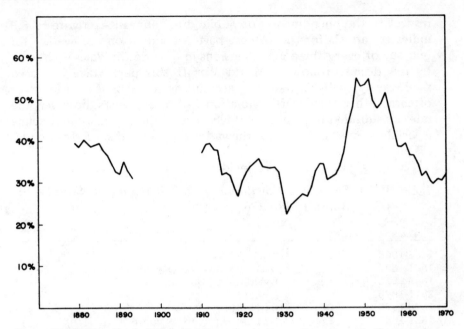

Figure IV.6.9 New South Wales: Drunkenness arrests as percentage of all arrests for offenses other than traffic violations, 1879-1970

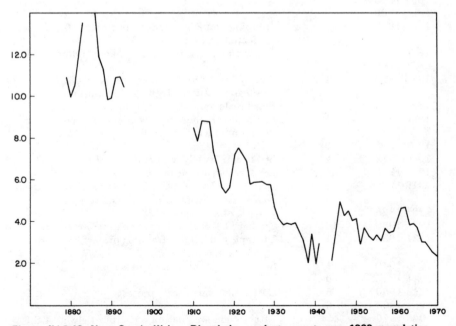

Figure IV.6.10 New South Wales: Disorderly conduct, arrests per 1000 population, 1879-1970

respect to the phenomenon of public drunkenness. As Figure IV.6.9
indicates, arrests for this offense have accounted on the average for
one out of every three apprehensions in New South Wales each year.
In the decade following World War II this percentage increased
significantly, with drunkenness accounting for half of all arrests for
offenses other than traffic violations. In recent years, however, the
rate has subsided to its normal (high) level. A more consistent decline
is visible in rates of arrest for the various forms of disorderly conduct
(Figure IV.6.10).

Changing patterns in the incidence of civil strife in New South

Table IV.6.1 Scope and Magnitude of Civil Strife in New South
             Wales, 1788-1970

Years	Score	Events
1788-1800	0	
1801-1805	11	Irish convict conspiracy and revolt
1806-1810	3	Overthrow of Governor Bligh
1811-1825	0	
1826-1830	2	Bushranging
1831-1835	1	Small-scale protest by convicts
1836-1840	4	Aboriginal massacres
1841-1845	2	Sydney election riot
1846-1850	2	Sydney New Year's Eve riot
1851-1855	0	
1856-1860	0	
1861-1865	5	Lambing Flat riots; Sydney unemployed demonstration
1866-1870	1	Attempted assassination of Duke of Edinburgh
1871-1885	0	
1886-1890	11	Anti-Chinese protests; maritime workers' & shearers' strikes; 1890 demonstration
1891-1895	1	Small scale harassment of Chinese
1896-1900	1	Street disturbances between working-class youth and military
1901-1905	0	
1906-1910	2	Strike activity, Sydney & Broken Hill
1910-1915	1	Small-scale antiwar protest
1916-1920	12	General Strike 1917; strike of 1919; Sydney arson activity; antiwar protest; soldiers' riot
1921-1925	1	Postwar street fighting
1926-1930	10	Timber Strike; Rothbury Lockout; street protests
1931-1935	11	Unemployed demonstrations; protests; eviction riots; street fighting
1936-1940	1	Small scale Communist protest
1941-1945	0	
1946-1950	5	Coal Strike; small scale protest
1951-1965	0	
1966-1970	11	Attempted assassination of Arthur Calwell A.L.P. leader; numerous antiwar protests; antiapartheid demonstrations

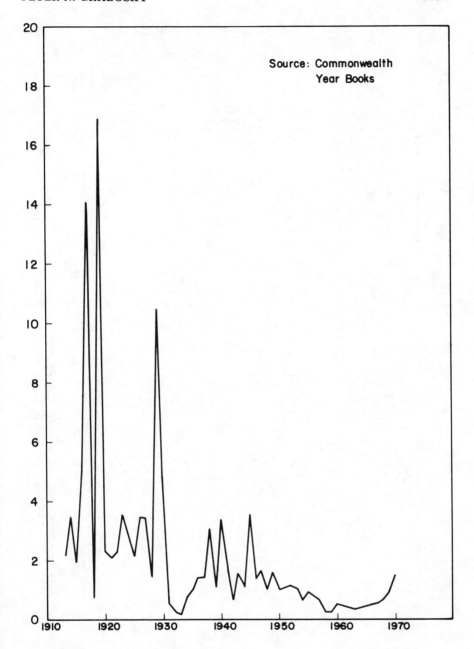

Figure IV.6.11 New South Wales: Number of working days lost in industrial disputes per
1000 trade unionists, 1913-1970

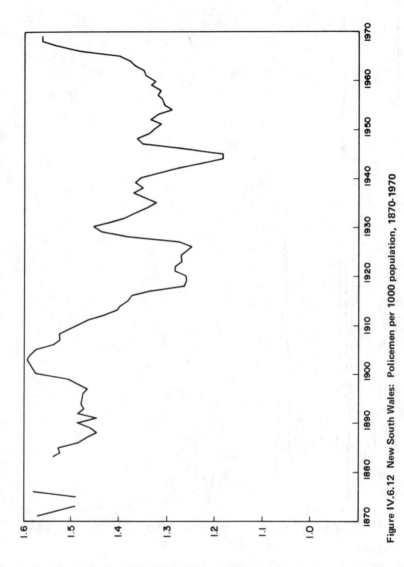

Figure IV.6.12 New South Wales: Policemen per 1000 population, 1870-1970

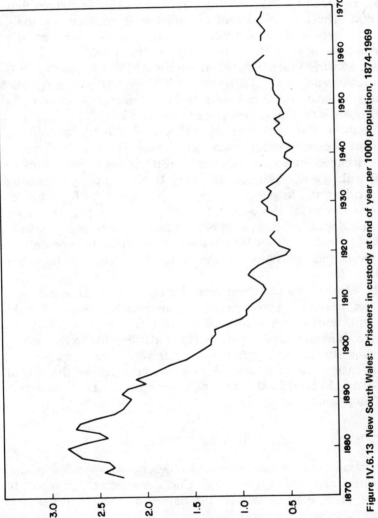

Figure IV.6.13 New South Wales: Prisoners in custody at end of year per 1000 population, 1874-1969

SYDNEY: CONCLUSION

Wales are portrayed in Table IV.6.1.[2] The unsuccessful revolt of the
Irish convicts and the overthrow of Governor Bligh at the beginning
of the nineteenth century were followed by a relatively tranquil
period of about fifteen years. The middle years of the century were
marked by turmoil as varied as bushranging in the 1820s and 1830s,
aboriginal massacres in the late 1830s, urban riots or protests in
1843, 1850, and 1861, and the attacks on Chinese at Lambing Flat
in 1862. The last decades of the nineteenth century saw the emergence of large-scale labor protest; this form of collective activity was
to reappear with greatest intensity during World War I, the late
1920s, and the years before and after World War II (Figure IV.6.11).
The 1950s and early 1960s were relatively tranquil, but collective
protest against military[3] and racial[4] dimensions of the federal
government's foreign policy arose in the late 1960s.

Trends in the evolution of the New South Wales police establishment are even more easily described.[5] Whereas the size of the
force declined after consolidation in 1862, it has grown steadily since
1870 with the exception of the early 1930s and the years during the
two world wars. In per capita terms, the size of the force has tended
to keep abreast of the general rate of population growth, except for
the first decade of the twentieth century and the war years (Figure
IV.6.12). In the 1960s it increased sharply but did not quite reach
the levels that prevailed at the turn of the century (also see Ch.
IV.4).

The aforementioned long-term decline in rates of arrest for most
offenses has been accompanied by an even steeper decline in the
apparent reliance on incarceration as a treatment method. Figure
IV.6.13 illustrates this trend, which is attributable to the practice of
awarding shorter and proportionally fewer prison sentences during
the twentieth century than in previous years. Since the end of the
long-term decline in the prison population in 1920, the rate has
fluctuated only slightly.

DETERMINANTS OF LONG-TERM TRENDS

Previous chapters have provided a descriptive overview of the eras
and forms of public disorder and official reaction that are part of the
history of Sydney. Although the nature of the study has made it
necessary to sacrifice depth for breadth, it is possible (indeed imperative) to attempt an integration of the themes discussed. In a few
situations we can use statistical techniques to explain trends and
variations in criminality. Otherwise, less formal means of explanation
can be employed. Certain general patterns are readily discernible, and

spelling them out will facilitate the task of those who wish to undertake more intensive historical study or to compare the Sydney experiences with those of other cities.

Despite the questionable validity of available criminal statistics, multiple regression analysis can be used to examine possible causes of some of the long-term trends in crime indicators, outlined previously. Measures of proportional male population, economic conditions, urbanization, police force strength, and police appropriations were regressed on Supreme Court conviction rates for three major offense categories for the period 1826-1893.[6] The resulting equations explained from 61 to 86 percent of the variance in the conviction rates (Table IV.6.2). In these analyses masculinity of the population emerged as the most significant determinant of rates of conviction for serious offenses against the person and against property. Police force manpower level, on the other hand, made the most significant contribution to indicators of crimes against sexual morality.[7] The possibility that these relations result from the presence of a trend component in the data series was tested in subsequent analyses by introducing time as an explicit variable. Results indicate the dominant influence of a trend component in all but the serious property crime model; in this instance the estimate of the effect of population masculinity continued to dominate the equation well within the .05 limit of statistical significance.

The reader is cautioned that these findings are only suggestive. Aside from the aforementioned problems of validity, discontinuities

Table IV.6.2 Determinants of Selected Supreme Court Conviction Rates on New South Wales, 1826-1893

	Standardized Regression coefficients		
Variable	Serious aggressive crime	Serious crimes of acquisition	Serious crimes against sexual morality and custom
Economic conditions	.03	.13	.38
Population masculinity	.85**	.84**[b]	.22
Urbanization	−.07	.07	—[a]
Police force strength	—[a]	—[a]	.67*
Police appropriations	.06	.05	—[a]
	.86	.77	.61

a. Variable not entered in equation.
b. Only this coefficient remained significant once trend was controlled.
**Significant at .01.
*Significant at .05.

in the data series precluded the application of more rigorous econometric techniques. Fortunately the availability of continuous data series beginning in 1914 permitted a more thorough analysis of the same sort. Additional independent variables employed in the analysis of twentieth century arrest and conviction rates include a measure of industrial unrest and two "dummy variables" representing years of war and of Labor Party control of the state government.[8] Population masculinity was excluded from this analysis because it is virtually invariant during the present century. The regression equations, based on Cochrane-Orcutt iterative transformations to correct for autocorrelated residuals, contain the parameter estimates listed in Table IV.6.3.[9] Three of the six equations listed explained more than 90 percent of the variance in the respective crime indicators, with the weakest of the six still accounting for 52 percent. The measure of urbanization dominates all but one of the six and appears to have been particularly influential with regard to rates of arrest for crimes against the person and against property. When time was introduced as an explicit independent variable to control for the effects of trend, the urbanization measure continued to exert significant influence on rates of arrest for acquisitive crime and remained a discernible but no longer statistically significant determinant of the remaining crime measures.

Finally, we tested the possibility that there may have been time-lagged or cumulative effects between factors such as urbanization and increased crime rates. Lagrangian polynomial interpolations were used, and the results revealed the presence of a significant five-year cumulative effect between urbanization and each measure of acquisitive and sexual crimes.[10] These findings are generally consistent with the simultaneous time-series analysis summarized in Table IV.6.3.

The substantive implications of these statistical analyses can be summarized as follows. During the convict era and the later colonial period, crimes against persons and property tended to be highest when the male population was proportionately largest, declining as the sex structure of the colony became more balanced. Since the disproportionately large numbers of males were mostly convicts, the results signify the importance of their criminal inclinations, or official efforts to restrain such inclinations, for generating the high crime rates of the earlier part of the nineteenth century. In the twentieth century offenses against the person, against property, and against sexual morality have increased as urbanization has increased, and it appears that this is a real and cumulative relationship, not simply a statistical artifact: Periods of especially rapid urban growth have been accompanied, and followed, by high rates of property and sex crimes in particular. But there is little evidence that variations in

Table IV.6.3 Determinants of Selected Arrest and Conviction Rates in New South Wales, 1914-1969

Standardized regression coefficients

Variable	Arrest rate: crimes against the person	Conviction rate: serious aggressive crime	Arrest rate: acquisitive crimes against property	Conviction rate: serious acquisitive crime	Arrest rate: crimes against sexual morality and custom	Conviction rate: serious crimes against sexual morality and custom
Economic conditions	-.02	-.05	-.08	-.09	.06	.08
Industrial unrest	.02	.19*	.00	-.00	.01	.03
Police force strength	.04	.08	.03	.17	.06	-.07
Urbanization	.52*	.06	.83**a	.63*	.86**	.95**
Police appropriations	.05	.40*a	-.10	-.04	.03	.03
Labor Government	.15	.03	.03	-.02	.01	.03
War	-.02	-.29	.09	.08	-.01	.03
Durbin-Watson statistic	2.37	1.96**	1.84*	2.39*	2.54*	2.04*
R²	.85	.60	.90	.52	.94	.93

a. These coefficients remained significant once trend was controlled.

b.

** Significant at .01.

* Significant at .05.

number of police or police resources have had systematic effects on the levels of any kind of offense, with the possible exception of sexual offenses.

VICTIMLESS CRIME

Among the most interesting patterns of criminality in the history of New South Wales have been the drastic fluctuations in rates of arrest for many of the less serious offenses. These periodic phenomena, already discussed in some detail, have been strikingly visible since the mid-1930s as is evident in Figures IV.6.14 to IV.6.16. Interpretation of these data is difficult, and regression analyses reveal no significant structural determinants; contextual materials suggest, however, that although the fluctuations may have been partly attributable to changes in the incidence of offenses per se, they were largely the results of changes in police enforcement policy.

The criminal law of New South Wales has imposed difficult burdens on the police. Under persistent conditions of manpower shortage, they must control a vast array of criminal behaviors, some so widely practiced that (as in the case of SP betting before the advent of the Totalisator Agency Board) they may not properly be described as deviant. The police are thus faced with a fundamental dilemma; whereas a laissez-faire approach to victimless crime would permit the police to pay more attention to more serious forms of criminality, it runs the risk of antagonizing those members of the elite with strong propensities to moral indignation. Alternatively, more rigorous enforcement policy has tended to weaken support for police among members of the public at large.

The police of New South Wales have adapted to this dilemma with sporadic enforcement policies, dramatically attending to certain specific offenses from time to time, while relaxing enforcement in intervening years. Such a situation of de facto licensing punctuated with periodic crackdowns appears to have relieved, at least in part, this dimension of conflict within New South Wales society. The conflict nevertheless lingers, since wealthy citizens of New South Wales can indulge their deviant inclinations in private or in the more permissive jurisdictions. Less affluent citizens who lack privacy or mobility, however, still live under the shadow of official proscription.

One interesting but largely invisible aspect of these enforcement policies concerns the attitudes of the police themselves to various "victimless" crimes. Members of the force have on occasion alluded to the virtual impossibility of suppression, but they do not publicly support proposals for decriminalization. Whether this reflects the

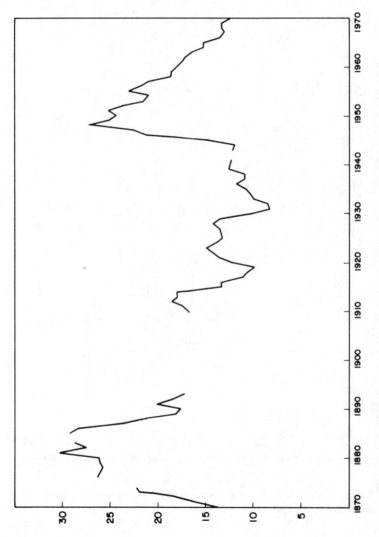

Figure IV.6.14 New South Wales: Drunkenness and related offenses, arrests per 1000 population, 1870-1970

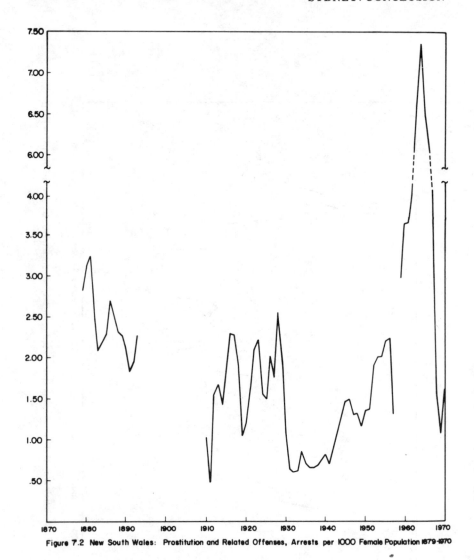

Figure 7.2 New South Wales: Prostitution and Related Offenses, Arrests per 1000 Female Population 1879-1970

Figure IV.6.15 New South Wales: Prostitution and related offenses, arrests per 1000 female population, 1879-1970

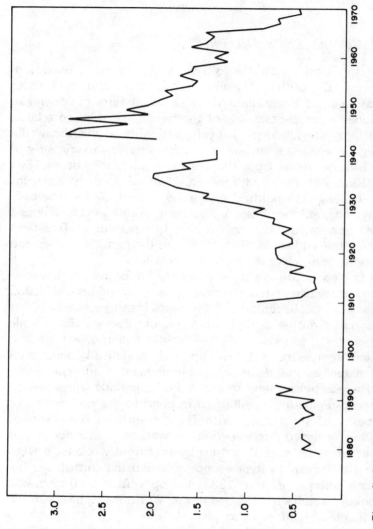

Figure IV.6.16 New South Wales: Gambling offenses, arrests per 1000 population, 1879-1970

moral judgment of high-ranking members of the force or the desire to maintain conditions that help justify greater appropriations is open to question.

COLLECTIVE VIOLENCE AND PROTEST

Dissident political activity in Sydney, visible in such "unconventional" forms of political behavior as rebellion, riot, and street protest, has been relatively rare. Although the absence of systematic data precludes a precise mapping of the trends and their correlates, certain patterns are apparent. Forceful attempts to overthrow the existing regime occurred on only two occasions, both very early in the city's history. Aside from the Irish convicts' rebellion of 1804 and the "Rum Rebellion" of 1808, residents of Sydney have not sought to challenge the political system by violent means. The only noteworthy incipient revolutionary activity, visible in the IWW and New Guard movements, occurred during two periods of twentieth century economic and social dislocation, but the periods of crisis and the movements themselves proved to be short-lived.

Rioting in New South Wales, whether for fun or protest, has been very infrequent; when it has occurred it has been of brief duration and low magnitude. Regardless of the participants' motives, it has tended to occur during periods of economic distress. Large-scale collective protest, generally in the form of nonviolent protest marches and demonstrations, has appeared sporadically since such behavior emerged as a mode of political expression in mid-nineteenth century. These activities tend to occur during periods when government has been unable or unwilling to respond to the preferences of large segments of the public. With few exceptions, the events in question have occurred during periods of war, economic decline, or labor-management tension. Reactions by organized workers to what they viewed as threats to their economic well-being constituted the bulk of such activity prior to 1935, and opposition to foreign and military policy, which surfaced first during World War I, has been the dominant theme of contemporary protest.

The relative rarity of collective disorder during the first half-century of Sydney's history appears to have been the product of two conditions: The coercive capacities of the regime and the prevalence of relatively favorable economic conditions. Colonial authorities commanded an impressive monopoly of coercive force, and though the threat of lash and scaffold could not suppress all dissident inclinations, they appear to have inhibited most forms of collective protest. Moreover, those convicts who demonstrated the greatest propensities to deviant or dissident activity were sent to isolated penal "subsettlements" at some distance from Sydney; the most notorious of these was Norfolk Island.

In addition to the obvious disincentives to dissent, conditions existed in early New South Wales that encouraged political legitimacy. Although authorities in London originally viewed transportation as a punishment only slightly less dreadful than execution, existence for convicts in early New South Wales was not uniformly miserable. At best, an industrious individual could take great advantage of the opportunities afforded by a developing economy; at worst, material deprivation in Sydney was less severe than in the slums of London. Thus the political system of early New South Wales was as effective as most others of that time in providing a tolerable existence for the majority of its citizens.

Perhaps the most plausible explanations for the lack of persistent public disorder in Sydney since the convict era have to do with the overwhelming racial homogeneity of the population and the relative responsiveness of existing institutions and authorities to citizens' demands. After the immigration of Asians was ended in the late nineteenth century, racial minorities have been numerically negligible and communal conflict has been minimal. Issues that have drawn Sydneysiders to the streets, or have moved them to undertake more subtle noncooperative forms of protest, have seldom lingered. When erosions of legitimacy have occurred, they have not been cumulative or enduring. Prolonged, severe disaffection has been limited to numerically insignificant groups, and aggregate public support has remained quite strong.

The last two decades of the nineteenth century were a crucial period in the history of New South Wales because the development of labor organizations constituted a significant force for social change. Although labor movement met with a less than cordial reception from the economic elite, the violent repressive practices that characterized American labor history were rare. Strikes and protests over union recognition and working conditions in 1890 were followed by extensive working-class activity in conventional channels; this shift from industrial to political action constituted one of the more abrupt changes in the political history of New South Wales.[11] The Labor Party provided formal institutional machinery for the aggregation and articulation of working-class demands; it held the balance of power in the New South Wales Parliament by the turn of the century and was instrumental in the enactment of legislation improving working conditions and instituting such social reforms as old-age pensions. There was little lag between the extension of working-class political consciousness and participation and the subsequent adaptive response of existing institutions.

The emergence of working-class political participation in New South Wales tended to alleviate rather than to generate class conflict. Labor parliamentarians in the 1890s opted for bargaining and compromise at the expense of revolutionary purity. Subsequently, as electoral success remained their paramount concern, Labor Party leaders maintained their posture of compromise, seeking the piecemeal satisfaction of nonelite demands rather than a drastic restructuring of political and economic institutions. The spread of revolutionary consciousness was thus limited to numerically small factions such as the IWW, and a moderate Labor Party was accepted as a fact of political life by those who might otherwise have resisted such developments.

Australian forces have been involved in overseas combat on four separate occasions during the twentieth century, with consistent consequences for domestic dissent and official response. Support for the various war efforts was generally quite strong within the New South Wales public, although opposition to Australian participation in Vietnam had grown substantially by 1972. When dissident activity has not been broadly based, it has tended to elicit a harsh repressive response from state and federal governments. Regardless of whether or not federal authorities have appeared responsive to popular sentiment, protest has subsided after the end of international hostilities.

Few residents of Sydney are perfectly satisfied with the distribution of wealth and freedom in their society, yet absolute deprivation is experienced by very few. The occasional annoyance seems always to have passed on; inequalities in the standard of living have endured, but only the small aboriginal population may be regarded as severely deprived. Meanwhile, symbols as diverse as the monarchy and a viable and enduring Labor Party are sufficient palliatives for members of a polity who might otherwise engage in more heated conflict. The vast majority of Sydneysiders view their governments as effective: Thus within an increasingly urbanized and cosmopolitan society, resort to violence by citizen or state has been minimal.

TRENDS IN LAW ENFORCEMENT AND CORRECTIONS

The evolution of law enforcement and correctional institutions in New South Wales has featured significant structural change and increases in scale. Nevertheless certain chronic problems in each of these components of the criminal justice system have been perennial sources of complaint.

That the policeman's lot has improved greatly over the past century and a half is beyond dispute; one need only look back at the abysmal working conditions and paltry (often nonexistent) compensation that characterized police work in the early nineteenth century. Yet relative to the general level of well-being in the society at large, improvement in the nature of law enforcement work has been modest at best. Indeed, it may be argued that economic expansion and diversification in New South Wales has provided an ever widening range of alternative vocational opportunities, inhibiting recruitment and facilitating frequent turnover within police ranks. Thus if law enforcement officials no longer have to contend with a force comprised of irresponsible drunkards, they must work with policemen who may be less qualified or, optimally, with individuals who remain at their work under conditions of personal sacrifice.

Another chronic burden on the police of New South Wales has been the necessity of performing extraneous administrative duties; police complaints concerning such matters have been heard since the 1830s. Despite the expansion of the state civil service, such claims on police resources remain substantial. The problem is exacerbated by the broad scope of the law the police are charged with enforcing. The issue of victimless crime has been addressed already; it appears that throughout the history of New South Wales, the extent of crime as legally defined has exceeded the ability of the police to identify and control it. This has produced not only problems of resource allocation, but on occasion has also invited corruption and strained relations between police and public.

Police surveillance of political dissidents has further detracted from conventional law enforcement functions and has tended to tarnish the image of the force. Fortunately, this practice seems to have been less visible in recent years, if for no other reason than the expansion of domestic intelligence operations at the federal level. Otherwise, police involvement in political issues appears to have been limited to crowd control activities which periodically provoke charges of unwarranted use of force.

One of the more welcome innovations in New South Wales law enforcement, the 1862 centralization of police forces, eliminated previous problems of communications and control and has spared New South Wales the difficulties inherent in the fragmented organization of law enforcement found in the United States. Yet despite this step in the direction of organizational efficiency, such practices as promotion based on seniority and the maintenance of antiquated physical requirements for police service have had an inhibiting effect on the modernization and improvement of the force.

Among the more perplexing and enduring problems faced by elites in New South Wales is the treatment of convicted criminals. In general, trends in correctional philosophy have evolved from retribution to isolation to rehabilitation; these themes have been evident in the operational treatment strategies of physical punishment, incarceration, and noncustodial treatment. The convict era was, of course, a unique period in the history of the colony. The difficulties of controlling a large convict population were great; capital and cor-poral punishment were inexpensive, easily administered, and consis-tent with the moral sensibilities of the times. Secondary transporta-tion, a costlier alternative, served the purpose of isolating the more troublesome convicts. Ironically, the early years of settlement were not without innovative themes. Policies of convict assignment and the granting of tickets of leave, encouraged by the necessities of economic development, were embryonic examples of community-based treatment programs.

Changes in New South Wales correctional practices resulted from the diffusion of British humanitarian thought and from the changing nature of the colony's social structure. Free immigration and natural population growth lessened the need for convict labor; incarceration provided a convenient way of coping with deviance after corporal punishment fell into disuse. For most of the following century, penal retribution remained the dominant correctional strategy. Increasing attention was paid to matters of rehabilitation, modifications were implemented in piecemeal fashion, and prison conditions improved gradually, but with little change in the overall structure of the prisons system. Incarceration became an increasingly expensive treat-ment strategy during the present century, however, and its effective-ness as a deterrent and as a method of rehabilitation grew more questionable. Thus began a period of investment in such non-custodial alternatives as probation, parole, work release, and periodic detention, a new treatment strategy that seems destined to dominate correctional practice for some time to come.

THE MEDIA, POLITICS, AND PUBLIC INSECURITY

The impact of the media on public perceptions of criminality in New South Wales may not be assessed with precision. However, journalistic focus on the more sensational crimes (particularly violent crime and sexual offenses) may have produced a slightly distorted view of the insecurity of society over the past century. This phenom-enon may be attributed to a number of factors. Public response to dramatic stimuli has always been strong, and the media may devote disproportionate attention to crime in order to enhance audience appeal. Moreover, the need for exploitable issues is characteristic of most political systems; the tendencies of candidates in New South Wales to identify with the theme of law and order, and of opposition members to take issue with the crime control policies of the govern-ment, are reinforced by the ready access to the news media enjoyed by politicians.

Yet there is evidence to suggest that, in spite of continued media attention to crime, the New South Wales public has usually regarded other matters as more pressing. At the very peak of the most recent "crime wave," Wilson and Brown's survey revealed education to be an issue of greater concern among the respondents.[12] More recently, as Australia experiences the inflation now prevalent on a worldwide scale, prices rather than crime loom largest on the citizen's mind. Accordingly, political discourse has shifted to economic matters, and exploitation of law and order themes for political advantage has subsided.

PUBLIC ORDER: THE FUTURE

As has been the case throughout much of the history of New South Wales, future trends in crime and conflict will more than likely be influenced by demographic and economic factors. Although the age cohort whose members were born in the aftermath of World War II are now passing beyond the "crime prone" or "high-risk" range, a drastic drop in levels of crime appears unlikely. Subsequent annual birthrates in New South Wales have declined, but at a very gradual rate. Meanwhile, the actual number of births has increased, as has the overall population of the Sydney metropolitan area. The inferences to be drawn from these trends are uncomplicated; high levels of theft appear destined to remain a fact of life in New South Wales for the foreseeable future.

With few exceptions (Switzerland and Japan among them), high levels of acquisitive crime appear to be endemic to modern capitalist societies. The years since World War II have seen Australia move consistently toward mass consumption society. As New South Welshmen enjoy creature comforts to an unprecedented extent, and, more importantly, become increasingly socialized into intense materialism, common theft and white-collar crime may be expected to increase. Such tendencies, moreover, are likely to be enhanced by the inflationary pressures of the current economy of New South Wales.

We are confronted here not with sporadic and isolated attempts to gratify impulses, but with a society's fundamental value patterns. As long as intensely materialistic values prevail, and insofar as they increase, New South Welshmen will be likely to seek to improve their material well-being—most through means defined by authorities as legitimate, others extralegally. Propensities to theft might conceivably be lessened by a massive restructuring of social and economic relationships, or, alternatively, by the implementation of Orwellian methods of social control. It seems safe to say that both these possibilities are remote.

New South Wales is peaceable by tradition, and only the most drastic social dislocation could precipitate a significant outbreak of collective violence. Barring war, severe economic contraction, and the economic or political persecution of class or ethnic groups, it seems probable that the grievances harbored by New South Welshmen will not be expressed in the streets. Even if such forms of disorder did arise, they would not likely exceed the relatively low magnitude of those that have occurred in Scandinavia. The possibility that collective violence in New South Wales would begin to approach the levels of the United States during the 1960s is almost nil.

The phenomenon of inelasticity in the less serious forms of criminal behavior also merits mention here, for members of New South Wales society may be expected to continue indulging their appetites for drink, gambling, and illicit sex as they have since the landing at Sydney Cove. The aforementioned problems in controlling these forms of behavior are likely to continue in the immediate future; in the long run, however, as the increasing heterogeneity of the New South Wales population is accompanied by a greater tolerance of human differences, some form of de facto, then de jure decriminalization seems likely. Diversion of habitual drunkards from the criminal justice system to detoxification centers, state regulation of gambling and prostitution enterprises, and official tolerance of homosexual behavior have been instituted in other Western societies without a corresponding collapse of the social order. The success of these social experiments overseas will not go unnoticed in New South Wales. Indeed, precedents have already been set in New South Wales with the establishment of state lottery and off-track betting systems. Further innovations are likely within a decade or two.

From prison camp to advanced industrial society, the history of Sydney has been a colorful one, and though problems of public order have rarely dominated the larger picture, they provide an interesting reflection of contemporary attitudes and institutions. Over the years Sydney has enjoyed a level of tranquility exceeding that in many, probably most, of the world's large cities. As long as state and federal governments continue to provide conditions of freedom and comfort for the vast majority of its inhabitants, Sydney should remain a relatively orderly place.

NOTES TO CHAPTER IV.6

1. The terms "high court" and "higher court" refer to the Supreme Court of New South Wales sitting in Sydney and on circuit elsewhere throughout the colony or state. This body is not to be confused with the High Court of Australia, a federal institution established in 1903.

2. The scoring procedures were patterned after those of Ted Robert Gurr and Muriel McClelland, *Political Performance: A Twelve Nation Study* (Beverly Hills, Calif.: Sage Professional Papers in Comparative Politics, 01-018, 1971).

3. See Henry Albinski, *Politics and Foreign Policy in Australia: The Impact of Vietnam and Conscription* (Durham, N.C.: Duke University Press, 1970).

4. See Harris, op. cit.

5. Police and prisons statistics have been drawn from the annual reports of those departments.

6. The indicators of the independent variables regressed on the various measures of criminality were constructed as follows. (a) *Economic conditions.* Averaged standard scores of (1) percentage change from mean of preceding two years, N.S.W. overseas export revenues per capita, 1909-1971; (2) percent of N.S.W. labor force unemployed, 1907-1971 (sign inverted); (3) petitions in bankruptcy per capita, N.S.W. 1860-1910 (sign inverted); (4) percentage change from mean of preceding two years, index of export prices, N.S.W., 1861-1905; (5) percentage change from mean of preceding two years, colonial revenue per capita, N.S.W., 1821-1856; (6) percentage change from mean of preceding two years, intercolonial and overseas export revenues per capita, N.S.W., 1826-1908. This composite indicator thus represents short-term economic fluctuations, in addition to the general state of the economy in a given year. It does not purport to measure long-term changes in material well being. (b) *Population masculinity.* Percentage of the New South Wales population of the male sex. (c) *Urbanization.* Percentage of the New South Wales population residing in the Sydney metropolitan area. (d) *Police force strength.* Number of law enforcement personnel per 1,000 inhabitants of New South Wales. (e) *Police appropriations.* Percentage of the New South Wales annual budget allocated for police operations.

7. There exist a number of plausible explanations for the latter relationship. On the one hand, an expansion of law enforcement resources may have enabled police to devote closer attention to sexual offenses. Alternatively, the growth of the police force may have occurred coincidentally with an increase in the behaviors in question. It is also possible that an increasing moral rigidity on the part of colonial elites was accompanied by an expansion of the police force and by a more indignant official attitude toward sexual deviance.

8. Independent variable measures regressed on twentieth century rates included (a) industrial unrest (man-days of work lost in strikes and lockouts per 1,000 trade union members, N.S.W.), (b) Labor government (years in which the Australian Labor Party controlled the government of New South Wales for the entire calendar year) and (c) war (years in which Australian troops were engaged in combat operations overseas).

9. David Cochrane and Guy Orcutt, "Applications of Least Squares Regression to Relationships Containing Autocorrelated Error Terms," *Journal of the American Statistical Association*, 4 (1949), 32-61.

10. On the method used see Shirley Almon, "The Distributed Lag Between Capital Appropriations and Expenditures," *Econometrica*, 33 (January 1965) 178-196.

11. Gollan, op. cit.

12. Wilson and Brown, op. cit.

Part V

CALCUTTA: THE POLITICS OF

CRIME AND CONFLICT,

1800 TO THE 1970s

Richard C. Hula

AUTHOR'S NOTE: The author would like to acknowledge the many individuals who read portions of this manuscript. Particularly helpful were the careful readings by Ramkrishna Mukherjee, David H. Bayley, and John McLane. As always any errors of fact or interpretation remain the responsibility of the author. Thanks are also due Doreen Ellis who helped with the early collection of data; to Tina Peterson who aided in the analysis of the data; and to Joan Johnson, Dowla Hogan, and Cheryl McKinnis who helped type the manuscript. Special thanks are due to Catherine Hula who both helped collect the data that made this work possible and gave the moral support needed to complete the task.

A number of libraries and other institutions have been very helpful as well. They include the library at the India Office, London, the British Museum, and the libraries of the University of Chicago, Northwestern University, and University of Illinois.

The history of civilization in India, and more specifically in Bengal, begins many centuries before the intrusion of the European powers during the sixteenth century. We begin our narrative at the latter point because our aim is not a history of India or of Bengal but of Calcutta, a city created at the expanding edge of British economic imperialism. This study focuses on the history of public order in Calcutta, leaving to some future historian the task of writing a complete social and political history of the city. We inquire into the political circumstances of public order in Calcutta: the changing foci of official concern, the nature of the institutions charged with the development and implementation of the official definition of public order, and, at the center, the forms of public disorder in the city and the magnitude of the events. We also hope to explore, though less thoroughly, some correlates of changes in this "public order system." Much attention must be given to the history of nationalism in Bengal, because nationalism was responsible not only for changing patterns of disorder but for the transformation of the institutions by which public order is defined and maintained.

Calcutta has a nearly irresistible attraction to the student of public order because in the contemporary era it is widely thought to be one of the most "disorderly" cities in the world. There can be little doubt that in the twentieth century the city has endured a level of social and collective violence unmatched in most societies. To study Calcutta is not to examine a representative of some larger class of cities, but rather one that may be unique. Because of its high and sustained level of social disorder, many commentators regard the city as a negative model, exhibiting all that is to be avoided in future urban development. Indeed, obituaries for the city have been written since the seventeenth century.[1] They have all proved to be premature, and a central concern of this study is why and how Calcutta persists.

Although Calcutta has distinctive and extreme problems of public order, it also has liabilities as a research site. Many of these disadvantages are closely related to features that attract the researcher in the first place. For example, since Calcutta seems to be an extreme case, it may be of limited value in discovering generalizations that

467

might help us to understand public order in a range of different societies. If we are committed to the development of social theory, it may be that a case study of Calcutta will have little long-term payoff. A closely related, if somewhat more practical consideration, is the relative lack of data and information. One would not expect a society exposed to massive social violence to be terribly concerned with bookkeeping. Thus data such as crime statistics may have even less value here than elsewhere.

One particularly difficult problem associated with Calcutta is the need to abstract the relevant history of the city from the much broader history of Bengal and India, while retaining a proper cultural context. India is, after all, beyond the experience of most Western social scientists. Assumptions commonly made in the study of Western cities can be made here only at some peril.[2] There are, of course, points at which some of these broader issues must be discussed. Certainly it is hard to understand the development of violence in Calcutta without consideration of the political climate in Bengal. We have made these contextual discussions as brief as possible, however, partly because of practical limits on how much information can be contained in a short study. There is a more important theoretical reason as well. A critical assumption of the larger research, of which this study is a part, is that the social phenomena of disorder are not due simply to idiosyncratic characteristics of a particular society. Our goal has been to isolate some of these more general social variables.[3]

We begin with a brief survey of the early history of the city, with special reference to its economic basis and the consequences of colonial rule for Indian politics and society. Following is a more detailed history of the period from 1800 to the 1970s, which deals with economic, political, and social factors in general and the origins of nationalism and communal tensions in particular. The third and fourth chapters deal specifically with the history of public order and the institutions established to maintain it in the nineteenth and twentieth centuries, respectively. A summary chapter examines some correlates of public order and disorder in Calcutta and assesses the city's future prospects.

NOTES TO INTRODUCTION, PART V

1. For the most recent example of such literature see Geoffrey Moorehouse, *Calcutta* (New York: Harcourt Brace Jovanovich, 1971).

2. For example, in a study of a North American city it would not be unreasonable to assume a general knowledge of the class structure of American society. Obviously this is not likely to be true for an Indian city.

3. A general characteristic of the literature on Bengal and Calcutta is a focus on particular individuals. Such an approach does not readily suggest broader social variables.

A GENERAL HISTORY OF
CALCUTTA, 1690-1800

The locale of what was to become Calcutta was long recognized by European trading powers as a critical point from which to tap the vast commercial potential of Bengal.[1] The initial European penetration in the area was some miles down the river Ganges at Garden Reach, where the Portuguese annually traded with the Bengalis. Eventually the Portuguese attempted to establish a permanent settlement further up the river at Hooghly, a point only 25 miles from the modern site of Calcutta. The Portuguese had poor relations with the Mughal rulers of India, however, and in 1632 the Mughal ruler Shah Jahan attacked the settlement. Although the Portuguese appeared to have the advantage in terms of both men and material, they were routed and the town was sacked. It was a defeat that eliminated the Portuguese as significant participants in the coming struggle for economic dominance in Bengal.

The ready defeat of the Portuguese tends to overstate the inner vitality of the Mughal empire. Hindsight suggests that in the early decades of the seventeenth century the empire was in its twilight. Throughout the later decades of the seventeenth century the authority of the Mughals was in decline. Increasingly the Mughal governorship in Bengal came to resemble a local dynasty.[2] The British learned this firsthand in their attempts to implement favorable trade agreements negotiated at the Mughal court in Delhi. Major Indian challenges to the British in Bengal during the eighteenth century came increasingly from Bengal itself.

With the Portuguese driven from the area, Bengal witnessed the invasion of what was to be a much more potent force. The vehicle by which the British began their penetration of India was the East India Company, a government-regulated corporation formed by a charter granted by Elizabeth I in 1600. The aim of the company, described in requesting the charter, was the establishment and maintenance of "quiet trade" with the East Indies. The royal charter not only established a trading company, it also outlined the creation of an essentially independent political power in the area in which the company chose to do business. Thus the royal charter charged the company as follows:

> To make, ordain and constitute such and so many laws, constituting orders and ordinances to them [the company] or the greater part of them, being then and there present, shall deem necessary and convenient to the good government of the Company and all factors, mariners, and other officials employed or to be employed in their voyages, for the better advancement and continuance of their trade and traffic.[3]

Throughout the latter half of the seventeenth century, the East India Company cautiously probed the possibility of extending its rapidly growing Indian commercial interests into Bengal. The initial penetration occurred in 1636. As a reward for treating a daughter of the Mughal emperor, a British doctor asked for and received permission for the company to establish trading areas, or factories, in Bengal.

In 1689 Job Charnack was appointed as Governor of the Bay of Bengal. His dominion included a number of small settlements scattered around the area of Hooghly. That the Bengal settlements still constituted a minor element within the East India Company is suggested by Charnack's subordinate position to the directors in Madras. As the British began to develop their position in Bengal, a number of other European powers with similar commercial aspirations made their appearance in the area. About the time the British set up their first factories in Bengal, the Dutch settled at Chinsurah, some 25 miles upstream of Hooghly. This settlement was later ceded to William IV of Britain following a series of European wars. In 1673 the French established themselves at Chandernagore, only a few miles from the British settlements. Thus at the end of the seventeenth century it was by no means certain who would come to dominate Bengal in the coming years. It was clear, however, that there was no lack of aspirants.

Ambiguity regarding the source of political authority in the whole of Bengal notwithstanding, within British settlements there was little question. Although the British would claim a lack of territorial aspirations for another 100 years, the royal charter on which they based their commercial enterprise revealed that there was no intention of placing any European under the authority of the "host" government. British settlements in Bengal always claimed and always received at least de facto extraterritoriality. It is clear that English subjects, and probably Indians who found themselves in the British settlements, were never under even token jurisdiction of indigenous political authorities. Thus, as early as the seventeenth century, the British made and enforced their own law.

As the British presence expanded in the seventeenth century, an increasingly hostile attitude on the part of the Muslim leadership in Bengal developed. In 1688 the British were forced to withdraw from Hooghly. Following their evacuation, the British engaged in a series of negotiations in which they attempted to legitimize their position with the Mughal authorities. In 1689 these negotiations broke down, temporarily forcing the British to leave Bengal altogether and retire to Madras.[4] Further negotiations resulted in an invitation to the British to return to Bengal. Thus a year later Charnack returned. Rejecting past sites for the company's factories, Charnack selected a new location. It was a settlement that later evolved into Calcutta.

In many ways the Bengal factory was located in a most unpleasant place to live. According to one tradition the site was chosen without much thought, but it seems unlikely that the decision was a casual one. Charnack's major considerations were the site's usefulness for trade and its ease in defense. Calcutta met both these requirements. Located on the east bank of the Hooghly, it was the closest area in which goods could be disembarked from the Bay of Bengal that had a continuous supply of fresh water. It could be reached by ocean-going vessels, although movement up the river was by no means easy. It had clear access to and from a vast hinterland that included not only the Ganges Delta, but the Gangetic plains and the Assam valley to the north, and the resource-rich zones of Bihar, Orissa, and Madhya Pradesh on the west. It was also easily defensible. To the north of the site was Chiput Creek, to the south the Adi-Ganga River, and to the east a vast salt lake. It is also evident, however, that in the decision-making calculus employed by Charnack, considerations of residents' health and comfort were not given much weight.

During the first years of the settlement, survival was the most important goal for many of the European residents. The climate was such that the British could adjust only with the utmost difficulty. Between March and September temperatures average from 82 to 87 degrees. Temperatures higher than 100 degrees are common, and the climate seems even hotter because of the very high humidity that generally accompanies the heat. July ushers in the monsoon season, and the average rainfall in that month is 13 inches. The rainy season extends through September, with an average rainfall each month of

10 inches. During other months it seldom rains in the area, and one characteristic of the dry season is the drying up of portions of the salt lakes. The prevailing winds carried the pungent odor of rotten fish into the city. For the Europeans the climate of Calcutta was more than unpleasant, it was positively unhealthy. European mortality during the early years of the settlement was very high. A Captain Hamilton reports:

> One year I was there and there was reckoned in August to be 1200 English, some military, some servants to the company, some private merchants residing in the town, and some seamen belonging to the shipping of the town, and before the beginning of January there were 460 burials registered with the Clerk's Book of Mortality.[5]

Nonetheless it appears that most Englishmen thought the gains to be made by locating in the town were worth the obvious risks, for there does not seem to have been any serious demand that the Calcutta settlement be relocated to a more healthful site.

Perhaps the most important point to be made in discussing the early history of the city is that the policy of the British in the city of Calcutta itself differed from the policies followed in the rest of Bengal. Within the city the British immediately assumed direct political control. The initial de facto assumption of power was sanctioned by the Mughal of Bengal only a few years after Charnack landed in the city. In 1689 the company was allowed to purchase the zamindar rights to three small villages in the area of what was to be Calcutta. Although the British often described the role of zamindar as if it were simply that of landholder, it implied a good deal more.[6] A zamindar resembled a feudal lord; although he held title to the land, those who worked the land were not subject to his arbitrary dismissal because the right to work the land was also a hereditary right. In addition, the responsibilities of the zamindar were far more extensive than those of a simple landowner. He was expected to provide a wide variety of governmental services to the people who lived on his land, including the maintenance of a legal system. The only formal link between the zamindar and the Mughal authorities was the payment of an annual tax.[7] In the case of the British even his obligation does not seem to have been met.

With the acquisition of the three villages, the British gained formal control over an area approximately three miles long and extending about one mile inland from the river. It is clear that from this time the function of administration in the city was distinctly British, in sharp contrast to the case of the rest of Bengal, where the British went to some lengths to avoid the direct assumption of administration. It was not until 1772, long after Mughal authority had ceased to exist, that Warren Hastings assumed formal control of the province. Much of the province had been subject to no authority above the village level for anywhere from 25 to 100 years, and it seems likely that the British adopted an imperial territorial policy only when the lack of order in the countryside threatened their lucrative economic imperialism.

Three general characteristics of the social system that evolved in Calcutta during the seventeenth and eighteenth centuries have very direct implications for the study of the city in later centuries and are explored in detail below. First, at a very early date the city became a way station for removing wealth from Bengal to Britain. A second characteristic of the early city is the beginning of a general restructuring of elites in the whole of Bengal as well as in the city itself. The third early and persistent attribute of the city was the incapacity of the city's political system to respond to the demands placed on it, even those requisite for collective physical survival. At times the city's rulers and economy were unable to make available enough food to its population to avoid mass starvation.[8]

THE DEVELOPING ECONOMIC SYSTEM

There can be little doubt that the city of Calcutta was created by the East India Company as a device for removing wealth from India. A good deal of support for this interpretation can be drawn from a consideration of the people who were attracted to company service. Company clerks were often of aristocratic backgrounds, and for them India was seen as a means of replenishing a dissipated family fortune or as an avenue of advance for a second-born son. For the most part positions in the service were filled through a system of patronage and were not available to those who were not "well connected." The demand for such positions was great despite the small salary formally offered for the positions.

A more systematic view of the early economic substructure of the city can be derived by examining the trade between India (in particular Bengal) and Great Britain. The form of the relation is suggested by the construction of the city's first dry docks in 1710 to facilitate the loading of saltpeter, which the British needed for the manufacture of explosives for their European wars. These increasing levels of exports did not stimulate the Indian economy, however. For the most part the wealth that flowed from Britain in payment for natural resources was channeled into consumption of the British traders, and often it returned to Britain.[9]

The increasing boldness of the British in the exploitation of Bengal brought on a final attempt by the Muslim authorities to restrain British influence. After a series of confrontations, the Nawab of Bengal attacked Calcutta and in 1756 captured and sacked the city. Once again, however, an apparent defeat of a European power masked the real weakness of the Indian political structure. A year later Colonel Robert Clive marched from Madras to recapture the city. He succeeded, and in the subsequent Battle of Plassey, the issue of who was to dominate all of Bengal was settled in favor of the British. From this point the Mughal authorities were simply figureheads for the British, subject to removal if they developed notions of independence.

A good test of British dominance is the case of Mir Qasim, who became nawab in 1760. Following Plassey, Indian traders faced a number of taxes that applied only to them. To reduce the advantages of the British, the Nawab did away with the taxes for all traders. In response to this move toward free trade, the British promptly deposed the nawab and his replacement reimposed the taxes. This was part of a general British strategy of destroying any potential competition to be found in the Indian economy. Thus by the beginning of the nineteenth century indigenous industry, particularly weaving, had been largely destroyed.[10]

A number of writers have suggested that the Battle of Plassey ushered in the period of the most massive removal of wealth from Bengal. The initial settlement following the battle called on the nawab to deliver 7.5 million silver rupees as compensation to the East India Company. Two weeks later another 4 million silver rupees were demanded and delivered. Clive himself was granted a payment of £234,000 for his trouble and also was given an annual payment of £30,000 for the rest of his life. In addition to monetary payment, the company annexed 900 square miles around Calcutta. As a prelude to the direct assumption of power by British authorities, the emperor restored an ancient distinction in the administration of political authority in Bengal between the nawab and the dewan: The dewan had the formal authority for revenue collection. Following Plassey, the company was given the option of "standing as dewan," that is, of assuming direct responsibility for the collection of land revenues. Some internal resistance to the assumption of the dewan developed, however, and the option was not exercised until seven years later.[11]

Administration in the countryside had almost completely collapsed in the aftermath of the Battle of Plassey. In this state of near anarchy, the East India Company moved into the rural area in search of trade. It was a trade whose terms were most often defined at the barrel of a gun. The numerous large fortunes being made in Bengal set off a furor in England. To some extent the anger was an outrage against the behavior of the British in Bengal. It was also the reaction of "old wealth" as it faced the possibility of a challenge to its place in society. Whatever the cause, the importing of enormous personal wealth to England was not well received. In a parliamentary debate Burke declared:

> Here were not tradesman, here was conquistadors, animated with avarice of age and impetuosity of youth, they roll in one year after another; wave after wave; and there is nothing before the eye of the native but an endless prospect of new flights of birds of prey with appetites continually renewing.[12]

Criticism of the behavior of its servants in Bengal was by no means the only serious problem faced by the East India Company at the start of the second half of the eighteenth century. In spite of the expanding levels of trade and the personal wealth flowing from India, the company found itself in financial difficulty. In particular, famine conditions in much of Bengal had served to restrict the land revenue. In 1765 the company persuaded Clive to return to India as Governor of Bengal. Granted a wide range of powers, Clive instituted a number of reforms aimed at maintaining behavior that was more consistent with company objectives. Thus the value of gifts company servants could accept was greatly reduced, and private trade was suppressed with previously unknown vigor. Although two years of authoritarian rule by Clive cut down on some of the more spectacular excesses by the company servants, he failed to produce a dramatic increase in revenues. The officials of the company in London offered two general explanations for this performance. First was the extraordinary overhead in maintaining a colonial empire as a business expense. Tripathi reports that possible revenue to the company was diverted into numerous expeditions to "pacify" areas of the Indian subcontinent.[13] The second major problem continued to be posed by private trade. Numerous strategies were adopted by the directors to control it, but none seemed to be effective.

In 1770 Bengal was stricken by a massive famine. It is estimated that Calcutta lost as much as a third of its population, which was then certainly in excess of 100,000. The most important result of the famine for the East India Company, however, was that revenue dropped even more. In the early 1770s the East India Company applied for a million-pound loan, which was needed to allow payment of a dividend on the company's investment. The Bank of England refused, the company was forced to apply for relief directly to Parliament, and the result was a thorough examination of the management of the company by Parliament. In 1772 the East India Company was granted its million-pound loan. There were, however, a number of conditions attached. Perhaps the most important was the creation of a Royal Governor of Bengal who was charged with the administration of the province. From this point the British Parliament assumed more and more power in the administration of the Indian empire, a trend that climaxed in 1858 with the direct assumption of royal administration in India.

THE DISRUPTION OF TRADITIONAL ELITES

A second aspect of the changing social system in Calcutta was the extensive disruption of traditional patterns of organization. The effects on the economic system have already been suggested. Traditional village industry was largely destroyed as a result of a flood of imported English goods. Weaving, which later became a symbol of the struggle against British domination, was severely retarded by the large-scale importation of cheap cotton goods from the mills in England. The British also would move to forestall the development of modern industry, which might offer competition to English industry.

Perhaps the most obvious disruption of the Bengali social system involved the emergence of a European, particularly British, privileged class. To the extent that there was any provincial government at all, the authority of that government rested with the European community in Calcutta. Within the city all aspects of administrative authority were explicitly reserved for Europeans. For example, of the nine seats on the municipal board, seven were reserved for British Christians. As the social power of this group increased, so did its tendency toward conspicuous consumption. By the middle of the eighteenth century, British society in Calcutta was generally more ostentatious than that found in London. As late as 1785 a number of Europeans owned slaves. An average family might well have 40 servants. Moorehouse reports that one family of four had 110 servants, and the bachelor William Hickey had 63. The community developed a minor culture of its own. It was for the most part encapsulated from other European communities, and, as would be expected, there was little desire to move outside European circles. The social isolation of the European community in Calcutta was reinforced by physical distances: The trip to Benares up the Ganges River took 75 days, Dacca was 35 days' travel, and the trip to Murshidaban took almost a month. Thus the European community in Calcutta turned inward.[14]

The "official" community, both within the East India Company as well as later representatives of the crown, was by no means always impressed with Calcutta society. If there were indeed a norm, it seems to have been one of distrust of and distaste for the perceived provincialism and ostentatious display of wealth of the private entrepreneurs. Nevertheless, the political influence of the community in the administration of the city was very great. This strength was revealed after Clive placed a tax on the transfer of house deeds as a means to secure urban improvements. The European community objected strenuously, and shortly thereafter the tax was removed from Europeans, although it remained collectible from Indian residents.

British policy also served to bring about a resurgence of a Hindu elite, in many cases at the expense of the Muslim community. In fact, hindsight reveals a sharpening of the division between these two communities that would one day lead to untold violence throughout India. The basis of this social change rests broadly with two British policies. The first dealt with land, the second with the recruitment of Indians into lower levels of the British administrative system.

As noted earlier, land ownership in Bengal was based on the zamindar relationship. From the British point of view the single most important role of the zamindar was the collection of land revenue, yet the traditional system struck the Europeans as totally inefficient. In the eighteenth century falling land revenues led the East India Company to consider how the entire system might be rationalized (i.e., how more revenue might be collected on a regular basis). In 1793 Lord Cornwallis, then governor, late of Yorktown, put into effect what has since been referred to as the Permanent Settlement, a key to which was the British demand that the zamindar rights to the property be forfeited if taxes on the land were not paid. Although there had been some provision for the punishment of those who did not pay taxes in the Muslim period, the notion that zamindar rights might be revoked was nothing short of revolutionary.

The Permanent Settlement had the effect of introducing on a wide scale the idea of land ownership in Bengal. Property became a commodity that could be bought and sold. Given the decline in Bengal industry and commerce, land became an increasingly attractive investment in the nineteenth century. As old zamindars were forced to sell their holdings, a new landed aristocracy began to emerge.[15] This new elite was largely Hindu and based in Calcutta. There is strong evidence that the distribution of wealth in Bengal became even more skewed during the period. The importance of the rural money lender increased as the level of rural indebtedness grew, and it became more and more difficult for the small landowner to maintain his land.[16] Increasingly, such landowners either were forced to assume tenant status or were driven off the land. Those who had to leave were likely to add to the population of urban areas.

Coupled with the change in the land tenure system, there was a substantial effort by the British to develop a Bengali market economy during the eighteenth and nineteenth centuries. The extent to which the British authorities maintained their commitment to the market model is revealed in the numerous periods of famine during the 1700s and 1800s. Many of the famines were brought on by the inability of peasants to pay for the food that was available, rather than by lack of food. The problem was compounded by a good deal of pressure to commit agricultural land to nonfood products. The most important of these new cash crops was indigo. Indigo plantations spread through Bengal and soon assumed a major place in the export economy. The shifting to indigo as a crop was often resisted by the peasants, however, and the use of force against them was not at all uncommon. The reservoirs of ill will thus created served as a basis of widespread rural agitation against the British in the nineteenth century.

The second major British policy that disrupted traditional elites in Bengal can be attributed to the process of recruiting Indians for the lower levels of their administrative apparatus and to the Western-style education that was generally made a requirement for such employment. In their patterns of recruitment, the British did not seek a representative sample of the Bengali population but centered recruitment on one particular segment, the Hindu Bhadralok. The Bhadralok were traditionally the Bengali elite; literally, the word "Bhadralok" means "respectable people" or "gentle people." For the most part, the Bhadralok formed a cultural entity in Bengal.[17] The most distinguishing characteristic of the Bhadralok was a strong aversion to manual labor, which was to be avoided even at the price of severe reduction in material well-being. Thus the administrative positions opening up under the British were of enormous appeal to the Bhadralok. Other elites, particularly Bengal's Muslims, were much less aggressive in seeking Western education and entering the British administration. By the end of the nineteenth century the Bhadralok dominated the Indian imperial service, not only in Bengal but in most surrounding provinces as well.[18]

The movement of the Bhadralok into the "mainstream" of the European administrative system of Bengal was based largely on the acquisition of Western skills, principally the learning of English. However there was also an implicit need for rejection of a number of traditional Hindu values. In particular there was a whole set of caste restrictions that were impossible to maintain. The extent to which many young Hindus did reject such values was noted with concern within the Bhadralok community itself.[19] There were examples of aping of what young Bhadralok perceived to be a European lifestyle. Ironically, such behavior led a number of European observers to question the worth of Hindu society.

The penetration of the Hindu Bhadralok into the British administrative services occurred at first only at the very lowest level. During this early period there was scarcely any suggestion that the Bengalis, or any other Indians for that matter, were capable of more demanding work. Even this notion of limited participation was by no means uncontroversial. As Governor of Bengal, Warren Hastings had displayed a good deal of racial arrogance but still seemed to hold the opinion that Bengal offered an example of a viable civilization that demanded a degree of respect. By the time the Marquess of Wellesley assumed power in 1798, it was the official view that Indians were shiftless and lazy, and some effort was made to reduce the Indian influence in the administrative services. The outline of British policy toward the inclusion of Indians in governmental service continued to vacillate into the twentieth century. As late as 1905, serious attempts were made to reduce Indian penetration.

THE LACK OF GOVERNMENTAL CAPACITY

From the data available, it appears that the city itself grew rapidly if somewhat erratically. In the eighteenth century the city was expanding in terms of geographic size and the proportion of the city that was devoted to actual urban settlements. Table V.1.1 lists some of the population estimates available for the city. Once again, very rapid population increase is suggested. This is perhaps all that can be concluded, given the very poor quality of the data. It is known that almost all the population estimates were based on counting residences in the city and multiplying by some factor that was taken to represent occupancy. How that factor was calculated is seldom known, and indeed the factor used in many of the population estimates is often not given. A source of particularly gross error in the post-1752 estimates has been suggested by Ray.[20] He argues that the estimates obtained in 1789, 1796, and 1800 were essentially guesses. He devotes some energy to analyzing the notes from which the 1750 estimates were derived and suggests a number of ways in which a large error might have been introduced.

As one might expect, early Calcutta can be thought of as two cities.[21] Contemporary observers point out that the distinction between the two was very great indeed. Price has described the European section of the town: "Round their little fort and close to it, by degrees they built themselves neat, if not elegant houses, a church, a

Table V.1.1 Population Growth in Calcutta in the Eighteenth Century

Year	Area owned by British	Area owned by other zamindars[a]
1704	15,000	30,000
1706	22,000	41,000
1708	31,000	62,000
1710	41,000[b]	82,000
1710	12,000[b]	
		Zamindars under British influence
1752	104,860	209,720
1789-		
1790		600,000
1796		500,000
1800		500,000

a. The grant of the Nawab in 1689 was actually not a direct grant of the zamindar rights to the areas. Rather it was a grant of permission to purchase those rights. Resistance was general to the takeover, and it was well into the 18th century before the British had formal control of the zamindar rights to the entire area.

b. The unreliability of the data can be seen from the wide divergence in two separate estimates of the populations within British Calcutta in 1710. There is no information as to how the authors of these estimates reached their conclusions.

Source: These data are reported in the introduction to *The Census of India, 1901.* The original source of each of these estimates is reported there.

courthouse, and laid out walks and planted trees and made their own little district neat, clean, and convenient." [22] The description contrasts very sharply with conditions in the Indian portions of the city. McIntosh, who visited the city in 1780, wrote of the Indian section of Calcutta:

> It is a truth, from the western extremity of California to the eastern coast of Japan, there is not a single spot where judgment, taste, decency, and convenience are so grossly insulted as in the scattered and confused chaos of houses, huts, sheds, streets, lanes, alleys, windings, gutters, sinks, and tanks, which, jumbled into an undistinguished mass of filth and corruption, equally offensive to human sense and health, compose the capital of the English Company's Government in India. The very small portion of cleanliness which that city enjoys is owing to the familiar intercourse of hungry jackals by night, and ravenous vultures, kites, and crows by days. In a like manner it is indebted to the smoke raised in public streets, in temporary huts and sheds, for any respite it enjoys from mosquitos, the natural production of stagnant and putrid water. [23]

This very grim view of the Indian portions of the town even at this early date were reinforced by Grandpre, who visited Bengal in 1798:

Such animals that die in the streets or in the houses are thrown into the drains and there they lie and putrefy. From sickness or accident many a poor wretch of the human species also expires in the street. I have seen the body of a poor creature lying dead at my door serve for two nights for food to some hungry animals.[24]

Thus few urban services were provided in the eighteenth century. Health and sanitation measures were also scanty in most other cities of that era, of course, but the living conditions in Calcutta must have been nearly unspeakable even by contemporary standards.

The low performance of the urban system also is revealed in its repeated failure to supply enough food to maintain the population, the most dramatic example being the famine of 1770. The British themselves reported that to undertake any kind of relief program was "economically unfeasible" and simply left those who were starving to die. What relief efforts did exist were all private and very small. Some thirteen years later the city experienced yet another serious famine, again with no response from the British. This lack of governmental activity in the face of famine suggests the general orientation and the incapacity of the British administration within the city. There was little effort to control the growth of the city or to provide even a minimal level of urban services. It was not until 1798 that a commission was established to develop some improvements in the city, and it soon collapsed owing to lack of interest.

NOTES TO CHAPTER V.1

1. A thorough treatment of the early history of India is found in a rather long volume edited by Narendra Krishna Sinha, *The History of Bengal* (Calcutta: University of Calcutta, 1967).

2. See Vincent A. Smith, "India in the Muslin Period" (revised by J. B. Harrison), in Vincent A. Smith, *The Oxford History of India* (edited by Percival Spears) (Oxford: Clarendon Press, 1958).

3. Cited in Raja Binaya Krishe Deb, *The Early History and Growth of Calcutta* (Calcutta: Romesh Chandra Ghose, 1905).

4. For details see Smith, op. cit., pp. 431-427.

5. Cited in Moorehouse, op. cit., p. 18. Captain Hamilton's authenticity as a historical source is also vouched for by Deb, op. cit.

6. An overview of the role of the zamindar in Bengal society is found in J. H. Broomfield, *Elite Conflict in a Plural Society: Twentieth Century Bengal* (Berkeley: University of California Press, 1968).

7. Traditionally, a zamindar was held to be hereditary. For the most part it was not tied to the ability of the zamindar to collect taxes. Needless to say this was one of the elements of the traditional Indian system that exasperated the British.

8. The problem of recurring famines in Bengal have been treated in a number of sources. See, for example, Bengal Publicity Board, *Famines in India* (Calcutta: B. G. Press, 1933); Kali Ghosh, *Famines in Bengal 1770-1943* (Calcutta: Indian Association Publishing Co., 1944); and T. C. Narayan, *Famine Over Bengal* (Calcutta: The Book Company, 1944).

9. For example, Deb, op. cit., argues that from 1708 to 1756, 75 percent (by value) of all imports into Calcutta were in the form of gold. This gold would have been unlikely to stimulate the development of the Indian economy. The importance of treasure as an import continued well into the nineteenth century. *The Statistical Abstract for British India* reports that for 1891 approximately seven percent of all imports into Bengal were in the form of treasure.

10. See N. K. Sinha, "Administrative, Economic and Social History: 1759-1793," in Sinha, op. cit., pp. 76-128.

11. The controversy over the assumption of the dewan has been described more fully by Vincent Smith (rewritten by Percival Spear), "India in the British Period," in Smith, op. cit., pp. 455-473.

12. Cited in Moorehouse, op. cit., p. 33.

13. Amales Tripathi, *Trade and Finance in the Bengal Presidency: 1793-1833* (Calcutta: Orient Longmans, 1956).

14. See Moorehouse, op. cit., and also R. Pearson, *Eastern Interlude: A Social History of the European Community in Calcutta* (Calcutta: Thacker Spink, 1933).

15. The impact of this changing status of land was to reinforce and greatly expand the influence of the Hindu elite, generally at the expense of the traditional Muslim landholders.

16. Data on rural indebtedness are given in B. M. Bhatia, *Famines in India* (Calcutta: Asia Publishing House, 1967).

17. The validity of the concept of the Bhadralok is by no means universally accepted. A number of authors argue that it was largely a British fiction that did not describe Bengal culture. As an example, see Leonard A. Gordon, *Bengal: The Nationalist Movement* (New York: Columbia University Press, 1974), pp. 7-8. For a counterview see Marcus Franda, *Radical Politics in West Bengal* (Cambridge: MIT Press, 1971), pp. 7-41.

18. It is important to note that the Bhadralok dominated only the portion of the British service open to Indians, which at this point was small and limited to the lowest levels of the bureaucracy.

19. The Hindu Bengalis' role within the British service and its effects within their community are discussed in Nemal Sadhan Bose, *The Indian Awakening and Bengal* (Calcutta: Firma Mukhopadhyay, 1969).

20. A. K. Ray "A Short History of Calcutta," *Indian Census 1901*, Vol. VII part I.

21. See E. H. Edwards, *Crime in India* (New York: Oxford University Press, 1924). Though Edwards is a biased source, he does offer a useful physical interpretation of the early city.

22. Cited in the revised edition of H. Beverley, "Report of Census of the Town of Calcutta, 1876," in *Indian Census 1951*, Vol. 6 pt. 3, pp. 4-20.

23. Ibid.

24. Ibid.

THE DEVELOPMENT OF
CALCUTTA, 1800-1974

A number of general features of Calcutta emerge from the following survey of the city's history during the nineteenth and twentieth centuries. The most obvious feature for the present study, and in some respects, the most important, is Calcutta's role as a source of intellectual and social development for not only Bengal but to some degree much of India. Development in this case is not necessarily to be understood in the positive sense of improvement. It is clear, however, that a great deal of social agitation complete with justifying ideology emerged from the city, with profound implications for all India. At the same time, of course, the city was the seat of administrative power, first for the British and, after independence, for West Bengal. Of the three main groups in Bengal (Muslims, Bhadralok, and Europeans), only the Muslims did not center their influence in the city.

A second important characteristic of the city has been identified in the preceding discussion of its economic structure. Although economic development is often taken to be a unitary concept, economic growth in Calcutta was of a special and directed type. It did not generate self-sustaining growth; rather, it was largely a conduit for channeling wealth from India, and for this purpose it was "well developed." Thus a good deal of caution is needed in interpreting economic indicators, which probably overestimate the level of "development" as the term is more commonly understood. This may explain the apparent decline of the city's economy after independence, when the pattern of extraction was no longer a principal concern of the elite.

The period under study falls rather naturally into four periods. The first runs from 1800 to 1857, the second from 1858 to 1905, the third from 1906 to 1947, and the fourth dates from independence onward. Our first era begins with an arbitrary date and ends in the year of the Sepoy mutiny. With the mutiny came the official end of the East India Company and the direct assumption of political power in India by the British crown. To be sure, 1857 does not represent a break with the past quite as sharp as one might expect. The drift toward official royal political authority had been clear for more than a century. Nonetheless a number of trends reached their climax during the period of transition. The end of the second period marked the beginning of intense political conflict, which finally led to the British relinquishment of India. The struggle within Calcutta was often vicious and violent. The peaceful ideology of Mohandas Gandhi was not the model for the revolution in Bengal. The post-independence period has proved to be one of difficult transition for the city. Not only was its major source of raw materials lost through partition, but a radical reassignment of priorities by political decision makers put the city for the first time on the losing side in a battle with rural areas for the distribution of political influence. The results have included general decline in the city and increased radicalization of the politics of the city (and in fact of all Bengal).

As one examines the periods, the factors that seem to dominate shift from the economic to the political. Where the early history of the city seems to have been shaped by the products moving through the port, later emphasis is much more on the political agitation exported to and by the city. There were concurrent and closely related changes in the forms and issues of social disorder. Throughout most of the nineteenth century the concern of relevant elites focused on the more traditional and conventional forms of individual deviance and crime. In the twentieth century the elites faced escalating collective disorder whose motivation was a desire to destroy a particular normative order rather than evade it, as is more often the case in "normal" criminal behavior.

1800-1857

In the first half of the nineteenth century most of the protagonists in the struggles that later characterized social life in Bengal were already visible. The extreme factionalization of the society has led John McLane to speak of it as a society of dualisms:

> The dualism between the Europeans who owned the managing houses, banks, factories, and the Bengalis who worked for the Europeans as clerks but seldom rose to managerial positions; the dualism between Europeans

who dominated the upper echelons of the administrative and military services and the Bengalis who were generally confined to subordinate positions; the dualism between the large, non-Bengali element in the factory labor force and the domestic labor force and the Bengali professional class of lawyers, doctors, teachers and clerks; and the dualism of the Marwaris and Europeans who dominated the wholesale distribution industry and the small scale Bengali merchants and traders. In other words, Calcutta had a plural society in which racial and regional devisions were reinforced by economic specialization.[1]

Although McLane was concerned with the Calcutta of the late 1800s, the general outline of the social division was similar almost a full century earlier. At this earlier period, however, the European community's advantage was so great that overt, rancorous conflict was rare. Fears of unrest were focused outside the city. There exists a vast narrative literature about the efforts of the British to control bands of dacoits (thieves and murderers in the countryside), but problems of social control in the city were hardly mentioned.[25]

Table V.2.1 Level of Trade Moving through the Port of Calcutta

Year	Shipping value[a] (£000 sterling)		Ships entered[b]	
	Imports	Exports	Number	Tonnage
1801				
1811			224	86,336
1813	2,120	5,390	240	97,686
1814	2,610	5,610		
1815	3,440	6,660		
1816	5,840	6,990		
1817	6,850	7,810		
1818	7,620	7,090		
1819	5,650	6,950		
1820	4,520	6,710	271	112,729
1821	4,670	7,790		
1822	4,300	8,710		
1823	3,880	8,040		
1824	4,040	7,750		
1825	3,600	7,600		
1826	3,400	6,800		
1827	4,150	8,730		
1831				
1840			256	96,439
1845			612	208,000
1850			688	255,000
1855			876	369,000
			1,097	647,681

a. From the Third Report of the Select Committee of the House of Commons, 1831.

b. From Report of the Port Commissioners to Improve the Port of Calcutta (serial).

The major concern of the British was not the control of social behavior. Rather, their goal was to increase the level of economic activity. In general the economic trends described in the earlier history of the city were maintained. Trade through the port was principally of goods imported from or being exported to Britain. The absolute level of trade continued to rise at a fairly brisk pace. Table V.2.1 gives an indication of how quickly this trade was increasing. Two features of the Port of Calcutta trade are noteworthy. First and most obvious, the overall level of economic activity within the port increased throughout the period. What is perhaps more interesting is the continuation of a very large trade surplus. This strongly suggests that the various experts of India were being transformed into foreign wealth rather than being exchanged for wealth that would flow into the Bengali economic system.

In addition to the general increase in the level of British trade with India, other trends in the economic development of the country were maintained. For example, the large-scale destruction of indigenous industry apparently continued, though this is difficult to document in a systematic manner. Available data, however, suggest that throughout the first half of the nineteenth century India became increasingly dependent on European sources of goods that were once produced in India.[3] One of the most important, particularly in symbolic terms, was cotton cloth. The data presented in Table V.2.2 show that by the middle of the nineteenth century the domestic spinning industry had all but collapsed.

One can cite other direct manifestations of the emphasis on the development of the British economy irrespective of its effects on the development of the Bengal economy. A Calcutta-based shipbuilding industry developed in the late eighteenth century. In 1814, because of pressure from domestic shipbuilders in Britain, all Indian-built shipping was banned from the India-Britain trade. The result was a death blow to the nascent shipbuilding industry.[4] Some years later the economic privileges of the East India Company were restricted by the Regulating Act of 1833, in which the company was ordered to cease commercial activity. The need for a license to trade in the area was abolished, and henceforth trade with India was open to all. It was claimed that the act would place Bengal in the free market system—but it was a free market only if one were British. Although the act of 1833 also called for an increase in the level of Indian participation in the governing of India, it was generally understood that such participation would be only at the lowest level of the bureaucracy. The major significance of the act was surely to further the demise of the company rather than to expand the role of Indians in the administration of Bengal.

Table V.2.2 Decline of the Bengal Cotton Industry, 1813-1832

	Cotton goods (000 Rs)	
Year	Exported	Imported
1813	5,291 [a]	9
1814	8,490[a]	45
1815	13,151	263
1816	16,594	317
1817	13,272	1,122
1818	11,537	2,658
1819	9,030	1,582
1820	8,540	2,559
1821	7,664	4,678
1822	8,009	6,582
1823	5,870	3,720
1824	6,017	5,296
1825	5,834	4,124
1826	3,948	4,346
1827	2,876	5,252
1828	2,203	7,996
1829	1,326	5,216
1830	857	6,012
1831	849	4,564
1832	822	4,264

a. The Napoleonic war checked exports to Europe.
Source: Nilmani Mukherjee, "Foreign and Indian Trade," in N. K. Sinha, ed., *The History of Bengal* (Calcutta: University of Calcutta, 1967).

The Development of Nationalism

A number of indigenous social movements that questioned the British occupation of Bengal arose in the first half of the nineteenth century. The one that was to have the greatest long-range political significance in Bengal was a largely intellectual social movement among the Bengal Bhadralok. Throughout the early 1800s the Bhadralok continued to reassess the validity of Hindu tradition as well as their social position vis-à-vis the British administration. An excellent example of the early intellectual ferment is to be found in the work of Rammohan Roy. Roy argued that through an accommodation of Hindu and Western thought it would be possible to expand the role of the Hindu in the political life of Bengal. Some of Roy's best-known writings were tracts challenging the practice of suttee. He argued that numerous practices that were "offensive" to Europeans were offensive from a Hindu point of view as well. Roy also was extremely critical of the British administration of Bengal and the obviously low opinion the British held of Bengalis. Roy published a series of tracts in 1827 objecting to various discriminatory aspects of the British legal system—for example, any Christian had the right to demand a jury comprised of Christians, but the Hindu had no such right.

Much of the intellectual development begun by Roy was maintained at the Hindu College. Here a band of students gathered around the person of H. Derozio, a Eurasian instructor at the college. Collectively this group came to be known as the Derozians, or more popularly, Young Bengal. The group's members were considered radical both in their anger at perceived maltreatment at the hands of the British and in their scorn for many Hindu traditions.

In 1842 Young Bengal began to publish the *Bengal Spector*, marking the beginning of the nationalistic press in Calcutta. Members of Young Bengal put a good deal of effort into the publication of pamphlets and newspapers arguing against the discriminations heaped on the Hindu in the British political order. Once again a common theme was the inadequacy of the judicial system. Rasik Krishna Mallik, a prominent member of Young Bengal, stated the general feeling of the group in an 1835 publication: "The administration of Justice in India is so much characterized by everything that is opposed to the just principles of government, we offer no apology to introduce it to the notice of our readers."[5] Mallik continued the argument by suggesting that a government organized and run as a profit-maximizing business was not likely to promote social and economic development. In concluding, Mallik appealed to the better nature of the British to right the wrongs some of their countrymen had committed in Bengal. This conclusion reveals the implicit irony in the point of view of Young Bengal. Despite anger at the way the Bengali Bhadralok were treated, there remained a strong attachment, even an idealization, of British society. The strong rhetoric notwithstanding, Young Bengal never seriously challenged the concept of British rule. Rather, the demands centered on increased participation in a British-ruled Bengal.[6]

Many of the perceived excesses within Young Bengal produced a reaction in the more conservative elements of Hindu society. Many were appalled at the lengths to which members of Young Bengal and their fellow travelers seemed to be prepared to go in an attempt to win the approval of the British. Sinha points to the scorn held by many toward these people:

> They became very much anglicised and had an inordinate fondness for everything English. They adopted Western ideas and habits, dresses and mannerisms, and openly indicated their repugnance to everything Indian. They spoke in English, thought in English, and as humorously remarked by Bhudeb Mukherjee, probably even dreamed in English.[7]

Throughout the 1830s and 1840s a number of intellectual societies formed with the aim of counteracting the effects of Young Bengal. However in 1851 many of these organizations joined with the remnants of Young Bengal to establish the British Indian Association, with the specific goal of agitating for favorable changes in the Indian Charter (Parliament's charter for the East India Company), which was to be renewed in 1853. In particular, it was hoped that support could be generated for the so-called black acts, which would have allowed the trial of Europeans by juries composed at least in part of Indians. The reaction of the European community to the general outlines of the black acts was swift and nearly hysterical. It appears that the issue was postponed in the rewriting of the charter and was dropped completely following the Sepoy mutiny in 1857.

A comparison of the pattern of social agitation in the Bhadralok and the Muslim elites in Bengal is quite instructive. The most obvious difference is that the Islamic response to British pressures in the early part of the nineteenth century was reactionary. There was a good deal of commitment to the notion of a "return to glory."[8] For the Hindu, by contrast, there was more social change and adaptation, although much of the "reformist" ideology of this period was often simply a rejection of that which was Indian or Bengali. In retrospect, however, it can be seen that the currents of social change in the first half of the nineteenth century accentuated the difference between Muslims and Hindus. The values held by adherents of the two religions became even more distinct.

The revolt of the Indian Sepoy regiments in 1857 affected much of northern India. Both sides practiced and experienced a high level of savagery. In Calcutta, however, there was no violence at all. The Sepoy regiment stationed in the area was quickly and peacefully disarmed. The major result of the mutiny in the city was the unleashing of a tremendous amount of abuse from the Europeans on everything considered Indian. The general reaction of the Hindu Bhadralok to the mutiny also was one of shock and disgust. This indicates that the developing feelings of national identity among the Bhadralok did not spread far beyond that class.[9]

The Capacity of the Urban System

It is difficult to make any general characterization of the population growth reported in Table V.2.3. Ray argues that available population estimates through 1815 represent a set of guesses that ultimately were based on a greatly inflated estimate of population published in the eighteenth century.[10] According to Ray, the earliest

Table V.2.3 Estimates of Population in Calcutta, 1800-1857

Year	Population
1800	500,000
1802	600,000
1814	700,000
1815	500,000
1821	179,917
1822[a]	230,552
1822[b]	300,000
1831	187,081
1837	229,714
1850[a]	361,361
1850[b]	413,182

a. Data from A. K. Ray, "Short History of Calcutta," in *Indian Census, 1901*, Vol. VII, pt. I.
b. Indicates multiple estimates.

estimate of population that can be trusted at all is that reported for 1821. The variation between census estimates for the same years (two each for 1822 and 1850) suggest that the later estimates probably represent little more than guesses themselves.

Given the state of the data, it is hardly surprising that there is no reliable breakdown of population in terms of either sex or ethnicity. However two facts emerge from the narrative literature. First, Calcutta was very much a male society. Most estimates suggest that perhaps two-thirds of the population was male. Commitment to the city was low because many of these men had migrated to the city in the hope of earning money to enable them to return to the rural areas of the province. A later census (1866) reports that the city had a "floating" population of perhaps 50,000, continually drifting between rural areas and the city. Proportional ethnicity is not known, except that the European community, although very small numerically, dominated the city. The Bhadralok, also few in number, occupied a second level within the city. Lower-class Hindus and Muslims, clearly in the majority, had little influence on any aspect of the social and economic development of Calcutta.

There is little evidence to suggest any improvement in the conditions of urban life for most of the residents of the city by the beginning of the nineteenth century. City government remained rudimentary.[11] Most of the urban governmental functions that had been assumed by the East India Company were in the hands of the Municipal Council, which was appointed by and reported to the East India Company. In addition to the normal administrative functions, it served as a court of record for the European residents of the city.

For the native population, the council appointed a company civil servant to the post of zamindar. Although the procedures adopted by the zamindar are not very clear, this official was charged with both administering law and collecting land revenues in the town. The available information indicates that the latter responsibility took precedence over the former.

Within the city itself there was growing concern about the state of administration during the latter half of the eighteenth century. We have noted the lack of official response to the 1770 famine. In addition to failure to act in emergency situations, the unsanitary condition of the city was reaching the danger point. Finally in 1793 Parliament provided for the appointment of a number of justices of the peace who were given responsibility beyond their judicial duties for maintaining streets and a minimum level of sanitation. To finance the latter function, the justices were given limited assessment powers as well as the power to impose a municipal liquor tax. The positions were generally reserved to honor citizens of "distinction." However the political and administrative impact of the justices was minimal. One reason was the sharp restrictions on the level of funds that could be raised and how they could be spent.

1858-1905

The second half of the nineteenth century was a period of basic social transformation in Bengal society, although the direction of many of the changes had been evident earlier. Bhadralok society gained much from an unprecedented outflowing of cultural achievements. Buoyed by self-confidence, elements of the Bhadralok stood on the brink of issuing a revolutionary challenge to the British empire at the beginning of the twentieth century. In addition, a number of violent rural agitations suggested a greater basis than had previously existed for uniting the interests and goals of the Bhadralok and the lower-class Hindus. Splits within the society were also growing, however. The fateful division between Hindus and Muslims appeared to widen, heralding the approach of the confrontations that became so common in the next century.

Economic Developments

The economic dominance of Calcutta over all the Lower Provinces of British India led more than one official source of British trade statistics to argue that data relevant to the city were an index of economic conditions in the entire region.[12] A number of major changes in the economic system occurred outside the city, however.

Of particular importance was the peasant agitation over the planting of the indigo. As discussed in the previous chapter, a large-scale shift to raising indigo was brought about at the insistence of British landlords. Peasant discontent coalesced in a series of violent uprisings during 1850-1860. For a time much of rural Bengal was subjected to periodic outbreaks of collective violence. The relatively spontaneous peasant uprisings could not be maintained, however, and were generally under control by the end of 1860. Even though they were quickly put down, the indigo revolts had important implications. In short-run economic terms, the planting of indigo was greatly reduced, and this crop never recaptured its position of economic dominance in Bengal. By the 1880s and 1890s the worldwide demand for indigo was much reduced through the introduction of artificial dyes.

The indigo revolts had a second effect, a social one. For the first time since the British occupation of Bengal, the Bhadralok could identify with the lower-class peasants of Bengal. This suggested further the possibility of enlisting these classes in the struggle with the British, but most later attempts of the Bhadralok to organize the lower classes for political purposes failed.

With the decline of indigo as a cash crop, the importance of jute increased (Table V.2.4). Once again the expansion of a cash crop was

Table V.2.4 Production of Jute in India, 1832-1905

Years	Exports (Average of five years, cwt.)
1832-1836	11,000
1837-1841	67,000
1842-1846	111,000
1847-1851	234,000
1852-1856	439,000
1857-1861	710,000
1862-1866	969,000
1867-1871	2,628,000
1872-1876	4,858,000
1877-1881	5,362,000
1882-1886	7,274,000
1887-1891	10,194,000
1892-1896	11,183,000
1897-1901	12,356,000
1902	13,036,000
1903	13,721,000
1904	12,875,000
1905	14,480,000

Source: Statistical Abstract for British India, various editions.
Bengal was the principal source of jute.

Table V.2.5 Exports of Food Grains form India

Year	Rice and paddy (cwt)
1867	12,698,000
1868	15,377,000
1869	10,615,000
1870	16,079,000
1871	17,311,000
1872	23,294,000
1873	20,245,000
1874	17,393,000
1875	20,416,000
1876	19,914,000
1877	18,429,000
1879	22,166,000

Source: B. M. Bhatia, Famines in India (Calcutta: Asia
Publishing House, 1967), p. 38. Bhatia includes data for a
number of other food grains as well. Bengal was the
principal source of exported food grains.

encouraged even in the face of chronic food shortages. In terms of
general trade, Bengal (indeed all India) remained a primary source of
raw materials to Britain; the exportation of foodstuffs continued,
widespread food shortages notwithstanding. Table V.2.5 gives an idea
of the magnitude of the export figures on food grains from India for
a number of years. The major conclusion drawn from the table by
Bhatia is as follows:

While there was an all around scarcity in the country and prices were
about four times the normal price, the exports not only continued but
even showed an increase.[13]

It is important to point out that although the aggregate level of
trade that passed through Calcutta increased throughout the nineteenth century, the pattern of that development was quite restrictive.
Since the British were not interested in fostering internal economic
delivery systems, in terms of trade Calcutta remained linked much
more closely with Great Britain than with most of India. Between
1830 and 1905 the quinquennial value of the coastal trade of Bengal
was never more than 25 percent of the value of foreign trade and
often was less than ten percent. The massive foreign trade imbalance
in favor of Indian exports also continued. The value of exports was
nearly double that of imports in the 1830s and 1840s, and during the
last three decades of the century was consistently about 50 percent
greater.[14]

In the latter half of the nineteenth century another aspect of the
Calcutta economic system became evident, namely, its extreme

volatility. That volatility had two major sources. The first was the instability of the Indian currency. Tied to the value of silver, the value of the rupee dropped sharply with the price of silver throughout the latter half of the century, particularly in the 1870s. The rate of inflation rose, and it became difficult to agree on even the terms of short-run contracts. In 1893 the rupee was taken off the silver standard and pegged to the pound. A second source of instability was the very limited and unstable character of the capital market. In particular, banks that were allowed to deal in foreign exchanges often failed. For example, there were 22 such exchange banks in Calcutta in 1866, but only seven in all India survived a financial panic that year.[15]

The Development of Nationalism

The seeds of racial pride planted by Roy in the intellectual circles of Bhadralok society continued to flourish throughout the latter half of the nineteenth century, a period of great literary production. The crowning achievement of this intellectual development came in 1913 when Rabindranath Tagore was awarded the Nobel prize for literature.[16] The Bengali renaissance had profound political and implications for the Bhadralok. In social terms it suggested that the inferiority complex displayed by the adherents of Young Bengal was not warranted. The notion that Hindu society had a right to enter on its own the mainstream of political authority in Bengal received new support. In fact, much of the literature and poetry of the Bengali renaissance had distinctly political implications. Often the material extolled the virtues of the Indian society in general and the Bhadralok in particular.[17] At the same time there also developed a popular press that offered a Bengali point of view. In 1878 protests over the transfer of funds from a famine relief fund to the Afghan War led the British to impose the Vernacular Press Act, under whose terms the freedom of the press to criticize the government was drastically restricted.

One obvious effect of the Bengali renaissance was to create more anger at the barriers constructed against Indians in all phases of economic and social life in Bengal. Particular objection was raised against administering Indian Civil Service (ICS) examinations in England alone. In 1876 Surendranath Banerjea and a small number of associates formed the Indian Association to demand that the examinations be given in India as well as in England. The issue was of special concern to Banerjea because he was one of the few Indians ever to have passed the ICS exam. Shortly after being accepted into the service, however, he was sacked for what was generally agreed to be a minor error. The British government then made Banerjea's humiliation complete by refusing him entry to the Indian bar because he was a "dismissed government employee."[18]

For a time the growing aspirations of the Bhadralok received a degree of support from the upper echelons of the official British administration. This does not include, of course, members of the unofficial community or the rank and file of the ICS. Nevertheless, when Lord Ripon arrived in India to serve as viceroy in 1880 he made what was to many the rather bold assertion that it was his goal "to spur the small beginnings of an independent political life." In 1882 Ripon repealed the Vernacular Press Act and in the same year offered the Ilbert Bill, which would have largely implemented the terms of the "black acts" suggested some 50 years earlier. The European community again opposed such legislation and managed to delay consideration of the bill. Indian opinion, however, was a good deal more organized at this time. Protest meetings were held throughout Bengal, and during the agitation Surendranath Banerjea was arrested. Response to the arrest was unprecedented. Some 10,000 persons marched in Calcutta in a protest that marked the beginnings of mass agitation in the city.

In 1883 the Indian Association moved to assume control of the stirring of nationalism at the all-India level. In that year they called for a national meeting in Calcutta to discuss the state of political rule in India. A second national meeting held in 1885 was largely overshadowed by a meeting in Bombay of the newly formed Indian National Congress. The Congress excluded a number of prominent Bengali nationalists who were viewed as too radical by the more conservative leadership of the Congress. Although Bengalis later joined the Congress and, through the end of the nineteenth century, dominated it, this early distance and distrust came to typify the relation between the nationalist leadership in Bengal and the Congress. Throughout the twentieth century the Congress regarded the Bengalis as extremists and renegades within the national movement.

As the Bengalis began to assert themselves politically, the need to create institutions to further the economic interests of the Indian community was perceived. The Bengal National Chamber of Commerce was formed in 1887 as an alternative to the European association that was generally taken as the spokesmen for all "commercial interests" in the city, although it represented only a limited sector of the city's commercial classes. The new chamber was dominated by Bengalis, but there were for a time delegates from a number of Indian communities. In particular, Marwari businessmen were involved in the formation of the group, but in the twentieth century, when the Marwari achieved something like their current economic dominance of the city, they left the National Chamber and formed a separate trade organization.[19]

It is important to note that almost all the political, social, and cultural developments discussed thus far are those of a single community, the Bengali Bhadralok. The nationalist organizations offered a rationale for their programs in a distinctly Hindu framework, and a number of half-hearted attempts to recruit others, particularly Muslims, into the growing social movement were generally unsuccessful. The Muslim community in Bengal began to develop a quite different political style. Muslims preferred to work quietly with the British in an informal consultative relationship, which allowed them to gain a number of concessions from the British for their community. Increasingly the Muslim elites perceived the Bhadralok, rather than the British, as the major competitors for position and privilege.[20]

The increasingly militant expression of Bhadralok interests can be associated with the strengthening of a number of other social groups as well. Both the unofficial European commercial classes and members of the ICS began to press the government to protect what they defined as their interests. It was a political struggle they could hardly lose in the short run, and hardly expect to win over the long term. Certainly early victories over the Bhadralok in the twentieth century were dramatic and seemingly convincing. The net effect, however, was to create conditions for revolution and to ensure the Europeans' downfall.

The Capacity of the Urban System

The general demographic makeup of the city did not change greatly during the latter half of the nineteenth century; both the composition and the overall level of population remained relatively stable (Table V.2.6). The censuses also provide quantitative evidence

Table V.2.6 Calcutta: Population By Social Community

Year	Total	% Hindu	% Muslim	% Christian
1850	415,345	66	27	3
1866	380,924	58	30	6
1872	447,601	65	30	6
1876	429,535	65	29	6
1881	433,219	64	29	6
1891	681,997[a]	66	29	4
1901	847,796[a]	—	—	—

a. Including suburbs.
Sources: Census of 1850, 1860, 1870, 1876, 1881, 1891, and 1901.

Table V.2.7 Population by Sex and Religion (% Male)

Year	Hindu	Muslim	Christian	Total
1850	60	65	62	62
1866	58	67	53	61
1872	65	60	60	67
1876	64	72	57	66
1881	65	73	59	67

Sources: Census of 1850, 1860, 1872, 1876, and 1881.

on the continuing sexual imbalance of the city's population, which was predominantly male throughout the remainder of the century. If anything, the proportional male population increased. It is especially interesting to note that the imbalance was found in all social communities, but in varying degrees (Table V.2.7). The Muslims had the highest sexual imbalance in the city, their population often reported as more than 70 percent male. The data are consistent with the common description of the Muslim community as a depressed, impoverished one. At least in terms of family and related institutions, the Muslim community would seem to have had the least stake in the city. It is important to hold two points in mind, however. First, the overall level of male preponderance is so high that doubts are raised about the accuracy of the data. Second, and even more important, the view that the lack of family organization has malign social implications rests on generally untested sociological assumptions.

Although the general demographic characteristics of the city changed little during the last half of the nineteenth century, a number of basic alterations in the society were occurring. Many of these changes can be described in the context of modifications in the Calcutta Corporation. In 1876 the government of Bengal established the first partially elected municipal corporation. An earlier proposal had attempted to deal with the inevitable communal antagonisms by a direct awarding of communal seats. Although the proposal was dropped in the face of widespread Hindu objections, the plan served as a prototype for the communal representation that was introduced into the all-Bengal Council in the twentieth century. The 1876 reforms provided for a corporation of 76 members, two-thirds of whom were to be elected from eighteen wards. Wards that had European voters were allowed to send three commissioners to the corporation. Other wards were awarded two seats. The lieutenant governor of Bengal was charged with the selection of the remaining 24 commissioners. In 1888 the structure of the Calcutta Corporation was revised once again as the city was merged with some of its suburbs. The number of wards grew to 25, but the number of commissioners was increased only to 50. This was accomplished by allocating each ward a maximum of two seats. In addition, nine of the 24 appointed positions were dropped. The remaining seats had been allocated to organizations thought to represent certain interests in the city. These organizations included the Bengal Chamber of Commerce, the Calcutta Trade Association, and the Calcutta Port Trust.

The implementation of an electoral system within the city further divided Hindus and the Muslims of Calcutta.[21] For the Muslims it represented a disruption of their established lines of consultation with the British, offering in its place the very dubious prospect of electoral politics. It was generally assumed that the best the Muslims could hope for was approximately ten percent of the seats, and this level was indeed reached in 1886. The Hindus, however, regarded the corporation as a potential avenue toward greater political influence. Throughout the 1880s and 1890s the debate over whether or not the principle of elected leadership ought to be expanded in both the city and the rest of Bengal became increasingly bitter. The Muslims saw their communal interests threatened by the more aggressive Hindus. Eventually much of the visible Muslim elite came to support a series of proposals aimed at reducing the participation of the Bengali Bhadralok in the administration of Bengal.[22]

In 1898 Lord Curzon arrived in Bengal to assume the position of viceroy. Curzon embraced the philosophy of the European community in Calcutta that the movement toward "Indianization" had gone beyond proper bounds and a period of retrenchment was in order. Supported by the Muslims, Curzon moved in 1899 to transfer the political authority of the Calcutta Corporation from the elected council to a state-appointed board that was dominated almost entirely by the European elements of the city. Later a similar bill was proposed for the governance of Calcutta University. The most important element of the Curzon strategy, however, involved a subsequent proposal to divide Bengal into two provinces. The effect of such a partition seemed certain to weaken gravely the social power of the Bhadralok. The province of East Bengal would contain an overwhelmingly Muslim majority; thus it was expected to come to be dominated by Muslims. Even in the remainder of Bengal, the Bhadralok would find themselves a minority surrounded by the Oriyas and Biharis, who were also Hindus but who were isolated from the Bhadralok culturally and socially. Throughout the early years of this century, the Bhadralok engaged in what was at the time the "traditional pattern of protest." Letters were written, angry but polite speeches were delivered, and petitions were signed and posted. By

1905 it was clear that protesting had little effect and that plans for the partition were proceeding. At this point there occurred a truly critical break with tradition. To support their position that Bengal ought to remain one province, the Hindu Bhadralok appealed for mass participation in a boycott of British goods. Bengal and Calcutta had entered the age of mass agitation politics.

1906-1947

On July 19, 1905, final plans for the partition of East and West Bengal were announced. On the same day Bhadralok leaders in Calcutta called on the people of Bengal to boycott all British goods until the partition was revoked. For a time the response to that call was very impressive. The Marwaris, who increasingly dominated commerce in the city, refused to handle any British goods. Numerous strikes were called, and production dropped sharply. However the effectiveness of the boycott was short-lived. The Marwaris resolved a number of contractual disputes with British merchants and were soon dealing with that community again. Most of the strikes were either settled or quickly broken. Increasingly, radical students were pressed into service as the shock troops of the movement. As the support for the boycott waned, a number of attempts were made by students to force shopkeepers and traders to maintain the action. A number of shop owners were attacked, and some stores were burned or looted. In addition, there were violent attacks on British nationals. An official government report later claimed some 200 "outrages" in Bengal for the years 1906-1907.[23] The emergence of violence brought a stern response from the British, who had broken the back of the boycott movement in Calcutta by the end of 1907. The movement as a whole, however, continued in the rural areas of Bengal, where British influence was a good deal less pervasive.

Throughout Bengal large numbers of *samitis* (associations) were simultaneously established to enforce the boycott and to create pressure for the *swadeshi* (home) industries. As in the city, students played an important role in the samitis, which increasingly assumed a paramilitary character. One outgrowth of the movement was the formation of a large number of "national" schools. The national schools were useful ideologically as well as practically, since more and more students in British-supported institutions were being expelled for political activity. By 1908 there were 46 such national schools in Bengal with between 2,500 and 3,000 students. The politicization of students remains characteristic of Indian education today.

Although the effectiveness of the samiti movement varied across districts, almost everywhere the movement was an irritant to those who did not wish to be a part of the protest. This is particularly true of many Muslims who, in fact, supported the partition. In addition, much Muslim antagonism was aroused by antipartition rhetoric that was phrased in terms of explicitly Hindu symbols. Thus there developed substantial pressure within the Muslim community to counter the growing power of the Hindu Bhadralok. The perceived need for such a demonstration grew with the forced resignation of Governor Fuller of East Bengal in 1906. Fuller was known for his general sympathy for the Muslim point of view, and most Muslims believed that Fuller had been removed because of the growing Hindu dislike of his pro-Muslim policies.[24]

Throughout the latter months of 1906, Muslims gave vocal support to the partition. The Muslim League, founded in 1906, sponsored a public meeting in Dacca that was attended by 25,000 to 30,000 persons. More than 20,000 Muslims marched in Calcutta to show their support for the partition. Increasingly, Hindus perceived danger in Muslim political organization. The fear was greatest in areas having large Muslim majorities. The general fears of Hindus were further increased by the support British authorities gave such Muslim efforts. The British were weary of Hindu agitation and saw in Muslim organization a source of countervailing power with which they might finally end the problem. In several instances British authorities allowed Muslim violence against Hindus to go on unchecked, so to "teach the Hindu a lesson." It was a very dangerous game to play, and unfortunately it was one the British eventually were unable to control.[25]

A whole series of direct Hindu-Muslim clashes was set off in 1907 as the Muslim League expanded its support for the partition.[26] Not surprisingly, such racial and ethnic confrontations brought about a transformation within the Hindu community. In much of East Bengal the samiti, which were originally defined as an agency to enforce the boycott, began to be considered as defense units. The danger of being attacked led many to the conclusion that demands for the British to leave India were foolish because such a vacuum would expose the Hindu minority to the ravages of Muslim persecution. Thus the British were viewed somewhat ambivalently as a necessary evil, at least in the short run.

By late 1907 the rapid spread of violence, both communal and anti-British, led the authorities to conclude that strong steps were needed. Among other actions, the British created a secret police, instituted widespread press censorship, introduced preventive detention, and deported a number of alleged terrorists without benefit of trial.[27] By the end of 1908 violence seemed to be largely under control. However the actions taken by the British had led to a good deal of antagonism between them and even the most moderate Bengali nationalists. As an attempt to reduce this tension, the Indian Councils Act of 1909 modified provincial consultative councils to give them an Indian majority. The councils were now empowered to "discuss any matter of general public interest and to move resolutions on the budget."[28] Most Bhadralok leaders refused to assume any role in the councils. However the revocation of the partition in 1911 served as a basis for entry of the moderate wing of the nationalist movement into the reconstructed legislative council in 1912. In the elections held to fill the council, a number of the more prominent Bengali nationalists who stood for election were rejected by the voters. This result was due partly to the restricted electorate that had been created by the British, but mainly it reflected lack of political organization and expertise. As the British increased the size of the electorate, the Hindu nationalist politicians found it increasingly difficult to maintain their position. At one point, in fact, the British adopted the policy of expanding the Indian electorate as a deliberate strategy to reduce the disruptive influence of the Bhadralok.

At the same time that a number of nationalist leaders were entering the British councils, others were becoming convinced that collaboration with the British would bring about very little meaningful change in the distribution of political authority. The period from 1912 through 1915 saw another steady rise in the level of political violence reported in Bengal. Lord Charmichael, the British governor, was convinced that an all-out attempt to repress the violence was at best a short-run solution and argued that the only feasible course would be to strengthen the hands of the more moderate nationalists who now served in the British councils. Charmichael recognized that much of the political terrorism had a good deal of popular Bengali support. Ultimately, however, pressure from the central government as well as from London forced Charmichael to abandon this more moderate course and to institute the traditional strategy of mass repression. The year 1915 saw the implementation of the Defence of India Act, whose provisions were very much like the series of laws that had been used against the terrorist violence in 1908. The result was just as Charmichael had predicted. In the short run there was a reduction of political violence, but in the long run the moderate wing of the Bengali nationalist movement proved to have lost most of its appeal and was never able to regain it. The Indian independence movement, at least in Bengal, was radical and violent from this point forward.[29]

In 1916 the Lucknow Pact, an all-India agreement, was concluded by the Indian National Congress and the Muslim League. It sought to unite Hindu and Muslim to press the British for responsible provincial governments and dominion status for India. The heart of the agreement was an a priori allocation of communal representation within the provincial legislatures.[30] Within Bengal, the effect of the pact was exactly opposite to its purpose. The formula of representation adopted for Bengal represented a compromise at the national level that pleased no one at the Bengal level. The terms of the Lucknow Pact were seized on by a number of extremists in both communities as a means to increase popular support. Since such support did increase, the level of communal tension rose dramatically. In 1918 Calcutta experienced the heaviest rioting in its history to that date. The worst riot lasted three days and virtually shut off the city from the rest of the world. Relative order was restored only when the British army occupied most of the city.

In 1920 Gandhi withdrew his support from continued Congress participation in British legislative councils. He argued that if the nationalist movement were to succeed, it would have to turn inward, to make society more "worthy." Specifically, Gandhi called members of Congress to withdraw from all British institutions, be they political, educational, or economic. [31] Gandhi's arguments were not well received in the Bengal Congress. Nevertheless the national strategy of noncooperation was eventually endorsed by the Bengal Congress leadership. The result was reminiscent of the boycott protests following the partition of Bengal. From 1920 to 1922 there was a sharp rise in political violence and communal confrontations.

In 1920 the British moved once again to crush the violence, and massive arrests were made under the Prevention of Seditious Meetings Act. The response was a series of demonstration in Bengal of unprecedented size, and violence was so intense that Gandhi called a halt to the entire civil disobedience movement in 1922. Gandhi himself was arrested shortly afterward.

Within the Bengal Congress there developed a vociferous argument over what policy would be followed after the collapse of the civil disobedience movement. Finally it resolved that the radicals would reenter the Bengal Legislative Council. The aim, however, was not to share the power with the British but rather to assume an obstructionist position and destroy the dual system of governance the British were attempting to implement in the province. It was thought that this approach would force the British to make further concessions, and a new party, the Swaraj party, was formed. The Swaraj leadership realized that there could be no majority in the newly elected councils without Muslim support. In 1923, after a long series of negotiations, the general outline of a Hindu-Muslim alliance was reached. Thus in the elections of 1923 there appeared a strong, unified political organization. It was a phenomenon without precedent in Bengali elective history. The strength of the Swaraj party was demonstrated when their candidates beat well-known, more conservative politicians in many districts.

In 1924 the Swaraj Party captured a large majority on the newly constituted Calcutta Corporation. Based on reform legislation, the strong executive organization of the corporation had been abolished and an expanded number of commissioners were charged with the administrative responsibility for the city. The corporation was allowed to choose both its own mayor and, subject to a state veto, its own executive officers. The capture of the corporation gave the Swaraj a source of political patronage, previously lacking because of its obstructionist stance in the Bengal council. Thus the municipal administration began to take on a number of characteristics of a social organization familiar to a North American political scientist, the political machine: The government began to function on the basis of material benefits granted in exchange for support. Increasingly, city jobs became the reward for nationalist activity. A full-scale patronage system was evolving. As Weiner has noted:

> Payrolls padded with the names of nationalist prisoners, under-qualified men appointed to many posts within the municipal administration, and councillors more powerful than the municipal administration became features of the municipal government in the pre-independence era. Municipal government in Calcutta has been severely attacked for its poor performance in terms of those familiar with American urban politics, but the fact is that the Congress movement was strengthened by its control of the municipal corporation.[32]

As would be expected, this period was also characterized by increased tension between the elected and appointed members of the corporation, paralleled by a good deal of friction between the corporation and the British-dominated civil service.

Increasingly frequent acts of political terrorism by Hindi extremists constituted a major threat to the shaky unity of the Swaraj party. The terrorists maintained that they had full support of the Swaraj party, and indeed they had substantial support in the Bhadralok elements of the party. The Bhadralok who tended to reject violence were hardly in a position to take such a position publicly, given the very broad support for the terrorists displayed in the Bhadralok community as a whole. The violence by Hindu samitis had the opposite effect on the Muslim members of the party, who were becoming very suspicious of the goals and tactics of their coalition partners. The strain within the party became even greater when a party conference in 1924 adopted a resolution that appeared to lend support to the terrorist movement. The resolution also gave the Bengal government the evidence it needed to gain special powers from the central Indian government. Under this grant of special power, the Bengal government moved against the samitis. Included in the mass arrests were most Hindu leaders in the Swaraj party, including some of the Bengal council.

By 1924 the tactic of the nationalists in the Bengal legislative council had brought that institution to the verge of collapse. Throughout the year the council refused to appropriate funds to pay the ministers' salaries. Finally the lieutenant governor suspended the constitution on which the councils were based. The council did not meet from August 1924 to January 1925, and in January the demand for salaries was again rejected. Once again the constitution was suspended. The British decided that there would be no further meeting of the council until after new elections planned for late 1926. British officials also decided to devote this period to an explicit attempt to drive a wedge between the Muslims and Hindus in the Swaraj Party. In practical terms it was a strategy of fostering the organization of Muslims who placed communal advantage over the possible gains from intercommunal cooperation.

The policy had heavy support, and British district officials were instructed to give aid to any Muslim organization professing to be loyal to the British government. Increasingly, the Bengalis saw the possibility of a Muslim-dominated council as the result of the up-coming election. Reaction in the Hindu communities was even more agitated as it became clear that the British were acting to expand the electorate, thus enfranchising more Muslims. Communal tensions soared. In 1926 there were serious communal riots throughout the province, and the elections of 1926 were fought for the most part on distinctly communal lines. Of the 39 Muslim representatives selected for the new councils, only one was a member of the Swaraj Party. All the others had stood for the proposition that they were dedicated to obtaining advantages only for their own communal groups. The formation of the new Muslim-dominated ministries marked a radical decline in the legislative power of the Bengali Bhadralok: In the past he had been the master, both in terms of appointments and the ability to obstruct. From this point he could do neither. Thus Bhadraloks were to retreat to the power of "communalism and terrorism."[33]

By 1930 support within the Hindu nationalist movement for any sort of British-dominated democratic institutions seems to have collapsed. There was a general demand for revolution. When the

Congress declared for civil disobedience in 1930, the response was widespread and violent. Mass demonstrations and large-scale picketing occurred throughout the province. A raid on the Chittagong District Armory supplied arms and made possible open warfare in some Bengal districts. In Midnapore District the Congress established a shadow government including police and other civil forces. British administration in the area had virtually ceased as three successive district magistrates were assassinated. Continuing what was by this time a familiar pattern of meeting force with force, the British outlawed the Bengal Congress and proceeded to jail more than 10,000 Hindu nationalists. By 1934 the civil disobedience movement was largely crushed, and the Bengali national movement was in chaos. Within the jails a remarkable political transformation was occurring. Large numbers of those imprisoned during the British crackdown were converted to some form of Marxism. Almost all the major leaders of the various postindependence communist parties were in British jails during this period.[34]

That the Bengal Legislative Council no longer operated in the interests of the Bengali Bhadralok is indicated by the mass arrests conducted through the early 1930s. These arrests were based on legislation that had been approved in the Bengal Legislative Council with Muslim support. In the entire history of the council the British had never been able to secure support for such measures. From 1927 to 1935 the government moved in a number of areas that seemed to challenge the position of the Bhadralok. The first, in 1929, was a rural education bill whose aim was to extend education to the peasants in the countryside. In 1932 the Muslim ministries reserved communal representation on local administrative bodies. In Calcutta they also moved to increase their level of representation, and by 1935 the Calcutta Corporation had elected its first Muslim mayor. Finally, throughout the 1930s the Bengal government had to reduce the indebtedness of peasants to money lenders. This generally reduced to a conflict between Muslim debtors and Bhadralok capital. The Government of India Act passed in 1935 accelerated this trend as the elective power of the Bhadralok was reduced even further through the increased representation of both Muslims and scheduled (untouchable) castes.

As the Muslims became more adept at political organization, they began to resort to some of the organizational techniques long employed by Hindus. A challenge to Muslim government in 1938 was partially made in the streets. Muslim shop leaders were urged to close their shops and demonstrate for the government. A number of Congress representatives were picketed in their homes, and a number of assaults were reported. As the session of the Bengal Legislative

Council was convened, thousands of Muslims were outside awaiting the results of the voting. The government did not fall, and communal tensions worsened. Communal violence struck the city on a large scale once again in 1940 and quickly spread. For the next ten months the violence flared throughout Bengal.[35]

The government of Bengal was nearing collapse by the beginning of the 1940s, and the pressures on it continued to grow. The Japanese occupied Burma at the outset of World War II, posing a possible military threat to the city. The more immediate effect of the war, however, was to cut off supplies of Burmese rice, traditionally a major food source for the Bengalis. In 1942 the Indian Congress called on the British to commit themselves to Indian independence. Until such a declaration was made, the Congress advocated a wave of civil disobedience and resistance to participation in the war effort. Under emergency war powers the British once again began to arrest prominent members of the Congress—and once again the effect was to throw the province into revolutionary turmoil. In the early 1940s there were reported 301 cases of police firing at civilians, 2,000 police injuries, and 322 jails and more than 2,000 government buildings destroyed. In a number of areas within Bengal the system of British administration broke down altogether.

As the political situation grew more critical, so did the lack of food. Not only was Bengal deprived of supplies from Burma, much of the rice crop in West Bengal had been destroyed in a cyclone. In fact, the entire 1942 crop in India was very poor, and refugees flowed into the city as food became more and more scarce in the countryside. By 1943 Bengal was firmly in the grip of perhaps the worst famine in its history. The response of both British and Indian officials was to deny the problem, a policy that was pursued until there were literally too many bodies to be ignored. The port was clogged with Allied shipping, and movement of food through the port proved to be nearly impossible. For a time the port was subject to Japanese bombing as well. At this point the British had neither the will nor (most probably) the resources to stop the dying. Estimates of the number who died in the 1943 famine vary. The official government figure, 1.5 million persons throughout Bengal, is almost certainly too low. The number offered by the Communist Party of India is 12 million, which is certainly too high.

The crisis was met with almost incomprehensible stupidity on the part of the relevant governmental agencies, all of which followed the passive strategy of denying the existence of a problem. The most callous example of this attitude is found in the 1943 British report that, in the face of tremendous starvation, 80,000 tons of foodstuffs were exported from Calcutta. In the city food was stockpiled only for munition workers. In the rest of the province, nature was allowed to take its course. At this point, perhaps 11,000 deaths a week were "nature." The famine was ended only with a fine rice crop in 1944.[36]

As independence came nearer, Hindus and Muslims became increasingly concerned with making its terms as favorable to their respective communities as possible. The change in the political order is revealed by the Muslims' loud assertion that Bengal ought to remain a single entity as a part of an Islamic nation. Of course this was the ultimate nightmare to many Bengal Bhadralok, who argued the need to partition Bengal between a free India and an independent Islamic state. Massive violence throughout 1947 brought almost everyone to the conclusion that partition was unavoidable. The terms of the new partition largely traced those of the hated partition of 1906. Thus Bengal moved toward independence, divided once again.

INDEPENDENCE AND AFTER, 1947-1974

The Republic of India came into existence on August 17, 1947. As the nation celebrated, the mood in Calcutta and throughout Bengal was clearly one of ambivalence. Although great pride was felt about the Indian role in forcing the British to give up the rule of India, victory had been achieved at a very high cost to Bengal. The creation of Pakistan had reduced Bengal to an area only one-third its preindependence size. The extent of the economic dislocation was generally assumed to be great, although its true magnitude was appreciated only in the coming decade. Calcutta itself was still tense from the massive communal violence of the early 1940s. The final irritant to radical Bengali nationalists was the failure of independence to bring them to power. Almost to a man, the leadership of the Bengali terrorist movement was denied access to positions of authority in the new Bengal government. Thus the political cleavages in Calcutta remained similar to those of the preindependence period.

Economic Developments

The partition had the effect of separating Calcutta from both its major source of materials and its major markets. In 1947, 92 percent of all jute grown in Bengal came from areas that were ceded to Pakistan. However all 108 jute mills were located in West Bengal. In the same year 61 percent of Bengal's paddy crop, 70 percent of its cotton, and 61 percent of its oil seed were grown in East Pakistan. In West Bengal there were 80 percent of the oil mills and 76 percent of the cotton mills. Some 80 percent of the hides and skins tanned in

Bengal were from the east, but all the tanneries were located in the west. Calcutta faced grave problems of transport as well.[37]

The effects of partition precipitated yet another period of decline for the Calcutta economy, which at the time of independence was none too healthy. Throughout the 1950s and 1960s, the economic system does not appear to have grown at a rate equivalent to the increase in the subsistence requirements of the city. Between 1951 and 1961 the level of registered factory employment rose by 0.9 percent a year.[38] Meier has estimated that since independence the resources generated for reinvestment in the Calcutta metropolitan area have at best increased at the annual rate of five or six percent.[39] This reinvestment, however, tends to occur outside the city, in the form of monies earned in the city and transmitted back to families remaining in the villages. Throughout the postindependence period, Calcutta continued to have the highest per capita rate of outgoing money orders of any major city in India.[40]

Although it is impossible to reach an exact conclusion regarding the level of public and private investment in Calcutta, it is clear that the trend in the 1960s was downward. Meier suggests that the trend reached something approaching a limit in 1969.

> Last year the situation had deteriorated to the point that only about 1% of the gross regional produce was being invested in the infrastructure of the district. This compares with an estimated 8-10% just to stand still, and proportions around 15-20% in those cities which have carefully constructed welfare development such as in Singapore. In Calcutta industrial employment has been dropping, and industrial investment in the private sector has stood still, with a few thousand luxury and middle income units completed while an equal number have disappeared in floods and the collapse of tenements.[41]

This lack of investment in the public sector of the Indian economy is reflected in the policy that seems to have been adopted by the authorities in Delhi. A general inclination to "write off" the city may account for the distribution of resources within the national Indian political system. For example, in 1963 West Bengal received only 11.5 percent of its assessed annual requirements of copper, only 17.5 percent of its tin requirements, and only 3.2 percent of its lead allocation.[42] The state government has generally taken a similar position with regard to the city, preferring to channel available resources into rural development. This governmental policy differs rather sharply, of course, from that of the British. It was of primary importance to the British that the city be maintained well enough to carry out its extractive function. During the famine of 1943, for example, it was only in the city that "national interest" demanded the creation of a minimal relief effort.

The worsening physical condition of the port has compounded the economic stress on the city. The harbor continues to silt up in spite of widespread dredging operations, hence the movement of ships into and out of Calcutta has become increasingly difficult and dangerous. The consequent loss of trade has greatly reduced the level of foreign exchange available to India. The poor long-range prospects for the port led the Calcutta Port Commission to suggest the development of a new port further downstream, at Haldia, where the silting problems might be controlled. In 1969 plans for this new facility were drawn up and submitted to the World Bank for a loan to cover the foreign exchange requirements of construction. A modified plan was approved, but the impact of the new port on Calcutta at this point is problematic. On one hand, it offers a mechanism that will bring a good deal of wealth and trade into the region. On the other hand, the port will be two or three hours from Calcutta, and the separation may reduce the viability of the city even further.[43]

The shrinking economic base of the city coupled with a high rate of inflation has created much labor agitation. The number of strikes rose steadily throughout the period. Moorehouse reports that in 1967 there were 438 industrial disputes in West Bengal involving 165,000 workers at a loss of 5 million man-hours. By 1969 totals had risen to 710 industrial disputes involving 645,000 workers and 8.5 million man-hours.[44] From the numerous labor agitations a new form of protest emerged as well, the *gherao*, in which a target individual is surrounded for a prolonged period by a group making demands on him. The person facing the gherao must either give in to the demands of the group or hope for rescue from the police. It is most unlikely that he will be able to escape unaided. The gherao is generally nonviolent, but the target may or may not be permitted to have food and water. For a time the gherao was widely used in the city.[45]

Political Developments

At independence the political leadership of the state of West Bengal was in a state of disarray. Unlike other Indian states, there was no established Congress government to assume political power. The preindependence ministries in Bengal had, of course, been firmly controlled by the various Muslim political organizations. Most of this leadership cadre left for Pakistan after the partition was announced. Following independence a Congress government was created and imposed by the federal government in Delhi. At the time of independence the Congress had very little organization in West Bengal, and its political strength was based on the generally high level of prestige accorded to the national Congress organization. Many people, however, did not regard the Congress highly and viewed the creation of a Congress government as a continuation of a "foreign" regime.

The major center of opposition to the "established" political order in West Bengal centered, as in the preindependence period, around the Bengali Bhadralok. The discontent of the Bhadralok was mobilized through a number of leftist groups, the most important being the Communist Party. That these groups remained alienated from the new political order was illustrated by the Communists' refusal to join the various independence celebrations that occurred throughout Bengal. Rather, the party attempted to assume (or perhaps more accurately, maintain) an insurrectionary posture. There is ample evidence to suggest that, following independence, the Communist Party was engaged in a number of incidents calculated to create revolution, at least in Bengal.[46] The response of the new Bengal government was both rapid and highly reminiscent of earlier British policies. The Communist Party was declared illegal, the printing of any party material was outlawed, and all major party leaders were arrested and jailed without trials. The strong response of the government and the lack of general support for the revolutionary stance within Bengal caused a good deal of reevaluation of the violent strategy that had been chosen by the party. As the leadership began to be released from prison toward the end of 1951, the party came to place increasing emphasis on developing organizational strength to contest the planned 1952 general elections.

It soon became clear that the two major political factions within Bengali politics would be the Congress and a somewhat more diffuse "leftist bloc." Within the two major groupings, however, there has been a great deal of factionalism. This was most apparent in the leftist bloc throughout the 1950s. The leftist disagreement involved the fundamental question of whether or not elective politics offered a viable means for the creation of a socialistic state. Those who argued a leftist strategy of insurrection seemed to hold the upper hand. Throughout the 1950s and early 1960s the factions within the Communist Party became increasingly institutionalized, creating the conditions for a split. The schism in the communist movement was increased by four major events: The Tibetian revolt in 1959, the Sino-Indian border clashes that began in 1957, the declaration of President's rule in Kerala state, and the food crisis in West Bengal. To support India in the clashes against China would be to challenge the leftist notion of communist solidarity. Although such a policy was adopted by the all-India Communist Party, the leftist-dominated Bengali party refused to endorse it. Similarly, the assumption of political power by the central government of a Communist-dominated government in Kerala suggested to many that the capture of a state government by way of electoral politics might be a hollow victory. Finally, the large-scale and successful protests organized by the party indicated to many that agitational politics was the most useful tool. In 1962 the Indians were faced with even greater military pressure from the Chinese, but the Communist Party in Bengal continued to refuse to condemn the Chinese action. Because of this stance almost all the party's leaders were arrested on the basis of the Defence of India regulations, and during their internment the right wing assumed control of the party. The leftists were unable to reassume their dominance the following year and moved toward an open split, which became final in 1964. The result was not two homogeneous parties, however, but two new parties, each plagued by factionalism.

The internal dissension that characterized the leftist parties also surfaced in the Congress Party in 1966. In this year the Bangla Congress was formed by dissident members of the Congress Party. Sacrificing ideological purity for electoral expediency, the leadership of the new party began negotiations for electoral alliances with the leftist parties. By the time of the 1967 elections, the Bangla Congress had generated enough support to prevent the regular Congress from receiving a majority of the votes for the first time. The United Front coalition that assumed office was Communist dominated, but was in fact made up of thirteen different parties, three votes short of an actual numerical majority. The coalition was shaky and collapsed within nine months.[47]

The political situation in Bengal became even more unsettled in 1967 with the outbreak of widespread peasant agitation in the Naxalbari area of Bengal.[48] The movement itself, though violent, was crushed by the United Front Government in a relatively short time. The agitation was a good deal more significant than is evident from its immediate effects, however. First of all, the agitation generated a good deal of popular support, which was translated into the formation of a largely covert terrorist organization, the CPML (Communist Party of India, Marxist-Leninist), and the heart of the CPML appears to be drawn from the Calcutta-based Bhadralok. Thus the Bhadralok assumed the position of directly challenging the official government, even though the particular state government was a Communist-dominated coalition. Within the city widespread guerrilla warfare broke out. The political and economic situation in West Bengal, accompanied by large-scale labor unrest, moved toward collapse. Finally, in November 1970, the central government in Delhi assumed direct control of the state. Elections in 1971 returned the United Front to power, this time with a substantial numerical majority. The new coalition was associated with increasing levels of disorder and economic deterioration. It soon broke down, and President's rule was reestablished.

The Capacity of the Urban System

The generally high level of stress on the administration of Calcutta continued throughout the postindependence period. The economic decline of the city has been exacerbated by a steady increase in the population, generally higher than in other parts of India. Table V.2.8 reports available population estimates through 1961. As with other census data, there exist serious questions of reliability. Particularly suspect is the 1941 figure, which seems to have been inflated by both Hindu and Muslim communalists in an attempt to create the impression that their respective religious communities were much larger than they really were. [49] A second problem in interpreting the population figures is one of scope. As the table reveals, the area of Calcutta began to increase in 1931. Since we cannot be certain which areas the increase refers to, however, the comparability of such estimates with earlier ones is suspect. [50] Even with such serious reservations, however, it can be said that the population of the city has continued to grow through much of the twentieth century. Of particular importance in this increase is the flood of refugees from East Bengal that began in the 1940s and has continued through the 1970s. The fluctuations of this movement are shown in Table V.2.9. This flow of refugees into the city has radically changed the population mix within the city. As Table V.2.10 indicates, the relative number of Muslims in the city has declined dramatically since independence. [51]

The period described in this section represents a time of profound transformation for the city. Political events and conditions now seem

Table V.2.8 Population Estimates for Calcutta, 1901-1961

Year	Population	Reported geographic size of city (square miles)
1901	847,796	32.1[a]
1911	896,067	32.1[a]
1921	907,851	32.1[a]
1931	1,196,734	44.8[b]
1941	2,108,891	33.7
1951	2,548,677	32.3
1961	2,927,289	39.8

a. Our calculations are from data given in square acres (20,547).
b. Our calculations are from data given in square acres (28,694).

Table V.2.9 Influx of Refugees into West Bengal

Year	Number
1946	44,624
1947	377,899
1948	419,018
1949	275,592
1950	925,185
1951	
1952	477,186
1953	60,647
1954	105,850
1955	211,573
1956	246,840
1957	9,133
1958	4,285
1959	5,539
1960	8,629
1961	10,095
1962	12,804
1963	14,601
1964	667,125
1965	159,989
1966	4,214
1967	6,895
1968	6,589
1969	11,068
1970	140,000

Source: Bengal Chamber of Commerce, West Bengal: An Analytical Study (Calcutta: Oxford and IBH Publishing Company, 1971).

Table V.2.10 Relative Size of Hindu and Muslim Communities in Calcutta, 1901-1951

Year	Total Hindus	Total Muslims	Muslim population, % of Hindu population
1901	603,310	270,797	44.9
1911	671,206	275,280	41.0
1921	725,561	248,912	34.3
1931	796,628	281,520	35.3
1941[a]	1,531,512	497,535	32.5
1951	2,125,907	305,932	14.4

a. There is a good deal of evidence that the 1941 figures are greatly inflated as the result of systematic efforts in both communities during the census.
Source: Census of India, 1951, Vol. 6 Part 3, p. xv.

to have a much greater impact on social change than the economic factors that were so important in the earlier history of the city. Most striking of all is the evolution of a pattern of social violence that may be unmatched elsewhere in the contemporary world. We turn next to the more systematic examination of civil conflict and crime. Although it is unlikely that definitive causal assertations can be made, we hope to have provided here some general perspectives on the social, political, and economic conditions that have been associated with major changes in the forms and extent of disorder in Calcutta.

NOTES TO CHAPTER V.2

1. John McLane, "Calcutta and the Mofussilization of Bengali Politics," in Richard L. Park, ed., *Urban Bengal* (East Lansing: Asian Studies Center, Michigan State University, 1969), pp. 63-64. "Mofussilization refers to the process by which Bengal politics spreads from Calcutta to the rural portions of the province."

2. There is a great deal of popular literature on Indian dacoits, almost always sensational. Examples include: George Bruce, *The Stranglers* (New York: Harcourt Brace Jovanovich, 1968); James Huiton, *A Popular Account of Thugs and Dacoits* (London: W. H. Allen, 1857); Nila Kanta Sastri, *The Cholas* (Madras: Madras University Press, 1955); James Slerman, *The Thugs* (London: Low & Marston, 1933); and Francis Tuker, *The Yellow Scarf* (London: Dent, 1961).

3. One attempt to prove this point is Nilmani Mukherjee, "Foreign and Inland Trade," in N. K. Sinha, ed., *History of Bengal.* See also Kissen Mohum Mullik, *A Brief History of Bengal Commerce* (Calcutta: Hindoo Press, 1871).

4. For an outline of the British economic strategy in Bengal see N. K. Sinha, *The Economic History of Bengal* (Calcutta: Roy and Gossian, 1956), 2 vols.

5. In N. K. Sinha, *Economic History*, p. 165.

6. See Amit Sen, *Notes on the Bengali Renaissance* (Calcutta: National Book Agency, 1957).

7. N. K. Sinha, *Economic History*, p. 189.

8. N. K. Sinha, "The National Movement," in Sinha, ed., *History of Bengal.*

9. See Broomfield, op. cit., and Moorehouse, op. cit.

10. A. K. Ray, op. cit.

11. For a further discussion of the structural evolution of the urban government, see a series of publications issued by the Institute of Public Administration, in particular Monograph 1, M. Bhahacharya, M. M. Singh, and Frank Tysen, *Government in Metropolitan Calcutta: A Manual;* and Monograph 9, Ali Aschrat, *The City Government of Calcutta.* See also Christine Furedy, "A Neglected Minority: Muslims in the Calcutta Municipality, 1876-1900," in Barbara Thomas and Spencer Lavan, *West Bengal and Bangladesh: Perspectives from 1972* (East Lansing: Asian Studies Center, Michigan State University, 1973).

12. For example, this position is reflected in a number of the tables in the *Statistical Abstract of British India.*

13. Bhatia, op. cit., p. 39.

14. Mukherjee, op. cit.

15. Ibid.

16. A number of sources deal with the Bengali renaissance at some length. See op. cit.; Amitabna Mukerjee, *Reform and Regeneration in Bengal 1774-1823* (Calcutta: Rabindra Bharaii University, 1968); Bose, op. cit.

17. For a discussion of the impact of one such writer see Rachel R. Van Meter, "Bunkimcondra's View of the Role of Bengal in Indian Civilization," in Edward C. Dimock, ed., *Bengal: Literature and History* (East Lansing: Asian Studies Center, Michigan State University, 1970).

18. Banerjea eventually became the first Indian Chief Minister of Bengal.

19. The Marwaris first emigrated to Calcutta from northern India during the late nineteenth century. The flow steadily increased through the twentieth century. Originally the Marwari community focused on moneylending and trade. Many have now branched out into property and industry. See Thomas Timbers, "The Origin of Marwari Industrialists," in Robert and Mary Jane Reech, eds., *Bengal: Change and Continuity* (East Lansing: Asian Studies Center, Michigan State University, 1971).

20. The revolving political strategies of both Hindus and Muslims have been well described in Broomfield op. cit.

21. See Furedy, op. cit.

22. McLane has pointed out that "in 1901 only 22 out of every 10,000 Muslims in Bengal knew English compared to 114 out of every 10,000 Hindus. Muslims held only 41 of the 'high appointments' under the government while the Hindus, who were less than twice as numerous, held 1,235." John McLane, "The 1905 Partition and the New Communalism," in Alexander Lipski, ed., *Bengal East and West* (East Lansing: Asian Studies Center, Michigan State University, 1970), p. 46. Also see Broomfield, op. cit.

23. The official government committee on revolutionary violence was titled the Sedition Committee but was known better as the Rowlatt Committee in recognition of its chairman, S.A.T. Rowlatt. A more balanced view of the period is provided by Broomfield, op. cit.

24. That perception was almost certainly correct; see McLane, "The 1905 Partition and the New Communalism."

25. Ibid.

26. Ibid.

27. See Broomfield, op. cit., p. 39. Relevant police reports for the city give the official view.

28. See Broomfield, op. cit., p. 34.

29. A more rigorous examination of the trends in disorder is offered in a later section.

30. The Lucknow Pact was concluded by this Muslim League and the Indian National Congress. The pact sought to create a common framework that would allow both Hindus and Muslims to press the British for representative government and dominion status for India. The heart of the agreement was a prearranged communal distribution of seats in the various provincial councils. See Broomfield, op. cit., p. 114.

31. Among Gandhi's goals was the political reconciliation of Hindus and Muslims. To make this possible Gandhi attempted to mobilize the Indian National Congress to support Muslim concerns over the fate of the Turkish caliphate after World War I.

32. Myron Weiner, "The Politics of Patronage: Calcutta," in Myron Weiner, ed., *Party Building in a New Nation* (Chicago: University of Chicago Press, 1967).

33. Broomfield, op. cit.

34. Franda, in *Radical Politics in West Bengal*, treats the transformation within the British jails at some length.

35. See Moorehouse, op. cit.

36. All major sources on Calcutta that cover this period discuss the impact of the famine. A number of sources dealing specifically with famine were cited in note 8 to Ch. V.1.

37. See Marcus Franda, "West Bengal," in Myron Weiner, ed., *State Politics in India* (Princeton, N.J.: Princeton University Press, 1968), p. 241.

38. It is generally agreed that these official statistics underestimate the extent of industrial growth because firms are reluctant to register. This is discussed in "Calcutta and Delhi," in Richard Meier, ed., *Observations Upon the Developmental Character of Great Cities* (Berkeley: Institute of Urban Planning, University of California, 1969), p. 57.

39. Meier, op. cit.

40. Ibid., p. 58.

41. "Groundswell in West Bengal," in Richard Meier, ed., *Developmental Features of Great Cities of Asia, Vol. 2, Japanese, Chinese, Indian* (Berkeley: Institute for Urban Planning, University of California, 1970), p. 58.

42. Moorehouse, op. cit., p. 283.

43. On balance the conclusion seems to be that Haldia will help. See "Haldia New Port: New Growth for Calcutta," in Meier, *Developmental Features.*

44. Moorehouse, op. cit.

45. There is little doubt that the tremendous upsurge in gheraos was due to the sympathy of the United Front governments with such action. After the Front Government fell, reported gheraos also dropped.

46. The activities of the various elements of the Bengali left wing after independence are described in Franda, *Radical Politics in West Bengal.*

47. See Marcus Franda, "Radical Politics in West Bengal," in Paul R. Brass and Marcus Franda, eds., *Radical Politics in South Asia* (Cambridge: MIT Press, 1973), pp. 183-222.

48. For a more complete discussion of the Naxalbari agitation see Franda, *Radical Politics in West Bengal,* pp. 149-179, and Moorehouse, op. cit., pp. 309-312.

49. For a discussion of the probable error in the India census data, with particular reference to the 1941 census, see *Indian Census, 1951,* "A Note on Population Growth in the City," in Vol. 6, pt. 3.

50. Source: *Annual Report on Administration of Justice in Bengal.*

51. There is, of course, the further problem of whether such census districts have any relation to the Calcutta police district, which is of primary interest in this study. For years in which there are estimates of population in the police reports, it appears that the population covered is similar, although only for the early years of the twentieth century are precisely the same figures reported in the census and the police reports. The sources of later police estimates of population within the police districts are not reported and may be little more than guesses based on the census data.

52. One demographic aspect of the city that appears not to have changed much is the predominance of males in the city. Postindependence data suggest, however, that the relative proportion of women in the city is gradually increasing. The *Census of India, 1961* reports that there were 580 women in the city for every 1,000 men in 1951. In 1961 the relative number of women had increased to 612. This compares with 518 and 492 women in 1901 and 1911, respectively.

CRIME, CONFLICT, AND PUBLIC ORDER
The Nineteenth Century

BENGAL AND CALCUTTA UNDER THE EAST INDIA COMPANY, 1800-1840

The Levels of Public Disorder

Official data on public disorder during the East India Company era are sparse and in general tell more about the expanding scope of the company's administrative control than about the patterns of social disorder per se. Most of the data refer to all Bengal and the Lower Provinces, an area of variable boundaries that was at its greatest extent, much larger than Bengal in the twentieth century. Population data for this area have an apparent precision that is belied by the results of the first comprehensive census, taken in 1872, which revealed a population about 80 percent greater than previous estimates. We can say only that the data on crime refer to a population that probably numbered between 30 and 60 million; where we have risked the calculation of rates, it is on the basis of the company's population estimates, which fall toward the lower end of that range.

Tables V.3.1 and V.3.2 give some data on specific offenses in the 1820s and 1830s. On the average there were only 700 offenses against the person known to officials per year in all Bengal, or about 0.2 per 10,000. Crimes against property were more than ten times as numerous and, like crimes of violence, were highly variable from year to year. The lesser violations known as "offenses" were two to four times more numerous than property crimes. The data are too unreli-

Table V.3.1 Known Crimes Against the Person in Bengal, 1823-1836

Year	Total	Offenses per 10,000 Population
1823	322	.087
1824	441	.120
1825	749	.200
1826	807	.200
1835	1,634	.420
1836	940	.240

Source: G. T. F. S. Speede, The Criminal Statistics of Bengal (Calcutta: W. Thacker, 1847).

Table V.3.2 Known Crimes Against Property and "Offenses" in Bengal, 1823-1836

Year	Crimes against property per 10,000 population	"Offenses" per 10,000 population
1823	3.8	8.1
1824	1.8	9.3
1825	2.7	7.7
1826	3.3	8.7
1835	6.1	10.2
1836	3.5	7.4

Source: G. T. F. S. Speede, The Criminal Statistics of Bengal (Calcutta: W. Thacker, 1847).

able to sustain any inferences about the "true" extent of social disorder—if that concept has any meaning in a dual society—and too sparse to permit an assessment of trends. It is worth mentioning, though, that the order-of-magnitude difference between numbers of property crimes and violent crimes that attracted official attention is characteristic not only of later crime data for Calcutta but also of the data from the three Western cities in this study throughout the nineteenth and twentieth centuries.

Table V.3.3 indicates the total magnitude of official efforts to deal with "crime" and the impact of these activities on the Indian population. The data are a compilation of most of the available series from 1800 to the 1850s. Their interpretation is problematic, but the early data (1807-1814) suggest that proportionally very few persons were tried for serious offenses. The series on "total persons concerned" and "total arrested" are probably comparable, and though the absolute numbers are large—from 65,000 to more than 100,000—they work out to rates of about 25 per 10,000, a figure that is very small by comparison with the later experience of Indians in Calcutta.

Table V.3.3 Statistics on Criminal Justice in Bengal and the Lower
            Provinces, 1807-1852

Year	Total prisoners held for trial[a]	Total persons concerned[b]	Total arrested[c]	Total convicted[d]	Total cases
1807	7,012				
1808	7,756				
1809	7,750				
1810	5,787				
1811	5,447				
1812	5,289				
1813	4,833				
1814	4,901				
1823		93,605			44,372[e]
1824		96,142			41,502
1825		99,980			39,237
1826		102,575			45,012
1833		68,589			
1834		64,693			
1835		66,756			39,748
1836		65,626			28,805
1843			86,543	40,280	44,774[f]
1844			82,987	45,025	43,487
1845			86,623	50,135	117,001
1846			87,302	52,204	119,932
1847			89,789	53,454	129,708
1848			93,975	56,648	134,200
1849			97,645	59,246	141,895
1850			92,342	54,683	90,154
1851			90,483	52,053	90,743
1852			87,549	53,351	87,788

a. Report on East India Affairs in Parliamentary Papers, 1816; Appendix F to
"Administration of Justice in Bengal," p. 719.
b. From G. T. F. S. Speede, The Criminal Statistics of Bengal (Calcutta:
W. Thacker, 1847).
c. Parliamentary Papers, 1856; "Papers Relating to the System of Police in
Bengal," p. 358.
d. Ibid.
e. Ibid., 1823-1836.
f. Ibid., 1843-1852.

The image of a tranquil Bengal that might be inferred from these
statistics of dubious validity is contradicted by many narrative
reports in which officials expressed concern about the poor state of
public order. In 1798, for example, the Governor General of Bengal,
Lord Cornwallis, summarized the prevailing view in a minute to the
board of directors of the East India Company:

The magnitude of the criminals with which the jails in every district are now crowded, and the numerous murders, robberies and burglaries daily committed and the general insecurity of persons and property which exist in the interior parts of the country are melancholy proofs of their having long and too generally existed. Having experienced the inefficiency resulting from leaving all the criminal courts and their proceeding being left dependent on the Nabob Muhammad Reza Khan, and the objections he might be naturally disposed to feel, on the ground of his religion, to any innovation in the prescribed customary rules and application of Mohammedan law, we ought not, I think, leave the future control of so important a branch of government to the sole discretion of any native, or indeed any single person whomever.[1]

The apparent contradiction between accounts of pervasive social disorder and low rates of criminality can be resolved if we remember that frequency of illegal behavior is only one variable in the generation of criminal statistics. A second critical component is the level of resources given to the control of such behaviors by political elites. In the case of Bengal, particularly outside Calcutta, there were few resources committed to the control of social disorder. The operating standards of order and their enforcement were largely left to local elites, generally landowners. Nowhere was this more true than with respect to the British landowner. This condition is perhaps best captured by the following excerpts from a set of judicial proceedings, filed in a report to the East India Company in 1810.[2]

The Case of Mr. J. L. Turner

Mr. Turner was indicted for murder. The depositions state that Mr. Turner, having sent peons to seize and bring other royats before him, and having inquired why they had not sown indigo, according to their engagements, Mr. Turner's dewan alleged that the deceased would not sow unless he were punished. On this Mr. Turner struck the deceased several times with his fists and kicked him, and then ordered him and two other royats into the stocks for the night, during which the deceased died. The place where the stocks stood was infested with snakes, and the jury appear to have given credit to the evidence brought forth that the deceased was bitten by a snake, and died in consequence. They acquitted Mr. Turner accordingly.

The Case of Mr. Gardiner

It would appear that his master was not satisfied with his activity, and had him and another seized and brought before him, and punished by stripes with a rattan. . . . He died toward the latter part of the third night after the day he was flogged. The grand jury threw out the bill.

The Case of Mr. T. Clark

Mr. Clark was charged with the murder of a royat. . . . The deceased died the next morning in consequence, as the depositions state, of [the] beating. Verdict, manslaughter; sentence, a fine of 400 Rupees and 12 months imprisonment.

It appears that the behavior of the British toward Indians was regulated only in the most general way. These findings are of direct relavance to the study of the city because the trials all took place in Calcutta's Supereme Court. No European could be tried on any charge in an interior court. Thus it seems likely that the attitudes manifested in the cases just described also characterized interactions across communities in the city.

Although the evidence is far from complete, it appears that the level of disorder within Calcutta itself is similar to that shown by the all-Bengal data: The reported levels of disorder seem low. Within the city all "serious" criminal cases were tried by the Calcutta Supreme Court as a court of original jurisdiction. The reported committals to the court of the years 1833-1842 (Table V.3.4) suggest that serious crimes came rather infrequently to the attention of officials.

Apparently official efforts to control crime in Calcutta exceeded those in rural Bengal. This might be an instance of the general

Table V.3.4 Cases Committed to Trial by the Calcutta Supreme Court, 1833-1842[a]

Year	Cases	Persons	Cases per 10,000 population	Persons per 10,000 population
1833	91	172	4.5	8.5
1834	62	132	2.9	6.3
1835	73	163	3.4	7.6
1836	68	142	3.1	6.4
1837	59	88	2.6	3.8
1838	146	179	6.1	7.5
1839	134	181	5.4	7.2
1840	104	161	4.0	6.2
1841	139	217	5.2	8.1
1842	118	191	4.1	5.9

a. The raw data for the table are taken from Report of the Police, Calcutta, for 1842. The population figures were obtained by averaging population estimates taken in 1831, 1837, and 1851 over the appropriate periods. The population estimates must, of course, be considered with the utmost caution. Commitments are for "serious" crime. A more complete description of what constituted a serious crime is not available. However, the returns of the Supreme Court overestimate the level of criminal prosecution because it also served as a court of original jurisdiction for Europeans charged with criminal offenses anywhere in Bengal.

phenomenon that urban areas have higher rates of criminal behavior. In the present case, however, a much more likely explanation is the difference in the level of penetration of the judicial system, which was clearly greater within the city. Support for this proposition appears in Table V.3.5, which gives the reported cost of maintaining courts within Calcutta and in rural Bengal for the early years of the nineteenth century. Not all the costs of the Supreme Court can be considered an "urban" cost because the court also acted as an appellate court for the rural areas. The narrative evidence suggests, nevertheless, that most cases before the Supreme Court were urban ones. The differential in resources devoted to the two courts remains striking. The Bengal courts, which were supposedly serving 35 million persons, received about five times as much as a court primarily concerned with a jurisdiction of perhaps 500,000. The general trend in the level of expenditures (up for rural areas, down for the city) suggests that the British were in the process of expanding their judicial system in rural Bengal.

Though it is quite likely that the order-maintenance activity of the British was a good deal more intensive in Calcutta than in most of Bengal, we have already observed that the absolute numbers of committals to trial were rather low (cf. Table V.3.4). This can be

Table V.3.5 Index of the Costs of Courts in Bengal and Calcutta, 1792-1809[a]

Year	Supreme Court (Calcutta)	Adawalts (Bengal)
1792	129	
1793 (base year)	100[c]	100[b]
1794	90	115
1795	95	124
1796	74	134
1797	67	124
1798	106	126
1800	92	138
1801	79	131
1802	82	133
1803	82	143
1804	85	163
1805	85	149
1806	87	153
1807	73	
1808	70	
1809	74	

a. Raw data from *Parliamentary Papers,* Report of the Select Committee: 1810.
b. Actual value is £314,766.
c. Actual value is £66,063.

related to earlier descriptions of the physical isolation of the European community from Indians in Calcutta. Behavior in the native areas was of little concern to the European authorities. Just as the European community had insulated itself physically from the Indians, the judicial apparatus served to maintain social distance. This would be consistent with much contemporary research which indicates that police and judicial authorities in certain circumstances adopt a containment strategy. Thus persons of "known disrepute" are not bothered by authorities so long as they stay within "their" neighborhood.[3]

Although it is virtually certain that the low level of British surveillance of Calcutta's Indian areas was a major factor in the low rate of reported crime, most narrative sources suggest that violent crime was fairly uncommon in the city. When violent crime did occur, it was often in the form of an assault on prostitutes to gain the jewelry they were in the custom of wearing. A second major source of social violence lay in the tendency of European sailors to engage in riotous behavior. The police reports of the period mention that attacks on Indians were often considered to be something of a sport on the docks. Armed dacoit attacks of the kind that plagued the countryside were rare in the city itself. However, Europeans were careful not to stray outside the "safe" areas of the town at night. The riverways leading into the city were favorite staging areas for attacks by dacoits on boats moving into and out of the city.

The Evolution of Structures

The Police and the Court: When the British were first granted zamindar rights to the area of Calcutta, they were also charged with the responsibility of maintaining public order. This was, of course, consistent with traditional Indian practice. There was no immediate call for structures to administer either the European or native population. The first publicly supported watch force was not established until 1704. Apparently the force was inadequate, for the following year a British corporal and six soldiers were sent to help reduce the growing level of crime in the city. The zamindar, usually a minor company official, was charged with the administration of justice for Indians, and it appears that the Council of the East India Company acted as a court of Europeans.

In 1726 more permanent institutional arrangements were attempted. The chief merchant of the East India Company was named zamindar, and he served as a court for the Indian population. He was also charged with control of the watch force, which by this time had grown to 143 persons. A night patrol had been established as well. A number of company officials complained to the directors in London that this was an unreasonable expense for the company to assume and argued that the population of the city ought to pay for the watch service. This recommendation was not accepted by the directors. During the same period a mayor's court was established to try Europeans accused of criminal offenses.

The most distinctive aspect of the early institutional arrangements for public order in the city was the distance the British sought to maintain between Europeans and Indians. Much of the jurisdiction of the chief zamindar was traditionally delegated to a native "black zamindar." Gobinram Mitra, who served in the post from 1720 to 1756, was legendary for his ability to engage in graft and corruption.[4] The important consideration for the British, however, was that the natives' problems not weigh on the company's ledger books. By 1753 Indians were not allowed to engage in litigation before the mayor's court.

A second characteristic of these institutions in Calcutta was their diffuse functional character. That is, the process of adjudication, maintaining police, collecting revenues, and providing minimal urban services generally fell to the same governmental office. After Plassey (1757), the major administrative officer of the city, as well as of the newly acquired areas of 24-Parganas, was the collector. This functionary had enormous power; during a reconstruction project in Calcutta in 1760 the incumbent was able to order the impressment of 8,000 men from the interior of Bengal for the project. In 1774 the power of the collector was challenged by the arrival of a royal court in Calcutta, the Supreme Court. The members of the Supreme Court were inclined to view themselves as the ultimate source of authority in Bengal, a proposition that was not well received by either the Council of the East India Company in Bengal or the directors in London. A power struggle resulted in statutory limitations being placed on the Supreme Court by Parliament, which decreed that the administration of justice in the rural areas of Bengal was to remain in the hands of the Company and was to be based on English interpretation of traditional law. Within the city itself, however, the Supreme Court was to have jurisdiction over criminal offenses. The law the court was charged to enforce varied according to both the ethnicity of the defendant and the nature of the accusation that brought the individual before the court. In the case of Europeans, English common law was to be applied. For Indians the relevant body of law varied. Crimes against persons—particularly violent crimes—and generally crimes against property were treated in the context of English law. Crimes against public morality were most often defined by some variety of "traditional" law.

In the nineteenth century a process of structural elaboration and differentiation began in Calcutta. In 1806 three of the justices of the peace were granted magisterial powers. Under the chief magistrate a number of police and judicial departments were set up. From this date minor legal infractions were tried within the misdemeanor and felony departments, but major criminal cases continued to go before the Supreme Court. Within the police there was a similar pattern of structural differentiation. The force was composed of a *thandari* force, boundary police, the town guard, and the river police. The primarily Indian thandari force carried out the general police functions of the city. From 1800 through 1860 a number of Europeans were added to this force to operate within European neighborhoods. The boundary police regulated traffic into and out of the city, the river police maintained order in the river wards of the city, and the town guard was an armed force held in ready reserve. This was how the Calcutta police system was organized until major structural reforms were undertaken by the British in 1866.

Numerous commentators and a number of official studies have reported that the conduct of the police in Bengal and Calcutta left much to be desired. One common charge was that the police obtained confessions through the use of torture. The charge gains credence from the admissions of a number of British officials in Bengal. Challenged on this point in Parliament, the Governor of Bengal admitted that the official policy against the use of torture was not being implemented because, he said, torture was so embedded within Indian tradition. After reviewing attempts to eradicate police torture, the governor concluded:

> It is no wonder, then, that all the influence and exhortations of the British government, though honestly, seriously, and constantly directed to that purpose, have not yet been able to eradicate from the mind of our Indian subjects the notion of its [i.e., torture's] efficacy and expediency.[5]

It was generally accepted by the British that the native population of Bengal did not have a favorable impression of the evolving British legal system. Writing in 1832, the Select Committee on East India frankly concluded, about the Calcutta Supreme Court, that "There is a good deal of dread of this court. They [Indians] seek never to go inside the city so as not to be subject to it. At times blackmail is paid to avoid prosecution."[6] Writing about the Bengal police in 1834, the Governor of Bengal admitted: "The whole of the police is abhorred and detested by the people, who never apply for its aid, and think those most fortunate who [by] circumstances are placed from its influence."[7]

By 1842 the strength of the Calcutta police had grown to 1,838, including sixteen Europeans. A constant problem in expanding the force, however, was the very low wages the East India Company was willing to pay either Indian or European police officers.[8] Throughout the nineteenth century the wages offered the Calcutta police were below those offered manual laborers. A number of early police reports lament the fact that police were forced to accept the city's "scum."

Treatment and Prisons: Consistent with the apparently low levels of crime throughout British Bengal, official sources suggest that the number of persons imprisoned in Bengal was also low. For example, in June 1840 there were only some 18,901 men and 469 women in British jails; these amounts can be compared with the figure of 40,280 convicted for all offenses in 1843 (Table V.3.3). What the official statistics do not capture, of course, is the large-scale reliance on "informal" order maintenance of the type discussed earlier. At any rate, the earlier conclusion that much of Bengal was not greatly affected by the British judicial apparatus is reinforced by this evidence.

Data from earlier years of our next period suggest a very grim picture of Bengal prisons. It is clear that the East India Company was even less interested in diverting resources into prison maintenance than in the establishment of effective police systems. Mortality rates in Indian jails reached staggering levels. As late as 1852 and 1853 the annual mortality rates of the Presidency Jail, to which most native prisoners from Calcutta were probably sent, were 13.3 percent and 13.6 percent, respectively.[9] This compares with a mortality rate of less than two percent in most contemporary British jails. The grim picture of the prisons of this period is further reinforced by a consideration of the punishments commonly used in the jails. A prison report of the 1850s offers a partial list: handcuffs, solitary confinement, stoppage of diet, whipping, leg irons, and iron rings. The conditions in the jails help explain the short sentences commonly given by the British courts. As the next section demonstrates, the sentencing of an individual to a five-or ten-year term approached a capital sentence.

The Development of Criminal Law

At the beginning of the nineteenth century, criminal law throughout Bengal was in a rudimentary state. A basic confusion centered on the British attempt to enforce a variety of "traditional" laws as well as British criminal law. This is not to suggest that the British were always unclear as to the nature of the laws they sought to enforce. A good example is dacoity. The legislation used to control dacoity suggests that while the threshold determining whether or not to regulate a behavior was quite high, the resulting engagement of the British legal system tended to be rather brutal. In the eighteenth century legislation prepared in Calcutta defined dacoity as a capital offense and placed sanctions on the dacoit's entire family. In the nineteenth century district magistrates were authorized to designate a person a "known thief," and on the basis of this designation the individual could be jailed.

One area of concern for authorities in Calcutta was the development of mass communications. The first newspaper in the city was published in 1780. Within a few years the editor had offended so many people that his newspaper was closed, and he was shipped back to England. This pattern was repeated on a number of occasions during the closing years of the century. In 1799 the first comprehensive set of regulations concerning the press was passed. Among its provisions were the following:

1. All published material had to indicate its author.

2. Every editor and printer had to register with the government.

3. No paper could be published on Sunday.

4. All printed material had to be inspected and certified by the government before it could be circulated.

5. There was no appeal for those found in violation of these regulations.

The heart of the press regulations was, of course, the system of prior censorship. Based on the cases with which the authorities were most concerned, it is clear that the aim of the regulations was to enforce homogeneity of political expression in the city.[10]

In 1818 the Bengal administration suspended the provision for prior inspection of all printed material, without limiting the material for which a publisher might be held responsible. This experiment was not highly regarded by the directors of the East India Company. Nevertheless, the change had little impact in the city. In 1835 this liberalizing trend was continued when prohibitions against certain forms of publication were reduced. The authorities' concern about the potentially disruptive nature of newspapers—of the native press in particular—by no means disappeared. Thus the "liberalized" regulations of 1835 provided that nothing should be printed "which might create division in society."

THE ERA OF REFORM, 1840-1870

The years 1840 to 1870 represent a period of transition. The most notable development was the formal demise of the East India Company as the ruling body in British India. In addition, various other aspects of the government were formalized, including the implementation of criminal and civil legal codes. A police structure was established whose general form continues to exist in Calcutta today. The period saw an increasing penetration of the British legal system into Bengal, and reasonably systematic record keeping developed along with the increasing scope of police and judicial activity.

The Levels of Public Disorder

During the middle years of the nineteenth century, several enduring features of crime in Calcutta began to emerge. The most important feature was the extremely low level of "formal" arrests. In 1852, for example, the Calcutta jails held only 1,790 persons. Although information on the social characteristics of violators is quite limited, the available data indicate that crime was largely a male-native phenomenon (Table V.3.6).[11]

During the period 1840-1870 the Calcutta police reported two types of crime: "heinous" and "miscellaneous." The first was broken down into more specific subcategories of offense; the second was not. The primary criterion separating the two was the seriousness of the act. The distinction is similar both to that between cognizable and noncognizable offenses (incorporated into Indian law at a later date) and to the North American distinction between felonies and misdemeanors.

The magnitudes of the various categories of serious crime in the city itself in this era are shown in Table V.3.7.[12] Figures V.3.1 to V.3.4 reveal that levels of the more serious categories of crime tended to increase through the late 1860s, after which there was a rather sharp decline. A similar pattern is evident in the incidence of less serious "miscellaneous" crimes (the term used in the sources), although the peak was reached somewhat later. The peak of reported crime coincides roughly with the famine of 1870, and much of this increase was likely due to attempts to secure food. The general

Table V.3.6   Race and Religion of Offenders in Calcutta Jails, 1852

	Europeans	Hindus	Muslim	Other
Male	312	656	680	44
Female	—	48	38	12

Source: Report of the Police Commissioner, 1852.

Table V.3.7 Serious Crimes Known to the Calcutta Police per
10,000 Population, 1840-1870[a]

	Mean	Maximum	Minimum
Crimes of Individual Violence	.83	2.2	.31
Murder	.11	.19	0
Serious assault	.14	.41	0
Minor assault	.66	1.72	.14
Assaults on public officials	.006	.11	0
Property crimes	67.1	110.4	44.3
Major theft	9.2	13.7	6.6
Minor theft	54.9	72.2	35.6
Fraud	2.3	9.2	.4
Assaults on property	.06	.23	0
Crimes of group violence	.001	.19	0
Group murder	0	0	0
Group assault	0	0	0
Group theft	0	0	0
Rioting	.002	.19	0
Sexual offenses	.17	.45	0
Obstruction of justice	.41	1.58	0
Regulatory offenses	.08	.27	0
Total serious crimes	71.6	112.1	45.0

a. For selected years.

increase in the level of official records of crime in the 1850s and
1860s also suggests, however, that the trend was more than a
response to the extreme stress of famine. Crimes of group violence
and regulatory offenses display a similar increase in the 1860s but
fail to level off in the early 1870s. Neither of these categories of
crime adds much to the total crime rate during this period, though;
as Table V.3.7 shows, both were quite rare.

A more detailed analysis of the data for serious crime reveals that
the reported increase was by no means a general phenomenon;
instead, it was the result of a change in the levels of particular forms
of crime. There was little change in the reported levels of major
violent crimes such as murder and serious assault. There were, however, some increases in the number of minor assaults and very large
increases in the numbers of thefts and frauds. In fact, changes
within the categories of major and minor theft account for the
most significant portions of variance in overall levels of crime in
the city.

Figure V.3.1 Calcutta: Known cases of individual violence per 10,000, 1840-1870

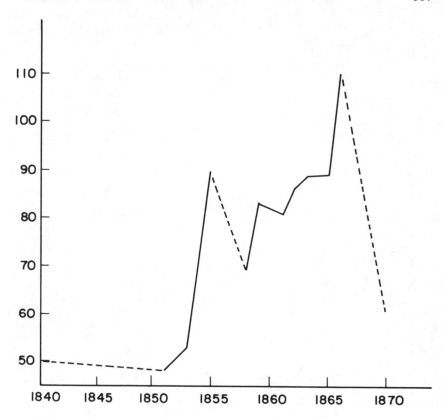

Figure V.3.2 Calcutta: Known property offenses per 10,000, 1840-1870

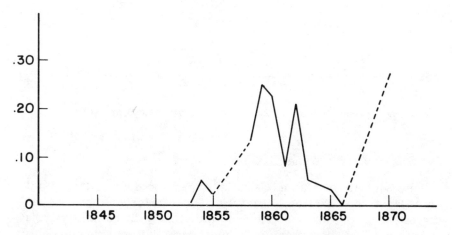

Figure V.3.3 Calcutta: Known "minor" offenses per 10,000, 1840-1870

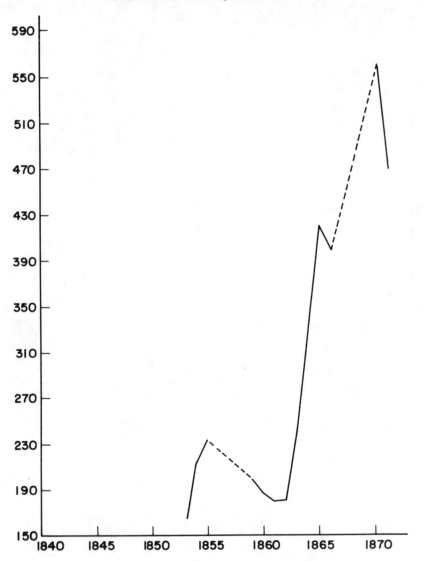

Figure V.3.4 Calcutta: Known "miscellaneous" offenses per 10,000, 1840-1871

Patterns in Violent Crime: A Closer Analysis[13]

Few violent crimes in Calcutta were recorded in the middle decades of the nineteenth century. Those reported, however, are suggestive of the kinds of violence most likely to come to official attention. First, consistent with most cross-cultural criminological findings, victim and assailant tend to be from the same social stratum. For example, in 80 percent of crimes for which there is information, both parties were of the same communal grouping. For European assailants alone, however, the picture is rather different. In almost 40 percent of the cases in which Europeans were charged with violent crimes, their victims were Indians or other non-Europeans. The prima facie interpretation is that the European community directed more violence toward non-Europeans than vice versa.

Another distinctive difference between the European and Indian communities was that European defendants were less likely than Indians to be convicted for major offenses. The data in Table V.3.8 show that almost half the Indian defendants in cases of serious violent crime were charged with murder or attempted murder, whereas this was true of only 23 percent of cases involving a European defendant. There are varied explanations for the differences shown in the table. The "official" explanation is that the European community was less likely than Indians to be involved in the most heinous crimes of violence. Descriptions of specific cases imply that sailors' brawling was the major source of crimes of violence by Europeans, a circumstance that also may help account for the relatively high incidence of assaults by Europeans on Indians. There are, however, at least two major alternatives to the official interpretation. First, British institutions of public order penetrated Indian society less completely than they did European society. One likely consequence is that the weight of British law was brought to bear mainly on the most serious of violent crimes among Indians, and perhaps not all those. Second is the possibility that crimes by Indians were treated more harshly than those by Europeans. We know from the police reports that sentences for Indian prisoners in the Calcutta jails were longer than sentences for European prisoners by ratios of 10: 1;[14] it is quite possible that similar racial discrimination was practiced when charging offenders. Therefore the intercommunal

Table V.3.8 Ethnicity of Persons Accused of Violent Crimes, 1840-1870

	Accused (%)	
Charge	Indians (N=118)	Europeans
Murder	39	23
Attempted murder	9	—
Homicide/manslaughter	25	39
Criminal assault	26	39
		(N=39)

Source: Annual Report of Police Administration in the Town of Calcutta and Its Suburbs.

difference in crimes of violence evident in Table V.3.8 may reflect an indeterminate mix of behavioral reality and differential policies of public order.

To what extent was the legal and judicial system "stacked" against the Indian defendant? There is no definitive answer to this question, but a number of indicators suggest that penalties were differentially applied to defendants. An index of sentences given to defendants in cases of violent crimes was constructed and separately applied to cases involving Indian and European offenders. It showed that the sentences given to Indian defendants were on the average almost 50 percent greater than those given European defendants. [15] A similar pattern of differential sentencing emerges when we compare prison sentences of those convicted of crimes of violence, controlling for the social community of the targets of the violence. There is a clear pattern of harsher sentencing in cases in which the victim was European.[16]

The Evolution of Structures . . . Public Order

Following the Sepoy mutiny in 1857 the East India Company was abolished, and formal responsibility for the administration of British India was vested in Parliament. In 1859 the Code of Civil Procedures was enacted, followed a year later by the Indian Penal Code and, in 1861, by the Code of Criminal Procedures. The Police Act of 1861 established the structures that continue to operate in West Bengal today. The most intense period of structural change of the political system in Bengal also occurred between 1858 and 1861. In many respects the institutional changes that came about during this period were more fundamental than those that accompanied independence nearly a century later.

The Development of Criminal Law

Griffiths observes that three major documents supplied the basis for the operative criminal law in Bengal.[17] The first is the Criminal Code, which defined the entire range of criminal acts. The code explicitly held that British common law was not to be invoked in most cases, and the development of the English legal system in India turned sharply away from that which existed in Britain. In particular, the British in India were henceforth consistently more concerned with explicit codification.

The second "pillar" of Indian law was the Code of Criminal Procedures, which attempted to specify the process whereby police and other judicial officials would implement the Criminal Code. A number of features of the Code stand out. First, it provided a basic distinction between cognizable and noncognizable offenses. Cognizable offenses were the only ones for which a police officer could arrest a person without a warrant. In fact, the police were not allowed to investigate a noncognizable offense without the express order of a magistrate. The code sought to define the powers of the police in the course of investigating an alleged crime, authorizing them to require any person to respond to questions, with the exception of self-incriminating ones. The police were allowed the power of search without a warrant, although the code stated that a warrant should "generally be secured." The code also limited the formal authority of the police to detain a suspect to 24 hours, after which he had to be presented before a magistrate. However, the magistrate might order that the man be held for up to fifteen days while the police continued the investigation. At the end of this period the suspect had to be either charged with an offense or released. [18] These provisions remain in force today.

The Code of Procedures also gave the police a number of "preventive" powers. The first was the requirement that police arrest any person, whether the officer had a warrant or not, if there were grounds to believe that the person was about to engage in a cognizable crime. A much more important section of the code dealt with unlawful assemblies. Under its provisions the officer in charge of any police station could declare any assembly of five or more persons to be "threatening to the public order," thus illegal. This provision became very important in the twentieth century and has been invoked quite often. A third preventive power, also frequently invoked, granted magistrates the power to demand the placement of bonds to guarantee good behavior by individuals. The code authorized a magistrate to demand a bond from a person who was "a habitual robber, thief, forger, receiver of stolen property, or habitually commits cheating, mischief and certain other crimes, or is so desperate and dangerous as to render his being at large hazardous to the community." [19] Once the demand for a bond was made, the individual either had to post the necessary amount or go to jail. The code also provided for judicial review of these cases. Magistrates in the twentieth century began to show reluctance to allow such "bad livelihood" cases, but the provisions were widely used against political prisoners.

The third major source of penal law was the Indian Evidence Act, first passed in 1872, in an attempt to reduce what was believed to be a widespread police practice of forcing confessions from suspects. The major provision of the act prohibited the use of any confession made to the police as evidence in a court of law. The only exceptions were cases in which collaborating evidence existed confirming the validity of the confession, for example when a weapon was produced from information contained in the confession. At any rate, the matter of confessions posed a difficult problem for the Indian courts, and confessions were held in very low esteem.

Within this broad context of developing criminal law, some trends specific to Calcutta emerge. The greatest increases in serious crime were in fraud and various types of theft, but most regulatory statutes were invoked very infrequently.[20] This suggests that regulation of everyday social and economic activities was not of primary interest to the authorities in Calcutta. The number of "miscellaneous" crimes, however, continued to rise. Given the regulatory character of many of these offenses, it appears that the scope of the legal system was expanding. One particularly important new subject of regulation was political expression. In the late 1860s a number of Indian (Hindu) newspapers appeared, politiely expressing the view that Bengal might be governed in ways more beneficial to the Indian. This development was not well received in the European community, whose members often demanded that the native newspapers be better controlled. The Sepoy mutiny strengthened these demands, and after the mutiny an earlier trend toward more liberal press laws, relating in particular to the native press, was reversed.

The Evolution of Structures

The Police: From 1840 to 1860 the general structure of the Calcutta police remained unchanged. Although information is very scant, it appears that the number of persons employed in the Calcutta force actually dropped. The police report of 1842 gives a force size of 1,838, whereas in 1863 there were reported to be only 1,400 police. This is consistent with a general retrenchment of government activities by the East India Company in an attempt to reduce the costs of its Indian civil administration. In 1864 the first metropolitan police force in India was formed in Calcutta, pursuant to enabling legislation. It was responsible for most of the suburbs as well as the city of Calcutta itself. By 1871 this new police force was composed of 3,434 men, including 113 Europeans. The evidence is not clear on this point, but it appears that the increase in manpower was the result of both the amalgamation of the suburban police and an increase in the number of police in the city.

In structural terms the metropolitan police of 1864 provided the basic pattern for the police in Calcutta today. There were and are two noteworthy aspects of the organization. First, the Commissioner of Police of Calcutta was not even formally under the control of the Bengal Inspector General of Police. The existence of two separate police systems in Bengal continued to be a source of controversy throughout the nineteenth century. Repeated attempts to merge the two under a single high-level authority were unsuccessful. A second aspect of the new metropolitan police was the commissioner's position as chairman of the justices, a continuation of the linkage between the city's judicial and police systems. This arrangement also came under a good deal of scrutiny and criticism but remained in effect throughout the nineteenth century.

The public estimation of the police does not seem to have improved very much, either before or after the formation of the metropolitan police. The internal state of the force is suggested by the constant complaints of the police commissioners about extremely high turnover rates in the force. For example, of the 1,400 men on the force in 1863 there reportedly were 800 changes in personnel. At the beginning of the 1870s, the annual turnover rate continued to be well over 50 percent. Complaints about the quality of the police, voiced throughout the nineteenth century, included widespread accusations of police use of torture to gain confessions. That such claims were accepted as accurate in official circles is revealed rather strikingly in the Indian Evidence Act of 1872, which made confessions virtually nonadmissible in a prosecution.

It was the general consensus that the poor state of the police was largely attributable to their very low pay. Throughout the period the wages paid to the native police remained less than the prevailing rates for manual labor, and the police seemed to be more than willing to augment their salaries through bribes and other corrupt practices. A number of police officials admitted that the wages paid to the police barely reached subsistence level. Much the same can be said for the wages paid to Europeans, although their rate of pay was seven to ten times greater than that of the native police. The annual turnover rate for Europeans on the force apparently was even higher than that for natives, generally in the area of 70 percent.[21]

Table V.3.9 Prison Population and Prison Mortality in Bengal

Divison	Prison Population		% Mortality	
	1852	1853	1852	1853
Presidency	1,653	1,607	13.3	13.6
Barracpore	7,460	7,303	7.0	9.1
Dacca	6,641	5,499	7.3	7.1
Dinapore	6,385	6,747	9.3	12.8

Source: Report of the Jails of the Lower Provinces, 1852 and 1853.

Treatments and Prisons: One part of the public order system that was largely unaffected by the numerous structural revisions of the late 1860s was the penal system. Prisons remained largely punitive and primitive, with very few resources devoted to their operation. Mortality continued at very high levels throughout Bengal's prisons but appears to have been worse in the Calcutta jails. Some evidence is given in Table V.3.9. The jail reports themselves attribute the very high level of prisoner mortality to poor sanitation facilities and the meager rations.

THE PRELUDE TO NATIONALIST REVOLT, 1870-1905

As the previous chapter pointed out, the last decades of the nineteenth century were a time of profound change in Bengali society. Change was not immediately manifest in the political and racial conflict that nearly destroyed the city in the twentieth century. Nevertheless, a number of clear and important trends in the level of civil strife became evident.

Patterns of Social Disorder

Perhaps the most important aspect of social order in Calcutta between 1870 and 1905 was the continued lack of civil strife. The major act of political violence was the assassination of the Chief Justice of the Calcutta High Court in 1870. Although it was generally assumed that the assassin had political motivations, the crime was clearly an individual act and was greeted with scorn and disgust in the native sections of Calcutta. However the beginnings of political unrest were surfacing in the city. At the end of the nineteenth century there were a number of street demonstrations demanding greater political authority for Bengalis, but for the most part these were small and peaceful.

A notable change is evident in this period in the components of the overall rate of crimes recorded by the police. The most numerous cognizable offenses are violations of a number of "special laws" applicable only to Calcutta. Their aggregate is referred to in the accompanying figures and tables as "regulatory offenses." The special laws that defined them reflect an official response to growing urban problems and include a variety of public and local nuisance acts, police acts, port acts, and jail acts. At no time between 1870 and 1905 did these regulatory offenses comprise less than 69 percent of all cognizable crimes in the city, and at the highest they constituted 91 percent of all cases. Since the format of the police reports changed at the beginning of this period, there is no basis for direct

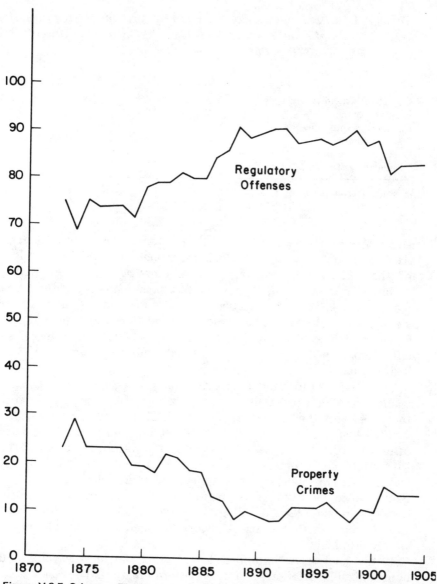

Figure V.3.5 Calcutta: Regulatory and property offenses as percentages of all known cognizable crimes, 1873-1904

comparison of these regulatory offenses with those of earlier periods. Our interpretation is that the high absolute and relative frequency of these offenses, and their detailed presentation in police reports, reflect an increasing concern by officials with such urban problems.

Figure V.3.5 shows the percentages of the total rate of reported crime contributed by the two largest categories, regulatory offenses

*Table V.3.10   Percentage Contribution of Particular Categories of
Crime to the Overall Level of Cognizable Crime,
1870-1905*[a]

Category	Mean	Maximum	Minimum	S.D.
Crimes of individual violence	1.8	.82	4.1	.86
Property crimes	15.3	29.0	8.1	5.8
Crimes of group violence	.06	.13	.01	.03
Sexual offenses	.05	.15	.006	.04
Obstruction of justice	.1	.35	.004	.08
Regulatory offenses	82.7	91.0	68.5	6.6

a. For selected years.

and property offenses. The overall proportion of regulatory offenses
rises until about 1890, then declines, though not to the lowest levels
of the 1870s. For property crimes there is an inverse pattern.
Although not shown in Figure V.3.5, the same inverse pattern holds
for almost all major categories of offenses, including individual
violence, sexual offenses, obstruction of justice, and crimes of group
violence.[22] The absolute proportions of each of these categories of
crime are very different (Table V.3.10), but their trends are strikingly similar.[23]

The 1870s and 1880s apparently were periods of significant
change in public order in Calcutta. Behavior changed less than did
the policies of the authorities, however. The Calcutta police reports
for 1874 and 1893 state that the declining numbers of regulatory
offenses were the result of direct orders from police administrators
to restrain enforcement activities. Indeed, the "overuse" of such
statutes was considered important enough in 1893 to force a redefinition of a number of regulatory laws aimed at controlling
carriages in the streets of Calcutta. The net effect of this legal reform
was to decriminalize some behaviors that had been considered marginally criminal.[24]

If the analysis is extended to cases of the least serious kinds,
noncognizable offenses, a similar pattern emerges. The relative contribution of noncognizable crime to total cases (cognizable and
noncognizable) peaks in 1886, a few years earlier than the peak in
public order offenses. It is important to note that the relative
contribution of noncognizable cases to the total is small. A decline in
the resources of the system of public order is likely first to affect the
number of minor offenses dealt with, and, while there is no direct
evidence to this effect, we suspect that this happened with respect to
noncognizable crimes in Calcutta in the late 1880s.[25]

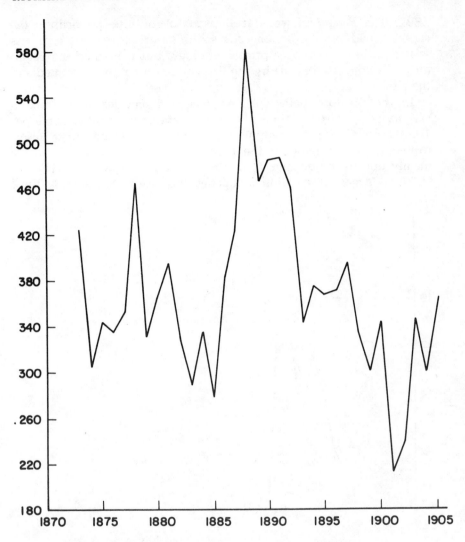

Figure V.3.6 Calcutta: Known regulatory offenses per 10,000, 1873-1905

Although attempts were made throughout the period to reduce the relative effort devoted to enforcing minor regulatory statutes, official control was expanded in another direction not directly revealed by the criminal statistics—namely, censorship of the growing Indian press. The Indian press assumed an increasingly critical attitude toward the British during the latter decades of the nineteenth century, and the first official closure of a Bengali newspaper came in

1891. The *Bangabasi* was not allowed to continue publication because it had printed "numerous seditious articles." This case was settled rather easily by a printed apology, but it marked the beginning of a concerted effort by the British to control the mass media in the city.

In the previous paragraphs we analyzed changes in the mix of various categories of crimes. When the rate of cognizable crime per 10,000 population is examined, we find a downward trend, interrupted by an increase in the early 1890s. The overall decline is mainly due to the decline in numbers of regulatory offenses (Figure V.3.6). Crimes of individual violence increase rather sharply until

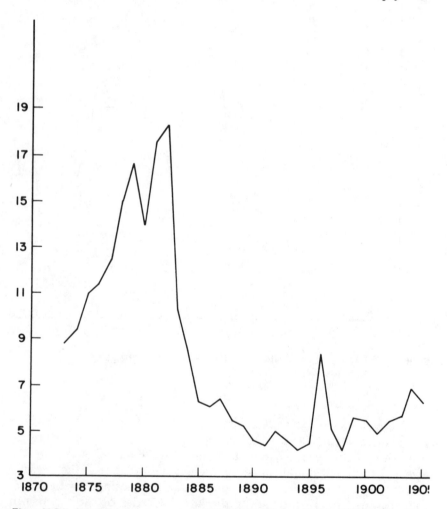

Figure V.3.7 Calcutta: Known cases of individual violence per 10,000, 1873-1905

1882 (Figure V.3.7); the dramatic "improvement" thereafter probably is due to the reclassification of lesser offenses. More detailed
data, not separately graphed, show that the most serious forms of
individual violence increase steadily throughout the period. Property
crimes, on the other hand, manifest a sharp downward trend that
reversed only after the beginning of the twentieth century (Figure

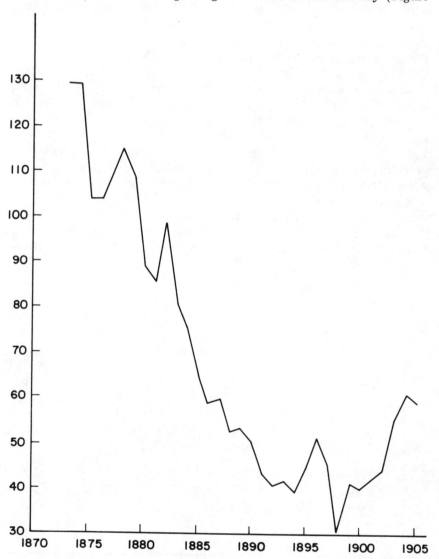

Figure V.3.8 Calcutta: Known property offenses per 10,000, 1873-1905

V.3.8). Other types of serious crime—sexual offenses, obstruction of justice—were relatively stable during the first part of the period and then began steep increases. Crimes of group violence, including dacoity and rioting, were relatively few in number and varied irregularly during the entire period, with a hint of a downward trend (see Figure V.3.9). Thus the general decline in the total rate of cognizable crime in Calcutta in the last part of the nineteenth century is a misleading function of the diminution of official attention being given to regulatory offenses. The rates of a number of more serious crimes, which were much smaller in absolute numbers (see Table V.3.11), increased markedly.

As in the preceding period, the reports of Calcutta's police commissioner for 1871 through 1905 discuss specific violent crimes, but with decreasing detail. Data on criminal assaults, which were surveyed in the reports of 1840 through 1870, were no longer given, and by 1905 only unsolved murders were listed. The practice of providing narrative descriptions of particular crimes also was ended. After 1905 the major narrative sections of the reports tended to focus on civil strife, a telling indication that official concerns had shifted in response to the advent of new forms of disorder. Changes in content of the police reports over time suggest that it is probably dangerous to draw general conclusions based on the data and infor-

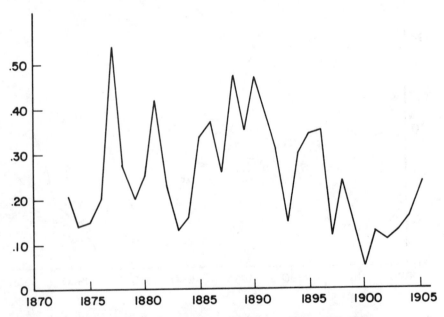

Figure V.3.9 Calcutta: Known cases of group violence per 10,000, 1873-1905

Table V.3.11 Cognizable Crimes Known to the Calcutta Police
per 10,000 Population, 1870-1905[a]

Offense	Mean	Maximum	Minimum	S.D.
Crimes of individual violence	8.2	18.4	4.2	4.2
Murder	.14	.27	.04	.05
Serious assaults	1.5	2.9	.78	.51
Minor assaults	4.9	14.1	2.3	3.4
Assaults on public officials	1.6	4.2	.56	.8
Property Crimes	68.2	129.3	30.3	29.3
Major thefts	.07	.29	0.0	.05
Minor thefts	60.1	119.9	27.4	26.9
Fraud	7.2	19.4	2.6	3.7
Assaults on property	.006	.06	0.0	.01
Crimes of group violence	.26	.54	.05	.13
Group Murder	.004	.05	0.0	.011
Group assault	.007	.07	0.0	.015
Group thefts	.002	.035	0.0	.007
Rioting	.24	.54	.02	.13
Sexual offenses	.2	.6	.03	.17
Obstruction of justice	.47	2.0	.01	.42
Regulatory offenses	370.1	580.6	214.8	74.7
Total cognizable cases	447.4	639.6	263.0	79.6

a. For selected years.

Table V.3.12 Communal Variations in Charging Patterns, 1870-1905

Charged	Indian (N=233)	European[a] (N=32)
Murder	.55	.41
Attempted murder	.20	.16
Homicide/murder	.25	.44

a. Does not add to 1.00 because of rounding error.
Source: Data compiled from Annual Report of Police Administration in the
Town of Calcutta and Its Suburbs.

mation presented in them. Some such conclusions are drawn in the
following analysis, but their uncertain validity should be kept in
mind.

Much of the particular information contained in the police reports
is consistent with the more complete data available from 1840 to
1870. Violent crime still is generally intracommunal rather than
intercommunal, as measured by the crude indicator of the relative
proportion of violent crimes involving European versus European,
Indian versus Indian, and European versus Indian. In only five
percent of cases were victim and attacker of different communal
groups. As before, the probability of a European aggressor selecting

an Indian victim was much greater than that of an Indian attacking a European. In almost 27 percent of the cases in which Europeans were identified as the attacker, the victim was an Indian. Only five percent of attacks by Indians were directed at Europeans.

A second pattern in violent crime that continues from the earlier period is the tendency for Indian defendants to be charged with more serious offenses than Europeans when arrested for a violent crime. This is apparent from the data in Table V.3.12, which also suggest that the pattern of differential sentencing continued. This conclusion is reinforced by comparison of prison sentences, which indicate that Indian defendants received sentences almost 50 percent longer than those given to Europeans. The sources of these differentials remain unknown: They reflect some combination of differential behavior between the Indian and European communities, differential policing, and discriminatory charging and sentencing practices.

No less significant than the changing pattern of criminal behavior and official policy during this period is the concurrent change in the population accused of criminal behavior. Data about the religious backgrounds of criminal offenders are available beginning in 1870, at which time Muslims were overrepresented among offenders. Fully 54 percent of all the persons in Calcutta jails were Muslim, though they comprised only 30 percent of the city's population. Less than 40 percent were Hindus. By 1903, the last year in which these data were published, the two communities had exchanged positions: 39 percent of the prisoners were Muslims, and 56 percent were Hindus. The proportion of Europeans in prison declined through most of the period. We can suggest two complementary interpretations to the changing communal composition of Calcutta's jail population, although both would require a verification of more complete data. The growth of nationalism, which occurred principally among the Hindu population, may have provoked more Hindus to challenge colonial laws. The same circumstance may also have made the authorities more attentive to Hindu crimes. The most likely explanation is that both hypotheses are valid.

Institutions of Public Order

The most fundamental constraint on the British legal and judicial system in Bengal during the late nineteenth century was its lack of funds. Thus the colonial administrators had the same problem experienced by the East India Company in the first half of the century. One consequence is the condition we have repeatedly noted, namely, that the low level of reported crime in Calcutta was due at least as much to British decisions about the apportionment of very limited resources as it was to the "law-abiding" behavior of the native Bengalis. The effects of limited resources on each institution can be examined in turn.

The Police: Few colonial institutions received as much attention as the police in official studies by the Bengal government. From the time the British assumed official responsibility for the governance of India through 1905, no fewer than six major studies of the police in Bengal were undertaken, and these often were made with particular reference to Calcutta.[26] In general, almost all the study groups denounced the state of the police forces throughout the province. Although recommendations varied among study commissions, consensus existed that the police offered little protection for anyone. The charge of corruption was nearly universal and was often accepted by police officials with the declaration that such a situation seemed inevitable with police wages below subsistence level.[27] Although the rural police appear to have been worse than their urban colleagues, there were few if any words of praise for the Calcutta police.

Despite widespread official criticism of the urban police system, its resources were not increased. To the contrary, the level of institutional support dropped during most of the last three decades of the nineteenth century. This is evident in the number of men on the Calcutta police force and in the amount of money spent in maintaining it. In 1886 the cost of the police was some Rs 13,010 per year per 100,000 population. By 1899 the figure had dropped to Rs 9,500 per 100,000 population. Similarly, in 1866 there were 44 police per 100,000 persons, but by 1899 there were only 35 per 100,000. This lack of support can be traced to a number of factors within the city itself. First of all, the apparent lack of crime meant that there was no convincing demand for more complete or extensive protection. Those most adversely affected by the ineffectiveness of the police, the native Indians, were in a poor position to make demands on the European-dominated political system.

A second long-standing characteristic of the city has been resistance by those with wealth or social position to use their wealth or power to support programs of social benefit. From a very early date, Calcutta's economic elite displayed either inability or unwillingness to tax their own wealth.[28] Throughout this period the principle was applied to various civic improvement schemes as well as to the police. As Ch. V.2 illustrated, there were very few "urban services" during this period.

At the turn of the century many of these trends were reversed. By 1905 expenditures on police had increased to 10,600 Rs per 100,000 persons. Although there was no immediate increase in the number of men on the force, the 30-year downward trend in resources clearly had ended. One cause of the reversal was the rise in crime rates in almost every major category, which seems to have led to some popular demand for an improved police force. Just after the turn of the century, an equally important factor in Calcutta was the stirring of a strong and increasingly militant nationalist movement. By 1905 Calcutta had been the site of a number of street demonstrations that had political connotations. Such events had been unknown during the years that were coming to be remembered as the tranquil 1880s and 1890s. The importance of the police in the evolving strategy to contain what the British viewed as a dangerous politican development is illustrated by the extension of police responsibility to a number of new regulatory areas. The most important of these areas was the censorship of a variety of mass media.

The Courts: Two major courts operated in the city. All major criminal offenses were tried by the Calcutta High Court; minor offenses—by far the majority of all criminal violations—were disposed of by some type of magistrate's court. As indicated in the police reports, the level of judicial activity declined throughout the nineteenth century. The number of cases tried in magistrates' courts in 1880, approximately 710 per 10,000 population, had declined by 1900 to about 275 per 10,000. A similar trend existed in the High Court, where rates per 10,000 dropped from their 1880 high of about 1.0 to less than one-tenth of that in 1900.

Consistent with the decline in cases before the courts was a sharp drop in the level of punishments assigned in the various courts. For example, an index of the revenue brought in from fines in the magistrates' courts is correlated - .74 with the passing of the years in the period. [29] After 1900 there was an upturn in court activity, particularly in the High Court, where the number of cases increased rather quickly. However, by 1905 per capita rates were not nearly as high as those of the 1880s.

One important aspect of the political system in Bengal, which by the end of the nineteenth century was under constant criticism from the Bengalis, was the bias of the judicial system toward the protection of European defendants. It will be remembered, for example, that Europeans throughout Bengal could be brought to trial only in the High Court of Calcutta (which replaced the Supreme Court in 1862). In addition, Europeans had the right to demand juries composed completely of Europeans, whereas Indians had no comparable right. Interestingly, at the beginning of this period the conviction rate for European defendants was very high, about 78 percent, but it declined sharply thereafter. By 1905 the rate was under 45 percent.

Despite the apparent trend in the conviction rate, it ought to be pointed out that in no year were there more than 290 cases involving Europeans.[30]

The data concerning European defendants are susceptible to different interpretations. But whatever else they reflect, it surely can be concluded that the judicial system in Calcutta and throughout Bengal favored Europeans over Indians.

The Prisons: The British disinclination to spend money on public order in India is nowhere more clearly revealed than in the conditions of the prisons. Jails were large, overcrowded barracks in which scant attention was given to sanitation and prisoner well-being. In most of the years under study, mortality rates were high enough to suggest that even a moderate prison sentence could easily result in the death penalty. The average mortality rate (around six percent) was generally admitted to be far higher than that of the general population.

The jail system, like the Bengal police, was the subject of a number of critical studies. Often these investigations took the form of critical commentaries from the surgeon general suggesting that the conditions in the jail ought to be improved to at least a minimum level of healthiness. More often than not the British officials offered the countertheory that the extraordinary mortality was not caused by the conditions of the jails at all but occurred because "persons of poor quality" were placed in the prisons. Writing in 1878, the Lieutenant Governor of Bengal responded to a charge that the conditions in the jails were resulting in the deaths of convicts. The report read:

> The Lieutenant Governor doubts whether our knowledge of the cause and origin of disease is yet sufficiently developed to justify such a conclusion. He has noticed that the highest death rate is not in the most crowded jails or those considered to be the most defective from a sanitary point of view. Much of the mortality in the jails is beyond doubt attributable to the fact of imprisonment alone. Criminals in all countries are men of short lives and many die in jails engendered by the dissolute lives they have led before their convictions.[31]

It is abundantly clear that there was little thought of rehabilitation within Indian jails: They were defined and maintained as punitive institutions. A number of officials argued that the conditions ought not be improved because prison might then be too "pleasant." In fact, officials often suggested that the jails already might be too well developed. The Lieutenant Governor of Bengal in 1881 remarked in a conclusion to the annual Report on Jails that Indian jails were "palatial palaces when compared with native huts."

The extremely punitive orientation of the British prison is perhaps best illustrated by the manner in which discipline was enforced. Authorities used corporal punishment, penal diets, solitary confinement, handcuffs, and fetters. Indeed, reliance on these rather primitive treatments seemed to increase between 1870 and 1905, as did the relative proportion of physical to other punishments. For example, the use of solitary confinement and reduced diet rose from three to more than ten percent of the total number of punishments administered. The use of handcuffs and corporal punishment similarly rose.

Treatment favoring Europeans is evident in the administration of the prisons as well as in charging and sentencing. For example, corporal punishment was much less used for European prisoners, and there were tremendous differentials in the cost per prisoner of maintaining people in prisons. For 1882-1883 the expenditure data show that the Presidency European jail had expenditures per inmate which were 4.6 times the expenditures at Presidency North, which was strictly a native institution.

NOTES TO CHAPTER V.3

1. Cited in W. R. Gourlay, *A Contribution to the History of Police in Bengal* (Calcutta: Bengal Secretariat Press, 1916).

2. Judicial Proceedings of the East India Company, 1810.

3. For example, see James Q. Wilson, *Varieties of Police Behavior* (New York: Atheneum, 1970).

4. N. K. Sinha, *History of Bengal.*

5. *Parliamentary Papers 1854-1855*, Vol. 40, paper 183, p. 541.

6. Report of the Select Committee, *Parliamentary Papers, 1831-1832*, Vol. 8, paper 734, p. 7.

7. Cited in Gourlay, op. cit.

8. In 1842 the total cost of the police in Calcutta was Rs 10,639. This included Rs 9,841 for the Indian branch of the force and Rs 798 for the European branch. On a per capita basis, the European force was ten times as expensive to maintain.

9. Taken from the Report on Jails, 1853.

10. Report of the Select Committee on the Calcutta Journal, *Parliamentary Papers, 1833.*

11. In general, early police and judicial reports did not devote any attention to the race or religion of offenders. One exception was the Report of the Police Commissioner, 1852, which is the course of these data.

12. Beginning in 1864 the police of Calcutta were responsible for a number of suburban areas as well as the city itself. However, data for the suburbs are not introduced until analysis of the post-1870 period because until then data for the suburban areas were scattered.

13. The data for this section were collected from various police reports, 1840-1870. During these years it was the habit of the police commissioner to present a brief narrative on serious violent crime in the city. However, the criteria for a "serious assault" were never explicated in the reports.

14. The Report of the Police Commissioner, 1852, points out that the average prison sentence of Indians in Calcutta jails was 4,447 days. The average sentence for European prisoners was 447 days. The reports of the East India Company cited in the last section also lend credence to the notion that Indians were treated much more harshly than were Europeans for similar offenses.

15. The index was constructed from the following formula:

Average Sentence = (number of sentences less than five years) +
(number of sentences greater than five years) +
(number of sentences of transportation) +
(number of sentences of execution)

The index was computed over all violent crimes for Indian and European communities separately.

16. It could be argued that much of the sentencing differential is based on the difference in charging procedures. That is, the differentials in sentencing may add no additional evidence to the charge that the judicial system was weighted heavily against Indians.

17. Strictly speaking, the code of Criminal Procedures was not applied to Calcutta. For details see Percivel Griffiths, *To Guard My People: The History of the Indian Police* (London: Ernst Benn, 1971).

18. Once charged with an offense, a person could be held until his trial.

19. Griffiths, op. cit., p. 150.

20. The police report for 1842 states that there were 358 and 625 conservancy cases (a principal class of regulatory offense) in 1841 and 1842, respectively. The "miscellaneous" cases charged under the penal law, which seem to consist mainly of regulatory offenses, totaled 2,595 in 1842.

21. These data are offered in various police reports.

22. The categories are not defined because, except for the regulatory offenses, they are self-explanatory. The sexual offenses consist almost entirely of rapes, very few of which came to official attention. The concern with homosexuality and prostitution, which was intense in most European societies in this period, was entirely absent in Calcutta in the nineteenth and twentieth centuries.

23. There were no reported assaults on property until the mid-1890s. From this point, the incidence of such offenses follows the general trend.

24. The 1874 figure for minor offenses was also reduced as a result of changes in the regulations concerning shipping in Calcutta's harbor.

25. As the general summary showed, the resources devoted to the prosecution of noncognizable crime were very small when measured by indicators such as numbers of persons taken to trial and numbers of persons convicted.

26. The major source for a discussion of these various reports, most of which have not survived, is Gourlay, op. cit.

27. Gourlay, op. cit.

28. Writing in 1970, Meier, op. cit., has made a similar complaint.

29. Particular indices we examined included number of cases in magistrates' courts, number of cases in High Court, number of fines assigned in magistrates' court, index of sentence length assigned in magistrates' court, index of prison sentence assigned in High Court, and number of whippings assigned in magistrates' court.

30. Perhaps even more striking is the scarcity of serious crimes charged to Europeans. Cases involving murder, assault, and similar offenses were in no year more than three percent of the total number of cases charged against Europeans.

31. *Report of the Jails of the Lower Provinces*, 1873.

CRIME, CONFLICT, AND
PUBLIC ORDER
The Twentieth Century

FROM THE BIRTH OF NATIONALISM TO INDEPENDENCE

Civil Strife, 1906-1947

The years from 1906 to 1947 were a strife-torn, violent epoch in Calcutta, worse than any other era in its history.[1] Few other cities of the twentieth century have experienced such protracted conflict over so many issues—political, economic, and communal. In the early years of the period agitation for independence became increasingly common throughout Bengal, and by the middle 1940s many areas of the province were in open rebellion against the British. Cyclical waves of revolutionary violence in the city were followed by similar waves of British oppression and mass arrests. The city was also swept by large-scale episodes of communal strife and numerous violent labor agitations. As might be expected, these issues of conflict were seldom distinct but tended to merge with one another. Since the general history of the period has already been reviewed, we now consider in more detail the principal civil disorders that occurred in the city during these years. The next section analyzes crime and its relation to collective conflict.

The first instances of collective disorder in the twentieth century belong by date to the previous chapter but are discussed here because they foreshadow the deeper, "modern" conflicts of the coming decades. The civil order of the opening years of the twentieth century was briefly disrupted by two strikes, both expressing griev-

559

ances against police actions. In 1901 there was a general strike of the cart and hackney drivers. One of their major complaints was alleged harassment and extortion by the police in the application of the various municipal acts that regulated hackneys. In 1904 the Marwari dock merchants went on strike in protest over a police decision to remove their wares from the footpaths. Settlements were reached in both cases when the police were instructed not to be overzealous in enforcing the law.[2]

The age of mass agitational politics came to Calcutta in 1905 with the announcement of the final plans for the partition of Bengal. As we have seen, the response of many Bhadralok leaders was to call for a boycott of all British goods until the partition was revoked. In Calcutta the result of this call was impressive. The Marwari commercial community, which controlled much of the wholesale distribution of goods in Calcutta, endorsed the boycott. In addition, there were numerous strikes and labor disturbances throughout the city. This show of support, however, turned out to be very short-lived: "Yet, while the Congress leaders were involved and workers did shout about 'Bande Mataram,' the strikes were inspired more by economic and work grievances than a dislike of the partition. By the end of 1905, the first round of strikes had ended."[3]

Although there were complaints about the excessive demands made on the police, the first year of the boycott seems to have passed without a great deal of violence in the city. One of the minor consequences was an apparent decline in the level of petty crime; officials in fact, were reluctant to divert time and resources to such matters, given the high degree of unrest in the city. In addition, the police faced security problems posed by a visit of the Prince of Wales—a visit of some historical interest because of its influence on the future King's conclusion that the partition was a mistake.

As the boycott weakened through 1907, the rhetoric in its favor began to increase in intensity. The police commissioner reported that 1907 had been marked by "a good deal of radical agitation." A number of overtly political arrests were made, including ten prosecutions for seditious speech. On October 2, 1907, the police were greeted with a shower of rocks and sticks when they attempted to disperse an antipartition rally. For the next three days police were subject to such attacks throughout the city, although the most intense attacks were in North Calcutta. The (mixed) evidence suggests that the police, tiring of constant molestation, decided to take private action against the Bengalis. What ensued was essentially a police-directed riot in which a number of upcountrymen and urban goondas were prodded by the police to attack Bengalis and their property. The exact involvement of the police in the affair is not known, but substantial evidence indicates that at the very least widespread looting occurred in the presence of the police and no action was taken. In the affray one Bengali was reported killed. An investigation decided simply that the man had been killed by persons unknown. A later report by the police blamed the entire affair on the criminal classes.[4]

The violent and tense atmosphere of the city continued through 1908. In November of that year the police raided a home bomb factory, and the informer who had made the raid possible was subsequently murdered in the Calcutta jail. In addition, a senior Calcutta deputy magistrate, who had been assigned to a well-known bombing case that had occurred outside the city, died after nitric acid was thrown in his face. Later in the year an attempt was made on the life of the Lieutenant Governor of Bengal as he entered the city.[5] In 1909 political violence declined, although a prosecutor was shot and killed in open court while engaged in a trial concerning political bombing.

In 1910 the city was struck by a very different kind of violence, that of communal conflict. Early in the year Marwari businessmen had become concerned with the increasingly hostile attitude of the Muslim community, with whom they shared the area of Calcutta known as Burra Bazar.[6] They began to hire numerous guards and goondas to protect their property. An isolated fight set off a clash that lasted until elements of the British army were called into the city. The communal tension that nearly destroyed the city in 1946 had begun, although the hostilities associated with this early outburst seem to have been basically economic.

The British began to move strongly against nationalistic terrorism in 1908 and were largely successful in reducing its level. However, in 1910 a police inspector whose major responsibility was the control of political crime was murdered. The following year the superintending engineer of the Writer Building was the target of a bomb that failed to explode. The pace of the terrorist attack picked up again in 1914 with assassination attempts, one successful, on two inspectors in the political branch of the Calcutta police. A number of parcel bombs were found to be in circulation, although their quality was such that they did little damage. One could view all these events as precursors of the storm of violence that was to hit the city in 1915.

The year 1915 saw a spectacular increase in the level of political crime. There evolved an unprecedented form of motor dacoity in which robbers struck and escaped by motor car. Six such dacoities occurred in 1915. The stakes were large, with robberies of Rs 18,000 and Rs 19,000 reported. It is likely that much of these funds was channeled into the revolutionary underground to supply guns, munitions, and other materiel needed in the "war" against the British.[7] A second feature of these robberies was an increasing reluctance of those who were victimized to offer aid to the authorities. It is likely that the noncooperation was based on fear rather than growing Bengali nationalism. Nevertheless, the ability to create such fear points to the growing strength of the terrorist movement in the city. In addition to the various dacoities, four police assassinations were attributed to Bengali terrorists. The response of the British to this outburst was much the same as in 1908. Repressive legislation was drafted and applied in the city, and the police reported in 1916 that the recent outbreak of disorder was well under control.

During the next few years political violence declined in the city. Through 1918 there were no more assassination attempts, nor were any dacoities reported. Generally it was believed that the transformation was due to strict enforcement of the Defence of India Act. The extent to which a revolutionary situation had prevailed in previous years was officially acknowledged in 1918 in a report documenting that between 1906 and 1918 there had been more than 200 "political outrages" in the province of Bengal.[8] The report concluded that the British faced a well-developed revolutionary conspiracy:

> Our examinations of the cases have impressed us of the alliance and interconnectiveness of these groups, formed into one revolutionary movement with one common object, viz, the overthrow of His Majesty's government in India by force. All the individual cases stand out as interconnected parts of a whole, which they form, both as to the personnel, and as to the acts of crime, one continuous movement of revolution, which must be regarded as living and prolonged in all its parts until the movement is completely extinguished.[9]

Although the level of violence had declined, police continued to discover stores of arms and explosives and to intern suspected political agitators. Thus, although the level of violence was at a low point, the British had little cause to be optimistic about the long-range prospects for civil order.

If revolutionary activity was at low ebb in 1918, communal conflict reached a new high. The history of tension between Hindus and Muslims was reviewed in Ch. V.2, and reference was made to the Lucknow Pact of 1916, which attempted to resolve political differénces between the two communities. In Bengal, however, both Hindus and Muslims were convinced that its provisions were unfair, and throughout 1918 agitators from both groups stirred up opposition. The Islamic newspapers in Calcutta made a particular issue of the fact that Muslims elsewhere in India had been physically attacked, arguing that security could be had only by preparing for self-defense. Into this tense atmosphere a Muslim paper introduced the charge that a Hindi paper had made a derogatory remark about the Prophet. This inspired a large and angry public meeting several days later, at which a call was issued for an all-India meeting of Muslims in Calcutta to protest their allegedly inferior status.

Plans for the proposed meetings were made throughout August, and it became evident that the gatherings would be in the control of Muslim extremists. Finally the more moderate Muslim leaders joined Hindus in asking that the government forbid the meetings. By early September most Muslim leaders had agreed that the rally ought not be held. On September 8 a large crowd gathered but dispersed on being told that the leadership was still negotiating with the British. Another crowd formed on the following day and tried to march on the Government Building. The procession was finally turned back by armed Calcutta police, but the marchers returned to the neighborhood that many of them shared with a number of Marwari businesses. Fearing damage to their property, the Marwari once again called out a number of armed guards to clear away the crowd from their warehouses. Some blows were exchanged, and the police were called. Greeted by a barrage of bricks, the police responded with gunfire. Soon much of the city was caught up in rioting and looting that continued for three days, until the British army was called in to reestablish control. In all 490 persons were arrested; scores were killed or injured.

The rioting of 1918 represented a new development in Calcutta politics. There had been communal riots in the past, though not as extensive; this was the first time that communal unrest had been stimulated for political purposes. The rioting made it clear that extreme talk could bring extreme responses in the city. It also demonstrated that the Muslims of Bengal—like the Bengalis almost twenty years before—were increasingly disposed to take uncompromising positions. In the aftermath of the riots, the potential for intercommunal cooperation in the future seemed slight.[10]

An apparent increase in criminal behavior in 1918 was attributed by the authorities to a number of factors. One was economic: The cost of living had gone up without a similar rise in wages. In point of fact, the economy of Calcutta was in a rather severe postwar recession. The police also cited the return to the city of a large number of men who had been prisoners during World War I, especially those from disbanded labor gangs in rural Bengal. Reference also was made to the general atmosphere of the city and to the "wild radical press." Problems of public order were especially pronounced in Calcutta's troublesome north end. The practice of Marwaris in the Burra Bazar area of hiring armed goondas was a chronic source of tension, and according to police reports, many of the goondas were involved in illegal activity. Toward the end of 1918 the police mounted a campaign against the goondas, sweeping through the area a number of times and arresting their leaders and "other known criminals."

Nationalists' activity in the years following the war began to take new forms, as they discovered that strikes were a useful means of opposing British rule. There were a number of very small strikes in 1919, none of them politically consequential, and at the beginning of 1921 there was a walkout of taxi drivers and drivers of personal cars. This was followed by a much more serious strike of the Calcutta tramway workers, lasting from January 27 to February 14. When the Calcutta Tramway Company attempted to utilize Anglo-Europeans as strikebreakers, a violent confrontation occurred between the strikers and would-be strikebreakers. The police were called in a police firing ensued in which one striker was killed. The police also were assigned to guard the company's property throughout the city against the attacks to which it had been subject during the strike. The strikers returned to work on the understanding that there would be further negotiations; these talks failed, however, and the strike resumed on October 25 and lasted into November.[11]

Simultaneously with the tramway strike, the Indian National Congress launched the swadeshi movement.[12] Once again the city was enmeshed in the tactics of boycott: Shops that did not cooperate with the boycott risked looting or burning, and their owners were subject to physical abuse. Rising political tension reached a critical level in late November when the All-India Congress Committee called for nationwide civil disobedience. The dangers facing the British were compounded because, at least at the all-India level, there was once again a tenuous alliance between Muslim and Hindu nationalists.[13] Thus, as the Prince of Wales (the future George V) landed in Bombay on his long-awaited goodwill tour of India, a total hartal, or general strike, was called in Calcutta. Broomfield describes the result:

> All shops were closed and no private or public transport was allowed to move in the streets. The police lost control of the city to the volunteer brigades, but they in turn found they were unable to manage the gang of factory labourers who had been brought into the city from the outlying mills by the Khilafatists. Assisted by Goondas, these gangs looted shops, molested pedestrians and in South Calcutta fought a pitched battle with the police.[14]

The British authorities knew that if the Calcutta hartal were not quickly broken up, the visit of the Prince of Wales would have to be postponed. This the British fervently hoped to avoid. More important, however, the British saw a challenge to their government of unknown but serious magnitude in the civil disobedience movement. Consistent with past policy, the British chose a strategy of rapid and decisive repression. All public meetings were banned. The head-quarters of both the Congress and the Khilafat committee of the Muslim community were raided and their leaders arrested. The trans-portation strike was broken, and the trams moved again under armed guard. Every attempt to protest the banning of public meetings was met with massive arrests. The once-successful tactic of placing women and children at the head of processions to forestall arrests proved to be of little value. Suspected goondas were rounded up and held under a variety of vague charges, often that of "bad liveli-hood."[15] To aid the police during this period, a civilian Calcutta guard composed of European residents was established.

The British imposition of repressive policies in Bengal set in motion a now-familiar pattern. In the short run political order was restored to the city. The much more important effect of this clash between the British authorities and Bengali nationalists, however, was a final collapse of the Bengali moderates who saw a possibility of working with the British. The British response had other results that paralleled earlier sequences of events. For example, as the level of disorder dropped in Calcutta, there was an apparent increase in such disorder in rural Bengal. It was this rising level of disorder in rural areas that led Gandhi in 1922 to call off the civil disobedience movement. As in the earlier periods, those arrested by the British underwent a period of socialization and radicalization in British jails. In fact throughout the 1920s the British were plagued with protests, many of them violent, within their jails.

As the Swaraj party moved toward its sweeping election victories in 1923, the Bengali terrorist movement again began to assert itself in the city. Police announced the discovery of an organization they called "Red Bengal," whose program was described as the systematic execution of police. In 1924 an attempt on the life of the police commissioner failed because a confused assassin killed the wrong man. The political ends of the Swaraj party were reached in that year, however, as the British were forced to suspend the constitution. The Swaraj party had by then become so radicalized that there appeared to be general support of the Bhadralok elements of the party for the terrorists. Citing a number of party resolutions that suggested as much, the British arrested most of the Swaraj leadership in 1924. Several members of the Bengal Legislative Council were interned in Calcutta.

As the level of Hindu violence against the British increased, the always-shaky alliance between Hindus and Muslims began to totter.

Although events brought tension between the two communities to a new peak throughout Bengal, the situation was especially bad in Calcutta. On April 2, 1926, the musicians in a Hindu religious procession passing a mosque were asked by the Muslims within to cease. All did so except a single drummer. The Muslims took this as a challenge and pelted the procession with debris, precipitating a series of riots that engulfed the city for two weeks. Rioting centered in North Calcutta, where numerous temples and mosques were destroyed along with much other property. The principal weapon of the rioters was the lathi, a stout stick used as a club; 50 were killed and more than 700 injured. The rioting stopped only after British troops using automatic weapons and armored cars occupied the city.

Scarcely a week later, on April 24, a drunken brawl in North Calcutta spread rapidly into another riot. This time firearms were widely used, and the ranks of the rioters were swelled by goondas who again had been brought in from rural Bengal by worried property owners. The police reported that this second wave of riots involved more extensive looting and property damage than the first. It was also more deadly: 70 persons were reported killed and more than 400 injured. Once again the army had to be called in to restore order. Calcutta's paroxysm of violence was not yet over, for late in July there was another ten-day series of riots, followed by a fourth episode in September.

The inability of municipal authorities to forestall or even control rioting in 1926 is evidence of the breakdown of city administration. The British administration was also more directly under attack by political terrorists. A special superintendent of police was assassinated in the Alipore Jail while attempting to interview persons convicted of possessing explosives, and throughout the year the police made many raids seeking explosives and firearms.

The attempt of the British to divide Bengali Hindus and Muslims at the provincial level had dramatic impact on the level of disorder in Calcutta. Although the levels of civil strife in the city varied from year to year, there was to be no real reduction in intercommunal tension until after independence—if then. The tone of the communal press was particularly vitriolic after the 1926 riots, and the British soon reinstituted strict regulations on all religious processions in the city. The aim was a simple one—to keep Muslims and Hindus separate. The city authorities had some success in reducing the level of violence between Calcutta's communal groups but not in controlling political terrorism. The Bhadralok of Calcutta were intensely frustrated by political developments in the province as a whole, and one consequence was a sharp increase in attacks on the British. There were numerous politically motivated dacoities and a rash of assassinations. In 1928, for example, an attempt was made on the life of the police commissioner, and the Superintendent of Prisons for Bengal was killed.

Labor unrest provided variety if not respite for the authorities. In 1927 a general strike by employees of the Calcutta Port Commission, accompanied by scattered violence, closed both the docks and jetties. A general strike in Howrah, Calcutta's industrial suburb on the Hooghly's west bank, was broken the following year only after a police firing. These strikes often had political overtones, as in 1928 when a general hartal was called to coincide with the arrival in Calcutta of the British Statutory Commission, which was to rewrite the constitution governing India. The hartal was marked by large-scale violence and, as in 1926, was controlled only by military occupation. In 1929 a general strike in the jute mills paralyzed that industry for much of the year. The Calcutta carters and transport workers struck to protest a new set of regulations concerning the treatment of animals. The strike was broken after a police firing. Shortly thereafter the police made mass arrests in a successful effort to forestall a general strike that had been proposed to protest the firings.

In 1930 Gandhi called for a new wave of civil disobedience, and one response was a fresh surge of political violence in the city. In that year the Inspector General of Police for Bengal was assassinated, and two attempts were made on the life of Charles Tegart, commissioner of the Calcutta police. In 1931 Edgar Villar, president of the European Association, was murdered by terrorists, and Alfred Watson, editor of the British *Statesman*, had two narrow escapes. British governmental buildings were bombed, and the police continued to be preoccupied with uncovering plots and arresting Indians for possession of guns and explosives. As in the past, the British enacted repressive legislation, in this case the Bengal Criminal Amendment of 1930.[16]

1. Provision for preventive detention of "known" revolutionaries.

2. A mechanism by which "subversive" organizations could be outlawed. The major target of this feature of the law was, of course, the Congress.

3. Provision that property held by banned organizations would fall to the government.

4. Provisions requiring persons considered to be "probable" trouble-makers to register with the police.

One of the first applications of the act was the outlawing of the Bengal Congress. The Congress nonetheless attempted to proceed with a party conference in Calcutta, and 200 of its members were arrested. In anticipation of a similar attempt of 1933, the police detained 930 persons and served orders on 4,017 others forbidding them to participate in any event related to the civil disobedience movement. A meeting was attempted again in 1934 and was dispersed with a good deal of official violence, although a later governmental inquiry concluded that all the injuries sustained were accidental.[17]

Strikes were common in the 1930s, in response to both economic and political grievances. In consequence of the worldwide Depression, a number of industries attempted to reduce wages, and bitter strikes resulted. One side effect was an increase in Communist influence in the labor movement. Often economic issues became entangled with political ones, especially since the British tended to see and respond mainly to the political aspects of growing labor unrest. In 1933 there were strikes by the tramway workers, the carters, and scavengers; all were marked by a police firing. The jute mills were again closed. Late in 1934 the dock stevedores tied up 73 ships in Calcutta port for more than 21 days over issues that were chiefly political. To break the stevedore strike, the government declared the union seditious and jailed its leaders. The British also applied themselves to the task of creating dock unions that were more friendly to the British point of view.

Most but not all the agitation and mass protest in Calcutta during the 1930s involved the Hindu rather than the Muslim population. An exception in 1932 centered on the execution of two Punjabi youths who murdered the Hindu author of a tract thought to be offensive to Islam. On the appointed day, some 50,000 persons protested near the site of the execution. Police forestalled their attempt to carry the bodies through the city, and little violence ensued.[18] The nationalist awakening of the Muslim population dates from the middle 1930s. As with the Hindu Bhadralok community, Bengal's Muslims increasingly placed nationalism in a religious context. A number of demonstrations were held to voice concern for such pan-Islamic issues as the Arab position in Palestine and the fate of the Punjabi Muslims. By 1936 the Muslims had turned their attention to specific political issues in the city. That year's elections to the Calcutta Corporation were boycotted to protest the small number of Muslims working for the city. As a consequence the elected seats that were reserved for Muslims had to be filled by governmental appointment.

The Bengali Hindus were by no means politically quiescent in these years. In 1937 there was a fresh outpouring of nationalist activity, inspired by a hunger strike begun by a number of prominent Hindu political figures in August. As the strike progressed there were widespread meetings of support and protest throughout Bengal, including more than 100 public meetings in Calcutta in five weeks. The police moved to control protest by outlawing public meetings of any kind in many areas of the town. This restriction set the stage for the violent suppression of a number of meetings that were held in spite of the regulation. As political unrest increased, so did the level of labor agitation. The police report of 1937 lists 55 major strikes, and during the summer of 1937 a partially successful general strike was called.

The ability of the colonial political system to administer the city continued to decline throughout the 1930s. Increasingly the official concern was the control of the European sectors of the city; the rest of the city was left to take care of itself. Although there were periods of relative tranquility, the general increase in social violence—be it political agitation, communal violence, or labor unrest—was unmistakable. In 1938, for example, Muslims rallied more than 250,000 persons in the city to protest a Congress-inspired vote of no confidence in the Muslim ministry of the Bengal Government. In 1939 there were 78 major strikes, up by nearly half from 1937. Serious attempts at intercommunal cooperation had long since been given up, and both groups began demanding independence on their own terms. The first street demonstrations that explicitly advocated an independent Muslim state occurred in 1940.[19]

The extent of the administrative breakdown in the city was evident in a number of areas. At various points in the 1940s the police function within the city had to be taken over by the army.[20] During the 1943 famine officials declared themselves unable to collect the numerous corpses that were accumulating in the streets. No program could be devised to deal with the thousands of beggars who lived in the city streets. The prevailing view was expressed by the police commissioner, who observed that there was simply "no place to put them."

The last effort of the British to reestablish some measure of public order in Calcutta was the implementation of a new and much more drastic Defence of India Act in late 1940. The act gave authorities extremely broad powers to deal with sedition. In response to this challenge, Gandhi organized the Quit India movement. The response of the British was yet another roundup of Congress leaders, which precipitated another round of revolutionary turmoil in Bengal. During the early 1940s there were reported 301 police firings. 2,000 police injuries, and the destruction or serious damage of more than 200 police stations, 322 jails, and 2,000 other government buildings. In some areas of Bengal British administration nearly collapsed. The end of the British political structure in Bengal can be traced, however, to the catastrophic famine of 1943.[21]

It is difficult to comprehend much less describe with any precision the impact of the famine on Calcutta.[22] One finds, for example, that between August 15 and October 15 almost 10,000 persons were admitted to Calcutta hospitals suffering from malnutrition, and 2,757 of them died. On a single day, September 28, 325 persons were reported to have died of starvation in the city hospitals. Of course these figures represent only a small fraction of those affected, since hospitals were limited in scope and effectiveness in such a situation. On October 27 a volunteer relief organization reported having collected 176 bodies that had been rotting in the streets. Perhaps the circumstances of urban life are conveyed in a single account from the *Hindustan Standard* of March 26, long before the famine reached crisis proportions:

> The dead body of a destitute woman was found yesterday morning in a vacant house by the District Board road off Sarish Station. The body was seen lying all day without any arrangement for removal. At night, jackals dragged the body out and mostly devoured it up. The remaining part of the body is being devoured by dogs and crows in the front of the eyes of hundreds of passers-by this morning.[23]

The authorities engaged in the ultimate act of denial with the passage of the Bengal Destitute Persons Ordinance, under whose terms some 43,500 starving persons were rounded up in the latter months of 1943 and sent out of the city. The pressure of the famine eased only with the good rice crop of 1944.

Once the famine passed, the survivors turned their regained energies to attacking the ineffectual British administration. In 1945, well before the end of the war, there was a sharp rise in anti-British sentiment and violence, though directed more against property than persons. In February a number of British and American military vehicles were the targets of mob action, and armed Gurkha paramilitary police were unable to contain the rioting, despite repeated use of automatic weapons. On February 12 the police were replaced by military units, which required two days to restore a semblance of order to the city.

It is noteworthy that there was little intercommunal violence during the war years. In March 1946, however, it was announced that a cabinet commission would come to India to consider the bases on which India would gain independence. The announcement raised questions about the future status of Bengal and its Hindu and Muslim communities, bringing latent communal tension to a boil. Tension was increased by another food shortage. In late March 65,000 workers left the jute mills to protest a reduction in rations. At the same time a large number of weapons, most of them American war surplus, began to enter the city. According to British sources the Americans were not particularly concerned about whether military materiel reached Indian hands.[24] The British reacted to rising tensions by sending more troops into the city, and by mid-1946 Calcutta was an armed camp. By July there were four British battalions, one artillery regiment, and five Gurkha and Indian regiments in the city: Troops were not simply stationed in the city but were in fact viewed as "serving in the city."

The "great killing" of Calcutta was the result of a Direct Action Day held in the city on October 16, 1946. The demonstration was called by the Muslim ministry of the Bengal Government to demand that a Muslim state be created, independent of India. The communal rioting that ensued was probably the most extensive and deadly civil strife in the city's history. One cannot be certain because, as in the past, the official function of recording and reporting failed as disorder increased. Griffiths argues that more than 20,000 people were killed or seriously wounded, but Tuker asserts that the casualties numbered only 500.[25] Whatever the human costs of the rioting, it is clear that it never ceased for long but continued sporadically until independence in August 1947. Labor conflict also was rife, with 115 major strikes being reported in 1947. Probably the most consequential was a strike of 22,000 employees of the Calcutta Port Trust, an action that closed the port for three months. Nor was independence day to see the end of strife. There were celebrations in Calcutta on August 17, 1947, but communal and revolutionary violence soon reappeared.

Patterns of Individual Crime, 1906-1947

The low rates of reported crime in Calcutta between 1906 and 1947 are documented in Table V.4.1. In the major categories of individual crimes of violence and property crimes, there is an actual decline compared with the previous period. For the most serious crimes of personal violence, murder and serious assaults, the trend is downward throughout the period. Less serious assaults increased until 1923 and declined thereafter; since they were relatively more numerous, the graph of crimes of individual violence (Figure V.4.1) reflects the incidence of these minor offenses. A similar rise and decline is evident for property crimes (Figure V.4.2). The downward trend after 1923 was so great that the 1946 rate of these offenses was less than the rate in 1906. The aggregate measure of regulatory offenses shows a similar pattern, too, except that the peak was steeper and occurred somewhat later, in 1930 (Figure V.4.3), coinciding with Gandhi's call for a new wave of civil disobedience. The incidence of crimes of group violence (Figure V.4.4) was more variable, with peaks in years of great social tension: 1926, 1930, and 1932.

As Table V.4.2 shows, regulatory offenses continued to be by far the most common type of cognizable offense known to police. On the average they comprised 92 percent of all cognizable cases, an increase of nine percentage points from the 1870-1905 period.[26] In general, these offenses increased as a proportion of total offenses until 1930, when they accounted for almost 97 percent. Subse-

Table V.4.1 Cognizable Crimes Known to the Calcutta Police
            per 10,000 Population, 1906-1947[a]

Category	Mean	Maximum	Minimum	S.D.
Crimes of individual violence	6.6	10.4	3.5	1.9
Murder	.27	2.2	.08	.36
Serious assaults	1.5	2.4	.75	.48
Minor assaults	3.8	6.2	2.2	1.0
Assaults on public officials	1.8	2.3	.16	.7
Property crimes	63.8	100.9	30.9	20.5
Major theft	.40	1.6	.07	.46
Minor theft	59.2	93.8	28.9	19.0
Fraud	3.7	6.6	1.5	1.4
Assaults on property	.04	.11	0.0	.03
Crimes of group violence	.43	2.2	.12	.42
Group murder	0.0	0.0	0.0	0.0
Group assault	.05	.71	0.0	.12
Group thefts	.002	.02	0.0	.005
Rioting	.38	1.5	.12	.33
Sexual offenses	.22	.35	.08	.06
Obstruction of justice	.52	1.0	.12	.25
Regulatory offenses	933.5	1633.3	313.7	303.7
Total cognizable cases	1005.	1697.3	395.8	302.6

a. For 34 years.

Table V.4.2 Percentage Contribution of Particular Categories of
            Crime to the Overall Level of Cognizable Crime,
            1906-1947

Category	Mean	Maximum	Minimum	S.D.	N
Crimes of individual violence	.74	1.5	.34	.35	34
Property crimes	7.2	18.6	2.7	3.9	34
Crimes of group violence	.05	.56	0.	.09	34
Sexual offenses	.02	.05	.01	.007	34
Obstruction of justice	.06	.01	.01	.03	34
Regulatory offenses	92.0	96.7	79.3	4.3	34

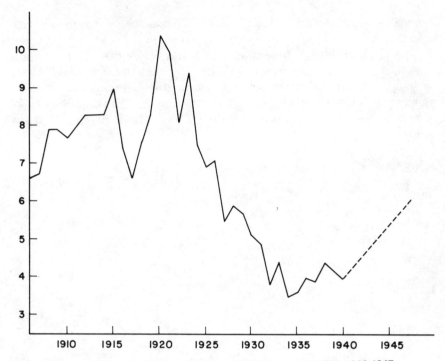

Figure V.4.1 Calcutta: Known cases of individual violence per 10,000, 1906-1947

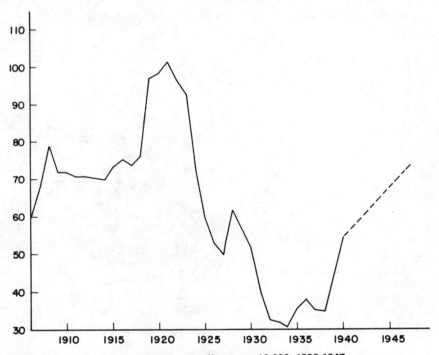

Figure V.4.2 Calcutta: Known property offenses per 10,000, 1906-1947

quently the percentage of regulatory offenses began to drop somewhat.

The data presented in Tables V.4.1 and V.4.2 present a seeming paradox. Our narrative survey of collective disorder clearly describes a long-term rise in strife and governmental efforts at control in Calcutta. Yet official crime statistics reveal that most serious categories of crime declined during most of the period. Even regulatory

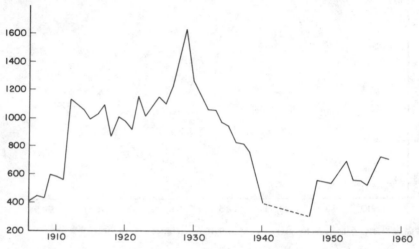

Figure V.4.3 Calcutta: Known regulatory offenses per 10,000, 1906-1958

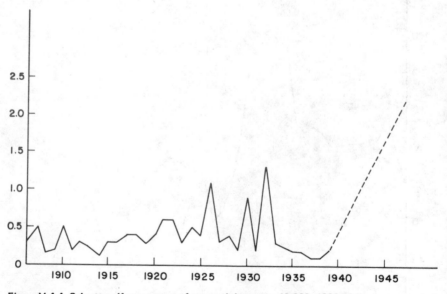

Figure V.4.4 Calcutta: Known cases of group violence per 10,000, 1906-1947

offenses, which rose until 1930, began to fall after this peak was reached. One is tempted to question these data as flights of fancy of police administrators. The second alternative, however, is that factors other than objective citizen behavior are once again playing a major role in the social definition of crime. Given the extreme pressure put on the Calcutta police during this period, it is not surprising that the resources devoted to common crime were cut back severely. If such resources were reduced, the level of crime detected would also drop. Criminal statistics then would decline, not in spite of high levels of social disorder, but precisely because of them.

Structures: The Police, the Courts, and the Prisons

According to a number of narrative sources, by the 1930s it was implicitly understood that the British struggle to remain in India had been lost, and colonial withdrawal was simply a matter of time. Efforts by the British establishment to reduce or at least to control the more serious kinds of disorder continued, but officials appeared to forego attempts to enforce the European normative order that had guided British rule during the previous century. There are two phases to the history of British institutions of public order during this period. In the first they attempted to cope with enormous external pressure; in the second, a phase that might be called "deinstitutionalization," the institutions were so weakened by stress that they could no longer deal with the condition.

The institutional breakdown in Calcutta is perhaps best revealed by the fate of the police. In 1942 the army had largely assumed direct responsibility for the maintenance of social order in the city. Accounts generally agree that the police had become ineffective. Francis Tuker, who headed the British troops in the city during this period, wrote:

> It is interesting to note the large numbers of troops that we were keeping in and about Calcutta solely for the maintenance of law and order in the city and its suburbs. . . . That is, thirteen big units, yet civil officials were on the tenth of July clamouring for more troops.[27]

Although Tuker makes questionable judgments about causes, the fact of the police collapse seems uncontrovertible. There is evidence, in indicators of manpower and cost, that the deterioration of the police system had in fact begun a good deal earlier. It will be recalled that the turn of the century saw general increases both in the number of police and in their budgetary resources in proportion to population. This trend continued until the late 1920s, but thereafter both indicators began to decline sharply. By 1940 per capita expenditures on the police were below the 1910 levels, despite the enormous growth in civil strife.

It also is important to point out that at no time was the quality of the Calcutta police high. Although official police reports state that the police were well equipped to deal with the tasks that challenged them, most other sources, including a number of British study commissions, concluded that the overall quality of the police was very poor indeed. Perhaps the most thorough examination of the police in British India was made by the Police Study Commission of 1905. The Calcutta police were condemned with a curt observation: "Corruption and inefficiency are rampant in the city as well as in the district. They are in the main due to the same causes."[28] The causes enumerated by the commission included ill-trained police or those poorly suited to police work, the inefficiency of the district and city police, and the lack of what the commission called a "living wage" for the lower ranks.

It is perhaps ironic that while the quality of the police was generally decried, there was a tendency throughout the period to arm the force with greater authority. For example, during the 1910s and 1920s the following legal powers were established:

(1) Persons who were judged by police to be habitual offenders, vagrants, and suspected persons could be required by a magistrate to post a bond to indicate that they would display "good behavior." Failure to post such a bond would result in imprisonment.

(2) Any person released from jails might be subjected to police supervision for up to five years.

(3) By the authority of the Criminal Tribe Act, particular tribes might be required to register and be subject to surveillance by the police. The act further required that the tribe members be confined to a reservation.

(4) For a time the police could demand a security for good behavior independent of any court. In the 1930s this power was restricted, over the strong objections of the police establishment.[29]

The criminal courts in Calcutta trace a similar reduction in levels of activity. The numbers of criminal cases presented both to the Calcutta High Court and the lesser magistrates' courts decline in almost linear fashion through the period. For example, there were six criminal trials per 10,000 persons in the High Court in 1910. By 1940 this rate was below one per 10,000. In a similar time period the number of cases before magistrates' courts dropped from a high of 1,000 per 10,000 to a low of 230 per 10,000.[30] These totals do not reflect, however, the thousands of individuals who were interned during the various British campaigns to control the independence movement. If any systematic records were kept of such internments, they have not been made public.

Although the number of cases before the courts declined steadily, there was an increase in the average severity of sentence, and this trend persisted into the 1920s. Thereafter the severity of punishments, measured by average fine and average prison sentence, began a steady decline.[31] None of the anti-British agitations of the 1930s or 1940s appeared to have had much effect on the trend, but the issue is obscured because we lack information on the sanctions imposed by the special tribunals that administered the internment programs.

Within the prison system there is little evidence of change in basic orientation: Convicts were to be punished, not rehabilitated. There was, however, a detectable shift away from physical punishment and toward simple custodial treatment. This is evident in the increased reliance on "warnings" as a response to the perceived misbehavior of both Indian and European inmates. By comparison with the earlier period, all kinds of physical punishment declined, both absolutely and in proportion to the total number of punishments meted out to convicts.[32]

In summary, virtually every indicator points to the decline of colonial institutions for maintaining public order in Calcutta between 1906 and 1948, and especially after the late 1920s. Police resources declined and so did the number of reported cases and the severity of sanctions administered by courts and prisons. The latter trends might under other circumstances be regarded as evidence of a growing humanitarianism, and perhaps that motive was present. In the context of rising social disorder, however, we are inclined to interpret them as further evidence of the dissolution of British will and ability to rule a hostile population. The only surprising feature of the final collapse of British institutions in the 1940s is that it did not happen sooner.

CALCUTTA SINCE INDEPENDENCE

The coming of independence did not reduce social tension in either Calcutta or what was now the state of West Bengal. The leaders of the Bengali terrorist movement remained excluded from political power, and communal tensions were exacerbated by reports of slaughters on both sides of the India-Pakistan border. Labor agitation continued at a high level, and there was a new source of potential conflict as well: The population of the teeming refugee camps increased daily and seethed with discontent. Political authorities braced themselves for a new outbreak of violence after independence was declared. It appears likely that the emphasis on public order rather than crime control per se was maintained throughout the province, particularly in Calcutta.

Civil Strife, 1947-1974

With the coming of independence many of the left-wing elements within the Bengali nationalist movement redirected their agitation to the Congress governments at the national and state level. Led by the Communist Party of India (CPI), Bengal remained in revolutionary turmoil.[33] The activities of the CPI have been discussed at some length by Franda:

> The most intense party activity in West Bengal took place in an eighteen-month period that extended from October 1948 until March 1950, during which time innumerable trams, busses, trains, and buildings were either bombed or set on fire. Demonstrations by students, mass organizations, and cultural front groups took place at the rate of at least one or two a week in Calcutta, and deaths from the activities of the revolutionaries were estimated to be in the hundreds.[34]

Acts specifically traced to the CPI or to related organizations included an attack on the home of the Bengal labor minister, an attack on a public meeting held by the same minister, the complete destruction of the Calcutta telephone exchange, an attempt to blow up the Calcutta water works, a number of raids on the home of the president of the state Congress party, attacks on a number of Congress officials, an attack on Prime Minister Jawaharlal Nehru, and large-scale raids on Dum Dum Airport in which a number of airline employees were killed. Late in 1950 Calcutta was again racked with communal violence in which some CPI units were throught to be involved.[35]

As the forms of political struggle continued from the colonial period, so did the governmental response. The new Congress Government quickly armed itself against the growing challenge. The CPI was banned, as were a number of militant Muslim communal organizations. Shortly after independence the West Bengal Government also offered the West Bengal Security Act to the state Parliament. In its general outline the bill continued the tradition of repressive legislation by which the British had ruled for the last 40 years. It allowed the government to detain any person for up to three months without a trial or charges and provided that internment could be renewed. For the first fifteen days of confinement those interned did not even have the right to be told why they were being held. Within the

Bengal Assembly only the Communist representatives offered serious objection to the bill. Outside the assembly the police marked the passage of the bill by firing 30 rounds into a protesting crowd. By 1950 the police had a formidable arsenal of laws they might use to justify their attempts to maintain order in the city. Among those invoked by the Special Branch of the Calcutta police were the Indian Criminal Law Act, the Indian Press Act, the West Bengal Special Ordinance, the Indian Arms Act, the Explosive Substance Act, the Indian Telegraph Act, the Indian Penal Code and Arms Act, and the Influx from Pakistan Act.

The leftist parties, particularly the CPI, had created a good deal of social disorder during this period, but a true revolutionary situation had not been generated. After the Communist leadership was released from jail toward the end of 1951, the party began to interest itself in electoral politics. An electoral policy in Bengal, however, does not always imply non-violence. In fact violence has proved to be an effective vote-getting technique for the Communists throughout Bengal and most particularly in Calcutta. Thus, the Communists continued to devote a great deal of effort to agitational politics. In July 1953 the Communists, along with the Socialists and some minor Marxist parties, organized a Tram Fare Increase Resistance Committee in response to the British-run tram company's announcement that there would be an increase in the second-class fare on the city's trams. Failing to obtain their goals through negotiation, the committee called for a hartal. In North and South Calcutta only about ten percent of the shops remained open. A boycott of the trams began, and demonstrators frequently dragged those who attempted to ride the trams off into the street. Students blocked streets until driven by the police into university compounds. In general the police chose not to follow the students onto campuses and opted instead for a containment policy. On July 10 mass arrests were made at a demonstration in Dalhousie Square, and five days later the police commissioner invoked section 144 of the Bengal Criminal Code to ban gatherings of more than five persons in any section of Calcutta or its suburbs. Mass demonstrations greeted the declaration, and over the next few days there appear to have been numerous police firings. The police reported the situation to be completely out of hand and requested that the Indian military move into the city. By July 18 much of North and South Calcutta was under the control of mobs. The violence was not reduced until the next day, when the government and the tram company capitulated on the issue of the fare increase.[36]

In addition to political agitation over the tram fare issue, there were demonstrations by Hindu refugees from East Pakistan. The police report for 1953 suggests that disorder in the bustee communities (registered slums) was a potential threat to the maintenance of order in the city.

In 1954 there was another episode of violent agitation. The immediate issue was the All-Bengal Teachers Association rejection of a wage offer made by the Bengal Government. To dramatize dissatisfaction, the union staged an illegal sitdown strike in Dalhousie Square, and some attempts were made to stop legislators from entering the Assembly. Widespread vandalism broke out throughout the city. Buses and trams were burned, private cars were attacked, street lights and traffic signals were destroyed, roads were barricaded, and shops were looted. During the affray four persons were killed and more than 65 hurt. The strike and the accompanying agitation were called off only when the government granted substantial concessions to the union.

As Myron Weiner has pointed out, however, violence in Calcutta does not always have a formal organization base. In 1955, 400 students attacked a number of examination centers in a spontaneous protest against a difficult examination question. The same year saw a similar occurrence when thousands of unemployed persons appeared to apply for a handful of positions announced by the Calcutta Fire Brigade.[37]

Labor difficulties increased sharply in 1955 as the economic situation in the city worsened. Inflation was substantial in the early 1950s and had continued to increase. For much of 1955 Calcutta's port was crippled by violent labor strife. Early in the year seamen began a slowdown, and later they were joined by the dock workers. There were three separate reports of police firings at the crowds gathered at the docks during the slowdown. Finally the chairman of the Port Commissioners was granted emergency powers, 44 union leaders were arrested, and the slowdown ended.

An environmental element was added to Calcutta's chronic crises in 1957 when there was serious flooding in parts of the city. Most of the problems remained human ones, however. The year began with a general strike in the city's banks, called to protest the detention of sixteen bank employees under the terms of the West Bengal Security Act for engaging in "subversive labor organising."[38] The strike ended when the men were released. Toward the end of the year a more dangerous situation developed when the city's firemen went on strike. The deteriorating economic situation revealed itself in a number of areas other than strikes. Numerous large, though generally peaceful, demonstrations were held to protest the scarcity of food. One result was increased attention by the Communist Party to food agitation. In 1957 the CPI and a number of other left-wing organizations set up the Price Increase and Famine Resistance Committee (PIFRC), which called for massive protests over the lack of food supplies in the city. A general strike was planned to stop activity in the city and the entire state of West Bengal. In response the West Bengal Government arrested 250 Bengali leftists, setting off a wave of demonstrations in which 12,845 persons were arrested. Within Calcutta, some 39 persons were killed during the food demonstrations, and a number of police stations were attacked as well. [39] Simultaneously with the food agitations of the PIFRC, a series of demonstrations erupted in the refugee camps. A demonstration demanding increased benefits for refugees saw the Bengal government forcibly remove more than 6,000 refugees from the city.

Several years of relative calm followed, but in the early 1960s political tensions within the city intensified again. The 1964 decision of the national government to arrest much of the CPI leadership under the provisions of the 1962 Defence of India Act was decidedly unpopular in much of West Bengal. On their release from prison, the left-wing members of the Bengal communist movement engaged in a truly massive agitational campaign throughout the state, most particularly in Calcutta. Although a variety of issues on which to attack the government were chosen, the major one was again the scarcity and high price of food. A coalition similar to the original PIFRC was established, and as protests spread throughout the state, the level of violence increased. In early 1966 there were a number of police firings reported outside the city, and a number of food protesters in 24 Parganas were killed. The result was a series of violent demonstrations, first in 24 Parganas and then throughout West Bengal. Several students were killed in a student demonstration in Calcutta. A further demonstration called to honor the dead shut down the city as well as much of the state for three days. Over these three days at least 39 people lost their lives and some 550 arrests were made. Order was restored only through the use of auxiliary police from nearby states, plus elements of the Indian army. Eventually the West Bengal Government made a number of concessions to the leftist front. Although the concessions were of relatively minor substantive value, the Congress Party had clearly lost its ability to govern Bengal. Its formal right to govern was removed in the election of 1967, whereupon a leftist coalition formed a non-Congress United Front state government.

We have seen that with the assumption of power by the United Front Government there was a tremendous rise in labor unrest, particularly in the incidence of gheraos. Moorehouse has described some of them:

They were held to force the reinstatement of workers who accepted a scheme of voluntary retirement and had already collected compensation. They were held to support a demand for recruitment of more staff when management held there was already too many staff; to back a demand for wages during an unauthorised absence; to force the dropping of an inquiry into theft by workmen; to demand the promotion of certain people and the removal of others; to demand the reinstatement of workers who had been dismissed for misconduct two-and-a-half years previously after an official inquiry.[40]

Accompanying this economic disruption, Calcutta once again saw the emergence of organized armed insurrection. The Naxalite Movement, which waged a sort of guerrilla war within Calcutta for a number of years, succeeded in making a number of areas within the city very dangerous indeed.[41] With the return of a Congress Government a measure of stability had been restored to the city. The economic condition of the city was further reduced, however, with a second flood of refugees reaching the city during the 1971 conflict that led to the creation of Bangladesh.

Crime Since Independence

It is important to determine whether or not criminal statistics for the years since 1947 are in any way comparable with the data for the colonial period. This is partly a question of legal definition and official policy, partly a matter of social behavior. As for the criminal law, it changed little at or after independence.[42] We also know that some of the more dramatic forms of public disorder persisted, notably revolutionary activity. Evidence about a more common, marginally criminal kind of behavior is provided by the Indian railroads. During the colonial period riding the railroads without a ticket had been viewed as an act of defiance and Indian disdain for British rule. However, the new Indian government shortly found itself faced with the same difficult policing task that had confronted its colonial predecessors. For the years 1951 to 1962 there were never fewer than 14,000 persons sent annually to Bengali prisons for riding the trains without a ticket.[43] A peak was reached in 1960, when nearly 35,000 persons were imprisoned for this offense. Such cases declined in 1961 and 1962, but it is impossible to say whether this represents change in behavior by the public or the police.

A more concrete difficulty in assessing crime rates in the post-independence period is the paucity of data. From the 1950s to the present the Indian government has been reluctant to make statistical information for Calcutta available. For example, by the 1960s annual police reports for the city were no longer being issued.[44] Such difficulties are magnified by general hostility to Western social science research. Much of this hostility has stemmed from international events, but the sensitivity of Indians about Calcutta was heightened because Western research often put the Indian government and people in a bad light. For whatever reasons, data on crime in the postindependence period are meager.

Two sets of crime statistics are available, nonetheless. For nine years between 1948 and 1958 we have detailed information from the annual police reports. They are not examined separately in this chapter except for regulatory offenses, which were included in Figure V.4.3. They were as numerous after independence as they were in the later 1930s and made up more than 90 percent of all cognizable crimes known to the Calcutta police in the decade after independence. They also were highly variable, in response to peaks in civil strife. Evidently the emphasis of colonial authorities in Calcutta on the general maintenance of order carried over after independence, and the same legal tools were employed. On the other hand, relatively little attention was given to the detection or prosecution of individual crimes.

To analyze trends in official attention to crime over the entire period after independence, we must rely on more summary data reported in publications of the West Bengal and Indian Federal

Table V.4.3 Reported Criminal Offenses per 10,000 Population 1939-1972

Category	Mean	Maximum	Minimum	S.D.	N
Murder	.35	2.2	.53	.44	24
Violent group crimes[a]	1.0	2.4	.60	.54	18
Rioting	1.3	4.1	.53	1.0	22
Dacoity	.13	2.2	.09	.44	24
Crimes against property[b]	34.9	68.0	17.5	14.9	30
Robbery	.3	1.6	.02	.32	30
Theft	27.7	46.7	14.4	9.6	30
Burglary	6.9	25.1	1.6	5.8	30
Coining offenses	.02	.03	0.	.01	18

a. Violent group crimes were calculated by adding reported rioting and dacoity cases.
b. Crimes against property is the simple sum of robberies, thefts, and burglaries. Coining offenses were not included because of their small number.
Sources: Data through 1955 were obtained from various issues of the Report of the Police Commissioner, Calcutta. The data for the 1960s were obtained from the *Statistical Abstract for West Bengal* and various issues of *Crime in India*. The late 1960 and 1970 data are taken from the relevant issues of *Crimes in India*. The sources generally agree on the levels of crime, but there are variations among sources in particular categories.

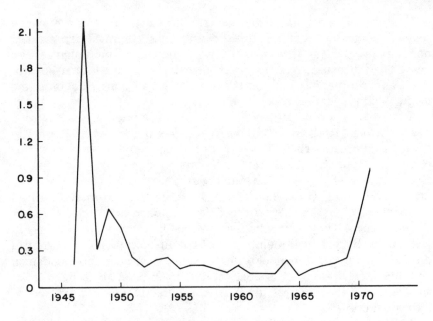

Figure V.4.5   Calcutta: Known cases of murder per 10,000, 1946-1971

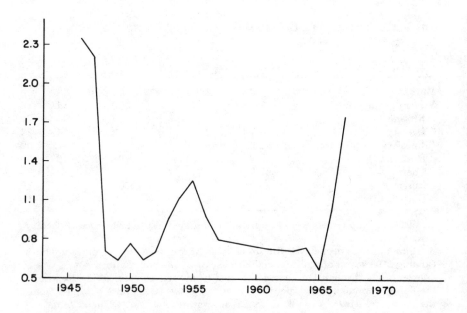

Figure V.4.6   Calcutta: Known cases of group violence per 10,000, 1946-1966

governments. These sources include data on murder, violent group crimes, robbery, theft, burglary, and coining offenses, among others. [45] In some instances they can be linked to the police data; in others this is not possible. Our data on these offenses from various sources are summarized in Table V.4.3 and are graphed in Figures

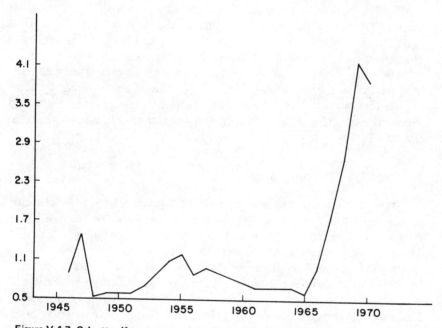

Figure V.4.7 Calcutta: Known cases of rioting per 10,000, 1946-1970

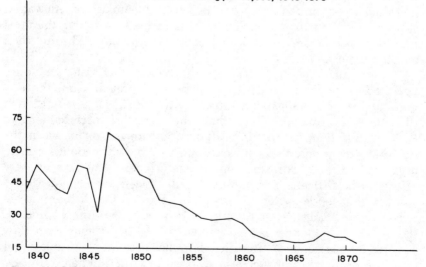

Figure V.4.8 Calcutta: Known property offenses per 10,000, 1939-1971

V.4.5 through V.4.8. Figure V.4.5 shows that the peak in murders associated with the 1947 riots was followed by an abrupt decline and then a more gradual one into the early 1960s; an increase began in the late 1960s and was particularly pronounced after 1969. A similar reversing pattern is evident in the aggregate measure of crimes of group violence (Figure V.4.6). Cases of rioting increased greatly after 1965 (Figure V.4.7) as well. The increase in these group offenses is obviously correlated with the general rise in social and political agitation in the late 1960s that culminated in the first United Front Government. The rising murder rate appears to be due to the more specific outbreak of urban terrorism by the CPML. The summary measure of property crimes (Figure V.4.8) declines consistently after independence, but this is somewhat deceptive because the rarer and more serious offenses of robbery and burglary increase markedly in the late 1960s.

Institutions of Public Order

There was a remarkable degree of continuity between the criminal justice system of colonial Bengal and the institutions on which the new Indian government relied to maintain order. Article 372 of the 1950 Indian Constitution stated that all laws in effect prior to the enactment of the Constitution were to remain in effect until changed by political authorities. Earlier we argued that independence did not generate basic changes in the criminal law. The dualities common in British enforcement continued. Thus the claims of particular communal groups in the area of "private law" such as marriage and inheritance continued to be recognized. A similar generalization applies to the various agencies that applied the law. For the most part structures from the British period were maintained, only their names were changed.

The Police: The basic features of the colonial Calcutta police persisted throughout the present period. In organization, the Calcutta police are still under the direct control of the Home Ministry of the state government rather than the Bengal Superintendent of Police. Thus there is no formal basis for cooperation between the Calcutta police and those of surrounding areas. The police remain organized in ranks corresponding roughly to the American military distinctions: officers, noncommissioned officers, and men. Finally the postindependence police maintains the British distinction between unarmed and armed sections. However, the armed forces of the police are no longer held in reserve as in earlier years but are now assigned a wide range of "traditional" police activities.[46] Table V.4.4 gives the proportion of such armed forces in several Indian states. By

Table V.4.4 Size of Armed and Unarmed Police Forces for Selected Indian States

	Utter Pradesh	Bihar	West Bengal	Orissa	Assam
Total					
1950	58,591	17,763	44,412	12,226	8,923
1960	64,874	32,566	49,034	14,553	16,769
% Armed					
1950	39	5	39	40	44
1960	40	33	35	33	58

Source: Data derived from David H. Bayley, *Police and Political Development in India*, (Princeton, N.J.: Princeton University Press, 1969), p. 64.

Table V.4.5 Reported Surveillance Activities of the Special Branch of the Calcutta Police

	Events observed and noted	
Year	Meetings[a]	Processions
1952	2,805	n.d.
1953	2,598	604
1954	2,618	415
1955	2,685	466
1956	3,105	399
1957	3,893	243
1958	2,889	773

a. The police reports characterize such meetings as "antigovernment or antinational in character."

1960 the proportion of police assigned to the armed divisions was 33 percent or more in every state, and it is evident that West Bengal is not exceptional with respect to the relative size of its armed police reserve.[47] There is other evidence, however, to suggest that throughout the post-independence period a major focus of the police in Calcutta has been in areas other than those of "traditional" police functions. The Special Branch of the Calcutta police force, which had been created by the British to control political and subversive agitation, had a high rate of activity in the 1950s (Table V.4.5).

Another basic characteristic of the colonial police system that has been perpetuated since 1947 is the castelike nature of divisions within the force. Some movement through the ranks is possible, but advancement is rare. The officer corps of the Indian police is drawn almost exclusively from the ranks of the Indian Police Service (IPS), which is organized and controlled by the Union government. The

Table V.4.6 Cost and Strength of the Calcutta Police

| Year | Size of force | | Cost per officer |
	Number	per 10,000	
1951	15,404	60.4	Rs190
1956	14,765		Rs238
1961	14,850	50.7	Rs295
1966	18,628		Rs419

Source: Statistical Abstract of West Bengal.

emphasis on IPS recruitment of officers is clearly analogous to the British practice of restricting the officer ranks to Europeans.[48] The effect of this policy was, of course, to create a tremendous social distance (social, cultural, and often even linguistic) within the force, with consequent problems for administrative control.[49]

A final similarity of the pre- and postcolonial police force is that both received little in the way of resources from political elites. As Table V.4.6 indicates, the absolute size of the Calcutta police actually declined from 1951 to 1961. The increase in the per capita cost of the police can be largely explained by high rates of inflation in the 1960s. The last year for which data are available (1966) suggests that in absolute size the force had begun to grow, though proportionally it remained smaller than in 1951. Perhaps even more fundamental than the lack of material support has been an apparent lack of political support. Much of the suspicion and distrust of police created during British rule continued, even though Calcutta now had an "Indian" police force.

The antipolice orientation of political authorities was most extreme during the United Front Governments of the late 1960s and early 1970s. This lack of support was dramatically revealed in the tendency of Front Governments to support apparently illegal activity rather than the police, if that behavior were "politically correct." Especially good examples of this were the initial attitude of the Bengal Government toward the Naxalbari agitation and their support for gheraos. Police resentment against this lack of political support broke out in violence in Calcutta in 1971 when there was a police riot in the state assembly. The protest stemmed from the killing of two policemen during street rioting in the city. A small band of the police first ransacked the offices of the police superintendent, then proceeded to the state Assembly, where they smashed more furniture and assaulted several politicians before being subdued.

Since the fall of the United Front Governments there is evidence that the level of support for the police has increased both within the new Congress Government as well as the general population. There is agreement that the Naxalite terrorism in Calcutta generated widespread demands for a more effective police within the city.

The Courts: As with the police, the basic structure of the postindependence system of courts in the city was not greatly different from its colonial counterpart. Initially, the same two-tier system of courts was maintained. In 1957 an intermediate court, the Court of Sessions, was added. The magistrates' courts remain lowest in the court hierarchy, generally limited to imposing prison sentences of not more than two years and fines up to Rs 1,000. The Sessions Court deals primarily with the more serious crimes and can deal in any point of law, subject to review of the High Court. However, all death sentences imposed by the Sessions Court must be reviewed by the Calcutta High Court, which stands at the head of the state court system. At present it is almost exclusively an appellate court, although unlike its counterparts in Madras and Bombay it has retained at least formal jurisdiction for a number of serious crimes. The structure and jurisdiction of the state high courts can be traced to the supreme courts which were established by the British in Calcutta, Madras, and Bombay in the 1860s, a point widely acknowledged by the Indian officials. Yet another interesting similarity between the postindependence judicial system and the colonial system is that administrative responsibility for the state courts is retained, not by any administrative agency, but rather by the Union Parliament in Delhi.

The number of cases processed by particular Calcutta courts is very much a function of their respective jurisdictions. As would be expected, the post-1955 increase in regulatory offenses is reflected in a steady increase in the number of cases taken up in the magistrates' courts. In 1955 there were a total of 150,000 cases disposed of in the magistrates' courts. By 1965 that number had risen to more than 250,000. The official reports that are available show that this upward trend was not a general one but is rather confined to offenses relating to health, safety, and a number of municipal and local ordinances.

As the number of cases disposed of in the magistrates courts rose, the number and severity of sentences assigned by these courts declined. From 1957 to 1963 the total number of persons sentenced to prison in the magistrates' courts dropped from a total of approximately 8,200 persons to about 1,870. Despite a sharp increase in the number of persons sentenced to prison in 1965, there was an immediate decline the following year. A similar reduction in punitiveness is evident in the number of fines assessed. Except for a short upturn in the early 1960s, the number of persons fined in the magistrates' courts declined steadily after the mid-1950s.

The criminal returns of the Sessions Court are similar. The number of cases committed to the Sessions Court decreased only slightly during this period, but there was a substantial drop in the numbers of persons convicted and sent to prison. There were 48 persons sentenced to prison by the Sessions Court in 1959, compared with nine in 1968. During the same period the conviction rate dropped from 58 percent to 17 percent. [50] A similar decline in the cases assigned to the Calcutta High Court can be largely explained by the administrative transfer of cases to the new Sessions Court after 1957. It appears that in the category of most serious crimes reserved for the High Court there was no dramatic decrease in conviction rates. Even in the High Court, however, sentences tended to be less severe: There was a distinct drop in the proportion of those convicted who were sentenced to transportation or capital punishment.

The Prisons: Consistent with colonial practice, administrative oversight of the Bengali prison system remained at the state level. Since there was no Calcutta jail system per se, inferences about the nature and conditions of the Calcutta jails must be drawn from data for all West Bengal. There is little to suggest that Bengali jails have undergone any substantial improvement since independence. For example, the per capita cost of maintaining prisoners rose from Rs 644 in 1951 to just Rs 653 in 1960, despite considerable inflation. Narrative sources do suggest, however, that the preindependence trend away from the more inhumane practices continued. The prison reports of the 1950s and 1960s mention ever fewer physical and corporal punishments. [51] Although there was ideological commitment to rehabilitation, the prisons evidently lacked resources for anything more than custodial care. Attempts at reform were centered on new schemes for classifying and segregating the prison population. Beginning in 1946 prisoners were classified by age, physical and mental health, and according to whether or not they were habitual offenders.

The intention of classificatory reform was to facilitate separate treatment of prisoners, and at present the Bengali jail system distinguishes, in theory if not necessarily in practice, such categories of inmates as under-trial prisoners, security prisoners, civil prisoners, those suffering from certain illnesses such as leprosy and tuberculosis, lunatic prisoners, condemned prisoners, those sentenced to simple imprisonment, superior-class prisoners, and women. Most of these categories are self-defining, but a few need a bit of elaboration. Under-trial prisoners include not only those whose trials are actually in progress, but also those who were either denied bail or were unable to post bail. Such prisoners are numerous, and available reports show that on the average they spend two to three months in jail. There is some attempt to segregate these prisoners, and the prison reports make repeated reference to the dangers of continuing to treat the under-trial prisoner as a convicted felon. A security prisoner is one who has been convicted of an offense against the state or who is being detained under a preventive detention law. Superior-class prisoners are those who, in the opinion of the presidency magistrates, are accustomed to a style of life superior to that of the average convict. A person so classified is segregated from other convicts, given better food and clothing, and allowed more privileges. Evidently this is an adaptation of the British practice of maintaining superior prisons for Europeans.

Given the relative rarity of convictions for serious offenses, it is hardly surprising that the number of convicts in Bengali jails closely parallels fluctuations in the frequency of regulatory offenses. Following independence the number of persons confined dropped, reaching a minimum in 1955. Five years of steady growth ensued, followed by a decline after 1960, although data are insufficient to determine whether the trend continued. Moreover the data show that most inmates were imprisoned for very minor offenses: Most prisoners served sentences of less than three months.[52]

NOTES TO CHAPTER V.4

1. The material utilized for the following discussion on the history of collective disorder in the city is drawn from fragmentary accounts in various sources. These sources include: Moorehouse, op. cit.; Franda, *Radical Politics in West Bengal;* Broomfield, op. cit.; Griffiths, op. cit.; David H. Bayley, *The Police and Political Development in India* (Princeton, N.J.: Princeton University Press, 1969). The quality and amount of information in these sources is quite uneven. A primary source which greatly supplemented these secondary sources was the series of Calcutta police reports. In addition, a number of governmental reports, usually reproduced in the *Parliamentary Papers,* were of great help.

2. The order that police ought to be less enthusiastic in their enforcement of these laws is made quite explicit in the Calcutta police report of 1904.

3. McLane, op. cit., p. 67.

4. Almost all sources at least mention the 1907 riots. The most useful, however, is McLane's "Calcutta and the Mofussilization of Bengali Politics." The police reports of the period supply the "official" version of the disorders.

5. The sentences eventually handed down in these two cases serve to support a hypothesis suggested earlier (i.e., it is important not only what you do but to whom you do it). The assassin of the Indian magistrate was given seven years. The would-be assassin of the lieutenant governor was given ten years.

6. The Burra Bazar is an area of North Calcutta. Although the neighborhood is heavily Marwari, there exist a number of other social communities in the area, particularly Muslim. See Moorehouse, op. cit., pp. 171-172.

7. Conclusions about the level of underground revolutionary activity are based almost entirely on a reading of official government sources, particularly police reports.

8. This is the famous Rowlatt Report, which itself generated a great deal of political controversy. Its conclusions on the extensiveness of the conspiracy were not unanimously accepted. Most controversial, to Indians at least, was the report's call for extensive implementation of repressive legislation of the sort implied by the Defence of India Act.

9. Rowlatt Report, p. 81.

10. All the major sources discuss the 1918 riots, but Broomfield, op. cit., offers the most perceptive discussion of their political implications.

11. Most quantitative information on labor unrest in this period comes from the police reports, which deal with strikes in some detail. Police attention to the subject of strikes is an indicator of sorts of the extent of British concern with the labor situation.

12. "Swadeshi" literally means "of one's own country." See the discussion in Ch. V.2.

13. See Broomfield, op. cit., for details.

14. Khilafat Committees were established throughout Bengal in 1919 to mobilize Muslim support for the Turkish Khaifat. To increase Hindu-Muslim cooperation, Gandhi argued that Congress ought to support the Khilafat movement. See Moorehouse, op. cit., p. 222.

15. The rationale for the "bad livelihood" charge has already been mentioned. This charge was used frequently; for example, there were 902 cases reported in the city for 1922.

16. In 1930 the Muslim Bengal government ratified the Bengal Criminal Amendment. This marked the first time the British were able to secure the support of Indian ministers for a policy of preventive detention and suspension of due process.

17. Report of Disturbances, 1934.

18. See Moorehouse, op. cit.

19. At this point it was thought possible that the whole of Bengal including Calcutta might be ceded to a Muslim state. This was the ultimate fear of the Bengal Hindus, and it inspired attempts to negotiate with the Muslims.

20. The role of the army during this period is discussed in Francis Tuker, *While Memory Serves* (London: Cassell, 1950).

21. Moorehouse provides a general overview of the 1940s in *Calcutta* but there is very little information on the period. British records and commentaries are scanty. Indian sources are almost completely silent on the famine period.

22. There are a number of descriptions of the famine available. In particular see Ghosh, op. cit.; A. Mahalanobis, *The Effects of Famine* (Calcutta: Statistical Association Publishing Company, 1944); Narayan, op. cit.

23. Cited in Moorehouse, op. cit., p. 112.

24. Official British reports are quite critical of the lax procedures under which the American military disposed of surplus arms.

25. Tuker, op. cit.; Griffiths, op. cit.

26. The second most common category of offenses was crimes of acquisition, which on the average accounted for 7.2 percent of arrests during these four decades. No other category of offenses accounted for more than 1 percent of arrests in any year and most averaged between 0.1 and 0.2 percent.

27. Tuker, op. cit., p. 377.

28. Report of the Police Study Commission, 1905.

29. At times these powers were subject to the formal review of a magistrate. It does not appear that this was an important restraint on police.

30. The magistrates' cases included a great many noncognizable offenses that have not been added into the indices of crime in this study. Data for the number of trials in all levels of Calcutta courts have been taken from the annual report, Report on Justice in the Lower Provinces.

31. Our index of severity of punishments was generated by weighting categoric data in the various Reports on Justice in the Lower Provinces.

32. Data on punishments assigned in the jails are from the annual jail reports, Report on Jails in the Lower Provinces.

33. A basic factor in the isolation of the communist movement from other nationalist organizations had been the decision of the Communists to support the British effort in World War II, in direct opposition to the position espoused by the Indian National Congress.

34. Franda, *Radical Politics in West Bengal*, op. cit., p. 48.

35. An official description of the violence is *Communist Violence in India* (Calcutta: Government Printing Office, 1948).

36. The events surrounding the tram violence are discussed in Moorehouse, op. cit., as well as the Calcutta police report of 1953.

37. Myron Weiner, "Violence and Politics in Calcutta," *Journal of Asian Studies* 20 (May 1961), 275-281.

38. See the Calcutta police report of 1957.

39. Franda, op. cit., p. 312, says there are no reliable estimates of injuries or the extent of property damage in this period. Once again the level of strife in Calcutta exceeded the capacity of the system to record, much less control it.

40. Moorehouse, op. cit., p. 312.

41. The urban Naxalites claimed an ideological affinity with the perpetrators of the land agitation that broke out in the Naxalbari area of Bengal in 1967. There is little evidence that the two groups were closely related, however.

42. This point is made a number of times in the *Indian Yearbook* in describing the Indian legal system. Also, the 1950 Constitution explicitly states that all colonial laws were to remain in effect until such time as they were reviewed by the Indian government.

43. These data were reported in Report on Jails in West Bengal (various years).

44. If these reports were compiled, they do not appear to have been made generally available. For example, the crime returns reported in *West Bengal Statistical Abstracts* are said to be taken from unaggregated police data.

45. These more limited data are available in both the *Statistical Abstract for West Bengal* (serial) and *Crime in India* (serial).

46. Bayley, op. cit.

47. Ibid., p. 66.

48. See ibid. for a more complete discussion of the IPS.

49. The relative distance between upper and lower levels within police is a phenomena that has been noted in a number of settings. Wilson, op. cit., has argued that such distance makes executive control of the police more difficult.

50. Report of the Prisons in West Bengal.

51. Ibid.

SOCIAL DISORDER AND
SYSTEMIC CHANGE
IN CALCUTTA

This concluding chapter provides an overview of long-term trends in public order and explores possible linkages between levels of public order and other characteristics of the Calcutta social system. The first section summarizes various quantitative measures of public order, several of which were not considered in the main narrative sections of the study; it also probes the relationship between various categories of crime and collective violence. In the second section we turn to several possible correlates of crime. Initially we focus on the institutions most directly involved in the implementation of elite policies aimed at the control of social disorder: the police, the courts, and the prisons. The analysis suggests that these institutions are not discrete causal factors in the generation of public order but rather are a set of additional dimensions in a general decline in the capacity of the Calcutta political system to regulate and control individual behavior. In addition to these institutional variables, we have investigated the relationship between public order and economic conditions. To suggest that economic conditions are related to levels of public order is, of course, a well-established tradition in both the criminological and economic literatures.

The third section examines the question of system transformation, specifically the impact of independence on the level of public order in the city. We are interested not only in whether independence was associated with significant change in the levels of various forms of disorder, but also whether independence brought about any restricting of fundamental social relationships within the city. The last section, an epilogue, goes beyond fact and data to speculate about what the sheer existence and persistence of Calcutta implies for our understanding of the conditions of urban society.

A SUMMARY OF TRENDS

Throughout this study we have relied on criminal cases known to the police as our measure of crime. From these data we have inferred the extent of elite concern with regulating social behavior. Although we do not suggest that objective citizen behavior is unimportant in creating elite demands and expectations, it is assumed that citizen behavior is but one of several important influences.[1] For example, we would expect that assaults would increase during periods of very high collective disorder, and indeed they almost certainly do increase in an objective sense. Nevertheless, we find that there is a negative correlation between collective disorder and personal assault. This apparent paradox is resolved if we remember that during the period of most intensive collective violence, the major goal of political elites was simply to restore a minimum level of order in the city. The enumeration of particular criminal cases, including assaults, was of decidedly secondary importance. Thus the inverse relation between riots and personal assault cases is evidence that the Calcutta crime rate represents a political variable quite distinct from the "true" crime rate.

A visual inspection of crime returns suggests a number of politically and socially significant trends in crime. There appears to have been no clear linear trend during the 1870s and 1880s, but in about 1890 total cognizable crime began to drop, reaching its lowest level in 1905. In 1906 crime began to rise again until a peak was reached in the mid-1930s at a level approximately three and one-half times the rate of the early twentieth century. Reported crime dropped sharply thereafter and by the late 1940s had fallen nearly to nineteenth-century levels. Although there is some evidence of a rise in crime after independence, the rate was never more than 50 percent of that of the late nineteenth century.

As might be expected, if the total crime rate is disaggregated into component categories, we find that the trends just described generally apply only to the regulatory offenses that comprise the greatest number of cases in the overall crime rate (Figure V.5.1). More serious crimes, which constitute only small portion of the total crime rate, follow quite different patterns. The distribution of sexual offenses is reported in Figure V.5.1, and Figure V.5.2 reviews the distributions of crimes of personal violence, property crimes, and obstruction of justice cases. The most striking feature of these figures is that each of the categories reached its highest rates in the nineteenth century, generally in the 1880s. Only for crimes of personal violence does an index based on 1873 crime returns (1873 = 100) exceed 100 in the twentieth century. Thus there is a clear decline within almost all these categories of serious crime. To be sure, however, there are significant deviations about this trend. The lowest levels of reported crime were around the turn of the century. Crimes of personal violence then increased until a peak was attained in the early 1920s, whereupon they began to decline once again. A minimum was reached in the early 1940s. Independence seemed to be associated

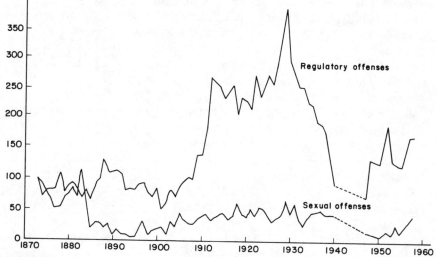

Figure V.5.1 Calcutta: Index of regulatory and sexual offenses per 10,000, 1873-1958 (1873 = 100)

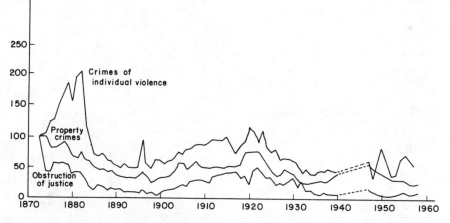

Figure V.5.2 Calcutta: Index of individual violence, property crimes, and obstruction of justice per 10,000, 1873-1958 (1873 = 100)

with an increase that continued into the 1960s. We have seen some evidence that this upward trend became much sharper in the late 1960s (see Figure V.4.5). For the other categories of crime the trend prior to independence is similar, although the local peak for sexual offenses occurred somewhat later, around 1930. The postindependence period is more variable. Obstruction of justice cases are fairly stable. Sexual offenses seem to be on the rise. Property crimes, however, have dropped throughout the postindependence period (see also Figure V.4.8).

One exception to the general trends already described is the changing incidence of group crimes of violence. This category, consisting mainly of riot cases, shows the most extreme variation of any crime aggregation thus far examined. Again using an index with 1873 as a base year, Figure V.5.3 reports the distribution of these group offenses over time. Values of the index range from 23 to more than 1,000. There is a general upward trend in reported cases that is most pronounced in the postindependence period and particularly in the late 1960s (see Figure V.4.6). To balance this apparent extraordinary variation, we need to keep in mind that in absolute terms there were never a great number of such offenses.

In addition to the absolute levels of reported crime, the relative contribution of particular categories to the total crime rate is of interest. Since regulatory offenses make up such a large proportion of all reported crimes, we would expect changes in the total rate to be chiefly a function of these offenses. Large changes within other categories will be reflected neither in the total crime rate nor in the

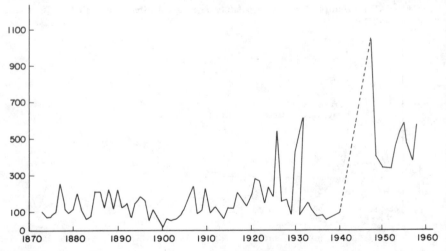

Figure V.5.3 Calcutta: Index of crime of group violence per 10,000, 1873-1958 (1873 = 100)

Table V.5.1 Annual Percentage Contribution of Selected Categories
            of Crime to the Overall Rate of Cognizable Crime
            Known to the Police, 1870-1959[a]

Category	Mean %	Minimum %	Maximum %	S.D.
Crimes of individual violence	1.2	3.4	4.1	.83
Property crimes	10.6	2.9	29.1	6.2
Crimes of group violence	.07	.01	.56	.07
Sexual offenses	.03	.006	.15	.03
Obstruction of justice	.07	.004	.35	.06
Regulatory offenses	88.0	68.5	96.7	7.0

a. Data for 76 years.

Table V.5.2 Percentage Contribution of Selected Categories of Crime
            to the Overall Rate of Serious Cognizable Crime Known
            to the Police, 1870-1959[a]

Category	Mean %	Minimum %	Maximum %	S.D.
Crimes of individual violence	8.7	3.7	14.3	2.5
Property crimes	85.3	74.0	94.8	4.1
Crimes of group violence	.68	.10	3.31	.74
Sexual offenses	.27	.05	.67	.15
Obstruction of justice	.57	.03	1.38	.26

a. Data for 76 years; regulatory offenses excluded.

ratio of that category to the total. This is clearly shown in Table
V.5.1. To discover whether there were indeed significant changes in
the composition of more serious crime, a new index was computed
from which regulatory offenses were deleted. The results of this
analysis are reported in Table V.5.2, which reveals significant variation in the relative magnitude of the various crime categories.

Alternative Measures of Crime and Official Concern

There might be objections raised against the practice of using
crimes known to police as an indicator of elite concern about
regulating social behavior. In Western societies this datum is usually
regarded as the best measure of "true" crime or alternatively, as a
measure of citizens' perception of crime (see Part I), since it derives
mainly from the people's reports. In Calcutta we suspect that there is
a good deal less voluntary reporting of common crimes, if only

Table V.5.3 Mean Annual Values of Alternative Measures of Calcutta's Crime Rate[a]

Category	Reported cases	Total arrests	Taken on magistrate's order	Total convictions
Crimes of individual violence	7.1	9.1	1.5	3.9
Property crimes	63.0	44.4	7.0	24.9
Crimes of group violence	.42	9.7	.19	1.0
Sexual offenses	.20	.21	.00	.002
Obstruction of justice	.46	.69	.34	.01
Regulatory offenses	652	717.5	16.3	666.6

a. Based on rates per 10,000 population, ca. 1870-1960.

Table V.5.4 Correlations Among Alternative Measures of the Cognizable Crime Rate, 1870-1960[a]

Category	Reported cases	Total arrests	Taken on order of magistrate	Total convictions
Crimes of individual violence				
Cases	1.0			
Arrests	.98	1.0		
Magistrate's orders	.29	.36	1.0	
Convictions	.89	.90	.27	1.0
Property crimes				
Cases	1.0			
Arrests	.91	1.0		
Magistrate's orders	.17	.93	.07	1.0
Convictions	.78	.93	.07	1.0
Crimes of group violence				
Cases	1.0			
Arrests	.81	1.0		
Magistrate's orders	− .46	− .04	1.0	
Convictions	.54	.82	− .03	1.0
Sexual offenses				
Cases	1.00			
Arrests	.95	1.00		
Magistrate's orders	.53	.52	1.00	
Convictions	.43	.43		1.00
Obstruction of justice				
Cases	1.0			
Arrests	.93	1.0		
Magistrate's Orders	.16	.17	1.0	
Convictions	.63	.78	.26	1.0
Regulatory offenses				
Cases	1.0			
Arrests	.99	1.0		
Magistrate's orders	.41	.37	1.0	
Convictions	.98	.98	.39	1.0

a. Pearson product-moment r's are reported in this and later tables.

because of distrust of the police, and that many of the "known" offenses are likely detected through active policing. This is obviously true of most regulatory offenses, but it may be true for others as well. In any case we have alternative measures of officials' efforts to control crime, in the form of indicators based on arrests and the number of convictions. We now consider the substantive differences among these alternative measures.

Data are available from four decision points for most years from 1870 to 1960: Reported cases, arrests, convictions, and number of cases taken up on order of a magistrate. The first three need no definition. The last refers to a rather small number of criminal cases, initially held by the police to be groundless, that were later investigated on the direct order of a court. Although it is not clear from the statistical sources, it appears that these cases were included in the reported totals we have reported throughout this study. The relative magnitude of these indicators within various categories of crime are reported in Table V.5.3. As we would expect, there is a considerable difference in the magnitude of the indicators. Of greater interest, however, is the extent to which they display different patterns or trends over time. No a priori logical relationship can be expected among them, though reported crime might be expected to impose a ceiling on arrests. However, as Table V.5.3 shows, multiple arrests for a single criminal offense were quite common. Yet the number of arrests do supply an upper bound for the number of convictions, and within these very broad constraints, the data are free to vary. Table V.5.4 reports the correlations among the various indicators of crime. Except for magistrates' cases in some categories of crime, all the correlations are highly positive, which strongly suggests that there is indeed a common dimension to these indicators.[2] This unidimensionality is particularly clear for regulatory offenses, where the values of r exceed .98—except for orders. We interpret the general dimension as a measure of the varying extent of elites' concerns and efforts at control.

Civil Conflict

The most salient aspect of public order in Calcutta in this century is the extraordinary level and frequency of large-scale collective violence. We have noted a number of instances in which intense episodes of mass violence brought "normal" enforcement activities near to collapse. On several occasions, both before and after independence, the military was forced to assume police powers to restore the city to a nonchaotic state. Table V.5.5 lists the principal episodes of three general forms of violent civil conflict most common to the

Table V.5.5 Major Episodes of Civil Conflict in Calcutta, 1900-1970[a]

Year	Event
	Political terrorism and revolutionary activity
1906-1908	Antipartition agitation
1912-1915	General political unrest
1920-1924	Noncooperation movement
1930-1934	Civil disobedience movement
1942-1943	Quit India Movement
1948-1949	Communist violence
1967-1971	Urban Naxilites
	Communal violence
1918	First major communal violence
1926	Major riot
1946	Worst riot in history of city
1950	Major riot
	Violent labor agitation
1921	Large-scale political strikes
1928	Large-scale political strikes
1934	Large-scale political strikes
1953	Major strikes: economic and political
1954	Major strikes: economic and political
1957	Major strikes: economic and political
1960-1970	Entire decade marked by repeated large strikes; often having political as well as economic goals

a. Prior to 1900 there were no reports of major instances of violent civil conflict. Specific events reported in the table are discussed in more detail in the narrative sections of the study.

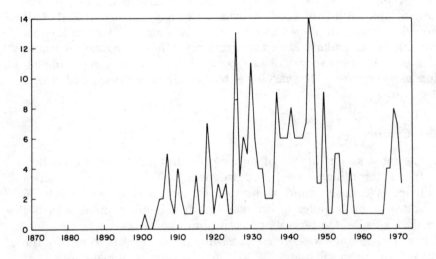

Figure V.5.4 Calcutta: Index of violent civil conflict, 1870-1971

city: political terrorism and revolutionary activity, communal strife, and violent labor agitation.

The narrative and tabular information on episodes of disorder can be translated into an ordinal index of the magnitude of violent conflict. We used a model developed by Gurr and McClelland to construct such an index,[3] which is graphed in Figure V.5.4. Scores were obtained by assigning numerical weights to particular episodes of collective violence, taking into account both frequency and intensity. The figure reveals that civil conflict tended to increase throughout the four decades before independence, with local maxima occurring in 1918, 1926, 1930, 1946, and 1971. The historical events of these years are well known and have been discussed in the narrative sections of the study.

Table V.5.6 reports the correlations between this index of civil conflict and categories of crime measured at different decision points within the Calcutta system of criminal justice. (Cases on magistrate's orders are not included because they are few in number and have weak and inconsistent correlations with the other measures of crime.) There are consistently positive relations between civil conflict and two categories of crime: Group violence and regulatory offenses. The first is to be expected, since most of the offenses in question are defined by antirioting laws. The second supports the interpretation that the police made extensive use of regulatory statutes in "street-clearing" operations. High levels of civil conflict are associated with low levels (indicators) of individual violence, though. Most interesting of all, perhaps, is that reported property crimes tended to increase in times of extensive strife, while arrests and convictions were likely to fall. This is the most general evidence we have found that the control of "common crime" was de-emphasized in periods of high social disorder.

Table V.5.6 Correlations between Civil Conflict and Selected Indicators of Cognizable Crime, 1870-1960

Category	Reported cases	Total arrests	Total convictions
Crimes of individual violence	−.30	−.28	−.30
Property crimes	.22	−.35	−.44
Crimes of group violence	.52	.45	.22
Sexual offenses	−.06	−.06	.22
Obstruction of justice	−.14	−.09	.01
Regulatory offenses	.43	.42	.40

CORRELATES OF CRIME AND CIVIL CONFLICT

In this section we turn to a number of social variables that may influence levels of public disorder. Although there is no well-articulated social theory from which to posit causal linkages, a wealth of conventional and academic wisdom suggests relevant social variables. Two kinds of causal connection are considered in this section: The effects of characteristics of the criminal justice system on crime and conflict, and the impact of economic change.

The Criminal Justice System

The criminal law serves as a skeleton for institutions of public order and suggests the "operational definition" of crime and disorder as it exists in the street. We have seen that the criminal law in Calcutta took quite different developmental paths in the nineteenth and twentieth centuries. The nineteenth century was a period of rudimentary development and modification of criminal law, having the main goal of controlling individual behavior. The present century has been characterized by a tremendous expansion of regulations, and their functional use by the new Indian Bengal Government suggests that the emphasis on order relied on by the British has continued into the postindependence period. To be sure, one can easily overemphasize the dichotomy between the nineteenth and twentieth centuries. Certainly there was some official concern with the possible disruptive influence of emerging Bengali nationalism in the 1800s. On the other hand, efforts to control individual criminal behavior obviously continued throughout the twentieth century and were given up only in periods of the most extreme social unrest.

Table V.5.7 identifies the major legislative additions to the criminal law applicable to Calcutta during the nineteenth and twentieth centuries. Particular emphasis has been placed on the development of law aimed at curbing disorder and political agitation. Although Table V.5.7 may seem to imply that the scope of the criminal law was increasing in a linear fashion, it is more accurate to refer to cycles of repressive legislation followed by periods of moderation. It is unlikely, however, that in any period of moderation the scope of the law returned to its prior level. Thus there was a clear if somewhat uneven linear expansion of the scope of the criminal law throughout the twentieth century. The only possible exception to this general trend occurred during the short-lived United Front Governments of the late 1960s and early 1970s.

We also need to explore the relationship between levels of public disorder and characteristics of those institutions most central to

Table V.5.7 Major Developments in Criminal Law for Calcutta

Year	Law or Code	Provisions
Development period		
1862	Indian Penal Code	Codification
1872	Indian Evidence Act	In general disallowed the use of a confession given to the police.
Repressive period		
1908	Criminal Law Amendment	Outlawed a number of political organizations; specified a set of crimes for which a jury trial did not have to be provided
1910	Press Act	Demanded a security from anyone distributing printed matter
	Bengal Code: Act III	Banned all public meeting one hour before sunset; allowed to expire in 1912
1911	Prevention of Seditious Meetings Act	Outlawed meetings declared seditious.
1915	Defense of India Act	Allowed ban on public meetings, preventive detention, and suspension of due process
1918	Cinemagraphic Act	Extended prior controls on press to plays and movies
1919	Rowlatt Act	Wide powers to control terrorists
1921	Indian Criminal Law amendment	Preventive detention; also allowed greater control of public meetings
1924	Ord. 1: Criminal Law Amendment	Reduced the limitations on police searches
	Sea Customs Act	Tightened controls on imported printed matter for "seditious" material
	Goonda Act	Allowed the deportation from Calcutta of "known" goondas
1926	Indian Penal Law Amendment	Created special courts to deal with political crimes
1929	Press Act	Reimposed requirement that all publishers post a security as a promise against publishing seditious material
1930	Bengal Amendment	Allowed the suspension of civil rights; provided for preventive detention; created a special tax for areas having very high

Table V.5.7 Continued

Year	Law or Code	Provisions
		terrorist activity to aid in paying for police and army patrols
1942	Emergency Powers Act	Allowed the banning of political organizations and the detaining of their leadership; main target was the Congress
1946	Defense of India	Expanded detention and control of subversive organization
1948	West Bengal Criminal Code	In general a continuation of the British legal codes
	West Bengal Security Act	Reimposed most of the repressive law used by the British, including preventive detention
1949	Section 144: Bengal Criminal Code	Allowed the banning of all public meetings
1962	Defense of India Act	Preventive detention

Relaxation of repressive measures
1967-1972   Informal United-Front Government policies

Calcutta's criminal justice system: The police, the courts, and the prisons. For the police we consider two major attributes, social investment and efficiency. "Social investment" refers to the level of resources allocated to an institution by political authorities. "Effi-

Table V.5.8 Correlations Between Police Efficiency, Investment, and Rates of Cognizable Crimes Known to Police, 1870-1960

Category	Correlations with Efficiency[a]	Correlations with social investment in police	
		Expenditures per capita	Police per capita
Crimes of individual violence	−.08	.04	.64
Property crimes	.10	−.02	.37
Crimes of group violence	−.18	.65	.16
Sexual offenses	−.27	.12	.12
Obstruction of justice	−.15	.06	.61
Regulatory offenses	−.13	.33	.57
Index of violent civil conflict	−.18	.21	.32

a. The measure of "efficiency" for each category of crime is the ratio of arrests to offenses known for that particular category. The measure of "efficiency" correlated with the conflict index is the ratio of total arrests to total cognizable offenses.

ciency" refers to an institution's success in meeting demands placed on it. Police efficiency is measured here by the ratio of arrests to total reported crime. For the courts, efficiency is measured by the ratio of convictions to the total number of arrests. Our discussion of prisons must be more impressionistic because of the paucity of quantitative data.

Table V.5.8 shows that there was little relation between police efficiency, measured by capacity to make arrests for known offenses, and the levels of crimes known or the magnitude of violent conflict. For example, violent crimes were neither more nor less common in years in which the police were particularly successful in clearing them through arrests. There is, though, a moderately positive relation between social investment in the police, whether measured by their numbers per capita or their per capita cost, and levels of reported crime. These "social investment" variables also are positively related to collective disorder. The simple explanation is that more police record more, but it should be kept in mind that for most of the 90 years police resources and manpower were declining—as were most kinds of recorded offenses. The positive correlations are evidence of the general diminution in the capacity of the criminal justice system to sustain itself or to detect crime.

The effects of court efficiency are presented in Table V.5.9: There is a fairly strong negative relation between the conviction rate and the total number of reported cases in each crime category. This is particularly true of the more serious crimes of individual violence. In the context of Calcutta, these findings imply that as the incidence of violent crimes decreased, it became more likely that persons arrested for these offenses would be convicted. This almost certainly reflects

Table V.5.9 *Correlations Between Efficiency of the Calcutta Courts and Rates of Cognizable Crimes Known to Police, 1870-1960*[a]

Category	Correlation
Crimes of individual violence	−.08
Property crimes	−.54
Crimes of group violence	−.23
Sexual offenses	−.28
Obstruction of justice	−.42
Regulatory offenses	−.22
Index of violent civil conflict	−.15

a. The measure of "efficiency" for each category of crime is the ratio of convictions to arrests for that particular category. The measure of "efficiency" correlated with the conflict index is the ratio of total convictions to total arrests for cognizable offenses.

an increase in the selectivity of the police when making arrests during periods when rates of known crime were low.

In the prisons there was a detectable shift of institutional emphasis from retribution and punishment to custodial care. Although there has been official endorsement of the ideal that prisons ought to be involved in rehabilitation and training efforts, there is no evidence that this endorsement has been transformed into increased resources. Reinforcing this custodial emphasis is the large number of persons sentenced to very short terms for minor offenses. For example, jail officials have bitterly complained that their facilities are greatly overtaxed by the many persons sentenced to a month or two in jail for riding the railroads without a ticket. Such pressures, coupled with very low levels of resources, leave prison officials few policy choices.

One interesting impact of the evolving custodial emphasis in Indian jails has been the creation of an environment conducive to the development of political consciousness, often radical political consciousness. Enforced leisure often has led to political discussion and the formation of informal study groups. Indeed, the British often encouraged such study groups as a means of keeping prisoners "quiet." The most dramatic of several examples of this kind of political evolution was, of course, the conversion of much of the Bengali left to Marxism while in British jails during the 1920s.

There is a major gap in our knowledge of Indian prisons, both before and after independence. We know that during much of the twentieth century there were "shadow" prisons for political prisoners and detainees. However, we have no systematic evidence on the size or condition of these prisons. Our only source of information is personal remembrances of persons held in such prisons, sources which are often of doubtful validity. We do know for certain, however, that functionally the shadow prisons were almost completely custodial.

Cost of Living and Public Disorder

We have already observed that economic growth and political development in Calcutta have been closely intertwined. Indeed, the city was created by the British as a means of extracting wealth from India. In this section we consider the much more specific question of whether changing economic conditions in the city can be related to measures of public disorder independent of the political environment. We restrict the analysis to cost of living, using it as a surrogate measure for individual economic well-being in the city.[4] The major deficiency of this approach is that we have no comparable measure of personal income. The offsetting advantage is that the cost-of-living

Table 5.10   Correlations Between Inflation and Selected Categories
              of Crimes Known, 1873-1958[a]

Category	Correlation
Crimes of individual violence	−.31
Property crimes	−.20
Crimes of group violence	.61
Regulatory offenses	.16
Index of violent conflict	.44

a. Data for 76 years.

data are available for virtually the entire period from 1860 to 1960.
Moreover the narrative sources suggest that there were a number of
periods of inflation not matched by increases in wages.

The simple correlations between our cost-of-living index and the
levels of reported crime are listed in Table V.5.10. On first inspection
the results may seem to be counterintuitive. For example, property
crime tends to decrease in periods of inflation. One would expect the
opposite to be true if the cost-of-living index does tap economic
well-being. The paradox is partly resolved by the evidence on collective disorder. Table V.5.10 also shows that inflation is positively
correlated at a high level with crimes of group violence and our index
of violent conflict. The economic distress caused by inflation
apparently has been a contributing factor to large-scale outbreaks of
civil conflict, a phenomenon that has been shown repeatedly to
reduce reports of individual crime.

STEP CHANGE: THE IMPACT OF INDEPENDENCE

The previous section was primarily aimed at assessing the impact
of a number of variables on crime and conflict over a fairly long
period. We implicitly assumed a static pattern of relationships among
the variables of interest. Without suggesting that such relationships
are invariant over time, we do assume that changes in social systems
are largely incremental. In this section we test some effects of step
change, a concept that refers to a restructuring of relations within a
system, as distinct from more or less continuous changes in particular
variables. In this instance we wish to explore the impact of a change
in political regime on the level of public order.

There is little evidence to lead us to believe that independence
brought about any dramatic transformation of the criminal justice
system in Calcutta. Indeed, the literature indicates that colonial

political and social structures persisted after independence. Data discussed in Ch. V.4 (Figures V.4.5 to V.4.8) reveal that some categories of crime were very high in 1946 and 1947, but not for long.

There is some evidence that independence was associated with less dramatic but more persistent changes in trends in various categories of crime. Table V.5.11 reports the simple correlations between selected categories of crime and time during the periods from 1873 to 1947 and from 1948 to 1958 or 1948 to 1971, depending on the availability of data. In most categories there is evidence of a strong linear trend whose direction sometimes changes after independence, particularly with respect to crimes of individual violence. In the preindependence period there was a strong negative trend that reverses to strongly positive after independence. This is also true of group violence, sexual offenses, and cases of obstruction of justice. The reported rate of regulatory offenses continued to rise, and the number of property crimes continued to decline. For some offenses, including regulatory ones, conclusions must be very tentative because the time span for which there are data is very short. The results for the data series extending to 1971 warrant more confidence. In both instances, though, two interpretations are possible. One is that the city became more "disorderly" after independence. In view of the de-emphasis on controlling individual crime in the latter part of the colonial era, the increases might also be taken as evidence of a rise in the city's ability to police itself. To support this hypothesis, we can note that violent civil conflict in the city was relatively low during most of the 1950s and 1960s. There also is evidence of more intensive policing in the middle 1960s. But a resurgence of disorder

Table V.5.11   *Correlations Between Time and Selected Reported Crimes per 10,000 Population in Pre- and Post-independence Calcutta*

| | Preindependence | Postindependence | |
	1873-1947	1948-1958	1948-1971
Category			
Crimes of individual violence	−.51	.81	nd
Serious assault	−.32	.53	.07[a]
Minor assault	−.42	.84	nd
Property crimes	−.44	−.87	−.88
Crimes of group violence	.32	.61	.35
Sexual offenses	−.19	.57	nd
Obstruction of justice	−.26	.05	nd
Regulatory offenses	.71	.34	nd

a. Murder only.

*Table V.5.12   Public Order and Inflation: A Comparison of the Pre-
and Postindependence Periods*

Correlation of inflation with: Category	Preindependence (67 years)	Postindependence (7 years)
Crimes of individual violence	-.12	-.68
Property crimes	.06	.22
Crimes of group violence	.64	-.54
Sexual offenses	-.13	-.85
Obstruction of justice	.06	-.55
Regulatory offenses	.46	-.29

in the late 1960s shattered any short-term possibilities for a new
social order.

Perhaps the most interesting, if most speculative, possibility is that
system transformation leads not to trend changes but to fundamental
modifications in the nature of social causality. It might be proposed
that the creation of an independent India, midwifed by postwar
stress and massive collective violence, led to a readjustment of the
social system that defines Calcutta, and the city became better able
to cope with future stresses. A typical example of such a readjustment is the de jure or de facto decriminalization of behaviors authorities are unable to control. Examples range from the American
experience with prohibition to the inability of the British to control
the nationalist press in Bengal. To explore this kind of possibility in
Calcutta, we computed a series of correlations between our indicator
of cost of living and the various categories of known crime. Separate
coefficients were estimated for the pre- and postindependence
periods. If step changes had occurred at the point of independence,
there should be a changing pattern of parameter estimates. In some
instances this is precisely what happens (Table V.5.12). Whereas
inflation was a positive correlate of group violence and regulatory
offenses before 1947, it was a negative correlate thereafter. The
results are only suggestive of what might be accomplished in an
analysis using other variables and data for longer periods. We report
them here not for their substantive importance but to indicate a
direction for future analysis.

EPILOGUE: REFLECTIONS ON A DISORDERLY CITY

Almost from the moment Job Charnack selected Calcutta as the
base for the operations of the East India Company in Bengal, the
future of the city has been debated. Since the 1750s, if not earlier, it
has been widely assumed that conditions in the city were intolerable

and that it simply could not long survive. Calcutta has become an antimodel—it represents what no city ought to be. For the more pessimistic commentators, the city defines the direction of all future urban life, a future that is very bleak indeed. It is an example of a social system in which extreme poverty, disease, and violence are the conditions of normality. Questions of urban development and reform seem curiously out of place in a city that has sometimes been unable to clear the streets of its dead in the morning. How does one approach the problem of improving housing in a city where perhaps a quarter-million persons have no housing at all? The enormous scale of Calcutta and its problems has led many to turn away in despair. Indian officials tend to vary between episodes of rage in which the supposed ills of the city are equated with the overactive imagination of intellectuals (particularly Western intellectuals) and a desperate hope that the objective horror of the city will not overtake all India. The latter attitude is reflected in a policy of "benign neglect" in which the central government has focused on the development of rural Bengal. And yet the city remains. It continues to be not only a source of great wealth to a very few of its citizens, but also a major center for Indian society and culture. Calcutta refuses to collapse or "go away." How it manages to survive forms a fundamental question for anyone who is interested in social development.

Perhaps the most obvious lesson to be drawn from the social history of Calcutta is the remarkable extremes to which human collectivities seem to be able to adjust. It is a certainty that the vast majority of Calcutta's population has never found life pleasant, yet the city continues to attract immigrants. What has evolved in Calcutta is largely outside the Western experience and severely strains our ability to understand it. Models of development are largely inappropriate. Calcutta is neither the society of expanding social scale described by Scott Greer nor the simple collection of villages that is often thought to represent urbanization in many "underdeveloped" countries.[5] If there is ever to be a general theory of urban development, surely the challenges posed by the case of Calcutta will have to be addressed.

Calcutta also provides a critical test for what social science thinks it knows about the relationship between deprivation and social violence. Although we have spent a good deal of time discussing the city's high levels of collective violence, one might wonder why such violence is not even more common, given existing conditions. Even more curious is the minimal impact of collective violence on political structures. The formal government of Bengal often seems to have been immune to it. The British did not leave Bengal until 1947, after more than 40 tumultuous years, often marked by violent resistance on a massive scale. Similarly the sovereignty of the independent Indian government over West Bengal and Calcutta has not been shaken by severe and protracted episodes of political violence in the late 1940s and late 1960s. This apparent political stability raises again the more general issue of the nature of the formal social organization by which Calcutta maintains itself.

Calcutta is an extremely fragmented society. Although this fragmentation, particularly that based on religion and class, is the source of much collective violence, it also provides a measure of social and political stability. The extent of social fragmentation within the city mitigates against the formation of any group that might be able to enforce its will on the entire society. Thus we can say, perhaps paradoxically, that the great divisions within Calcutta society act as a source of strength to current political elites. At the same time it needs to be recognized that the severe social fragmentation within the city restricts the scope of potential action for the elite. There are numerous examples of such constraints. For example, there have never been any general laws on inheritance applicable to all Calcutta. Hindus and Muslims were left largely to create their own legal systems for this and other matters. We would argue that this devolution extends into a number of areas to which the criminal laws are formally applied. Indeed, one explanation of the low crime rate in the city is that much of the responsibility for enforcing social norms has remained with informal social groups. Any complete study of public order in Calcutta would have to examine these informal social controls as well as the formal political institutions, which have largely been our focus. Such a study is far beyond the scope of this work, of course.

Investigation of the role of crime and violent conflict in Calcutta yields a further important lesson to the student of comparative politics. Some of these actions are similar in an objective sense to behaviors we observe in other political systems, but they turn out to be quite different functionally. For example, collective violence has played a major role in the history of North American cities as well as that of Calcutta. It is impossible to summarize 200 years of American urban history in a few sentences. It can be said, however, that in the political system of the United States, mass protest has in general proved to be an inefficient way of making political demands. To be sure some groups, most notably organized labor, have utilized collective action as a means of gaining access to political power: Modern organized labor was born and tested in conflict.[6] Once entry to the mainstream of American politics was achieved, though, disruptive tactics were rejected as a primary strategy. Where mass protest has not opened wide the gates to power, as with black unrest of the

1960s, the payoffs of disruptive tactics for the challenging group have been much more uncertain.[7] Success in American politics rest on money, organization, and expertise. Such a political order implies an environment relatively rich in resources. Calcutta provides a counterexample of a resource-poor environment in which violence has become an institutionalized form of political demand. In Calcutta street violence tends to establish a political balance much like the balance that might be observed around a conference table in a resource-rich political system. Throughout the twentieth century political violence has served to secure governmental response for social groups that had very little else in the way of political resources. In Calcutta the link between violence and decision makers is a direct one. To draw an analogy from economics, collective violence as it is practiced in Calcutta represents a labor-intensive form of politics, as contrasted to the capital-intensive interest group politics more familiar in the West. One further implication of a resource-poor environment is the resulting emphasis on symbolic rather than material rewards. We have some evidence that the process of bargaining for material rewards creates pressures for moderation in political demands.[8] Where symbolic issues are deemed more important, there appears to be a tendency toward radicalization, as in Calcutta politics.

There is a commonality between Calcutta and Western cities in that widespread collective disorder creates elite demands that such behavior be controlled and eliminated, if possible. In twentieth-century Calcutta these demands had the consequence of diverting limited resources that had been allocated to the control of individual behavior (i.e., crime). Thus we have consistently argued and cited evidence that falling rates of serious crime do not imply an increase in the personal safety of city residents. Rather, the scope of public control of social disorder was declining. Changing crimes rates were due more to changes in policing than to modifications of social behavior. Thus we have the implication that it is inappropriate to compare Calcutta's crime rate with that of other cities, especially prosperous Western ones. There is an obvious lack of equivalence. Indeed, the problem of equivalence imperils our attempts to compare crime rates over time within Calcutta. If comparative work on public order is to be undertaken, it must be recognized—as it is in this study—that crime statistics are not a simple mirror of disorderly behavior in the society that generates them. In the extreme case of Calcutta, the relative level of resources allocated by political elites to the control of individual crime is a critical factor in the production of crime statistics.

Although we have been able to offer what is hoped to be an

accurate description of the changing state of public order in Calcutta, we have avoided the much more difficult task of explaining the process by which the city reached its present state. Even more important questions might be raised concerning the future of the city. Unfortunately there is little to guide us in either investigation. Certainly the economy of the city has become, in Clifford Geertz's phrase, "involuted."[9] The word signifies that the economy of the region, although it may be expanding in an aggregate sense, is not creating conditions for long-range and self-sustaining growth. Instead, the resources generated by the developed sector of the dual economy tend to reinforce the maintenance of the traditional social and political elite. Only those directly involved in the developed sector of the economy benefit from the exchanges in it. This not only describes the economy of Calcutta through most of the present study, but it is also an abstract of British economic policy throughout Bengal for much of the period in which they were rulers of India. This emphasis has largely been maintained by the indigenous Indian leadership since 1947. There is little evidence that the dual economy has been weakened.

There is, of course, the very real issue of whether or not there is much potential for long-range development in the city, and a variety of indicators suggest that the future is far from bright. As we have already seen, Calcutta suffers with a port of dubious quality, an obsolete and shrinking manufacturing base, and an uneven pattern of industrial development. More fundamental perhaps is the human problem, which to an extent is simply one of numbers. It would require an enormous level of investment, far more than India could possibly mount, to raise the standard of living in any meaningful way. Even if it were possible to secure a minimum increase in the city's standard of living, the improvement would quite likely fail to have a stabilizing effect. More probable would be an increase of expectations and political demands, which would quickly surpass any capacity to deliver. In addition to rising expectations, a general improvement in the economic condition of the city would bring about more interactions among hostile social groups. Unfulfilled expectations and increased competition in Calcutta have similarly violent implications. Thus even if economic improvement were possible, it might well result in an increase in collective violence. A much more likely future for the city is found in the developmental pattern of its immediate past; a gradual economic decline coupled with increased social and political devolution. The consequences of devolution for urban survival, and the circumstances under which it might be reversed, are major challenges to theories of urban development and decay.

NOTES TO CHAPTER V.5

1. Reported crime is not a simple function of citizen perception of criminal behavior for several reasons. One is that citizens rarely report "victimless" offenses. Where crimes against persons and property are concerned, the victim must feel that it is worthwhile to report the crime. One factor affecting this perception is the belief that something will be done about the complaint, which in turn depends on the resources and capabilities of the police.

2. These cases on magistrates' orders were considered at some length during the data analysis to determine whether they were related to such system characteristics as the level of civil conflict, or whether they consisted of particularly sensitive or "political" cases. The results of these analyses were negative. Since these cases were relatively uncommon, the results of their analysis are not reported further.

3. This index was derived from one used by Ted Robert Gurr and Muriel McClelland, *Political Performance: A Twelve-Nation Study* (Beverly Hills, Calif.: Sage Professional Paper in Comparative Politics, 01-018, 1971).

4. The inflation index was constructed from several overlapping statistical series. The period 1861-1931 relies on reported food costs in Calcutta from *Index Numbers of Indian Prices 1861-1931* (Calcutta: Department of Commercial Intelligence and Statistics, 1933). This series was continued in various editions of *Statistical Abstract for British India.* Following independence a more general cost-of-living index reported in the *West Bengal Statistical Abstract* was used.

5. See Scott Greer, *The Emerging City* (New York: Free Press, 1962).

6. Michael Lipsky, "Protest as a Political Resource," *American Political Science Review*, 62 (December 1968).

7. See Susan Welch, "The Impact of Urban Riots on Urban Expenditures," *American Journal of Political Science*, 19 (November 1975).

8. Lipsky, op. cit.

9. Clifford Geertz, *Agricultural Involution: The Process of Ecological Change* (Berkeley: University of California Press, 1963).

Part VI

THE COMPARATIVE ANALYSIS

OF PUBLIC ORDER

Ted Robert Gurr

Chapter VI.1

THE BEST OF TIMES,
THE WORST OF TIMES
Trends in Crime in Four Societies

The four cities have had different experiences of crime and strife during the past century and a half. In London, Stockholm, and New South Wales the official indicators of common crimes of violence and theft all trace a declining trend during the second half of the nineteenth century and into the early decades of the twentieth century. But no later than the 1950s, most of them begin a dramatic ascent. One might almost conclude that some common social and political dynamics created public order over the course of a century in Western societies, then went crazily unsprung in a single generation. When we examine the regulation of social conduct, though, evidence of common trends in behavior is overshadowed by many indications that the tides of official concern with deviant and disorderly behavior have periodically risen and subsided. Civil conflict in the Western cities also has been episodic. A recurrent issue of conflict has been the demands of rising classes for a greater share of goods and power; but open combat over these and other issues has erupted at different times, displaying differing forms and intensities, and bringing varied consequences. Calcutta represents another world with a vastly different history. Its orderly colonial existence at the turn of the twentieth century disintegrated in a welter of crime, conflict, and repression in the first half of the present century. The "creative" uses of disorder that won Indian independence endured in Calcutta long after their initial goal was achieved. Reported crime, prosecutions, and convictions oscillated wildly in the first 25 years after independence, in a complex response to the ebb and flow of political combat.

The evidence for these generalizations, and many qualifications of them, are the subject of this chapter and the next. We begin by examining the trends in official indicators of crime, and we also deal with the critical question of interpretation: Are the trends a reflection of changing social behavior or changing institutional policies? The next chapter surveys the comparative history of civil conflict in the four cities, with special reference to its national political context, and identifies the principal periods of crisis in public order in each of the societies.

The grist for the analysis that follows is provided by indicators constructed from offical data on several categories of crime, using both offenses known to police and convictions, whenever both are available. Interpretation is problematic, however for reasons spelled out previously. Depending on their types, indicators of crime are directly informative about the volume of citizens' reports to police, the extent of police activity, and the extent and severity of public sanctions applied. But virtually no one who studies crime statistics is content to stop there. Where there's smoke there's fire, they assume, and differences in the volume of smoke should tell us where the fire is greatest. We think the assumption is tenable under certain strict conditions. Differences in crime indicators from one locale to another permit inferences about differences in social behavior only if the locales have very similar policing agencies, operating with similar legal codes, procedures, and methods of accounting. The greater the differences in any of these institutional factors, the less reliable are inferences about differential social behavior. In this study these conditions for comparability do not obtain. As a result, few conclusions can be drawn about differences among the cities in absolute levels of crime.

Differences in crime indicators within one locale over time are more promising, provided the offense in question is a "visible" one. Crimes that have victims usually are more consistently recorded than those whose detection depends on active policing: People who are assaulted or plundered complain; gamblers, addicts, sexual deviants, drunks, and abortionists generally keep a low profile. Therefore the trends in common crimes against persons and property offer potential evidence about changes in social behavior. Additional evidence is found by reference to different indicators of the same kind of offense: If change is similar in indicators of both reported crime and convictions, or indicators of similar kinds of offenses (both murder and assault, or robbery and larceny), we gain confidence about the social reality of change. Another test is whether substantial changes have occurred in the institutions and practices of policing and judicial administration, and if so, whether they may account for recorded changes in crime. Small or abrupt changes in the indicators are suspect on these grounds. Changes that are both large and cumulative are more convincing evidence of behavioral change.

Our analysis focuses on long-term trends in representative indicators of murder and assault, theft, white-collar crime, sexual deviance, and drunkenness. The primary concern is to describe the trends, the secondary is to interpret them in the light of what we know about changing policies of public order. The question of interpretation is only begun here; the analysis of legal and institutional innovation in later chapters yields additional evidence.

A preliminary note on methods is needed. The graphic comparisons below are based, wherever possible, on ten-year moving averages of annual crime data, weighted per 100,000 population. All subsequent references to crime "rates" and "indicators" are to these population-weighted measures. They convey no direct evidence on the absolute number of offenses or on year-to-year variations. Since our objective is to include the longest time span possible for each type of offense for each city, it is generally necessary to use several different kinds of measures on a single chart. Where possible, we use two parallel kinds of indicators, one based on offenses known (or arrests, in New South Wales), the other on convictions. The meanings conveyed differ greatly. "Offenses known" signifies the number of criminal acts that come to official attention. "Convictions" signifies the number of offenders actually processed and punished. A single individual may be responsible for a large number of offenses, especially theft. The magnitudes of the two indicators thus are often vastly different: Known thefts, for example, exceed convictions by about 10:1. The amplitudes of changes in different indicators of a crime usually are different too: Known offenses tend to decrease and to increase with more volatility than arrests and convictions. But in most sets of parallel indicators we have examined, including many not reproduced here, the direction of their long-term trends is the same.[1]

TRENDS IN MURDER AND ASSAULT

Murder and serious cases of assault are more likely than any other category of common crime to receive official attention. They also are subject to relatively little definitional variation from one time and jurisdiction to another.[2] Thus a prima facie case could be made that the trends depicted in Figures VI.1.1 through VI.1.4 represent real changes over time in the propensity for private mayhem. Some grounds for skepticism are considered below.

In London the rates of convictions for indictable offenses for murder, manslaughter, attempted murder, and grievous assault (Figure VI.1.1) were at their highest recorded levels in the 1840s. They

declined between then and the 1920s by a ratio of about 8:1. The
decline in attempted murder and assaults was more precipitous than
the drop in murder and manslaughter. Convictions for the latter
offenses, which are much less numerous, declined by a ratio of 3:1,
from a high of about .70 per 100,000 population in the 1820s to .25 in
the late 1920s. Comparisons for the last 50 years must be based on
crimes known to the police. Reported attempts at murder and assaults
(not shown in Figure VI.1.1) began to rise in the 1920s and more than
doubled by the late 1940s. The increase in the next 25 years, though,
reduced the earlier one to insignificance: In the early 1970s Londoners
were more than ten times as likely to be victimized by serious assaults
as they were in the late 1940s. It is conceivable that some of this
increase was due to changing police reporting procedures, but the rising
rate of reported murder during these decades (see Figure VI.1.1)
suggests otherwise. In 1950-1951 the murder rate was .48 per 100,000,
by 1971-1972 it had tripled to 1.47 per 100,000. The nineteenth
century decline and the mid-twentieth century increase in indicators of
aggressive crime thus have similar properties: Attempted murder and
serious assaults declined, then increased simultaneously with murder,
but more sharply. And the century-long decline in the murder
conviction rate, by a ratio of about 3:1, was equivalent to the 1:3
increase in known murders since 1950.

London's experience of violence against persons is paralleled by
that of Stockholm. (Note that since the data for Stockholm and for
London are aggregated somewhat differently, the absolute rates
cannot be directly compared.) In Stockholm the rate of convictions
for murder, attempted murder, and manslaughter declined by a ratio
of 7:1 between the 1830s and the early 1900s, though the decline is
broken by a temporary doubling in the early 1880s—a period marked
by numerous attacks on police and the beginnings of organized labor
protest. Data on known offenses document the same long-term
decline and temporary increase. The big decline between 1916 and
1917 reflects a change in recording procedures. As in London, we
rely on reports rather than convictions to document the rate of
mayhem thereafter.[3] The rates are consistently low through the
1920s and 1930s but begin a distinct and persistent increase around
1940. The increase in reported offenses between the 1930s and the
1960s is about 1:9, but part of the increase and subsequent decline
after 1969 is a function of changes in the recording of manslaughter.
No such procedural ambiguity affects the rate of reported assault
(not shown graphically), which increased 500 percent between the
1940s and the early 1970s.

In New South Wales we rely on composite indicators of serious
crimes against the person, including murder, manslaughter, attempted
murder, and armed assault. The extraordinary nineteenth century de-

(text continued page 41)

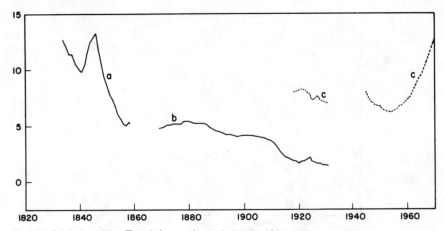

Figure VI.1.1 London: Trends in murder and assault, 1834-1972

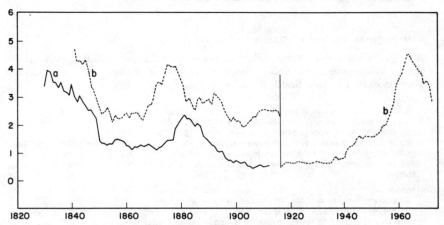

Figure VI.1.2 Stockholm: Trends in murder and assault, 1830-1971

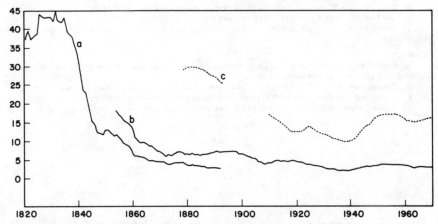

Figure VI.1.3 New South Wales: Trends in murder and assault, 1820-1970

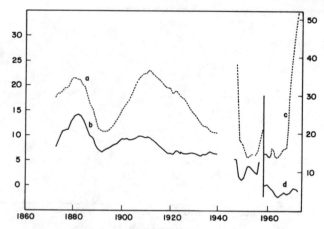

Figure VI.1.4 Calcutta: Trends in murder and assault, 1873-1971

Notes to Figures on Trends in Murder and Assault

All figures show ten-year moving averages of rates per 100,000 population, except where specified. Solid lines are convictions; dashed lines are reported offenses except in New South Wales, where they signify arrests.

London
a. Convictions for murder, manslaughter, attempted murder, and serious assaults, Middlesex County, five-year moving average, 1834-1858.

b. Convictions for same offenses as in a, MPD, 1869-1931.

c. Reported murders and manslaughter, MPD, 1918-1931, 1938, 1945-1972, per million population. Reports of all offenses in a increase so greatly after 1950 that they cannot be fitted on the same graph: the rate circa 1950 is 13 per 100,000, circa 1970 it is 90 per 100,000.

Stockholm
a. Convictions for murder, attempted murder, and manslaughter, 1830-1912.

b. Reported murders, attempted murders, and manslaughter, 1841-1971. The series is broken in 1916-1917 to reflect a change in reporting procedures.

New South Wales
a. Supreme Court convictions for serious aggressive crimes, 1820-1892.

b. All higher court convictions for serious aggressive crimes, 1854-1970.

c. Arrests for aggressive crimes against persons, 1883-1897 and 1914-1970, per 10,000 population.

Calcutta
a. Reported murders and serious assaults, 1873-1940 (ten-year moving average) and 1947-1958 (three-year moving average).

b. Convictions for murder and serious assault, same years and moving averages as in a.

c. Reported murders, 1959-1971, per million population, five-year moving average.

d. Convictions for murder, 1959-1971, per million population, five-year moving average.

cline in conviction rates is partly attributable to the declining proportion of convicts in the population, since this group was prone to
violence and subject to harsh judicial sanctions. However the decline continued long after the end of transportation in 1840,
though.

The index of convictions by the higher courts declined by 9:1
from the 1850s, when transportation was a fading memory, to the
tranquil years of the 1930s. Another persuasive comparison is provided by the arrest and conviction rates for serious aggressive crimes
between 1880s and the late 1930s: Arrests declined by a ratio of 3:1,
convictions by 2:1. The postwar increase has been much less pronounced in New South Wales than in London or Stockholm, however. Arrests and higher court convictions both increased about 50
percent between 1940 and 1970, but most of the increase occurred
in the first decade after the war. Reported homicides and serious
assaults increased by 40 percent between 1960 and 1970. If Sydney
traces the London and Stockholm pattern, steeper increases are in
the offing.

The trends in murder and serious assault in Calcutta differ greatly
from those of the European cities. The pattern of both recorded
offenses and convictions is cyclical, with peaks in the 1880s,
1906-1915, the mid-1940s, and the early 1970s. The last three peaks
coincide with periods of violent strife, generated by nationalism in
the first instance, Hindu-Muslim conflict in the second, and left-right
political combat in the last. The inference is that the officials
knowingly included in the crime data some, perhaps all of the deaths
and injuries that occurred in strife. This would also help account for
the markedly greater discrepancy between offenses known and convictions between these three periods and other times: The perpetrators of murder and assault in riots are rarely caught and brought to
trial. Quite a different explanation of the trends is that they reflect
the extent of police activity. The ratio of police to population in
Calcutta from the 1870s to 1940 traces a curve very similar to that in
Figure VI.1.4 (see Figure VI.4.4 on p. 711, below). Since the Indian
population of Calcutta was reluctant to report offenses to police,
whom they commonly feared for their venality and brutality, it is
reasonable to expect that "offenses known" depended more on the
extent of police patrolling than on real trends in behavior as reflected
elsewhere in citizen reports. The two explanations are complementary, not inconsistent, and we examine more evidence for them
in the next section.

Distinctive long-term trends or cycles are evident in the indicators
of murder and assault in all four societies. Some show tenfold
decreases and increases. The second quarter of the nineteenth century and the third quarter of the twentieth were periods of intense

public concern and high levels of official effort to control violent crime in the Western societies; in Calcutta four more closely spaced peaks are evident. To what extent do the indicators also reflect a changing social reality? Murders and assaults are visible and universally abhorred; thus the more serious of these offenses are likely to reach the attention of officials in any city having a rudimentary police and criminal justice system. But alternative explanations must be considered. Have police and public sensitivities about minor cases of assault changed enough over time to account for some of the trends? The sensitivity of such offenses in Western societies no doubt has increased during the last century and a half, yet for the 1800s the trend in indicators of assault was down. Moreover the 150-year trends in murder and assault are the same; both declined for a century, both increased in the last 30 years. This alternative explanation thus is not convincing; at most it may account for part of the skyrocketing increase in reported assault since 1950 in London and Stockholm.

Part of the evidence for trends in violent crime consists of conviction ratios, which may be influenced by changing judicial policies. Declining conviction ratios from the 1820s to the 1930s might be explained by arguing that judicial standards of proof have changed, making convictions on a given body of evidence decreasingly likely. The evidence against this interpretation is substantial. (a) Indicators of committals to trial (not shown here) are available for the same periods as convictions and document the same trends. (b) Where data are available on offenses known and arrests, they show the same trends as convictions. (c) The greatest expansion of defendants' rights has occurred during the last 50 years, and conviction ratios have risen, not declined, during the last part of this period. This does not rule out another possibility, though, that court jurisdictions for offenses of a given degree of seriousness have changed systematically over time. Trends in murder convictions do not admit of such an explanation; trends in assault might be more amenable. Part of the precipitous decline in convictions for crimes of violence in New South Wales between the 1820s and the 1860s, for example, is probably due to a shift of lesser offenses from the jurisdiction of the higher courts to magistrates' courts. In London summary jurisdiction over assaults was extended in 1827-1828 and again in 1926; neither had a visible effect on the rate of convictions by the higher courts. In Stockholm and Calcutta, where we have data on the activities of the lower as well as higher courts, the trends in minor assaults approximate those in serious cases.

Some of the nineteenth century decline in the indicators of violent crime in the three Western societies may be due to the altered workings of the police and courts. The same reasoning may be applicable to some of the recent increases. But not even the most skeptical multiple pleading can explain away the trends themselves. The only simple explanation that is consistent with the body of historical and statistical evidence is real change in social behavior. In these three societies, we ·conclude, interpersonal violence did decrease very substantially during the century that ended in the 1930s, and in London and Stockholm such behavior increased greatly in the last 30 years.

TRENDS IN THEFT

Even in the worst of times murder and assault affect only a handful of people compared to the number victimized by theft. A few statistics from London and Stockholm document the relatively high frequency of theft and thieves. In London in 1840 a total of 2,271 people were convicted for indictable crimes of robbery, burglary, larceny, and receiving stolen goods;[4] only 134 were convicted for murder and serious assault. In Stockholm in the same year 490 people were convicted for all kinds of theft compared with 75 for murder, assault, and breach of the peace. The discrepancies in reported offenses are considerably greater. In 1971 there were 266,200 indictable thefts reported in London's Metropolitan Police District, contrasted with about 8,000 murders and serious assaults (mostly the latter). The figures for Stockholm were 68,564 thefts and 2,932 cases of murder, assault, and breach of the peace. These figures are comparable within each city but not between them, because the London data are for indictable offenses only. By any standard, though, the volume of contemporary property crime is impressive: in Stockholm in 1971 there was one recorded theft for every 11 persons, in London one serious recorded theft for every 29 persons.

The social significance of the 150-year reversing trend in crimes of violence might be minimized if we could demonstrate an enduring improvement or simple persistence in trends in theft. Some comfort might even be taken from a finding that property crime has increased in lockstep with increasing prosperity. Unfortunately neither of these patterns is evident in the data on theft. In all four societies the trends and cycles are very similar to those for crimes of violence.

In London the rate of convictions for indictable (serious) crimes of theft, lines a and b in Figure VI.1.5, was very high in the mid-1830s and mid-1840s but fell by a ratio of 3:1 by the beginning of the 1870s. The decline continued through the 1920s, and by the onset of the Great Depression the conviction rate was less than a tenth of what it had been a century earlier. The only reversal was a 50 percent increase between 1899 and 1908, after which the decline resumed. The trends were not identical for all forms of theft, though.

For robbery, the most serious form of theft in English law, the decline was about 7:1. Convictions for indictable larcenies declined by about 10:1. Burglary more than doubled, however, and by 1930 that crime accounted for two-thirds of all convictions for indictable theft. This changing "mix" is attributable to two factors. One was a real shift from armed robbery to burglary as the preferred method of theft, a trend that is readily explained by the progressive "disarmament" of the English citizenry and increasing penalties for crimes committed with guns. The other was officials' increased reliance, evident as early as the middle of the nineteenth century, on summary justice for larcenies that were nominally indictable. By the middle of the twentieth century virtually all larcenies, regardless of whether formally indictable, were disposed of summarily. Thus conviction trends a and b in Figure VI.1.5 document a decline in the overall rate of what English officials regarded as "serious" property crimes (i.e., those worth prosecuting as indictable offenses), but they only tell us something about the changing volume of total property crime when considered in conjunction with summary convictions. Line c in Figure VI.1.5 shows the trend in summary convictions for property crime between 1869 and 1931. Summary convictions were three times as numerous as indictable convictions, though they also declined between 1870 and 1930 by a ratio of about 2:1, compared with a 3:1 decline in convictions for the more serious offenses combined.

The indicator of known indictable thefts for London, beginning in 1918, shows a decade-long decline followed by a reversal that corresponds approximately with the onset of the Great Depression and continues without interruption until after World War II. The postwar improvement proved to be temporary—it lasted less than a decade. The total increase in the rate of known indictable thefts between 1935 and 1970 was about 400 percent. In 1935 there was one indictable theft reported per 120 Londoners, in 1970 there was one for every ·32. The increase is not uniform across all forms of theft, any more than was the decrease. From the early 1930s to the early 1970s the robbery rate increased by 3000 percent (mostly after 1955), burglary by 700 percent, and indictable larceny by 300 percent.

The trends of theft in Stockholm (a and b in Figure VI.1.6) trace a familiar pattern. Moreover they pose fewer problems of comparability or interpretation than those of London, since they represent all forms of theft and are continuously available for more than a century. Convictions per 100,000 for all thefts declined by a ratio of 5:1 between the early 1840s and the 1930s; there were sharp but temporary interruptions in the trend around 1870 and during World War I. (Sweden was a noncombatant in both world wars, but espe-

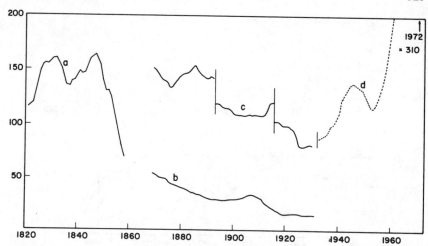

Figure VI.1.5 London: Trends in theft, 1820-1972

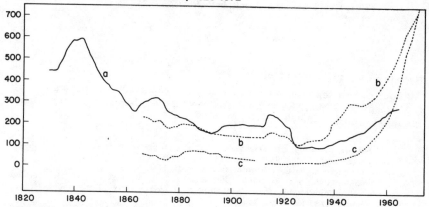

Figure VI.1.6 Stockholm: Trends in theft, 1830-1971

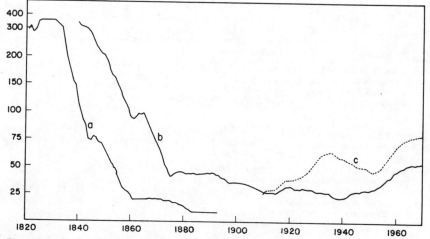

Figure VI.1.7 New South Wales: Trends in theft, 1820-1970

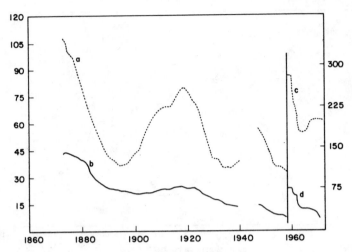

Figure VI.1.8 Calcutta: Trends in theft, 1873-1971

Notes to Figures on Trends in Theft

All figures show ten-year moving averages of rates per 100,000 population, with the exceptions noted. Solid lines are convictions, dashed lines are reported offenses (arrests in New South Wales).

London
a. Convictions for indictable offenses of robbery, burglary, larceny, and receiving stolen goods, Middlesex County, five-year moving average, 1820-1858.

b. Convictions for indictable offenses as in a, MPD, 1869-1931.

c. Summary convictions for indictable larceny (not included in b) plus summary convictions for nonindictable theft and similar offenses, 1869-1930. Breaks represent changes in aggregations used in 1893 and 1915.

d. Reported offenses for indictable offenses as in a, MPD, 1933-1971, per 10,000 population.

Stockholm
a. Convictions for all categories of theft including robbery, burglary, larceny, and pickpocketing, 1830-1963.

b. Reported offenses as in a, 1866-1971, per 10,000 population.

c. Reported robberies, 1866-1972.

New South Wales   (Note that the vertical scale above 100 is compressed.)
a. Supreme Court convictions for theft and similar offenses, 1820-1893.

b. All higher court convictions for theft and similar offenses, 1840-1970.

c. Arrests for all forms of theft, 1910-1970, per 10,000 population.

Calcutta

SOURCE: Data for 1878-1958 are from annual reports of the Calcutta commissioner of police, later data are from annual editions of **Crime in India** (New Delhi: Ministry of Home Affairs) and are not comparable in inclusiveness to earlier data.

a. Reported noncognizable (minor) thefts, 1873-1940 and 1947-1958.

b. Convictions for noncognizable thefts, same year as in a.

c. Reported cognizable thefts (robbery, dacoity, burglary, ordinary theft), 1959-1971, five-year moving averages.

d. Convictions for offenses as in c.

cially severe economic difficulties during World War I brought food riots in Stockholm, and a rise in theft.) The trend in thefts known to police per 10,000 is similar to convictions; that is, it declines irregularly from the 1860s to the mid-1920s by somewhat more than 2:1. Known thefts began to increase in the late 1930s and continued upward with scarcely any interruption into the 1970s. The 50-year increase is about 1:7. In London we observed that the more serious property crimes declined and increased more rapidly than the total volume of theft. A comparable phenomenon is evident in Stockholm: The rate of reported robbery per 100,000 (c in Figure VI.1.6) increased, especially after the 1950s, at a much more rapid rate than total theft. From 1940 to 1970 the ratio of increase was 1:20. In absolute numbers, there rarely were as many as a dozen robberies a year in Stockholm in the 1920s; in 1971 there were 615.

In New South Wales the higher court conviction rates for thefts dropped very sharply after the convict era ended. Between 1840 and 1880 they fell by a ratio of 10:1, then in the next 50 years declined by half again. The upward trend set in during World War II, and by 1970 the conviction rate had doubled. The trend in arrests for all kinds of theft, represented by line c in Figure VI.1.7, shows that they have increased since 1909, with upward spurts during the Depression and after 1950. Data on known offenses are too fragmentary to trace over a long period, but they show an extraordinary rate of increase in the 1960s. Between 1960 and 1970 the rate of larceny more than doubled; breaking and entering tripled, and armed robbery increased 800 percent. In property crime, if not crimes of violence, the postwar experience of New South Wales is the same as that of London and Stockholm.

In Calcutta the trends in theft since the 1870s (Figure VI.1.8) are generally similar to the city's experience of violent crime, through the 1950s. The distinct decline in known thefts and convictions from the 1870s through the 1890s may be a colonial manifestation of the processes and policies that reduced property crime in England. The subsequent increase in reported theft, though, is unique to Calcutta and coincides with the rise of the nationalist movement and a rapid expansion of the Calcutta police. There is little doubt that theft did increase during the decades after 1905: There is documentation of dramatic robberies by nationalists and looting by Moslim and Hindu rioters. But there is less reason to think that theft declined after 1920. Rather, there was a halt in police expansion and an increase in official preoccupation with the control of civil strife. We infer that the decline in reported thefts and convictions between 1920 and 1940 reflects a relative decline in police and court activity that bears no necessary relation to behavioral change. A test of this proposition is provided in Figure VI.1.9, where reports of theft and convictions are calculated per policeman rather than per 100,000 population over a period of 50 years. Known thefts per policeman have the same general trends as the population-weighted trend in Figure VI.1.8 but convictions per policeman do not: They steadily decline, by a ratio of about 2:1 between 1900 and the 1930s. Violent crimes per policeman show the same divergent patterns. The proposition seems to be accurate: Trends in crime indicators in Calcutta during the nationalist era were as much a function of police activity as they are of criminal behavior.[5] The data on theft after 1946 are suspect on the same grounds. Two very different series of data must be used, before and after 1958, but each shows irregular declines. The high initial level of reported theft in 1947 probably reflects the disorder that followed the partition riots. The decline thereafter, though, is almost certainly due to the diversion of official attention from common theft to more threatening problems of public order. Between 1960 and 1971 we find that common thefts known to police fall by nearly 2:1 and convictions by 4:1, whereas known robberies and dacoities (group robbery) increase by 1:4. We have observed no comparable inverse trends in any of the Western cities with respect to the forms of theft, and we regard the tendencies cited as prima facie evidence of a narrowing of the focus of official concern. Additional evidence on the general point is provided in the next chapter.

The behavioral reality of Calcutta's trends in theft is open to serious question. Is it necessary to express the same doubt regarding the three Western societies? We think not, for the same kinds of reasons that led us to infer that a changing behavioral reality underlies the trends in indicators of crimes of violence. The direction of trends in known offenses, arrests, committals to trial, and convictions are all in the same direction. So are the trends for different categories of theft, with the exception of burglary in London from 1870 to 1930. Some of the decline in higher court conviction ratios in the nineteenth century is due to a transfer of jurisdiction for petty cases from higher to lower courts. But wherever we have data on the total volume of cases of theft—in Stockholm throughout its history, in London beginning in 1869—the direction of trends is the same. The substratum of petty theft in Western societies apparently declined less than more serious forms of theft during the century of improvement, but it did decline. The rising tide of theft manifests the same internally consistent pattern: The more serious offenses have increased much more rapidly than less serious ones.

TRENDS IN WHITE-COLLAR CRIME

Theft and assault are mainly crimes of the young, the poor, and the desperate. Fraud and embezzlement are mostly crimes of middle-

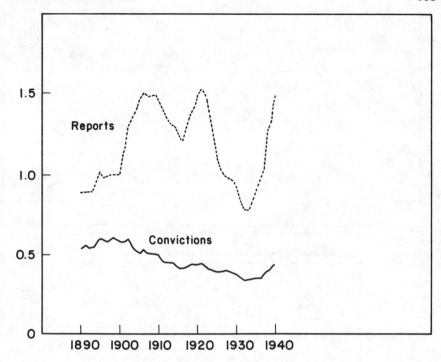

Figure VI.1.9 Calcutta: Theft reports and convictions per policeman, 1890-1940, five year moving average

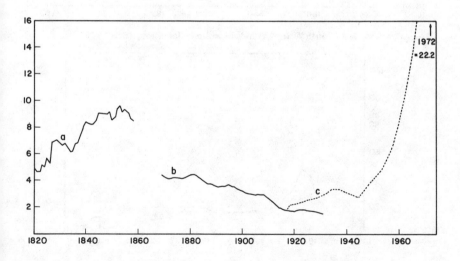

Figure VI.1.10 London: Trends in white-collar crime, 1820-1972

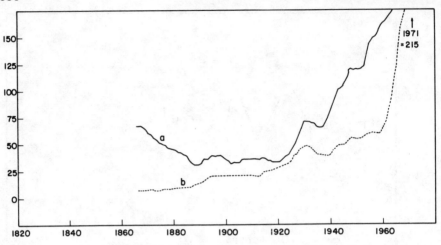

Figure VI.1.11 Stockholm: Trends in white-collar crime, 1866-1971

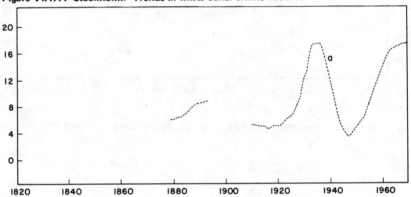

Figure VI.1.12 New South Wales: Trends in white-collar crime, 1879-1970

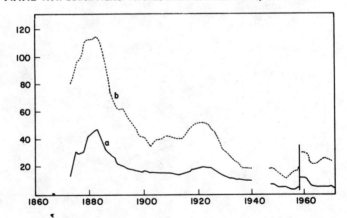

Figure VI.1.13 Calcutta: Trends in white-collar crimes, 1873-1971

Notes to Figures on Trends in White-Collar Crime

All figures show ten-year moving averages of rates per 100,000 population, with the exceptions noted. Solid lines are convictions, dashed lines are reported offenses (arrests in New South Wales).

London
a. Convictions for indictable fraud and embezzlement, Middlesex County, five-year moving average, 1820-1858.
b. Convictions for indictable fraud and embezzlement, MPD, 1869-1931.
c. Reported cases of fraud and embezzlement, MPD, 1918-1972.

Stockholm
a. Convictions for fraud, embezzlement, forgery, and offenses by officials, 1866-1964.
b. Reported cases of fraud, embezzlement, and forgery per 10,000, 1866-1971.

New South Wales
Arrests for fraud, embezzlement, forgery, and similar offenses, 1879-1893, 1910-1970.

Calcutta
SOURCE: Data for 1878-1958 are from annual reports of the Calcutta commissioner of police, later data are from annual editions of **Crime in India** (New Delhi: Ministry of Home Affairs) and are not necessarily comparable to earlier data.

a. Convictions for cognizable (serious) cheating, breach of trust, counterfeiting, and similar offenses, 1873-1940, 1947-1958 (three-year moving average), 1959-1971 (five-year moving average).
b. Reported cases of cognizable offenses, as in a.

class employees and business men. Theft and white-collar crime are motivated by avarice, but the embezzler has the advantages of skills and opportunities of a different order from those of the common thief. Since the class position and opportunities of thieves differ markedly from those of white-collar criminals, we might expect the social dynamics of white-collar crime to be different and its trends to differ as a consequence.

The trends in indicators of white-collar crime in London (Figure VI.1.10) prove to be familiar. Conviction rates are highest in the 1840s and 1850s; from 1870 to 1930 they decline gradually but consistently by a ratio of about 3:1. Known offenses increase by about 50 percent between the two wars; after 1945 they increase more rapidly, by 700 percent as of 1972. The only significant difference between these trends and those for theft is the trend from 1820 to 1858, when the rate of convictions for white-collar offenses nearly doubled. This probably reflects the rapid expansion of commercial enterprise in London during the first half of the nineteenth century, hence an equally rapid expansion in opportunities for white-collar crime.

The nineteenth century Stockholm data (Figure VI.1.11) show a 2:1 decline in convictions for white-collar crime during the last third of the nineteenth century followed by several decades of little change. A rapid increase begins in the 1920s, about a decade earlier than the turning point for common theft. The rate of convictions increases by 600 percent in the next 40 years. Offenses known show a steady, gradual increase from the 1860s onward. The ratio of increase between the 1860s and the 1920s is 1:4. In the next 50 years the offenses increase by another 700 percent. The evidence from Stockholm thus is ambiguous about whether a decline in white-collar crime occurred during the nineteenth century: Convictions declined, known offenses increased. An "opportunity" explanation best fits the data. Large-scale commercial development did not begin in Stockholm until the last decades of the nineteenth century; before that opportunities for fraud were fewer and offenders more easily detected. The twentieth century increase in known offenses and convictions can be attributed to the rapid expansion of opportunities and commensurate official efforts at control.

White-collar crime in New South Wales apparently has been cyclical, on the basis of the fragmentary arrest data in Figure VI.1.12. During the Depression arrests increased by 400 percent, and a 400 percent increase following World War II substantially outstripped the simultaneous 200 percent increase in common theft.

In Calcutta the long-term trend in white-collar crime from the 1880s to the 1970s has been irregularly but consistently downward (Figure VI.1.13). The indicators are aggregated from a diverse set of offenses such as forgery, cheating, use of false weights and measurements, and giving false evidence. The noticeable increase from about 1915 to 1925 coincides with a much greater increase in common theft, but the interpretation is ambiguous. Since policing had increased in previous years, the apparent rise in white-collar crime is probably due less to behavior change than to better reporting. The subsequent decline almost surely reflects a decline in policing. The beginnings of Calcutta's commercial decline, which can be seen in the 1930s, surely were not yet sufficient to restrict the opportunities for fraudulent activities.

In the Western societies the opportunities for white-collar crime have increased as a function of economic growth generally and commercial expansion specifically. We suspect that the trends depicted in Figures VI.1.10 to VI.1.12 provide a somewhat distorted version of an underlying behavioral reality. The "century of improvement" in public order had the effect of keeping white-collar crime at relatively low levels despite the expansion of opportunities. The Depression that began in the late 1920s was a strong inducement to hard-pressed members of the middle class to bend and break the economic rules. By no means all sharp commercial practices are illegal, and only some of the illegal ones led to convictions. Thus when it was perceived that breaking the rules contributed to the economic betterment of those who did so, more and more people began to take advantage of the ample opportunities available in expanding urban economies. The hypothesis—we have no direct evidence for it—is that practices that caught hold during times of austerity were so successful that they were widely imitated during the subsequent periods of prosperity. They may even have provided cues that helped stimulate the dramatic increases in common theft.

THE REGULATION OF SOCIAL CONDUCT

Many kinds of deviant social conduct have been treated as crimes in Western societies. Some, like adultery and drunkenness, are so common that they are not "deviant" at all but are regulated nonetheless. A sketch of the criminalization and decriminalization of different kinds of social conduct is offered in a later chapter. Here we examine the evidence of trends in the public regulation of sexual conduct and the consumption of alcohol. It is unreasonable to expect trends in indicators of these offenses to correspond to a changing behavioral reality. Patterns of sexual behavior and alcohol consumption obviously have changed over time, but the amount of official attention given them has changed even more, and there is no warrant for assuming that the two kinds of change are correlative. The trends examined here are, first and foremost, reflections of change in official interests and policies.

Rather different kinds of sexual conduct have been regulated in Western societies.[6] The indicators in Figures VI.1.14 through VI.1.16 represent a mixed bag of offenses ranging from rape and homosexual acts to indecent exposure—often an official euphemism for public urination. The evidence of the conviction ratios suggests that the regulation of these offenses is cyclical. Both the London and New South Wales data include convictions for only the most serious offenses. In London the conviction ratio peaks in the 1830s, a time of intense concern about theft and violence as well; a spillover effect may have been at work. Convictions for sex crimes increased dramatically between 1880 and 1900 without a corresponding rise in conviction rates for other offenses, and it is tempting to interpret this as an official manifestation of Victorian morality. In New South Wales there appear to be localized peaks in convictions at the same two periods: in the 1830s and around 1890. The same interpretations are applicable. The first corresponds with the extremely high levels of official action against theft and violence, the second signifies the judicial response to vociferous public and legislative concern about sex crimes, amply documented in our study of public order in New South Wales.[7]

The conviction data for Stockholm are more difficult to interpret because the kinds of offenses included are not specified. Evidently minor offenses as well as more serious ones are incorporated. The decided downward trend in convictions from the 1890s through the 1930s is consistent with what we know of the history of decriminalization of sexual offenses in Sweden. A separate series of data on convictions for adultery, not included in Figure VI.1.15, shows that these too declined markedly during the latter part of the nineteenth century; the last conviction for adultery in Stockholm was in 1917. Data on sexual offenses known trace quite a different pattern, though; they rise in the late nineteenth century, then decline into the early 1920s. We know only that these are "gross sexual offenses," that is, offenses more serious than those represented by the declining trend in convictions.

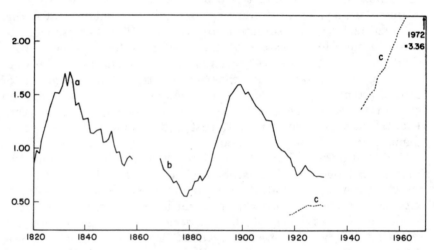

Figure VI.1.14 London: Trends in regulation of sexual conduct, 1820-1972

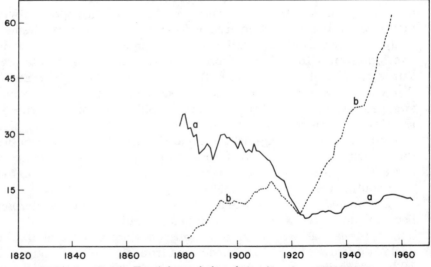

Figure VI.1.15 Stockholm: Trends in regulation of sexual conduct, 1879-1964

All three societies show evidence of rising concern about sexual offenses during the past 40 to 50 years. Offenses recorded by police began to increase in the 1920s in London and Stockholm; arrests in New South Wales rise after 1940. Convictions increase slightly in Stockholm and very substantially in New South Wales. Social histories provide considerable documentation of the changing sexual mores of Western societies during this period. The rising trend in known offenses and arrests through the 1950s thus reflects both the growing diversity of sexual conduct and the fact that official criteria

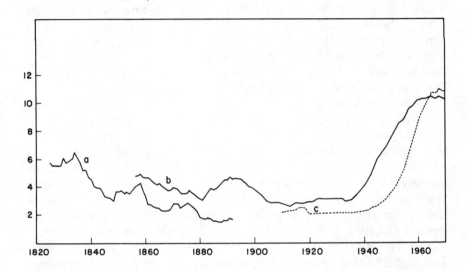

Figure VI.1.16 New South Wales: Trends in regulation of sexual conduct, 1825-1970

Notes to Figures on Regulation of Sexual Conduct

All figures show ten-year moving averages of rates per 100,000 population, with the exceptions noted. Solid lines are convictions, dashed lines are reported offenses (arrests in New South Wales).

London
  a. Convictions for indictable rapes and attempts, homosexual acts and attempts, indecent exposure, and similar offenses, Middlesex County, five-year moving average, 1820-1858.
  b. Convictions for indictable offenses as in a, MPD, 1869-1931.
  c. Reported offenses as in a, MPD, 1918-1931, 1938, 1945-1972, per 10,000 population.

Stockholm
  a. Convictions for indecent behavior and similar sexual offenses, 1879-1964. Specific kinds of offenses are not identified in the sources.
  b. Reported gross sexual offenses, including rape, 1882-1967. Specific kinds of offenses are not identified in the sources before 1952, but the aggregation is less inclusive than in a.

New South Wales
  a. Supreme Court convictions for rape and attempts, homosexual acts and attempts, bestiality, bigamy, and similar offenses, 1825-1896.
  b. Higher court convictions for offenses as in a, 1857-1970.
  c. Arrests for all sexual offenses, 1910-1970, per 20,000 population.

of sexual criminality had not yet adapted to changing social standards. In the 1960s in Stockholm and New South Wales all the indicators appear to have peaked out (unlike the indicators of assault and theft), suggesting that official standards were being modified. We know from our detailed studies that this period was characterized by formal decriminalization and informal relaxation of enforcement.

The mood of toleration of sexual diversity has limits, however. Rape and other kinds of sexual assault are not on the verge of being decriminalized in any Western society. The incidence of these offenses has increased in recent decades at a rate comparable to other sexual offenses: In Stockholm the increase in reported rapes was 300 percent between 1951 and 1971, in New South Wales it was 200 percent between 1960 and 1970. The decriminalization of benign offenses like homosexuality and the use of mild narcotics may facilitate official efforts at controlling the kinds of sexual attacks that continue to be universally condemned in Western societies.

Public drunkenness provides a larger volume of police business in most Western societies than any other nontraffic offense. In Stockholm in 1910 about 80 percent of all sentences meted out by the courts were for drunkenness, and in 1960 the figure was about 70 percent. In New South Wales 50 percent of all nontraffic arrests in the late 1940s were for drunkenness; 20 years later the proportion was about one-third. In London during the last century, drunkenness and disorderly conduct has been the occasion for 30 to 45 percent of all arrests. The data in Figures VI.1.17 to VI.1.19 reveal the variability of the regulation of drunkenness over the long run in all three places. The highest rates are recorded in Stockholm, where the conviction rate in the first decade of this century reached a peak of 4,100 per 100,000. Since virtually all the guilty were adult males, this means that about one man in eight was convicted of the offense each year, though no doubt there were many repeaters. The rate of nineteenth century increase in sentences for drunkenness in Stockholm is also misleading about the actual incidence of the offense. The sixfold, 60 year increase from the 1840s to 1910 is an official testimonial to the influence of the temperance movement. The trends in the last 60 years, though, trace with some accuracy the changing availability of beer and aquavit. The sharp decline in sentences after 1910 coincides with the imposition of strict rationing policies. Rationing ended in 1955, and public drunkenness apparently tripled.

In London arrests for drunkenness have been proportionally fewer than in Stockholm and New South Wales, except during the 1830s when arrests annually exceeded 2,000 per 100,000 population. Enforcement appears to have been episodic, with 10- to twenty-year periods of intensified enforcement around 1850, in the 1870s, and from the 1890s to World War I. The new licensing laws may help account for the low arrest rates during the decades between wars, and relaxed standards of police enforcement may have contributed to this effect. Since 1945 there has been a steady increase in arrests, by 300 percent in three decades. The upward movement has been so consistent that it is more likely to be due to real change in public behavior than to differences in police enforcement.

In New South Wales arrests for drunkenness also have varied cyclically. The peaks in the 1880s and the late 1940s correspond with periods of public concern and stepped-up police enforcement. Whether these episodes reflect behavioral change as well is unknowable. The most recent peak began almost immediately after the end of World War II, and it is at least plausible that the increase in drunkenness arrests, along with the simultaneous rise in arrests for assault, reflects official efforts to control the activities of discharged servicemen.

THE COMMON TRENDS IN COMMON CRIME IN WESTERN SOCIETIES

Though lacking crime indicators to reinforce or undermine their perceptions, the articulate people who lived through the 1830s and 1840s in London, Stockholm, and Sydney left ample testimony in their writings and in the policies they pursued of their conviction that they lived in dangerous times. Their descendants, however, became increasingly certain of the security of their persons and property in the course of the next three generations. Virtually every

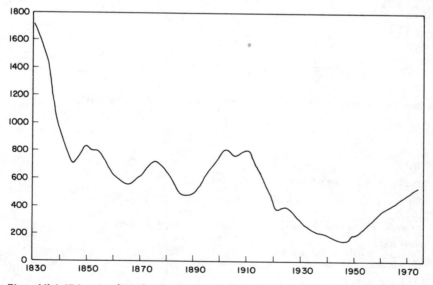

Figure VI.1.17 London (MPD): Trends in regulation of alcohol abuse, 1831-1974

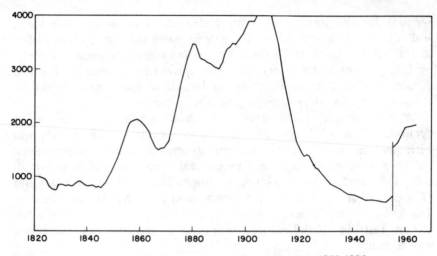

Figure VI.1.18 Stockholm: Trends in regulation of alcohol abuse, 1822-1964

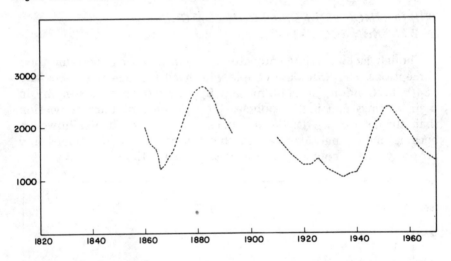

Figure VI.1.19 New South Wales: Trends in regulation of alcohol abuse, 1820-1970

Notes to Figures on Regulation of Alcohol Abuse

All figures show ten-year moving averages of rates per 100,000 population.

London
    Persons arrested for drunkenness and disorderly conduct, 1831-1974.

Stockholm
    Persons sentenced for drunkenness, 1822-1964. The series is broken in 1955-1956 to
show the impact of the end of liquor rationing in 1955.

New South Wales
    Persons arrested for drunkenness, 1859-1893, 1910-1970.

indicator we have examined, whether of police or court activity, of theft or assault, of serious or petty offenses, testifies to the social reality of improving public order during the latter half of the nine-teenth century and the early decades of the twentieth century.

The downward trends in crimes of violence and theft among the three Western cities are similar enough to be plotted on a single graph (Figure VI.1.20) representing the relative decline in convictions for crimes of violence and theft. The decline from eight around 1840 to just over one in 1930 signifies that the conviction rates declined, on the average, by a ratio of 8:1. In New South Wales, for example, in the early 1850s the higher courts convicted about eighteen persons per 100,000 population of murder or grievous assault, whereas in the early 1930s only about two per 100,000 were convicted. The 9:1 decline in New South Wales was slightly higher than the average; the vertical bars represent the range of variation around the common trend.[8]

The reversal in the common trend begins in the late 1930s. The timing was somewhat different among societies; in some it was detectable as early as 1930, in others not until 1945. By the mid-1960s the conviction rates had increased, on the average, more than 100 percent from their low point between the wars and were at about the same level they had reached at the turn of the century.

The fateful question is what these trends signify. In the conven-tional or "official" view they are a direct reflection of changes in criminal behavior, which are shown here to be common to three cities. But conviction data present at best a diffracted image of social behavior that has passed through the distorting lenses of differential public concern, selective reporting and enforcement, and bureau-cratic processing. Then we must ask whether the trends are due to changes in the institutions of public order. They cannot be attributed to the changing scope of criminal law because, as we show in a later chapter, there has been little substantive change in legal definitions of offenses against persons and property. The century-long decline in the conviction rates cannot by any stretch of the imagination be attributed to declining police efficiency. Instead the decline coin-cides with the establishment of effective, centralized police forces in all three cities. A third possibility is that the judicial disposition of cases has shifted. To the extent that offenders are dealt with sum-marily, they do not appear in data on convictions in serious crimes. Historical evidence suggests that some of the decline in conviction ratios in London and New South Wales can be attributed to a shift of jurisdiction of cases from higher to lower courts. But wherever we have data on convictions for all offenses, serious and petty (in Stockholm for 130 years, in London for shorter periods), the decline is less pronounced but the same trends are evident. It seems that only a small part of the reversing trend in conviction rates is due to institutional change. The inference is that the changing conviction ratios trace approximately, the institutional response to changing patterns of social behavior.

Trends in the courts' disposition to convict are less persuasive as evidence of social change than are trends in offenses known, because the latter are based on the reports of police and citizens who are most likely to know firsthand about the incidence of assault and theft. Their reports are not widely available until after 1900. During the 60 years across which we can trace them for all three societies (Figure VI.1.21) they show the same trends as the conviction data. There are only two differences. One is that the offenses known begin to increase in the late 1920s, a decade before the reversal of the trend in convictions. The second, and more significant, is that known offenses fell more rapidly than convictions during the last of the era of improvement and accelerated much more rapidly after 1950.

Part of the recent increase in known crime might be a function of two social facts: People in contemporary Western societies have access to telephones, an easy means of reporting offenses to the police, and the prospect of insurance claims is an added incentive to make known losses, especially serious ones. Positive feedback also

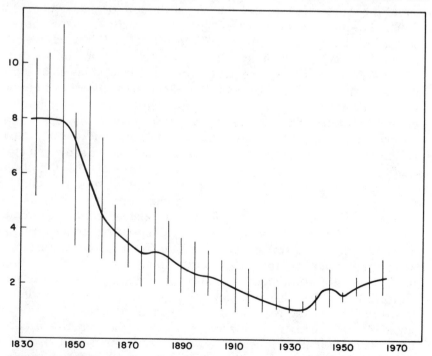

Figure VI.1.20 The common trend in convictions for crimes of theft and violence in Western societies, 1835-1965

may be at work. Crime reports are grist for newspaper accounts and indicators of rising crime, which reinforce the common perception that we live in disorderly times. The effect may be to encourage people to report offenses, especially petty ones, that earlier might not have been reported. Or, equally plausible, increased awareness of crime may breed public cynicism, which reduces the disposition to report small losses that are not covered by insurance. Another possibility is that police today are less selective in reporting offenses than previously. Systematic changes of this type are easily detected, though. Modifications in London in 1931 and in New South Wales in 1970 caused step-level increases in recorded crime which are readily distinguishable from the cumulative, year-by-year increases that characterize the three cities in this study since the 1950s.

Some but not much of the average fivefold increase in known assaults and thefts during the past 40 years may be explained by a growing disposition to report offenses. Murders have increased as well as assaults. Reports of the more serious forms of theft have increased much more rapidly than indicators of petty theft. White-collar crime and serious sexual offenses, especially rape, have escalated at the same rapid rates. Victimization studies show a large reservoir of unreported offenses even in the late 1960s and early 1970s; it is scarcely likely that the reservoir would be so large if it had been the source of reports that had already increased by multiples of 3, 5, 10, and 20. We suspect, in fact, that crime indicators understate the true rate of increase in minor theft in recent decades. Cynicism is one reason; another is growing prosperity, which makes a

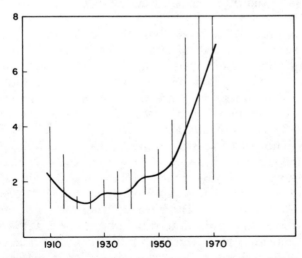

Figure VI.1.21 The common trend in known crimes of theft and violence in Western societies, 1910-1970

small loss scarcely worth reporting. If this is true, it helps explain both the large "dark figure" (the European term for unreported crimes) revealed in recent victimization surveys and the fact that serious theft reportedly has increased more than petty offenses. We conclude that social behavior obviously has changed in these societies in the last 30 to 40 years, and although the crime indicators may reflect those changes in a distorted way, they reflect it nonetheless.

Reversing trends in public order have proved to be remarkably similar across three different and distant cities. Other studies of long-term trends in common crime provide evidence that this reversal is by no means unique to the cases investigated. The nineteenth century trends in conviction rates for London are paralleled by the data for all England and Wales: committals to trial for all serious offenses increased from 1805 to the 1840s by a ratio of about 1:4 but declined by 3:1 during the next 50 years. The trends, though not these precise ratios, characterize both property crime and crimes against the person. Gatrell and Hadden attribute part of the increase in the first part of the century to institutional changes, but they conclude that the subsequent decline probably understates the true reduction in criminal activity.[9] In France the rate of persons accused of property crime declined by a ratio of 10:1 between 1826 and the 1930s and remained relatively low until the 1950s. Crimes of violence fluctuated over this period without any clear trend.[10] Our examination of recent French data shows a doubling in property crime rates between 1955 and 1970. A study of crime in Canada from 1901 to 1960 gives contrasting results: Crimes against property nearly tripled, and offenses against persons increased 800 percent, with particularly sharp increases during 1910-1915, 1935-1939, and 1955-1960.[11]

National trends in crime rates are not necessarily the same as those in cities, however. A number of cities in the United States, but few elsewhere, have undergone such studies, and most of them exhibit trends similar to those of London, Stockholm, and New South Wales. Studies of Boston reveal a pronounced decline in indicators of various kinds of serious crime between the middle of the nineteenth century and the 1930s or 1940s.[12] A study of Buffalo, N.Y., from 1856 to 1946 shows that known crimes against persons and property peaked around 1870 and declined irregularly thereafter. By 1946 violent crimes were down by a ratio of 5:1, property crimes by only 1.5:1.[13] A final comparison is provided by a century of arrest data for Chicago (Figure VI.1.22). There was an irregular 4:1 decline from the 1870s through the 1940s, interrupted by two sharp reversals, the second one coinciding with the Prohibition era. The increase from 1950 to 1970 was about 300 percent.[14] Similar increases in crime indicators in almost all American cities after 1950 are well known and they need no documentation here.[15]

The reversing 140-year trend in indicators of crimes against persons and property in London, Stockholm, and New South Wales reflects profound changes in public concern about threatening social behavior and official efforts to control it. Real changes in social behavior evidently underlay altered perceptions of public disorder, though the indicators probably exaggerate the nineteenth century decline in assault and theft and understate the recent increase in

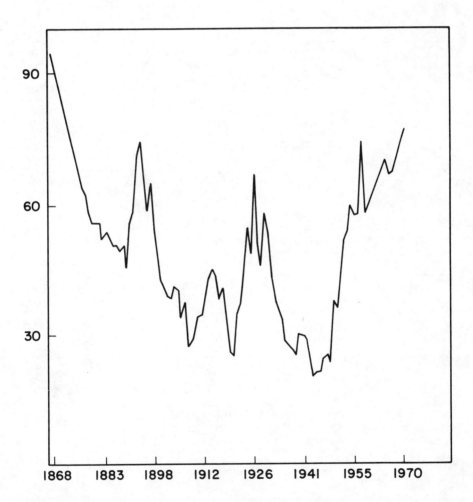

Figure VI.1.22 Chicago: Total arrests per 1,000 population, 1868-1970

theft. In Calcutta the trends in crime indicators permit few firm inferences about changing patterns of individual behavior. Most of the fluctuations noted are due to changes in the scope of official efforts at social control and to the impact of civil strife.

NOTES TO CHAPTER VI.1

1. Annual data on general and more specific categories of offenses are portrayed in the separate city studies, as are some of the statistics on arrests and trials.

2. Dr. S. Mukherjee of the United Nations Social Defense Research Institute, in Rome, has made a systematic, unpublished study of the formal definitions of murder, manslaughter, and similar offenses in nineteen countries, representing all world regions. The elements of the definitions prove to be closely comparable.

3. Data on convictions for murderous offenses are available in Stockholm through 1951 but are not comparable with earlier data because they include, without separate tabulation, sentences for procuring abortions. The aggregation is instructive about changing Swedish values (since 1975 abortion has been legal under almost all circumstances) but not about the changing incidence of convictions for murderous assault.

4. In the lexicon of crime in English-speaking countries, robbery is the most serious form of theft and involves the use or threat of force against the victim. Burglary involves surreptitious entry, usually into homes or commercial establishments. Larceny is the theft of property from public places (e.g., bicycle theft and shoplifting). One or more classes of larceny are typically distinguished (grand vs. petty, indictable vs. summary, etc.), based on the value of goods stolen. The aggregate measures of theft used in our analyses also include a variety of less numerous theft-related offenses such as attempted robbery and burglary, receiving stolen goods, and pickpocketing.

5. This proposition applies only to Calcutta. The Western cities experienced several periods, identified in the later chapter on police and policing, during which increased policing led to rising crime rates, but these are short-term phenomena and are not comparable to the enduring pattern in Calcutta.

6. Sexual offenses and drunkenness were so rarely recorded in Calcutta that little is to be gained by examining the statistics. What is significant is that neither British nor Indian officials though it necessary to police these activities.

7. See also Peter N. Grabosky, *Sydney in Ferment: Crime, Dissent, and Official Reaction, 1788-1973* (Canberra: Australian National University Press, 1976).

8. This is the procedure used to determine the common trend in Figures VI.1.20 and VI.1.21. For each city, the moving ten-year average for convictions was recorded for every fifth year for which data were available (as shown in Figures VI.1.1 through VI.1.7): for 1830, 1835, 1840, and so forth. The lowest rate in each series was set equal to 1.0 and the other rates expressed as a ratio of that one. In London, for example, the lowest average conviction rate recorded for indictable murders and assaults between 1820 and 1930 was 1.36 per 100,000 in 1930, the highest was 12.5 in 1845. The 1930 ratio was set at 1.0; the 1845 ratio therefore was $12.5 \div 1.36 = 9.2$. The procedure was repeated for the trend in indictable thefts, and for both kinds of convictions in New South Wales (higher court convictions) and Stockholm (all convictions). Since all the series have a common minimum of 1.0, they can be plotted on the same graph. The graph covers only the period for which at least four ratios were available. New South Wales is excluded before 1850 because of its exceptionally high rates

during the convict era; if these data were included, the 1830s average would
exceed 10. The vertical bars represent the range of variation around the mean. In
1880, for example, the highest ratio score was 4.8 (aggressive crimes in Stockholm), the lowest was 2.0 (theft in New South Wales), the average of six ratios
was 3.2. Neither kind of offense and no one city has a consistently higher or
lower rate of decline.

   9. V. A. C. Gatrell and T. B. Hadden, "Criminal Statistics and Their Interpretation," in E. A. Wrigley (ed.), *Nineteenth Century Society* (Cambridge: The
University Press, 1972), pp. 372-379.

   10. A. Q. Lodhi and Charles Tilley, "Urbanization, Crime, and Collective
Violence in 19th-Century France," *American Journal of Sociology*, 79 (September 1973), pp. 296-318.

   11. P. J. Giffen, "Rates of Crime and Delinquency," in W. T. McGrath, ed.,
Crime and Its Treatment in Canada (New York: St. Martin's Press, (1965), ch. 4.

   12. Sam Bass Warner, *Crime and Criminal Statistics in Boston* (Cambridge:
Harvard University Press, 1934); Theodore N. Ferdinand, "The Criminal Patterns
of Boston Since 1849," *American Journal of Sociology*, 73 (July 1967),
688-698; Roger Lane, *Policing the City: Boston, 1822-1885* (Cambridge: Harvard University Press, 1967); Roger Lane, "Urbanization and Criminal Violence
in the 19th Century: Massachusetts as a Test Case," in Hugh Davis Graham and
Ted Robert Gurr, eds., *Violence in America: Historical and Comparative Perspectives: A Report to the National Commission on the Causes and Prevention
of Violence* (New York: Praeger and Bantam Books, 1969), ch. 12.

   13. Elwin H. Powell, *The Design of Discord: Studies of Anomie* (New York:
Oxford University Press, 1970), ch. 8.

   14. From Wesley G. Skogan, *Chicago Since 1840: A Time-Series Data Hand-
book* (Urbana: Institute of Government and Public Affairs, University of
Illinois, 1975).

   15. See Fred P. Graham, "A Contemporary History of American Crime," in
Graham and Gurr, eds., op. cit., ch. 13, for national data. For a comparison of
data for all the large American cities see Wesley G. Skogan, "Law, Order, and the
Transformation of Urban Society," paper presented to the Midwest Political
Science Association, Chicago, 1974.

CIVIL STRIFE AND
CRISES OF PUBLIC ORDER

Our assessment of trends in crime has relied mainly on indicators of the official attention given to crimes and criminals. Civil strife leaves more substantial tracings in the journalistic and historical accounts of its time. A review of narrative and official evidence about the incidence of strife in the four cities provides the basis for a comparative interpretation of changing magnitudes, issues, tactics, and forms of group conflict. In the second part of the chapter we juxtapose the evidence about short-run increases in official data on common crime and episodes of civil strife and demonstrate that these phenomena coincide with remarkable frequency.

TRENDS IN CIVIL STRIFE

The Historical Record

The cities differ widely in the timing, circumstances, and severity of civil conflict.

Calcutta: Undoubtedly Calcutta has been the most turbulent of the four cities in the twentieth century, but its nineteenth century history contains very few references to serious episodes of protest or rebellion. Most collective disorder in Bengal before 1905 occurred away from Calcutta. Traditional Islamic resistance to British rule in the early nineteenth century had few urban manifestations. Colonial forces made strenuous efforts to control thugism and dacoity, which were rife in the rural areas of Bengal, but these murderous forms of banditry came no closer to the city than the nearby riverways.

Peasant revolts in the 1850s had even less impact on public order in Calcutta, and the Sepoy Mutiny of 1857 had none at all.

The first serious strife in Calcutta proper was distinctly modern in purpose and form: It was a manifestation of Bengali nationalism, which had begun as an intellectual and social movement among urban middle-class Hindus in the 1820s. Polite opposition to British policies throughout the century gave way gradually to mass agitational politics. The first episodes occurred in the 1880s but were infrequent and limited in scope; in 1905, however, British plans to partition Bengal stimulated the first wave of the widespread nationalist resistance that was to continue until independence. During those years strife took every form conceivable in an urban setting, including boycotts, strikes, protracted terrorism, massive demonstrations, and large-scale riots. The peaks of nationalist activity in Calcutta occurred at intervals of roughly a decade: 1906-1908, 1912-1915, 1920-1924, 1930-1934, and 1942-1946. It is noteworthy that serious communal conflict between Hindus and Muslims followed rather than preceded the onset of militant nationalism and was exacerbated by the growing schism in the political sympathies of the two groups: Many Muslim leaders were co-opted into the apparatus of colonial rule, most Hindus opposed it. Communal strife was chronic after the first major episode of communal violence in 1918, and there were particularly virulent outbreaks in 1926 and in 1946, the single most ·bloody year in Calcutta's history. Strikes over economic issues did not become common until the early 1920s, but they too soon took on a political cast.

A crescendo of political, communal, and labor violence speeded Britain's formal withdrawal in 1947 from a province and a city she no longer controlled. But independence failed to resolve hostilities that had been exacerbated by decades of conflict between radical and conservative politicians, Hindus and Muslims, workers and employers. Quite the contrary: The success of protest and rebellion as means to independence appears to have increased the attractiveness of these activities to antagonistic groups. Since most of the radical nationalists were excluded from the postindependence governments of Calcutta and West Bengal, they continued open rebellion and sporadic campaigns of terrorism and sabotage for some years, though with declining amplitude until the onset of Naxalite terrorism in the late 1960s. The most durable tradition has proved to be mass agitation. Every divisive political, economic, and communal issue in Calcutta's postwar history has been marked by rallies, strikes, demonstrations, and riots that have become what might well be called an "alternative urban lifestyle."

Stockholm: The Swedish city reverses the Calcutta pattern. Its history between 1700 and 1900 was rather tumultuous, albeit on the small scale to be expected in a small city, but for most of the past 50 years it has been notably free of civil strife. In the earlier period strife had two quite different components: Stockholm was the arena in which national political conflicts were fought out, and it also had a fractious citizenry given to spontaneous street protest and fighting inspired by the sociochemical interaction of group antagonisms and aquavit. Strife focusing on unpopular soldiers or police, without specific ideological content, was particularly common during the late 1780s and 1790s, and again from the 1860s through the 1890s.

Explicitly political conflict evolved through three stages, each characterized by substantial strife. Struggles between the monarchy and nobility were manifest in coups of 1772, 1789, and 1809, and the assassination of King Gustav III in 1792. The political interests of the growing middle and artisan classes fueled serious political riots in 1809, 1838, and 1848. Working-class demands were evident in the events of 1848, but significant organized strife by the working class did not develop until the 1890s, when workers initiated frequent strikes and demonstrations aimed at resolving economic issues and securing the franchise. These issues were the source of much open conflict that continued into the second decade of the twentieth century.

Issues of class political and economic conflict were largely resolved by the early 1920s. The years of World War I were turbulent in Stockholm, though, first because of demonstrations for and against Swedish neutrality, and later because of strikes and riots inspired by severe economic depression, occasioned by the wartime disruption of trade. Since the 1920s strife in Stockholm has taken the form of substantial strike activity in 1924-1925, 1932, and 1952; demonstrations against American involvement in Southeast Asia in the late 1960s and early 1970s; and occasional apolitical street clashes. Demonstrations have been by far the most numerous of these events: Swedish sources indicate that some 260 occurred in Stockholm between 1961 and 1970. Virtually all demonstrations had foreign not domestic political objects, and few were disruptive. The most substantial issue of domestic political protest in Stockholm in recent years, in fact, seems to have been opposition to removal of a stand of elm trees. On this issue, as in many others in Sweden's history, the protestors ultimately won the day.

London: Apparently London experienced in the nineteenth century conflict as widespread as that of Stockholm, but less violent. In the twentieth century London has had strife of greater magnitude and seriousness. The heyday of the "London mob" was in the eighteenth century; by the nineteenth century the urban proletariat was unorganized and usually quiescent. No popular support was attracted by the Cato Street conspirators, for example, who attempted a revolutionary seizure of power in London in 1816 and plotted another in 1820. The great movements for political reform of the nineteenth century included agitation over the first Reform Bill in 1830-1832, the Chartist movement from 1835 to 1848, and the demonstrations over the Second Reform Bill in 1865-1867. The major support for the first two causes came from outside London, and when the London workers did participate in rallies and demonstrations on behalf of reform they were almost always peaceable and careful to avoid potentially violent confrontations. Nonetheless the English elite greatly feared rebellion during the first half of the century and responded to popular protest by employing a network of spies and informers, massive shows of force, and harsh judicial sanctions. The cautious tactics of London protestors also characterized the labor movement. London was affected by fairly widespread strikes in 1859-1861 (in the building trades), in 1888 (among dock workers), in the years immediately before and after World War I, and in 1926—the year of the nationwide general strike; but on the whole the tenor of labor disputes in London was peaceful, one is tempted to say deferential.

Parallel to the activities of organized labor, a vociferous socialist movement emerged in the last quarter of the nineteenth century. The socialists' favorite public activities were outdoor rallies and processions, events they organized in substantial number over a period of many years. In times of economic distress these occasions were sometimes disruptive, but as a rule they were all of a piece with the tradition of orderly protest that has inspired hundreds of demonstrations a year in London—the war years excepted—over almost every domestic and international issue imaginable. The most threatening manifestations of strife in London during the latter part of the nineteenth century were episodes of Fenian terrorist activity, which continued sporadically in the twentieth century.

The last battles in the campaign for universal suffrage were fought by the feminists between 1900 and 1914. The militant suffragettes, mainly a middle-class group, were neither deferential nor afraid to employ violent tactics. The streets of London were their principal battleground, and they made calculated and dramatized use of mass demonstrations, physical confrontations with police, and campaigns of arson, bombing, and the kind of property destruction lately called "trashing." Suffrage was extended to women in 1918, after a wartime suspension of domestic hostilities, and the decades of the 1920s and the 1940s were largely free of group conflict in London. In the 1930s, however, the activities of Sir Oswald Mosley's British Union of Fascists were a serious threat to public order, mainly because of their success in provoking their many opponents into brawls.

Since the mid-1950s civil strife in London has increased markedly. The increase has four dimensions, all manifestations of national problems. One is labor conflict, which has grown significantly during each period of Conservative government and has contributed to the early demise of one of those governments. Second is the rise of civil disobedience, which began with the "Ban the Bomb" movement of the 1960s and spilled over into protest against the Vietnam war and a variety of other international issues in which Britain was scarcely implicated. The third is ethnic conflict, observable in recurring small-scale attacks on nonwhite immigrants from the Commonwealth—and, most recently, attacks by black youths on white police. Last is the rise in the 1970s of protest and terrorist violence by or on behalf of Irish nationalists. The protagonists in these conflicts have few interests or tactics in common, but their cumulative effect has been to make contemporary London the most strife-ridden of the Western cities in this study.

New South Wales: This Australian state deserves the sobriquet of "quiescent polity,"[1] thanks to a remarkably strife-free history since its founding in 1788. Virtually the only episodes of strife in nineteenth century Sydney before the rise of the labor movement were a revolt of Irish convicts in 1804 and a few "issueless riots" in the 1840s and 1860s. Workers demonstrated against immigration of Chinese in the 1880s and organized some substantial strikes, notably in 1890 and 1917, but by and large labor demands over both economic and political issues were accommodated by the commercial and political elites. In the twentieth century there have been only three periods of significant strife: during World War I, over war-related issues; during the Depression of the 1930s, which inspired protests by workers and the unemployed, eviction riots, and the mobilization in response of a conservative paramilitary group, the New Guard (it took no action); and the late 1960s, when many antiwar demonstrations apparently contributed to the federal government's decision to begin withdrawing troops from Vietnam in 1970.

The Official Records: Public Order Offenses

There are good reasons for expecting that the hostilities evident in civil conflict will also appear in some official indicators of crime. Whereas the vast majority of crimes against persons and property are committed on private account, some are manifestations of collective hostilities and objectives. Individual and group assaults on police and other officials often arise out of political antagonisms. The incidence of such offenses is regularly reported in crime statistics; in some circumstances the offenses so recorded are direct responses to police

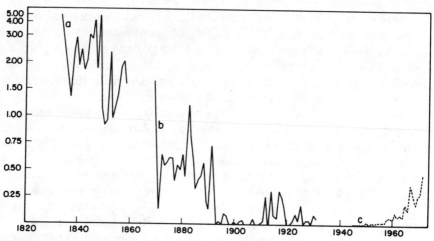

Figure VI.2.1 London: Public order offenses, 1834-1972

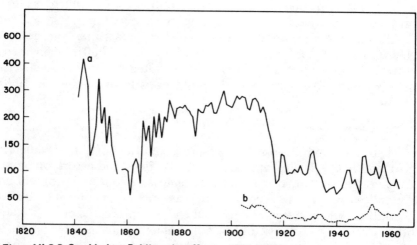

Figure VI.2.2 Stockholm: Public order offenses, 1841-1967

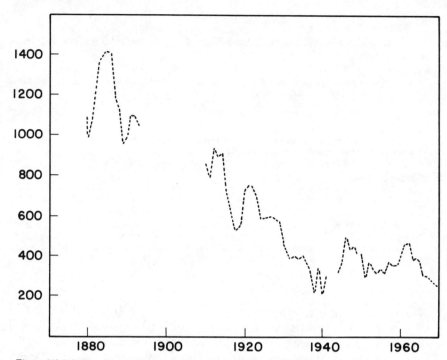

Figure VI.2.3 New South Wales: Public order offenses, 1879-1970

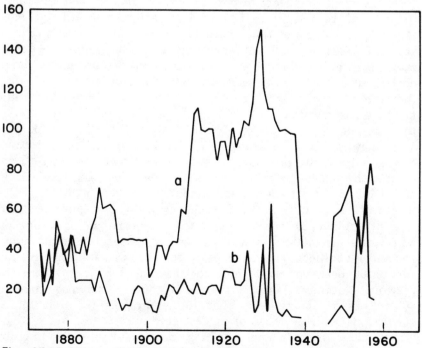

Figure VI.2.4 Calcutta: Public order offenses, 1878-1958

Notes to Figures on Public Order Offenses

All figures show annual data weighted per 100,000 population except where noted.

London
    a. Convictions for all indictable cases of assault on the police, riot, treason, unlawful assembly, and similar offenses, Middlesex County, 1834-1858.
    b. Convictions for offenses as in a, MPD, 1869-1931.
    c. Known offenses as in a, MPD, 1945-1972.

Stockholm
    a. Convictions for violence or threats against officials, resistance to officials, and other offenses against public authorities, 1841-1964.
    b. Known offenses of violence or threats against officials, 1904-1967.

New South Wales
    Arrests for assaults on officers and resisting arrest; riot, unlawful assembly, and treason; riotous, offensive, and threatening behavior and language, etc., 1870-1893, 1910-1970.

Calcutta
    a. Convictions for noncognizable offenses against public order per 1,000 population, 1873-1940, 1947-1958. These are minor offenses against a variety of regulatory acts.
    b. Convictions for assaults on public persons, obstruction of justice, group action against authority, and offenses against the state, same years as in a. These are more serious offenses.

efforts to disperse rioters and protestors.[2] Other categories of offense explicitly register the extent of official response to strife and dissent: Some common and obvious examples are arrests and convictions for such offenses as rioting, unlawful assembly, and treason.[3]

The changing incidence of public order offenses in the four cities is indicated in Figures VI.2.1 to VI.2.4. In each instance we aggregated the offense categories that appeared most likely to reflect acts of political dissent and official repression. Since the graphs give annual rather than averaged data, any correlation with historical episodes of civil strife can be readily seen. The data for London comprise only the more serious (indictable) offenses. They were far more common in the nineteenth than in the twentieth century, and highest of all in the conflict-ridden decades of the 1830s and 1840s. The peak in 1834 may well be a consequence of the Reform Bill demonstrations of the early 1830s; one such occasion in 1833 involved a significant clash with police. Chartist conventions were held in London in 1839 and 1842; only the first corresponds with a blip in the graph. A massive Chartist rally in 1848 coincides with the highest recorded level of public order convictions in the 140-year span. Some but not all peaks in convictions later in the century also can be attributed to particular conflicts. The 1888 peak, for example, follows a bloody encounter between police and socialists in Trafalgar Square the previous November. In the twentieth century the magnitude of convictions is much lower, but the approximate correlation of convictions with episodes of protest continues to be evident. The violent phase of the women's suffrage movement shows up in rising convictions, and so does the tide of antiwar protest of the 1960s.

For Stockholm the data on convictions for public order offenses, line a in Figure VI.2.2, include minor as well as serious cases of resistance to police and officials. In the nineteenth and early twentieth centuries it is sometimes possible to associate a peak in offenses with particular events: Major political riots in 1848 and 1864-1865 and the general strike of 1909 are cases in point. But the graph is more informative about the general level of hostility between rulers and citizens. The rising trend that begins in the 1860s coincides with the growth of acute class conflict in Sweden following the limited parliamentary reforms of 1866. That conflict was manifest in a growing number of strikes and protest demonstrations, which subsided after the entrance of the Social Democrats into a ruling coalition in 1917. Universal franchise was introduced between 1918 and 1920; thereafter both measures of public order offenses are much lower and fluctuate irregularly. Increases around 1930 coincide with the increased economic tensions and strike activity of the Depression. In the 1950s substantial strike activity and a number of "issueless riots" seemingly combined to push up the offense rates. The data come to an end shortly after the onset of anti-American protest in the mid-1960s but show no evidence of an upturn. We know from narrative sources that such protest was regarded by Swedish authorities as legitimate, and vestiges of criminal sanctions that might have been applied to it were stricken from the criminal code. In short, the indicators of public order offenses in Stockholm are not surrogate measures of civil strife, but they probably trace the changing intensity of class economic and political tension better than any other available index.

The incidence of arrests for public order offenses in New South Wales (Figure VI.2.3), does not seem to be a valid indicator of strife or of class tensions. During each of three periods of significant strife in the twentieth century—1914-1918, the early 1930s, and the late 1960s—the index is low. The index is comprised largely of arrests for assaults on police and for various offenses in language and behavior. Its 7:1 decline over a period of 85 years speaks plainly about improvements in civility of public behavior and citizen-police interactions in Sydney but is mute about the tensions that underlie civil conflict.

The Calcutta police evidently relied very heavily on regulatory penalties to maintain social control. The upper line in Figure VI.2.4 traces the conviction rate per 1,000 for a great variety of offenses against regulations governing public order. Although few of these regulations appear to have had specific political content, they were invoked much more often during periods of civil conflict. The conviction rates are extraordinarily high, too: during the 1920s and 1930s there were rarely less than 100,000 convictions per year, and in years of peak disorder convictions were nearly twice as numerous. In ratio terms, between 1910 and the 1930s the annual conviction rates for these offenses averaged about one for every ten residents of the city. The lower line in the figure traces the conviction rate per 100,000 for a set of uncommon political crimes. Before the turn of the century these rates were relatively high despite the lack of significant civil strife, and convictions for petty public order offenses were relatively low. The inference is that in orderly times criminal sanctions were used to control some kinds of behavior that later were treated as regulatory offenses. In any event both indicators register the principal epochs of twentieth century strife in Calcutta. Both increase beginning in about 1904 and continue upward, irregularly, during two decades of recurring political dissent, communal violence, and the beginning of large-scale strike activity. The peak of police efforts to control opposition apparently came between 1926 and 1934. Among the events of these years were a major communal riot (1926), large-scale political strikes (1928, 1934), and most significant, the Civil Disobedience movement from 1930 to 1934. There was less strife after 1934, and convictions for offenses of both kinds declined accordingly. Data for Calcutta after 1958 indicate that numbers of riots and persons arrested for rioting increased greatly after 1965. These figures are examined in comparison with data on crime later in this chapter.

The principal value of indicators of public order offenses is that they trace rather accurately (except in New South Wales) the extent to which elites use the instrumentalities of the criminal law to maintain political order. Yet these indices should not be expected to mirror exactly the historical episodes of civil strife because open opposition is usually sporadic, whereas official sanctions reflect both elites' ongoing efforts to forestall strife and their intensified efforts to reassert control once open conflict does occur.

Issues, Forms, and Outcomes of Strife:
A Comparative Analysis

Lack of quantified information precludes precise comparisons of magnitudes of civil strife among the cities or within them, but the general patterns emerging from the evidence just summarized are clear enough. Calcutta passed from civil tranquility during the middle years of colonial rule to intense revolutionary resistance and mass agitational politics during the twentieth century. The numbers of people mobilized in these conflict situations, the casualties suffered, and the extent of physical and economic losses sustained far exceed those of the three Western cities in any period we examined. The Western cities are by no means identical in their experience of civil

conflict, however. Stockholm experienced episodic conflict throughout the nineteenth century and into the early twentieth century.
Such conflict was often deadly in the first half of the nineteenth
century, but rarely thereafter. The last 50 years have been largely
peaceful ones. Strife in London has been episodic and sometimes
pervasive in both centuries but seldom has led to fatalities. Sydney's
most turbulent years were in the early twentieth century, from
around 1915 to 1935, but the scope and intensity of strife have been
so low in the entire history of New South Wales that (aside from
clashes with aborigines) we can document no more than a dozen
deaths in collective confrontations.

There is, in short, no common long-term trend in magnitudes of
civil strife among the cities. Three points of twentieth century
similarity in the three Western cities are worth mentioning, however.
One is a high level of internal conflict between 1914 and 1918: The
combination of war-related issues and preexisting conflicts generated
particularly intense economic and political strife in all three cities.
This was in marked contrast with the experience of each during
World War II. Strike activity remained low during and after that war,
and international conflict precipitated few divisive political debates
in any of the societies. Last, the international youth "movement" of
the 1960s was represented in all three cities. University students and
sympathetic members of the middle classes carried out a series of
mass protests in which similar tactics were used to oppose groups and
policies associated with nuclear armament, the Vietnam war, and
apartheid in South Africa. By the middle 1970s such protests had
become less frequent and less well attended. They also took on
ritualistic qualities evident in an anti-American demonstration held at
the United States embassy in Stockholm on July 4, 1975.

Comparisons of the timing and magnitudes of strife may be less
instructive than comparisons of parties, issues, tactics, and forms of
conflict. Two widely cited generalizations about changing manifestations of conflict in Western societies can be tested against the
evidence provided by these cities. One is the observation that
"revolutionary" conflict has given way to the politics of reform,
compromise, and co-optation.[4] The other, which has been proposed
by Charles Tilly, is that collective violence in Western societies has
evolved through several stages, from "primitive" communal-based
conflict, through reactionary resistance to the demands exacted by
expanding national states and economies, to "modern" demands by
associational groups for rights and benefits due them.[5]

We have documented the emergence of revolutionary politics in
Calcutta in the twentieth century. In the other societies there was
very little "revolutionary" conflict even in the nineteenth century,
except perhaps in the nightmares of the English elite during the

uncertain decades after the French Revolution. Coups in Stockholm were not revolutionary in any contemporary sense; rather, they revealed the existence of factionalism within the elite. Other classes took part in or responded to them only as a function of their affinities for particularly popular or unpopular members of the nobility. London was the site of an isolated incident of revolutionary "putschism" in 1816 in which class interests were at issue, but no class-based support was inspired. In New South Wales a group of disgruntled military officers in 1808 staged a successful coup against Governor William Bligh (who had suffered a similar misadventure at sea a few years previously) because Bligh had tried to stop their trade in smuggled liquor. The principal instance of "revolutionary" activity in twentieth century Sydney was the agitation of a small group of Industrial Workers of the World during the years 1907 to 1916. When Commonwealth legislation declared the IWW to be an unlawful association, 80 of the most active "radicals" presented themselves for arrest. It probably is accurate to say that there has been more *talk* of revolution among intellectuals in the three Western cities in the last decade than at virtually any time in the last two centuries, but not much more action.

Revolutionary activity did not "decline" in these three Western cities, it never was present to a significant degree in the nineteenth or twentieth centuries. The periods we have examined were characterized instead by cycles of group protest and elite resistance to it, followed sooner or later by compromise. There was, moreover, a common thread: Major episodes of protest in these cities usually developed out of the demands of subordinate classes and categories of people for greater political rights and economic benefits. It is tempting to fit such movements into the procrustean bed of economic class analysis. In Stockholm and London the locus of protest shifts over time from the expanding middle class to skilled workers to the new industrial working classes. But the protests of suffragettes, Irish nationalists, and pacifist students cannot readily be described in class terms. The most that can be said is that these diverse groups were all of lower or middle social status, all had distinctive interests and felt that these were being thwarted by the (in)action of powerful others, and all chose tactics of protest, confrontation, and selective violence to advance their interests. It certainly is the case that class-based conflict has declined in Stockholm and Sydney, indeed has all but disappeared as a source of civil strife. Only in strike activity in England is there a substantial element of class hostility. The new issues of protest, especially in the 1960s, have centered not on the distribution of economic benefits or the attainment of political rights but rather on the uses and abuses of political power.

The nature of elite response to protest in the Western societies has had a good deal to do with the issues and forms of urban strife. The immediate response—to demonstrations, riots, and widespread strikes—has rarely been accommodating. Protestors usually have been dispersed, their leaders arrested or harassed, the activists and their organizations subjected to legal and economic sanctions. In longer perspective, though, most of the basic issues of protest have been met by substantial concessions and reforms. Certainly this was true of demands for the extension of the franchise and for the rights of labor to organize and to bargain collectively. All three of the Western societies in the early twentieth century developed powerful labor-based political parties that singly or in coalition have held national power for substantial periods. Viewed individually, the steps by which these changes came about may seem to merit such belittling descriptions as "concession" and "co-optation." Looked at over a 150-year span, however, it is evident that they have been cumulative and little short of revolutionary in their impact: The locus of political power undeniably has moved down the class ladder, and the power of capitalistic enterprises has been sharply constrained by organized labor and prolabor governments, respectively. These separate histories of conflict and accommodation have had two kinds of consequences for civil strife. On the one hand they have preempted revolutionary conflict, by undermining its rationale, incentives, and social bases. On the other, they have created political cultures in which protestors anticipate compromises and elites believe that they are obliged to comply. These mutually reinforcing expectations allow many conflicts to be managed and minimized short of civil strife, and they give a ritualistic quality to incidents that can be called strife.

These generalizations are not necessarily a forecast of civil peace for the indefinite future in these three Western cities or societies. We have pointed out the high level of serious strife in London and have referred to the prevalence of talk of "revolution" among radical intelligentsia. The prevailing methods of conflict management that bind elites and citizens, workers and employers in these societies, are not necessarily applicable to new kinds of issues raised in the last decade or so. Coping with problems of international conflict, persisting inequalities, and alienation and the demand for autonomy in complex societies may be beyond the capacity of elites. In any event such issues may be "nonnegotiable" for growing numbers of the discontented. Indeed, incapacity and intractability may exist side by side. And persisting grievances over irresolvable issues are the seedbed of revolutionary conflict. This is the final objection to generalizations about the conflict-minimizing effects of modernization and urbanization.

The assertion that civil conflict in Western societies has evolved

through "stages" characterized by different types of social organization and motives also needs qualification in light of our evidence.
The categories themselves can be used for describing most of the civil
strife in the three cities. Most strife in all three cities has been what
Tilly would call "modern" and has been initiated by associational,
class-based groups. Illustrations of his "primitive" category of violence are the various small riots and skirmishes between Anglo-Saxon
Londoners and Irish immigrants in the nineteenth century and
"coloreds" in the twentieth; the brawls and riots between Stockholmers and soldiers in the nineteenth century might fall into the
same group. There are few instances of "reactionary" violence, as
Tilly defines the category, but one would not expect to find many in
the urban centers of national expansion; these events are more
characteristic of people on the periphery. Riotous protests against
police actions are one kind of urban example. It also is tempting to
use the same classification for the recent protests of alienated youths
and intellectuals, because of the presence of a substantial element of
reaction to the impersonal and seemingly impervious power of the
modern state. There remain instances of civil strife in the cities that
do not fit well any of these three categories. The violent struggles
of elite factions for power (limited mainly to early nineteenth-
century Stockholm) are one kind of example. Also to be considered
are the riotous outbursts of anger and exuberance sprinkled through
the histories of all three cities, which have neither explicit rationale
nor any target other than the people and property closest to hand.
They seem to merit the characterizations of "issueless riots" used by
Gary Marx, or "rioting for fun and profit," *pace* Edward Banfield.[6]
Such riots were never particularly common in these cities, though,
and rarely if ever resulted in the mobilization of the crowds who
turned out on the occasion of specific political and economic
confrontations.

The assertion that these forms of civil strife evolved in sequence
does not seem to be supported by the evidence of these cities over
the last 180 years or so. Our judgments are necessarily impressionistic, but protest based on associational groups appears to have been
about as common in the early and middle nineteenth century as it
has been in the twentieth. Instances of "primitive" violence are as
easily found in the twentieth century as in the nineteenth; they have
declined markedly in Stockholm, but the same is true of other forms
of civil strife. And nothing in history points to the existence of an
intervening stage of "reactionary" violence in these three cities.
Tilly's generalization is based on data from France, at the national
level. Thus we can identify two sources of the discrepancy. The
political and social histories of our three societies, especially Sweden
and New South Wales, differ markedly from the case of France and

give us little reason to expect civil strife to have similar social forms and bases in the same historical sequence. Equally important, we would expect strife in dominant cities to have different characteristics from strife occurring elsewhere. We suggest, on the basis of limited evidence, that with great historical consistency civil strife in the Western cities has arisen mainly from the demands of "associational" economic groups and political factions. The generalization applies with some certainty to London, Stockholm, and Sydney during the past 180 years.

There is little point in testing generalizations about civil strife in Western cities against the experience of a non-Western city like Calcutta because no one has claimed those generalizations to be relevant. In Calcutta civil strife evolved from protest to rebellion and revolution, under conditions that are familiar from a general theoretical perspective: Each successive round of Bengali nationalist agitation was met by coercive response of sufficient severity to bring it to a gradual halt. In the ensuing periods of relative tranquility the suppressive measures were gradually relaxed. Since few substantial concessions or adjustments were made by the colonial elite during the lulls, nationalist agitation reemerged more or less quickly, usually with more adamant and less negotiable demands. These cycles continued until the British capitulated, having lost the will and means to resist further. The general principle is that the mix of inconsistent repression and lack of reform is usually fatal to the elites who employ it.[7] Another generalization can be drawn by contrasting the political cultures that have evolved in the four cities, with special reference to conflict and conciliation. Certain patterns of mutual expectations of compromise have evolved among most groups in the three Western cities and societies, in sharp contrast to the readiness of contending groups in Calcutta to use mass agitation and violence in all conflict situations. The difference need not be attributed to some vague "cultural difference" between Eastern and Western or "modern" and "underdeveloped" societies. It is more simply explained by the very different historical experiences of these societies: In three of them traditions of gradual elite accommodation emerged, whereas in the fourth victory has gone to the groups whose reliance on force has been most persistent and uncompromising.

The last issue addressed here is whether there is anything distinctively "urban" about the patterns of civil strife we have traced. A number of features evidently are dependent on the urban setting. The prevalence of associational groups in conflict, even in Calcutta, is a function of urban occupational and mobility patterns, which cut across and erode the primary ties that bind communal groups together. Moreover, a "critical mass" of disaffected citizenry is more often to be found in cities than elsewhere, which means also that cities are promising places to organize agitational politics. This relationship holds true regardless of whether there is proportionally more disaffection among city dwellers than among their counterparts in the towns and country: People are more readily organized in the cities. By the same token, people also are more easily observed and policed in the cities than the country. In the face of modern armies and police forces, dissidents who initiate conflict in urban areas are likely to select less violent and provocative tactics, and they are unlikely to be able to carry out sustained "revolutionary" action. A fourth distinctive property of urban settings, especially metropolises such as those we studied, is that the agents who are responsible for grievances, or capable of resolving them, are more likely to be found there. Thus targeted protest accompanied by carefully formulated demands is more likely to occur in cities, too. In addition to these generalizations it is evident that the concerns and grievances of city people usually differ from those of the rural element. The former are less concerned with land than with jobs, less with separatism or resistance to government agents than with sharing or seizing power. It is tempting to use these generalizations as a basis for proposing that many of the typical characteristics of civil strife in "modern" societies—limited demands, associational base, high degree of organization, relatively nonviolent and nonrevolutionary character—are partly a function of their urban setting. The evidence examined here is only suggestive; it provides no test of the assertion.

CRISES OF PUBLIC ORDER: THE COINCIDENCE OF CONFLICT AND CRIME

We have documented the trends in individual crime and the episodic nature of civil strife in four societies. The next question is one we posed earlier. Does any correlation exist between the outbreak of civil conflict and short-term increases in common crime? Our use of the portmanteau concept "public disorder" presumes some correspondence between the two faces of disorder. In later chapters we review evidence that both conditions have often stimulated similar kinds of official response, especially the expansion and reform of police forces. Calcutta has furnished suggestive evidence on the point: Almost all indicators of crime rose sharply at about the time of the onset of nationalist agitation.

There are at least three reasons for expecting to find a general relationship between high crime and civil conflict. One of the most pervasive assumptions of theories of crime and conflict is that both are rooted in social tensions that are manifest in a prevailing sense of individual anomie, alienation, or discontent. It is plausible to suppose that such states of mind will motivate some to join in collective action and others, depending on their needs and opportunities, to take more individualistic courses of action. A second line of argument is that widespread and prolonged group conflict causes or increases the breakdown of moral order. People in disorderly times are more likely to do what they feel like doing than what others say is right and proper. A third factor is that elites faced with real or threatened resistance probably intensify efforts at social control across the board, increasing policing, prosecuting, and punishment. The changing incidence of public order offenses, reviewed earlier, offers one proof of this connection. The additional evidence summarized below neither tests nor assumes the accuracy of any one of these arguments. Together, though, they give us more than sufficient reason for expecting a positive but less than perfect connection between conflict and crime.

The first step in testing the crime-conflict nexus was to identify systematically what are popularly called "crime waves." We decided to include each period in which the crime rate increased in three successive years at an average rate of ten percent a year or more. The procedure was applied separately to indicators of violent crime and theft for each of the four societies. Four to eight "waves" of increases in each type of crime were identified in each city, most of them three to four years in duration, a few lasting ten years or more. Then the extent of strife in each period of rising crime was assessed, based on the narrative accounts reviewed earlier in this chapter. Whenever two or all three kinds of disorder increased simultaneously, we label them a "crisis of public order." The results are summarized in Tables VI.2.1 to VI.2.4, which we discuss separately, then comparatively.[8]

In 150 years of London's history there were seven instances of sharp increases in crimes of violence and eight in theft (Table VI.2.1). A number of these periods coincided approximately or precisely with serious conflict, constituting six distinct crises of public order. Their approximate dates are 1830-1832, 1842-1848, 1874-1882, 1916-1920, 1925-1931, and 1956-1972. With the exception of 1874-1882, which corresponds with a sharp economic decline, all are marked by increasing crime and strife. Both theft and violent crimes usually increased during one of these episodes (1830-1832 is the single exception), lending added force to the argument that the two facets of disorder are closely interconnected. The relationship is by no means perfect, however. There are four periods of sharply rising crime rates (one in the 1820s, three between 1890 and 1907) during which no significant strife occurred. And the five years before the outbreak of World War I—a time of intense political protest in London, especially by the suffragettes—had no noticeable effect on the rate of common crime.

Table VI.2.1 Crises of Public Order in London, 1820-1972

Years of rising crime rates[a]	Average increase in violent crime (%)[b]	Average increase in theft (%)[c]	Evidence of civil strife
1825-1827		24	None in London; economic riots elsewhere, 1826-1827
1830-1832	49		Agitation for Reform Bill of 1832; widespread riots and strikes throughout England
1842-1845	13	14	Major Chartist demonstrations in London, 1842 and 1848, in context of national workers' movement 1838-1848
1845-1848	16		
1874-1876	16	11	No significant strife; 1875-1880 was a period of sharp economic decline
1877-1882			
1891-1899		10	No significant strife
1901-1903		17	No significant strife
1905-1907	14		No significant strife
1916-1920	37	26	Widespread strikes, 1919-1921
1918-1920			
1925-1928	16	26	General strike of 1926; significant strike activity 1929-1932
1928-1931			
1956-1972	12	12	Large-scale political protest over various issues; small-scale ethnic clashes; substantial strike activity 1957, 1969-1971

a. Periods in which crime rates increased for at least three consecutive years at an average rate of at least 10 percent per year.

b. Average annual percentage increases for indictable offenses of murder and assault, convictions before 1920, known offenses thereafter.

c. Average annual percentage increases for indictable theft, convictions before 1920, known offenses thereafter.

Table VI.2.2 Crises of Public Order in Stockholm, 1840-1971

Years of rising crime rates[a]	Average increase in violent crime (%)[b]	Average increase in theft (%)[c]	Evidence of civil strife
1850-1852		11	No significant strife
1866-1868		26	No significant strife
1874-1876	24		Serious clashes with police and soldiers, three in 1875 alone
1880-1876		12	Substantial labor protest, continued clashes with police. In the decade five riots, twelve demonstrations, and numerous strikes were recorded
1881-1890	83		
1899-1905	49		High level of strike activity; serious clashes between police and strikers in 1900 and 1905
1916-1918		43	The "hunger years"; many demonstrations and a food riot
1938-1942		25	No significant strife
1938-1945	46		
1947-1949		14	Minor street clashes
1952-1958	26		Minor street clashes, significant strike activity
1961-1963	26		
1963-1970		10	Numerous antiforeign protests, few strikes or clashes
1965-1967	28		

a. Periods in which crime rates increased for at least three consecutive years at an average rate of at least 10 percent per year.

b. Average of annual percentage increases for known offenses of murder and attempts. The percentages are high because such offenses are few in number and subject to great annual variation.

c. Average annual percentage increases for all known offenses of theft, including burglary, robbery, larceny, and auto theft. Figures before 1870 based on conviction data.

In Stockholm fifteen epochs of rising reported crime also qualify as "crime waves," across a span of 130 years (Table VI.2.2), and ten of them were associated with significant strife. We have already referred several times to class tensions in Sweden during the latter decades of the nineteenth century and the early years of the twentieth. Stockholm's crises of public order of 1874-1876, 1880-1890, and 1899-1905 are related to these tensions. The next crisis, in 1916-1918, was directly a consequence of economic collapse, for the economy of neutral Sweden suffered even more in World War I than in the next war, which was also accompanied by rising crime rates. In the years after 1945 there are three identifiable surges in crime rates, the last two coinciding with significant strife. The distinctions among them may be arbitrary, for the trend in crime rates has been up since 1947. The onset of strife came well after the rise in crime, however, and touched on seemingly unrelated economic and political issues. When we turn the situation around and identify major periods of conflict that were not accompanied by rising crime rates, we find two: the struggle of the middle class for greater political rights, which lasted into the 1840s (there were devastating riots of 1848), and the strike-ridden years of the 1920s and early 1930s (just under half of the 685 strikes recorded in Stockholm between 1900 and 1970 occurred in these two decades).

New South Wales provides another set of tests (Table VI.2.3). Between 1830 and 1970 there were nine marked increases in conviction rates for violent crime and five for theft. We already have remarked on the low level of civil conflict in New South Wales during most of its history, and it is not surprising that six of these fourteen "crime waves" occurred independently of strife. It is perhaps more surprising that eight of the fourteen do coincide with strife. The first episodes of large-scale working-class protest, in 1886-1888, coincide precisely with a rise in convictions for both kinds of common crime, and a similar pattern is repeated in 1918-1923. The effects of the Depression also are evident in the form of a simultaneous rise in economic crime and economic protest. When the relationship is examined from the perspective of strife, we find that there are eight five-year periods of detectable strife between 1850 and 1970, and only one—economic protest in the early 1860s—is not matched by rising crime. On the whole, the correlation between rising crime and civil conflict in New South Wales is as strong as it is in the two European cities.

The evidence from Calcutta on this issue is mixed. In the span of 99 years for which we have convictions data (Table VI.2.4) there is evidence for six distinct crises of public order: 1876-1879, 1906-1910, 1918-1920, 1923-1926, 1931-1933, and 1956-1959. Convictions for crime and strife rise simultaneously in all but the

Table VI.2.3 Crises of Public Order in New South Wales, 1830-1970

Years of rising crime rates[a]	Average increase in violent crime (%)[b]	Average increase in theft (%)[c]	Evidence of civil strife
1853-1855	27		No significant strife
1871-1873	33		No significant strife
1886-1888[d]	32	28	First large-scale labor protests and strikes, 1885-1888
1898-1900	21		Minor apolitical street clashes
1907-1914	37		Significant strike activity, 1907 and after
1918-1923	19	14	Major strikes in 1917, 1919, some postwar street fighting
1929-1931[d]		15	Major strikes in 1929; recurrent demonstrations, eviction riots, street fighting in early 1930s
1937-1939		19	No significant strife
1940-1942	30		No significant strife
1946-1950	11		Significant strike activity, small-scale protests
1954-1961		10	No significant strife
1967-1969	19		Many antiwar and antiapartheid demonstrations

a. Periods in which crime rates increased for at least three consecutive years at an average annual rate of at least 10 percent. There were no periods of substantial increase between 1830 and 1852.
b. Average of annual percentage in higher court convictions for murder and assault.
c. Average of annual percentage increases in higher court convictions for theft.
d. Period includes two years of very substantial increase and one year of slight decline.

first of these six instances. Three crises coincide with three of the four principal nationalist campaigns, and crime data are lacking for the fourth one, the Quit India movement of 1942-1943. Most of the major episodes of communal violence in the city's history also coincide with short-term increases in crime. The exceptions are posed by strike activity. Widespread political and economic strikes in 1921, 1928, 1934, and 1953-1954 are not matched by rising rates of violent crime or theft.

An examination of more detailed evidence for the 1960s, though, shows relations among strife, crime, and official behavior that are different and more complex. Some of the relevant data are set out in Figure VI.2.5; since the time span is short and population estimates are unreliable, the data are not weighted by population. It is strikingly evident that during these years the recorded levels of crime and official efforts at control were greatest when strife was low. From 1963 through 1966 more than 20,000 cognizable (serious) offenses were recorded per year, and officials were able to obtain convictions for more than two-thirds of them. (For India's eight largest cities in 1965, by contrast, the average conviction rate for cognizable offenses known was 41 percent.) The most serious offenses—murder, armed robbery, and dacoity—numbered less than 100 per year during this period, and "riots" (collective disturbances by five or more individuals) were at a relatively low level of 200 to 300 per year.

Beginning in 1966 riots and arrests for rioting began a five-year increase of 400 percent, paralleled by a sevenfold increase in the most serious individual crimes. These are the official tracings of a crisis of public order of the most serious magnitude, precipitated mainly by the Communist Party of India (CPI), which in 1966 organized a massive series of food agitations, strikes, and violent demonstrations aimed at toppling the Congress Party Government of Bengal. After the 1967 elections the CPI joined the new left-wing United Front Government, whose effects on public order are evident in the official statistics. By 1971 (following a period of direct rule by the central government) the total number of serious offenses known to police had dropped by more than half, arrests and trials declined by ratios of 5:1 or more, and convictions were obtained for scarcely 20 percent of what was now a much smaller number of "known" cases. The phenomenon was peculiar to Calcutta. In India's other large cities there were no comparable declines in known offenses, and in 1971 convictions were obtained in an average of 44 percent of all known cases.[9]

The impact of civil strife associated with the rise and fall of the United Front Government on crime and the criminal justice system in Calcutta was very great. Evidently a concerted effort was made to improve public order in the city under the Congress Party regime in

Table VI.2.4 Crises of Public Order in Calcutta, 1873-1971

Years of rising crime rates[a]	Average increase in violent crime (%)[b]	Average increase in theft (%)[c]	Evidence of civil strife
1876-1879	48	15	No significant strife
1906-1908		13	Antipartition movement, first overt nationalist strife, 1906-1908
1906-1910	15		
1918-1920	26	14	First major communal riots 1918, otherwise a quiet period characterized by economic recession
1923-1926	15		Last phase of noncooperation movement, 1920-1924; major communal rioting, 1926
1931-1933	13		Civil disobedience movement, 1930-1934
1957-1958		44	Major economic and political strikes 1954-1957 but not in 1958 or 1959
1956-1959	107		

a. Periods in which crime rates increased for at least three consecutive years (except 1957-1958) at an average annual rate of at least 10 percent.

b. Average of annual percentage increases in convictions for murder and assault.

c. Average of annual percentage increases in convictions for noncognizable (minor) theft.

the early and mid-1960s. During that time the police and courts were very assiduous in detecting offenses, arresting suspects, and securing convictions. Because of altered political circumstances thereafter, the institutions of public order suspended most of their routine control activities and, apparently, did little more than record and react to the rising incidence of rioting, murder, and robbery.

The immediate conclusion to be drawn from these comparisons is that sharp increases in indicators of crimes of violence and theft usually coincide with episodes of strife. Objective criteria have been used to identify 29 substantial increases in violent crime, measured mostly by reference to changes in conviction rates. Nineteen of the 29, or 66 percent, coincided with serious internal conflict. Of the increases in theft, thirteen of 25 also coincided with civil strife. Since neither "crime waves" nor episodes of strife are particularly common in these cities (except for strife in Calcutta), there is not much doubt that the correlation reflects the existence of a pervasive and important social phenomenon. The simplest explanation—that periods of strife provide greater opportunities for crime—is probably insufficient. When social tension is widespread and intense, it is likely to provoke different forms of disorder at the same time that it spurs elites and officials to intensified efforts at control. In extreme cases disorder rises to such a pitch that the authorities are reduced to impotence. Two examples of this occurred in Calcutta, in the mid-1940s and in the late 1960s.

This study does not specify the more remote social causes of crime and strife, which would be necessary to test this kind of hypothesis. The three chapters that follow are concerned instead with how the law, police, and judicial institutions have defined, reported, and responded to the diverse conditions of public order. As institutions have changed, so has public disorder, exhibiting a recurring pattern of interdependence that is as enduring as it is antagonistic.

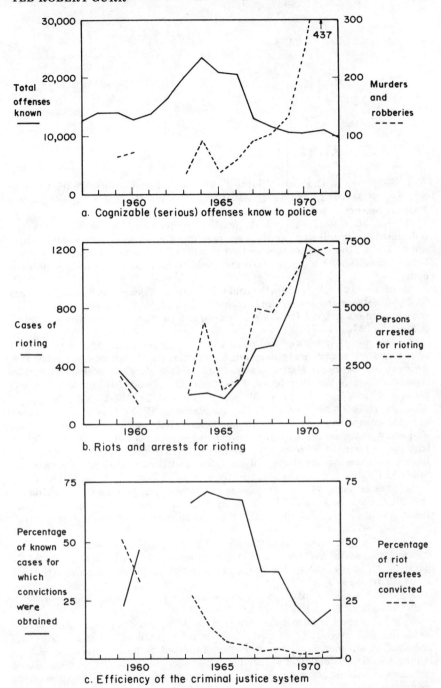

a. Cognizable (serious) offenses know to police

b. Riots and arrests for rioting

c. Efficiency of the criminal justice system

Figure VI.2.5 Calcutta: Indicators of crime, conflict, and the administration of justice, 1957-1972

NOTES TO CHAPTER VI.2

1. See Peter N. Grabosky, "Protest and the Quiescent Polity: Public Order in Sydney, 1788-1973," paper given at the Annual Meeting of the American Political Science Association, Chicago, September 1974.

2. Not all rioters act out of political conviction, and many attacks on policemen are motivated by the common impulse to resist or retaliate against arrest. Unlike the other crimes we have examined, however, a significant proportion of the offenses so categorized are likely to have diffuse or specific political content.

3. In a study of "protest" crimes in nineteenth-century England, George Rudé so categorizes arson, riot, machine-breaking, high treason, sedition, and breach of the peace, in "Protest and Punishment in Nineteenth Century Britain," *Albion*, 5 (1973), 1-23.

4. The debate over the "end of ideology" includes as one of its elements the subsidence of revolutionary demands and tactics by the urban proletariat. See, for example, Seymour Martin Lipset, *Political Man: The Social Bases of Politics* (Garden City, N.Y.: Doubleday, 1960), chs. 2, 3, and 7; Mostafa Rejai, ed., *Decline of Ideology* (Chicago: Aldine, 1971), and C. I. Waxman, *The End of Ideology Debate* (New York: Funk and Wagnalls, 1969). Contemporary cross-national comparisons of the characteristics of civil conflict document the high frequency and intensity of internal wars and conspiracies in non-Western countries by comparison with Western countries, from which historical trends away from revolution are sometimes inferred. See Ted Robert Gurr, "A Comparative Study of Civil Strife," in Graham and Gurr, eds., *Violence in America*, ch. 17.

5. Charles Tilly, "Collective Violence in European Perspective," in Graham and Gurr, eds., ch. 1, and "The Changing Place of Collective Violence" in Melvin Richter, ed., *Essays in Social and Political History* (Cambridge: Harvard University Press, 1970).

6. See Gary T. Marx, "Issueless Riots," *Annals of the American Academy of Political and Social Science*, vol. 391 (September 1970), 21-33, and Edward C. Banfield, "Rioting Mainly for Fun and Profit," *The Unheavenly City* (Boston: Little, Brown, 1970), ch. 9.

7. The argument is made and various examples cited in Gurr, *Why Men Rebel* (Princeton, N.J.: Princeton University Press, 1970), esp. ch. 8.

8. More precise comparisons require more complete and precise data on the incidence and magnitude of strife than could be gathered in this study. The principal disadvantage of the procedure followed is not imprecision but its failure to test systematically for the occurrence of strife without correlated increases in crime. Observations on this point are included in the subsequent discussion.

9. The data on Calcutta and other Indian cities during this period are from annual editions of *Crime in India* (New Delhi: Ministry of Home Affairs).

ELITE INTERESTS AND THE
DEFINITION OF PUBLIC ORDER

The nature of elites' concerns about public disorder is most concretely revealed in the institutions they establish and the policies they follow in the ongoing effort to manage conflict and control crime. The next three chapters compare the evolution of institutions and policies in four societies, with particular reference to the nature and scope of criminal law, the development of police forces, and the judicial and penal treatment accorded offenders. Of special interest are the timing and circumstances of changes in these institutions, and the ways in which such changes appear to have affected the extent and severity of public disorder.

Most of the discussion is concerned with national or colonywide policies and institutions rather than with those of the four cities alone. With some exceptions, however, the policies and institutions we examine were devised in response to metropolitan interests and problems and were implemented at least as quickly and thoroughly in primary cities as elsewhere. Therefore a "national" analysis is fully and often especially applicable to the cities.

ELITE INTERESTS

We begin with a consideration of the kinds of values and objectives that elites apply to questions of public order. The "elites" of concern are the groups and individuals—mainly political leaders and officials, but also the spokesmen for powerful economic and social groups—who make the fundamental decisions about public order policies. By focusing on elites we are not assuming that their interests and values are necessarily different from or antithetical to those of other social strata. As far as we can tell, the elites of all the societies examined here have shared some values and norms with other major social groups—even in Bengal during colonial rule. The differences are variable over time and become apparent both in the patterns of strife and crime and in public demands for changes in law and policy. Those demands sometimes have substantial effects, and this reveals another aspect of our conception of the role of elites in defining and policing public order: They are not autonomous but rather are subject to various kinds of influences and constraints. The values and social beliefs held by elites in common with other members of society are one latent kind of constraint. The bureaucratic inertia of established police, judicial, and penal systems is another. It is evident, especially in contemporary societies, that many well-intentioned elite attempts to alter, say, police and penal policies, are thwarted by the passive resistance or incapacity of lower echelon members of those institutions. External pressures for change, on the other hand, come from a variety of sources: sometimes from the general public, concerned about crime or pernicious policy, sometimes from special interest groups, sometimes from the intellectuals and experts who mold opinion, elite as well as public. Thus it is too simplistic to maintain that changing policies of public order are merely manifestations of an elite's class interests or narrow desire to retain power. Class and conservative interests are often evident in public order policies, but so are many other conditions.

The following summary of the most salient elite concerns about public order in the four societies makes reference to two major dimensions of variation: first the extent to which issues of public order have been of primary concern to elites, and second, the extent to which elite interests in defining and policing public order appear to have diverged from the concerns of other social groups.

Public order issues were of the greatest salience for the British who ruled Bengal. The achievement of British economic ends in Bengal depended in the most fundamental way on eliminating or at least controlling organized Indian resistance to British rule. Individual crime was of less concern, except insofar as it affected the British population and their clients and employees. The control of crime among Indians was a low-priority item during most of the colonial period, as is evident from the scanty resources devoted to the relevant institutions of public order, as well as from the retrenchment of ordinary crime prevention activities during periods of heightened nationalist activity. Circumstances have not changed greatly since independence. The persistence of revolutionary opposition to the new Indian rulers of West Bengal and the enduring tradition of mass agitational politics in Calcutta pose a real and continuing threat to both political and economic elites. The city's economic decline has increased the need and reduced the resources for public services of all kinds. It is not surprising, given these conditions, that the control of common crime receives fewer resources and more perfunctory attention than in Western societies.

The rulers of (West) Bengal have had relatively little to fear from individual Indians compared with the uneasiness caused the authorities of New South Wales by convicts during the first half-century of the colony. The maintenance of order among a population comprised substantially of transported convicts and Irish nationalists was a paramount end in itself in the early years. The necessity for tight and punitive control was reinforced by the prevailing British belief in the inherent depravity of the "criminal class." In the early nineteenth century the development of labor-intensive agriculture, employing convict and ex-convict labor, furnished an explicitly economic incentive for maintaining, even tightening coercive control. By mid-century, however, public order was no longer a dominant issue, thanks to three factors: the end of transportation in 1840, the upsurge in the number of voluntary immigrants, and the rising agricultural prosperity of a colony that "rode the sheep's back" through the rest of the century. It probably is accurate to say that for the past century and more, the principal concerns of the New South Wales and Commonwealth elites have been continued economic prosperity and the provision of public and social services, with the relative emphasis varying according to whether working-class or middle-class parties were in power. Public order has become a salient issue only when disorder seemed to threaten the economic system or middle-class conceptions of proper social and sexual conduct.

The threat of crime and revolution weighed very heavily on the English elite from the end of the Napoleonic wars well into the 1840s. Beginning late in the eighteenth century, Britain, like most other European societies, suffered from the first phase of the population "explosion" that has continued to the present. For several decades the consequence was a labor surplus and the progressive immiseration of the urban and rural lower classes. By contemporary standards—and, what is more important, by the standards of the previous century—the poor were "overworked, atrociously housed, undernourished, disease-ridden and lived in a misery that defies the modern imagination."[1] Many were forced into beggary and petty thievery to exist at all, and a few were both desperate and well-nourished enough to cherish hopes of revolution. The English elite's fears of revolution proved to be illusory, partly because of the expanding economic opportunities that accompanied the "take-off" of the Industrial Revolution. The problems of crime were more obvious and pervasive, but they too proved tractable. This period of crisis coincided with what Asa Briggs has called "the age of improvement," during which most of the leaders of English society became supremely confident of their capacity to create a moral, industrious, prosperous—hence orderly—society. The conditions that bred the "criminal class" and crime were thought to be remediable, along with other social ills, and the developments of the Victorian era, during which public order improved dramatically, seemed to justify a positive attitude.[2]

In some contrast to this early optimism is the mixture of toleration and resignation with which most members of English society seem to regard rising disorder in recent decades. Officials, journalists, and ordinary citizens are concerned, some of them intensely, but there are at least two noteworthy characteristics of elite and popular attitudes toward crime and strife in English society. The fear, hysteria, and advocacy of draconian measures that typify the North American reaction to the problem have been rare in England for over a century. Even the political bombings in the 1970s have evoked responses much more defensive than repressive. Second, there are no major episodes of public moralism in our study of London comparable to those we observed in Sydney (of which more later). That is, whereas the New South Welshmen have often made intense but short-lived elite, legislative, police, and judicial efforts to control particular kinds of offenses—usually having to do with sex, drugs, or public behavior—the tides of English concern have risen and fallen more gently. Our conclusion is that since the 1850s public order in English society generally, and in London in particular, has rarely been any more than a secondary concern for most of the elite or the public at large. The principal exception to this generalization came during the years immediately before World War I, as discussed in the next chapter.

Several themes are evident in the history of elite concern about public order in Stockholm. The rise of liberal middle-class dissent in the first half of the nineteenth century was perceived as a threat calling for legal and judicial response by the monarchy and the nobility. In the last two decades of the nineteenth century and the first years of the twentieth, the economic and political demands of the working class stimulated substantial efforts at controlling strikes and other kinds of protest. In the aftermath of the Russian Revolution there was considerable concern about revolutionary prospects in Sweden, and these fears may have contributed to the decision to grant universal suffrage in 1921. A second, recurring issue has been public behavior, drunkenness and vagrancy in particular. Both economic and social motives were evident in official efforts to control such activities: Vagrancy, mainly a nineteenth century problem, was usually synonymous with unemployment; the personal and social costs of alcoholism have attracted the concerted efforts of reformers representing various strata of Swedish society for well over a century. Notably absent is apparent, intense concern by the Swedish elite about "ordinary" crimes of violence or theft. The marked differences over time in the reported incidence of these crimes have not inspired comparable official efforts at control. To the elite, they seem to have appeared less threatening then either civil strife or disorderly individual behavior.

Thus far we have assessed the salience of civil strife and crime for the elites in these four societies, making only passing reference to the views of non-elites. The interests of the latter have been very diverse and mostly undocumented, and our conclusions and comparisons on this issue are more tentative. We suggest, first, that dissent and civil strife have been the subjects of the greatest divergence of opinion in all the societies. The reasons are obvious: Most political and economic strife in the societies has had a class basis and the objective of curtailing some of the powers and privileges of the dominant classes. In the three Western societies there has also been a gradual convergence of interest between rulers and ruled on the issue of strife and dissent. One does not have to accept the "end of ideology" thesis to recognize that there has been a significant increase in the political and economic power wielded by working-class organizations. The old upper classes have largely dissolved, and the old and new middle and professional classes are generally acquiecent about power-sharing. As a consequence the social basis for strife has lessened, and something like consensus exists on the need for cooperation and conflict management. These assertions are most applicable to Sweden and New South Wales, they need some qualification with reference to Britain, where important segments of the labor movement intransigently hold to revolutionary objectives (if nationalization can still be said to be "revolutionary") and disruptive means to that end. Radical student and intellectual protest in England and in Australian society is also outside the consensual pale, not necessarily in its objectives but certainly in its reliance on tactics of civil disobedience. Strife of this kind has only a small social base and is rejected by most other social groups. The foregoing generalizations do not apply in West Bengal, where elite and popular opinion remain acrimoniously at odds over what public order ought to be and which groups should define and maintain it.

The realm of social behavior and morality continues to divide social opinion in the three Western societies. One distinctive consequence of the growing influence of the middle classes in the nineteenth century was their attempt to impose their standards of behavior on other social classes. The list of behaviors that have been the subject of recurrent attempts at regulation is highly similar across all three societies. It is also long and sometimes ludicrous, and

includes idleness, lack of regular employment, infidelity, homosexuality, abortion, prostitution, public urination and profanity,
gambling, alcohol consumption, the private distilling of alcohol, and
the use of drugs other than alcohol. The first few items on this list
now largely escape attempts at official regulation; most of the others
are the subject of sporadic or persistent, and often strenuous, efforts
at control. What is at issue, of course, is the conflict between the
desires of people with the least stake in society to "do what feels
good" and the desire of those who have more stake, and are armed
with moral tenets of religious origin, to limit what they perceive as
the socially corrosive effects of indulgence. The nineteenth century
Victorians were remarkably successful in persuading most of the
working class of the rightness of their views on these issues, and we
infer from limited evidence that middle-class values on most of these
matters became pervasive in Swedish and Australian society too.
Coincident with World War I, however, some well-documented
changes began to occur in middle-class notions of morality and
deviance, followed by modifications in demands for public order and
the definition of it. To simplify grossly what has happened in the
past 50 years, attempts to regulate sexual conduct have largely
ceased in London and Stockholm (though not in New South Wales);
drug use is of intense concern in Stockholm and Sydney; while
public drunkenness is both common and rather consistently policed
in all three Western cities. Sydney appears to be the most "moralistic" of the three in the Victorian sense, London is distinctly the
least. Both Sydney and Stockholm seem to be characterized now by
consensus across classes about such issues, though there are definite
differences between the cities. English opinion seems to be more
sharply divided, with the professional and intellectual classes leading
the libertarian way over the resistance of much of the lower middle
and skilled working classes.

In Bengal the British imported their version of social morality
beginning in the eighteenth century and in some instances attempted
to apply their standards not only to the foreign community but to
Indians as well. The British were particularly offended by the Indian's use of infanticide as a form of birth control and did what they
could to discourage the practice. It seems to have been resorted to
more in rural than in urban areas, and rarer than contemporary
accounts imply. Another offensive practice was suttee, the immola-
tion of widows with the bodies of their husbands. In the early
nineteenth century there were several hundred instances each year in
Calcutta. The major impetus for outlawing the custom did not come
from the British, though, but from Bengali Hindus who found the
practice morally objectionable. For the most part one receives the

impression that "deviance" among Indians went unpoliced or was left to indigenous courts and traditional patterns of control. British attempts to ensure the humane treatment of animals in the city, for example, were given up for want of police resources. We have no direct evidence about contemporary Bengali opinion on these matters, but the rates of arrests and convictions for offenses of the types just listed are very low or nonexistent. Offenses against standards of social conduct are not necessarily rare in Bengal society, but they seem to be under informal social control much more than in Western societies.

The kinds of crime about which social consensus is probably greatest in all four societies are murder, assault, and the various forms of acquisitive crime. In Part I we observed that there is some social relativity in what constitutes theft or crimes against the person, but these kinds of offenses are what most people have in mind when they excoriate crime. We have no evidence of substantial disagreement across classes in the four cities about the undesirability of these behaviors, with two kinds of exceptions. Some small revolutionary groups in twentieth century Calcutta and London have justified certain kinds of murder and theft as political tactics. It also could be argued that high rates of theft are prima facie evidence that some groups, otherwise voiceless, value stealing other people's property. Yet it is safe to say that these groups have not been tolerant about assault and theft when they are the victims. The social differences of opinion about murder, theft, and assault in the Western cities (we lack evidence for Calcutta) have centered not on whether these behaviors are social evils, but rather on how to deal with them.

We conclude this commentary on elite and popular interests in public order by pointing out that recent increases in public disorder in the Western cities have been most pronounced in offenses that are both commonly abhorred and widely felt. The agreement of ordinary citizens, police, judges, and elites on the reality of ascending statistics on assault and theft is further evidence of the behavioral as well as social truth of this phenomenon. But there is something paradoxical about public response to the issue. One would expect this kind of commonly perceived problem to stimulate concerted public demands and programmatic official response. In fact the elite and governmental response has been relatively tolerant. At least two plausible explanations come to mind. One is paralyzing lack of agreement among interested parties about the most effective policies to follow. Second, elites and officials are in fact relatively little concerned about these kinds of crime because their costs—unlike the costs of civil strife—are sustained mainly by ordinary citizens, who are most likely to be assaulted and who bear, directly and indirectly, most of the costs of personal and commercial theft.

THE EVOLUTION OF CRIMINAL CODES

Criminal law establishes the framework within which policies of public order are carried out. Much of the criminal law on the books at any one time is only selectively applied or has been allowed to lapse into disuse. But changes and reforms in criminal codes reflect the evolution of elite and public attitudes toward public order. In Western societies, and others that have accepted the Western legal tradition, changes in law are telling manifestations of shifting goals and values of the elite, and of changing patterns of group influence on policies of public order. Even if legal changes are made for the sake of show rather than action (a motive we think has been relatively uncommon in the four societies during the era we studied), they reveal much about the values and social interests to which decision makers believe they must be symbolically responsive.

The criminal laws of all four societies have been recurrently revised and modernized during the last 200 years. This is the chronological skeleton. English criminal law at the beginning of the nineteenth century consisted of a core of uncodified common law overlaid by a hodgepodge accumulation of acts of Parliament prescribing criminal penalties for a great many specific activities—e.g., stealing from bleaching-grounds, appearing armed and disguised, consorting with gypsies, and participation in a combination of workers seeking increases in wages. All but the last were punishable by death; as of 1820 so were at least 200 other offenses, minor as well as serious. This reliance on the death penalty was a fixture of seventeenth and especially eighteenth century political thought and criminal law throughout Europe: Capital punishment was widely regarded as the most effective deterrent to crime. English juries and judges often were reluctant to convict because they thought the death penalty too severe in specific cases, and throughout the eighteenth century a great many sentences of death were commuted to transportation, the second pillar of English penal practice at the time.[3] Attempts at reform early in the nineteenth century culminated in a series of acts in the late 1820s and 1830s that consolidated and simplified criminal law. The number of capital offenses was greatly reduced during the same period, and transportation to all penal colonies was finally ended in 1867. A set of acts passed in 1861 effected a further consolidation and ended capital punishment for crimes other than murder and treason. Throughout the nineteenth and twentieth centuries many specific acts have modified aspects of the criminal law, but there have been no eras of change comparable in scope to those just cited. Two liberalizing changes in the 1960s worth special mention were the abolition of capital punishment and the decriminalization of homosexuality between consenting adults. There was also, in 1968, a general consolidation of statutes applying to the various kinds of theft.

The criminal law of New South Wales derived from English common law also, but a great many acts have been added. Only two wholesale revisions have been made, in 1883 and 1900, and neither constituted a comprehensive criminal code. The act of 1900 was modified by no less than 37 amending acts through 1972, though most of the modifications have been procedural not substantive. The severity of sentences prescribed has declined markedly, as in Britain. Capital and corporal punishments were less often specified in law and much less often applied after the end of transportation in 1840. It was not until 1955, however, that capital punishment was formally abolished (for all offenses except treason and piracy), and whipping remained a legally permissible penalty until 1974. Virtually all the enactments of criminal law in New South Wales during the last 75 years remain on the books; there has been almost no formal decriminalization. The only substantial exception was the establishment of state-run off-track betting in 1965, which in effect legalized a durable and popular pastime that the police had never effectively controlled.

Bengal was governed by the East India Company through 1858, and its patchwork of European and "native" courts applied both English and Indian law, depending on the case. Among the first reforms introduced after the Crown assumed the government of India were the introduction of civil, penal, and criminal codes, 1859-1861, which were explicit and tailored to Indian circumstances. The principal additions thereafter included more than a dozen acts introduced between 1908 and the 1930s, which provided the formal basis for combating nationalist activity. The 1950 constitution of independent India stipulated that previous laws, including colonial ones, would remain in effect until modified. The 1948 West Bengal Criminal Code was mainly a rewriting of colonial law, and in the same year the West Bengal Security Act reestablished legal tools, including preventive detention, which the British had used to combat nationalism. Fragmentary evidence suggests that severe penalties were prescribed in the law administered by the East India Company, whereas the 1859-1861 codes reflected the somewhat less punitive orientation of prevailing English criminal law. There has been no subsequent easing of sanctions, however: Both capital and corporal punishment continue to be administered in independent India.

The evolution of Swedish criminal law appears to have been a more orderly process than was found in the English tradition, if only because it was punctuated by three comprehensive recodifications, the first in 1734. But the difference is more apparent than real because most of the substantive and procedural changes in Swedish law have been introduced piecemeal; the recodifications of 1865 and 1965 were consolidations rather than fundamental innovations. The eighteenth century code resembled English law in its reliance on the threat of death to restrain offenders—there were 68 capital offenses, including many kinds of theft. Torture and other forms of corporal punishment also were prescribed. Liberalization of punishment began earlier than in England; the use of the death penalty was significantly limited in 1779 and abolished for most other offenses in the 1850s. Only fifteen executions took place after 1865, and the penalty was taken off the books in 1921. The comparatively early decline in reliance on capital and corporal punishment in Sweden was paralleled by the expansion of legally prescribed options for treatment, as reviewed in a subsequent chapter.

DEFINING DISORDER: ELITE INTERESTS AND SOCIAL ISSUES

The foregoing chronicle of changes may obscure recognition that the nineteenth century was the principal era of rationalization and consolidation in criminal law in all four societies. The basic definitions of individual criminal behavior that apply today were largely established in the years between 1825 and 1885. But the generalization does not extend to the regulation of collective behavior, and it masks considerable variation in the definition of particular kinds of offenses. We focus more closely now on historical changes in the nature and especially the scope of formal definitions of "criminal" behavior. Such changes reflect evolving social interests in public order, as we have observed. They also potentially influence the volume of reported crime, the number of persons prosecuted, and the burden on penal and rehabilitative institutions: As the boundaries of criminal behavior expand, more people and activities are subject to arrest and sanction, and vice versa. The comparisons to follow deal with the nature and social origins of definitional change; institutional embodiments and consequences are examined subsequently.

"Common Crime"

The legal definitions of murder, assault, rape, malicious destruction of property, and similar crimes of aggression have changed little during the last two centuries in the societies investigated. But there has been some expansion in the social groups and circumstances to which the definitions apply: Attacks on and physical abuse of "natives," servants, employees, wives, children, and inmates are more likely to be specified in law as criminal offenses now than in 1800. Special status for superordinates in criminal matters was long a feature of law in medieval and renaissance Europe. Even in the sixteenth century the upper classes of some European societies continued to enjoy the privilege of carrying on feuds, and under cover of these legal hostilities they used to hire people to commit acts of assault and robbery that were capital offenses when indulged in by members of subordinate classes. The reduction of such privileges for powerful groups was part of a broader movement to reduce the imprecision of criminal law and the arbitrariness of its application. The movement arose in the eighteenth century, stimulated by the intellectual thought of the Enlightenment and by the interests of the rising middle classes in securing their rights vis a vis their rulers.[4] The "rationalization" of criminal law was one manifestation of this movement; there were many others as well and in fact the desire for fairness and exactitude underlies many of the reforms in policing and judicial and penal policies to be cited presently.

While old immunities have been dissolved by the principle of equality before the law, new forms of aggressive and acquisitive behavior have inspired legal modernization. Some additions have been devised in response to the evolving technology of mayhem, giving police and courts the authority to sanction the carrying and use of razors, firearms, bombs, and so forth. But these are essentially new means of regulating behaviors whose general character has been long proscribed; they are responses to the changing "opportunity structure" for physical attack. More substantial modifications in the criminal law governing theft have the same kind of origin. Because of economic and technological change, there are new things to be stolen; hence criminal codes have been elaborated to prohibit, for example, the theft of bicycles, autos, aircraft, bank notes, securities, and credit cards. In addition, new and more devious ways of stealing things have inspired a great expansion of criminal laws bearing on fraud, embezzlement, and other white-collar crimes. But these changes signify no alteration of the basic principle that personal, commercial, and public property is supposed to be secure from seizure by force, stealth, or subterfuge. This principle is the basis of the contemporary criminal codes of all Western societies and most others.

We note one small step that may portend the decriminalization of some kinds of theft, however. In Sweden in 1971 an official commission coupled a recommendation that penalties for petty shoplifting be reduced with the proposal that merchants warn first offenders rather than report them to the police. In 1974 the police were instructed not to record thefts from stores with a value of less than 20 kronor (about $5 U.S.) nor to arrest their perpetrators. Many different strands of social change come together in this small innovation. One is the long-standing trend toward "liberalization" in Swedish criminal law and treatment, another is the general prosperity of Swedish society (i.e., commercial victims of $5 thefts are not seriously discommoded). The effect of the Swedish policy is to give the sanction of law to a prevalent commercial practice in other Western societies—to accept the costs of pilferage and pass them on as a kind of generalized tax to consumers. A third feature of the Swedish policy is that it relieves the bureaucracy of the burden of dealing with a host of petty matters at a time when more serious offenses also have increased substantially. The Swedish policy may have some appeal to hard-pressed officials and intellectual reformers. If applied in less egalitarian and prosperous societies, however, its effect would be a regressive "tax" on those least able to afford it. In the United States it is the urban poor who are most victimized by theft and high prices.

Social Conduct

The legal regulation of social conduct has varied more in the last two centuries than has the regulation of assault and theft, especially in the three Western societies. Control of employment and unemployment was of serious concern to the propertied classes of European societies during the eighteenth and nineteenth centuries, and class economic interests are clearly evident in much of the applicable criminal legislation. In England the Masters and Servants Acts, of medieval origin but much revised, prescribed criminal penalties for workers who broke contracts or left work unfinished; they were widely used in the early nineteenth century, notably against workers who resisted the reductions in their wages that were a consequence of the labor surplus of the period. These acts remained on the books in vestigial form even after a reforming act in 1875. Of the same genre was the Masters and Servants Act of 1828 in New South Wales, which was enacted during a severe labor shortage and created the offenses of neglect of work, absence from work, and the destruction or loss of an employer's property. Another body of relevant legislation having an equally ancient pedigree was aimed at vagrancy, that is, lack of regular employment. The first English legislation on the subject dates from 1349, with numerous subsequent modifications. In 1743 legislation broadened the definition of people who could be treated as vagrants, the Vagrancy Act of 1824 added new penalties, the Vagrancy Act of 1935 modified them. Initially such laws were used in combination with workhouses to provide relief for the poor;

later, especially in the eighteenth and nineteenth centuries, they were relied on for social control of the classes thought to be dangerous. Generally the vagrancy laws of the nineteenth century had the effect of obliging the lower classes to accept private employment on any terms or be forced into public employment. An example from New South Wales is an act of 1835 that created a whole range of "idle and disorderly" offenses, for which the penalties were terms at hard labor—the penal practice being to hire out such individuals to private employers. In Sweden during the same period the authorities were especially concerned about the costs, and the strife potential, of rampant unemployment in Stockholm. A half dozen ordinances requiring military service, and later forced labor, for those without other means of support were passed between 1802 and 1846. In the latter part of the nineteenth century vagrancy was made a civil rather than a criminal matter, but this meant in practice that administrative bodies could—and regularly did—intern vagrants in agricultural colonies. Laws against vagrancy were still being applied in Sweden in the 1920s, though apprehensions by then were but a tenth of what they had been 50 years earlier.

Another facet of social conduct much subject to regulation in these societies is the use of alcohol and drugs. It is possible to impute economic motives to these efforts on the argument that intoxicated people make poor workers, but there are more potent and direct explanations. From the official point of view drunkenness has been a nuisance, to say the least. It was and is a chronic source of private brawls and attacks on police, and during the periods for which arrests data are available, it usually has been the single most common offense in all three Western cities. From a social welfare perspective alcoholism was devastating to the family life of its victims, and members of large and broadly based prohibition movements in the three Western societies in the nineteenth and early twentieth centuries sought to reduce these costs.

Efforts at the control of alcohol abuse in this period did not elicit major changes in the scope of the criminal law, however, because being drunk and disorderly was a criminal offense virtually throughout the period and new legislation affected mainly private distilling, bootlegging, and the retail trade. In New South Wales controls on the liquor trade were established in the earliest days of the colony. The heyday of the prohibition movement in the 1880s saw some expansion of administrative restraints (fewer licensed public bars, Sunday closing laws), but neither then nor later has the relevant law been substantially modified. The Swedish emphasis also has been on drying up the source of the problem, beginning with prohibition of household distilling early in the last century, restrictions on numbers of taverns, the establishment of a state monopoly on retail sale of liquor, and rationing from the 1920s to 1955. The temperance movement, begun in the 1830s, actively promoted its policies for a century but failed to secure complete prohibition in a national referendum in 1922.

The Swedish approach to drunkenness differs in emphasis from the prevailing official view in England and the antipodes, where public drunkenness is treated first and last as a criminal offense. In Sweden, though a major emphasis of law and policy since the 1920s has been to treat and rehabilitate alcoholics, arrest rates continue at a very high level in Stockholm because not all drunks are alcoholics. The Swedish preference for decriminalization was evident in the end of rationing in 1955, which was expected to end widespread but small-scale bootlegging. Judging from arrest data it seems to have stimulated bootlegging instead, and it certainly contributed to a marked increase in arrests for drunkenness thereafter. Drunken driving, however, has been a criminal offense since 1934. Moreover the scope of the relevant law has been increased by extending it to moped drivers (1952) and by reducing the threshold of blood alcohol concentration required for criminal sanctions (1941, 1957). Imprisonment is mandatory for most drunken driving offenses, and ten percent of those in prison on any given day in contemporary Sweden are there for that reason.

Regulation of the use of drugs other than alcohol has been a more recent development. The first major English legislation dates from 1920. In Sweden, incremental controls on prescriptions and on other facets of drug use began in the late 1930s and were extended in the next two decades. The growth of drug use in the late 1960s stimulated new narcotics legislation in 1968 and 1969, significantly broadening the scope of related offenses and prescribing penalties that are quite severe by contemporary Swedish standards. It is evident from this example, and also from the Swedish policy of mandatory jail sentences for drunken driving, that whereas Swedish law and society may be "tolerant" about sex and theft, other kinds of deviance meet a firm legal and penal response.

Sexual behavior is the last area of social conduct to be considered here. The legal description of "sex crimes" has changed unmistakably over time in the Western societies. Male homosexuality, a criminal offense of long standing in all three was decriminalized in Sweden in 1944 and in England in 1967; but this move has not been made in New South Wales. Prostitution per se has never been an offense in England and Sweden, but it has been the object of a great deal of law-making and regulatory activity. The English approach was to restrict prostitution by imposing criminal penalties on soliciting, procuring, brothel keeping, and other ancillary activities. A high pitch of public morality was reached in 1885 when a consolidating act was passed by Parliament to close loopholes in earlier statutes; further restrictions were imposed by acts of 1912, 1922, and 1959. The Swedish approach emphasized regulation rather than criminalization, though in Stockholm as in London procuring and brothel keeping were criminal offenses. Regulation in Stockholm took the form of obligatory registration and medical checkups, practices in force for most of the nineteenth century. Prostitutes who failed to register or violated regulations (e.g., by wearing sensational clothing) were subject to criminal penalties. In this century the trend in Stockholm has been toward deregulation and decriminalization. Police registration of prostitutes ended in 1918, and a program to control venereal disease was established. The Vagrancy Act was applied to prostitutes during the next decade, but since 1930 the official policy has been one of toleration. During the same era, from the second to fourth decades of the century, adultery and other kinds of consensual sexual activities were also decriminalized.

The New South Wales experience again offers a sharp contrast. The nineteenth-century legal strictures on sexual behavior were substantial and emphasized criminal sanctions rather than regulation. In this century new sex-related offenses have been added, and there has been no legal decriminalization. A 1967 act, for example, establishes criminal penalties for those frequenting premises used by prostitutes, as well as for prostitution in massage parlors. Most laws related to sexual conduct seem to be enforced more selectively now than they were in the past, but there is persisting political and official resistance to formal decriminalization.

Abortion is another aspect of sex-related behavior that has generated considerable social debate, criminal legislation, and official action in all the Western societies. In England the termination of pregnancy was made an offense punishable by life imprisonment in 1861. In the 1920s abortion was sanctioned in cases where the mother's life was endangered. Proabortion groups secured the liberalization of the law in practice in the late 1930s, but not until 1967 were the legal grounds expanded significantly. In Sweden abortion was regarded as a very serious offense during the nineteenth and early twentieth centuries, and the first step toward decriminalization was not made until 1939. Since then the trend has been to increase the circumstances under which legal abortions can be obtained. One important expansion occurred in 1968; seven years later abortion by a licensed practitioner during the first trimester was entirely decriminalized. In New South Wales, interestingly, there was little public or official concern with abortion until the turn of the century, when a number of "abortion scandals" were denounced by press and from pulpit, and an official commission blamed the state's decline in birthrate on contraception and abortion. A spate of legislation accompanied this public furor, in which abortion and related activities (advertising abortion services, selling abortion-inducing drugs, etc.) were criminalized. These activities, like most other crimes of social conduct in New South Wales, have not come to the point of formal decriminalization.

Other significant areas of social conduct that are sometimes subject to criminal law have not been discussed here. One is public behavior: Numerous statutes in the Western cities prohibit a variety of raucous, insulting, and indecent actions. Anxiety over such conduct increased markedly during the nineteenth century, mainly as a reflection of evolving middle-class concern about decorous behavior, and the prohibiting laws generally remain in force. Two areas that merit more serious attention are traffic and commerce. The first is the object of familiar regulations about who can drive what, where, and how; trade and banking activities come under a host of mainly administrative regulations about who can sell what to whom, from what premises under what terms and circumstances. We have not separately analyzed these spheres of official action, or similar ones, because they have rarely posed critical issues for the public or officials in the societies we studied. They are part of the more or less routine control that has become essential to the functioning of complex societies. From a general perspective on public order, though, they may deserve more attention than we have given them. The number and scope of traffic and commerce regulations has expanded exponentially over time, and their net effect in restraining human behavior and interaction is no doubt much greater—because they affect more people more of the time—than all the body of law relating to common crime and social deviance. Moreover if such regulatory activities were curtailed or suspended, the unbridled interests of drivers and businessmen, among others, would very likely give rise to nasty and pervasive social problems that in turn would generate substantial pressures for the restoration of "public order."

Nothing has been said here about the regulation of social conduct in Calcutta. Although our sources make frequent references to attempts to regulate public behavior and commercial activity of the types just mentioned, there is little evidence that questions of sexual morality ever occasioned a great deal of legislative or official concern.

Collective Behavior

The legal definitions of assault, theft, and similar crimes have been modernized and rationalized during the past 150 years, but the underlying legal conception of violations of person and property is little changed. "Criminal" social conduct has varied more widely in

definition, among and within societies, mainly in response to changing middle-class and official perceptions of vital social and moral
issues. The most distinctive indications of changing class interest in
public order, though, are apparent in the shifting legal ground rules
of permissible collective behavior. There is a pattern of spasmodic
legal response by dominant social groups to threatening collective
behavior from others, followed in the Western societies by political
accommodation that is reflected in legal reform.

An enduring feature of the legal codes of virtually all Western
societies is a set of statutes authorizing officials to control such
collective actions as riotous behavior, unlawful assembly, and acts of
mutiny, rebellion, and sedition. Some of the variation in these legal
controls is a function of the development of new repressive means.
Yet most changes sharpen and expand, or contract, the definitions of
criminal collective behavior, in response to the emergence of new
forms and methods of dissent and opposition. Growing use of sabotage by English workers and Irish nationalists, for example, promoted the passage of the Malicious Damage Act of 1861. This law
imposed severe penalties for causing damage with explosives, and for
a wide range of other actions that previously had not required
itemization: setting fire to churches, flooding mines, damaging quays
and locks, and destroying bridges. Instead of reviewing all instances
of legal response to collective behavior in the four societies, we
present sketches of the legal efforts to control the activities of
organized labor in England, mainly in the nineteenth century, and
the legal manifestations of the colonial authorities' response to
nationalism in Bengal in the twentieth century.

The emergent trade unions of eighteenth century England began as
local "clubs" or "societies" and were tolerated as long as they
remained parochial in scope, making no demands of employers. If
they united over larger areas (hence the word "union"), they were
very likely to encounter legal and judicial repression. The same kinds
of response usually met protests over wage rates, which by custom
were sometimes directed at magistrates (who traditionally regulated
wages) and the House of Commons, as well as at employers. By the
end of the century some forty acts prohibited workers' organizations
in particular trades. Concerted legislative action was first taken in the
Combination Acts of 1799 and 1800, which prescribed a general
"remedy." The penalty for a first offense was "three months in gaol,
or two months' hard labour [for] any working man who combined
with another to gain an increase in wages or a decrease in hours, or
solicited anyone else to leave work, or objected to working with any
other workmen."[5] It is worth pointing out that the immediate
occasion for the 1799 act was a petition by master millwrights to the
House of Commons seeking the suppression of a combination of

millwrights in the London area; though no more threatening than many past instances, the circumstances coincided with a "reformist" interest in Parliament to deal in a general and systematic way with a problem previously treated piecemeal. Whereas the Combination Acts were indicative of a rationalizing spirit rather than a change in social or political interest, their repeal 24 years later was the result of the actions of a group of radical members of Parliament. The repeal, which spurred an almost instant explosion of trade unionism, and also strikes, was promptly amended (in 1825) to restrict the activities of the unions, but not to outlaw them again. The trend from then to the present century was one of gradual expansion of the rights of organized workers, punctuated by episodes of increased restraint. Picketing, decriminalized by an act of 1859, was effectively criminalized again—along with other strike actions—in the early 1870s. Later acts resumed the liberalizing trend; one in 1875 made an employee's breach of contract a civil rather than criminal matter. The right to strike was significantly expanded in 1906 by the new Liberal Government, and in 1913 the Liberals also legalized political action by trades unions.

It is important to note that the gradual decriminalization of labor activism in England was not the work of working-class representatives in Parliament; the Labour Party elected its first MPs in 1906 and formed its first government in 1924. Reform was mainly the work of middle-class politicians who were sympathetic to workers' interests and demands and also concerned with general issues of social and economic progress. Their objectives were not to pave the way for working-class political control or state socialism—outcomes most of them would have abhorred—but rather to improve the operation of the capitalist system. Moreover there were limits to the kind of collective action that the elite was prepared to tolerate from workers. The London police went on strike in August 1918, and the next year Parliament passed an act prohibiting trade unionism among the police. A protest strike by the London police was crushed, as was their union. In 1927, the year after the Great Strike virtually paralyzed British industry, a Conservative Government passed a Trade Disputes and Trade Unions Act specifying heavy penalties for general and sympathy strikes and restricting picketing. In contemporary Britain it is a matter of paramount importance to restrain wage demands and limit local, unsanctioned ("wildcat") strikes. The necessity of limiting the scope of collective action by workers is accepted even by Labour Governments, but the use of criminal law and penalties to attain that end has fallen into disrepute.

In Bengal the demands of Indian nationalists in the twentieth century were intrinsically more extreme than the demands of English labor, and the British legal responses to them were comparably harsher and less compromising. Table VI.3.1 shows more clearly than a narrative account the timing of major episodes of nationalist activity in Bengal and additions to Bengal and Indian law between 1906 and 1946. Three general observations may be made about the information summarized there. First, the correlation in timing between peaks of strife and legal response is approximate rather than precise partly because some of the legal response was aimed at all-India problems rather than those of Bengal specifically.

Second, there are several dimensions to the legal response: (1) control of the propagation of nationalist sentiments, (2) expansion of police powers, (3) expansion of judicial and penal procedures, especially the use of special tribunals and preventive detention, and (4) limits on certain kinds of collective behavior, public meetings in particular. Only the first and last dimensions formally expanded the scope of criminal behavior; the others gave officials the means to implement repressive policies within the boundaries of old and new definitions.

The third observation is that although the policies carried out within this expanding legal framework produced some periods of respite from strife, they only postponed the nationalist victory. In the short run they sometimes seemed to work; in the long run they did not. One can only speculate whether more compromising and less repressive responses would have made any difference. Given the gulf between Indian and British values and interests, it is unlikely that accommodation would have affected the final outcome, but it would have made the struggle less costly for all concerned.

Some briefer observations about the Swedish and New South Wales experience of legal control of collective behavior conclude this section. Both governments experimented with censorship laws in the early nineteenth century to muzzle liberal criticism (Sweden 1812, New South Wales 1827). But the attempts were soon abandoned in the face of middle-class opposition. Laws aimed at suppressing labor activity in Sweden appeared mainly between 1887 and 1900 and included fresh resort to censorship. Little used after universal franchise was granted in 1921, the controls were repealed in the late 1930s. The rise of the labor movement in New South Wales generated less intense conflict than parallel developments in the other societies. Masters and servants laws against "conspiracy" to raise wages were on the books but were not updated after 1840. More to the point, there is no evidence that they were widely used to control the new labor movement. The first legislation specifically aimed at modern labor conflict, passed in 1901, required compulsory arbitration of disputes. Accommodation to early labor demands in New South Wales may be attributed to two reinforcing factors: The colony had no entrenched upper class, and labor was a scarce and

Table VI.3.1 Nationalism and British Legal Response in Bengal, 1906-1946

Manifestations of nationalism	Years	Additions to criminal and civil law
Agitation against partition of Bengal	1906-1908	
	1908	Criminal law amendment: various political organizations banned
	1910	Press Act: security deposit required for distribution of printed matter
	1910	Bengal Code Act III: public meetings limited
	1911	Prevention of Seditious Meetings Act
Intensified nationalist agitation, large-scale terrorism	1912-1915	
	1915	Defence of India Act: preventive detention, suspension of due process, ban on public meetings
	1919	Rowlatt Act: wide powers to control terrorism
Noncooperation movement, political strikes	1920-1924	
	1921	Criminal law amendment: preventive detention, control of public meetings
	1924	Criminal law amendment: greater police powers
	1924	Sea Customs Act: controls on import of seditious material
	1924	Goonda Act: deportation of known goondas [professional thugs] from Calcutta
	1926	Penal law amendment: special courts for political crimes
Large-scale political strikes	1928	
	1929	Press Act: security deposit required for publication
	1930	Bengal law amendment: suspension of civil rights, preventive detention
Civil disobedience movement, political strikes	1930-1934	
Quit India movement	1942-1943	
	1942	Emergency Powers Act: banning of political organization, detention of leaders
Worst communal rioting in Calcutta's history	1946	
	1946	Defence of India Act: expanded detention, control of subversive organizations

precious commodity. Legislation passed during World War I outlawed the International Workers of the World, not for economic reasons but because of the labor organization's outspoken pacifism. Class tensions and labor surplus increased during the Depression, and in 1929 a predominantly conservative state assembly passed punitive antistrike legislation. The immediate internal stimulus was a timber workers' strike, the external model was the repressive labor legislation passed in England 1927. Like much other criminal legislation in New South Wales, the 1929 act remained formally in force long after it ceased to be applied.

All the foregoing examples of legal response to collective behavior predate the upsurge of protest and terrorism in the past decade. The Swedish legal response is instructive, though not typical. The widespread toleration of peaceful protest in Swedish society is reflected in two recent legislative actions. Strikes by public servants were legalized in 1965. After 1970 it was no longer a criminal offense to insult Swedish or national foreign symbols nor to advocate rebellion. The net effect of the 1970 changes was to legalize political demonstrations, notably those directed at United States foreign policy since 1965. Swedish toleration of dissent stops well short of violence, however. Strict measures enacted in 1973 gave the police broad powers to deal with the terrorists, mainly Croatians and Palestinians, who had become active in Stockholm. On both these issues, innovation in Swedish law reflects not narrow class or elite interests but a broad spectrum of public opinion.

On the basis of the evidence reviewed here, criminal law represents very different sets of interests, depending on the "criminal" behavior in question. The class-interest explanation of the criminal law fits best the legislation aimed at controlling collective behavior. The changing fears and sympathies of the political elite and the rising political influence of new classes are traced in legislation governing collective behavior, as surely as a seismograph records earthquakes and tremors. The laws governing social and sexual conduct are more ambiguous cases. Most of the relevant law in Western societies is an outgrowth of historical efforts to codify the standards of middle-class morality and to apply them to all social groups. Such laws are, or were, manifestations of class social interests rather than narrowly political or economic ones. The standards applied now are not only or mainly those of the middle classes, however. Some are almost universally accepted, and one probably would find less tolerance for drug and alcohol abuse, and sexual deviance, in the working-class neighborhoods of the three Western cities than among the politicians, officials, and intellectuals of the new ruling class. Consensus was and continues to be greatest about common crimes against persons and property. No vocal group seems ever to have argued that such acts should be tolerated. The class issue with respect to these offenses has been how theft and violence should be dealt with.

NOTES TO CHAPTER VI.3

1. William L. Langer, "Europe's Initial Population Explosion," in Carl E. Schorske and Elizabeth Schorske, eds., *Explorations in Crisis: Papers on International History* (Cambridge: Harvard University Press, 1969), p. 439. For a comparative analysis of the consequences of this immiseration for criminal law and penal practice see Georg Rusche and Otto Kirchheimer, *Punishment and Social Structure* (New York: Columbia University Press, 1939), ch. 6.

2. The reference is to Asa Briggs, *The Age of Improvement* (London: Longmans, Green, 1959), which deals with the period 1784-1867.

3. Other common penal practices in eighteenth and early nineteenth century England were sentences to workhouses and corporal punishments such as whipping. The evolution of penal practices is examined in a subsequent chapter.

4. On these points see Rusche and Kirchheimer, op. cit., esp. pp. 15-16, 72-83. For a detailed study of English law on theft which emphasizes the social and economic circumstances of its evolution, see Jerome Hall, *Theft, Law and Society,* 2nd ed. (Indianapolis: Bobbs-Merrill, 1952).

5. A paraphrase, not a quotation from the act, from G. D. H. Cole and Raymond Postgate, *The Common People 1746-1946,* 4th ed. (London: Methuen, 1949), p. 173.

Chapter VI.4

THE POLICE AND POLICING

Criminal laws cannot be systematically enforced without specialized policing agencies. Such bodies can be identified in many European cities as early as medieval times, but the history of police and policing in Europe up to the nineteenth century, insofar as it is known, shows more diversity than similarity. Policing was sometimes a local sometimes a national function; usually it was carried out by organizations whose roles differed widely. Some bodies were concerned with patrolling, others with apprehending known criminals, still others (or sometimes the same ones) with controlling political dissidence and riotous crowds. Contemporary European police systems have some organizational and operational features in common, but these are more readily explained by convergence through imitative response to similar problems, especially in the last century, than by common dynamics of development. Diversity among contemporary European police systems, Bayley suggests, is due partly to the different patterns of national political conflict and development, partly to a kind of organizational inertia that permits the culturally distinctive traits of police organizations to persist over time.[1]

The institutional development of the police is important to our analysis because the quality and extent of public order, and the official indicators of disorder, depend very directly on what the police do and how they do it. At the same time we are concerned with the social and political forces that have shaped police organization and activities. Institutional changes in the police, like changes in the criminal law, are influenced by larger political and social circumstances and particularly by the shifting interests and concerns of dominant social groups. The sections that follow trace the development of police forces in the four cities with special attention to external influences on their growth and operations. Many of the characteristics of police organizations are also subject to the internal, system-maintaining dynamics of bureaucratic organizations, but they are not analyzed here; the main concern is the external sources of constraint and change.

PREMODERN URBAN POLICING

Some form of policing was carried out in all four cities from early times, but the activities were fragmented, limited in scope and function, and mostly nonprofessional. Official and public dissatisfaction culminated in major police reforms in the middle decades of the nineteenth century: in London in 1829, Stockholm in 1850, New South Wales in 1862, and Calcutta in 1864. In all four societies there were substantial changes in policing before and after the dates given, but during these years public police organizations began to acquire their contemporary forms, ethos, and methods of operation. Their prior development had been diverse and discontinuous; it became more similar and evolutionary. We begin by sketching the character of policing in the four cities before these transitions.

London, which was already a large city in the early eighteenth century, made do with uncoordinated policing arrangements at the parish level. Householders typically served as constables, and watchmen were employed and supervised by notoriously venal local justices of the peace and officers of the watch. It was regarded as a signal improvement when magistrates Henry and John Fielding, in the 1750s, established a small cadre of professional "thief-takers" who operated throughout the metropolis. Another advance occurred with the introduction of annual stipends for some justices, who had previously been subsisting on what they could extract in fees and fines from their clientele. The first professional force in London was the Marine Police Establishment, founded in 1798 by private merchants but soon taken over by the Home Office. As of 1800, when London had about 900,000 inhabitants, there were roughly 500 professional police, including the river police, the Bow Street Runners established by the Fieldings, and constables attached to district magistrates' offices, plus perhaps 4,500 watchmen at the neighborhood level. Watchmen aside, the primary task of the police was to capture known offenders. Reformers in and out of the House of Commons advanced proposals for a centralized, professional police force from the 1750s through the 1820s, on grounds that existing bodies were often corrupt and generally were ineffective in preventing crime. The proposals came to nothing, however. Two recurring themes of political opposition were the fear that the police would become an instrument of repression, and resistance to spending public funds on policing. In addition London's aldermen and magistrates were concerned about the possible loss of control of a function that traditionally had been theirs. It should be pointed out that Londoners lacked neither models nor precedent: A centralized and increasingly professional police force had functioned in Paris since the late seventeenth century, and the British government had seen to the establishment of a salaried, centralized police force in Ireland in 1786. It was the activities of these forces, especially in Paris, that inspired influential members of the urban middle classes to fear a centralized London police as a threat to their liberties.

In Stockholm, with less than a tenth of London's population, policing in 1800 was divided among a city guard of sixteenth century origin, a fire guard, and a military garrison, each having some law enforcement functions (mainly patrolling), and a newly reformed (1797) police force of about 90 men whose principal task was to arrest offenders. In 1812 the total strength of these bodies, excluding the garrison, was about 400 for a city of some 75,000. This works out to a ratio of about 50 men per 10,000 population compared with a ratio of about 55 per 10,000 in London at the same period. The major changes in policing in the first half of the century were consolidation of the fire guard and garrison into the Military Corps and increases in police patrolling. Merchants' concern about rising theft in the early 1830s inspired some of these changes; riots in 1838 were followed by the inauguration of intensive patrols by the Military Corps and, later, the opening of the first three neighborhood police stations. ·Criticism of police services was particularly pronounced in the 1830s and 1840s, partly because of high levels of public disorder, partly because the police and the Military Corps were a rough lot who used harsh methods. The reports of the governor of Stockholm in the 1840s expressed strong dissatisfaction with the Military Corps, and the liberal press was also critical; otherwise voiceless ordinary citizens expressed their antagonisms in individual and collective assaults on police and patrols.

In Sydney a night watch was established a year after the colony was founded, and in 1810 a permanent force of 35 constables was created to police a settlement of about 7,000 inhabitants. Separate forces were later set up to patrol the native population, rural and border areas, and the Sydney waterfront, and by 1850 the colony had six separate and uncoordinated forces. The City Police were very badly paid by standards of the time; many were ex-convicts, and most were untrained men who left the force after brief service. Colonial and municipal authorities contributed to these problems by curtailing police expenditures as public order improved in the 1830s; thus by 1844 the force numbered only 95 men for a booming town of some 40,000—a ratio of less than 25 per 10,000 compared with a ratio nearly double that just five years earlier. There were many

demands for police reform from the 1830s on, including the
recommendations of a succession of official committees. Some were
inspired by relevations of corruption and incompetence on the force
(three successive chiefs of police were dismissed for malfeasance),
others by urban riots.

In Calcutta the first public watch force of 68 Indians was established in 1704 and was supplemented by a tiny military contingent
the next year. By the beginning of the nineteenth century responsibilities for public order were divided among the river police, the
boundary police, and the town guard, each with specialized duties,
and the primarily Indian *thandari* force, which provided general
police services. Europeans on the latter force served mainly in the
city's European neighborhoods. By 1842 the Calcutta police numbered 1,838 men, sixteen of them Europeans, for a city of about a
quarter million—a ratio of about 75 per 10,000. Though relatively
numerous by comparison with the other cities, the Calcutta police
were similarly untrained, underpaid, and unloved. Little skill could
be expected of police whose wages throughout the nineteenth century were below those paid to manual laborers and whose turnover
rates were 50 percent a year or more. They were known to be
corrupt and brutal; police officials acknowledged widespread use of
torture to secure confessions. The governor of Bengal bluntly reported in 1834 that "The whole of the police is abhorred and
detested by the people. . . ." However his judgment and the criticisms and pleas of several police commissioners failed to move the
East India Company to reduce its profits by increasing the funds
devoted to civil administration.

These sketches illustrate a number of points about premodern
police services. Their "fragmented" character, for example, reflects a
contemporary value judgment. By the standards of the societies in
which they evolved, they were typical of public response to social
problems: Specific problems were met with specific responses; thus
policing services, like criminal laws, were numerous and narrow in
scope. This may throw some light on one aspect of the "modernization" process, which prevailing academic opinion holds to involve a
shift from functionally diffuse to functionally specific organization.
In fact eighteenth and early nineteenth century European police
organizations (and many others) were a good deal more specialized in
function than are modern forces. Modernization has been more a
matter of coordination, integration, and professionalization than
specialization.

Another distinctive characteristic of premodern police is that in
most respects they were indistinguishable from those whom they
policed. Police organizations were staffed by men drawn from the
lowest ranks of societies, the same groups whose criminality was of

greatest official concern. They were frequently corrupt, brutal, and as fond of alcohol as those whose drunkenness warranted police attention. They rarely had uniforms or special equipment, nor did they receive special training except for those enlisted in paramilitary units. The men most likely to remain on police and watch forces for any length of time were those whose personal limitations—infirmity, age, lack of skills—prevented them from taking more attractive employment. Norms of professional conduct were highly unlikely to develop and be maintained in such circumstances. It is little wonder that the police were detested and scorned by ordinary citizens.

These characteristics of premodern police cannot be explained by attributing to elites a clever scheme of setting thieves to catch thieves. Their motives, insofar as we can judge by what they said and did, were simpler: Maintaining public order was a dirty job that was to be done as cheaply as possible. Economic motives were repeatedly evident in elite decisions about policing. Where possible, the costs of policing were put off onto private citizens, merchants, and local communities, or met by paying fees to "thief-takers" (with funds derived from the confiscation of criminals' property). The police reforms of Stockholm in 1850 were financed by new taxes on the liquor trade—poetic justice, since drunks were the policeman's principal clients. When public funds had to be expended, they were grudgingly allocated and subject to pressures to cut them back.

THE TRANSITION TO MODERN POLICING

Criticisms of police services and demands for reform were common in all four societies for decades before the moves toward centralization in the 35 years between 1829 and 1864. Thus it is worth asking what kinds of circumstances contributed to reform. In three of the four societies the new forces were established in and for the capital city (the exception is New South Wales, where policing was colonywide). Only later were the new police systems extended to other cities, towns, and rural areas. Therefore it is reasonable to assume that the distinctive problems of metropolitan public order provided one incentive to reform. Which problems were most important remains to be shown, however. One possibility that can be dismissed at the outset is pressure arising from the scale and anonymity of urban life. The cities' approximate populations at the dates of transition were as follows:

Greater London, 1829:   1,800,000
Stockholm, 1850:   92,000
Sydney, 1862:   100,000 (New South Wales 370,000)
Calcutta, 1864:   365,000

There is no basis here for an argument that there exists a threshold of urban size beyond which centralized policing becomes essential. The distinctive urban problems of public order have more to do with the ideas, interests, and circumstances of urban social groups.

One source of demands for police reform was intellectual and social. The same spirit of rationalization and reform that led to legal recodification in European societies was applied to policing: The search for order and security by the urban middle classes and the political elite could not be satisfied by legal reform alone but required new and more efficient institutions capable of enforcing the new laws. The idea of professional police forces was widely advocated on the Continent, especially by those impressed with the efficacy of the French and Prussian police in maintaining political and social order. Continental visitors often expressed surprise at the toleration of the English for high levels of urban crime and vice that could easily be lowered, they thought, by police methods already in use abroad. The relative success of the English system, once inaugurated (in London in 1829, countrywide in 1839), increased the likelihood of imitation elsewhere.[2]

The middle decades of the nineteenth century brought rapid commercial expansion to all the cities. Prosperous urban merchants and middle-class householders were more numerous and had more to lose from theft than in earlier times. In London and Stockholm the middle classes also were politically more influential than their forebears had been. But there is no precise correlation between the increasing prosperity and political influence of rising classes and the timing of police innovations. These factors, like "the police idea," provided at best a general disposition to police reform, not an explanation of when or how it occurred.[3] For that we must examine specific circumstances in the four cities.

In London the fear of disorder was particularly great in the 1820s: Acquisitive and aggressive crime were thought to have increased sharply and civil strife was much feared, though little in evidence in London itself.[4] The Home Secretary, Sir Robert Peel, who earlier had supervised the Irish police and had long advocated police reform in London, was able in these circumstances to engineer parliamentary approval of an act establishing the Metropolitan Police, soon nicknamed "bobbies" or "peelers" in derisive acknowledgement of their founder. In Stockholm the telling factor was rioting in 1848, part of the wave of revolutionary and protorevolutionary activity set in motion all across the Continent by the February revolution in France. The Stockholm riots led the royal government to heed previous criticisms of the Military Corps and city police and the governor's proposals for reform. In New South Wales the final impetus for reform was not urban at all. An outbreak of bushranging and disturbances on the goldfields in 1862 gave the colonial assembly what proved to be definitive evidence of the need for an adequately financed, colonywide force. The New South Wales Police Force was established within the year, and all the Sydney police were incorporated into its Metropolitan Division. Police reorganization in Calcutta was one of the steps taken in the period of legal and penal reform that followed the introduction of royal government, that is, after the Sepoy Mutiny of 1857 had precipitated the end of private government by the East India Company. Calcutta had no immediate crisis of public order per se in the early 1860s; the principal aspect of reforms was integration of the city and suburban police under the direct authority of the government of Bengal.

We suggest, on this evidence, that crises of public order in these four societies catalyzed the implementation of police reforms that had long been sought by forward-thinking officials and, at least in the three Western cities, by some members of the middle classes. Our hypothesis is that what the middle classes wanted, and finally got, was more certain protection of person and property; what the political elite apparently desired was increased security against collective behavior by the lower classes. In support of the second part of this explanation we note that the new police forces were removed from local or metropolitan control and were made directly responsible to national or colonial governments, except in Stockholm where they continued under the governor's aegis. This is too pat to constitute a complete explanation; all the underlying intellectual, political, and economic conditions cited previously pointed in the same direction. But the evidence just reviewed makes a prima facie case that the convergence of middle-class and elite interests in the European societies eventually overcame the middle classes' fear of police forces that might be used against them, as well as both groups' reluctance to spend more public monies on routine policing.[5]

THE GROWTH OF MODERN POLICE FORCES

The new police organizations were similar in all four cities, and they followed parallel lines of development. All were centralized from the outset and were given responsibilities for policing most if not all of their metropolitan areas. All employed a precinct or district type of organization in which police were assigned to and patrolled from local station houses. The central police organizations, immediately or within a few years, assumed virtually all functions of their more specialized predecessors. Gradually they were given new responsibilities as well. Early on, all created detective branches, now much expanded, whose activities are designated "criminal investigation." Other kinds of specialized divisions were established to deal with such matters as prostitution, drugs, political dissidence, police training, communications, and traffic control. Stockholm's experience of police specialization is probably typical: In 1850 almost all its men were assigned to district patrol stations, but by 1924 its central and specialized divisions employed nearly 40 percent of the force. The Sydney and New South Wales police, who have been proportionally the smallest of the modern forces, were given especially broad responsibilities. At various times they were required to carry out such duties as licensing public houses, dogcatching, compiling electoral lists, registering motor vehicles, and counterespionage. The London police also were assigned quite broad responsibilities in the nineteenth century but later ceded many of them, not least because police commissioners complained that such tasks as the abatement of smoke nuisances and regulation of weights and measures were not properly police matters. In the present era the functions of the Stockholm police seem to be the most narrowly defined.

The new police forces absorbed not only the functions of their predecessors but many of their personnel as well, except for London where the Metropolitan Police recruited their first 1,900 men largely from the civilian population. Gradual improvements in pay and conditions of employment in the three Western forces, plus the zealous professionalism of the new police officials, led to improvement in the character and abilities of men recruited and retained in the ranks. Internal training programs for recruits began to appear later in the nineteenth century (in Stockholm in 1876; in England not until 1907). One immediate consequence of modernization was a shrinkage in the absolute number of police, but the long-run trend has been a tremendous increase in police manpower in all the cities. The data in Table VI.4.1 show that all have doubled and redoubled since their reformation, and the Sydney force is 27 times as large now as it was a century ago. The police services of all these cities are now large-scale bureaucratic organizations.

The strength of police forces is usually compared in proportion to the population they control. The ratios in Table VI.4.2 show that police reform invariably had the effect of reducing the relative size of police forces. In the three Western cities the force ratios had declined by 1870 to less than half their levels at the beginning of the century. It also is evident that the Western cities have had approximately similar police-to-population ratios in different eras. As best we can tell from imprecise data, all had about 50 police per 10,000 population in the early nineteenth century, and all the twentieth century ratios given are between sixteen and 33 per 10,000. Calcutta offers a substantial contrast. In both centuries its police force has been proportionally larger than any of the others.

Table VI.4.1 Police Manpower in Four Cities, 1800 to 1970[a]

Time	London	Stockholm	Sydney	Calcutta
Nineteenth century				
First quarter	5,000[b] (1800)	400[a] (1812)	35	No data
Second quarter	4,500[b,c] (1830)	390 (1850)	114 (1839)	1,838 (1842)
1870	9,160	314	180	3,434
Twentieth century				
1920	21,546	903	1,508	5,314
1970	17,380	2,435	4,862 (1969)	18,628 (1966)

a. Solid bars signify the occurrence of comprehensive police reform.
b. Estimates.
c. Including 3,000 men of the Metropolitan Police Force, an estimated 1,000 watchmen in the City of London, and an estimated 500 constables plus Thames River Police.

Table VI.4.2 Police per 10,000 Population in Four Cities, 1800-1970[a]

Time	London	Stockholm	Sydney	Calcutta[b]
Nineteenth century				
First quarter	55[b,c] (1800)	53[b,c] (1812)	50[b] (1810)	No data
Second quarter	24[c] (1830)	42.4 (1850)	33[b] (1839)	74[b] (1842)
1870	25.3	23.1	13.3	65[b]
Twentieth century				
1920	29.7	21.6	16.7	59[b]
1970	21.4	32.9	17.9 (1969)	62[b] (1966)

a. Solid bars signify the occurrence of comprehensive police reform.
b. Population data are estimated or of questionable reliability.
c. Police data are estimated.

The easiest explanation for the decline in police size following modernization is "efficiency." Integrated and professional police forces needed less manpower to carry out their duties. But economic factors also were at work, because the modernized police imposed a greater burden on the public purse than their predecessors. Pay tended to be higher, and there was substantially greater investment in training, facilities, and equipment. There also is recurring evidence that politicians and officials tried to keep postmodernization police costs down. In the Western cities, in short, reform may have bought more professional police services, but it also bought fewer police. The Calcutta police, by contrast, continued to rely on large numbers of men employed at the lowest possible wage. A series of critical government reports in the colonial period and the fiscal data of

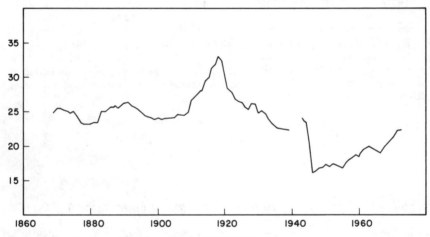

Figure VI.4.1 London: Police per 10,000, 1869-1972

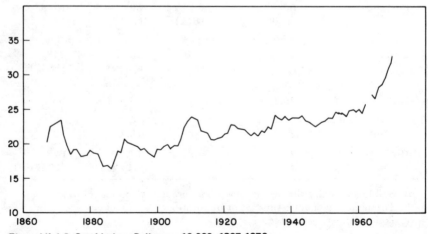

Figure VI.4.2 Stockholm: Police per 10,000, 1867-1970

Calcutta police reports testify that the great bulk of the force continued to consist of untrained and underpaid Indians. In the years following independence, perhaps a third of the Calcutta police have been kept as an armed reserve to deal with civil strife. This circumstance helps account for the continued high level of police manpower, yet fragmentary data on police finances indicate that costs, hence wages and investment in training or facilities, remain low.

More precise evidence on the changing size of the urban police forces during the last century is provided in Figures VI.4.1 through

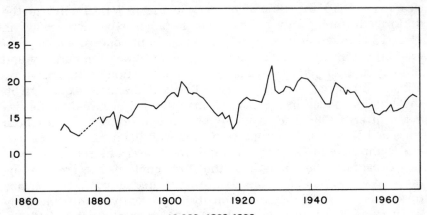

Figure VI.4.3 Sydney: Police per 10,000, 1869-1969

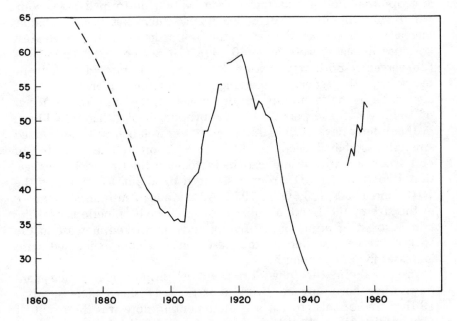

Figure VI.4.4 Calcutta: Police per 10,000, 1870, 1890-1940, scattered years 1952-1966

VI.4.4. There are persisting pressures, especially from the police services themselves, to increase the number of police commensurate with urban growth and police specialization. Despite these pressures for continuity, all cities record substantial and sometimes abrupt changes in ratios of police to population. Both the trends and the timing of the highs and lows differ greatly from one city to another and are suggestive about the impact of public disorder on urban policing.

In London the Metropolitan Police varied little in proportional size from 1870 to 1909. (The data in Figure VI.4.1 refer to the uniformed force only.) The one notable expansion came in 1882-1884 and followed a marked increase in concern about property crime: Between 1876 and 1882, convictions for burglary and robbery and for petty theft per 100,000 population had increased by 75 and 50 percent, respectively. The most dramatic expansion in the London police in the last century, though, occurred in the five years after 1909. The absolute and proportional increases both exceeded twenty percent and coincided with the peak of the suffragette campaigns in London and the highest level of strike activity in two decades.[6] The strength of the force continued to grow during the war years, but after the Armistice it gradually declined in size (absolutely as well as proportionally), apparently uninfluenced by widespread labor turmoil in 1919-1921 and 1926. By 1946 the Metropolitan Police had fewer than 13,000 uniformed men, compared with 22,000 in 1919. Since 1946 there has been a gradual increase in the relative size of the uniformed force; the greatest absolute increases were in 1946-1948 (10 percent) and 1955-1971 (25 percent). Both were periods of rising crime rates—the first one temporary, the second coinciding with London's highest levels of civil strife in the twentieth century. Even so, the uniformed force as of 1974 was smaller, absolutely and proportionally, than it had been in the orderly days of the 1930s, and it was well below its authorized strength, as it had been for 30 years. A more telling indicator of police concern with crime was the increase of the Criminal Investigation Department (CID) from a strength of about 1,300 during the 1940s and 1950s to 3,500 in 1974. All periods of substantial increase in the size of the London police prove to have been periods of rising crime, strife, or both; and of five periods of marked increase in the two kinds of disorder in the past century, four coincided with increases in police strength.

In Stockholm the long-term trend in proportional police manpower has been upward, with a particularly sharp increase after 1961. Some of this growth was incremental; more was the result of five unmistakable short-term increases in the absolute size of the force in 1886-1890 (40 percent), 1904-1910 (32 percent), 1918-1922 (14 percent), 1928-1935 (27 percent), and 1965-1970 (16 percent). The last increase occurred while the city was losing population to suburban growth. In the late 1870s and early 1880s Stockholm experienced a substantial (40-60 percent) increase in reports of and convictions for theft, assault, and disorderly conduct, all of which declined sharply after 1886. Labor unrest also was significant in the 1880s but not a great deal more than previously. The four most conflictive periods in twentieth century Stockholm were 1904-1909 (strikes and demands for suffrage), 1916-1920 (strikes, political demonstrations, food riots), 1924-1932 (strikes, more serious elsewhere than in Stockholm), and 1965 to the present. The most substantial increases in common crime in this century occurred in 1917-1919 and from 1955 to the present. The correlation between crises of public order, especially civil strife, and enlargement of the Stockholm police is precise.

The trend in Sydney police manpower has been more variable, almost cyclical. The force increased in proportional size from the 1870s until 1904, declined until 1918, increased by more than 50 percent to 1929, then declined irregularly until about 1960, when it began to increase once again. Similar peaks and valleys are evident in the data for the entire New South Wales force (not given). The periods of greatest absolute increase in the Sydney police were 1875-1881 (73 percent), 1889-1892 (30 percent), 1918-1929 (116 percent), 1945-1947 (21 percent), and 1963-1969 (28 percent). No pronounced increase in either crime or strife preceded or coincided with the years 1875-1881. Large-scale protest by organized labor emerged between 1885 and 1890, the 1890 strike being particularly severe. The most intense periods of civil strife in twentieth century Sydney were from 1917 to 1920 and from 1926 to the early 1930s. There was no consequential increase in serious crime or strife in the mid-1940s. The rise of crime and political demonstrations in the 1960s has been documented. In Sydney the correspondence between crises of public order and expansion of the police is not as precise as in London and Stockholm, but it is substantial nonetheless.

The size of the Calcutta police force varied with remarkable regularity during the colonial period. After centralization in 1864 the police-to-population ratios declined steadily until 1904, when the force was about ten percent smaller in absolute numbers and 40 percent smaller in proportion to population than it had been in 1870. Then, in lockstep with rising Bengali nationalism, the force was swiftly and regularly increased through 1917, by 73 percent in absolute numbers. In the next two decades the city's population more than doubled, but since no increments were made to the force, by 1940 the force ratios were half what they had been in the early 1920s. The inference is that the British chose to rely on means other than police manpower to deal with endemic disorder; we have already commented on their use of emergency powers, detention camps, and troops to quell the most serious outbreaks of strife. There are two different, fragmentary series of postindependence data for Calcutta; neither is directly comparable to the earlier figures but both show a distinct proportional (and absolute) increase. The data appear to indicate attempts by government to control resurgent strife; there is no recorded evidence of a concurrent increase in crime.

Thus for the four cities in the century beginning about 1870 we have identified sixteen periods in which police manpower increased at a much greater rate than urban population: four in London, five in Stockholm, five in Sydney, and two in Calcutta. In only two cases had there been no prior or concurrent increase in civil strife or recorded crime. In three other instances police manpower was increased following an increase in crime alone, and in six cases manpower was strengthened during or immediately after a period of increased strife. In the five remaining instances the manpower increase followed or coincided with a simultaneous rise in crime and strife. It could be argued in principle that augmentations in police strength lead to increases in reported crime and stimulate popular resistance. The data are not consistent with this kind of explanation, because in virtually every instance of correlation between increased disorder and an increase in police, disorder came first. In the case of strife there is typically a year's lag between a major episode and police expansion; the indicators for crime usually register increases for five years or more before police expansion. It is not necessary to base the argument solely on temporal correlations, either. In a number of instances we have statements of contemporary officials and others that the police were expanded in response to rising disorder. The sequence is best documented for the expansion of police forces in the three Western cities in the 1960s.

There is one paradoxical aspect of this evidence. The primary rationale and duty of urban police forces is to control crime, whereas more of the police expansions have occurred in response to strife (eleven of sixteen) than to crime (eight of sixteen). To resolve the paradox, we suggest that collective disorder is more threatening to elites than is crime, and this discrepancy has been sufficient to render elites more willing to invest additional resources in standby forces that can be used for crowd control than in manpower for crime control per se.

THE EFFECTS OF POLICE REFORM
ON PUBLIC ORDER

The circumstances of police reform and expansion provide consistent and convincing evidence that these changes were intended to improve public order during years when influential social groups felt particularly threatened by rising strife and crime. But whether public order improved as a consequence is not nearly as certain. A number of factors combine to make the matter problematical.

The control of strife has been one apparent object of police expansion, but since urban strife is episodic by its nature, the passing of a particular crisis is inevitable and might be attributed to almost any prior change in circumstance or policy. In any event officials and groups who are threatened by strife are likely to regard police success in minimizing its disruptive consequences as an improvement in public order. Therefore the criteria of successful control lie in the characteristics and consequences of strife as much as in its occurrence. By this kind of standard, on the whole, the modern police in the Western cities have been quite successful. Except for incidents in Stockholm in the mid-nineteenth century, there have been virtually no instances of protracted or widespread rioting, crowds have never threatened to topple a political regime, and the police have rarely inflicted serious or fatal injuries in conflict situations. The typical police role has been to restrain crowds of demonstrators and strikers, and to disperse rioters, with a minimum of force. The success of the police in the Western cities is due partly to the circumspection of those they are attempting to control, partly to police confidence that force displayed, but used in moderation, will work in crowd-control situations. This is one of the principal consequences of police modernization and expansion for public order in these three cities; the modern police are sufficiently numerous, well-trained, and confident of their abilities to have been able to control collective protest without using force in ways that would discredit them or intensify opposition.

In contrast, we have the failure of police policies in Calcutta to control either nationalist resistance or communal rioting during the last 40 years of colonial rule. The Calcutta police, though more numerous than their European counterparts, were badly trained. The critical limitation on their performance, however, was the fact that they served illegitimate masters. The political liabilities under which they operated all but assured the failure of any meliorative influence that might have followed from police reform and expansion. If the London, Stockholm, or New South Wales police had operated in similar political circumstances, it is not likely that they would have fared better.

The problems of assessing the impact of policing on crime are still more difficult. Expansion of police manpower may lead to detection of more crime and to more arrests, thereby masking evidence of deterrent effects. Changes of crime indicators in either direction after a manpower increase may be attributable to social and economic reasons quite unrelated to increased policing. It is also possible that criminal behavior is more influenced by what police do than by their numbers or organization. Our data about changing police procedures are insufficient to permit assessment of such an explanation. Nonetheless there is enough evidence to make some limited but suggestive comparisons of the impact of police reform and expansion on crime rates.

The years of nineteenth century police reform and subsequent periods of rapid police expansion in the three Western societies provide a set of seventeen social experiments whose impact on crime rates can be compared by examining the short-term trends in summary indicators of aggressive and acquisitive crimes during and after these police changes. In the case of reforms the trend was observed during the subsequent five years. For example, the Stockholm police were reformed in 1850. Our test of the effect on crime rates is to calculate and average separately the annual rates of change in convictions per 100,000 for assaults and for thefts between 1850 and 1854. In the case of expansions we use overlapping periods, beginning with the first year of increased police strength and continuing for two years beyond. The first pronounced increase in the Stockholm force occurred in 1886-1890; our measures of effect are the average of annual rates of change in convictions per 100,000 for assaults and theft, separately, between 1887 (the first year in which any effect might be expected) and 1892 (two years after the last year of expansion). For London and New South Wales we used indicators of serious (indictable) crimes of aggression and acquisition. Because of varying availability of crime data, all pre-1940 tests use convictions per 100,000; tests after 1940 use crime known to police per 100,000. When both kinds of data were available, we made separate tests of effects (not reported here) and found them to be consistently in the same direction and of similar magnitudes.

As Table VI.4.3 indicates, the principal police reforms in the nineteenth century ordinarily were followed by increased convictions. The reorganized police evidently were more zealous than their predecessors in arresting offenders. Committals to trial increased as a consequence (not shown), and so did convictions. The nine significant expansions of police strength between 1870 and 1940 had quite different kinds of results. They rarely were followed by increases in convictions; in most instances the indicators of one or both kinds of crime declined substantially thereafter.[7] One might conclude from these findings that the effect of increased policing on public order was what officials and ordinary citizens expected it to be. Since 1940, however, there has been a distinct reversal. In only two of ten comparisons was police expansion followed by a significant decline in recorded crime. In the others crime indicators continued to rise. This does not mean that increased policing is likely to have "caused" the concurrent increase, however. Most of the manpower increases in question occurred in the 1960s, and all were designed to cope with crime rates that had been rising for some years; our results for 1941-1970 simply reflect the fact that increased police manpower did not affect the rising trend.

The short-term effects of improved policing on crime (indicators of crime) differ from one time and circumstance to another. One interpretation of the findings cited is that the reformed police of the nineteenth century were in fact effective in creating public order,

Table VI.4.3 The Effects of Police Reform and Expansion on Crime Indicators in London, Stockholm, and New South Wales

Average annual change in crime indicators[a]	Number of expansions		
	1829-1862[b]	1870-1940[c]	1941-1970[d]
Greater than 7% increase	3		4
4-6% increase	2	1	1
1-3% increase		2	3
No significant change		3	
1-3% decrease	1	4	
4-6% decrease		5	1
Greater than 7% decrease		3	1
Mean change[e]	+10.0%	-3.9%	-3.8%

a. Changes in indicators of aggressive and acquisitive crimes are examined and counted separately (see text).

b. Percent changes in convictions per 100,000 in the five years following police reform in London (1829), Stockholm (1850), and New South Wales (1862).

c. Percent changes in convictions per 100,000 during and immediately after years of rapid police expansion, nine instances (see text).

d. Percent changes in reported crimes per 100,000 during and immediately after years of rapid police expansion, five instances (see text).

e. Mean of averages for all recorded instances.

and the experience of the last several decades is the result of a basic change in social causality or in the institutions of public order themselves.

We earlier showed that the long-term trends in crimes of violence and theft in all three societies are remarkably similar; they declined irregularly but persistently from high levels in the second quarter of the nineteenth century to much lower levels in the 1920s and 1930s. Yet only in London did the modernization of the police in 1829 correspond approximately with the beginning of decline. Convictions for serious assaults declined by half in the two ensuing decades; indictable thefts did not taper off noticeably until after 1850. In Stockholm and New South Wales the decline came first, then police reform. Police reform in Stockholm was in fact followed by a temporary abatement of decline. In New South Wales convictions per 100,000 declined at a rate ten times as great in the two decades before police reform in 1862 as they did in the two decades after.

The apparent success of modern police in minimizing the effects of civil strife in the three Western cities was tentatively attributed to the political circumstances of protesting and policing. Had governments been illegitimate, or had they adamantly resisted accommodating protest, police policies of restraint probably would not have worked, assuming they had been implemented in the first place. The same general explanation applies to the divergent effects of police reform and expansion on the incidence of common crime. Increased policing can reduce criminal behavior when it reinforces improving socioeconomic conditions. But policing alone cannot counter the corrosive effects of such criminogenic conditions as economic dislocation, social fragmentation, and cultural decay. The "failure" of modern policing to cope with rising levels of disorder is not due to institutional failure but to societal change.

THE FUTURE OF URBAN POLICING

The capacity of the police to maintain public order in the three Western cities probably is more subject to question now than at any time during the past century. Increases in police manpower during the last ten to twenty years have not appreciably slowed rising rates of common crime. Waves of strife during the 1960s and early 1970s appear to have subsided in each city, even in Calcutta, but strife in all the cities has been episodic even in the most turbulent periods. New issues of collective conflict are no doubt in the offing, and some old ones are likely to surface again. We can summarize the factors that most affect present and future policing in these cities under two rubrics: organizational response and social support.

New Responses to Disorder

The prevailing response to crises of public order is "more of the same": more police, more intensive patrolling, improved equipment, and so forth. At some point, however, more substantial and innovative changes are generally attempted.

One such approach is decriminalization. Formally this is a legal response; in practice the police, and courts, are able to selectively criminalize and decriminalize particular kinds of behavior. When serious offenses increase, the police can spare less attention for petty ones. Police organizations also are subject to a variety of formal and informal pressures from other agencies, legislatures, and elite and nonelite interest groups to "tilt" their enforcement activities in one direction or another, or to adapt them in response to shifting judicial policies. The courts, by modifying procedural restraints and by treating particular types of offenses leniently, discourage the policing of certain behaviors and groups. The history of New South Wales is rich in examples of selective police crackdowns (especially on so-called victimless crimes) followed in a few months or years by renewed tolerance. We suggest that the rise in serious disorder is often followed, not by crackdowns, but by police inattention to particularly widespread and nonthreatening offenses. In Sydney, London, and—as far as we know—Calcutta, this kind of adjustment is largely informal. In Stockholm, where there is more insistence on congruence of legal form and police practice, the extensive decriminalization of deviant social behavior, cited previously, reveals a formal shift. We also noted the decriminalization of petty larceny from stores in Sweden. In the other cities police apparently continue to record such offenses, when informed of them, but they evidently lack resources to take effective countermeasures: we showed earlier that reported offenses of this kind have increased far more rapidly in recent years than either arrests or convictions. It may be objected that decriminalization of petty offenses, whether de jure or de facto, is a non-response. On the contrary, it may have the practical positive consequence of freeing scarce police resources for direction toward more serious offenses. Police also may gain in public acceptance if they take a tolerant line to behaviors that are now widespread and, to many, socially tolerable (e.g., abortion, sexual deviance, gambling, loitering, and some kinds of disorderly conduct). Probably more important than either of these factors, though, are the symbolic effects of decriminalization on perceptions of disorder. The public view of crime and deviance involves a good deal of symbolic manipulation and elite persuasion of non-elites about the definition of acceptable behavior. Insofar as crime is created by these symbolic means, it can also be reduced by symbolic means, leaving only that core—no doubt a substantial one—of serious aggressive and acquisitive offenses that are universally abhorred.

There also are more major structural innovations in prospect. The forms created in the nineteenth century police reforms are not necessarily suitable to contemporary circumstances. In Sweden in 1965, for example, the police were nationalized. The immediate stimuli for the reorganization were rising crime rates, a desire for efficiency, and the growing need for directed coordination among diverse local police forces. Two important consequences for policing in Stockholm have been an increase in police size, already remarked, and more effective communication and cooperation between city and suburbs. The English police forces continue to be locally controlled, except for the Metropolitan Police, and nationalization may be in the offing.[8]

The use of private guards and security services is a frequent response to the inability of the police to control property crime. In Sydney, Stockholm, and London, more and more businesses are employing their own guards or obtaining police services on contract from private security agencies. In Stockholm in the early 1970s private police outnumbered public agents, and the government contracted with private institutions to provide guards for foreign embassies. Private police are not new, of course. They are widely used in non-Western societies and, historically, were found in many Western cities. What is exceptional is their rapid expansion now and the possibility that they may have the resources and flexibility to innovate in ways that are closed to public police forces.

Another alternative to public policing is reliance on military and paramilitary organizations, which often are called on to control civil disorder and have been much used in Calcutta throughout the twentieth century. Less frequently, such forces provide more routine police services. They rarely have seen action in twentieth century London, Stockholm, or New South Wales, and when they were used in earlier times in these societies they were the object of intense public hostility, as they are in India today. Any contemporary government that relied on paramilitary police would almost certainly lose a measure of its legitimacy, and such forces surely will not be called on while fear of public disorder in the three Western cities remains at its present level.

Social Support for Policing

That popular police are effective police is an article of liberal faith. Marked differences past and present in the style of policing and in the popularity of the police in the four cities allow us to test this proposition. The London police work individually and unarmed, as they have since 1829, depending heavily for their success on citizen respect and cooperation. Support had to be earned in an atmosphere of public hostility that was particularly intense in the 1830s and again in the 1860s, but an official opinion poll in the early 1960s showed that the English police were generally perceived as they wish to be seen: honest, helpful, and trustworthy.[9] In the last decade, however, the hostility of many youthful activists as well as a sizable segment of the London press, combined with widely publicized instances of corruption, has made a dent in that image.

The police of Stockholm had more difficulty than their London colleagues in living down an unsavory nineteenth century reputation. Riots against police, especially in reaction to arrests, were common for some decades after 1850; the incidence of individual offenses against officials (mainly assaults on police) increased from the 1850s until after 1910. Some of this hostility was no doubt due to the role of police in controlling working-class protest between the 1880s and 1920. In the last 50 years, however, there has been a fundamental change in Stockholmers' attitudes toward the police. Recruiting standards are high, police are well trained and well-paid (equivalent to secondary school teachers), and accusations of corruption or brutality are virtually nonexistent. Recent opinion polls supply convincing evidence of strong public support, though youths in Sweden, as elsewhere, are more hostile toward the police than are other groups.

The police of New South Wales were also unpopular in the nineteenth century, but they seem to have been less actively disliked than members of Stockholm's force. They have had relatively broad functions and considerable discretion in applying the law—more, that is, than the police of London and Stockholm. Since the 1890s they have been armed, and from World War I until 1949 they also had counterespionage and surveillance responsibilities. Moreover police are still recruited largely from the working class, and salaries remain relatively low. The net effect of these factors is that the New South Wales police have never enjoyed a high degree of support. Public suspicion and hostility is apparent in accusations that police are sometimes corrupt, use "basher tactics," and are indiscriminate in making arrests. Polls in the 1960s gave evidence of mixed and declining public support for the force.

There are no opinion polls about police in Calcutta, but it was noted earlier that the common policeman was generally deficient in training and rectitude, underpaid, and unrespected, throughout the years of colonial rule. The continued use of these agents to control strikes and demonstrations is unlikely to have won much public support for the force in recent decades. The police also lacked official support during the years of leftist United Front government in the late 1960s. Like many another group with a grievance in Calcutta, some of them protested in 1971 by rioting at the police superintendent's office and in the state assembly.

High levels of public support for the police in London and Stockholm have had no discernible dampening effect on instances of public disorder in either city. Indeed, public respect for the police in those cities may have encouraged victims of crime to report such incidents to the police, thereby increasing one indicator of public disorder. In New South Wales the rise in crime indicators has been less pronounced, though the police are less popular there—not necessarily by coincidence. In general we have little support for the view that police popularity per se has much to do with keeping crime down. It is certain only that being a policeman, and dealing with one, is somewhat better in London and Stockholm than in Sydney, and much better there than in Calcutta. For the future, two positive consequences may depend on popular respect for the police: Ordinary people may be patient longer with rising disorder, and they may be more likely to accept innovative responses to it—if and when they are devised.

NOTES TO CHAPTER VI.4

1. David H. Bayley, "The Police and Political Development in Europe," in Charles Tilly, ed., *The Formation of National States in Western Europe* (Princeton, N.J.: Princeton University Press, 1975), pp. 328-379. Bayley's generalizations are based on a study of the national development of the English, French, German, and Italian police.

2. The history of uniformed policing in the United States begins in 1853, when the New York City police were reorganized on the model of London's Metropolitan Police: see James F. Richardson, *The New York Police: Colonial Times to 1901* (New York: Oxford University Press, 1970). In the next 40 years virtually every one of the 100 largest cities in the United States followed suite, the most populous cities first; see Eric H. Monkkonen, "The Uniformed Police: A Dispersion Model" (unpublished paper, Department of History, University of North Carolina, Charlotte, 1976).

3. A study emphasizing the importance of the middle classes' quest for order as a source of professionalization of the police is Allan Silver, "The Demand for Order in Civil Society: A Review of Some Themes in the History of Urban Crime, Police, and Riot," in David J. Bordua, ed., *The Police: Six Sociological Essays* (New York: Wiley, 1967).

4. Bayley, op. cit., p. 357, argues that since domestic turmoil in England had largely subsided by 1820, disorder played little role in the establishment of the Metropolitan Police. This interpretation seems to ignore the widespread fears of strife voiced by the English elite during the 1820s and the elite's great concern about crimes of violence and theft, reflected in high and rising rates of committals to trial and convictions for these offenses. Moreover the 1839 act requiring all English cities and counties to establish police on the London model was passed at the height of the Chartist movement.

5. There is considerable debate among American historians about the circumstances of police modernization in cities in the United States. Monkonnen, who has reviewed the debate (op. cit.), shows that the timing of modernization depended primarily on the size of cities and, implicitly, on the need for rationalized and efficient urban services. Neither ecological factors such as ethnic composition and industrial base nor episodic ones like rioting had any significant role. But this evidence bears on the diffusion of the police idea in a single society. We want to determine what circumstances led to the introduction of modern police organization in the metropolises of societies that had not previously used it.

6. On the intensification of class conflict in England in these years, see Standish Meacham, "The Sense of an Impending Clash: English Working-Class Unrest Before the First World War," *American Historical Review*, 77 (December 1972). Some of the concurrent increase in police strength had a more prosaic purpose: It was made necessary by the decision to give policemen one free day a week rather than one per fortnight. But this required only 1,600 new men, whereas the force was expanded by about 4,100.

7. A broader but more impressionistic study has come to very similar conclusions about the impact of police professionalization on property crime in nineteenth century Canada, the United States, England, and France: The short-

run effect usually was a recorded increase, the long-run effect usually was a decline. See Charles Tilly, Allen Levett, A. Q. Lodhi, and Frank Munger, "How Policing Affected the Visibility of Crime in Nineteenth-Century Europe and America," in Theodore Ferdinand, ed., *The Criminal Justice System* (forthcoming).

8. There have been successive amalgamations of the English police forces, which (including Wales) numbered 49 as of 1966; roughly half their financial support has been provided by the national government, which uses the power of the purse to ensure uniform practices. Greater efficiency of police work nonetheless might follow from formal nationalization. See T. A. Critchley, *A History of Police in England and Wales, 1900-1966* (London: Constable, 1967).

9. Royal Commission on the Police, *Final Report* (London: Her Majesty's Stationery Office, 1962).

TRIALS, PUNISHMENT,
AND ALTERNATIVES

The fate of those charged with criminal offenses has varied remarkably depending on the time and place. In the eighteenth and early nineteenth centuries a good many people were sentenced to hang for offenses that in some of the four societies would now bring a fine, on evidence that would now result in acquittal. This chapter surveys some of the reforms in courts and court procedure, criminal sanctions, and correctional practices that have contributed to a fundamental change in the consequences of crime for most of those accused of it.

The evolution of punishment in Western societies was much influenced by class and economic considerations.[1] Class interests and cost efficiency are implicated in a good many of the changes reviewed below, but these factors operate in the context of a more fundamental transformation in social values and beliefs about crime and punishment that began in the eighteenth century and is still in train. This is no place for a history of Western social thought, but two changes are strikingly apparent in any review of evolving policies of "law and order" during the last two centuries. One is the decline of brutal and inhumane treatment of offenders, the other is the rise of the belief that crime has mainly social origins, therefore calls for rehabilitation as well as or instead of punishment. These humanitarian views are by no means universally held or applied. The institutions of public order of the four societies we studied embody such principles in differing degrees. One theme in the comparisons to follow is the extent to which humanitarian values and practices have supplanted the repressive ones of past centuries; the underlying issue is to determine the kinds of social and political circumstances that have encouraged the implementation of humanitarian policies.

It is fashionable among liberal scholars and reformers to castigate officials in Western societies for their failure to eliminate substantial residues of repressive law, procedure, and punishment that remain in the bodies politic. This kind of critique often assumes, implicitly or explicitly, that consistent application of humanitarian principles would lead to improved public order. We make no such a priori assumptions. We prefer humanitarian policies, but we think it is an open question whether such policies do in fact reduce threatening social behavior. The evidence to be surveyed may suggest partial answers.

One other initial qualification is needed. The criminal justice system is widely assumed to be the keystone of social defense against individual crime, but in the times and places we studied it has had only an adjunct role in maintaining civil peace. Response to strife has been first of all a political, police, and military matter. The courts and penal institutions have played a significant role in relation to strife only when and where there were political decisions (usually embodied in laws designed to control collective behavior) that rioters, protesters, and revolutionaries be charged, judged, and sentenced like ordinary criminals.

JUDICIAL SYSTEMS

Western systems of defense against crime depend on the courts because they decide the crucial questions of guilt and punishment for almost all major offenses and many petty ones as well. In most medieval societies they weré the only regularly constituted institutions of public order; those who arrested offenders and imposed penalties were for the most part agents of the courts. The development of specialized institutions for policing, punishment, and rehabilitation has meant that some quasi-judicial functions are performed elsewhere; for minor offenses, arrest may be tantamount to conviction, and parole boards have much discretion to vary sentences. But the critical decisions for most people accused of crimes are made in court.

Despite their central role in maintaining public order, the courts have rarely been the object of intense controversy or politically motivated reform in the four societies we studied. Crises of public order have seldom been blamed on sins of commission or omission by the courts, as in the United States today, and rarely have led to substantial reform in judicial structure or procedure. The judicial systems of these four societies have been changed fairly often, and there has been a marked expansion in the rights accorded defendants before the courts; but most of these developments have been evolutionary and have occasioned little political debate. There is no paradox here. The judicial function seems to have virtually universal acceptance in Western political theory and practice. From time to time, there have been controversies over which people are brought to court by whom and for what offenses, and over the standards and sanctions to be applied. As a consequence, most efforts and reform in the three Western societies, and even in Bengal, have been directed at the criminal law, policing, and treatment, but not at the existence of the courts or their jurisdication.

The Structure and Jurisdiction of Criminal Courts

The contemporary criminal courts of the four societies have a number of common structural features. All are multitier systems in which petty cases are tried before lesser courts and others are assigned to higher courts according to their nature and seriousness. In the three societies that share the English tradition, the lowest tier is comprised of magistrates' courts. In England the system of magistrates, or justices of the peace, had medieval roots. Traditionally the justices were drawn from the local gentry and unpaid (as they still are in much of the country), and they had responsibility for civil administration as well as summary jurisdiction over a variety of criminal and civil cases. In London in the eighteenth century they had become notoriously venal; reforms in 1792 established a new system of paid (stipendiary) justices having police as well as judicial powers. Magistrates assigned administrative and judicial functions were established in the early years of the New South Wales Colony and in Calcutta in 1793, with further reforms in 1806. In Calcutta these officials supplanted or supplemented a system of East India Company courts in which a mayor's court administered English law and corrupt Indian zamindars administered traditional law for the Indian population. In Stockholm police and judicial responsibilities also were commingled at the lowest level, though not as in London: Petty cases were tried in a police court, which was presided over first by the governor, then by the police commissioner, and after 1864 by a special judge.

In the eighteenth and nineteenth centuries the magistrates' and police courts often exercised jurisdiction over fairly serious (rarely capital) offenses. In the twentieth century, although they deal mainly with petty and administrative offenses, these institutions remain the foundation of the court systems in all four societies. Offenses that carry significant criminal penalties are disposed of by various higher courts. In England the first tier of courts beyond the justices of the peace is the Quarter Sessions, consisting of a number of justices sitting as a panel. The centerpiece of criminal justice in London was and is the Central Criminal Court, a court of assizes whose justices are appointed by the Crown. New South Wales has had a similar three-tier system, but until 1839 its highest court was the Court of Criminal Jurisdiction whose members were military officers; as befitted a penal colony, this was, in effect, a court martial. In Calcutta a Supreme Court established in 1774 was the court of original jurisdiction for all Europeans in Bengal accused of serious crimes, and also for Indians in Calcutta. It applied English common law to European cases and to crimes of violence and theft by Indians. A third, intermediate level of courts was not added until 1957. Stockholm, the smallest city of the four, has the most complex court system. In the nineteenth century it had two courts, later one, for serious offenses, and the High Court of Justice held review powers previously exercised by the king. A major reform in 1942 created the present system, which has three levels beyond the police court. The least serious criminal offenses are tried by a single judge, graver crimes by a three-judge panel, and the weightiest cases by a single professional judge and seven to nine lay judges.

This is sufficient background on the structure of the courts for the comparisons to follow. Note that the dates of court reform given here, and others given in the four city studies, do not coincide with crises of public order. Of the restructurings just cited, the only one known to have been an issue of public controversy was the 1792 act that reformed the London magistracy, and this was simply one part of a long struggle for legal, judicial, and police reform.

The Rights of Defendants

At least four characteristics of court procedure are important from a defendant's point of view. One involves the question of equity versus discrimination in the court's application of the law. In all the societies the young, the poor, the less-educated, the immigrants, and members of subordinate ethnic groups have been more likely than others to be arrested and committed to trial. But how equitably are they treated once brought before the courts? We managed to gather all too little evidence on this question in the course of so general a study. There are two substantial examples of inequity, though. The case studies provide ample evidence that the courts gave harsher sentences to convicts and ticket-of-leave holders in early nineteenth-century New South Wales, and to Indians in Calcutta during colonial rule, than to other defendants.

The traditional English means of ensuring a fair trial was to permit the accused to be judged by a jury of his peers. However the principle was not immediately extended to New South Wales; jury trials were not used until 1833, and military courts were not abolished until the end of transportation seven years later. Europeans accused of crimes in Calcutta had the right to trial by European juries; Indians lacked a comparable right. There was no such Scandinavian tradition, but a functional equivalent exists in the contemporary Swedish use of panels of judges to decide serious cases. The same kind of principle is evident in the use of panels of justices in Quarter Sessions in both England and New South Wales. The person accused before these courts is not being judged by his peers, but decisions made by a panel of judges presumably moderate the effects of individual judicial bias.

Another mechanism for checking the arbitrariness of individual justices is the right of appeal. Stockholm had an appeals court at least as early as 1614, and it was traditional for the monarch to review all death sentences. In the other three societies death sentences also were subject to review, not always systematically, and often they were commuted. Provisions for appeal of other kinds of sentences were slow to be institutionalized, however. England had limited provision for appeals in 1873, but the first formal criminal appeals court was not established until 1907. New South Wales followed suit in this as in so many other innovations by establishing a Court of Criminal Appeals in 1912. Since 1957 the High Court in Calcutta has served almost exclusively as an appeals court, though it had exercised that function for some time previously. The evidence we have suggests that appeals are not particularly common in any of these societies now, and the decisions of lower courts usually are sustained.

Jury trials and appeal courts aside, the last decades of the nineteenth century saw a general and growing tendency to strengthen the rights of defendants. Some of the steps were procedural. In England the rules of evidence were revised, for example, by permitting the accused to examine witnesses and to testify in his own defense. Similar rights were accorded New South Welshmen in 1891. In India an act of 1872 prohibited the use of confessions to police as evidence in court—a reform whose importance was due to the police practice of coercing confessions. The Swedes have been particularly insistent that courts' decisions take account of the individual's circumstances and characteristics, and since 1964 detailed presentencing investigations have been required.

These reforms theoretically have benefited all defendants. The provision of free legal services to the poor was another thrust of reform having great practical impact, and the Swedes were pioneers. The city of Stockholm paid a lawyer to assist poor defendants beginning in 1884 and in 1913 established a bureau to offer the same services. An act of 1919 made free legal services generally available, at the courts' discretion. At first these services were furnished mainly in civil cases, but after 1919 in a number of defendants in criminal cases also were given help. In 1972 Sweden established a comprehensive system of legal aid in criminal, civil, and administrative cases in which receipt of assistance was a function not of judicial discretion but of the individual's ability to pay.

Despite the repeated urgings of reformers, England and New South Wales made legal services available slowly and grudgingly. Judges were empowered to support the defense of persons on trial for indictable offenses beginning in 1903 in England and in 1907 in New South Wales. In both places political sentiment has consistently opposed the establishment of a public defender's office, though it has been more than 50 years since the first legislative proposals in this regard were tabled. Piecemeal reforms have extended aid to defendants before the magistrates' courts, beginning in England in the 1930s, but use of such assistance continues to be constrained in both law and practice. In New South Wales an act that extended legal aid in 1969 excluded repeat offenders. The most recent English enactments (1964, 1974) require a means test, and it has been estimated that in the early 1970s only five percent of defendants were represented in their first appearance before magistrates' courts. Private agencies have provided some legal services in both countries. In New South Wales, for example, a special legal service was established for aborigines in 1970. Only in Calcutta do we lack evidence of special provisions for legal services for the poor. But in Calcutta almost everyone is poor, and the municipal treasury has no funds even for water and sewerage services; in such circumstances legal aid is neither relevant nor possible.

These illustrative instances of reforms that have improved a defendant's chances of a fair trial in the three Western societies, are more than sufficient to document a substantial trend. Defendants are much more likely now than a century ago to get a full hearing and to have their cases decided consistently and with attention to personal circumstances. It cannot be said that defendants are equals before the courts, but their status has improved greatly and their rights have been expanded. Considerations of economy and efficiency are a hindrance to any broad expansion, though. Legal aid and presentencing investigations are costly, adversarial proceedings in court are time-consuming, and appeals add considerably to the work load of the courts and their administrative agencies.

The increase in defendants' rights, combined with the rising numbers of arrests and committals to trial in the Western cities, are forces quite capable of overloading the criminal justice systems there. Plea bargaining is a popular North American response to such pressures; accused and accuser are partners to a pact in which the judicial system gains efficiency by reducing the defendant's risks and penalties. Plea bargaining is increasingly common in New South Wales but is virtually unknown in Sweden. In England plea bargaining per se is not practiced, but the same purpose is served by allowing the defendant in most criminal cases to opt for a summary trial before a magistrates' court rather than a jury trial before a higher court. Summary justice is speedier, and conviction is probably more certain; but most important for the defendants, the sentences magistrates can impose are limited in severity. The prosecution can give this option to the accused for all but the most serious crimes, and as a consequence about 90 percent of all cases legally triable by higher courts are now heard by magistrates. The system naturally invites comparison with plea bargaining in the United States. The English practice originated in the middle of the nineteenth century, when crime rates were declining, and it has always had explicit legal sanction and ground rules. Plea bargaining in North America has developed as an ad hoc administrative response to the increased number of cases; it has no formal legal basis, nor is it applied consistently.

Alternatives

Plea bargaining and summary justice are by no means the only administrative alternatives to full courtroom hearings of criminal cases. A much different approach is the creation of special bodies and procedures for dealing with particular offenses. This is done under two very different sets of circumstances. When public disorder is particularly great, and especially when political strife is prevalent, many societies resort to special tribunals that sentence dissidents to detention or imprisonment without the usual judicial niceties or rights of appeal. These tribunals are speedy and efficient, they need not be concerned about whether defendants are guilty according to criminal law and rules of evidence, and perhaps above all they function in privacy, out of political view. Such practices are alien to the Scandinavian and English temper, but the English nevertheless employed them against Bengali nationalists from the 1920s through the early 1940s. The Indians have continued to rely on such swift, nonpublic procedures for dealing with dissidents after independence; their imposition nationwide in 1975 was an extension of a means often employed at the state level during the previous 25 years.

The more important and humanitarian alternatives to criminal proceedings are based on the emerging belief that certain categories of offenders, and offenses, require special social treatment. Children who committed crimes were treated the same as adult offenders until well into the nineteenth century. In London in the 1840s, for example, persons aged nineteen and younger made up one-third of those committed for trial, while as late as the 1860s and 1870s between five and nine percent of the prisoners in London's notorious

Newgate Gaol were under sixteen, and a few were younger than twelve. Significantly different treatment of children accused of crimes began in the latter half of the nineteenth century and included the establishment of children's courts featuring special, usually private proceedings, a wide range of judicial discretion in disposing of cases, and special custodial care and home casework services. In Sweden local child welfare boards were given responsibility for such cases beginning in 1902. In New South Wales children's courts were established in 1905, in England in 1908. Women have occasionally been accorded special treatment by the law and courts, for example in New South Wales, but not at present as far as we know. Those who are mentally incompetent or ill also have benefited from special legal provisions; one of the significant thrusts of legal reform in twentieth century England has been to ensure that offenders medically judged insane are treated as such.

Certain kinds of offenses are also thought to warrant special social treatment, hence to require noncriminal adjudication. The Swedes have gone further in this direction than the other societies we studied, beginning with a program for interning vagrants in 1885. Local boards, not courts, passed judgment on persons accused of vagrancy and were empowered to commit vagrants to agricultural colonies for up to three years. Beginning in 1916 local temperance boards were given similar powers to take proceedings against alcoholics, who could be interned, for purposes of rehabilitation, for up to four years. The vagrancy boards no longer exist, and the temperance boards have been transformed; but the basic principle that some offensive forms of social conduct are not necessarily "crimes" but may be problems calling for rehabilitation remains a dominant feature of Swedish institutions of public order. Persons subject to quasi-judicial proceedings for such offenses are no more likely than defendants in criminal proceedings to be protected from capricious decisions, but at least they are not labeled and treated as criminals. New South Wales furnishes an instructive contrast: Drunkenness continues to be treated only as a criminal offense, there are no significant public programs for helping chronic offenders, and the political elite and police prefer to keep it that way, because by prevailing antipodean standards public drunkenness is immoral and public immorality is a crime.

THE TREATMENT OF OFFENDERS

The social ritual called criminal justice sorts people according to their degrees of guilt, and societies have evolved extraordinarily diverse ways of dealing with those judged guilty. The handling of criminals has changed more fundamentally, in these four societies and in Western civilization generally, than have the criminal law, the police, the courts, or perhaps all of them together. The long list of punishments includes execution, physical deprivation, and whipping; deportation; confinement in workhouses, prisons, and reformatories; public ridicule, fines, and loss of civil rights. Treatment of criminals also relied on many more "socially useful" practices: forced labor in galleys, penal colonies, farms, and industry; cautions like suspended sentences, parole, and community supervision; and programs of positive rehabilitation involving moral reeducation, counseling, and training. These treatments have been variously implemented, and there has been much disingenuous rationalization of the moral and social benefits of each. The four societies do not provide examples of all the approaches, but they do offer substantial evidence of the emergence of humanitarian practices, their differential distribution, and the kinds of social forces that have impelled and restrained reform.

Preferences and Possibilities for Treatment

The treatment of criminals in a particular time and place depends partly on what is socially preferable, partly on what is socially possible. Social preferences, infinitely diverse in detail, generally can be categorized as punitive and remedial. "Punitive" preferences and policies emphasize punishment of offenders and deterrence of potential offenders. "Remedial" preferences and policies, as we use the term, are those which seek to put criminals to social use—directly by exploiting their labor, or indirectly by resocializing them to become self-sustaining, productive members of society. Preferences of both kinds are expressed by different groups in contemporary and most historical societies, but we find that the same specific policies can satisfy both kinds of preferences, and many of the innovations in treatment of the last century and more have been devised precisely because they have both remedial and punitive effects. At the outset of this chapter we cited a trend away from callous and brutal treatment of offenders and toward humane policies. That trend is not identical or even highly correlated with a shift from punitive to remedial policies. Many policies designed to serve remedial ends have been incalculably cruel, and humanitarian sentiments have informed many punitive policies.

The policies actually used to treat criminals are constrained by the basic socioeconomic requirements and political dynamics of societies. On the economic front, labor scarcity is an incentive to exploit criminals' labor, even to create "criminals" to undertake unpleasant tasks. If labor is not scarce, other kinds of policies are needed, depending on levels of economic productivity. In poor societies it is preferable to rely on capital and corporal punishments, which are cheap. More prosperous conditions make possible more elaborate and expensive treatments, including both long-term imprisonment and rehabilitation. A potent political principle is that influential social groups can be counted on to oppose the use of punitive and inhumane treatments against themselves and those with whom they identify. The upper classes of most societies we know anything about have usually found ways to spare their deviant members the unpleasantness visited on criminals from other classes. The rise in political influence of the middle classes and, later, the working classes in the three Western societies is a dynamic force that underlies the evolution of humane and rehabilitative treatments. These observations do not explain treatment policies, however, because very substantial cultural and intellectual differences in treatment preferences have always existed independently of economic and class considerations. We think that the evidence reviewed below supports the position that humanitarian and rehabilitative ideologies in Western societies have exerted an independent force on the status and treatment of offenders. The most substantial innovations, of course, have come about when ideological preferences for reform have coincided with favorable economic and political circumstances.

Evidence from the four societies covers four kinds of policies and practices of treatment: the use of physical punishment, the labor alternative, the evolution of custodial care, and alternatives to imprisonment. The kinds of preferences reflected in each are discussed, and where evidence permits we comment on the intellectual and social circumstances that have led to the adoption or decline of each kind of policy.

The Passing of Capital and Corporal Punishment

Punishments for crime in eighteenth century European societies were nasty and cheap. Their nastiness was in large part deliberate, being intended first to deter others who might be tempted to crime, second to exact retribution from the guilty. Capital and corporal sanctions, the first line of social defense for crimes against persons and property, satisfied the prevailing preference for deterrence and punishment. They were not costly to administer, and there were no obvious reasons for thinking them ineffective. Hanging and mutilation were wasteful of manpower, it is true; but where labor was scarce physical punishments could be easily replaced by sentencing offenders to workhouses or transportation.

One measure of the brutality of punishment in the eighteenth and early nineteenth centuries was the frequency with which the death penalty was invoked. Execution was legally prescribed for a great many offenses, including petty ones, and judges had little discretion about whether to apply this penalty to people judged guilty. A seventeenth century writer reports, with reliability that is difficult to establish, that 72,000 thieves were hanged during the reign of the Tudor King Henry VIII, and that during Elizabeth's reign vagabonds were sometimes hanged by the hundreds.[2] But great opposition developed to executions on such a broad scale, not only by those who felt the noose at their neck but by intellectuals and many of the elite and middle classes. The elite in the eighteenth century tended to believe that the threat of capital punishment was necessary to deter crime; but little satisfaction was taken in the imposition of such sentences, and an increasing proportion of them were commuted. There was a growing liberal belief, first loudly voiced by European scholars in the seventeenth century, that capital punishment was needlessly cruel and socially useless, and by the 1780s this view had been incorporated into the new criminal codes of several continental states, where the death penalty was abolished. The declining incidence of capital punishment in England, Sweden, and New South Wales is represented in Figure VI.5.1, which indicates that by 1850 this sanction was rarely used.[3] Since the data are not weighted for population, they substantially understate the rate of decline. But it should also be noted that the crises of public order in the 1830s and 1840s are reflected in temporary increases in executions. The argu-

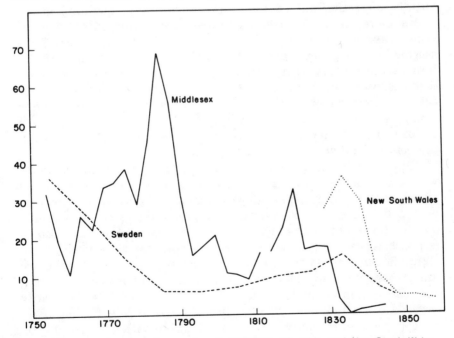

Figure VI.5.1 Average annual executions in Middlesex, Sweden, and New South Wales, 1750-1860

ments against capital punishment were not enough to dissuade officials under stress from stepping up reliance on the older methods.

One alternative to capital punishment was corporal punishment. Like executions it usually was administered publicly, both for its general deterrent effect and to contribute to the social embarrassment of the offender. Its use also declined in the nineteenth century, and by 1900 it had virtually disappeared as a judicially prescribed penalty in the three Western societies. Corporal punishment was regularly used to maintain prison discipline long after it had passed from public view, however. In Sweden and England whippings and other physical punishments were rarely imposed by the courts after the mid-nineteenth century. In Sweden they were not formally prohibited in prisons until 1925. In England the use of corporal punishment for disciplinary infractions in prisons was not abandoned until 1963. In New South Wales flogging and other physical punishments were used unstintingly during the convict era. Legislation passed in 1830, for example, prescribed up to twelve months hard labor in chains, or 100 lashes, for convicts convicted of drunkenness, neglect of work, or use of abusive language. The judicial bite was as sharp as its bark: In the mid-1830s 6,000 to 7,000 floggings a year were administered by the courts to a convict population of no more than 30,000. Corporal punishment was resorted to much less frequently after the end of transportation in 1840, but even in the 1890s there are police records of men being flogged in cases of wanton assault. Such physical punishments as bread-and-water diets, gagging, and floggings continued in official use in prisons until the turn of the century. The New South Wales tradition of relying on such chastisements was symbolically alive until very recently. A 1929 act broadened the circumstances under which judges could prescribe whipping, and a judge publicly urged a return to the practice in 1946. In fact the legal provisions have almost never been invoked in this century and were abolished by law in 1974.

Authorities in Bengal still rely on corporal punishment, as far as we know, but with the same diminution evident in Europe. Capital punishment has not been outlawed, but we lack recent information on the frequency of executions. Whippings were generously meted out by the courts not only in the nineteenth century but also in response to the early twentieth century episodes of Bengali nationalism. Prison reports from nineteenth century jails show extensive use of handcuffs and leg irons, whipping, and deprivation of food; and cases continued to occur, though less and less frequently through the 1950s and 1960s. During colonial rule Europeans in Bengal prisons received such treatment less often than did Indians, however.

The Labor Alternative

Capital and corporal punishment did no more than deter and punish. The alternative of putting criminals to work has an equally long European heritage, but the rationales vary from the exploitation of criminals' labor for public or private profit to the teaching to criminals of skills and habits they could profitably employ on release. A third rationale was punishment, by forcing prisoners to do work more rigorous and painful than they would voluntarily accept. Offenders were given many different tasks, depending on economic circumstances and prevailing views about punishment and rehabilitation.

Houses of correction were a common feature of European cities from the early seventeenth century. London's Bridewell was established in 1555, Stockholm's *spinnhuss* in the following century. Their inmates were mainly vagrants, beggars, and petty criminals who did routine work that was expected to turn a profit for the houses' public or private management. The contemporary view of these institutions is well summarized by Rusche and Kirchheimer:

> The essence of the house of correction was that it combined the principles of the poorhouse, workhouse, and penal institution. Its main aim was to make the labor power of unwilling people socially useful. By being forced to work within the institution, the prisoners would form industrious habits and would receive a vocational training at the same time. When released, it was hoped, they would voluntarily swell the labor market.[4]

The late eighteenth and early nineteenth centuries were a time of labor surplus in most European societies, however, and penal institutions run on capitalist principles illustrated in microcosm the Marxian thesis about the effects of declining profits on the immiseration of labor. Conditions for inmates, which in earlier times often had been tolerable by prevailing standards, sank to abysmal levels. In Stockholm some public attention and funds apparently were given to the workhouses during this period, and vagrants were offered the choice of military service.

The English had one attractive alternative to both capital punishment and unprofitable workhouses: transportation of offenders to the colonies, where labor could be put to good use. Transportation was a feature of English penal practice as early as 1597. The American colonies were planted with the help of tens of thousands of convicts, and the Botany Bay colony was founded in direct response to the need to remove the hundreds of prisoners who were stockpiled in convict ships in the River Thames after the American Revolution. By the 1830s the free settlers and emancipists of New South Wales were able to press for the end of transportation; they were successful in 1840, but the practice continued elsewhere in Australia until

1867. All told, an estimated 150,000 English and Irish convicts were transported to Australia. In New South Wales the prisoners were sometimes used for public works but more often were assigned to private employers, individually or in groups, as servants and laborers. Those who were unemployable or particularly dangerous were imprisoned, either in the colony or by secondary transportation to Norfolk Island. Convicts who had served their terms were released, and many remained to swell the colony's labor force. Sweden, lacking colonies to which convicts could be transported, experimented with the assignment of convicts to labor under private supervision. Stockholm maintained such programs through the 1890s.

One rationale for putting offenders to work shifted in the course of the nineteenth century when the economic incentives were undercut. Prisoners were proportionally fewer in the three Western societies as the century progressed, as is evident from the declining conviction rates reviewed previously. Probably more important was the growing capital investment needed to make profitable use of labor in all the societies, coupled with the opposition of private businessmen to cut-rate competition by prison workshops and, later, the objections of organized labor on the same grounds. The rehabilitative purposes remained, but they were best served through training programs rather than forced labor per se. One significant innovation began in London during the 1850s, when a new system of reformatories for child offenders was established. Previously children had been briefly jailed for each offense, then released to resume seeking their livelihood by the only means open to most of them, namely, petty thievery. The youngsters now were committed to reformatories long enough to receive basic education and work training.[5]

The concern for work-as-punishment remained and prompted a number of odious innovations. Prison authorities in England and New South Wales were particularly fond of treadmill labor—regardless of whether the mills' energies were harnessed. A committee in the New South Wales observed, after an investigation in 1825, that treadmill labor was a very effective punishment by virtue of its monotonous and irksome regularity and concluded "that if coercive labour and restraint is calculated to reform or deter from crime, no system of discipline can better be calculated for this purpose than that of the tread-wheel. . . ."[6] Prisons in most Western societies continued to require labor of some convicts in the twentieth century, but rarely was the rationale so punitive. The primary justification is rehabilitation; profitable productivity is secondary, and convicts in the three Western societies receive at least token payment for their work.

We have no evidence that prison labor was widely used or rationalized in Bengal in the period we studied.

Prison Reform and Custodial Care

The lessening reliance on physical punishment, the declining profitability of workhouses, the dramatic increase in crime and convictions in the 1820s and 1830s, and, in England, the restriction of transportation in the 1840s made it essential to devise different methods for treating offenders. The principal thrust of innovation in the three Western societies was prison expansion and reform. At least two different strands can be seen in the skein of reform. The same liberal sensitivities that championed reduction of capital and corporal punishment were aroused by the horrors of prison existence. Prisons in the late eighteenth century included the houses of correction, workhouses—which warehoused a motley crew of social undesirables, among them debtors, the insane, and petty criminals—and jails, which temporarily incarcerated people awaiting trial and execution of sentence for a great variety of offenses. These institutions typically housed without segregation people of all ages, both sexes, and every social category in ancient, cramped, unsanitary quarters. The inmates were ill-fed, their labor was exploited, and their money—if they had any—was extracted as fees by the goalers. John Howard, an English prison official of the 1770s, began what became an international movement for the reform of such conditions. The objects were to relieve the misery of prisoners and to improve their chances of rehabilitation.

The second strand of reformist thought was concerned less with implementing humanitarian principles than with establishing rational and efficient systems of custodial punishment. Criminals were to be sentenced to convict prisons in proportion to the seriousness of their offenses, and there was to be regular discipline, including especially the discipline of hard labor, both as punishment and as a source of moral regeneration.

The pace and substance of prison reform varied considerably from country to country. In Sweden efforts at improving prison conditions and treatment were inspired in part by John Howard's international movement and date from the 1780s. The effective impetus for prison reform came in 1840, and it came from the top down. In 1840 Crown Prince Oscar wrote a treatise *On Punishments and Prisons*, reflecting the most advanced thinking of the time. After he became king in 1844 Oscar encouraged the rapid introduction of a wide range of reforms in which the rehabilitation of the prisoner and his reintegration into society were the primary goals. Thirteen new

prisons were built by 1850, 34 by 1864, and placed under coordinated national management; prisoners were classified and assigned to
specialized institutions according to their offenses and prospects for
rehabilitation, and programs of vocational and religious training were
introduced. Citizens' aftercare societies, modeled on those of London and Philadelphia, were promoted with an eye to smoothing
ex-convicts' return to society. This early and programmatic start on
penal reform was followed by successive innovations that have continued to the present. Minimum-security institutions were established
late in the nineteenth century, and judges were given wide latitude in
sentencing by the 1865 criminal code. In this century a variety of
alternatives to imprisonment have been implemented. The most
recent (1974) reform in imprisonment per se guarantees rights to
inmates, including some form of participation in prison decision
making.

Prison reform in England was more gradual. Acts in 1823 and
1835 implemented some of the reformers' long-standing pleas for
more humane treatment in prisons, and houses of correction and
prisons came to be supported from public funds and inspected by
officials. Debtors' prisons were abolished in the 1840s as nonpenal
methods for dealing with these offenders were devised. The pressures
of a growing convict population inspired a spate of prison building
from the 1820s to the 1850s. In the 1830s and 1840s there was also
considerable experimentation with the "silent system," in which
prisoners were kept in isolation, forbidden to speak, and sometimes
prevented from seeing other prisoners, so that they could contem-
plate their sins in privacy and undergo a natural moral rejuvenation.
The reformers' good intentions foundered on two hard facts: such
systems were expensive, and the inmates, rather than finding inner
moral strength, all too often went mad. But nothing resembling a
comprehensive national program of treatment was designed until the
1853 Penal Servitude Act, which provided for hard and presumably
rehabilitative labor in convict prisons for men who before that date
would have been transported to Australia. English prisons were
centralized under Home Office control in 1877, but for the next two
decades the principal result was that imprisonment was made consistently harsh. The rigors of English prisons gradually began to abate
around the turn of the century, and especially during the tenure of
Liberal governments in the decade before World War I. The prison
population was reduced by more than half between 1905 and 1918,
for example, and the Borstal system for offenders aged 16 to 21 was
inaugurated and expanded. In the 1930s and since World War II
diversification has continued, with the development of open facilities
for adult offenders, the use of detention centers as alternatives to

conventional prisons, and creation of many specialized facilities. For the bulk of the prison population, though, the primary emphasis has not greatly changed: Prisons are designed to deter and punish as much as to rehabilitate.

The New South Wales prison system has had a strongly punitive orientation from the beginning. Nonetheless, serious efforts at devising positive programs of rehabilitation were made beginning early in the nineteenth century. During the penal colony days it was customary to grant "tickets of leave" to deserving convicts, but attempts to introduce incentive systems for well-behaved and productive prisoners were suppressed by higher authority when attempted in 1810-1820, the early 1840s, and again in the 1850s. A select committee in 1861 advocated substantial reforms, but few were made. In the 1880s and 1890s the prisons were overcrowded by drunks, vagrants, the aged, and the insane, and little money or attention was given to rehabilitation. The first wide-ranging prison reforms, introduced in the mid-1890s, included classification and assignment of prisoners according to type of offense, improvement of libraries, remission of sentences, probation for first offenders, and the establishment of associations for aiding discharged prisoners— much the same kinds of practices that had been initiated in Sweden some 50 years earlier.

The timing of the New South Wales reforms bears some explanation. Early reforms in Sweden had royal backing, and the initial English reforms were the result of a century of advocacy by liberal members of the middle class. The main impetus for prison reform and policies of rehabilitation in New South Wales has come from the working class—and organized labor did not gain substantial political influence until the turn of the century. Since then reforms have been slow and have met resistance from conservative, mainly middle-class and rural political groups. In 1905 provisions were made for indeterminate sentences (i.e., terms that could be varied according to the rehabilitative progress of the defendant), but this type of sentencing was rarely used because it challenged the dominant preference for punishment. Special facilities for juveniles were established as early as the 1880s, but the first minimum-security facilities for adult offenders were set up only in the late 1920s. Reforms since World War II have included better classification systems, the introduction of psychological counseling services, and in 1951 an institutionalized parole system—long after such systems were established in most of the West.

"Reform" seems to be inappropriate to describe what has happened in the prisons of Bengal during the past century, although there is some evidence of relative improvement. Prison sentences in

Bengal in the nineteenth and twentieth centuries were usually rather short, from a few months to a few years. An economic motive can be inferred: Prison costs are reduced by keeping sentences brief. Imprisonment had its risks, however. A prison report for 1852-1853 notes that the inmates of the Presidency Jail in Calcutta had a mortality rate of some thirteen percent per year (cf. two percent in English jails of the period); this was attributed to bad diet, unsanitary prison conditions, and the "poor health" of new prisoners. By the turn of the century prison mortality was down to perhaps six percent a year. Colonial commissions and officials sometimes recommended improvements in the jails, but the suggestions were generally rejected, one ground being that the institutions might become too attractive to impoverished Bengalis. In the twentieth century, and especially since independence, prison reports reflect an ideological commitment to rehabilitation; scarce resources presumably prevent the implementation of broadly effective policies. The practical penal "reform" in Bengal is this: From the 1920s on there has been a decline in the average length of sentence, and since independence fewer offenders have been committed to prison. The moral is clear enough. Custodial care and rehabilitation in a prison setting are a social luxury that poor societies now can afford no more easily than could their European counterparts three centuries ago.

Imprisonment became the principal means of punishment for serious crime in all three Western societies during an era when conviction rates were declining. At the dawn of the present century, prisons in England and New South Wales were grim places, and those of Sweden were only slightly less unpleasant. The existence and reputation of these institutions may have had a general deterrent effect for people outside them; their inmates certainly were kept out of circulation and mischief for longer periods than at present. Objectively, reforms have made prison existence less uncomfortable. Subjectively, however, prisons impose a loss of freedom and comfort that probably are as severe, by comparison with contemporary standards of life outside prison, as they were a century ago. If prisons now have lost their presumed deterrent effects, it is not because of their "comforts." The rapid increase in convictions during the last 25 years has far outpaced prison expansion, which means that fewer people can be sent to prison, and sentences are shorter. These constraints on officials fit hand in glove with reformers' urgings that more reliance be placed on noncustodial treatment. For officials, the immediate costs of noncustodial alternatives are lower. And from the point of view of the offender, the risks of prison are thereby reduced. The ultimate social costs of this calculus depend on the alternatives to punishment and their effects.

Alternatives to Imprisonment

One ancient alternative to imprisonment is the imposition of fines. Throughout the era dealt with in this study, offenders could pay fines in lieu of nastier punishments, especially for petty offenses but also for some more serious ones. The use of fines introduces a specific kind of class bias into punishment; those who are prosperous can pay their way out of trouble, and the poor (like debtors previously) are subject to imprisonment. In the three Western societies various reforms have been made to reduce this kind of inequity. In England, after 1914 when a law was passed giving individuals additional time to pay fines, prison admissions in default of fines declined by half. In 1972 a system of "community service orders" was inaugurated: Offenders could be required to give their free time to community projects in lieu of fines or imprisonment. In New South Wales, where many were imprisoned for nonpayment of fines, partial payment entitled the offender to partial remission of sentences beginning in 1899. Even so, as of 1919 two-thirds of new prisoners were jailed for default on fines. Sweden has followed the more equitable procedure: Beginning in the 1930s policies were introduced whereby fines are assessed in proportion to offenders' income and can be paid in installments. In Calcutta, in what appears to be a policy of growing leniency, the average fine assessed has declined since the 1920s.

Fines are an alternative to imprisonment but a punishment nevertheless. The most significant innovations of the twentieth century are those designed to encourage the reintegration of offenders into society. One of the earliest and most widespread practices of this kind is the suspended sentence, coupled with probation services: in a phrase, warning and help. In England after 1879, first offenders could be "bound over" (i.e., discharged on payment of security), and a system of supervised probation was introduced in 1907. Since 1972 courts are enjoined from imprisoning defendants who have not been in prison before, unless convinced no other measures are appropriate, and have been empowered to defer sentences for up to six months, then suspend them altogether if circumstances warrant. New South Wales provided probation for first offenders in 1894 and has continued to expand the system. In Sweden judges could award suspended sentences beginning in 1906, first for offenses that called for sentences of up to six months, later (1918) for sentences of up to one year, and now (since 1944) for sentences up to two years. Parole systems serve a similar function for prisoners who have served part of their sentence and are judged ready to return to ordinary life. New South Wales was late in devising regular parole procedures but expanded the new programs rapidly; between 1965 and 1971 the number of prisoners annually released on parole tripled. Sweden introduced regular parole procedures at the same time as probation, and 70 percent of the persons for whom the Corrections Board had responsibility were not in institutions by 1965; in 1975 the figure exceeded 80 percent. These policies work because there is an extensive system of community-based corrections and aftercare. In the mid-1970s Sweden had 12,000 volunteer supervisors of parolees and probationers.

The ultimate thrust of innovation in rehabilitation is to do away with imprisonment entirely. Nothing in the English, New South Wales, or Bengal experience suggests that these countries are on the verge of closing their jails, but Sweden has moved decidedly in that direction. The number of persons in custody in Sweden has declined steadily, and by 1975 they numbered only 4,000 in a population in excess of 8,000,000. About half of those were in minimum-security and youth facilities. The Swedish prisoners benefited from a furlough system, instituted in 1938 and since expanded, whereby about 10,000 home visits a year are granted. In addition there are holiday prisons where long-term prisoners spend time with their families. A number of prisoners also take advantage of a work release program (as they do in England and New South Wales), spending their working days away from prison. Despite this exceptional emphasis on reintegration, the current view is that institutional treatment remains a barrier to rehabilitation and increases recidivism. A number of Swedish officials and academics favor the elimination of custodial care for all but a handful of the most dangerous offenders.

Sweden has been in the forefront of the twentieth century movement toward noncustodial rehabilitation, but the same tendencies are evident to a lesser degree in England, New South Wales, and other Western societies. In 1976, for example, some members of Britain's ruling Labour Party proposed that imprisonment be abolished as a punishment for property crime. We may ask in conclusion what motives and interests underlie the tendency. The basic social purpose is not very different from the humanitarian objectives expressed by John Howard or for that matter by the middle-class nineteenth century advocates of the work ethic. Simply, it is to salvage the lives of offenders so that they can become "normal" and productive members of society. The "radical" innovations of Swedish and other penal reformers are based on the premise that imprisonment is an inhumane and inadequate means to an end that is better achieved by community-based rehabilitation. Like other intellectual currents of reform in policies of public order, this one has not come to fruition by sheer intellectual force. Two practical conditions have reinforced it, one economic and the other political. Prisons are expensive institutions, expecially when prison labor can no longer be exploited to public profit. Resistance to prison expansion evidently was an important consideration for those who established probation systems and partial remission of sentences in New South Wales at the beginning of the century. It also helped motivate the expansion of probation and parole in the three Western societies in the 1960s and 1970s. Given a rising number of convicted offenders, it is cheaper to release the least dangerous individuals than to build new facilities.

The political condition for policies of reform and rehabilitation is provided by the leaders and legislative spokesmen of labor parties, who usually have been more ready than middle-class parties in all three Western societies to support rehabilitative over punitive policies. The working classes have provided the bulk of the clientele of the prison systems of all societies we know anything about, and in these three societies in particular, working-class leaders are only a few decades removed from the era in which labor activists were often imprisoned. Thus the contemporary penal reforms advocated by liberal and radical experts and officials have an economic rationale that appeals to the more prosperous classes, as well as a natural political base of support. This interpretation—it is only that—is not necessarily applicable to other societies nor to the United States in particular, because evidence suggests that the American working class feels more victimized by crime than by punishment. The future prospect in all the Western societies is that ordinary citizens' growing fear of crime will erode support for policies of leniency and rehabilitation that do not seem to work. The empirical evidence, however, suggests that offenders dealt with leniently are not much more or less likely to show up again in court than those dealt with harshly.[7] The real roots of the problem seem to lie not in recidivism per se but in the growing number of people who indulge in crime in the first place.

NOTES TO CHAPTER VI.5

1. See especially Georg Rusche and Otto Kirchheimer, *Punishment and Social Structure* (New York: Columbia University Press, 1939).

2. Christian Henelius, *Tractatus politicus de Aerario* (Berlin, 1670), p. 325, cited in Rusche and Kirchheimer, op. cit., p. 19.

3. The data are averaged by decade for Sweden, and in five- and three-year intervals for New South Wales and Middlesex, respectively. The sources of the Swedish and New South Wales data are given in our studies of Stockholm and Sydney. The Middlesex data for 1750 to 1810 are from Leon Radzinowicz, *A History of English Criminal Law and its Administration from 1750*, Vol. I (London: Stevens, 1948). After 1811 they are our compilation from *Parliamentary Papers, Accounts and Papers:* 1818 (419) XVI 183; 1819 VIII 4; 1819 (62) XVII 295; 1830-31 (105) XII 461; 1837 (165) XLVI 255; 1842 (36) XXXII 545; 1846 (21) XXXIV 763.

4. Rusche and Kirchheimer, op. cit., p. 42.

5. See J. J. Tobias, *Crime and Industrial Society in the Nineteenth Century* (London: Penguin, 1972), pp. 88-107, 249-252.

6. New South Wales Legislative Council, "Extracts from the Report of the Committee on the Subject of Tread-Wheel Labour" (Sydney: 1825), p. 348.

7. Comparative evidence on recidivism was not gathered in this study. The empirical evidence up to the 1960s has been summarized in a series of reports prepared for the Council of Europe, e.g. Leslie T. Wilkins, *The Effectiveness of Punishment and Other Measures of Treatment for Adult Offenders* (Strasbourg: Council of Europe, Criminological Research Council, 1965, mimeo).

Chapter VI.6

TOWARD A THEORY OF
PUBLIC DISORDER

Thus far this study has hewed close to the historical facts of crime, civil strife, and the political context of such activities in four urban societies. The evidence has sometimes suggested interpretations and generalizations that challenge conventional wisdom, but always with the implicit qualification that they are based on less-than-complete information from a less-than-representative sample of societies. This chapter moves beyond the particulars of London, Stockholm, Sydney, and Calcutta to a more general understanding of the conditions on which public order and disorder depend. This effort takes the form of a theoretical model, not a formal theory. It specifies the kinds of conditions that cause disorder and maps their connections, but does not include the definitions and hypotheses required by fully elaborated theory. It draws upon the evidence of the four city studies to illustrate these causal connections, but does not claim that the evidence is a test of the model. The model came first, in the sense that the core of it was specified before the city studies were carried out. It was then a heuristic device, a guide to collecting and ordering information on a disorderly subject. Now there is sufficient information to amplify it, and we hope that others will find it worth using and testing.

THEORIES OF CRIME AND CONFLICT

Public disorder consists of threatening collective and individual actions that are subject to public control; the definition was elaborated in Chapter I.2. A general explanation or theory of public disorder as defined here should stipulate the conditions under which diverse kinds of social disorder become a matter of public concern, what kinds of interests and circumstances determine the shape of public response, and the effects of public control on disorder—as well as the impact of disorder on public policies. We know of no such theoretical explanation. Changes in the extent of social disorder obviously are one major source of change in public disorder, even though there is no one-to-one correspondence between the two. The etiology of social disorder therefore provides a well-explored point of departure for a theory of public disorder.

Criminogenic Theories

Studies that offer explanations of "crime"[1] address three rather different questions. First, what "causes" individuals to commit criminal acts? This is usually answered by citing some combination of the physical and mental characteristics of the offender and of his social experience and circumstances. Second, what determines whether an individual is labeled and treated as a criminal? The typical answer refers to the characteristics and interests of the enforcers. Third, why do the extent and type of criminal behaviors differ from one social group to another and from one time to the next?

The third question is more relevant to the determination of the causes of changes in public disorder, but most answers given draw on elements of the explanations offered in response to the first two questions. "Crime" is greater in some places and times because there and then are concentrated certain types of people. Or social conditions conspire there to generate frequent criminal behavior. Or at these junctures the enforcers are most interested in asserting their control.

There are numerous criminogenic theories in each category described, but none is universely accepted, and most are used by scholars and officials alike in eclectic combination with other theories. This tendency to devise multiple and ad hoc explanations for "crime" is reinforced by the great variety of "criminal" behaviors. Some explanations fit some kinds of threatening behavior better than others. Nettler has reviewed many current criminogenic theories that cite social factors and classifies them into four types.[2] Two focus on some form of culture conflict: The source of "crime" is said to be "some division within a society that is associated with differential acceptance of legal norms." Subcultural explanations attribute "crime" to the distinctive standards of behavior said to characterize lower class and ethnic groups; some of the "normal" behaviors of these groups are so deviant from the standards of dominant groups that they are labeled and treated as criminal. Structural explanations attribute "crime" to disparities between peoples' socially induced wants and the means available for their satisfaction; people whose social means are painful to use, limited, or ineffective are likely to resort to criminally deviant ways of getting what they want.[3] The two kinds of theory are not necessarily inconsistent. Entire social groups may be "structurally" handicapped in the pursuit of goals that other groups enjoy freely, and in response the former may develop deviant "subcultural" means to achieve satisfaction.

The other two kinds of explanation Nettler labels "sociopsychological." They "place more of the causal emphasis upon the individual actor, or upon 'kinds' of actors, and upon the interaction between these persons." Symbolic-interactionist theories attribute criminal behavior to what people learn from others about the relative desirability of different ways of acting, and how they learn to think of themselves from what others label them and do to them.[4] Control theories do not ask why people engage in criminal behavior, but why most people most of the time remain within the law. The answer in these theories is "discipline," both that which is internalized by children during socialization and that which is imposed by external social pressure and authorities later in life.[5] These two kinds of theory also are mutually compatible, at least at a very general level. People will do what they are encouraged to do and control what they are obliged to control; but if others' demands on them are too painful, they may react by living up to parents' and authorities' worst rather than best expectations.

The cultural conflict and sociopsychological approaches to explaining "crime" have enough common ground to justify joining them in a kind of universal social theory. Such a theory is likely to be too abstract to be tested or to inform policy, however. By attempting to explain everything in general, it would risk explaining nothing in particular. Moreover such a theory would be difficult if not impossible to assess in most kinds of historical and comparative research. Historical studies of crime and public order are limited to what can be observed mainly in records of public (especially official) policies and actions, and to aggregate measures of demographic and economic conditions. Information on the beliefs, social wants, and opportunities of less-advantaged historical groups is scanty. The same is true of information on such matters as how and how well or badly children have been socialized. What the sociological theorist should be testing—namely, the effects of cultural conflict and lacunae in social control on the extent of deviant or disorderly behavior—the historian will be disposed to treat as an assumption: Changes in criminality are visible evidence of shifting patterns of cultural conflict and social control that can best be detected by observing their consequences for public order.

The principal limitation of the sociological explanations of crime just reviewed is their inattention to crime's political circumstances. When political factors are weighed in, as in labeling theory, or in Richard Quinney's work, it generally is in the form of simplistic assumptions about the self-serving or class-serving operation of structures of authority. Political interests and institutions are a good deal more diverse, and have more variable effects on crime and public order, than is suggested by the criminogenic theories already surveyed. Some of these political conditions are incorporated in the preliminary theory of public disorder to be proposed. First, however, we review some of the explanations put forward for the other face of social disorder, civil strife.

The Etiology of Civil Strife

General theories about civil strife tend to concentrate on one of two areas. The first kind of theorizing considers why and how particular kinds of conflict occur. Revolution is the most popular subject here; coups d'état also have attracted a good deal of theoretical attention and so have riots, especially ethnic and communal riots. The second area involves the factors that determine the types and magnitude of civil strife in entire societies. The first kind of theory is concerned with a class of events, the second with the common properties of many kinds of events. Yet the two are complementary, the second kind of theory being the more general.

There are at least four distinguishable approaches to explaining civil strife, in particular forms or in general. Two share a concern with the psychological properties of people who participate in strife, the others explain strife solely in terms of properties of social systems. To give them labels, they are psychological, sociopsychological, social structural, and group conflict theories, respectively. In attempting to account for the behavior of participants in strife, some psychological theories specify the psychodynamic processes that make revolutionary leaders, others emphasize the extent to which rebels share such psychological properties as alienation and frustration.[6] The sociopsychological theories begin with premises about the conflict-disposing states of mind of rebels but put the weight of explanation on the social conditions that create or alter those states of mind. Some also specify the situational conditions that determine how men act on their motivations and attitudes. A premise common to a number of these theories is that strife is a collective response to discontent, which arises from discrepancies between peoples' expectations and attainments. To explain strife it therefore is necessary to identify the social conditions that increase men's expectations or frustrate their attempts to obtain satisfaction.[7]

The social-structural theories of strife differ in emphasis rather than kind from the more psychological theories. They assume that a fundamental social dislocation, sometimes called "strain" or "dysfunction," is the necessary precondition for strife. The origins of social dislocation are specified, as are the conditions influencing its outcome. But little or no attention is given to the psychological manifestations.[8]

These approaches to theory all purport to explain why groups resist or challenge the social status quo. A competing paradigm for theory asks, not "why men rebel," but how and why it is that groups in societies come into conflict. The group conflict theories in this tradition all assume that strife arises from competition between groups for valued conditions and positions. Some of them, like Marx's theory of revolutionary change, emphasize the class bases of conflict: They are concerned with contention between top-dog and underdog groups over their respective shares of goods, power, and status. Other group conflict theories attribute strife to differences of interest among groups and institutions generally, not just those bearing a hierarchic relation to one another.[9] The most consequential difference between the two approaches to conflict theory is that the former focuses on a more limited set of instances, namely, those involving repression and resistance.

Theoretical explanations of civil strife, like the criminogenic theories, can be shown to converge at a very abstract level. All assume that strife occurs because people, individually or collectively, are prevented from attaining their objectives by constraints imposed by circumstances—including what other groups have and do. The greater such constraints on a group of people, the more likely its members are to clash with other groups. Such an "explanation" is almost truistic, but it is useful in a theory of public disorder: Some such mechanism can be assumed to determine the extent of civil strife in any society at any time.

THE IMMEDIATE CONDITIONS OF PUBLIC DISORDER

Explaining why "crime" and civil strife occur is not the same as accounting for the extent of public disorder. Only some kinds of threatening behavior are regarded as a public responsibility, and the boundaries between "public" and "private" vary widely. Within the "public" realm some groups are much better able than others to translate their concerns into policies of public control. These two kinds of conditions are of equal and immediate importance in determining the effective scope of public disorder: the laws defining public disorder and the policies and institutions established to translate legal conceptions into practical control. The first delineate the formal boundaries of publicly unacceptable disorder, specify penalties, and in effect provide a warrant for collective action. The latter determine how much effort can in fact be given to detecting, controlling, and punishing those who violate the laws. Attempts at controlling disorder can increase because of a change in patterns of threatening behavior; they also can increase because legal redefinitions direct attention to new kinds of "criminality" and collective behavior. Moreover the extent of crime and strife that is officially recorded and policed has spinoff effects on the perceptions of disorder held by officials and their political public, and their willingness to countenance greater, or different, efforts at control.

To account for changes in public disorder we must understand not only why behavior changes, but why legal definitions and policies of public order are changed. One source of change is growing public concern about disorder: Authorities may formulate new laws and policies to give the appearance of action in response to increasing social disorder, and those laws and policies may ultimately reduce the activities that give rise to public concern. In other words there is a good deal of circularity in the processes that generate public disorder. This argument is summarized in Figure VI.6.1, where each

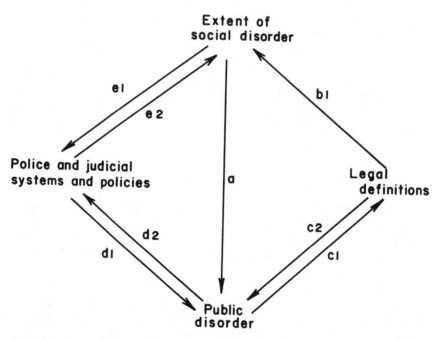

Figure VI.6.1 The immediate conditions of public disorder

arrow means "is one of the causes of." Each of the lettered arrows can be described, in general terms, and most of them illustrated with examples from the four city studies.

Definitions and Public Disorder (c_1, c_2)

Official definitions of crime vary considerably among societies and over time within them. Rising concern about disorder is one of the principal sources of change in definitions. A simple example of the authoritative redefinition of crime was the New South Wales Masters and Servants Act of 1828, which created the offenses of neglect of work and absence from work. There was presumably little change in real behavior, but authorities decided—during a severe labor shortage—to criminalize, sanction, and thereby reduce a particular kind of undesirable behavior.[10] In this instance elites' concern about disorder had impelled redefinition, a connection symbolized by the arrow c_1. The creation of a new kind of offense, in this example and in general, is usually followed by increased arrests and prosecutions, which all show up in criminal statistics as an upward trend in criminality, a consequence represented by arrow c_2. Thus the broadening of legal definitions ordinarily increases the extent of "public disorder" as measured by indicators of crime.

The interests that motivate expanding concepts of criminality are not necessarily those of a small elite. In Sweden a temperance movement established in the 1870s became one of the great popular movements of Swedish society, mobilizing members of the working class no less than middle-class and professional people. Holding that alcohol was the principal source of misery and poverty among the workers, the movement tried strenuously to restrict the sale of intoxicating beverages by controlling production and distribution and by outright prohibition. Public drunkenness had long been a criminal offense in Stockholm, but the laws enacted in response to the demands of the temperance movement created categories of offenses for those who distilled and distributed corn brandy and sold beer in violation of the new regulations. The rates of crime increased as a consequence. The temperance movement also led, eventually, to the treatment of alcoholism as a social disease rather than a crime.

Concern about civil strife also affects and is affected by legal definitions. When particular kinds of strife become issues of elite or general concern, a typical response is the passage of laws that criminalize some of the behaviors in question. In England in the nineteenth century (and earlier) a great many bills designed to eliminate or restrict what are now called trade unions were drafted especially to give magistrates powers to punish labor organizers and strikers. In Bengal between 1900 and the end of colonial rule there were approximately fifteen major modifications in the criminal law, of which eleven aimed specifically at controlling collective political action—by declaring associations illegal, banning various kinds of public meetings, providing for detention and the suspension of civil rights, and so forth. These laws were widely employed in efforts to control the nationalistic movement, and their effects are evident in indicators of public disorder.

Definitions, Crime, and Strife (b_1)

It is problematic whether changes in legal definition alone can change the patterns of social disorder, either "crime" or strife. Legal changes are supposed to depend for any deterrent effect they may have on the threat, and occasional actuality, of punishment. The case for a linkage of the sort represented in Figure VI.6.1 by arrow b_1 rests on evidence that in some societies, for many citizens, "the law" has a moral force sufficient to ensure that legal change brought about by legitimate authorities using legitimate procedures will discourage newly criminalized behavior. Direct evidence for this is very difficult to come by, but New South Wales affords one dramatic example. When legislation enacted during World War I made the International Workers of the World an illegal organization, its leaders suspended activities and presented themselves for arrest. The validity of the example is suspect, however, because the behavior was probably motivated as much by bravado as by acceptance of the legitimacy of the new law.

The extent of threatening social behavior affects legal definitions in more visible ways. As suggested previously, an increase in some kinds of strife or deviance increases public concern, giving rise in turn to elite or popular demands for legal redefinition. It is also possible that a decline in the sense of concern about particular kinds of behavior paves the way for their decriminalization, but there are relatively few examples of formal decriminalization in the four societies we have studied. One is the decriminalization of homosexuality in England during the 1960s; another is the Swedish relaxation of legal restraints on abortion. In both instances, however, it was not behavior that changed but prevailing notions of what behavior was acceptable, or anyway tolerable enough not to require public control.

Still another way in which the extent of crime and strife can affect legal definitions is illustrated by the "decriminalization" of labor organizations and strike activity, a process that occurred in all four societies, albeit at different times and in different circumstances. As the industrial labor force grew in size so did labor organizing and strike activity, despite vigorous and sporadically effective official efforts at suppression. Generally the workers redoubled their efforts with some redirection to political activity; as a result, efforts at control became too costly and in some instances downright impossible to continue. In terms of our model, the outcome in these societies was a redefinition of public disorder in norms and in formal-legal terms: Workers gained enough influence to ensure that most activities of organized labor became politically tolerable, whereupon the legal regulation of the activities in question was markedly relaxed. In the three Western societies the process involved no abrupt, fundamental political upheaval; in India workers were among the vanguard of the revolutionary movement that overturned, not the rules of the game, but the players.

In the examples just cited the effects of social disorder on legal definitions are mediated by political factors, notably the scope of public concern about what constitutes unacceptable individual and collective behavior. Is this principle general enough to be made a theoretical assumption? We symbolize our belief that this is true by showing no direct link in Figure VI.6.1 between the extent of social disorder on the one hand and legal definitions on the other. This is not a trivial assumption: It directs attention to the diverse political processes that intervene between changes in "disorderly" behavior and formal-legal specification of the behaviors that deserve public control.

Police, Punishment, and Public Disorder (d_1, d_2)

Police systems vary in their primary objective: They may be mainly concerned with controlling civil strife (as in Calcutta throughout the twentieth century), or with protecting a ruling class, rather than preventing and detecting individual crime—which is the conventional task of contemporary police. Whatever their principal tasks, police systems can be more or less comprehensive and efficient, and more or less self-serving, in detecting and recording illegal acts and in arresting suspects. How thoroughly they keep records and perform their duties is directly reflected in crime statistics, which provide our main indicators of "public disorder." Police efficiency is less directly reflected in the extent of public concern about crime. Victimization surveys and everyday observation demonstrate that a large volume of illegal behavior goes undetected, or at least unreported, in contemporary societies. This reservoir is an ever-present potential for "crime waves" arising from increased reporting by the public (linkage d_2) or from increased efforts at detection and apprehension by the police (linkage d_1). The publicity given "crime waves" has been a major reinforcement for public alarm about disorder in Western societies throughout this century, not merely in the last 25 years, and some of these phenomena have been much more a function of police action and journalistic incitement than of changes in social behavior. Examples involving crimes against sexual morality are particularly numerous. A case in point was a fivefold increase in arrest rates for prostitution offenses in New South Wales between 1958 and the early 1960s, followed by an equally precipitous decline, apparently due to a police crackdown preceded by considerable expression of moral opposition. The other side of the coin is represented by an abrupt temporary decline in arrests for soliciting in London in the early 1920s. Police made a particularly ill-advised arrest, creating such a public furor that some magistrates refused to convict and police enforcement was temporarily suspended.

The connections between police and judicial policies and public disorder can be even more complex. Growth in public concern about disorder often may stimulate more rigorous enforcement and lead to changes in the way the courts carry out business: Accused offenders may face greater likelihood of being found guilty and may receive sentences longer than heretofore given. In the history of New South Wales, for example, the following sequence of events is repeatedly observed. First is an increase in public concern, stimulated by the fulminations of clergymen, journalists, and/or citizens' action groups, about some dramatic type of crime—bushranging, Chinese opium dens, razor gangs, abortion, pack-rape, or what have you. One or a handful of publicized instances of the crime usually suffices to generate the wave of concern. What follows is a flurry of official pronouncements and legislative activity, prescribing heavy penalties for the crime, now more precisely defined, and also intensified police activity and the imposition of harsh sentences on offenders. Public concern soon subsides, usually paralleling a drop in the incidence of reported offenses as the police relax their vigilance; still later the courts begin to hand down less severe sentences.

A feature of these episodes of public disorder that bears special mention is the "placebo effect" of changing police and judicial policies in response to rising public disorder. Irrespective of whether or not the new policies affect social behavior—which is generally unknown anyway—"crackdowns" often are intrinsically satisfying to those who raised the alarm. Such episodes also furnish a rationale for increasing the resources of police and judicial systems. On a number of occasions, in all the four cities, increases in public disorder led to strengthening and reorganization of police forces. This is not a general warrant for a cynical "theory" to the effect that crime waves are generated by the police for self-serving purposes, but there is no doubt that crime reports and the sense of public disorder about both crime and strife are sometimes manipulated by officials and political groups to justify particular judicial and police policies. In a recent study of urban American crime rates, for example, Seidman and

Couzens demonstrate that rates of serious property crime in 1970-1971 were systematically deflated in eight of 30 cities by undervaluing larcenies; in the case of Washington, D.C., the "results" were used to demonstrate the "success" of the federal government's new anticrime program.[11]

Public Policies and Behavioral Control (e_1, e_2)

The last linkages in this part of the model are the connections between police and judicial policies and the objective extent of threatening social behavior. It is a token of popular and official belief that certain public order policies reduce crime and strife and others do not. Linkage e_2 symbolizes these multifarious connections. Neither officials, academics, politicos, nor ordinary citizens agree on which policies have which effect, but all believe that something works. It is likely that the more certain is punishment for crime, the lower is the "true" incidence of criminal behavior; and if certainty is fairly high, the more severe the punishment, the greater the deterrent effect. This equation does not necessarily hold for civil strife, however. The frequent escalation of demonstrations and strikes into violent confrontations in response to police intervention suggests what can happen on a small scale; the history of the nationalist movement in Bengal illustrates the point on a grand scale. The effectiveness of policies of public order for controlling strife rests more on dissuading potential participants than on punishing activists. If the participants are sufficiently numerous and serious, the existing institutions of public order can almost always be overwhelmed.

The hypothetical effects of punishment on crime cannot readily be demonstrated in the cities we studied because ordinarily the certainty of detection and arrest, and the likelihood of subsequent punishment, were too low to make much difference for the more common crimes—especially theft and "crimes against morality and custom." No doubt that is a principal reason for their commonness: Only by a massive and sustained investment in "order maintenance" and a Stalinist disregard for due process could the police and courts alone reduce substantially the incidence of the more frequently committed crimes. As a rule the intense efforts required to raise the risks of crime are devoted to offenses that are socially and politically most threatening—murder, kidnapping, terrorism, and a few others.

The new policies and reformed institutions of public order in the three Western cities in the nineteenth century apparently reduced the incidence of crime. We hypothesize that this occurred because policies and institutions were linked, by accident or design, with social changes that eroded the conditions responsible for threatening behavior. For example, the incidence of property crime in London in the second quarter of the nineteenth century was extraordinarily high. Much of it was perpetrated by homeless youths now labeled "delinquents." Those who survived the rigors of street life and numerous brief stays in poisonously unhealthy prisons graduated into the "criminal class" of adults, who were both victims and agents of much other social nastiness. Midcentury, however, brought the establishment of a system of reformatory and industrial schools where youthful offenders were confined for long periods, fed regularly, and given rudimentary training. This shift in penal practices coincided with a long-term expansion of economic opportunities; the two together appear to have been a major cause of the significant decline in theft that began in the 1850s and the eventual diminution of the distinctive "criminal class."

The general principle proposed here is that the policies followed by the police, judicial, and penal institutions have their intended effects on criminal behavior only in limited social circumstances. Once those rather narrow limits are exceeded, by larger cultural, socioeconomic, or political changes, established policies of public order have less and less effect and ultimately may be self-defeating. This brings us to the causal linkage labeled e_1 in Figure VI.6.1: the direct effects of social disorder on police and judicial systems and policies. An answer for strife has already been suggested: If it is sufficiently intense, widespread, and prolonged, it can overwhelm the institutions of public order. This is seemingly what happened in Bengal. The burgeoning nationalism of 1910-1946 eroded the capacity of the police and courts to deal with ordinary crime and ultimately their capacity to do anything at all, as long as they remained under British control. A sustained increase in serious "crime" is likely to have comparable effects. As it increases, conventional efforts at control are likely to be increased; insofar as they fail to work, the police and courts will put heavier emphasis on ritualistic responses and institutional self-preservation. Reform and renovation are not ruled out, but to be effective they need to be consonant with whatever changing social circumstances are responsible for the changes in patterns of behavior.

The immediate conditions of public disorder are so interdependent that it is difficult indeed to understand one without describing the others. And that is one of the points of the discussion just concluded. The causal connections among the conditions of public order can be neatly summarized in a model such as Figure VI.6.1, but that is no license for studying any one of them in isolation. It also bears repeating that this model is not explicit enough to be a "theory" of public disorder. Few hypotheses have spelled out precise connections among any of these conditions. Each refers not to one but a whole set of variables. Public disorder has several aspects, for example, and the efforts and effects of police and judicial systems comprise many characteristics. Formal theory would require that each be separately defined and linked by assumption or hypothesis with the others. It is too soon for this kind of detailed conceptualization. The general suggestion is that such connections are plausible and merit more careful empirical study and theoretical specification. Our city studies are a contribution to the first of these tasks.

THE INDIRECT CONDITIONS OF PUBLIC DISORDER

Time and again the discussion just concluded refers to factors like elites' interests and socioeconomic conditions that alter one or another of the immediate conditions of public disorder. The theories about the causes of "crime" and civil conflict, reviewed earlier, include much longer lists of social conditions thought to affect disorder, directly or indirectly. We now ask how we can think about and organize information on these conditions and their effects.[12]

The "exogenous" influences on public disorder are of three general types, here labeled "elite goals," "economic imperatives," and "social scale and cultural heterogeneity." The goals and interests of the political elite shape legal definitions of disorder and the nature of official responses to it. The structure and requirements of the eco-

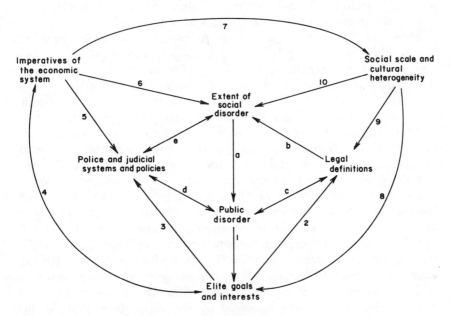

Figure VI.6.2 The indirect conditions of public disorder

nomic system influence the goals of the elite and limit the resources members of the elite can give to order maintenance. Far from least, much of the civil strife and some "crime" in contemporary societies flows from the onerous requirements of systems of production and the unequal distribution of their products. Social scale and cultural heterogeneity are also implicated as causes of disorder, according to some of the criminogenic and conflict theories already reviewed, as well as being interdependent with elite goals and economic imperatives. Proposals about the relations among these variables, and their effects on public disorder, can be discussed in relation to the schematization of Figure VI.6.2.

Goals and Interests of the Political Elite

Insofar as political elites are directly threatened by social disorder (linkage 1 of Figure VI.6.2), they are almost certain to attempt to control it by whatever means come to hand (linkages 2 and 3). If their personal property and safety are at risk, one can expect that at a minimum they will establish safeguards for themselves. If their position and perquisites are threatened by the collective action of other groups, those actions too will be restrained by any legal and institutional means available. The same two principles apply to non-elites, but these groups are not always able to give their views the force of law and the weight of official sanction. Insofar as non-elites are politically influential, their goals and interests are also directly relevant to the shaping of laws and policies of public order.

Elites have objectives and face problems other than those of maintaining their conception of public order. If their primary objective is to impose a particular moral or political orthodoxy on society, they will take one tack in defining and controlling disorder; if they are mainly concerned with such goals as economic growth, international conquest, or simply maintaining their own perquisites, they will take quite a different approach. There also are great differences in elites' assumptions about the appropriateness and effectiveness of different means for maintaining order—however that term is defined. Elites' views are vital on questions such as the following: What categories or modes of social activity are most valued and disvalued? How humanely or callously ought people to treat one another? Where does the locus of responsibility for deviance fall—on the individual, on his primary group, or on society at large? What are the relative merits of negative and positive sanctions as means of influencing behavior? Of course other groups in society have views on such questions, but it is the political elite whose norms are most directly translated into policies of public order. Thus there is virtually always an elite "tilt" to the laws and policies of public order, and the significant question is not "whether" but "how much."

The views of elites about the means and ends of social action are influenced by general economic and social considerations. They also are subject to modification as social and public circumstances change. An increase in the actual incidence of crime or strife is likely to increase the salience of order maintenance for the elite, and in any quasi-open political system, a rise in popular concern about disorder will likely have the same effect. The hypothesis can be stated explicitly: As official indicators of social disorder rise, the relative importance of order maintenance among elite goals also tends to rise. It is more doubtful whether there is a reverse process, whereby elites turn attention and resources away from order maintenance once their version of "order" has improved. The city studies afford numerous examples of ways in which those who define and police public order can "create" disorder. This possibility, combined with the tendency of specialized bureaucracies to perpetuate themselves, suggests that the institutions of public order are more readily expanded than contracted. The three Western cities treated here furnish ample evidence: Despite their common, long-term experience of declining common crimes from the mid-nineteenth century to the 1920s, their police forces continued to expand (commensurate with population) and to modernize. The scope of criminal law also was extended: A great deal of legislation was passed, defining and proscribing new kinds of offenses against sexual morality and public order especially. Such evidence is not definitive, of course, because these trends are backed by other factors as well—significantly, the functional necessity of regulating the increased traffic and commercial activities of growing cities.

Imperatives of the Economic System

The basis and structure of a society's system of production will directly or indirectly affect all other conditions of public disorder. First and most fundamentally, economic and ecological factors impose serious limits on the kinds of goals that can be pursued by elites (Figure II.6.2, linkage 4). They also constrain the kinds of institutions that can be maintained, including but not restricted to the institutions of public order (linkage 5). To take an extreme case, a society that produces only enough for bare subsistence of its members has no "surplus product" to support a specially privileged elite, much less to create specialized institutions of order maintenance. Highly productive capitalist and socialist societies enjoy a broader range of alternatives, but even Lyndon Johnson's "Great Society" of the late 1960s was unable to support both war and welfare. Moreover *any* division of labor and *any* pattern of distribution of goods create some kind of potential for conflict and social deviance (linkage 6). Division of labor creates differences of interest, over which groups will clash; and both produce a need for hierarchic control and coordination, which is always to some degree resented and resisted by those who are controlled.[13] Individually, men almost always aspire to more than they have, even when everyone has the same; and some in every society are driven or tempted to use "deviant" means to satisfy their aspirations.[14] Different modes of production and patterns of distribution generate different types and degrees of social disorder, but neither feudalism nor capitalism nor socialism nor utopian communism can be free of such dissonance.[15]

Certain kinds of connections are expected to exist between economic structures and the public order policies formulated by elites (linkage 4). For example, water diversion will be as heinous a crime in a hydraulic society as cattle theft is in a herding economy. If the economic system depends on the accumulation of material goods— whether for consumption or for capital investment—legal codes and public order policies will give especially close attention to crimes of acquisition. Civil strife involving workers will be of intense concern in economies that depend on large, docile supplies of cheap labor. Economic structures also will affect the specific institutions and policies chosen (linkage 5). The kinds of police systems established to carry out public order policies will be quite directly affected by a society's surplus product: Poor societies are likely to have small and weak police systems; the rich can devote large resources to the maintenance of public order. Thus a high level of public order may be a kind of social luxury, one that becomes a matter of elite concern only when surplus means for its attainment become available. Ways of treating offenders also are influenced by a society's modes of production and its fiscal status. Wealthy societies can afford to imprison and resocialize offenders; corporal punishment is more economically feasible for poor societies. And in societies where labor is scarce, or especially unpleasant economic tasks have to be performed, it is more likely that offenders will be put to forced labor than imprisoned or executed. Wealthy as the three Western societies in this study are, the evidence is that their elites at present would rather release offenders than invest additional resources in imprisonment or rehabilitation.

The characteristics of civil strife also are affected by modes of production, in at least three general ways (linkage 6). In any economic system that relies on a division of labor and authority, workers recurrently resist and contest the conditions of their servitude or employment. In slaveholding societies revolt was a dreaded occurrence, and feudal overlords faced always the threat of peasant rebellions. Colonial rulers and entrepreneurs must anticipate revolts, wars of independence, and crises of nationalization arising out of the ever-present resentment of indigenous clients and workers to the export of the fruits of their labor. Modern capitalists and managers of socialist economies are obliged to deal repeatedly with strikes, slowdowns, sabotage, and certainly in the United States and Britain, chronic theft by employees. These kinds of disorder are manifestations of "business as usual" in their respective economic systems. They are distinct from the exceptional episodes of resistance and rebellion by workers that accompany transformations from one type of economic system to another. Familiar examples of the latter in the Western historical experience are laborers' resistance to new economic arrangements, such as the English peasants who opposed the enclosure acts and, later, the machine-breaking Luddites, as well as the growing numbers of wage-earning laborers who struggled to gain economic bargaining rights and political suffrage. The third kind of economic-based conflict also occurs as a consequence of fundamental economic change, when rising economic classes—whether new feudal landowners, an urban bourgeoisie, or a new managerial elite— challenge the old political elite. Such challenges may be resolved by co-optation and accommodation, or by revolution.

Economic conditions, as distinct from economic structures, also have certain immediate effects on types and incidence of crime. Economic stress—declining productivity, rising unemployment—often is cited as a source of increased property crime and, depending on the society, as a cause of banditry, bread riots, or strikes. A second line of argument, which on its face is contradictory, is that increases in a society's wealth serve to increase the absolute and relative frequency of occurrence of property crime. There are two versions of the argument. One is that the affluence of rising classes inspires envy and deprivation in the less fortunate, who respond by taking what comes to hand. The other is simply that there is more to be stolen in affluent societies. The evidence of the city studies is that poverty *and* wealth are correlated with the incidence of common crime, not only theft but crimes against the person as well. In nineteenth century London, Stockholm, and New South Wales both theft and assault increased during periods of economic slump and declined when economic conditions improved again. Economic distress had very little effect on crime rates in either direction in the twentieth century, but as total productivity (wealth) increased, so did common crime. Evidently two separate causal processes were at work at different times. We can only speculate about whether the difference is due to the effects of a third variable or to a shift in the direction of social causality above some threshold in affluence.[16]

Social Scale and Cultural Heterogeneity

The economic structure of a society exerts a marked influence on the numbers and distribution of its population, the size and functions of its settlements, the diversity of interests among its members, the nature of social relations among individuals and groups, and the scope and complexity of its noneconomic institutions—in other words, almost everything (Figure VI.6.2, linkage 7). But it does not precisely determine these conditions. The scale and complexity of a society, and the extent to which it is comprised of diverse cultural groups, have important and independent effects on the conditions of public disorder. Two general kinds of connections of this kind are included in our model. The first is that social and cultural factors influence elite goals and interests (linkage 8). The priorities and preferred means of the elites will reflect the values and norms of the cultural groups from which they come; and their policies toward public order will vary depending on the extent of cultural heterogeneity. Socially heterogenous societies are characterized by two different approaches to public order. One defines the common public order narrowly and practices compromise and accommodation when formulating common laws and policies. The other imposes uniformity through coercive control of "deviant" cultural groups. The significance of social scale is that large and complex societies have much greater problems of public order than small and simple ones, because there are so many more people and activities to be coordinated and regulated. Large size and complexity cannot be maintained in a society unless these functional requirements are met.

Much evidence and theoretical speculation links social scale and cultural heterogeneity to the definition and extent of disorder (linkages 9 and 10). One general kind of argument is that the larger and more diverse a community, the less effective are informal, face-to-face methods of controlling and punishing deviance. Thus as cities and societies grow, the likelihood increases that the elites will find it necessary to define and proscribe unacceptable behavior, and the more likely they will be to rely on specialized institutions to maintain order. Moreover, as communities expand and become varied—conditions that usually follow on increasing specialization in economic activities—human interactions tend to become more complex and diverse, hence unpredictable. The typical, probably essential response of elites is to tighten legal definitions of acceptable behavior and to police such activities more carefully. A distinct trend in the four societies we studied here is the veritable explosion of laws and administrative codes designed to regulate day-to-day interactions, in domains as dissimilar as trade, public demeanor, and traffic.

One class of hypotheses especially relevant to social order in cities specifies ways in which increases in urban population and heterogeneity generate increased crime and strife (linkage 10). Four of the possible reasons are as follows.

1. Increasing cultural heterogeneity provides more varied standards of behavior, leading to erosion of the normative standards of behavior of the dominant social groups, hence fewer internal inhibitions to deviant behavior.

2. Increasing concentration of population leads to overcrowding, whose consequences may include physiological reactions that increase aggressiveness, or more social occasions for hostile interactions.

3. Increasing concentration of population contributes to "dehumanization" and anonymity of human relationships; the first of which helps justify aggressive and exploitative treatment of others, while the second makes it easier to get away with doing so.

4. Increasing size and heterogeneity together increase intergroup friction and provide more occasions for friction, which can lead to individual and collective attacks on members of opposing groups.

Still other paths from social scale and cultural heterogeneity to social disorder are mapped by the theories of crime and strife reviewed earlier. Cultural differentiation and conflict are important elements in Nettler's four types of criminogenic theories, and in all but the purely psychological kinds of explanations proposed for civil strife. This is not to claim that the concept of "social scale and cultural heterogeneity" comprises all the causal variables cited in explanations of crime and strife. It is possible, though, to map almost all the general socioeconomic and political conditions thought to affect social disorder onto the network of variables depicted in Figure VI.6.2. Those which are not aspects of scale and heterogeneity can be treated as aspects or consequences of the economic system, or of elite interests. Finally, most of the proposed psychosocial mechanisms by which social conditions are translated into "disorderly" behavior are consistent with the justifications offered previously for the connections indicated among the variables in the model.

The usefulness of the framework proposed here does not depend on its consistency with other theories: It has the similarities to others' arguments because some other theories have been incorporated into this larger framework. Its value depends on whether it facilitates further research on the nature and sources of public disorder. What it should do, and what it has done in this study, is to call attention to kinds of information not previously considered in this context, and to suggest new questions for precise theoretical treatment.

ON THE DECAY AND DISSOLUTION OF SOCIAL SYSTEMS

Social disorder, if sufficiently intense and prolonged, destroys social systems. A condition in which all are at war is a philosophical, empirical, and political definition of the absence of a social system. In developing the framework little has been said about the circumstances under which social systems can self-destruct. Some very tentative answers can be drawn out of the model, however, and two are mentioned briefly here. First, there is potential for "positive feedback" among the immediate conditions of public disorder (linkages a to e, Figure VI.6.2). That is, some kinds of policies of public order can have effects opposite from those intended for them; namely, they can increase rather than decrease social and public disorder. This is not only a theoretical possibility but one for which specific empirical examples can be extracted from the city studies, especially Calcutta. Second, positive feedback may develop among elements of the economic and social system and the extent of social disorder (linkages 6, 7, and 10). The expansion of economic systems tends to increase social scale and cultural diversity, which in turn can act to increase social disorder in a number of ways already suggested. Beyond some threshold, social disorder will undermine the economic system—directly by reducing the efficiency of production, indirectly by increasing the proportion of resources that must be drained off into order-maintenance activities.

Political elites play a crucial coordinating role in these processes; depending on their goals and their understanding of social causality, they may or may not be able and willing to make requisite adjustments in the economic system and policies of public order. Revolution is likely to ensue in the absence of such adjustments; yet revolution is no sure cure for social dissolution, since there is no guarantee that revolutionaries or anybody else possess the means and will to reconstruct a complex and orderly society. There has been no dramatic disintegration of social systems in recent Western history, which no doubt has reinforced the optimism about "social development" typical of Marxist and liberal scholars and ideologists alike. There are enough historical and non-Western examples, though, to suggest that theories founded on premises of irreversible social evolution are incomplete and suspect.

AN EPILOGUE ON POLICIES FOR PUBLIC ORDER

It is understandable if the reader, having journeyed through a dense thicket of facts, figures, and concepts about public order, feels dissatisfied that no formula or strategy has been offered by which public order might be improved in our time. The first antidote is the reminder that none was promised. Second, we note that the investigations of the four cities reveal a great diversity of policies that seemed at various times to improve public order; other policies whose effects left much to be desired are also identified. The more problematic question is whether the improvements that occurred, especially between 1850 and 1930, were due to the policies of public order themselves or to their coincidence with more fundamental cultural, economic, and political changes. The disquieting general conclusion of this study about "policies of public order" is that the effects of these policies depend on other circumstances, only dimly understood.

As a result there is little empirical basis for confidence about the contemporary effects of policies informed by humanitarian faith in equalization of opportunity and rehabilitation, or by conservative reliance on strict authority and firm punishment. It *may* be true that the reduction of urban poverty, the decriminalization of social offenses, and the creation of across-the-board programs of rehabilitation and social reintegration for offenders would turn back the surge in common crime that has marked the second half of this century. It *may* be true that systematic application by modern police and courts of the horrendous penalties prescribed 200 years ago would virtually eliminate common crime and civil strife—yet it is highly unlikely that such policies will be instituted in any Western society as now constituted. Since liberal reforms have always been resisted by substantial social groups on grounds of principle and economic self-interest, most implementations have been grudging and partial. Worse yet, the reformist principles are rapidly being discredited by their apparent failure to check rising disorder. On the other hand people today lack the callous acceptance of brutality that would be needed to administer the traditional solutions, and even if officials could be found to implement them, the policies in their pure form are utterly unacceptable to large segments of contemporary political and social opinion. If applied they would engender not order but disorder, in the form of resistance to oppression. Thus the possibilities for devising effective and broadly supported policies of public order are constrained by the same diversity of beliefs and purposes that becomes manifest in increased disorder. The people of Western societies simply are not of one mind about the most desirable behavioral standards or policies of social control.

The problem, and the inherent difficulty of solving it in modern democratic societies, can be put another way. The fundamental precondition for public order is congruence between the cultural values of the ordinary members of a society and the operating codes of order and opportunity maintained by political elites. Where common values and ruling codes diverge, for whatever reasons, disorder increases; and as they converge, order increases. Pressures for divergence, which arise from the inherently dissimilar interests of rulers and ruled, grow stronger as societies increase in complexity. Convergence, and a modicum of social order, are rare in complex societies. Where it is found, convergence is more likely to be the result of long-term social engineering, consistently applied, than the workings of natural social forces. The processes of "social engineering" are manipulative and often oppressive, a circumstance that raises a fundamental question: Are the costs of social disorder more bearable than the costs of order? This question has no empirical answer. For the time being, however, most of the citizens of three Western societies seem to be prepared to accept the costs of disorder; the citizens of West Bengal have little choice in the matter.

NOTES TO CHAPTER VI.6

1. In the remainder of this chapter "crime" in quotation marks refers to threatening individual behavior; when the word crime is used without quotes, the reference is to criminal behavior as legally defined.

2. Gwynn Nettler, *Explaining Crime* (New York: McGraw-Hill, 1974). Another survey of social theories of crime cited earlier is Hermann Mannheim, *Comparative Criminology* (Boston: Houghton Mifflin, 1965). For reviews of biological, psychological, and anthropological theories of crime and individual violence see Mannheim, Part 3, and Donald Mulvihill and Melvin Tumin, *Crimes of Violence* (Washington, D.C.: Government Printing Office, 1969), chs. 7-10.

3. Nettler, op. cit., chs. 6-7, quotation pp. 140-141.

4. Ibid., ch. 8, so classifies E. H. Sutherland's "differential association" hypothesis (see E. H. Sutherland and D. R. Cressey, *Criminology*, various eds., Philadelphia: Lippincott) and labeling explanations of criminality, initiated by Howard S. Becker, *Outsiders: Studies in the Sociology of Deviance* (New York:/Free Press, 1963).

5. The principal examples of control theory cited by Nettler (op. cit., ch. 9) are the "containment" theory proposed by W. C. Reckless in *The Crime Problem*, various eds. (New York: Appleton-Century-Crofts) and the analyses of defective social training by H. J. Eysenck, *Crime and Personality* (Boston: Houghton Mifflin, 1964) and G. Trasler, *The Explanation of Criminality* (London: Routledge and Kegan Paul, 1962).

6. This discussion follows the more detailed comparisons of theoretical approaches in T. R. Gurr, "The Revolution-Social-Change Nexus, Some Old Theories and New Hypotheses," *Comparative Politics*, (April 1973), 363-378. Examples of psychological approaches to the explanation of civil strife include E. Victor Wolfenstein, *The Revolutionary Personality: Lenin, Trotsky, Gandhi* (Princeton, N.J.: Princeton University Press, 1967) and David C. Schwartz, *Political Alienation and Political Behavior* (Chicago: Aldine-Atherton, 1973).

7. Three similar sociopsychological theories are James C. Davies, "Toward a Theory of Revolution," *American Sociological Review*, 27 (February, 1962), 5-19; Ivo K. Feierabend, Rosalind L. Feierabend, and Betty A. Nesvold, "Social Change and Political Violence: Cross-National Comparisons," in Hugh Davis Graham and T. R. Gurr, eds., *Violence in America*, and T. R. Gurr, *Why Men Rebel* (Princeton, N.J.: Princeton University Press, 1970).

8. Two influential theories emphasizing aspects of social structure are Neil J. Smelser, *Theory of Collective Behavior* (New York: Free Press, 1963) and Chalmers Johnson, *Revolutionary Change* (Boston: Little, Brown, 1966).

9. Aristotle developed a group conflict theory of political change in *The Politics*, Book V. The best-known contemporary theories of class conflict derive from Karl Marx's writings. Two influential non-Marxist theories are Johan Galtung, "A Structural Theory of Aggression," *Journal of Peace Research* (No. 2, 1964), 95-119, which parallels the Aristotelian argument, and Dahrendorf, *Class and Class Conflict in Industrial Society* (Stanford: Stanford University Press, 1959), which is concerned with the sources and consequences of group conflict generally.

10. This and subsequent examples are illustrative, not definitive.

11. David Seidman and Michael Couzens, "Getting the Crime Rate Down: Political Pressure and Crime Reporting," *Law and Society* (Spring 1974), 457-493. Specifically, the evidence is that the District of Columbia police, and apparently those of at least seven other large cities, began in the late 1960s or 1970 to value a significantly larger portion of larcencies at "under $50" and a smaller portion at "over $50." The total number of crimes is not affected, but the number of "serious" crimes declines as a consequence—and the latter are included in the summary Index of the FBI's Uniform Crime Reporting System. Such a change enabled the police commissioner of Baltimore to claim a 15.1 percent decline in major crime during the first half of 1971 by comparison with the first half of 1970 (cited in Seidman and Couzens, 480).

12. In the terms used to describe formal models in econometrics, the four variables shown in Figure VI.6.1 are "endogenous," and the relationships shown among them are too numerous for the equations expressing them to be identified. The additional variables shown in Figure VI.6.2 and discussed below are "exogenous." Of course any discussion of the formal status of such a model is premature because the variable aspects of most of the conditions are not specified here, and indices are not suggested for most of them.

13. Similar arguments, developed in more detail, include Dahrendorf, op. cit.; Harry Eckstein and T. R. Gurr, *Patterns of Authority: A Structural Basis for Political Inquiry* (New York: Wiley, 1975), chs. 15 and 16; and Arnold Feldman, "Violence and Volatility: The Likelihood of Revolution," in Harry Eckstein, ed., *Internal War: Problems and Approaches* (New York: Free Press, 1963).

14. For a formal, deductive theory about relations between actors' attainments and their expectations, and the consequences of different patterns of distribution for their potential for conflict behavior, see T. R. Gurr and Raymond Duvall, *Conflict and Society: A Formal Theory and Contemporary Evidence* (forthcoming), Part I.

15. The Marxian emphasis on the fundamental importance of a society's economic system in accounting for its other characteristics is accepted here, but not Marx's precise determinism: Economic factors limit the range of societal and political variation but do not exactly determine the shape of institutions and interests. The position here is that all conceivable economic structures create "antagonisms" that constitute a potential for social disorder.

16. Other studies also show evidence of an apparent reversal in causality. When compared with economic data, national crime data for the United States, Canada, England and Wales, and Scotland from 1900 to 1970 show positive correlations between unemployment and crime before World War II, and positive correlations between economic growth and crime thereafter. M. Harvey Brenner, "Effects of the Economy on Criminal Behavior and the Administration of Criminal Justice: A Multinational Study," paper presented to the Conference on Economic Crisis and Crime, United Nations Social Defence Research Institute, Rome, 1975. The results are more complex than this summary suggests, and Brenner puts a somewhat different interpretation on them.

Abel-Smith, B., 155n, 156n, 199n
abortion in comparative criminal law, 691-92
  See also criminal law under Britain, New South Wales, Sweden
Adler, M., 28n, 29n
Adlersparre, George, 247
af Forselles, Carl, 247
Ahnlung, N., 235n
Albinski, H., 463
Aldcroft, D. H., 57n
Almon, S., 464n
Almquist, G. F., 252n, 253n, 278n, 320n
Anand, V. S., 198n
Anderson, B., 235n
Anton, T. J., 236, 304n
appelate courts, compared, 729
  See also criminal courts under Bengal, Britain, New South Wales, Sweden
Arantz, Detective Philip, 428, 436n
Aristotle, 769
Aschrat, A., 519n
Askin, R., 421
assault, comparative trends, 621-27, 646-48
  See also trends in murder and assault under specific cities
associational groups and strife, compared, 664-65
  See also specific groups under specific cities, countries
Atwood, Thomas, 78
Australia:
  Commonwealth Police Force, 398
  Commonwealth War Precautions Act of 1914-1915, 391, 394
  Communist Party, 402, 414, 420, 421;
    suppression of, 404-05, 418-19

Communist Party Dissolution Act of 1950, 420
Labor Party, 333-34, 336, 374, 395-97, 398, 399, 402, 420, 421, 423, 428, 457-58
Liberal Party, 419, 421, 422-23, 427
Nationalist Party, 395-97, 402
Norfolk Island penal colony, 355, 377, 456
Security Intelligence Organization, 429
Van Diemen's Land (Tasmania), 344, 376-77
World War II, effects, 336, 404-05
See also New South Wales, Sydney
Avison, N. H., 197n

Babington, A., 156n
Backstrom, K., 252n
Bacon, R., 197n
Baltimore, 774n
Banerjea, Surendranath, 498-99
Banfield, E. C., 93n, 664, 676n
Bangladesh civil war, 582
Barker, T. C., 57n
Barry, J., 385n
Bayley, D. H., 592n, 594n, 725n, 701, 723n
Beattie, J. M., 58n, 62, 63, 104n, 203
Beccaria, Cesare, 82
Beck, Adolf, 145, 155n
Becker, H. S., 769n
Bell, D., 16, 30n
Benewick, R., 198n
Bengal:
  Bangla Congress, 515
  Bengal Assembly, 579
  Bengal Congress, 506, 509, 567
  Bengal Criminal Amendment of 1930, 567, 593n

TED ROBERT GURR is Payson S. Wild Professor of Political Science at Northwestern University. He is the author of *Why Men Rebel* (Princeton University Press, 1970), winner of the American Political Science Association's Woodrow Wilson Award as best book in political science published that year. He is coauthor (with Hugh Davis Graham) of *Violence in America: Historical and Comparative Perspectives* (prepared for the National Commission on the Causes and Prevention of Violence, 1969).

PETER N. GRABOSKY received M.A. and Ph.D. degrees from Northwestern University and is a member of the Department of Political Science at the University of Vermont. During 1976-77 he was a Russell Sage Foundation Resident Fellow in Law and Social Science at Yale Law School. He is the author of *Sydney in Ferment: Crime, Dissent, and Official Reaction, 1788-1973* (1976, Australian National University).

RICHARD C. HULA received his M.A. and Ph.D. degrees from Northwestern University. He has taught at the University of Illinois—Urbana, and is now a member of the political science faculty at the University of Texas, Dallas.